Chicago Portraits

Chicago Portraits
Biographies of 250 Famous Chicagoans

by June Skinner Sawyers

Foreword by Bill Kurtis

A Campion Book

Loyola University Press
Chicago

Loyola University Press
3441 North Ashland Avenue
Chicago, Illinois 60657

Library of Congress Cataloging-in-Publication Data
Sawyers, June Skinner, 1957–
     Chicago portraits: biographies of famous Chicagoans/June Skinner Sawyers.
          p. cm.
     Includes bibliographical references and index.
     ISBN 0-8294-0701-4 (hardcover) ISBN 0-8294-0700-6 (paperback)
     1. Chicago (Ill.)—Biography. 2. Chicago (Ill.)—Biography—Portraits. I. Title.
F548.25.S28   1991   91-24741
920.0773'11—dc20   CIP

Acknowledgments
Artwork by William Gorman pp. 26, 29, 62, 83, 84, 88, 144, 154, 161, 174, 190, 195, 234, 239, 272, 283, 286, and 292.
Electronic artwork (picture frames and symbols of professions) by Robert Voigts.
Cover and book design by Nancy Gruenke.
Cover artwork by William Gorman.

to Elizabeth Porter

Contents

List of Entries

Grace Abbott
Robert S. Abbott
Wallace C. Abbott
Jane Addams
George Ade
Nelson Algren
Saul Alinsky
Fran Allison
John Peter Altgeld
Arthur Andersen
Margaret C. Anderson*
Sherwood Anderson
Adrian Anson
Philip Danforth Armour
Louis Armstrong
Jacob Arvey
Ira J. Bach*
Barney Balaban
Claude A. Barnett
Mary Bartelme
Mathias "Paddy" Bauler
L. Frank Baum
John Belushi
Jack Benny*
Bruno Bettelheim
Frank Billings
Jesse Binga
Louise DeKoven Bowen
Preston Bradley
Myra Bradwell
James H. Breasted
"Big" Bill Broonzy
William Bross
Leo Burnett
Daniel H. Burnham
Edgar Rice Burroughs
Paul Butterfield
Frances Xavier Cabrini*
Al Capone
Anton J. Cermak
Leonard Chess
Nat "King" Cole
Charles A. Comiskey
Fairfax M. Cone
Jack Conroy
Sam Cooke
Jack L. Cooper
Paul Cornell

Charles Correll
and
Freeman Gosden
John Coughlin
Henry Crown*
Richard J. Daley
Arnold Damen
Clarence Darrow
Charles Gates Dawes
Eugene Debs
Floyd Dell*
Oscar De Priest
William E. Dever
John Dewey*
Walt Disney*
Michael Diversey*
R. R. Donnelley
Stephen A. Douglas
Theodore Dreiser
Finley Peter Dunne
Jean Baptiste Pointe du Sable
Mircea Eliade*
Elmer E. Ellsworth
Ada and Minna Everleigh
James T. Farrell
Edna Ferber
Enrico Fermi
Eugene Field
Marshall Field
John Fischetti
Morris Fishbein
Fahey Flynn
Bob Fosse
Bud Freeman
Henry Blake Fuller
Mary Garden
Hamlin Garland
Dave Garroway
Arthur J. Goldberg*
Maurice Goldblatt
Benny Goodman
Kenneth Sawyer Goodman*
Steve Goodman
Harold "Red" Grange
Walter Burley Griffin*
Samuel E. Gross
George Halas
Margaret Haley
Albert Halper*
Dina Halpern*

Alice Hamilton*
Fred Hampton
Lorraine Hansberry
William Rainey Harper
Sydney J. Harris*
Carter Harrison I
Carter Harrison II
William "Big Bill" Haywood*
Ben Hecht
Ernest Hemingway*
Robert Herrick
John Hertz
Sidney Hillman*
Earl Hines
Emil G. Hirsch
Julius J. Hoffman
William Holabird*
Joseph Holmes*
Henry Horner
Gurdon S. Hubbard
Robert Maynard Hutchins
J. Allen Hynek
Samuel Insull
Mahalia Jackson
William Le Baron Jenney
Jack Johnson
Jenkin Lloyd Jones*
John Jones
Florence Kelley
Edward J. Kelly
Michael Kenna
Otto Kerner, Jr.*
Charles H. Kerr
William W. Kimball*
John Kinzie
Herman Kogan*
James L. Kraft
Ray Kroc
Gene Krupa
Kenesaw Mountain Landis
Ring Lardner
Victor Lawson
Meyer Levin
Vachel Lindsay
Mary Livermore
Henry Demarest Lloyd
Rudy Lozano*
Charles MacArthur*

*Entry found in Appendix

George W. Maher*
Mary E. Marcy*
Jacques Marquette*
Vito Marzullo
Edgar Lee Masters
Oscar F. Mayer
Aloysius A. Mazewski
Cyrus H. McCormick
Robert R. McCormick
John T. McCutcheon
Mary McDowell
John McGreevy*
Joseph Medill
Charles E. Merriam
Ralph Metcalfe
Mezz Mezzrow
Albert A. Michelson
Ludwig Mies van der Rohe
Vincente Minnelli*
Harriet Monroe
Dwight L. Moody
William Vaughn Moody*
Joy Morton*
Archibald J. Motley, Jr.
Willard Motley
Elijah Muhammad
James Mulligan
George Mundelein
Paul Muni
Bronko Nagurski
Agnes Nestor
William Butler Ogden
Joe "King" Oliver

Francis O'Neill
James O'Reilly
Ruth Page
William S. Paley*
Bertha Honore Palmer
Potter Palmer
Francis W. Parker
Albert and Lucy Parsons
James C. Petrillo
Irna Phillips*
Allan Pinkerton
George Pullman
James Quigley
Leslee Reis*
Ben Reitman
Hyman G. Rickover*
Knute Rockne*
Carl R. Rogers*
George F. Root
John Wellborn Root
Julius Rosenwald
Barney Ross
Arthur Rubloff
Carl Sandburg
Abe Saperstein
Richard W. Sears
Ike Sewell*
Howard Van Doren Shaw
John G. Shedd
Philip Sheridan
John M. Smyth
Albert G. Spalding
Amos Alonzo Stagg
Ellen Gates Starr*
Melville E. Stone
Wilbur F. Storey
Louis Sullivan
Billy Sunday

Gustavus F. Swift
David Swing
Lorado Taft
Graham Taylor
Terence Teahan
Frazier Thomas
Theodore Thomas
Mary Harris Thompson
William Hale Thompson
Burr Tillstrom
Michael Todd*
Thorstein B. Veblen*
Bill Veeck
Charles H. Wacker
Charles Walgreen
Aaron Montgomery Ward
Harold Washington
Muddy Waters
Johnny Weissmuller
Ida B. Wells
William A. Wieboldt
Frances E. Willard*
Daniel Hale Williams
Sonny Boy Williamson I*
Howlin' Wolf
Frank Lloyd Wright
John S. Wright
Richard Wright
William Wrigley, Jr.
Charles Tyson Yerkes
Arthur Young
Ella Flagg Young
Florenz Ziegfeld

*Entry found in Appendix

Foreword

I've spent much of my life seeking out historical sites to see where John Dillinger was shot or where Abe Lincoln accepted the nomination for president or where the Hull-House complex stood in the era of Jane Addams.

And invariably I'm disappointed.

It's either been recently paved over or the fading paint seems so—ordinary. Maybe I expect the site to give some miraculous inspiration, like the grotto at Lourdes, or at least some clue to why history holds that particular square of earth so dear.

Instead, I inevitably realize that each location is unique in its revelation that people bring glory to a place. Individuals, in their time, consecrate a site with their achievement, for good or evil.

In this regard, Chicago has been generously blessed.

Immigrants, pioneers, merchants, and meatpackers flooded west with the expansion of a young growing nation. Why they would decide to stop and build homes in an onion patch will always amaze me. Suffice it to remain testimony to the developer's cardinal rule of success—location!

Chicago came alive with development. Transportation crisscrossed the continent but converged in Chicago's mammoth switchyard, an honor the city has never lost.

Commerce meant employment, which attracted a labor force from all cultures of the world and set the stage for a recurring theme of diversity in the city's fabled growth.

Giants of industry needed the strong shoulders of immigrants who in turn insured new life and culture for the city by mixing the customs of other nations with the wide-open atmosphere of a boom town.

Chicago's character was forged in the raw tension between labor's muscle and management's power, between the street fighter and the opera set. From this explosive mix came personalities who would meet the challenge of their times—and win.

Gustavus F. Swift is typical of these larger-than-life personalities; his name alone embodies an era in Chicago. Swift didn't come to Chicago a rich man. Not many Chicagoans did. He arrived in 1875 with an idea: to slaughter cattle in Chicago and ship the meat to the East in refrigerated rail cars. He didn't invent the new means of shipping fresh meat, but he was the first packer to fully understand its significance.

Swift's plan turned the Union stockyards into the world's capital of processing meat. By the late nineteenth century, seventy meatpacking plants were operating around the South Side yards. Swift's company had grown to 200 million dollars and employed 20,000. Other names like Armour would also become legendary in the meatpacking industry and in Chicago history.

It would be easy to choose only the giants in a selection of famous Chicagoans, but June Skinner Sawyers has been careful to fill in all perspectives of the city's life force. Alongside the merchants and robber barons are entertainers, musicians, and writers. She gives us real-estate developers and baseball players, mayors and hoodlums. They are all strong individuals who gave the city its style.

One man even gave the city its image. Alphonse Capone so caught the imagination of the public worldwide, helped along by television and movies, that we've been living it down for the last sixty years.

Some of the names found here are etched in their own living monuments within the city, names like Richard Sears, Montgomery Ward, Potter Palmer, Marshall Field, John G. Shedd, R. R. Donnelley, and Maurice Goldblatt. Others enter our lives through their music, which we can still hear—Muddy Waters, Bud Freeman, Gene Krupa. And many will surprise you for their world-class accomplishments that were born in the crucible of an urban experiment called Chicago. Jane Addams and her colleagues defined the very notions of social legislation.

The value of having such a collection of biographies is to negate the notion that past, present, and future are beyond our control. These human beings affected our lives and, in most cases, established standards that define our success and failure. You will find they almost universally emerged from modest beginnings to rise above their fellow travelers in achievement and success.

The message that emerges is overwhelming. If they could do it, so can we.

Chicago Portraits proves that a city's history is the sum of our lives. The men and women of this book are all Chicagoans, each representing millions of others whose dreams and sweat built one of the greatest cities in the world.

Bill Kurtis
Chicago, Illinois
July 1991

Preface

When Father George Lane asked me to put together historical sketches of prominent figures from Chicago's past, I thought it would be a fun and—truth be told—relatively fast and painless project. After all, how long could it take to write two hundred or so concise biographies? A few months? Surely no more than six months. Right? Wrong. Two years later, the last entry has been written, the last photograph secured, and I can finally see the light at the end of the tunnel.

Chicago has such a rich and varied history, so full of vivid and exciting characters, that the most difficult task was deciding who not to include. An even thornier problem was more fundamental: how exactly do you define "Chicagoan"? Must a person be born in Chicago to be considered a bona fide Chicagoan? How about someone who was born and raised elsewhere but spent many fruitful years here? Does that person qualify?

There were no easy, cut-and-dried solutions, so I had to rely on the counsel of valued colleagues and on the sound research of respected historians for guidance. Primarily, though, I used my own judgment. Not everyone will, of course, agree with my selections. Many undoubtedly will take issue (Why wasn't so and so included?). Those are the chances one has to take when assembling such a biographical encyclopedia.

Basically, I chose individuals who, either negatively or positively, made a substantial impact on the city. The entries fell primarily into two categories: those who were born and bred in Chicago and those who were born or raised elsewhere but, nevertheless, contributed to the vitality of the city.

The big names are here—Jane Addams, Nelson Algren, Charles A. Comiskey, Clarence Darrow, Richard J. Daley, George Pullman, Harold Washington, and, yes, Al Capone—as are the familiar ones that Chicagoans tend to take for granted, such as Field, Goldblatt, Kraft, Walgreen, Ward, and Wieboldt.

I've also made a sincere attempt to include people that the general reader may not immediately recognize but whose lives and deeds made a difference. Their contributions should be remembered. I'm referring to such people as Saul Alinsky, Mary E. Marcy, Albert and Lucy Parsons, and Ida B. Wells. Then there are those who we sometimes forget had strong Chicago ties, from Louis Armstrong to L. Frank Baum, from Nat "King" Cole to Sam Cooke, from Bob Fosse to Mahalia Jackson, from John Hertz to Knute Rockne.

Obviously, a work that contains almost two hundred and fifty names cannot possibly include every notable person who ever lived or worked in Chicago—that would require several hefty volumes and is beyond this book's scope and intention. Chicago Portraits does, however, strive to be representative of the people—to capture the essence of a life in a few paragraphs—who, at one time, made Chicago their home.

The book is divided into two sections: the main text and the appendix. The main text consists of biographical portraits of roughly four hundred to one thousand words in length. Each entry is followed by a brief bibliography and cross references and is accompanied by a photograph.

The appendix contains shorter entries, capsule biographies of native Chicagoans such as Walt Disney, Vincente Minnelli, and William S. Paley—people who left the city before their impact could be felt; people who made less of an impact on the city than those included in the main text; and people from the greater Chicago area. This latter category deserves further explanation.

Does one include only people from the city proper or does one adopt a more expansive approach and include individuals who lived and worked primarily in the suburbs? Granted, some of the older suburbs have a rich heritage of their own. Oak Park, for example, has claimed Ernest Hemingway. Frances Willard is associated primarily with Evanston, and Waukegan refers, and rightly so, to Jack Benny as its favorite son. In order to address the city/suburb dichotomy, I have included several entries describing the famous sons and daughters of the vast region beyond the city limits.

Franklin Rosemont, editor at the locally based Charles H. Kerr Publishing Company, once remarked that an entire book could be written about the scores of prominent individuals who visited the city for a few months, weeks, and days. How true. Their presence, no matter how fleeting, should be acknowledged. They include Rudyard Kipling, Oscar Wilde, Jesse Owens, Isadora Duncan, Joe Hill, Aleister Crowley, John Muir, Harry Houdini, "Mother" Jones, Eliot Ness, and John Dillinger, and countless others who passed our way.

The individuals portrayed in the following pages capture the many faces of Chicago's past. They were athletes and coaches, social workers and community activists, writers and editors, politicians and gangsters, pioneers and entrepreneurs, philosophers and musicians, judges and lawyers, priests, ministers, and rabbis.

These famous Chicagoans came from Glasgow and Rome; Niederselters, Germany, and County Cork, Ireland; St. Paul, Minnesota, and Galesburg, Illinois. They were descendants of people from lands all over the world. Generation after generation, they swept across the Illinois prairie, first by foot and wagon, then by train and automobile, and finally by airplane. They came from throughout the United States and from across the sea, all with their own heritage, all with their own dream, all with their own individual story to tell. Whether native or foreign-born, they shared one thing in common. They were all Chicagoans, as diverse and vibrant as the city itself.

June Skinner Sawyers
Chicago, Illinois
June 1991

Acknowledgments

A book of this scope could not have been written without the assistance of many individuals and institutions and the work of historians and journalists who have spent their time and talent chronicling Chicago's past. I would like to thank Elizabeth Adkins at Kraft, Inc.; Bill Church of Ernst and Young; Diane Dunne and Bill McDowell at R. R. Donnelley and Sons; Al Hall at WGN-TV; Richard Popp at the University of Chicago, Special Collections; Chuck Sadowski at the University of Chicago, Physical Education and Athletics Department; Barbara Winkelman at United Charities of Chicago; Linda Wedenoja at the Chicago Public Library Cultural Center; Walter Osborn, archivist at the Moody Bible Institute; Norma Spungen, archivist at the Asher Library, Spertus College of Judaica; Maryellen T. Thielen at Walgreen Company; the staff of the Chicago Tribune *library, especially Steve Marino, Donna Johnson, and Susan Miller, as well as the staffs of the Chicago Historical Society; the Museum of Broadcast Communications; Northwestern University library; the Frances Willard House; the Arthur Andersen library; and Abbott Laboratories.*

Those who suggested names or helped me with fleeting details include Kathy Anderson, Thom Bishop, Steven Gliwa (jazz and blues), Jill Kyriakopulos (Egyptology), Betsy Lannan (the Pinkertons), and Franklin Rosemont (labor). Thanks also to Frank Newell who thought no book about famous Chicagoans would be complete without the contributions of Fred Hampton, Julius J. Hoffman, and Elijah Muhammad. He was right.

Individuals who generously offered their advice and opinions include Tim Barton; Paul and Beth Garon of Beasley Books; Bucky Halker; Richard Lindberg; Dr. J. Fred MacDonald; Mark Newman; Chuck Schaden; Kenan Heise; Nathan Kaplan; Bill Reilly; Archibald J. Motley III; Mary Ann Johnson at Hull-House; Aloysius Mazewski, Jr., and the Polish National Alliance; and Paul Tyler, curator of the Scholl Museum of Folk Culture at the Old Town School of Folk Music.

Edwin Black, Bradley Kliewer, and Richard Kimmel helped me with computer problems.

Obtaining photographs was always a challenge. Those who made my task easier include Tom Sheridan and Earlene Spaulding at the Chicago Sun-Times; *Diana Haskell at the Newberry Library; Ray Flerlage; Richard H. Burnon and Joe Russo of the Hertz Corporation in Park Ridge, N. J.; Silvino da Silva of the Joseph Holmes Chicago Dance Theatre; Michael Baker at the Jackson-Madison County Public Library in Jackson, Tennessee; Glenn Lemieux at the Blues Archive at the University of Mississippi; Jim O'Neal; Dempsey J. Travis at the Urban Research Institute; Diane Richard at Holabird and Root; Chris and Tom Kastle; Kevin O'Donnell; Joe Segal; Lois Walker at the* Chicago Defender; *Lauren Bufferd at the Chicago Public Library Cultural Center, Special Collections; Eileen Flanagan at the Chicago Historical Society; Nancy M. Shawcross of the Special Collections Department at the Van Pelt/Dietrich Library, University of Pennsylvania; Terry Fife of History Works, Inc., in Oak Park, Illinois; Mark Moss at* Sing Out! *magazine; Wally Petersen at Leo Burnett Company, Inc.; Denyse K. Sturges at the University of Illinois at Chicago, Special Collections Department; Vicki Cwiok at Sears, Roebuck and Company; Franklin Rosemont at Charles H. Kerr Publishing Company, Les Orear and Al Stein at the Illinois Labor History Society; Rick Kogan; as well as the* Chicago Daily Law Bulletin, *WLS-TV, the Francis W. Parker School, the Theatre Historical Society, the Chicago Bears, the Chicago White Sox, and the Museum of Modern Art, Film Still Archive Department in New York. Grant B. Schmalgemeier, Chicago history buff extraordinaire, went above and beyond the call of duty.*

Special thanks to Randy Curwen at the Chicago Tribune *for giving me a chance.*

A personal thanks also to the staff of Loyola University Press, especially to Father George Lane for his faith in my ability to do the job, to Frederick Falkenberg and Nancy Gruenke in production, to Bill Gorman for his skillful drawings, and to my editor, Erin Milnes, for her patience and commitment to what, at times, seemed like a never-ending project.

Finally, I extend my deepest respect and gratitude to Ellen Skerrett for her knowledge, her insight, and her unfailing generosity.

Grace Abbott

Social Reformer

born: November 17, 1878
Grand Island, Nebraska
died: June 19, 1939
Chicago, Illinois

One of the illustrious women of Hull-House, Grace Abbott exposed the exploitation of immigrants and children to city officials and went on to have a distinguished career in both public service work and as a professor of public welfare at the University of Chicago.

Photograph courtesy of Special Collections, the University Library, University of Illinois at Chicago.

Grace Abbott came from an enlightened Quaker family that stressed social justice and social equality. Her mother, Elizabeth Griffin Abbott, told her daughter that "the rights of women belonged with the rights of the Indian and the Negro. Everyone must be free and equal, and everyone should be dealt with on the basis of equality and justice."

In 1898 Abbott graduated from Grand Island College, Nebraska, and later completed graduate work at the University of Nebraska. In 1908 she moved to Chicago to work at Jane Addams's Hull-House on the West Side. Her sister, Edith, was already affiliated with the University of Chicago's School of Social Work. Grace continued graduate studies at the University of Chicago and received her Ph.D. in political science in 1909.

Abbott became the director of the Chicago Immigrants' Protective League while she was at Hull-House. The league helped thousands of young immigrant families adjust to life in the New World. The league also established waiting rooms at railroad stations where new arrivals were greeted by men and women who helped them locate family members.

Soon after arriving at Hull-House, Abbott investigated private employment agencies in Chicago, many of which were located along Canal Street in an area referred to as the "slave market." Unsuspecting immigrants used these agencies only to be charged high fees for jobs that often didn't even exist. Abbott published her findings in the report, *The Chicago Employment Agency and the Immigrant Worker.* Her hard work led to the passage of a law in 1909 that controlled the unscrupulous practices of these agencies.

Abbott feverishly rallied for the passage of a fair and just immigration policy for the nation's "new" immigrants, a euphemism for immigrants from Eastern and Southern Europe. In January of 1912 she testified before a congressional committee in Washington, D.C, on their behalf.

Abbott joined the faculty of the Chicago School of Civics and Philanthropy in 1911 but left in 1917 to work for the government. From 1917 to 1919 she was the director of the Child Labor Division of the Children's Bureau in Washington, D.C. In 1918 she served as an advisor to the War Labor Policies Board. From 1920 to 1921 she was the executive secretary of the Illinois Immigrants' Commission, and she was chief of the United States Children's Bureau from 1921 to 1934. In this position she was able to ensure the passage of important child labor laws.

Following her departure from government work, Abbott returned to Chicago where from 1934 until her death she was professor of public welfare at the University of Chicago. She also edited the university's *Social Service Review* from 1934 to 1939.

In 1917 Abbott wrote *The Immigrant and the Community,* a sympathetic acount of the often shameful treatment of immigrants in Chicago, and in 1938 she completed the massive, two-volume *The Child and the State,* which discussed child labor and the role of the state.

Abbott died of cancer in Chicago in June of 1939.

See also: Jane Addams, Mary McDowell, Agnes Nestor

Further reading: Addams, Jane. *Twenty Years at Hull-House* (1910); Costin, Lela B. *Two Sisters for Social Justice: A Biography of Grace and Edith Abbott* (1983); Sochen, June. *Movers and Shakers: American Women Thinkers and Activists, 1900–1970* (1973).

Robert S. Abbott

Newspaper Owner/Publisher

born: November 28, 1868
St. Simon's Island, Georgia
died: February 29, 1940
Chicago, Illinois

By crusading against racism and urging the black community to fight injustice, Robert Sengstacke Abbott revolutionized black journalism and, in the process, became the city's first African-American millionaire.

Photograph courtesy of the *Chicago Defender*.

The son of slaves, Abbott was reared on the outskirts of Savannah, Georgia. His father, Thomas, died when Robert was an infant, and his mother, Flora, later married Joseph Sengstacke, the son of a German-born white merchant and a black slave. Sengstacke, an ordained minister, instilled in his stepson a love of books and learning. Young Abbott attended the Beach Institute, a small Congregational institution in Savannah, then transferred to Claflin University in Orangeburg, South Carolina, in 1887 before enrolling at the Hampton Institute in Hampton, Virginia, to learn the printing trade.

After graduation, Abbott returned to Georgia to help his stepfather publish the *Woodville* (Georgia) *Times* before deciding to study law at Chicago's Kent College of Law, where he graduated, the only African-American in his class, in 1899. Frustrated by the lack of opportunities for blacks—especially for a man as dark-skinned as he who had experienced rejection both by whites and by light-skinned African-Americans—Abbott toyed with the bold idea of starting his own newspaper.

"I wanted to create an organ that would mirror the needs, opinions, and the aspirations of my race," said Abbott. At that time there were three African-American newspapers in the city: Julius C. Taylor's *Broad Ax*, S. B. Turner's *Illinois Idea*, and Ferdinand L. Barnett's *Conservator,* but they functioned more as mouthpieces for their editors than as bonafide news-gathering organizations.

The *Chicago Defender* was different. It had a specific mission—the eradication of racial prejudice—and, in Robert Sengstacke Abbott, it had an indefatigible fighter. Abbott started from scratch. With 25 cents worth of capital (it cost $13.75 to print 300 copies, according to Abbott's biographer Roi Ottley, which he paid in

installments), a folding card table, and a kitchen chair as the sole equipment, he launched the first issue on May 5, 1905. Middle-class whites in positions of power and members of the black elite with strong economic ties to the white establishment dismissed it as inflammatory journalism, but to the vast majority of the African-American populace it was a source of pride. Although the *Defender* employed journalistic practices that would be considered rather dubious by today's standards to attract attention—such as the use of screaming yellow headlines—it was always taken seriously among its constituency. The *Defender* was there to goad, preach, and inspire.

Acutely aware of the widespread discrimination and severe unemployment in the South, Abbott encouraged rural blacks to migrate to the great industrial cities of the North. They came in droves, riding the Illinois Central passenger trains north from Louisiana, Mississippi, Alabama, and Tennessee. Abbott arranged for the Illinois Central to drop off copies of the paper along its route. Indeed Abbott would often hire railroad employees to distribute the paper in the South, notes historian James R. Grossman. In Chicago, the *Defender* was read in churches and in barber shops, anywhere people congregated. Through aggressive reporting and a vigorous advertising campaign, the *Defender* became known as the bible of the African-American community. By 1918 the *Defender* was able to boast a national circulation of 125,000, the largest selling black newspaper in the country. What's more, its passionate editorials and fearless reporting earned it the reputation as the most militant black newspaper in Chicago.

Abbott didn't forget his younger readers either. In 1929 he suggested the first Saturday in August be set aside as Bud Billiken Day. "Bud" was reportedly the nickname of Lucius Harper, executive editor of the newspaper while "Billiken" was named after a mythical Chinese figurine—said to be the guardian of children—that sat on Harper's desk. Whatever its origins, today Bud Billiken Day remains a durable and popular Chicago tradition and, indeed, has since grown to be the largest African-American parade in the country.

Abbott died in his sleep on February 29, 1940, in his home at 4742 South Parkway. In 1960 the *Chicago Defender* moved its offices from 3435 South Indiana Avenue to its present location at 2400 South Michigan Avenue. Although competition from other black publications has led to reduced circulation, the *Chicago Defender* continues to cover news and events of importance to Chicago's African-American community.

See also: Claude A. Barnett

Further reading: Drake, St. Clair and Horace R. Cayton. *Black Metropolis: A Study of Negro Life in a Northern City* (1945); Grossman, James R. *Land of Hope: Chicago, Black Southerners, and the Great Migration* (1989); Ottley, Roi. *The Lonely Warrior: The Life and Times of Robert S. Abbott* (1955); Spear, Allan H. *Black Chicago: The Making of a Negro Ghetto 1890–1920* (1967); Travis, Dempsey J. *An Autobiography of Black Chicago* (1981).

Wallace C. Abbott

Physician/Scientist

born: October 12, 1857
Bridgewater, Vermont
died: July 4, 1921
Chicago, Illinois

In 1888 Wallace Calvin Abbott founded what was to become Abbott Labs during a time when the pharmaceutical industry was in its infancy. From first year sales of $2,000, the firm has grown into a $6.2 billion global health-care company employing nearly forty-four thousand people in over forty countries.

Photograph courtesy of Abbott Laboratories.

Educated at Dartmouth College and the University of Michigan Medical School, Abbott came to Chicago in 1886 and settled in the Ravenswood neighborhood. In 1888 he started the People's Drug Store in the kitchen of his small apartment and began manufacturing "granules" or pills. Early medications were imprecise and unreliable and their side effects so severe—such as their nauseating taste—that Abbott borrowed the idea of using the "alkaloid," or active part of a plant, from a Belgian-born surgeon named Adolphe Burggraeve and compressed this into pill form (previously medicinal fluids were extracted from herbs or plants and given to the patient in liquid form). Initially, he bought the granules but then, frustrated by their inferior quality, he began to make his own.

He formed the Abbott Alkaloidal Company and hired family members and friends to assist him. His sister filled the orders and answered inquiries, his parents placed shipping labels on the bottles, and a boyhood chum, Henry Shattuck, kept the books. Abbott edited a professional medical journal, *Medical World*, and in 1892 produced his first catalog, which consisted of 14 pages of text and 150 advertisements. Two years later, he assumed the editorship of the *Alkaloidal Clinic*—later changed to the *American Journal of Clinical Medicine*—which became one of the leading medical and surgical journals in the country. In 1897 he collaborated with Dr. William Waugh on the *Text Book of Alkaloidal Therapeutics*, a standard reference work on the subject.

By 1914 the demand for alkaloids had peaked as the industry turned away from merely supplying remedies to actually manufacturing chemicals. Encouraged by members of his staff, Abbott entered the new field of synthetic medicines. Up until then, the manufacture of synthetic chemicals was confined to saccharin and aspirin, mostly manufactured by German companies. The outbreak of World War I forced the U.S. to manufacture its own products. Abbott began producing a new wonder drug called Chlorazene, an antiseptic developed by an English doctor that helped save the lives of countless soldiers. In later years, the company produced the anesthetic, Pentothal, and the antibiotic, erythromycin.

In 1921 all chemical manufacturing was transferred to a twenty–six-acre industrial site in the northern suburb of North Chicago. But the man behind the Abbott Labs was not to fully experience the fruit of his labor. In poor health and suffering from rheumatism and chronic kidney disease, Abbott walked home from his Ravenswood office one final time on July 1, 1921. Three days later, at the age of sixty-three, he died in his bed.

Some famous Abbott products include Murine eye drops, Selsun dandruff remedy, Similac infant formula, and Sucaryl sweetener.

Further reading: Kogan, Herman. *The Long White Line: The Story of Abbott Laboratories* (1963); Pratt, William D. *The Abbott Almanac: 100 Years of Commitment to Quality Health Care* (1987).

Jane Addams

Social Reformer

born: September 6, 1860
Cedarville, Illinois
died: May 21, 1935
Chicago, Illinois

As founder and director of Hull-House, Chicago's first settlement house, Jane Addams's fame has spread far beyond her native Illinois. Of all Chicago's historical figures, she is one of its most honored citizens.

By the time Addams enrolled at Rockford Female Seminary, where she met her life-long friend and colleague, Ellen Gates Starr, she had developed a deep-seated desire to do something meaningful with her life, although exactly what her calling would be was still unclear.

After the sudden death of her father in 1881, Addams decided to attend the Women's Medical College in Philadelphia, but, near physical collapse herself—due to back problems and emotional distress caused by her father's death—she returned to Cedarville to regain her strength. In 1883 she departed on her first trip to Europe. It wasn't until her second visit, almost four years later, that she, accompanied by Starr, visited Toynbee Hall, a settlement house in the London slum of Whitechapel. Returning to the U.S., the two women made plans to transfer this bold and novel idea to the streets of Chicago. All that was needed was a house in the right neighborhood.

They found it at the corner of Halsted and Polk Streets—a brick, two-story, dilapidated mansion built in 1856 by real estate developer Charles J. Hull and located in an overcrowded West Side neighborhood. On September 18, 1889, Addams, Starr, and a housekeeper, Mary Keyser, moved in.

Addams and Starr were not missionaries—they had no great desire to "uplift" the masses. Rather, Hull-House was an experiment in social living. Addams and her colleagues maintained that poverty and lack of opportunity—not racial or ethnic inferiority—determined a person's success or failure. Their goal was to improve the area and better the lives of their neighbors.

Inspired by Toynbee Hall in London, Hull-House was also part of a larger and indigenous American movement.

By 1911 more than four hundred social settlements existed in the United States—thirty-six in Chicago alone.

Serving an average of nine thousand people a week, Hull-House percolated with continual activity. There were lectures, art classes, and music lessons—Benny Goodman, Art Hodes, and James Petrillo were students. Laura Dainty Pelham's Hull-House Players, a professional theater group, pioneered the little theater movement in the U.S. Also on the premises was the Jane Club (a boarding club for working girls), a boys' club, an assembly hall, a coffeehouse, a dining room, a day nursery, a kindergarten, an employment bureau, a basketball team, and an orchestra. Cognizant of the need for physical fitness and good personal hygiene habits, especially since many homes lacked hot water and bathing facilities, Hull-House offered public baths, a public gymnasium, a public playground—Chicago's first, established in 1893—and a public swimming pool.

The women of Hull-House—Addams, Starr, Florence Kelley, Dr. Alice Hamilton, Grace Abbott, and Julia Lathrop, and others—were instrumental in the passage of much pioneering social legislation in the city and state, including the first factory inspection laws in Illinois, the first model tenement code in Chicago, and the first juvenile court in Chicago.

Blunt and outspoken, Addams's honesty often got her into trouble. During World War I, for example, she urged world leaders to end hostilities through arbitration. For this, she was branded a traitor and Hull-House chastized as a "hotbed of anarchism."

Despite such charges, Addams generally was venerated during her lifetime—some even called her a saint. Among her many accomplishments: she established the Women's International League for Peace and Freedom in 1915, wrote nearly a dozen books, received fourteen honorary degrees, and became the first American woman to win the Nobel Peace Prize (she shared it with Nicholas Murray Butler in 1931).

Addams died in May 1935 of cancer at the age of seventy-four. For two days, thousands of Chicagoans filed past her coffin on the Hull-House grounds to pay their last respects.

Other people have followed in her footsteps but Jane Addams remains a Chicago original—brave, kind, and resolute—and the institution she founded remains, in many ways, just as relevant today as when it first opened its doors in 1889.

Today the Hull-House Museum at 800 South Halsted Street, owned by the University of Illinois, attracts over twenty thousand visitors each year. The original 1856 house and the residents dining hall, added in 1905, are all that remain of the thirteen-building complex. In 1989 Hull-House celebrated its centennial with an exhibition, "Opening New Worlds."

In addition to the museum, the Hull-House Association operates six neighborhood centers, including the Jane Addams Center at 3212 North Broadway and the Uptown Center at 4520 North Broadway with twenty-one outposts involved in social service and community activism.

See also: Alice Hamilton [appendix], Florence Kelley, Mary McDowell, Ellen Gates Starr [appendix], Graham Taylor

Further reading: Addams, Jane. *Twenty Years at Hull-House* (1910); Addams, Jane. *The Second Twenty Years at Hull-House* (1930); Davis, Allen F. *American Heroine: The Life and Legend of Jane Addams* (1973); Davis, Allen F. and Mary Lynn McCree. *Eighty Years at Hull-House* (1969); Linn, James Weber. *Jane Addams, A Biography* (1935).

George Ade

Humorist/Playwright

born: February 9, 1866
Kentland, Indiana
died: May 16, 1944
Brook, Indiana

*George Ade was an American humorist whose wry commentary and gently satiric portraits of Midwestern types won national recognition. "Early to bed, early to rise and you'll meet very few of our best people," was a typical Ade remark. His biggest success was **Fables in Slang**, a collection of short sketches that poked good-natured fun at turn-of-the-century manners in the vernacular of the common man.*

Photograph reprinted with permission from the *Chicago Sun-Times.*

Ade arrived in Chicago in 1890 and joined the staff of the *Chicago Morning News* (later the *Chicago Record*). Within less than two years, the hardworking Hoosier rose from cub reporter to feature columnist.

From 1893 to 1900 Ade wrote a popular newspaper column, "Stories of the Streets and of the Town," illustrated by his friend and college chum, John T. McCutcheon. McCutcheon accompanied Ade on his rounds—in the courts, in the parks, at the theaters, in the shops, and down the alleys—and sketched what he saw. The prolific Ade churned out 1,500- to 1,800-word essays six days a week, creating broad characterizations of easily recognizable human beings in a colorful, slangy idiom. Like fellow columnists, Finley Peter Dunne, Eugene Field, and Ring Lardner, Ade convincingly captured the texture of American urban life—its nuances, its jargon, its milieu—and presented it in such a way that it appealed to a broad readership. He wrote about newly arrived immigrants striving to find their niche, about wayward souls living in rundown hotels, about brash young men eager to make their mark in the world. Artie Blanchard, Pink Marsh, and Doc Horne were some of his most popular creations. Many of Ade's characters were odd sorts and eccentric types who lived on the frayed edges of society, yet were able to maintain a sunny disposition.

In 1897 the *Morning News* published "The Fable of Sister Mae, Who Did as Well as Could be Expected," a humorous tale of two sisters from opposite sides of the track. The public liked what it read and wanted more. Ade responded with hundreds of these "Fables in Slang"—short and breezy morality pieces that ended with a flippant remark. This was the pattern he would follow the rest of

his career, and it served him well. Ten books of fables were eventually published and several were made into silent films.

Ade enjoyed the status that fame brought. A lover of theater, he and a group of local actors formed a supper club where visiting thespians could relax after work. He also wrote the comic opera *The Sultan of Sulu,* which opened at the Studebaker Theater in March 1902 and enjoyed a long run on the New York stage, and several plays including *The County Chairman* in 1903 and *The College Widow* in 1904.

Ade retired in 1920 to his 2,400-acre estate, Hazelden, near Kentland, Indiana, where he entertained his friends and enjoyed a life of leisure. Ade died in his home in 1944 at the age of seventy-eight.

Ade's unadorned writing style and essentially optimistic outlook brought him both fame and fortune, and he was praised in his time by the likes of Mark Twain and William Dean Howells.

See also: Finley Peter Dunne, Eugene Field, Ring Lardner, Victor Lawson, John T. McCutcheon

Further reading: Ade, George. *Chicago Stories* (1963); Coyle, Lee. *George Ade* (1964); DeMuth, James. *Small Town Chicago: The Comic Perspective of Finley Peter Dunne, George Ade, Ring Lardner* (1980); Kelly, Fred C. *George Ade: Warmhearted Satirist* (1947).

Nelson Algren

Novelist

born: March 28, 1909
Detroit, Michigan
died: May 9, 1981
Sag Harbor, New York

A realist in the tradition of Theodore Dreiser, Frank Norris, and James T. Farrell, Nelson Algren graphically portrayed the darker side of life. His gallery of characters included prostitutes, drug addicts, loan sharks, bookies, hobos, con men, and the other outcasts and rejects who haunted the pool halls, taverns, bowling alleys, and tenements of Chicago's underbelly. He wrote of betrayed dreams and lives lost, but the central theme of his work was, says his biographer Bettina Drew, "the failure of love."

Photograph reprinted with permission from the *Chicago Sun-Times*.

Algren's ambition was to be a great artist. Born in Detroit, Algren spent his early boyhood in a mostly Irish neighborhood on Chicago's South Side near 71st Street and Cottage Grove Avenue before moving with his family in 1913 to 4834 North Troy Street on the Northwest Side. In 1931 he graduated with a degree in journalism from the University of Illinois at Urbana-Champaign as the country learned to cope with the full brunt of the Depression. Unable to find work, he rode the rails and hitchhiked across the country laboring at various odd jobs—door-to-door coffee salesman, migrant worker, gas station attendant, carnival shill. Two years later, his first piece—" So Help Me"—ran in *Story* magazine.

On the basis of "So Help Me," Algren received a $100 advance from Vanguard Press to write a novel about hobo life in the Southwest. No stranger to the road, he hung out with thieves, petty criminals, and vagrants, asking questions, collecting stories, recording their observations, and listening to their patter. Bumming his way to Texas, he ended up serving a four-month prison term for stealing a typewriter from a rural college. From such experiences came his first novel, *Somebody in Boots*.

Along with novelist Richard Wright, Algren was an important member of the Chicago leftist literary establishment in the 1930s. He joined the Chicago John Reed Club, an intellectual social club that met at 1427 South Michigan Avenue, became secretary of the local chapter of the League of American Writers, and, with Jack Conroy, edited a literary magazine, *The New Anvil*. In 1936 Algren was hired as a field worker for the WPA Illinois Writers' Project, compiling neighborhood studies and case histories and later, in a similar capacity, roamed the streets tracking down infected victims for the Venereal Disease Control Program. From

1942 to 1945 he served in the army with tours of duty in Wales, Germany, and France.

Algren's career picked up with the publication of his second novel, *Never Come Morning*, a devastating indictment of life in Chicago's Polish-American slums, which the *New York Times* described as "brilliant." The deeply offended Polish community, however, condemned the book as Nazi propaganda. So unrelenting a portrait was *Never Come Morning* that the Polish Roman Catholic Union succeeded in banning it from the Chicago Public Library system for several years.

In 1950 Algren won the first National Book Award for Fiction for *The Man with the Golden Arm*, further securing his reputation as an important novelist. But by the time *A Walk on the Wild Side* was published in 1956, Algren's star had set. Critics, weary of his obsession with society's outcasts, dismissed it as a lurid, overly written potboiler, populated with stock characters and tired cliches and prompting one journalist to uncharitably ridicule him as "the bard of the stubblebum."

By the 1960s Algren had given up writing serious fiction and instead earned the bulk of his income from writers' conferences and lecturing. In 1968 he served an undistinguished stint as war correspondent in Vietnam for the *Atlantic Monthly*.

In 1973 *The Last Carousel*, a collection of stories and sketches, appeared to enthusiastic reviews but disappointing sales. His last novel, *The Devil's Stocking*, a fictionalized account of the life of boxer Rubin "Hurricane" Carter, was published posthumously in 1983. Other prominent Algren works include the short story collection, *The Neon Wilderness* (1947), featuring "How the Devil Came Down Division Street," and the lengthy prose poem, "Chicago: City on the Make" (1951).

In 1974 Algren moved to the East Coast. That same year he received the Award of Merit for the Novel from the American Academy of Arts and Letters. Several months before his death due to a heart attack in 1981, Algren was elected into the American Academy and Institute of Arts and Letters.

For a short period following his death, a segment of West Evergreen Street in the Wicker Park neighborhood was changed to West Algren Street. Residents complained so vehemently—many fumed at the inconvenience of changing their address and wondered, too, who was this Algren character anyway—that the city retained the original name.

In October 1989 a handful of Algren enthusiasts formed the Nelson Algren Committee. Its purpose is to "further the recognition of Nelson Algren as a major American writer of the twentieth century." Part of their mission is to have "appropriate" parks, streets, and libraries named in his honor and to urge the city to declare his birthday "Nelson Algren Day."

See also: Jack Conroy, Theodore Dreiser, James T. Farrell, Richard Wright

Further reading: Cox, Martha Healsey and Wayne Chatterton. *Nelson Algren* (1975); Drew, Bettina. *Nelson Algren: A Life On the Wild Side* (1989); Shay, Art. *Nelson Algren's Chicago* (1988).

Saul Alinsky

Community Organizer

born: January 30, 1909
Chicago, Illinois
died: June 12, 1972
Carmel, California

Opinionated, profane, and acid-tongued, Saul David Alinsky was called many things in his day—communist, atheist, fascist—but, above all, he was called an agitator and was proud of it. More than anyone, Alinsky put the occupation of community organizer on the map and aroused what many considered a radical, and dangerous, philosophy: that ordinary people could take charge of their own lives by working together.

Photograph reprinted with permission from the *Chicago Sun-Times.*

The child of Russian Jewish immigrants, Alinsky graduated from the University of Chicago in the early 1930s and developed into an ace criminologist who specialized in working with juvenile delinquents on the Near West Side.

Along with Joseph Meegan, Alinsky organized the Back of the Yards Neighborhood Council in 1939 under the banner: "We the people will work out our own destiny." It wasn't the first neighborhood-based organization in the city, but it was one of the most influential. With so many obstacles to overcome—a stubborn nationalist pride among area ethnics, and a fierce attachment to the local parish—it's remarkable that it got off the ground at all. Yet BYNC proved that by working toward a common goal neighbors could overcome even the most ingrained of Old World antagonisms. Holding its first meeting in July of 1939, Alinsky challenged the community to find its own solutions to inadequate housing, unemployment, and crime.

Throughout his career, Alinsky's strategy remained essentially the same. By throwing the enemy off-guard ("mass ju-jitsu," he called it) using the confrontational tactics of sit-ins, protest demonstrations, and boycotts, he hoped to force a showdown. "If the end doesn't justify the means," he would ask, "what the hell does?" His weapons were ridicule, sarcasm, and rudeness.

In the early 1940s, Alinsky established the Industrial Areas Foundation (IAF), an activist organization, whose initial aim was "to unite dispossessed peoples into power groups." Then he turned his attention to the racially troubled Woodlawn community, south of Hyde Park. When the University of Chicago announced plans to buy up property in Woodlawn, which would essentially uproot large numbers of poor black families, Alinsky raised funds from Catholic and Protestant churches and formed, in 1961, The Woodlawn Organization (TWO).

TWO's protests were marvelous examples of the power of negative publicity. When Woodlawn residents complained in vain to the school board of severe overcrowding in their elementary schools while classrooms in white neighborhoods stood half-empty, Alinsky mounted a "Truth Squad" campaign, which consisted of battalions of mothers armed with cameras who descended upon the schools and took pictures of the bare desks for all to see. On another occasion, caravans of black Woodlawn residents were bused to the homes of white slumlords on the North Side where they picketed up and down the streets, distributing leaflets, and generally making a commotion. Bluntly but effectively, Alinsky got his point across.

Alinsky traveled throughout the country organizing community groups—in Kansas City, Kansas; South Saint Paul, Minnesota; Lackawanna, New York; and Rochester, New York. He also wrote several books, including two primers of community organization—*Reveille for Radicals* (1945) and *Rules for Radicals* (1971)—and authored, in 1949, a sympathetic biography of union leader John L. Lewis.

In his last years, Alinsky began organizing among the white middle class, calling that vast group of Americans the most alienated in the country. "They don't have a spokesman and the values they were brought up with are gone," he said.

Although Alinsky died in 1972 of a heart attack, his legacy is very much alive. There are training centers and grass-roots organizations scattered across the country whose very existence would have been inconceivable without his work. The Industrial

Areas Foundation continues to train organizers by conducting intensive workshops, while the group Alinsky is most closely identified with, the Back of the Yards Neighborhood Council, celebrated its 50th anniversary in 1989. The Woodlawn Organization, with main headquarters at 6040 South Harper Avenue, and the Back of the Yards Neighborhood Council with branch offices at 1751 West 47th Street and 1950 West 51st Street, continue to offer social and economic advice to their respective communities. Today's generation of activists, organizers, and social workers, whether they realize it or not, owe a large debt to Saul Alinsky.

See also: Ben Reitman

Further reading: Finks, P. David. *The Radical Vision of Saul Alinsky* (1984); Horwitt, Sanford D. *Let Them Call Me Rebel: Saul Alinsky, His Life and Legacy* (1989); Slayton, Robert A. *Back of the Yards: The Making of a Local Democracy* (1986).

Fran Allison

Television Entertainer

born: November 20, 1907
LaPorte City, Iowa
died: June 13, 1989
Sherman Oaks, California

Along with Burr Tillstrom, Fran Allison formed the team that comprised Kukla, Fran and Ollie, one of the most popular shows in television history. Allison's warm personality and reassuring presence earned her the nickname of the "First Lady of Chicago Broadcasting."

Photograph reprinted with permission from the *Chicago Sun-Times*.

Allison made her singing debut at age four before a meeting of the Grand Army of the Republic in her native Iowa. She attended Coe College in Cedar Rapids, Iowa, where she earned degrees in music and education. While teaching the fourth grade, she began producing amateur contests and sang live on small Iowa radio stations. In 1937 Allison auditioned as a vocalist on Don McNeill's *Breakfast Club* program on the NBC radio network. Impressed with her singing voice and ebullient personality, NBC executives signed her to a long-term contract. On the *Breakfast Club* Allison began to develop further the character of Aunt Fannie, the town gossip, a character that she had originated on the Iowa stations.

When her husband, a music publisher representative, entered the service during World War II, Allison contributed to the war effort by selling war bonds at Chicago stage shows. At one of those shows she met a young puppeteer named Burr Tillstrom.

After the war, Tillstrom began developing a children's television program in Chicago that featured an unusual cast of puppets with rather exotic names: Kukla, Oliver J. Dragon, Beulah Witch, Fletcher Rabbit, Cecil Bill, and Madame Oglepuss. But he felt something was missing. What the program needed, said Tillstrom, was a human touch. He thought of the young woman he had met at the war bonds shows.

Kukla, Fran and Ollie premiered in 1947 on the ABC affiliate, WBKB. That same year it moved to the NBC affiliate, WNBQ-TV (which later changed its call letters to WMAQ). In 1954 the Kuklapolitans left NBC to rejoin ABC.

The program's nonhuman characters usually stole the show—Kukla, the earnest little Everyman; Ollie, the cocky, know-it-all dragon; pompous Madame Oglepuss; gossipy Beulah Witch, and an assorted collection of pranksters and tricksters. No matter how mischievous or outrageous Tillstrom's motley characters behaved, the calm figure of Fran Allison was always there to maintain control. Whether rolling her eyes at the latest antics of Oliver J. Dragon or feigning shock at a remark by Madame Oglepuss, Allison displayed ample doses of patience and wisdom. Although poor ratings eventually led to the show's cancellation in 1957, for ten years the television audience was willingly swept away by the humorous adventures and good-natured fun of Kukla, Fran, and company.

In 1961 Allison and the famous puppets returned to television—in a nationally syndicated show from New York—in five-minute installments on NBC five days a week.

Allison treated her nonhuman colleagues with the utmost respect and dignity. She never considered them mere cloth. "Kukla, Ollie, and the others are as real to me as people," she once remarked.

Allison continued to appear on Chicago television after the demise of KF&O. In the late fifties she hosted the Emmy-winning "Fran Allison Show" and occasionally appeared in local plays, commercials, and television specials.

Allison left Chicago in the late sixties, first settling in New Jersey, and later moving to Los Angeles, where she hosted a television program for senior citizens. Occasionally Allison and Tillstrom appeared in revivals of

KF&O at various Chicago theaters. In 1970 KF&O aired over public television stations for a five-week run. In 1978 the Chicago Historical Society staged a week-long KF&O festival and, the following year, the Kuklapolitans put together a holiday special, "Tis the Season to be Ollie," on Channel 5. For several years, beginning in 1979, Kukla and Ollie—without Fran—were a Christmas tradition at the Goodman Theater.

Allison died of leukemia in her Sherman Oaks, California, home at the age of eighty-one.

See also: Dave Garroway, Burr Tillstrom

Further reading: Brooks, Tim. *The Complete Directory to Prime Time TV Stars 1946–Present* (1987).

John Peter Altgeld

Politician

born: December 30, 1847
Nieder Selters, Germany
died: March 12, 1902
Joliet, Illinois

Honest, brave, and scrupulously fair, John Peter Altgeld was that rare breed of politician who stood by his principles, refusing to bow to public opinion. His accomplishments while in office were many—during his tenure, the University of Illinois was built, the public park system of Chicago was enlarged, and the powers of state government were extended—but he is primarily remembered as the man who pardoned the Haymarket "martyrs."

Brought to the U. S. as an infant by his German immigrant parents, Altgeld was raised on a farm in Ohio. Following a stint in the Union Army, he headed first to Cincinnati, then to St. Louis, and later to Kansas and Arkansas before settling in Savannah, Missouri, to study law. Admitted to the bar in 1872, he became a prosecuting attorney but departed suddenly in 1875 for reasons still uncertain to the rapidly growing city of Chicago to practice law. With no connections, however, he had a difficult time landing on his feet.

As soon as he accumulated sufficient savings, Altgeld began to purchase lots of land in the Lakeview neighborhood where he had settled, subdividing and selling the property at a considerable profit. In 1877 he married and moved into a two-story frame house on Wellington Street between Halsted and Clark Streets. As his financial status improved, so did his living conditions. Altgeld and hs wife moved into a brick house on West Grace Street. Altgeld then became a builder. His most ambitious project by far was the sixteen-story Unity Building in downtown Chicago. In 1890 he purchased a ninety-nine year lease on an expensive lot at 127 North Dearborn Street. This time, though, he wasn't so fortunate. A costly construction error forced him to sell his other property in order to pay for the construction of the structure. The Unity Building, which had been praised as Chicago's new "skyscraper," was demolished in 1989.

In 1884 Altgeld, a Democrat, ran for Congress representing the 4th District, a largely Republican area on the North Side, but lost to Republican George Adams. The publication of the booklet, *Our Penal Machinery and Its Victims,* however, soon brought him public attention. A brilliant indictment against the criminal justice system, it boldly claimed that incarceration not only failed to rehabilitate criminals, but actually turned them into repeat offenders.

In 1886 Altgeld was elected judge of the superior court of Cook County and served five years before resigning to devote his time to real estate matters, with which he accumulated a tidy sum. In 1892, bored with the business world, he returned to politics and was nominated as the Democratic candidate for governor of Illinois. His opponents branded him as a radical sympathizer and ardent socialist. Altgeld refused to respond to the accusations, choosing instead to run a low-key and cautious campaign. The strategy worked, for he won by a surprisingly large margin over the Republican incumbent Joseph Fifer. The victory earned him the honor of being the state's first foreign-born governor and the first governor to reside in Chicago.

Altgeld's term contained two of the most devisive moments in Chicago history. On May 4, 1886, a crowd of spectators gathered in Haymarket Square near Randolph and Desplaines Streets to protest the treatment by police of workers at the McCormick Harvesting plant the previous day. During the meeting, a bomb was thrown by an unknown figure, killing several people. Four men—Albert Parsons, August Spies, Adolph Fischer, and George Engel—were arrested, convicted, and on November 11, 1887, executed.

After reviewing the transcripts from the "Haymarket Riot" trial, Altgeld, on June 26, 1893, pardoned Samuel Fielden, Michael Schwab, and Oscar Neebe, the three surviving prisoners convicted of murder, including the murder of police officer Mathias Degan. In Altgeld's briefs, he denounced the selection of the jurors, presented irrefutable evidence that

the police had introduced perjured testimony, and concluded that Judge Joseph Gary had conducted the trial with "malicious ferocity."

Now viewed as a courageous act of justice, Altgeld's decision was immediately condemned as the work of an anarchist, except, of course, in labor circles where he was hailed as a hero. Across the country, the reaction was the same: "Governor Altgeld has encouraged anarchy, rapine and the overthrow of civilization," said the *Toledo Blade* while the *Chicago Tribune* charged that "Governor Altgeld has apparently not a drop of pure American blood in his veins." Residents of Naperville, Illinois, burned his figure in effigy. There was even talk of his impeachment.

Altgeld weathered the storm, but soon another crisis erupted. When wages were cut in the company town of Pullman without a commensurate reduction in rent, the employees voted to strike. Many joined locals of the American Railway Union which, led by Eugene Debs, agreed to boycott Pullman cars. To make matters worse, President Grover Cleveland ordered federal troops, stationed in nearby Fort Sheridan, into Chicago—despite the vehement objection of Governor Altgeld—to maintain order and ensure the delivery of the U.S. mail. Affronted, Altgeld assured the president that Illinois was able to take care of itself. The strike finally ended, but not until Debs and other union leaders were imprisoned, former Pullman employees blacklisted, and many lives lost.

Altgeld ran for reelection in 1896 but lost by an overwhelming margin to Republican nominee John R. Tanner. Virtually bankrupt, he settled into semiretirement. Despite losing his gubernatorial reelection bid, Altgeld was still recognized as the leader of the Democratic party in Illinois. One year after the loss, he

handpicked Carter Harrison II as the Democratic nominee for mayor of Chicago, an office that the young Harrison won handily. But Altgeld, who believed in public ownership of streetcar franchises, was persuaded to run for mayor in 1899 when Harrison retracted campaign promises and aligned himself with the Democratic ward bosses in support of private ownership of the streetcar franchise. Again Altgeld lost.

On March 11, 1902, Altgeld suffered a cerebral hemorrhage while delivering a speech in Joliet, Illinois, and died early the next morning. Ironically, the very same press that once damned him so vehemently during the Haymarket episode, mourned his passing as a great loss. Only in death did he earn the praise that was so rightfully his.

See also: Clarence Darrow, Eugene Debs, Carter Harrison II, George Pullman, Charles Tyson Yerkes

Further reading: Adelman, William J. *Haymarket Revisited* (1976); Avrich, Paul. *The Haymarket Tragedy* (1984); Barnard, Harry. *Eagle Forgotten: The Life of John Peter Altgeld* (1938); Carwardine, William H. *The Pullman Strike* (1973); Ginger, Ray. *Altgeld's America: The Lincoln Ideal Versus Changing Realities* (1958).

Arthur Andersen

Accountant

born: May 30, 1885
Plano, Illinois
died: January 10, 1947
Chicago, Illinois

Arthur Edward Andersen founded a public accounting firm that has branches throughout the country and, indeed, across the world. Andersen promoted the one-firm concept. From Chicago to London, San Francisco to Santiago, the firm applies uniform accounting principles. By the time of his death, Arthur Andersen and Company had branches in sixteen American cities as well as offices in London, Paris, and Mexico City. Today, it is one of the largest accounting firms in the world.

The fourth of eight children, Andersen was born in the town of Plano, Illinois, about fifty miles west of Chicago. His parents, John William and Mary Aabye Andersen, emigrated from Norway in 1882. After his birth, the family returned to Norway for several years and then came back to the United States and settled on Chicago's West Side.

In 1901 Andersen found work as a mail boy at Fraser and Chalmers Company, which later became a part of the Allis-Chalmers Manufacturing Company. He attended night school and received his high school diploma in 1903. By 1906 he had risen to the position of assistant to the controller.

In 1907 Andersen joined the Chicago staff of Price Waterhouse and Company. The following year he passed the Certified Public Accountant (CPA) examination, earning the distinction of being the youngest CPA in Illinois. At that time accounting was still a relatively new profession (it was not recognized by the state of Illinois until 1903). Andersen also enrolled in Northwestern University's night school program. He was such a conscientious student that the university asked him to teach a few accounting classes.

In 1911 Andersen commuted between his evening classes at Northwestern and his position as controller of Joseph Schlitz Brewing Company in Milwaukee. When several key faculty members left the university in 1912, the school appointed Andersen assistant professor and head of the accounting department. He reorganized the department. It was, he later recalled, a particularly stressful period as he was forced to prepare the courses on a weekly or monthly basis. "More frequently than not, the notes came off the mimeographing machine just before the class hour; there was not even sufficient time to allow them to dry," he confessed in his biography.

In 1913 Andersen and Clarence M. DeLany formed Andersen, DeLany and Company with offices at 111 West Monroe Street. From the beginning, they stressed professionalism by hiring a staff of full-time accountants at a time when the accounting profession felt that such a move would lead to soaring fees and dwindling clients.

While maintaining his practice in Chicago, Andersen continued to teach accounting at Northwestern. In 1915 he was promoted to professor of accounting. Four years later, his partner Clarence M. DeLany left and the name of the firm was changed to Arthur Andersen and Company. By 1922 the firm had grown so rapidly that Andersen felt it necessary to resign from the Northwestern teaching staff to devote more time to his own practice.

As the firm grew, so did its reputation. Andersen served an impressive list of clients including Goldblatt Brothers, Hershey Chocolate Corporation, Marshall Field and Company, Walgreen Company, Stewart-Warner Corporation, and Texaco. In addition, Andersen's expertise in federal tax laws and practices contributed to much of the firm's early success.

Andersen's one-firm concept streamlined the workload and made for smoother business practices among branch offices throughout the world. The one-firm concept integrated company policy, training, and operations so that all Andersen employees—no matter where they were located—learned the same principles. From office procedure to office design, Andersen stressed consistency in all matters.

After World War II, Andersen concentrated on establishing overseas branch offices to serve his international clients. In 1963, twenty-seven offices were operating outside the

United States. Today, Arthur Andersen and Company has 243 offices in 54 countries, employing over 51,000 people worldwide. Each member firm is privately owned and controlled by the partners in each particular country.

Andersen knew that a company is only as good as its employees. With that in mind, the firm established an employee training school in 1970 in west suburban St. Charles, Illinois.

Andersen was active in civic and philanthropic affairs such as the Chicago Home for the Friendless, the First Methodist Church of Evanston, the Salvation Army, and the American Red Cross. From 1936 to 1942 he served as president of the Norwegian-American Historical Association. In addition, he was chairman of the Illinois Board of CPA Examiners and was president of the Illinois Society of Certified Public Accountants from 1918 to 1919.

In 1939 King Haakon of Norway awarded Andersen the Commander's Cross of the Royal Order of Saint Olav. In 1953 he was elected posthumously to the Accounting Hall of Fame at Ohio State University.

A company history, *Arthur Andersen & Co.: The First Fifty Years, 1913–1963,* was published in 1963.

Andersen died in January of 1947 at St. Luke's Hospital in Chicago. He was sixty-one.

See also: Arthur Young

Further reading: Arthur Andersen and Company. *The First Fifty Years, 1913–1963* (1963); Heise, Kenan and Michael Edgerton. *Chicago: Center for Enterprise.* 2 vols. (1982).

Sherwood Anderson

Novelist

born: September 13, 1876
Camden, Ohio
died: March 8, 1941
Colon, Panama

Dreamer, hustler, businessman— Sherwood Anderson played many roles during his lifetime, but it is as hero of the Bohemian set during the Chicago literary renaissance of the early twentieth century that he is best remembered.

Photograph courtesy of the Chicago Historical Society.

Anderson's early years in Chicago were disappointing. He had come to the city in 1896 at the age of twenty to "make his mark" in life. Instead of finding easy street, he encountered drudgery and destitution, rolling barrels of apples in a North Side factory. Two years later he returned to Ohio when his regiment of the National Guard was called into active duty during the Spanish-American War, and he was sent to Cuba. In 1900 he moved once again to Chicago and found work as a copywriter for an advertising firm.

Bored with his job, Anderson returned to Ohio to establish a mail-order paint firm. As business waned, he retreated more and more into his writing—he had made a habit of scribbling down his thoughts and observations during the work day and in his spare time. He was careful to separate his creative identity from his practical side; he did not wish one to interfere with the other.

The strain of toiling at his day job and writing fiction at night proved too much for him. In November 1912 he suffered a nervous breakdown. He wandered for four days—no one knows exactly where—until he turned up at a Cleveland hospital, apparently suffering from amnesia brought on by nervous exhaustion.

Abandoning his wife and his business career in Ohio in order to pursue what he called "a life of truth," Anderson returned to Chicago, found an apartment at 735 Cass Avenue (now Wabash Avenue), and rejoined his old firm. In this quest he was encouraged by Floyd Dell, editor of the *Friday Literary Review* and the city's resident Bohemian. Dell took Anderson under his wing, referring to the businessman/writer as Chicago's "great unpublished author," and attempting to find a publisher for his first novel, *Windy McPherson's Son.*

With the publication of *Windy*, the story of a small-town dreamer who goes to the big city, Anderson began to be taken seriously as a writer. Although *Marching Man*, his second novel, received mostly bad notices and stalled the momentum, the release of *Winesburg, Ohio*, a collection of short stories published in 1919 that captured the numbing conformity of small-town America, changed everything. Not only was it hailed as Anderson's masterpiece—and it is still regarded as an American classic—it also confirmed Chicago's growing reputation as a literary center.

As his name grew, Anderson's link with Chicago loosened. Traveling to Paris in 1921, he discovered he was more famous abroad than at home.

In 1922 Anderson left Chicago altogether and began a peripatetic existence, lecturing and traveling across the country before finally settling in 1927 in Marion, Virginia, where he bought and edited two weekly newspapers. By 1933, he had become a national institution—though more celebrity than writer—whose time had come and gone.

In February of 1941 Anderson visited South America as the government's unofficial goodwill ambassador. He became sick en route and died from peritonitis in Panama on March 8, 1941.

See also: Floyd Dell [appendix], Edgar Lee Masters

Further reading: Anderson, Sherwood. *Sherwood Anderson's Memoirs* (1942); Kramer, Dale. *Chicago Renaissance: The Literary Life of the Midwest 1900–1930* (1966); Smith, Alson J. *Chicago's Left Bank* (1953); Townsend, Kim. *Sherwood Anderson* (1987); Williams, Kenny J. *A Storyteller and a City: Sherwood Anderson's Chicago* (1988).

Adrian Anson

Baseball Player/Manager

born: April 17, 1852
Marshalltown, Iowa
died: April 14, 1922
Chicago, Illinois

Adrian Constantine "Cap" Anson earned a reputation as baseball's greatest slugger and player/manager of the nineteenth century. He won four National League batting championships, five pennants for his Chicago team, and had the most wins in the White Stockings (which later became the Chicago Cubs) history.

Anson attended the University of Iowa but in 1869 switched to the University of Notre Dame, where he organized the school's first baseball team. Anson began his professional career with the Rockford Forest Citys. His friend and colleague, Albert G. Spalding, played with the same team. In 1871 the Philadelphia Athletics of the National Association, predecessor of the National League, acquired Anson. He stayed until 1875. The following year Spalding, then a pitcher for the Boston team, became manager of a new Chicago club, the Chicago White Stockings, and invited Anson to join as both player/captain. Dubbed the White Stockings (no relation to the present-day White Sox baseball club) because the players wore white hose, the team played at six different locations between 1870 and 1894, according to historian Steven A. Reiss, including the West Side Grounds bounded by Polk, Honore, and Taylor Streets.

In 1879 Anson became manager and switched from third base to first. Under his leadership, the White Stockings became baseball's "first dynasty." The team won four league batting championships and captured five league pennants.

Anson had an eye for talent. He signed Billy Sunday, who later became a popular evangelist, and groomed John G. Clarkson, considered by many to be one of baseball's greatest pitchers. In 1880, Anson and Spalding signed Larry Corcoran, Fred Goldsmith, Tommy Burns, and the great Mike "King" Kelly.

Anson retired in 1898 to become the nonplaying manager of the New York Giants. Shortly after, he finally decided to hang up his baseball mitt permanently. In 1900 Anson wrote his autobiography, *A Ball Player's Career*.

Anson introduced several key innovations into the game of baseball. He was the first manager to use two pitchers regularly, and he introduced the practice of spring training. Like Spalding, Anson was a stern disciplinarian. He imposed strict curfews and meted out heavy fines to transgressors. Sometimes he used his considerable clout to maintain the status quo, such as when he wielded his power to bar African-American athletes from playing major league ball.

Besides being a great coach, Anson was a gifted athlete. According to Chicago sports writers, Eddie Gold and Art Ahrens, Anson boasted a lifetime batting average of .333. By the time he retired, he had made 3,041 hits, 532 doubles, 124 triples, and 97 home runs.

Anson had other interests besides baseball. From 1905 to 1907 he served as the city clerk of Chicago. Later, he performed on the vaudeville stage with his two daughters, and then he opened a billiard hall. But baseball remained his first love. At one point, he formed his own semi-pro team, Anson's Colts.

Anson died in April of 1922. By then baseball had become such an indelible part of American life that it was difficult to imagine a time without it. Under Anson, Chicago had earned a solid reputation as a good baseball town. Anson was elected to the National Baseball Hall of Fame in 1939.

In 1907 the name of the White Stockings was changed to the Chicago Cubs. Seven years later, in April of 1914, the Cubs opened the 1914 season in their new home, Weeghman Park, at the corner of Clark and Addison Streets. In 1926 the name was changed to Wrigley Field.

See also: Albert Spalding, Billy Sunday, William Wrigley, Jr.

Further reading: Gold, Eddie and Art Ahrens. *The Golden Era Cubs 1876–1945* (1985); Names, Larry D. *Bury My Heart at Wrigley Field: The History of the Chicago Cubs* (1990); Reiss, Steven A. *City Games: The Evolution of American Urban Society and the Rise of Sports* (1989).

Philip Danforth Armour

Industrialist

born: May 16, 1832
Stockbridge, New York
died: January 8, 1901
Chicago, Illinois

Along with competitors, Gustavus Swift, Nelson Morris, and the Cudahy brothers, Armour helped make Chicago the meatpacking center of the country. Armour, a Yankee farm boy from upstate New York, firmly believed in the value of thrift, hard work, and perseverance. Keeping emotions in check also played a part in his attitude. "Most men talk too much," said the taciturn Armour. "Most of my success has been due to keeping my mouth shut."

In the early 1850s, Armour left up-state New York to pan for gold in California. Returning briefly to his hometown of Stockbridge, New York, he then moved to Milwaukee and entered the soap business. When his soap factory burned down, the restless Armour picked up again, this time settling in the 1860s in Saint Paul, Minnesota, where he stayed for two years selling hides. Not quite satisfied, Armour returned to Milwaukee to form a partnership with packer John Plankinton. With the Civil War raging and fresh meat in demand, business prospered.

Following the war, the packing industry, which had been centered in Cleveland, shifted to Chicago. Sensing that it was a city on the move, Armour transferred his base of operations in 1875 from Milwaukee to the booming metropolis and shrewdly began manipulating the pork market, buying when the price was low and selling at a handsome profit. Thus, Armour made a quick fortune—reportedly as much as $6 million during a twelve-month span. He expanded further into grain shipping, adding to his already impressive empire. An inventive businessman, Armour canned meat and exported it to Europe and shipped fresh beef to the East in the newly invented refrigerated cars.

In the early days of the packing business, animal wastes were promptly discarded but Armour realized that by-products could actually bring in additional revenue. In this way, nothing—save the squeal of the pig, as he reportedly once said—would be wasted. Thus, the fat of the cattle was turned into lard, the intestines cleaned and salted and used for sausage casings, the blood and animal refuse converted into fertilizer.

By 1892 Armour could observe his empire from afar and boast of offices not only in Chicago but also in Omaha and Kansas City with twenty thousand people in his employ. Still looking for ways to diversify, he began manufacturing toilet soaps, violin strings, medicines, and hospital accessories.

Armour harbored little sympathy toward unions and even less toward strikers. "As long as we are heads of our own houses," said Armour, "we shall employ what men we choose, and when we can't, why we'll nail up our doors—that's all."

Armour was a creature of habit who rarely veered from his rigid schedule. He would rise each morning punctually at 5 a.m. to eat a hearty breakfast and would arrive at his office by 7 a.m. After a full day's work, he would leave at 6 p.m. and was ready to retire by 9 that evening in his Prairie Avenue mansion. A humorless man, he had no time—nor the patience—for pastimes or hobbies. "What interests can you suggest to me?" he once asked. "I do not read. I do not take part in politics. What can I do? Making money. It is my vocation and my avocation." It was not, however, the money itself that appealed to him. Rather it was "the getting of it," according to biographers Harper Leech and John Charles Carroll.

A devout churchgoer, Armour always found time to attend services at the Plymouth Congregational Church. One Sunday, the popular pastor, the Reverend Frank Gunsaulus, delivered a sermon with the provocative title "If I Had a Million Dollars," in which he looked to the future and pointed out that a city such as Chicago was in dire need of educated, well-trained employees. Gunsaulus's lecture apparently struck a nerve with Armour, because afterwards the old man confronted the minister. "Young man do you believe what you have just preached?" he reportedly asked. "I

do, or I would not have preached it," replied Gunsaulus. Convinced of his sincerity, Armour offered the clergyman one million dollars in return for "five years of your life." With a clasp of the hand, the deal was sealed. From such an encounter emerged the Armour Institute.

In 1940 the Armour Institute merged with the Lewis Institute to form the Illinois Institute of Technology. Ludwig Mies van der Rohe, the renowned architect and an instructor at the school, carved a modern campus along South State Street between 31st and 35th Streets on what were once slum lands. Today IIT is a major institution that continues to specialize in architecture, science, and engineering.

Armour died in January of 1901. He was sixty-eight.

See also: Ludwig Mies van der Rohe, Gustavus F. Swift

Further reading: Leech, Harper and John Charles Carroll. *Armour and His Times* (1938); Wade, Louise Carroll. *Chicago's Pride: The Stockyards, Packingtown, and Environs in the Nineteenth Century* (1987).

Louis Armstrong

Musician

born: August 4, 1901
New Orleans, Louisiana
died: July 6, 1971
New York, New York

Louis Daniel Armstrong was a great jazz trumpeter as well as a marvelous improviser who exerted a major influence on several generations of jazz musicians. By bringing New Orleans–style jazz to Chicago, the Louisiana native contributed greatly to the local jazz scene. Indeed, "Satchmo" helped make Chicago the jazz capital of the world.

Photograph reprinted with permission from the *Chicago Sun-Times.*

Armstrong grew up on the streets of New Orleans. He received his first cornet at thirteen at the Colored Waifs' Home for Boys where he had been sent for shooting a pistol into a New Year's Day parade. After his release eighteen months later, he worked at an assortment of jobs—coalman, milkman, ragpicker—until he formed a six-piece band. His first break came when he secured a six-month gig with Fate Marable's orchestra aboard the New Orleans excursion steamer, *Dixie Belle.*

In 1917 Armstrong's idol, the famous cornetist Joe "King" Oliver, left New Orleans and settled in Chicago. Armstrong replaced Oliver in the Kid Ory band back in New Orleans. In 1922 Oliver sent a telegram asking Armstrong to come to Chicago to join his Creole Jazz Band as the second cornetist at the Lincoln Gardens nightclub at 459 East 31st Street, formerly the Royal Gardens.

According to historian George D. Bushnell, Jr., Armstrong wasted no time and headed north. Arriving in Chicago late at night, he took a cab to the cafe. From the street corner he could hear the music. Standing there in the dark, he paused and wondered if he was good enough to join the band that consisted of Johnny Dodds on clarinet, Honore Dutrey on trombone, and Lil Hardin on piano. No one else seemed to harbor such thoughts, however.

In 1924 Armstrong joined Fletcher Henderson's orchestra at the Roseland Ballroom in New York but returned to Chicago the following year. In late 1925 he joined the Erskine Tate orchestra at the Vendome Theater at 31st and South State Streets, switching from cornet to trumpet. A few months later he played with Carroll Dickerson's orchestra at the Sunset Cabaret at 35th and Calumet Streets, where he was first billed as the "World's Greatest Trumpet Player." Enjoying much success, Armstrong gained enough confidence to form his own band, the Hot Five which later became the Hot Seven. Their records, now considered classics, were made with some of the best jazz musicians of the day—Earl Hines on piano, Kid Ory on trombone, Johnny Dodds on clarinet, Lil Hardin on piano, and Johnny St. Cyr on banjo. Armstrong's star—and reputation—soared.

Armstrong formed a new outfit in Chicago in 1931. By this time, though, no one city could claim his prodigious talent. He already belonged to the world. During the 1930s he toured Europe, headlining the London Palladium in 1932.

In 1935 Armstrong moved back to Chicago and was forced to give up the trumpet temporarily due to lip problems. In 1937 he underwent minor throat surgery at Chicago's Provident Hospital. In 1956 he made a sweeping tour of Europe and Africa, which was filmed and released as *Satchmo the Great.*

Some of Louis Armstrong's most popular recordings include "Shine," "Chinatown," "Potato Head Blues," "When It's Sleepy Time Down South," "I Can't Give You Anything But Love," and "Ain't Misbehavin'." His compositions include "Sister Kate" and "If We Never Meet Again." In addition, Armstrong appeared or contributed musically to more than thirty films including *Pennies from Heaven* (1936), *Cabin in the Sky* (1943), *The Glenn Miller Story* (1953), and *Hello Dolly* (1969).

By the mid-1920s jazz in Chicago had reached its peak. The best musicians who had paid their dues in Chicago were ready to try their luck in the "Big Apple." Armstrong left Chicago in the late 1920s as did several other prominent figures on the local scene, including the Creole jazz pianist Ferdinand "Jelly Roll" Morton and the wunderkind from Iowa, Bix Beiderbecke.

To much of the world, Louis Armstrong epitomized jazz. As a band leader, he played, sang, and acted as the genial host. He developed a whole school of jazz singing called "scat," in which nonsensical sounds and phrases are used instead of words. During the Depression years when Armstrong played the "black and tan" clubs (nightclubs frequented by both African-American and white patrons) of the Northern cities, his popularity in Europe soared. Throughout the forties and fifties Armstrong became known as the "goodwill ambassador" of the United States and was a top concert and nightclub draw well into the sixties.

Armstrong's repertoire changed little over the years. Rather than compete with the bebop musicians of the forties, he continued to perform the straight-ahead melodic jazz that had made him so popular.

Armstrong died in his sleep in his New York home in July of 1971.

See also: Earl Hines, Joe "King" Oliver

Further reading: Bushnell, George D., Jr. "When Jazz Came to Chicago," *Chicago History* (Spring 1971); Collier, James Lincoln. *Louis Armstrong: An American Genius* (1983); Jones, Max and John Chilton. *The Louis Armstrong Story, 1900–1971* (1971); Shapiro, Nat and Nat Hentoff, eds. *The Jazz Makers: Essays on the Greats of Jazz* (1957).

Jacob Arvey
⋈
Politician

born: November 3, 1895
Chicago, Illinois
died: August 25, 1977
Chicago, Illinois

For many years, this son of a Maxwell Street peddler was one of the most powerful and influential politicians in Illinois politics. Arvey attributed his success to simple hard work and the old political system of handing out favors. "Put people under obligation to you," he said. "Make them your friends."

Photograph reprinted with permission from the *Chicago Sun-Times.*

Jacob Meyer Arvey was a self-made man. A graduate of John Marshall Law School in Chicago, he was appointed assistant state's attorney in 1918 and later served as prosecutor to the municipal court.

In 1922 Arvey joined the regular Democratic organization as a precinct captain. That same year Ward Committeeman Mike Rosenberg ran for Sanitary District trustee and asked Arvey to manage his campaign. Rosenberg won and Arvey rapidly rose to prominence. In 1932 he was elected 24th Ward alderman in the predominantly Jewish North Lawndale neighborhood. Arvey held this position for the next eighteen years. Historian Michael Funchion described Arvey as "the most powerful Jewish ward leader in the city." During the 1932 presidential election, Chicago chose a Democratic leader, Franklin Delano Roosevelt, for the first time since 1892. It was also the year that another Chicago Jew, Henry Horner, won the governor's seat. Arvey and his army of patronage workers in the 24th Ward helped carry the day for the Democratic party in Illinois. Four years later, the 24th Ward came through again, which prompted Roosevelt to call it "the best Democratic ward in the country."

When World War II broke out, Arvey was serving as finance committee chairman in the city council. Despite his age, he requested a leave of absence from his law practice and resigned from his aldermanic post to enlist in the 33rd Infantry Division of the Illinois National Guard as a judge advocate. He passed the physical only after faking an eye examination ("I memorized the chart," he later admitted). Arvey served admirably in the South Pacific, attaining the rank of lieutenant colonel and was awarded the Bronze Star and the Legion of Merit.

He then returned to Chicago, planning to retire from politics, but he couldn't resist the offer to succeed Mayor Edward Kelly as chairman of the Cook County Democratic Committee.

An innovative party chairman, Arvey slated such reform candidates as Martin J. Kennelly for mayor; Paul H. Douglas, an economics professor at the University of Chicago and later an alderman from the 5th Ward, for U.S. senator; and Adlai E. Stevenson for Illinois governor. Such choices earned Arvey a national reputation as a savvy and shrewd leader.

Arvey's success also lay in his ability to turn a handicap into an advantage. In 1948, convinced that President Harry S. Truman—who had fallen in the polls—couldn't win reelection, he tried unsuccessfully to persuade war hero, Dwight D. Eisenhower, to head the Democratic ticket. Eisenhower ultimately rejected the offer and chose to join the Republican party. Although some leaders expressed misgivings about Truman's candidacy, Arvey, reconsidering, became convinced that Truman could be turned into a winner. The real turning point came when Truman agreed to recognize the state of Israel in March of 1948. Arvey then gave his full, unconditional support. That November the scrappy Missourian toppled Republican front-runner Gov. Thomas E. Dewey of New York in one of the biggest upsets in American presidential politics.

Similarly, Arvey's quietly effective, behind-the-scenes influence convinced Gov. Stevenson, the "reluctant candidate," to accept the Democratic nomination for president in 1952 in his ill-fated run against Eisenhower. Other Illinois candidates that Arvey slated for public office included Sidney Yates for congressman; Abraham Marovitz for federal court judge; Otto Kerner, Jr., for governor; and Michael Howlett for secretary of state.

His power waned after Mayor Richard J. Daley assumed office in 1955. As Democratic national committeeman, Arvey was little more than a figurehead. By 1960 Arvey disagreed with Daley over the national leadership of the Democratic party, favoring Adlai Stevenson's third attempt for the presidency over Daley's choice, a young senator from Massachusetts named John F. Kennedy.

Arvey continued to serve on the Chicago Park District board until 1967 and was an Illinois member of the Democratic National Committee until 1972. He devoted his last years primarily to various Jewish philanthropic causes, serving on the boards of the Friends of Tel Aviv University, Israel Bonds Committee, and the World Jewish Council.

"I made mistakes," the dapper gentleman from Maxwell Street would later say. "I made a lot of them. But they're mistakes of judgment and not of the heart. I can live with them."

Arvey died in 1977 at the age of eighty-one. At the time of his death, the long-time West Side resident was living at 2300 North Lincoln Park West.

See also: Richard J. Daley, Henry Horner, Edward J. Kelly, Otto Kerner, Jr. [appendix]

Further reading: Berkow, Ira. *Maxwell Street: Survival in a Bazaar* (1977); Biles, Roger. "Jacob M. Arvey, Kingmaker: The Nomination of Adlai E. Stevenson in 1952," *Chicago History* (Fall 1979); Fremon, David K. *Chicago Politics Ward By Ward* (1988); Mazur, Edward. "Jewish Chicago" in *Ethnic Chicago,* Melvin G. Holli and Peter d'A. Jones, eds. (1984); Rakove, Milton. *Don't Make No Waves—Don't Back No Losers: An Insider's Analysis of the Daley Machine* (1975); Rakove, Milton. *We Don't Want Nobody Nobody Sent: An Oral History of the Daley Years* (1979).

Barney Balaban

Theater Owner

born: June 8, 1887
Chicago, Illinois
died: March 7, 1971
Byram, Connecticut

Barney Balaban got his start in the movie business in 1908 when he and members of his family opened their own theater on the Near West Side. From such humble beginnings would grow the city's largest movie theater chain, Balaban and Katz.

Photograph courtesy of the Theatre Historical Society of America-Archives.

Balaban grew up in the Maxwell Street neighborhood. His parents, Russian-born Jews, operated a tiny grocery store there. He left school at the age of twelve and went to work to earn money for the family. He held down many jobs—office boy in a hotel grocery shop, messenger, and clerk in a cold storage company. To escape the numbing squalor of daily life, Balaban and his brothers would visit the Yiddish theaters and the run-down nickelodeons strung out along Halsted Street and elsewhere. They weren't much to look at—usually old storefronts converted into theaters—but for young Balaban and his siblings they offered precious hours of entertainment and magical flights of fancy into another, seemingly perfect, world.

Barney's brother Abe, or A. J., as he was known, had a fine voice and secured a job singing at the Kedzie Theater at Kedzie Avenue and Roosevelt Road. It was an enjoyable way to make some money, and around the Balaban household the extra dollars were always welcome. Enticed by the aura of wealth that stood within easy reach outside their door, the Balabans talked boldly about going into the movie business, perhaps even buying their own theater.

Together they scrimped and saved until they had accumulated the tidy sum of $750, approached the owner of the Kedzie, and offered to buy it. To their surprise, he agreed to sell. They cleaned it up and hired a violinist for one dollar a night. The rest they did themselves—running the theater, managing the box office, even performing.

It worked. Gradually the receipts rose, and the Balabans borrowed money to build another theater one block away. The Circle Theater opened in 1909, considered the finest in its day. The Balabans installed a pipe organ, hired a four-piece orchestra, and began booking the best vaudeville talent available—from Groucho Marx to Sophie Tucker.

The Balaban Brothers acquired more theaters, and their income grew. Before long, business was so good that Barney quit his full-time job at the storage company to devote all his energy to life in the theater.

In 1915 Balaban teamed up with another entrepreneur named Sam Katz, and together they made plans to build a deluxe theater. The Central Park Theater could boast velour seats, chandeliers, and murals. In addition to offering movies, it presented stage shows, musical acts, and dancing. More theaters followed, each one more extravagant than the last—the Riviera (modeled after the chapel of Versailles), the Granada, the Century, the Paradise, the State-Lake, the Roosevelt, and finally, in 1921, the Chicago.

Moviegoing at a B&K theater was a special experience. The biggest theaters had exceptionally large staffs—sometimes as many as thirty ushers, uniformed and white-gloved, in addition to janitors, stagehands, projectionists, candy girls, cashiers, and ticket takers.

The success of the B&K chain piqued the interest of the owners of Paramount Pictures, who admired Balaban's hands-on management style and efficient fiscal policies. Eventually the studio bought two-thirds of B&K stock for $13 million. Balaban became a member of the stockholders' protective committee, and, in 1936, he became chairman of the board. He was named president of Paramount one month later.

Balaban was an able administrator. When other studios faced financial ruin, Paramount stayed afloat, earning a reputation as one of the best-run companies in the industry. Whereas some called Balaban a financial wizard, others were less kind. Noted director Frank Capra once referred to him as "money-wise" but "art-foolish."

As early as 1948, Balaban warned that runaway production costs could imperil the future of the motion picture industry. Indeed, he had arrived at the unfounded conclusion that no movie could—no matter how big a hit—gross more than $3 million. Accordingly, no Paramount budget could exceed $1.5 million.

Balaban dictated all policy decisions, business and creative, from the initial story treatment to the final hiring of cast and crew. Anything above the allotted budget required his approval in writing.

Unfortunately, Balaban's taste in movies was rather pedestrian. Movies, he thought, perhaps remembering the old days on Maxwell Street, should be entertaining. He had originally rejected *The Lost Weekend* before Paramount executives convinced him otherwise. Ultimately Ray Milland won the Oscar for best actor in this 1945 classic. Balaban much preferred films like *Gulliver's Travels* and *The Ten Commandments*.

In 1967 Balaban was named honorary chairman of the board of Paramount, a title that he retained until his death in 1971. B&K changed its name to ABC-Great States in 1968 and, in 1974, to Plitt Theaters, which eventually sold its interest to the Toronto-based Cineplex Odeon.

An Orthodox Jew, Balaban was active in the Jewish community and made major charitable contributions to many organizations, especially the Westchester Jewish Center. Philip Bregstone, in *Chicago and Its Jews,* quotes Balaban as saying, "We Orthodox Jews have a duty to perform, an obligation to pay. In the early period of Jewish immigration most of our people came here poor and destitute. Now that many of us possess wealth it is time that we take up the responsibility ourselves, to build and maintain the charitable and philanthropic institutions and to create such others as modern American Jewry may require."

Balaban died of a heart attack in 1971 at age eighty-three in his idyllic Connecticut home, far removed from the crowded alleys and pungent aromas of his native Maxwell Street.

Further reading: Balaban, Carrie. *Continuous Performance: The Story of A. J. Balaban* (1964); Berkow, Ira. *Maxwell Street: Survival in a Bazaar* (1977); Bregstone, Philip P. *Chicago and Its Jews* (1933); Meites, Hyman L. *History of the Jews of Chicago* (1924); Sentinel Publishing Co. *The Sentinel's History of Chicago Jewry, 1911–1961* (1961).

Claude A. Barnett

News Service Owner

born: September 16, 1889
Sanford, Florida
died: August 2, 1967
Chicago, Illinois

*A prominent leader in the black community for many years, Claude Barnett founded the **Associated Negro Press** in 1919 when race riots and other violence against blacks filled the pages of the mainstream press. "After World War I, there was practically no news about Negroes except lynchings and tragedy. I wanted to change that," he said. During its heyday, the ANP—the black equivalent of UPI and AP—supplied news stories, features, essays, columns, poetry, book and record reviews, cartoons, and photographs to scores of black newspapers across the country.*

Photograph courtesy of the *Chicago Defender.*

Claude Barnett was born in Florida, the son of a hotel worker, but he was raised in Illinois, where he attended elementary schools both in downstate Mattoon and later in Chicago. In 1902 he attended Oak Park High School while working as a servant in the home of Richard W. Sears, cofounder of Sears, Roebuck, and Company. Two years later he went back South and enrolled at the influential Tuskegee Institute in Alabama, where he became profoundly influenced by the black self-help principles of Booker T. Washington.

After graduating, Barnett got a job at the post office in Chicago before establishing his own advertising agency. He later formed a chemical company that manufactured cosmetics. For a short time, he sold advertising space for the *Chicago Defender,* Chicago's premier black newspaper.

In 1919, lacking capital but imbued with a personal vision, Barnett contacted black editors, civic leaders, and businessmen with the idea of establishing a news service of, for, and by blacks. Barnett called it the Associated Negro Press. Its watchwords were "progress, loyalty, truth."

The response was so good that by the end of its first year ANP had eighty-eight subscribers. At its peak, it provided news to 150 black newspapers across the nation, reaching an estimated 2 million readers per week. In addition, Barnett maintained a Washington, D.C., bureau, employed correspondents in New York and Los Angeles, and utilized scores of volunteer stringers.

Barnett was always looking for a black success story. He profiled black entertainers, politicians, clergy, and athletes—anyone who projected a positive image. He also ran national news stories but covered them from a black perspective. Later on, he carried some of the first news reports from the African continent.

Barnett wore many hats during his lifetime. In addition to his ANP duties, he acted as a special assistant to the secretary of agriculture, and from 1938 to 1942 he served as president of the board of Provident Hospital.

In 1947 Barnett and his wife, singer and actress Etta Moten, made their first visit to Africa, a land he would come to love and admire. Over the years, they made many trips there, establishing strong ties with African leaders, clergy, editors, and businessmen. Barnett and Moten became experts in African art and culture, collecting and exhibiting African crafts and delivering speeches before civic, religious, and fraternal groups.

Barnett's work on behalf of the worldwide family of blacks did not go unnoticed. In 1949 his alma mater, Tuskegee Institute, awarded him an honorary doctor of humanities, and the governments of Haiti and Liberia honored him in a similar way.

For decades, ANP fulfilled a need that was sorely lacking in the African-American community. It provided a national forum in which black leaders could express their views directly to their constituencies, and, equally important, it gave black journalists an invaluable opportunity to develop their skills.

All of that changed during the 1960s when the white mainstream media increased their coverage of issues affecting the African-American community. By this time, Barnett was in poor health, and he had neither the strength nor the time to devote to the news service. When he retired in 1964, the ANP ceased operations. He died three years later.

Barnett built a major news-gathering operation from scratch. Not only did the Associated Negro Press document the achievements of African-Americans, it fostered pride and self-esteem in black communities throughout the United States.

See also: Robert S. Abbott

Further reading: Evans, Linda J. "Claude A. Barnett and the Associated Negro Press," in *Chicago History* (Spring 1983); Hogan, Lawrence D. *A Black National News Service: The Associated Negro Press and Claude Barnett, 1919–1940* (1984); Wolseley, Roland E. *The Black Press, U.S.A.* (1971).

Mary Bartelme

Judge

born: July 24, 1866
Chicago, Illinois
died: July 26, 1954
Carmel, California

As the first woman judge in Illinois history and the second in the nation, Mary Margaret Bartelme was a pioneer in the field of helping underprivileged children. Nicknamed "Suitcase Mary" for the practice she had of providing young ladies en route to foster homes with suitcases packed with clothes and other necessities, Bartelme set new standards for treating wayward girls. Her philosophy was simple: "There are no bad children. There are confused, neglected children, love-starved and resentful children, and what they need most I try to give them—understanding and a fresh start in the right direction."

Mary Bartelme first planned to enter the medical profession. A woman doctor, however, advised her to consider law and set up an appointment for her with Myra Bradwell, founder of the *Chicago Legal News.* "One visit to her and I was determined to take up the study of law," Bartelme recalled.

Bartelme taught in the Chicago public schools for five years then, defying convention, enrolled at the Northwestern University law school. She was admitted to the bar in 1894 and appointed Public Guardian of Cook County by Gov. John Tanner in 1897—a post she held for sixteen years. In 1913 she was assigned to the Juvenile Court to hear girls' cases as an assistant to Judge Merritt W. Pinckney.

In 1923, three years after women won the right to vote, Bartelme was asked to run for the office of judge of the Circuit Court. In an unusual display of camaraderie, women from all walks of life rallied around her and provided the necessary margin for her victory. Bartelme was supported by various women's organizations, several of which even staged rallies on her behalf. Male voters also supported her, since many felt that a woman was the ideal choice for offering guidance to wayward girls.

Bartelme was a special friend to troubled girls everywhere who, through no fault of their own (generally due to divorce, death, or a separation in the family), found themselves homeless and with no place to turn. "I believe that the young girls of Chicago and of all of Cook County are entitled to at least one judge who can deal with them in terms of real sympathy and understanding rather than in terms of legal lore and technicalities," she explained.

Her unorthodox beliefs attracted worldwide attention. Social workers from around the globe wanted to visit the judge who spoke so eloquently on behalf of the nation's have-nots. Strong emotions were often played out in Bartelme's courtroom. It was not unusual for youngsters as well as jurors to lose their composure. Bartelme was prepared. She always had an ample supply of handkerchiefs on hand.

Rather than see unfortunate youngsters spend a night in jail, Bartelme formed what came to be known as "Mary clubs": institutions without bars, where girls were "helped, encouraged, corrected, but not reformed." In 1914 she converted her own house to the first "Mary club." Some girls stayed for as little as six months, some for as long as a year, and others for several years. Most went on to lead productive lives.

In 1927 Bartelme was unanimously elected president of the Women's Bar Association of Illinois. That same year she served as fund-raising chairwoman for the Women's and Children's Hospital, later named Mary Thompson Hospital.

In 1933 Bartelme retired from the bench and moved to Carmel, California, where she died in 1954. Today, six Mary Bartelme Homes in Chicago, serving young girls from the ages of nine to eighteen, carry on her work.

See also: Myra Bradwell

Further reading: Inglehart, Babette, ed. *Walking with Women through Chicago History* (1981); Kogan, Herman. *The First Century: The Chicago Bar Association 1874–1974* (1974).

Mathias "Paddy" Bauler

Politician

born: January 27, 1890
Chicago, Illinois
died: August 20, 1977
Melrose Park, Illinois

The last of the saloon-keeping politicians, Mathias J. Bauler was a true Chicago "character," a flamboyant and brash alderman of the old school who gained international notoriety when he uttered the immortal words, "Chicago ain't ready for reform." For over thirty years he ruled the 43rd Ward on the city's North Side from the back room of a saloon. As "clown prince" of the city council, he was more renowned for his wild parties than for any contribution he made to the public sphere. Instead, he drank, caroused, and reveled his way into Chicago folklore.

Photograph reprinted with permission from the *Chicago Sun-Times.*

Bauler's parents owned a saloon, and Paddy—nobody called him Mathias—early on learned the joys of poker, pinochle, and pool. When he was old enough, Paddy worked behind the bar. During Prohibition, he ran a speakeasy at the corner of Willow and Howe Streets where Chicagoans could rub shoulders with entertainers, politicians, and socialites, including Rudy Vallee, Anton J. Cermak, and Edith Rockefeller McCormick. But Bauler also pursued a political career, beginning as a part-time timekeeper in the Cook County treasurer's office.

After an unsuccessful run for alderman in 1925, Paddy Bauler was finally elected to the city council in 1933. When Prohibition was repealed, Bauler opened a saloon, the De Luxe Gardens, on the corner of North Avenue and Sedgwick Street. Bauler's saloon was the scene of wrestling matches, ribald storytelling sessions, and late night victory parties. When a political victory was assured, Bauler would don a silk top hat and frock coat, twirl a cane, and croon the opening lines of "Chicago, Chicago, that Toddlin' Town." An avid traveler, he and his long-time pal, Alderman Charles Weber of the 45th Ward, would fly off to Munich, Vienna, Paris, Hong Kong—it didn't really matter where—and return with an armload of gifts for their cronies. "Who knows where he got the money?" Alderman Leon Despres asked. No one seemed to care.

Controversy followed the rambunctious alderman in 1933 when he was indicted and charged with assault during a scuffle involving a Chicago policeman. Bauler, who fired two shots into the officer, claimed the shooting was in self-defense. All charges were eventually dropped.

Bauler, who always believed that one favor deserved another, had no patience with reformers, referring to them as "political science kids."

According to him, the duties of an alderman were simple: collect the garbage, repair the streets, and clean the sidewalks, and the citizenry will show their appreciation with their votes. The people, he said, want service, not reform.

Chicago has seen many dirty campaigns in its time, but one of the dirtiest occurred in 1939 when Bauler campaigned against Republican James B. Waller. Bauler was declared the winner in the April run-off by a scant 243 votes. Waller cried foul and listed a litany of transgressions, including bribery, fraud, and intimidation of voters. He demanded a recount. Bauler's colleagues in the city council thought otherwise and dismissed the plea by a vote of 37 to 6. "It was a victory for the people," beamed Bauler.

By the time Bauler stepped down from his aldermanic post in 1967, he was an anachronism, the last in a long list of colorful saloon-keeper–politicians such as Michael "Hinky Dink" Kenna.

During his later years, Bauler spent some time in New Mexico. In 1976 he returned to Chicago and moved into a high-rise retirement facility in Northlake. He suffered a stroke, apparently triggered by an earlier car accident in Santa Fe, New Mexico, and he died in August of 1977 at the age of eighty-seven in Melrose Park.

See also: John Coughlin, Michael Kenna

L. Frank Baum

Author

born: May 15, 1856
Chittenango, New York
died: May 6, 1919
Hollywood, California

*Lyman Frank Baum created the American children's classic, **The Wizard of Oz**. A prolific writer, Baum wrote adventure novels, fantasies, and some fourteen books about the magical land of Oz.*

The son of a Scots-Irish mother and a German-American father, Baum's childhood was spent in comparative luxury at his father's estate, near Syracuse, New York. Privately tutored, he briefly attended Peekskill Military Academy in New York.

Baum became a cub reporter for the *New York World* at seventeen. Two years later he opened his own printing shop in Bradford, Pennsylvania, where he established a newspaper called the *New Era*. For a while he managed a small chain of opera houses in New York and Pennsylvania, and one time he even acted with a traveling stock company.

Baum, a friendly and outgoing man, enjoyed telling stories to his children. Soon he began writing down Mother Goose rhymes. In 1877 a collection of these stories called *Mother Goose in Prose* was published by the Chicago firm Way and Williams with illustrations by Maxfield Parrish.

In 1881 Baum wrote an Irish musical comedy. *The Maid of Arran* enjoyed a respectable run in New York but didn't provide enough to live on. Baum then settled in Syracuse and established a small company that manufactured "Baum's Castorine," used for greasing axles. In the meantime, he wrote three more Irish melodramas: *Matches, Kilmourne,* and *The Queen of Killarney.* Only the first two were produced.

In 1887 Baum moved his family to Aberdeen, South Dakota, where he ran a general store, Baum's Bazaar, and published a weekly newspaper, the *Aberdeen Saturday Pioneer.* In 1891 the peripatetic writer moved to Chicago and found work as a reporter on the *Chicago Post.* He then worked as a salesman traveling throughout the Midwest selling china and glassware for a Chicago importing company. In 1897 he resumed his journalism career when he founded the *Show Window,* a monthly magazine for window trimmers. The following year he published, set the type, and printed in his own workshop another collection of children's stories, *By the Candelabra's Glare.*

Next, Baum composed a satire of the women's suffrage movement called *The Land of Oz.* In 1899 he wrote *Father Goose, His Book,* which was illustrated by Chicago cartoonist William Wallace Denslow and hand-lettered by Ralph Fletcher Seymour, another local artist. It sold well.

The turn of the century was a busy year for Baum. He wrote four children's books: *The Army Alphabet; The Navy Alphabet;* a fantasy called *A New Wonderland,* set in the beautiful valley of Phunnyland where it snowed popcorn and rained lemonade "and the thunder is usually a chorus from the opera of *Tannhauser*"; and *The Wonderful Wizard of Oz,* which he wrote in the summer of 1900 while living at what is now 1667 Humboldt Boulevard, on the city's Northwest Side. It was issued by George M. Hill, the small Chicago house that published *Father Goose.*

The Emerald City of Oz, the sixth in the series, reflected Baum's love of Ireland. It was a place where there was no illness or disease, where no one grew old, where animals could talk, where there were no rich, no poor, and was no need for money. There was no sickness, poverty, or death in Oz.

Initially Baum had great difficulty finding a publisher. Indeed, *The Wizard of Oz* was turned down by most of the local houses because, said Baum's wife, it was "too different, too radical." Hill agreed to distribute the book but Baum and Denslow shouldered all the printing expenses. By the end of the year, the adventures of Dorothy Gale from Kansas, who was blown into Oz by a twister, had become the fastest selling children's book in the country, and by 1902 it had sold five million copies.

Baum gave up his trade journal work to devote full time to creative writing. Collaborating with fellow Chicagoans Paul Tietjens, who wrote the music, and William Wallace Denslow, who designed the costumes, Baum wrote the book and lyrics to the musical, *The Life and Adventures of Santa Claus.*

Due to public demand, Baum returned to the Oz books. In 1903 he wrote *Enchanted Island of Yew* and in 1904, *The Marvelous Land of Oz.* Other books in the Oz series were *Ozma of Oz* (1907), *Dorothy and the Wizard in Oz* (1908), *The Road to Oz* (1909), *The Emerald City of Oz* (1910), and *The Patchwork Girl of Oz* (1913).

A prolific writer, Baum also wrote several adult novels (under the pseudonym Schuyler Staunton), two boys' adventure books, six novels about young fortune hunters, seventeen novels for teenage girls (under the pseudonym Edith Van Dyne), and six books of fantasy using the name Laura Bancroft.

In 1909 Baum moved to Los Angeles. Several years later, his musical, *The Tik-Tok Man of Oz,* opened. It enjoyed profitable runs in San Francisco and Chicago.

In 1914 Baum formed the Oz Film Manufacturing Company in order to produce movie versions of his fantasies. Five films were completed: *The Patchwork Girl of Oz, His Majesty the Scarecrow of Oz, The Magic Cloak, The Last Egyptian,* and *The Gray Nun of Belgium.*

In 1910 *The Wizard of Oz* was shot as a one-reeler by Chicago-based Selig Pictures, and, in 1925, a silent version starring Oliver Hardy as the tin man was released. The film version that is indeliby etched in the national consciousness is, of course, the MGM musical of 1939 starring a young Judy Garland as the lost Dorothy. Ironically, it was a commercial dud. Only later did it become the children's classic that we all know so well.

During his last years, Baum wrote *The Tin Woodman of Oz, The Magic of Oz,* and *Glenda of Oz. The Royal Book of Oz* was released posthumously.

Baum died in his Hollywood home, which he had named appropriately enough "Ozcot," in May of 1919, a week short of his sixty-third birthday.

In 1976 a local bookseller John Lenhardt proposed naming a North Side park under construction at Webster Avenue and Larrabee Street after the mythical land of Oz. Today Oz Park serves as the city's tribute to the man and his fantasy.

Further reading: Baum, Frank Joslyn and Russell P. MacFall. *To Please A Child: A Biography of L. Frank Baum* (1961); Gardner, Martin and Russel B. Nye. *The Wizard of Oz and Who He Was* (1957); Manguel, Alberto and Gianni Guadalupi. *The Dictionary of Imaginary Places* (1987).

John Belushi

Comedian/Actor

born: January 24, 1949
Chicago, Illinois
died: March 5, 1982
Los Angeles, California

John Belushi clowned his way through Chicago's Second City, the legendary Old Town comedy improvisation club and spent several sparkling seasons on NBC-TV's "Saturday Night Live" until attaining movie stardom at a relatively young age. Critics praised Belushi as a marvelous physical comedian who was also capable of great tenderness. He combined a robust blend of irreverent humor with a good-natured machismo filtered through a Midwestern sensibility. Belushi was a shooting star. He shone brightly for a few good years, and then he was gone.

Photograph reprinted with permission from the *Chicago Sun-Times.*

Born in Chicago but reared in west suburban Wheaton, Belushi was the son of Albanian immigrants. At Wheaton Central High he won praise as an outstanding athlete in football, wrestling, track, and baseball. He sang in the school choir and played drums in a rock band called the Ravins. Belushi, who attended several colleges in Illinois and Wisconsin, began his acting career performing in summer stock, including a part in *Anne of the Thousand Days,* in which he played Cardinal Wolsey.

Belushi then formed, along with two friends, Steve Beshekas and Tino Insana, a comedy group called the West Compass Players. In 1970, after graduating with an associate of arts degree from the College of DuPage, Belushi enrolled at the University of Illinois at Chicago and found an apartment on Taylor Street. Belushi, Insana, and Beshekas opened a coffeehouse in 1970 in the basement of the Universal Life Coffee House, one block from campus. This became the new home of the West Compass Players. Belushi wrote, directed, and starred in wickedly satirical skits. He auditioned for Second City and, in 1970, joined the cast.

Belushi was a popular member of the critically acclaimed troupe. His devastatingly funny and deadly accurate impressions of Mayor Richard J. Daley won favor. "You did eight performances a week," Belushi once remarked, "so you didn't have to get desperate . . . you learned to write on your feet."

In 1972 Belushi appeared in National Lampoon's *Lemmings* in New York. He wrote, directed, and performed in the "National Lampoon Radio Hour," a nationally syndicated FM radio program. In 1975 Belushi joined the cast of "Saturday Night Live," the ground-breaking NBC television show that revolutionized late-night programming.

SNL brought the Wheaton native fame and fortune. Among his most famous characterizations were a killer bee, a Samurai warrior, an imitation of rock musician Joe Cocker, and a waiter in a Greek diner—inspired by Chicago's Billy Goat Tavern—who constantly shouted "cheezborga, cheezborga!" Belushi and his colleague and best friend, Dan Aykroyd, left SNL in September of 1979.

Belushi scored a hit with his first motion picture, the frat house comedy, *National Lampoon's Animal House* (1978). The manic antics of "Bluto" Blutarsky grossed nearly $80 million. In *The Blues Brothers* (1980), another smash, Belushi and Aykroyd played their alter egos, Jake and Elwood Blues, two blues musicians on a "mission from God." In addition to the wildly successful movie, the Blues Brothers also spawned a hit album, *Briefcase Full of Blues* and a hit single, a rendition of Sam and Dave's "Hold On (I'm Comin')."

In *Continental Divide* (1981), Belushi played a gruff Chicago newspaper columnist reportedly modeled after Mike Royko. His last film, *Neighbors,* was released in December of 1981. Other Belushi films include *Goin' South, Old Boyfriends,* and *1941.*

A self-proclaimed "party animal," the beefy actor lived a life of excess. He overdosed on heroin and cocaine in March of 1982 at a Los Angeles hotel. He was buried on Martha's Vineyard, Massachusetts. At the time of his death, the thiry-three-year-old actor was learning a role for a Paramount picture, *Noble Rot.*

In 1989 the motion picture, *Wired,* based on Bob Woodward's best-selling biography of the same name, was released to largely disastrous reviews.

Further reading: Sweet, Jeffrey. *Something Wonderful Right Away* (1986); Woodward, Bob. *Wired: The Short Life and Fast Times of John Belushi* (1984).

Bruno Bettelheim

Psychologist

born: August 28, 1903
Vienna, Austria
died: March 13, 1990
Silver Spring, Maryland

"Most people don't really want children, they want little adults," the noted psychologist and child therapist Bruno Bettelheim once observed.

Born in Vienna, Bettelheim took over his family's lumber business after his father died, and at the same time he studied psychology under Sigmund Freud. He became interested in a then little-known disorder called autism, which at that time was considered incurable. In 1932 he welcomed an autistic child into his home. Bettelheim was convinced that, given the proper environment and support, an autistic child could learn to develop.

Bettelheim graduated from the Reform Realgymnasium in 1921 and received his doctorate degree from the University of Vienna in 1938. During World War II he was imprisoned in the Nazi concentration camps at Dachau and Buchenwald. Upon his release, he emigrated to the United States and became a researcher in progressive education at the University of Chicago until 1942. Then he transferred to Rockford College in Illinois as an associate professor of psychology.

Bettelheim gained international recognition in 1943 with his article, "Individual and Mass Behavior in Extreme Situations" in the *Journal of Abnormal and Social Psychology*. He based this article partly on his own experiences in the German concentration camps. The proper amount of tyranny, he wrote, produced complacency and conformity.

Bettelheim returned to the University of Chicago in 1944 and became a full professor in 1952. In 1944 he accepted the directorship of the Sonia Shankman Orthogenic School, a residential institution for the severely handicapped and part of the University of Chicago. He insisted that mentally ill children should be treated with respect and dignity. Bettelheim replaced drugs and shock treatment with ample doses of love, patience, and compassion. Still a strict disciplinarian, however, he refused to coddle the children. Instead, he attempted to create an environment as close to normal conditions as possible. He was rough on his students. "His class was a form of puberty rite," recalled one former student. "It was a terrifying experience, like climbing Mt. Everest."

In *The Uses of Enchantment: The Meaning and Importance of Fairy Tales* (1976), which won a National Book Award and a National Book Critics Circle Award, Bettelheim argued that fairy tales were an important component in the development of children. A love of fantasy, the psychologist held, is a child's way of coping and handling stress.

Bettelheim achieved his greatest success in treating autistic children, and many of his principles were adopted by psychologists throughout the world. By the time of his death at the age of eighty-six, however, an entirely different picture began to emerge.

In March of 1990 Bettelheim took his own life in a Maryland nursing home. In the weeks and months following his death, Bettelheim's methods—indeed his very career—came under attack from former students, patients, and staff members. Among his alleged transgressions are public humiliation, sexual degradation, and brutal beatings. The final verdict on the life and work of Bruno Bettelheim has yet to be rendered.

A prolific writer, among his many books were: *Dynamics of Prejudice* (1950), *Love Is Not Enough* (1950), *Truants From Life* (1954), *Symbolic Wounds: Puberty Rites and the Envious Male* (1954), *The Informed Heart* (1960), *The Children of the Dream* (1962), and *The Empty Fortress* (1967). In addition, he wrote many articles for both academic journals and mass circulation publications.

Frank Billings

Physician

born: April 2, 1854
Highland, Wisconsin
died: September 20, 1932
Chicago, Illinois

A noted physician, Dr. Frank Billings counted among his patients some of the leading citizens of Chicago. More importantly, Billings pioneered the study of medicine in the city with his greatest gift to medical education—the Medical School of the University of Chicago.

In 1832 Henry M. Billings migrated from New York State to southwestern Wisconsin, settling in Mineral Point and, with a partner, opened a general store. Frank Billings was born on farmland near Mineral Point. His father died in an accident when the boy was eight. Billings briefly taught in a country school before teaching at a public school for two years.

In 1878 Billings enrolled at the Chicago Medical College, which later merged with Northwestern University. In 1881 he graduated with a degree of Doctor of Medicine. Billings completed his internship at Cook County Hospital and joined the Chicago Medical Club, whose purposes were "the promotion of good fellowship, harmony, and unity among the members, the advancement of medical science, and the maintenance of high professional standards."

After three years of medical practice and teaching anatomy in Chicago, Billings went to Vienna in 1885 for a year of postgraduate study. He also attended lectures in London and Paris. It was in Paris where he met the great scientist Louis Pasteur.

In 1886 Billings returned to Chicago to resume his career. Before long he decided to restrict his practice to general medicine and some consulting work only.

In 1888 Billings joined the attending staff at Mercy Hospital, and he established a practice on the North Side where business flourished. As his reputation spread, he began to attract some of the city's wealthiest clientele, including many along posh Prairie Avenue. The meatpacker, Philip Danforth Armour, was one of his patients, as were George Pullman, Marshall Field, W. W. Kimball, the McCormicks, and the Palmers.

Billings served on the faculty of the Chicago Medical College as a professor of physical diagnosis from 1886 to 1891 and then as professor of medicine from 1891 to 1898. He was also attending physician at St. Luke's Hospital.

In 1898 Billings was appointed professor of medicine at Rush Medical College on the West Side. Billings then met with William Rainey Harper, the president of the University of Chicago to discuss a possible affiliation between Rush and the university. That year the two institutions agreed to merge. The new school, the Medical School of the University of Chicago, offered advance training in medical research, including anatomy, physiology, and biochemistry.

Billings was appointed professor of medicine at the school and served as dean until 1920. Among its distinguished faculty were surgeons Nicholas Senn and Christian Fenger. Billings also acted as chief physician at the Presbyterian Hospital for many years. Under his tutelage, both institutions earned a reputation as first-class centers for teaching, training, and research.

In 1917 Billings joined the medical corps of the Armed Forces at the age of sixty-three and was appointed chairman of the Red Cross Commission to Russia. In December 1921, he was promoted to Brigadier General in the Medical Officers' Reserve Corps of the United States Army.

Due to Billing's influence, the McCormick Institute for Infectious Diseases, which was located at 637 South Wood Street, was established by Harold F. and Edith Rockefeller McCormick. In addition, he fought for better quality health care at Cook County Hospital and helped improve the conditions of state mental institutions. He edited the second edition of the five-volume set, *Therapeusis of Internal Diseases* (1914) and, with collaborators, edited the *General Medicine of the Practical Medicine* series (1901–21).

In 1924 Billings retired from active teaching but was appointed professor Emeritus of Medicine at the University of Chicago. "The main contributions of medical science in the past may be said to have been made to youth in the prevention of infant mortality and in the victory over diseases to which children are susceptible," he said in 1929. "The next step is to aid adults in battling their physical enemies."

Billings slipped on a rug in his North Side home at 1550 North State Parkway and suffered severe internal bleeding. He died in September of 1932 at age seventy-eight.

Today four institutions comprise the University of Chicago hospitals: the Bernard Mitchell Hospital, Billings Hospital, the Chicago Lying-In Hospital, and Wyler Children's Hospital.

See also: Morris Fishbein, William Rainey Harper, Mary Harris Thompson

Further reading: Bonner, Thomas Neville. *Medicine in Chicago 1850–1950, A Chapter in the Social and Scientific Development of a City* (1957); Hirsch, Edwin F. *Frank Billings: The Architect of Medical Education, an Apostle of Excellence in Clinical Practice, a Leader in Chicago Medicine* (1966).

Jesse Binga

Banker/Realtor

born: April 10, 1865
Detroit, Michigan
died: June 13, 1950
Chicago, Illinois

Chicago's leading African-American businessman during the 1920s, Jesse Binga was also a successful real estate agent and banker and one of the city's wealthiest African-Americans. Binga symbolized a new type of black leader. His fortune came not from sports or entertainment—the typical route to African-American success—but from the business class.

Photograph reprinted with permission from the Urban Research Institute.

Born in Detroit, Binga was the youngest of ten children. After high school he studied law for two years in the office of attorney Thomas Crisup. Restless, Binga left in 1885 and wandered west as an itinerant barber. After working as a porter on the Union Pacific, he invested in real estate in Pocatello, Idaho. It proved a lucrative deal. In 1896 Binga returned to Chicago, and with a capital of only $10 he established a real estate business at 3331 South State Street in the heart of the city's "Black Belt." (During the early years of this century, most African-Americans resided in a densely populated strip on the South Side from 16th Street to 39th Street.) In 1908 Binga established the Binga Bank, the first African-American–owned bank in the city and the financial rock of the black community. In 1920 it became a state bank.

Proud, shrewd, and somewhat of a braggart, Binga was a controversial figure. Some called him a crook and an opportunist who used people whenever he had the chance. Others said he was simply an innovative businessman who wasn't afraid to take risks. A South Side booster and philanthropist, Binga helped scores of African-American families acquire homes in the burgeoning Black Belt.

In 1912 Binga married Eudora Johnson, the sister of the notorious gambling overlord, John "Mushmouth" Johnson. She had inherited $200,000 from her brother before the marriage. The match boosted Binga's social standing and income significantly.

In 1929 he built the Binga Arcade on the northwest corner of 35th and State Streets. The Arcade was a five-story building that included office space and a dance hall on the roof. That same year Binga became chairman of a successful insurance company.

Racial tensions flared during the summer of 1919 as African-Americans left the "Black Belt" and settled into the predominantly white neighborhoods of Kenwood and Hyde Park. Binga, who lived at 5922 South Parkway (now King Drive) and rented apartments to blacks in the area, received his share of attacks. His home and office, according to historian Allan H. Spear, were bombed seven times.

The Depression hit Binga and the African-American community particularly hard. On July 31, 1930, Binga's bank was shut down by the state examiner. Many members of Chicago's black community lost their savings and their hope. The bank, notes Spear, stood as a role model for a new confident generation of enterprising black businessmen. The collapse of the bank shattered the dream of black empowerment.

Binga was convicted in 1933 of embezzling $22,000 from the bank and sentenced to ten years in the Illinois State Penitentiary in Joliet. Many felt he was too harshly treated and requested leniency. Petitions from prominent men and women, including attorney Clarence Darrow, circulated calling for an early release in recognition of Binga's considerable contributions to the African-American community. Released in 1938, the once prominent citizen found work as a lowly handyman in a Catholic Church. He died penniless in June 1950 in St. Luke's Hospital. He was buried in Oakwood Cemetery.

Further reading: Commission on Chicago Historical and Architectural Landmarks. *Black Metropolis Historic District* (March 7, 1984); Logan, Rayford W. and Michael R. Winston, eds. *Dictionary of American Negro Biography* (1982); Spear, Allan H. *Black Chicago: The Making of the Negro Ghetto, 1890–1920* (1967); Travis, Dempsey J. *An Autobiography of Black Chicago* (1981).

Louise DeKoven Bowen

Social Reformer

born: February 26, 1859
Chicago, Illinois
died: November 9, 1953
Chicago, Illinois

As a child of privilege, Louise DeKoven Bowen could have had anything she wanted. Vast wealth and an easy, trouble-free existence were hers if she so desired. But Bowen was different. Imbued with a fierce social conscience and boundless energy, she chose instead to devote her life to helping the needy. As president of the Juvenile Protective Association, treasurer of Hull-House, and vice-president of the United Charities, she wielded great influence on social welfare programs in Chicago for almost sixty years.

Bowen was a member of many philanthropic, civic, and social organizations and was a leading figure in the woman's suffrage movement. Furthermore, she was instrumental in the formation of the Juvenile, Boys', and Domestic Relations courts. She was a founding member of the Visiting Nurses of Chicago and one of the organizers of the Woman's Board of Passavant Hospital.

Louise DeKoven was born at Wabash Avenue and Monroe Street, the only child of a wealthy Chicago pioneer family. She graduated from the Dearborn Seminary in 1875. As a young woman, DeKoven led a sheltered life. In her memoirs, *Growing up with a City* (1926), she recalled that: "The church . . . was the only outlet for social work."

Following her marriage in 1886 to Joseph T. Bowen, a successful financier and banker, Louise Bowen played the role of a socialite. But unlike other women in her position, she used her power and wealth to help those in need. She was greatly influenced by social reformer Jane Addams. During the 1890s Bowen and others brought about a statute establishing the first juvenile court in Chicago. When she became president of the Juvenile Court Committee, she convinced the city to erect a juvenile court building and a detention home.

In 1907 the Juvenile Court Committee became the Juvenile Protective Association whose function, said Bowen, was "to keep children out of the court by removing many of the demoralizing conditions which surrounded them." In many ways she was ahead of her time. For example, she advocated stronger punishment for rape offenders and proposed that couples be required to have a medical certificate when applying for a marriage license. Bowen was also an early advocate of improving the lives of African-Americans in Chicago.

In 1912, in memory of her late husband, she established the Bowen Country Club, a seventy-two acre summer camp near Waukegan, Illinois, for the underprivileged children of the Hull-House neighborhood.

Bowen was a leading figure in the cause for woman's suffrage. Not only was she president of the Chicago Equal Suffrage Association, she also acted as vice-president of the Illinois Equal Suffrage Association and served as auditor of the National American Woman Suffrage Association. In June of 1916 she led a march of five thousand women carrying placards that demanded votes for women. They marched on the Republican National Convention being held at the Coliseum in Chicago.

Bowen also championed improvements in women's working conditions and in the welfare of children and promoted efficiency and honesty in government.

At the time of her death, at the age of ninety-four, Bowen was still active in local affairs. She was the honorary president of Hull-House, of the Juvenile Protective association, and of the Woman's City Club.

In 1941 the Rotary Club of Chicago awarded her its gold medal for distinguished service, the first woman ever honored with this award.

See also: Jane Addams, Mary Bartelme

Further reading: Alter, Sharon Z. "A Woman for Mayor?" *Chicago History* (Fall 1986); Beadle, Muriel. *The Fortnightly of Chicago: The City and Its Women, 1873–1973* (1973); Bowen, Louise DeKoven. *Open Windows: Stories of People and Places* (1946); Bowen, Louise DeKoven. *Growing up with a City* (1962).

Preston Bradley

Minister

born: August 18, 1888
Linden, Michigan
died: June 1, 1983
Morrisville, Vermont

Author, columnist, and broadcaster, Preston Bradley served as pastor of the Peoples Church of Chicago at 941 West Lawrence Avenue in the Uptown neighborhood for sixty-five years. With his velvet baritone and unorthodox viewpoints, Bradley stood out from the crowd—he frequently departed from traditional Christian teaching—and indeed proved to be possibly the most controversial clergyman in Chicago history.

Photograph reprinted with permission from the *Chicago Sun-Times.*

Bradley's father was from County Antrim, Northern Ireland, and his mother was of English descent. Both were Presbyterian, and both believed that Christianity brought joy and cheer into the world. In their eyes, religion celebrated the spiritual and the earthly, the sacred and the profane. In his autobiography, Bradley admits that he cannot remember the time when he did not want to be a preacher—or an actor. "There's a little bit of the actor in every preacher, of course," he wrote.

Bradley attended Alma College in Alma, Michigan. After one year, he dropped out and studied law in Flint, Michigan. Inspired by a biography of evangelist Dwight Moody, he decided to move to Chicago to enroll at the Moody Bible Institute. In 1912 Bradley was ordained as a Presbyterian minister and installed as pastor of the Church of Providence on the North Side. At the same time, he enrolled at Hamilton College of Law. Later he received his doctor of laws degree from Lake Forest College and, in 1939, received his Doctor of Divinity from Meadville Theological Seminary.

"I am not orthodox about anything," he once remarked during a sermon in 1912. "I am thoroughly, completely, adequately, gloriously, and triumphantly a heretic." Charged with heresy for preaching that baptism is not a prerequisite for salvation, Bradley resigned and founded his own congregation, the Peoples Church of Chicago.

The Peoples Church was a progressive institution. From the day it opened its doors, it welcomed Chicagoans of all races, creeds, and nationalities. Bradley, a religious maverick, defied orthodox religion of any kind. Each Sunday he presided over a growing congregation of followers who were attracted by his provocative opinions, stirring speeches, and unconventional attitude toward established religion. Unlike most clergy, Bradley was not afraid to take a stand on controversial issues.

In 1923 Bradley became a Unitarian and the Peoples Church was accepted into the American Unitarian Association. The church, which remained nonsectarian, retained its unusual character. At its peak, the Peoples Church boasted a membership of four thousand people.

Bradley did not separate politics from religion. He believed that it was the duty of the clergy to become involved in political affairs, to be knowledgeable, and to express an opinion. He advocated birth control, for example, when only the most radical thinkers would venture such an opinion. In 1919 he marched with Jane Addams in a women's suffrage parade, spoke out against the Ku Klux Klan during the 1920s, defended the leftist policies of Roosevelt's New Deal in the 1930s, and during World War II spoke out against Hitler and the growing anti-Semitism that was spreading throughout the world. Bradley's followers urged him to enter politics and run for mayor. He declined.

The Peoples Church was the first in Chicago to broadcast regular services across the radio. Bradley acted as senior pastor at the church until 1968 and continued his weekly radio show until 1976 when failing health forced him to resign. A prolific writer, among his many books are *Courage for Today* (1934), *Mastering Fear* (1935), *Power from Right Thinking* (1936), *Life and You* (1940), *New Wealth for You* (1941), *Meditations* (1941), *My Daily Strength* (1943), *Happiness through Creative Living* (1955), and *Between You and Me* (1967). He also edited *Liberalist* magazine.

Bradley was also founder and president of the Izaak Walton League, a conservationists' club, and a charter member of the Chicago Human Relations Commission. Further, he served on the board of the Chicago Public Library for more than half a century. In 1962 the Chicago City Council awarded him its award of merit for distinguished service to the community.

Bradley died in June of 1983 at the age of ninety-four in a Vermont nursing home.

Today the Peoples Church continues to serve the diverse population of the Uptown community with social service programs, lectures, and consultation.

See also: Dwight L. Moody, David Swing, Billy Sunday

Further reading: Bradley, Preston with Harry Barnard. *Along the Way: An Autobiography* (1962).

Myra Bradwell

Legal Reformer

born: circa 1831
Manchester, Vermont
died: February 14, 1894
Chicago, Illinois

Although she never practiced law, Myra Bradwell was an articulate and passionate crusader for legal and other types of reform. As founder of the weekly **Chicago Legal News,** *Bradwell worked vigorously to improve the reputation of the legal profession and to encourage the highest standard of professionalism.*

Born Myra Colby in Vermont, Bradwell moved with her family to western New York State as a child. When she was twelve, the family settled in Chicago. She was educated in Kenosha, Wisconsin, and at the Ladies Seminary in Elgin, Illinois, eventually becoming a teacher at the latter institution. She also taught in the Memphis, Tennessee, school system before returning to Chicago. During the Civil War years, Bradwell raised funds for wounded soldiers and their widows and children by arranging and managing fairs.

In 1852 she married James B. Bradwell, a prominent member of the Illinois bar, and studied law in order to help her husband further his career. She, too, wished to practice law but because she was a married woman, her admission to the bar was refused by both the supreme court of Illinois as well as the United States Supreme Court. The nation's highest court held that "the peculiar qualities of womanhood, its gentle graces, its tender susceptibility, its purity, its delicacy, its emotional impulses, its subordination of hard reason to sympathetic feeling are surely not qualifications for forensic strife. Nature has tempered woman as little for judicial conflicts of the courtroom as for the physical conflicts of the battlefield. Woman is moulded for gentler and better things. The judges declared that a woman, especially a married woman, did not belong in a court of law because the "married condition" amounted to a "disability" that would somehow prevent a woman from maintaining the proper client confidentiality, according to historian Charlotte Adelman.

As a result of Bradwell's pioneering efforts, a woman—Alta Hulett—was finally admitted to the Illinois bar in 1873. Ironically, Bradwell had to wait more than fifteen years before the Illinois Supreme Court finally granted her a license in 1890. Due to poor health, however, she never actually practiced law.

Bradwell was the first woman in the U.S. to apply for admission to the bar, the first woman to become a member of the Illinois Press Association, and, according to contemporary newspaper accounts, the first woman to become a member of the Chicago Bar Association. In 1868 she established the *Chicago Legal News,* a newspaper intended for "every lawyer and businessman in the Northwest." The paper published a summary of cases heard in various U.S. courts as well as legal information and news items. Her constant attempts to further the legal profession inspired a group of men to found the Chicago Bar Association. Bradwell welcomed the new group and encouraged any organization that would elevate the standards of her calling and rid the profession of the "disreputable shysters."

An ardent feminist, Bradwell campaigned for women's suffrage and helped establish the Midwest's first women's suffrage convention in 1869.

Bradwell was one of the founders of the Illinois Industrial School for Girls and one of the first women to suggest an official Women's Department at the World's Columbian Exposition in Chicago in 1893.

The temper of the times changed gradually as did the conservative mindset of the male-dominated courts. In 1890 the Illinois Supreme Court granted Bradwell a license and, in 1892, the United States Supreme Court admitted her to the Illinois bar.

Other significant changes in the judicial system soon followed, notes historian Adelman. In 1894 the first African-American woman, Ida Platt, was admitted to the Illinois bar. During the next few decades great strides were made in the women's movement. In 1914 the Women's Bar Association of Illinois (WBAI) was formed and, in 1919, Illinois became the first state to ratify the Nineteenth Amendment, which granted women the right to vote. Finally, in 1939, Governor Henry Horner signed a bill that gave women the right to sit on Illinois juries.

Bradwell died in February of 1894 in Chicago at the age of sixty-three.

See also: Mary Bartelme, Henry Horner

Further reading: Adelman, Charlotte. "A History of Women Lawyers in Illinois," *Illinois Bar Journal* (May 1986); Kogan, Herman. *The First Century: The Chicago Bar Association, 1874–1974* (1974).

James H. Breasted

Archaeologist

born: August 27, 1865
Rockford, Illinois
died: December 2, 1935
New York, New York

A brilliant scholar of Egyptology, James Henry Breasted held the first chair of Egyptology in the United States. He was professor of Egyptology and Oriental History at the University of Chicago from 1894 to 1925 and founded the Oriental Institute Museum in 1919.

The second child of Charles and Harriet Newell Garrison, Breasted spent his early childhood in Rockford, Illinois. In 1873 his parents bought a seven-acre tract in Downers Grove and built a small house. He entered North-Western (now North Central) College in Naperville at the age of fifteen and then served an apprenticeship in a pharmacy owned by his brother-in-law in Rochelle, Illinois. From 1882 to 1886 Breasted attended the Chicago College of Pharmacy. In 1886 his brother-in-law offered him a position as prescription clerk at his store in Omaha, Nebraska. Breasted accepted. Not satisfied by the pharmaceutical profession, he returned to Downers Grove the following year and decided to pursue another line of study.

In 1888 Breasted enrolled at the Congregational Institute (now the Chicago Theological Seminary) to study Hebrew and the Scriptures under Dr. Samuel Ives Curtiss. Determined to master Hebrew, he also taught himself Greek, Latin, Babylonian and Assyrian cuneiform, ancient Egyptian, French, German, and a smattering of Italian. At this point, he realized that a life in the ministry was not for him, and he changed course again in order to devote his life to the study of Oriental history and languages.

In 1890 Breasted transferred to Yale to study under William Rainey Harper. Harper suggested Breasted accept a chair in Egyptology at the newly proposed University of Chicago, of which Harper had just been named president. Breasted graduated from Yale in 1892 and, two years later, received his Ph.D. in Egyptology from the University of Berlin. Berlin was, at that time, the teaching and research center of the world in Oriental languages. He was at the top of his field but he felt scared, lonely, and confused, according to his son and biographer Charles Breasted. Recalling his Berlin days forty years

later Breasted mused, "I shall never forget the dark shadow of uncertainty that always hung over me—uncertainty as to my own ability to make good and about following a science of which there was not a single professorship or post of any kind in any American university."

Breasted returned to the United States in 1894 and became an assistant in Egyptology at the University of Chicago. In 1905 he became professor of Egyptology and Oriental history, the first chair in that subject in America.

In the early days, according to Charles Breasted, Egyptology was, at best, a maddeningly inaccurate science, full of half truths and populated by a "handful of competent" scholars who often disagreed among themselves over even the most fundamental of matters.

During the early years of this century Breasted worked primarily in Europe, developing with other colleagues a dictionary of ancient languages. Collecting and collating some ten thousand historical documents, he produced *A History of Egypt* in 1905 and the five-volume *Ancient Records of Egypt* in 1907.

Breasted mounted his first major expedition to Egypt in 1905. In 1912 he published *Development of Religion and Thought in Ancient Egypt* and then wrote, with James Harvey Robinson, several high school textbooks: *Outlines of European History* (1914) and *Ancient Times: A History of the Early World* (1916). Following the excavation of King Tutankhamen's tomb in 1922 in Egypt, Breasted began working closely, mainly as a consultant, with the English archaeologist and noted Egyptologist Howard Carter and English aristocrat Lord Carnarvon, who financed the excavations. The discovery of the ancient Egyptian king's tomb fascinated the American public and, indeed, fired the imagination of people throughout the world. All the artifacts taken from the tomb are in the Cairo Museum in Cairo, Eygpt.

In 1919 the Oriental Institute at the University of Chicago was founded with a grant from John D. Rockefeller, Jr. In 1923 Breasted became the first archaeologist to be elected into the National Academy of Sciences. Two years later he began to devote all of his time to the institute and its various research projects.

His other writings include *Oriental Forerunners of Byzantine Painting* (1924), *The Conquest of Civilization* (1926), and *The Dawn of Conscience* (1933).

Breasted died from a throat infection at the Rockefeller Institute for Medical Research in New York City in December of 1935.

Breasted, who lived at 5811 South Dorchester Avenue in Hyde Park, played a significant role in the growth and development of Egyptology and the museum he founded, the Oriental Institute, is an internationally recognized pioneer in the history and study of Egypt and the Near East. The museum, located at 1155 East 58th Street, houses objects from Egypt, Mesopotamia, ancient Persia, Syria, and Palestine, and is considered one of the foremost centers of Egyptology in the world today. Most of the objects in the museum's collection were discovered by institute scholars during archaeological excavations.

See also: William Rainey Harper

Further reading: Breasted, Charles B. *Pioneer to the Past: The Story of James Henry Breasted, Archaeologist* (1943); Dawson, Warren R. *Who Was Who in Egyptology* (1972).

"Big" Bill Broonzy

Musician

born: June 26, 1893
Scott, Mississippi
died: August 15, 1958
Chicago, Illinois

One of the greatest musicians in the history of the blues, William Lee Conley Broonzy incorporated African-American spirituals and folk songs with country and urban blues to create a style that was solely his own. As the most popular African-American blues singer of his day, Broonzy dominated Chicago blues during the thirties. Indeed he came to epitomize the sound of big city blues: a guitar-driven, extremely rhythmic music with its roots in the Deep South.

Photograph courtesy of the Scholl Museum of Folk Culture at the Old Town School of Folk Music.

One of seventeen children, the Mississippi-born, Arkansas-raised Broonzy developed an interest in music at an early age. He learned to play the fiddle from relatives and a traveling blues singer named C. C. Rider. An uncle taught him such blues standards as "John Henry," "Midnight Special," and "Oh, Susanna." When still in his teens Broonzy began performing at local picnics and barbeques. From 1912 to 1917 he worked as an itinerant preacher in Arkansas. He served one year in the army and after his discharge settled in Chicago.

Broonzy arrived in Chicago in 1920 at the age of twenty-seven. He learned to play the guitar from "Papa" Charlie Jackson, performing nightly at house parties while working for the Pullman company as a porter during the day. House parties were an African-American tradition that were especially popular during the Prohibition era. Musicians would perform in a private residence in order to raise money for rent and would receive payment in the form of food and drink.

Within a few years, Broonzy had made several recordings, including "Big Bill Blues" and "House Rent Stomp" and played frequently in South Side clubs. Like most traditional musicians, however, Broonzy held many day jobs over the years—molder, cook, porter, and janitor at Hull-House.

During the thirties, Broonzy toured with country blues singer Memphis Minnie. A prolific composer, he reportedly wrote as many as 350 songs during his lifetime, including the blues standard "Key to the Highway."

During the folk revival of the fifties when traditional musicians were "discovered" by a young, generally college-educated audience, Broonzy performed frequently at folk festivals across the country. He also appeared and recorded with such national folk and blues figures as Pete Seeger, Sonny Terry, Brownie McGhee, and Leadbelly.

Broonzy recorded extensively after World War II—from 1925 to 1952 he made some 260 blues recordings on the Mercury, Chess, Folkways, and other labels.

Broonzy made his first trip to Europe in 1951 and visited the continent regularly thereafter. He was also a frequent guest on Studs Terkel's "I Come For To Sing" concert series at the Blue Note, a famous jazz and blues club of the forties and fifties originally located at 56 West Madison Street that reopened in 1954 at 3 North Clark Street before finally shutting down in June of 1960.

Broonzy died in August of 1958 from cancer at age sixty-five. He was buried in Lincoln Cemetery in Blue Island, Illinois. "Nobody gave us lessons," he wrote in his autobiography, *Big Bill Blues*. "It was just born in us to sing and play the blues."

Among his recordings are *Big Bill Broonzy: 1932–1942* (Biograph), *Big Bill's Blues* (Columbia), and *The Young Big Bill Broonzy, 1928–1935* (Yazoo). In 1990 Columbia issued a compact disc *Big Bill Broonzy—Good Time Tonight* as part of its Roots 'n Blues series.

See also: Leonard Chess, Muddy Waters, Sonny Boy Williamson I [appendix], Howlin' Wolf

Further reading: Broonzy, William and Yannick Bruynoghe. *Big Bill Blues: William Broonzy's Story* (1955); Clarke, Donald. *The Penguin Encyclopedia of Popular Music* (1989); Guralnick, Peter. *The Listener's Guide to the Blues* (1982); Harris, Sheldon. *Blues Who's Who: A Biographical Dictionary of Blues Singers* (1979); Rowe, Mike. *Chicago Breakdown* (1975).

William Bross

Editor/Politician

born: November 4, 1813
Sussex County, New Jersey
died: January 27, 1890
Chicago, Illinois

Often called the original Chicago booster, William Bross personified the spirit of the Midwestern frontier—that of a brassy, brazen, and confident citizen fueled by an indomitable optimism and an unswerving faith in the future of his adopted city.

Born in a log cabin in New Jersey, Bross moved with his family to Milford, Pennsylvania, when he was nine. In 1832 he entered Milford Academy. Two years later, he enrolled at Williams College in Williamstown, Massachusetts, where he graduated with honor in 1838.

He taught for several years before becoming principal of Ridgebury Academy, near his birthplace. In October of 1846 he embarked on a tour of the Western towns, including St. Louis and Chicago. Impressed with the settlement by the lake, he decided to stay and opened a bookselling company, Griggs, Bross and Company.

In 1849 he founded the *Prairie Herald* newspaper. Two years later he and John L. Scripps established the *Democratic Press*. Then, he began publishing a series of pamphlets that boasted the advantages of the city to potential settlers. "Go to Chicago now!" he exclaimed. "You will never again have such a chance to make money!"

In 1854 Bross published *The Railroads, History and Commerce of Chicago*, a pamphlet that contained extensive facts and figures detailing the rapid growth of the city from its pioneer days as a small settlement on the prairie to its incorporation as a city in 1833 and to what he considered its excellent prospect for further expansion.

As a prominent newspaper editor, Bross played an important role in Civil War history in Illinois. In 1858 the *Democratic Press* and the *Chicago Tribune* merged and the name changed to the *Press and Tribune* and, two years later, to the *Chicago Daily Tribune*. The *Tribune* was an early advocate of President Abraham Lincoln and, with the outbreak of war in 1861, Bross and his paper fiercely supported the Union cause.

Further, Bross raised the Twenty-ninth United States Regiment of Colored Volunteers, under the command of his brother, Colonel John Bross, by providing virtually all of the expense. Bross is credited with exposing a confederate plot to free prisoners at Camp Douglas on the South Side in November of 1864.

In 1864 Bross was elected Lieutenant Governor of Illinois. The following year he toured California and, in 1867, he spent six months in Europe visiting Ireland, Britain, France, Belgium, Germany, Austria, and Italy. Sketches from his European trip appeared in the *Tribune* and were widely read.

Even the devastating effects of the Great Chicago Fire of 1871 could not dampen Bross's enthusiasm for the city. "I tell you," he predicted, "within five years Chicago's business houses will be rebuilt, and by the year 1900 the new Chicago will boast a population of a million souls." The city did not disappoint him.

In 1876 Bross wrote *History of Chicago*, considered the most comprehensive history of the city at that time. He contributed generously to various cultural organizations, including the Chicago Library Association and the Chicago Academy of Science.

Bross died in Chicago in January of 1890 due to complications from diabetes. He was seventy-six.

See also: Henry Demarest Lloyd, Joseph Medill, Wilbur F. Storey, John S. Wright

Further reading: Andreas, A. T. *History of Chicago From the Earliest Period to the Present Time.* 3 vols. (1884–1886); Pierce, Bessie Louise. *A History of Chicago.* 3 vols. (1937–57); Wood, David Ward. *Chicago and Its Distinguished Citizens or The Progress of Forty Years* (1881).

Leo Burnett

Advertising Executive

born: October 21, 1891
St. Johns, Michigan
died: June 7, 1971
Lake Zurich, Illinois

Adman Leo Noble Burnett founded the Chicago advertising agency that bears his name in 1935. Today, with fifty-two branches in forty-three countries, it is the tenth largest agency in the United States and the fourteenth largest in the world.

Photograph by Yousuf Karsh, courtesy of Leo Burnett U.S.A.

Burnett attended the University of Michigan, where he was an editor of the student newspaper. He began his professional career as a police reporter for the *Peoria Journal* but soon left journalism to pursue the more lucrative field of advertising. In 1916 he became advertising manager at Cadillac Motor Company. After a stint in the Navy, he joined the Lafayette Motors Company as executive advertising manager, later accepting the position of vice-president at the Homer McKee agency in Indianapolis. In 1931 Burnett moved to Chicago to hold a similar title at the advertising firm of Erwin, Wasey and Company.

With eight associates, the young adman founded the Leo Burnett Company four years later and proved that great advertising campaigns did not have to originate in New York. His so-called "Chicago school of advertising" took the subtle approach, stressing the positive aspects of a product and allowing the "drama" to flow naturally. In essence, he wanted the product to sell itself.

During Burnett's long career, his agency created some of the best known characters in advertising for some of the industry's biggest clients: Charlie the Tuna, the Pillsbury Doughboy, the Jolly Green Giant, the Harris Lion, the Marlboro Man, Tony the Tiger, Morris the Cat, the Man from Glad, and the Keebler Elves.

Burnett strived to create an honest look, even going so far as to use Burnett employees rather than models in some of his ads. He abhorred phoniness in all its forms and encouraged employees to be themselves. "Any company . . . is too big when its ranks are riddled with cynicism," he said several months before his death. "When its heart pumps ink instead of blood and its arteries harden into bureaucracy. When it takes advantage of its bigness to become an economic bully. Especially, when its people feel that they shed their identity as individuals each working day from 9 a.m. to 5 p.m."

Burnett was a director of the Better Business Bureau of metropolitan Chicago and a trustee of the American Heritage Foundation. In 1963 he received the distinguished service award in journalism from the University of Missouri and that same year was given the Business Statesmanship Award of the Harvard Business School Association of Chicago. Burnett was also a director and former chairman of the national Advertising Council.

In 1967, at age seventy-six, Burnett stepped down from active management to take up the newly established post of founder/chairman. But he made it clear to his staff that he still intended to maintain a full schedule. "I expect to shave regularly and to remain fully active within the outer limits of my new status until senility clearly makes me either an old nuisance or a bench warmer."

He died four years later in June of 1971 of a heart attack at his Lake Zurich country estate.

In May of 1989, the Leo Burnett Company moved into its new international headquarters—designed by architect Kevin Roche—at 35 West Wacker Drive in Chicago's North Loop.

See also: Fairfax M. Cone

Further reading: Heise, Kenan and Michael Edgerton. *Chicago: Center for Enterprise.* 2 vols. (1982).

Daniel H. Burnham

Architect/City Planner

born: September 4, 1846
Henderson, New York
died: June 1, 1912
Heidelberg, Germany

More administrator than architect, Daniel Hudson Burnham was a bold visionary who dared to dream big. "Make no little plans; they have no magic to stir men's blood," he once said.

Of Yankee stock, Burnham moved to Chicago with his family in 1855 at the age of nine. During the Civil War he enlisted in the 19th Illinois Regiment of the Union Army, but his father protested that Daniel was too young and prevented him from serving. An excellent athlete and artist, Burnham, however, was no scholar—he failed the entrance examinations to both Harvard and Yale.

In 1867 Burnham became a salesman at a mercantile house in Chicago, a position he detested. Changing directions, he accepted a job in the architectural office of Loring and Jenney as a draftsman apprentice. Still uncertain, he took up a friend's suggestion to head west to Nevada, where, at age twenty-two, he ran unsuccessfully for state senator on the Democratic ticket. Disheartened by this latest failure, Burnham returned to Chicago to resume his architectural career, determined more than ever to become a great architect.

He found a mentor in Peter Wight, an innovative and successful architect who helped young Burnham to develop his drawing skills and bolstered his fragile ego.

In 1873 a rejuvenated Burnham formed a partnership with John Wellborn Root, a brilliant young architect originally from a prominent family in Georgia. It was a marvelous pairing of personalities—the outgoingness of Burnham complemented Root's serene intensity. For the most part, Burnham found the clients and Root designed the buildings.

Burnham and Root soon became one of the most famous architectural firms in the nation. During their eighteen-year partnership, they built residences, office buildings, railroad stations, hotels, churches, stores, hospitals, and some of the finest structures to be erected in the city of Chicago, including the Montauk

Building (1882); the Rookery (1886); the original Art Institute (1887); their most durable masterpiece and the tallest structure in Chicago made without steel reinforcement, the Monadnock Building (1891); and the Women's Christian Temperance Union (1892).

Burnham's greatest fame was as Director of Works for the World's Columbian Exposition of 1893, that mammoth celebration that commemorated the four hundredth anniversary of Columbus's discovery of America. Given complete artistic and creative control of the grounds and buildings, Burnham hired some of the greatest names working at the time—architects Dankmar Adler, Louis Sullivan, and Henry Ives Cobb; landscaper Frederick Law Olmsted; and sculptors Augustus St. Gaudens, Daniel Chester French, and Frederick MacMonnies.

Root died suddenly in 1891 before the designs for the exposition were finalized. Burnham chose as Root's replacement Charles B. Atwood, a draftsman in the New York architectural firm of Herter Brothers. Burnham's concept of a dream-like city painted uniformly white—hence the nickname "White City"—and designed in a mostly classical, or Beaux Arts, style supplanted Root's modern vision. Through rainstorms, blizzards, and strikes, Burnham and his crew of seven thousand created a magnificent vision on a site that only two and one-half years earlier had been marshy bog. But this achievement was at a high price. During the course of the construction, over seven hundred accidents occurred, and close to twenty men were killed.

The White City was universally admired for the timeless beauty and grandeur of its buildings. A great popular success, it attracted more than twenty-one million customers and inspired countless speeches and essays, several full-length histories, and a spate of novels, including Henry Blake Fuller's *With the Procession* and Robert Herrick's *Memoirs of an American Citizen*. Visitors who expected to see the achievements of contemporary Chicago architecture on display, however, were bound to be disappointed for the neoclassical structures faithfully imitated European models.

Despite the economic depression that gripped the city at the time, thousands of Chicagoans and visitors from around the country flocked to the grounds when the fair opened on May 1, 1893. Once inside, they simply couldn't believe their eyes. With its brilliant white color and neo-classical design, the exhibition earned the sobriquet "White City." Although certain people—ranging from Louis Sullivan to Harriet Monroe, Root's sister-in-law—criticitized Burnham for the fair's slavish imitation of classical ideals (in contrast to Root's vision of a bold, democratic style of architecture that would serve as a break with the past), the public was clearly impressed. Over twenty-one million people attended, according to Burnham's biographer, Thomas S. Hines, ringing up total gate receipts of $10,336,065.

Some time after the success of the Columbian Exposition, Burnham developed the monumental *Plan of Chicago*, published in 1909, an ambitious attempt to chart the city's future. Among other things, Burnham proposed the straightening of the Chicago River, the erection of a bridge across the river on Michigan Avenue, the widening and extension of Michigan Avenue, the construction of a double-decked drive that would skirt the congested downtown, the development of additional parks, the promise to protect the natural beauty of the city's lakefront, the creation of a civic center at the intersection of Halsted and Congress Streets, and, curiously, the halting of new skyscraper construction—twenty stories was the suggested maximum height.

The plan caused a sensation. Widely praised and accepted, it was officially adopted by Mayor Fred Busse in 1910. Charles H. Wacker, a wealthy brewer, was appointed chairman of the Chicago Plan Commission. Not all of Burnham's plans were realized—the civic center was never built and, of course, the Chicago skyline has continued to sprout skyscraper after skyscraper. But Burnham's vision was city planning at its best, an agile balance between the desire for growth and the need for continuity. He went on to create master plans for other cities—Washington, D.C., Cleveland, San Francisco, and Manila.

The Burnham Plan, however, was his greatest achievement. In the spring of 1912, he and his wife, Margaret, sailed for Europe. It was his seventh, and last, trip abroad. He died in Heidelberg, Germany, due to complications from colitis, food poisoning, and diabetes.

See also: John Wellborn Root, Louis Sullivan, Charles H. Wacker

Further reading: Condit, Carl W. *The Chicago School of Architecture: A History of Commercial and Public Buildings in the Chicago Area, 1875–1925* (1964); Hines, Thomas S. *Burnham of Chicago: Architect and Planner* (1974).

Edgar Rice Burroughs

Author

📖

born: September 1, 1875
Chicago, Illinois
died: March 19, 1950
Encino, California

Master storyteller Edgar Rice Burroughs didn't start writing until he was thirty-five years old, yet there was no denying his magical touch. Book after book, with one adventure story after another, he transported his readers from familiar surroundings to the exotic worlds of the African jungle, the landscape of Mars, and the center of the Earth. A prolific writer, Burroughs completed seventy-one books in his lifetime that were eventually translated into thirty-six languages and sold more than one hundred million copies. The popularity of "sword and sorcery" literature in recent years has led to a revival of interest, and to a reevaluation, of his work. Burroughs influenced many writers of this genre: from Robert E. Howard (creator of Conan) to Michael Moorcock (creator of Elric). One could even trace Burrough's spirit down to the present day in the persona of the dashing, globe-trotting archaeologist, Indiana Jones.

Photograph reprinted with permission from the *Chicago Sun-Times*.

Although not usually regarded as a Chicago writer, Burroughs was a native Chicagoan, born on West Washington Street, and he spent his boyhood years on the West Side. Occasionally he used the city as a setting. His best known Chicago novel, *The Mucker* (1912), describes the adventures of a wayward West Side street urchin named Billy Byrne. According to some accounts, Byrne, not Tarzan, was Burrough's favorite fictional character.

After graduating from a Michigan military academy, Burroughs wandered about the West, searching for gold and laboring at various occupations: cow puncher, policeman, salesman, railroad guard. Upon returning to Chicago, he ended up in a series of dead-end jobs. To relieve the boredom of his work, he would write wild adventure yarns. In 1912 he sold his first story, "Under the Moons of Mars" for $400 to *All-Story* magazine. Still secretive and apprehensive about his writing, he used the byline Normal Bean, which some conscientious copy editor changed to Norman Bean.

In December of 1911, confined to his tiny North Side apartment, Burroughs began writing the story that would earn him literary immortality. It was set in Africa and told the fantastic tale of an infant, John Clayton, raised by a family of apes. "Tarzan of the Apes" was published in the October 1912 issue of *All-Story* magazine.

The phenomenal success of Tarzan spawned sequels, movie and television interpretations, games, candy bars, and even an X-rated cartoon. The first Tarzan movie, *Tarzan of the Apes,* released in 1918, starred Elmo Lincoln as Tarzan and Enid Markey as Jane. Other screen Tarzans included Buster Crabbe, Johnny Weissmuller, and, on the small screen, Ron Ely.

Although the character of Tarzan was reportedly influenced in part by Rudyard Kipling's *Jungle Tales,* Burroughs always had an interest in mythology, and he admitted that the ancient story of Romulus and Remus, the founders of Rome, was the more likely inspiration.

Burroughs received much criticism for his casual approach to writing. He usually spent from one to three months writing a book. On the other hand, *The Chessmen of Mars,* took twenty-one months to complete. In the early days, Burroughs wrote his stories out in longhand, did little outlining or advance planning, and rarely any rewriting or polishing. With a wife and family to support, he was more concerned with paying the bills than courting critical acclaim. "I loathed poverty," he said later. "There is nothing honorable or fine about it."

In 1919 Burroughs moved to California and developed real estate in the San Fernando Valley. The community grew and eventually the residents had to choose a name. They voted to call it Tarzana in honor of the town's leading citizen.

Burroughs created thoroughly realized worlds and characters: John Carter, the Confederate officer who died on earth only to be reborn on Mars; and David Innes, the young man from Connecticut who traveled to an underground continent five hundred miles beneath the earth's surface. He encouraged his readers to become involved. In *The Chessmen of Mars,* he included a step-by-step description of how to play Jetan, or Martian chess ("The game is played with twenty black pieces by one player and twenty orange pieces by his opponent, and is presumed to have originally represented a battle between the Black race of the South and the Yellow race of the North").

In later years his attempts at serious fiction failed miserably. "I've often considered writing deeper stuff," he once said, "but why should I?"

During World War II, at age seventy, Burroughs covered the war in the Pacific from the Marshall Islands for the *Los Angeles Times.* He returned to California after the war ended.

On March 19, 1950, Burroughs died at his home in Encino, California, while reading the Sunday comics.

Other books in the Tarzan series: *The Return of Tarzan* (1914); *Tarzan and the Jewels of Opar* (1918); *Tarzan, Lord of the Jungle* (1928); *Tarzan at the Earth's Core* (1930). The Pellucidar series: *At the Earth's Core* (1922); *Pellucidar* (1923); *Return to Pellucidar* (1941). The Martian series: *A Princess of Mars* (1917); *The Gods of Mars* (1918); *The Warlord of Mars* (1919); *John Carter of Mars* (1964). The Venus series: *Carson of Venus* (1939); *Escape on Venus* (1946).

See also: Johnny Weissmuller

Further reading: de Camp, L. Sprague. *Literary Swordsmen and Sorcerers: The Makers of Heroic Fantasy* (1976); Johnson, Geoffrey. "Edgar, the Ape-Man," *Chicago* (December 1989); Lupoff, Richard A. *Edgar Rice Burroughs: Master of Adventure* (1965); Manguel, Alberto and Gianni Guadalupi. *The Dictionary of Imaginary Places* (1987).

Paul Butterfield

Musician

born: December 17, 1942
Chicago, Illinois
died: May 4, 1987
North Hollywood, California

Paul Butterfield, a white Chicago musician, played an amplified, rock-based version of the blues that influenced countless local bands and inspired rabid support on college campuses. Butterfield combined the virtuosity of jazz with the power of rock and the sensuality of the blues.

Photograph courtesy of *Sing Out!* magazine.

Butterfield grew up on the South Side, studied classical flute, and sang in the church choir. He taught himself how to play the harmonica and began gigging with such venerable Chicago bluesmen as Muddy Waters, Howlin' Wolf, Otis Rush, Magic Sam, Buddy Guy, Junior Wells, and Little Walter at various South Side clubs when he was still underage.

Butterfield attended the University of Chicago, where he met another musician, Elvin Bishop, and formed his own band. In 1964 he put together the Paul Butterfield Blues Band, which fused blues with folk, rock, and jazz and included Butterfield on harmonica, Bishop on guitar, and Mike Bloomfield on guitar.

Butterfield became a well-respected figure on the local club circuit, attracting a loyal following. Indeed, Butterfield and his band were the American equivalent of John Mayall's Bluesbreakers, that seminal English blues group of the sixties.

Their first album, *Butterfield Blues Band,* elicited largely favorable reviews. In 1965 the group appeared at the Newport Folk Festival in Newport, Rhode Island. The first electric band to play the festival, they also were the band who backed Bob Dylan's controversial foray into electric folk. In 1967 Butterfield added a brass section.

Band members fluctuated considerably during the late sixties. In 1969 the Paul Butterfield Blues Band played to thousands of fans at the famed Woodstock music festival in New York. Three years later Butterfield assembled yet another group, Better Days. In 1973, he recorded the soundtrack for the motion picture *Steelyard Blues* starring Jane Fonda and Donald Sutherland.

During the early 1980s, Butterfield experienced some serious health problems that were aggravated by his transient life-style and extensive drug use. In 1986 Amherst Records released *The Legendary Paul Butterfield Rides Again*.

Other Butterfield albums include *The Resurrection of Pigboy Crabshaw* (1968), *In My Own Dream* (1968), *Keep On Moving* (1969), *Butterfield Live* (1970), *East-West* (1971), *Golden Butter/The Best of the Paul Butterfield Blues Band* (1972), *It All Comes Back* (1973), *Paul Butterfield/Better Days* (1973), *Put It In Your Ear* (1976), and *North/South* (1981).

Butterfield, the white man who popularized the blues for a rock audience, died in his North Hollywood apartment in May of 1987 of an accidental drug overdose.

"Butterfield was certainly one of the pivotal figures in raising the consciousness of blues in what was a white-dominated '60s rock world," wrote *Los Angeles Times* pop music critic, Robert Hilburn, "and also helped make the idea of a white musician playing the blues credible."

See also: Muddy Waters, Howlin' Wolf

Further reading: Harris, Sheldon. *Blues Who's Who: A Biographical Dictionary of Blues Singers* (1979); Logan, Nick and Bob Woffinden. *The Illustrated Encyclopedia of Rock* (1977); Stambler, Irwin. *The Encyclopedia of Pop, Rock and Soul* (1989).

Al Capone

Gangster

born: January 17, 1899
Brooklyn, New York
died: January 25, 1947
Palm Island, Florida

No other name is more closely associated with Chicago than Alphonse Capone. Even decades after his death, his exploits still remain an endless source of fascination for millions of people worldwide.

Capone's father, Gabriel, had emigrated from the slums of Naples in 1893 to settle in a rough, working-class neighborhood of Brooklyn. Alphonse grew up on these mean streets, a big kid, cocky and hot-tempered. He quit school at fourteen, picking up odd jobs—a clerk in a candy store, a pin setter in a bowling alley—before joining a street gang, the Five Pointers, on Manhattan's Lower East Side. He then got a job as a bouncer and bartender before joining Johnny Torrio's gang. In 1918 he married Mae Coughlin, a salesgirl in a department store. The following year their first and only child, Albert Francis, was born, with Torrio acting as the infant's godfather. Within a short time, Capone had earned a reputation as an impulsive and fearless punk who used whatever means was necessary to get a job done.

In 1919 Torrio, who had moved to Chicago in 1909, sent for Capone to act as bodyguard, chauffeur, and bartender at the Four Deuces, 2222 South Wabash Avenue. When mob boss "Big" Jim Colosimo was murdered in his own cafe on May 11, 1920, Torrio took over the underworld.

The election of reform candidate William E. Dever as mayor of Chicago in 1923 forced Capone and his cohorts to lie low for awhile. At Torrio's behest, Capone set up shop in west suburban Cicero, where he ruled with an iron fist, eventually controlling the communities of Burnham, Chicago Heights, Melrose Park, Stickney, Berwyn, Posen, Blue Island, and Forest View.

In 1925 Capone inherited the ganglord throne from his mentor, Johnny Torrio when, Torrio, after surviving a near fatal assassination attempt, retired from the "business." Torrio transferred everything to Capone—brothels, breweries, speakeasies, and gambling houses. By that time Torrio had built quite an empire, reaping an annual income in the millions of dollars from bootlegging and prostitution and from the manufacture, distribution, and sale of liquor and beer. Capone then established headquarters in the Metropole Hotel at 2300 South Michigan Avenue. It was convenient to both city hall and the central police department. He marshaled his forces and began to methodically eliminate his enemies—a long list that included Dion O'Bannion, Hymie Weiss, and the O'Donnell brothers.

In 1928 Capone moved across the street to the imposing Lexington Hotel and occupied the entire fourth and most of the third floor. By this time the reelection of Mayor William Hale Thompson reasserted Chicago's status as a "wide-open" town. Capone took full advantage of the situation. Indeed, Capone enjoyed a rather cozy relationship with both the mayor and the men in blue. Daniel Serritella served as the gangster's "representative" in the city council, while his henchmen were furnished with offically stamped cards that read: "To the Police Department— You will extend the courtesies of the department to the bearer."

Meanwhile, gang killings continued unabated on the street. It took the deaths of several high-profile figures—the shooting of assistant state's attorney William H. McSwiggin in 1926, the killing of *Tribune* reporter Jake Lingle in 1930, and the ferocity of the St. Valentine's Day massacre in 1929—for the citizens of Chicago to demand that something be done.

For many years the public had simply looked the other way, refusing to acknowledge the daily horror that was taking place on the city streets. Many viewed Capone as a folk hero,

an underdog harassed by law enforcement officers. Almost despite themselves, ordinary citizens rather admired Capone's chutzpah, envied his wealth, and envied his apparently glamorous life-style. Indeed, millions of Americans actually sympathized with him. He reportedly received letters from all over the world. Many articles and books were written about him. But to a large number of Italian-Americans, Capone's exploits were a constant embarrassment and a reminder of how far removed they were from the mainstream of American society.

By 1930, at the age of thirty-one, Capone had reached the pinnacle of his blood-stained career. His personal income, according to Jay Robert Nash, was conservatively estimated at $50 million a year—by his accounts. He owned an extravagant home in Florida, and he was king of an immense criminal empire.

Bad bookkeeping led to Capone's fall. In 1931, due to the perseverance of Eliot Ness and his Department of the Treasury team—the fabled "Untouchables"—the government was able to gather enough evidence to indict Capone for conspiracy to violate the Volstead Act, which prohibited the manufacture, sale, or transportation of liquor within the U.S. More damaging were the charges of income tax evasion leveled against the gangster. Ultimately, Capone was sentenced to eleven years, first in a prison in Atlanta and finally in the federal penitentiary on Alcatraz Island. During his jail term, the syphilis he had contracted as a young man worsened, and due to poor health he was released from prison after serving only eight years. On January 19, 1947, Capone collapsed from a brain hemorrhage. Less than a week later, he developed bronchial pneumonia and died in the presence of his family at his

Florida estate. He was originally buried in Mount Olivet Cemetery at 2755 W. 111th Street, but his remains were later moved to Mount Carmel Cemetery in Hillside, Illinois.

See also: William E. Dever, William Hale Thompson

Further reading: Asbury, Herbert. *Gem of the Prairie: An Informal History of the Chicago Underworld* (1942); Kobler, John. *Capone: The Life and World of Al Capone* (1971); Nash, Jay Robert. *Makers & Breakers of Chicago* (1985); Nelli, Humbert S. *Italians in Chicago 1880–1930: A Study in Ethnic Mobility* (1970); Ness, Eliot with Oscar Fraley. *The Untouchables* (1969); Pasly, Fred D. *Al Capone: The Biography of a Self-Made Man* (1930); Peterson, Virgil W. *Barbarians In Our Midst: A History of Chicago Crime and Politics* (1952).

Anton J. Cermak

Politician

born: May 9, 1873
Kladno, Bohemia
(now Kladno, Czechoslovakia)
died: March 6, 1933
Miami, Florida

As Chicago's first and only foreign-born mayor, Anton Joseph Cermak took advantage of the city's changing demographics to organize the various groups into a cohesive political organization that led straight to city hall. It was a lesson that others—from Richard J. Daley to Harold Washington—did well to remember.

Cermak's family first settled at 15th and Canal Streets in Chicago, but they later moved to the small mining town of Braidwood, Illinois, some sixty-five miles away. Cermak attended elementary school there. After a short period of working in the coal mines in Will and Grundy counties, Cermak hopped a boxcar to Chicago. He found a job tending horses for the railway in the old Bohemian neighborhood of Pilsen. Soon he was able to buy a horse and wagon and began selling kindling wood. He moved to Lawndale on the West Side and dabbled in other occupations—trucking, banking, and real estate.

Like others before him, Cermak started his political career as a precinct captain. In 1902 he was elected to the Illinois state legislature. He then became secretary of the United Societies for Local Self-Government. A firm believer in personal liberties, Cermak was known around town as a staunch advocate in the fight against Sunday closing laws and state prohibition—the *Chicago Tribune* once referred to him as "the wettest man in Chicago."

In 1909 Cermak won the aldermanic seat from the 12th Ward (which later became the 22nd). Three years later he was elected to the office of municipal court bailiff. In 1918, however, he was defeated in his bid for election as sheriff of Cook County. A bit shaken, Cermak returned to the city council in 1919.

In 1922 he was elected president of the Cook County Board. During his tenure—he was reelected in 1926 and 1930—a new Criminal Courts Building and county jail were erected in his ward, new highways were constructed, and additional forest preserves were acquired.

In 1928 Cermak suffered two devastating blows. He was defeated in his bid for the Illinois senate and his beloved wife, Mary, died. Then, in a miraculous political recovery, Cermak clinched the leadership role of the Democratic party following the death of his friend and mentor, George Brennan. In 1931 he became Chicago's thirty-sixth mayor, sweeping past his Republican rival, "Big" Bill Thompson.

Cermak ran an efficient, cost-conscious, and well-oiled machine. He promised good government to all Chicagoans, and good government was what he delivered. Cermak was essentially a shrewd businessman and, like any good businessman, he learned the ways of acquiring power and played the role of the great compromiser very well. By pleasing his constituency and appeasing his enemies, he broadened his political base until anyone foolish enough to challenge his authority met with certain political death.

On the evening of February 15, 1933, Cermak was fatally wounded while appearing with President-elect Franklin D. Roosevelt in Miami, Florida. A disgruntled Italian immigrant, Giuseppe Zangara, had fired shots at Roosevelt but struck Cermak instead. As he was being taken to the hospital, Cermak reportedly uttered the famous line to Roosevelt, "I am glad it was me instead of you."

The city of Chicago and the nation stood vigil and waited as the mayor struggled valiantly for life. He lost the battle in the early morning of March 6. However, according to his biographer, Alex Gottfried, the direct cause of death was not the gunshot wound but ulcerative colitis.

Zangara, the self-proclaimed enemy of kings and presidents, was executed by the state of Florida two weeks after Cermak died. "Lousy capitalists," he reportedly uttered, as the switch was pulled.

Further reading: Gottfried, Alex. *Boss Cermak of Chicago: A Study of Political Leadership* (1962); Green, Paul M. "Anton J. Cermak: The Man And His Machine," in *The Mayors: The Chicago Political Tradition*, Paul M. Green and Melvin G. Holli, eds. (1987); Rex, Frederick F. *The Mayors of the City of Chicago* (1934).

Leonard Chess

Record Producer

born: March 12, 1917
Poland
died: October 16, 1969
Chicago, Illinois

Phil and Leonard Chess, Polish Jews who immigrated to the U.S. with their family, formed a record label that recorded some of the greatest names in the history of blues. Chess Records was a hands-on operation in which the brothers worked closely with the artists. Indeed, on at least one occasion, Phil reportedly played drums during a recording session. The label's roster of talent included Muddy Waters, Howlin' Wolf, Robert Nighthawk, Jimmy Rogers, Little Walter, Sonny Boy Williamson I, Johnny Shines, J. B. Lenoir, and Willie Dixon. In 1964, Chess even welcomed the bad boys of rock—the Rolling Stones—into its studios.

Photograph reprinted with permission from the *Chicago Sun-Times.*

Polish-born immigrants, Phil and Leonard Chess arrived in the United States in 1928—their father operated the Chess and Sons Junk Shop at 2979 South State Street—and developed a chain of nightclubs on the South Side. One of their most popular clubs was the Macomba Lounge at 3905 South Drexel Boulevard, which featured such artists as Billy Eckstine, Ella Fitzgerald, and Gene Ammons.

"We heard some of the music and we started recording it," said Phil. The label began in a garage as a strictly two-man operation. "I didn't know what I was doing," Leonard admitted in a newspaper interview in 1969, "but I was doing it all myself, working days at the record company, nights at the club. Pretty soon I had to get out of the club and I turned it over to Phil."

The Chess label had its own unique sound. By rigging a loudspeaker and a microphone at both ends of a sewer pipe, the now familiar echo effect was created.

Leonard spent much of his time on the road, in Detroit and in the South, delivering to the record stores himself. He became so busy that, finally, he told Phil to sell the Macomba to concentrate on running the record company. The Chess brothers frequented the city's taverns and juke joints in search of new talent.

Originally called Aristocrat, the label changed its name to Chess in 1950. Early releases on the Aristocrat label included polka music in addition to its stable of blues and jazz releases. The first record on the new label was "Union Man Blues" by Andrew Tibbs. However, the first release on the Chess label was Gene Ammons's "My Foolish Heart" and the second, Muddy Waters's "Rollin' Stone," which was a considerable hit.

Leonard made contacts with influential people while on the road. In 1950 he linked up with Sam Phillips, a record producer in Memphis, Tennessee. Chess had the opportunity to sign a young, unknown singer from Tupelo, Mississippi, named Elvis Presley but they weren't too impressed and turned him down flat.

Even after attaining nationwide commercial success, Chess remained a family business at heart. In the early years the label operated from a series of small storefronts at various locations on the South Side—at 49th Street and Cottage Grove Avenue between 1951 and 1954 and at 4750-52 South Cottage Grove Avenue between 1954 and 1957. In late 1956 Chess purchased a two-story building at 2120 South Michigan Avenue and converted it into offices with its own shipping facilities and a second floor recording studio. Chuck Berry recorded four of his seven top ten hits there, including "Johnny B. Goode" and "Rock 'n Roll Music," according to a Commission on Chicago Landmarks staff report. Another early rock 'n roller, Bo Diddley, also recorded at the studio.

Chess maintained a roster of jazz performers that included Ramsey Lewis, Ahmad Jamal, and Sonny Stitt in addition to its selections of Delta blues, country blues, jazz, doo-wop, gospel, and early rock 'n roll releases. Blues artist Willie Dixon also developed talent and acted as an arranger during the recording sessions.

With the growing popularity of rock and the widespread practice of white musicians covering the blues, Chess and other small independent labels went into decline. In an effort to appeal to a wider audience, the firm experimented with avant-garde and progressive rock in the late 1960s on the Cadet Concept label. One of the label's biggest successes was the Rotary Connection, a racially mixed group of four men and two women, which featured the expressive vocals of Minnie Riperton. Riperton turned solo and had a hit single in 1973 with "Loving You."

In addition to the record company, the brothers formed a partnership, L. and P. Broadcasting Company, that owned radio stations WVON-AM and WSDM-FM in Chicago and WNOV-AM in Milwaukee.

In 1966 Chess moved into larger headquarters at 320 East 21st Street. In 1969 the company was sold to a California firm, General Recorded Tape (GRT) and by the early seventies Chess had relocated to New York. Sugar Hill Records acquired the Chess catalog in 1979 and, in turn, sold it to MCA Records in 1986. MCA has reissued most of the Chess recordings making the music available for future generations.

Leonard Chess suffered a fatal heart attack in October 1969, two blocks away from the L. and P. Broadcasting Co. He was fifty-two. Phil Chess is now retired and lives in Arizona.

On June 7, 1990, the former Chess recording studios at 2120 South Michigan Avenue was dedicated as an official Chicago landmark.

"Blues," said Phil Chess, "is nothing but the truth."

See also: Muddy Waters, Sonny Boy Williamson I [appendix], Howlin' Wolf

Further reading: Commission on Chicago Landmarks. "Chess Records Office and Studio," (July 1989); Guralnick, Peter. *Feel Like Going Home: Portraits in Blues and Rock 'n Roll* (1981); Rowe, Mike. *Chicago Breakdown* (1975).

Nat "King" Cole

Musician

born: March 17, 1919
Montgomery, Alabama
died: February 15, 1965
Santa Monica, California

The smoky-voiced singer whose hits included "Mona Lisa," "Too Young," "Rambling Rose," and the timeless Christmas classic, "The Christmas Song," Nat "King" Cole was the first African-American to host his own weekly television program, which premiered on NBC in 1957 and ran for sixty-four weeks, and was the first African-American to cross over to the pop charts. The soft-spoken Cole was tops in his field in recording, night club performance, television, and motion pictures.

Photograph courtesy of the *Chicago Defender.*

Born Nathaniel Adams Coles (he later dropped the "s" in his last name), he moved with his family to Chicago from Alabama when he was four years old. His father became pastor of the True Light Baptist Church located at 7302 South Maryland Avenue, and young Nathaniel sang in the choir. Cole's mother was also a church singer. As a youngster, Cole played the piano and in high school organized a fourteen-piece band. He attended both Wendell Phillips and DuSable High School. Cole and his brother, Eddie, led a combo, the Rogues of Rhythm, in a tavern on 58th Street. Many evenings he would sit outside the Grand Terrace nightclub and listen to the likes of Earl Hines and Art Tatum. After graduating from high school, Cole went on tour with a musical revue called "Shuffle Along," and in 1937 he settled in Los Angeles.

Cole then began playing at California beer joints before forming the Nat "King" Cole trio, a strictly instrumental group that consisted of guitar, bass fiddle, and piano. The popular story is that during a show one night, a drunk shouted from the crowd, demanding that someone sing. Cole protested that there were no singers in the group. The heckler insisted, so Cole began warbling "Sweet Lorraine." Years later, Cole's widow, Maria, said the truth was a bit more mundane. Cole had been singing several songs per set and when the crowd responded positively to his voice, he simply began to sing more. Cole received his famous sobriquet when the manager of a club where he and his trio were playing was so impressed with the musician's nimble fingers on the keyboard that he christened him "King" Cole.

Although he first emerged as a jazz pianist of the first order, it is as a singer that Cole excelled. In 1942 Capitol signed the King Cole Trio and two years later they had their first hit, "Straighten Up and Fly Right." During the early 1950s, Cole enjoyed a string of solo hits that would make him one of the most popular stylists of his generation: including "Nature Boy," "Unforgettable," "Mona Lisa," "Too Young," and "Those Lazy-Hazy-Crazy Days of Summer."

Although Cole never injected politics into his music—he preferred to keep his personal opinions to himself—sometimes trouble followed him. At a show in Birmingham, Alabama, on April 10, 1956, members of the North Alabama White Citizens Council who were waging a campaign against bebop, rock 'n roll, and "Negro music," rushed the stage and knocked the singer to the floor, repeatedly kicking him. Understandably shaken, Cole said he couldn't continue and offered a refund. No one requested their money back.

Cole appeared in several motion pictures including *China Gate* in 1957 and the Academy Award–winning picture, *Cat Ballou*, in 1965. In 1958 he portrayed W. C. Handy in *The St. Louis Blues.*

Cole died in February of 1965 in Santa Monica after a two-month battle against lung cancer.

In 1968 School Superintendent of Chicago public schools, James F. Redmond, asked the board of education to name a school after Cole. The Nathaniel Cole Child-Parent Center stands at 412 South Keeler Avenue. In the same year, a park at 85th Street and South Park Avenue honored the late singer.

See also: Sam Cooke, Earl Hines

Charles A. Comiskey

Baseball Club Owner

born: August 15, 1859
Chicago, Illinois
died: October 26, 1931
Eagle River, Wisconsin

Baseball maverick Charles Albert Comiskey achieved many firsts in his life. He was the only player to become an owner, he changed first-base play by emphasizing the importance of fielding ground balls, and he introduced the idea of night games to a quizzical nation. Along with Byron Bancroft Johnson, he founded the American League and, in 1900, established a new baseball club, the Chicago White Stockings (not to be confused with the original White Stockings, which we now know as the Cubs). Two years later, he shortened the name to "White Sox." Comiskey revolutionized the game of baseball.

Comiskey's father, John, arrived in Chicago from County Caven, Ireland, in 1852, making his living first as a contractor and then as alderman for the old 7th Ward. A baseball fanatic from his youth, Charles played amateur ball on West Side sandlots before going off from Holy Family parish to St. Mary's College in Kansas to acquire a proper education. After signing up with the Dubuque Rabbits, a minor league team, as pitcher and reserve infielder, he acted as playing manager with the St. Louis Browns of the American Association, winning the team four straight pennants. In 1890 Comiskey joined the Pirates of the Chicago Brotherhood who played their games in an athletic field at 35th and Wentworth Streets.

From 1892 to 1894 Comiskey was captain, manager, and first baseman of the National League's Cincinnati Red Stockings (later called "Reds"). There he developed a friendship with "Ban" Johnson, sports editor of the *Cincinnati Commercial-Gazette*. With Johnson, he helped found the renegade American League, raiding other teams to recruit the best available talent.

The Chicago White Sox made their local debut on a cold and blustery April 21, 1900, in a wooden grandstand at the 39th Street grounds. Comiskey Park, however, didn't open its gates to the public until July 1, 1910, when the White Sox played the St. Louis Browns, losing the opener two to zero. The first night game was played there on August 27 of the same year.

Those were good days for Comiskey and his White Sox. In 1906 they battled the Cubs in the city's only crosstown World Series, winning four games to two. In 1913, always looking for ways to promote the sport and his team, Comiskey arranged for a series of exhibition games to be played in Japan, Australia, Ceylon, Egypt, Italy, France, and England.

Nicknamed "The Old Roman" because of his pronounced nose, Comiskey was a complex, curiously enigmatic figure. Although known as a tightwad around his players—indeed, he often treated them like chattel—he could be quite generous when it came to members of the press. He lavished gifts and words of praise on sportswriters and provided them with free meals after every home and road game. In many ways, an innovative and forward-thinking baseball strategist, he could just as easily be stubbornly conservative, as he was when he prevented blacks from playing in the major league.

In 1917 the White Sox brought home the pennant and the world championship aided by the powerful pitching of Eddie Cicotte, who won a dazzling twenty-eight games that year. As a result of their hard work, Comiskey had promised bonuses to the players, but he later changed his mind, rewarding them instead with bottles of champagne. Since their contract expressly forbade them from playing with any other team, they had little choice but to stay and endure. But their collective anger simmered.

In 1919 Comiskey assembled one of the greatest teams ever to play on a baseball diamond. There was pitcher Cicotte, outfielder "Shoeless" Joe Jackson, third baseman George "Buck" Weaver, center fielder Oscar "Happy" Felsch, southpaw pitcher Claude "Lefty" Williams, infielder Frederick McMullin, first baseman Charles "Chick" Gandil, and shortstop Charles "Swede" Risberg.

Frustrated and angry with the Old Roman's intransigence, Gandil approached Boston gambler Joseph "Sport" Sullivan and proposed for a promise of $80,000 cash to throw the upcoming 1919 World Series against the Cincinnati Reds.

Already suspicious, Comiskey had received anonymous tips and had even hired private detectives to uncover the truth. A grand jury was convened but, in a private meeting with the Old Roman, Cicotte tearfully confessed. The White Sox owner expressed little sympathy for the fallen ballplayer. "Tell it to the grand jury," he snapped.

The "Black Sox" trial began July 18, 1921. Although they were acquitted of any wrongdoing in court, the new baseball commissioner Kenesaw Mountain Landis banned the eight players from the game for life. "Regardless of the verdict of juries, no player who throws a ball game . . . will ever play professional baseball!" he insisted.

"The reason for the popularity of the sport," Comiskey said before the Black Sox scandal erupted, "is that it fits in with the temperament of the American people and because it is on the square. Everything is done in the open."

The scandal broke the spirit of the usually indomitable Comiskey. He died a recluse at his Wisconsin home on October 26, 1931, an emotionally drained veteran of the baseball wars.

On September 30, 1990, Comiskey Park hosted its last baseball game with a White Sox victory over the Seattle Mariners, 2-1. The new Comiskey Park opened across the street on April 18, 1991.

See also: Adrian Anson, Kenesaw Mountain Landis, Ring Lardner

Further reading: Asinof, Eliot. *Eight Men Out: The Black Sox and the 1919 World Series* (1963); Axelson, Gustaf W. *"Commy": The Life Story of Charles Comiskey* (1919); Lindberg, Richard. *Who's On 3rd? The Chicago White Sox Story* (1983).

Fairfax M. Cone

Advertising Executive

born: February 21, 1903
San Francisco, California
died: June 20, 1977
Carmel, California

Fairfax Mastick Cone, who cofounded the firm of Foote, Cone and Belding in 1942, was a major figure in Chicago advertising circles. Quick to condemn irresponsible advertising, he preferred to convey coherent and clear messages without the gimmicks. Above all, he wished to upgrade the much maligned reputation of advertising. "We believed that advertising should be thoughtful and honest, with no exceptions, and that no other kind of [advertising] should ever play a part in the affairs of Foote, Cone and Belding," he once remarked.

Photograph reprinted with permission from the *Chicago Sun-Times.*

Cone was born in San Francisco, the son of William H. Cone, a mining engineer and prospector, and Isabelle Williams, a teacher. Due to his father's peripetatic profession, Cone was tutored at home by his mother until the sixth grade. He attended high school in Oakland and at the age of sixteen went to sea for eight months on the S.S. *Haxtum,* a transatlantic freighter.

In January of 1921, at his father's insistence, Cone enrolled at the University of California at Berkeley to continue his education. He edited school magazines and enjoyed cartooning. One summer he was hired as a copy boy on the *San Francisco Bulletin.* He then worked on the *San Francisco Examiner* for three years as an advertising salesman, writer, and illustrator before jumping to the L. H. Waldron agency as an artist. He left after one year when he realized his color blindness—he had sketched primarily in monochromatic black-and-white previously—would limit his opportunity to advance.

In 1929 Cone joined the San Francisco office of Lord and Thomas as a copywriter. In 1939 he became manager and in 1941 transferred to New York as vice-president and creative director, working directly with the owner Albert D. Lasker. In 1942 Cone moved to Chicago where he became Lord and Thomas's executive vice-president. The firm dissolved when Lasker retired the same year.

The Chicago-based Cone, along with two other colleagues, Emerson Foote in New York and Don Belding in Los Angeles formed their own ad agency, Foote, Cone and Belding in 1942. Cone acted as chairman of the executive committee from 1942 to 1948, chairman of the board from 1948 to 1951, and president from 1951 to

1957. Under his leadership, the firm became one of the ten largest advertising agencies in the world.

FC&B was formed at a crucial time in the history of advertising. The war economy didn't offer much opportunity for luxury goods. Advertising was, in effect, a dispensable industry. Cone, who learned very quickly to adapt with the times, did the most logical thing—he devoted advertising space in magazines and newspapers to the war effort "as a truly unselfish public service." When television came into its own in the years following World War II, FC&B took advantage of the new medium by hiring cowboy Roy Rogers to sell Post Toasties and comedian Sid Caesar to promote Libby's canned pineapple.

Cone avoided anything that suggested even the slightest vulgarity or smacked of poor taste. FC&B clients included Sunkist Growers, Dole Pineapple, Kraft Foods, the Paper Mate Company, the Ralston Purina Company, Sara Lee, Hill Brothers Coffee, and Trans World Airlines. The agency's clever and catchy advertising slogans saturated the airwaves and entered into American popular culture. Some familiar FC&B campaigns were Raid, ("Raid kills bugs dead!") Dial soap ("Aren't you glad you use Dial? Don't you wish everybody did?"), Clairol ("Does she or doesn't she? Hair color so natural only her hairdresser knows for sure."), Hallmark ("When you care enough to send the very best"), Pepsodent ("You'll wonder where the yellow went"), the Toni Company ("Which twin has the Toni?"), and Zenith ("The quality goes in before the name goes on").

Cone typically worked sixty-hour weeks yet still managed to read five to seven books per week. He was also active in civic affairs. He was a member of the Board of Trustees of the University of Chicago and acted as its chairman from 1963 to 1970; was a director of the Chicago Better Business Bureau; and was general chairman of Chicago's Crusade of Mercy. Cone also served as chairman of both the American Association of Advertising Agencies and the Advertising Council.

Cone was somewhat of a purist. He believed that advertising was not only a respectable profession but also a noble one. An outspoken critic of offensive advertising methods, Cone denounced billboards ("The peace and beauty of the landscape is interrupted and, in effect, violated by jungles of unsightly advertisements") and abhorred the use of advertising to "sell" political candidates. The agency still refuses to accept political advertisements.

In 1975 Cone was elected into the Advertising Hall of Fame and in 1976 to the Illinois Business Hall of Fame. He wrote two autobiographical books *With All Its Faults* and *The Blue Streak.*

"Advertising always follows, it never leads," wrote Cone in *With All Its Faults.* "Nevertheless, it should be used in the best traditions of our society and not the very questionable postures that evolve from time to time. . . . Advertising should never stoop to conquer."

Cone retired to Carmel, California, in 1970. He died in June of 1977 at his home there after a prolonged illness. He was seventy-four.

Today Foote, Cone and Belding is the second largest advertising agency in Chicago—next in line after the Leo Burnett agency—the fourth largest in North America, and the seventh largest in the world, operating 153 offices in 40 countries. In 1986 FC&B moved into its new headquarters at 101 East Erie Street after twenty years at 401 North Michigan Avenue in the Equitable Building.

See also: Leo Burnett

Further reading: Cone, Fairfax M. *With All Its Faults: A Candid Account of Forty Years in Advertising* (1969); Cone, Fairfax M. *The Blue Streak: Some Observations, Mostly About Advertising* (1973).

Jack Conroy

Novelist

born: circa 1899
Moberly, Missouri
died: April 30, 1990
Moberly, Missouri

During the 1930s and 1940s Missouri-born Jack Conroy was the foremost practitioner of what came to be called the "proletarian novel." He wrote his most important work in Chicago, where he befriended and found inspiration from such kindred spirits as Nelson Algren and Richard Wright, both of whom, like the jovial and hard-drinking Conroy, harbored ambitions of becoming the "American Gorki," (referring to the Russian writer renowned for his Bolshevik sympathies).

Photograph reprinted with permission from the *Chicago Sun-Times.*

Jack Conroy was born in the mining town of Moberly, Missouri. His father, a former Jesuit, died in a mining accident. At thirteen Jack worked at a railroad car shop, and at fifteen he served as recording secretary for the local branch of the Brotherhood of Railway Car Men.

In 1922 Conroy led a column of laborers during the Great Railroad Strike of that year. When the strike was broken, Conroy lost his job and spent the next decade doing odd jobs throughout the country and living the life of a hobo. He worked in steel mills in Toledo and auto factories in Detroit, and in 1930 he returned to Missouri as a construction worker and there started *Rebel Poet* magazine. The "manifesto" of *Rebel Poet* eloquently expressed Conroy's leftist leanings. The magazine, he proclaimed, "championed the weak and defenseless" and condemned "the greed of industrial barons who are converting American laborers into abject serfs." His writing career received an additional boost when the Baltimore scribe, H. L. Mencken, published his work in *American Mercury.*

In May of 1933 he became editor of another small literary magazine, *The Anvil,* the first publication to print the work of African-American author, Richard Wright. Its motto was: "We prefer crude vigor to polished banality." In 1935 it merged with the *Partisan Review.* Conroy then came to Chicago in 1938 at the invitation of his friend Nelson Algren to edit the *New Anvil,* with Algren serving as managing editor. Conroy edited the *New Anvil* from 1938 to 1940. In addition to Wright and Algren, the *New Anvil's* list of contributors included James T. Farrell, Langston Hughes, and William Carlos Williams. Along with Algren, Studs Terkel, Saul Bellow, and others, Conroy was a member of the Illinois WPA Writers Project.

Conroy won critical acclaim in 1933 with his novel *The Disinherited,* a thinly disguised autobiographical work about life as a migrant worker in the 1920s.

Another novel about American laborers, *A World to Win* (1935), was not as succcessful as *The Disinherited.* In the same year Conroy was awarded a Guggenheim Fellowship to conduct research on African-American migration to the North. Ten years later, in 1945, his hard work paid off with the release of *They Seek a City,* coauthored with Arna Bontemps. An impassioned account of the mass exodus of rural blacks into the great Northern cities, it was the first literary collaboration between a white author and an African-American author. A revised edition was published in 1966 under the title *Anyplace but Here.*

Conroy also collaborated with Bontemps on several children's books including *The Fast Sooner Hound* (1942) and *Sam Patch* (1951).

In 1969 Conroy received the Illinois Literary Prize. In 1977 he won a National Endowment for the Arts grant.

Conroy also held important editing positions in Chicago: from 1946 to 1947 he was the literary editor of the *Chicago Defender,* and from 1947 to 1969 he was senior editor of the Chicago-based *New Standard Encyclopedia.*

Literary historian Doug Wixson, observed, "He was different from almost all the other proletarian writers. He wrote from within the experience. He was not an educated writer with political sympathies for the downtrodden and the worker. He was one."

In 1979 *The Jack Conroy Reader,* edited by Jack Salzman and David Ray, was published.

Conroy died in April of 1990 in Missouri. He was ninety-one.

See also: Nelson Algren, James T. Farrell, Albert Halper [appendix], Richard Wright

Further reading: Bontemps, Arna and Jack Conroy. *Anyplace But Here* (1966); Drew, Bettina. *Nelson Algren: A Life On the Wild Side* (1989); Salzman, Jack and David Ray, eds. *The Jack Conroy Reader* (1979).

Sam Cooke

Singer

born: January 22, 1935
Chicago, Illinois
died: December 11, 1964
Los Angeles, California

A pioneer soul singer, Sam Cooke was the first major gospel star to cross over to pop. Many critics now credit him with paving the way for a later generation of soul singers. His vocal style found favor with many performers from Otis Redding and Al Green to Smokey Robinson and Teddy Pendergrass. Rock star Rod Stewart has often cited Cooke as a major influence, and, indeed, Stewart recorded several of Cooke's songs, including "Twistin' the Night Away" and "Bring It on Home to Me."

Photograph courtesy of the *Chicago Defender.*

Sam Cook (he added the "e" later) grew up on the South Side of Chicago, one of eight sons of a Baptist minister. He began singing "as soon as he could talk," his father said in a newspaper interview. At nine, Cooke joined a gospel group, the Singing Children, and a few years later became a member of the Highway QC's. In the early 1950s, after graduating from Wendell Phillips High School, he sang with the gospel group, the Soul Stirrers, replacing lead singer, Rebert Harris. Later, he became the lead vocalist of the Pilgrim Travellers. A handsome and charismatic performer, Cooke considered switching to pop but hesitated for fear of offending his loyal gospel audience and disappointing his Baptist father. Hence, early pop recordings were released under the pseudonym, Dale Cook, including his first pop song, in 1956, "Lovable."

In 1957 Cooke recorded an original composition, "You Send Me," for Keen Records, which became his first million-seller, soaring to the top of both the R&B and the pop charts. In 1960 Cooke moved to RCA. Some of his more memorable hits include "Everybody Loves to Cha Cha Cha" (1959), "Only Sixteen" (1959), "Wonderful World" (1960), "Chain Gang" (1960), "Cupid" (1961), "Twistin' the Night Away" (1962), "Bring It on Home to Me" (1962), "Having a Party" (1962), "Another Saturday Night" (1963), and the posthumous "Shake" (1965).

An extremely likable performer, Cooke possessed a warm, sweet, and supple voice that soared, whispered, and lovingly caressed each syllable, giving even the most innocuous lyrics a depth that they otherwise lacked. Unlike many African-American artists who came into prominence during the 1950s and 1960s, Cooke maintained creative control over his material. He not only ran his own publishing company and his own management firm, he also owned a record company, Sar/Derby Records, where he gave a break to many up-and-coming singers, including Bobby Womack, Billy Preston, Mel Carter, and fellow Chicagoan Lou Rawls.

Cooke was shot to death in a Los Angeles motel room in December of 1964 by the night manager, Bertha Franklin, during a scuffle. The singer, dressed only in a topcoat, reportedly attacked Franklin in an effort to find the whereabouts of a young woman he had taken to the motel. Franklin shot Cooke three times during the altercation. His body was brought back to Chicago where thousands of screaming and crying fans at A. R. Leak's Funeral Home on South Cottage Grove Avenue tried to get one last glimpse of their fallen hero. He was buried at Forest Lawn cemetery in Glendale, California.

Despite the sordid circumstances surrounding his death, Cooke remained an idol to African-Americans. In early 1965 RCA released the prophetic, "A Change Is Gonna Come." It was an appropriate swan song, full of fire and righteous anger. It remains an enduring testament to Cooke's great talent.

Record compilations include *Feel It! Live at the Harlem Square Club* (RCA); *Two Sides of Sam Cooke* (Specialty); and *Sam Cooke—The Man and His Music* (RCA).

Further reading: Guralnick, Peter. *Sweet Soul Music: Rhythm and Blues and the Southern Dream of Freedom* (1986); Hirshey, Gerri. *Nowhere to Run: The Story of Soul Music* (1984); McEwen, Joe. Edited by Greg Shaw. *Sam Cooke: A Biography in Words and Pictures* (1977); Miller, Jim, ed. *The Rolling Stone Illustrated History of Rock & Roll* (1976).

Jack L. Cooper

Deejay

born: September 18, 1888
Memphis, Tennessee
died: January 12, 1970
Chicago, Illinois

Jack L. Cooper, a pioneer in his field, dominated black radio from the 1930s to the 1950s. The nation's first African-American radio personality, he was also the city's first black sportscaster on radio, the first black newscaster on radio, and the first black executive of a radio station. Although not the first black deejay on the air, he was the first to offer radio from an exclusively African-American perspective.

Photograph courtesy of the Chicago Historical Society.

Cooper left school in the fifth grade and found work as a gofer, traveling the racetrack circuit through the Midwest and the South. Later he moved to Cincinnati where he fought 160 amateur fights and won several championships including the Negro Welterweight Crown of Ohio. Cooper also played second base for a semi-pro baseball team, managed theaters in Florida and Arkansas, and wrote for several African-American newspapers, including the *Chicago Defender*. In 1924 he was hired as assistant theater editor at the *Defender*, and he wrote a regular column called "Coop's Chatter," which addressed issues of concern to the African-American community.

"Were we to spend half the time between the pages of good books that we spend between the curbstone and the building, there would be less crime, more business, and better understanding," he wrote. More than anything, Cooper wished to see the race advance. Black self-help, he believed, was the only road to success.

Cooper got his start in the entertainment business performing in minstrel shows. He then branched out into acting and comedy routines before forming his own theater troupe in the early twenties, the Cooper and Lamar Music Company.

While working as East Coast correspondent for the *Defender* in Washington, D.C., Cooper made his radio debut on a local musical variety program on a white-owned radio station hosted by a German bandleader. Since black broadcasters were not allowed to work on white radio stations, Cooper cloaked his African-American identity by performing comedy routines in various accents and dialects, including black dialect. The anonymity of radio thus offered African-Americans opportunities that otherwise did not exist in the entertainment field, yet it provided little outlet for self-expression. Frustrated with the program's restrictions and itching to reveal his true identity, Cooper returned to Chicago in 1926, determined to create a niche for African-Americans on the local airwaves.

On November 3, 1929, his first show, "The All-Negro Hour" premiered on WSBC, a live one-hour variety show that featured a diverse cast of characters as well as appearances from top local and national talent. In structure it resembled a vaudeville stage show. The program reflected the sentiment of its time. In response to the unprecedented success of "Amos 'n Andy," Cooper offered "Luke and Timber," about two black migrants. He also aired live gospel and spiritual concerts and produced a mystery-drama serial called "The Nitemare."

But Cooper's radio shows were not all just fun and games. In 1938 he launched a public service program, the "Search for Missing Persons," produced in cooperation with the Chicago Police Department.

Listeners who tuned into Cooper's various shows could hear advice about finding employment, learn about legal rights, and receive news from and about the African-American community. Each August, Cooper aired special coverage of the annual Bud Billiken parade—the biggest event in the black community. In the days before African-Americans were allowed to participate in the majors, Cooper aired play-by-play coverage of black baseball games. He also ran his own adverting agency and gave fellow African-Americans their start in radio. The crowning achievement of Cooper's radio career was a news discussion show called "Listen Chicago," says Mark Newman, author of *Entrepreneurs of Profit and Pride: From Black Appeal to Radio Soul.*

Cooper bought airtime from many stations, including at various times WSBC, WHFC, WEDC, WJJD, WAAF, and WBEF. By the late 1940s—at the height of his career—he boasted more than forty hours of air time on four different radio stations, notes Newman.

Cooper was extremely active in the black community, contributing time and money to various African-American groups and organizations, including the South Side Boys' Club and the Morgan Park Youth Association.

Cooper retired in 1961. He died in his apartment at 1335 West 111th Place at the age of eighty-one in January 1970.

See also: Robert S. Abbott, Charles Correll and Freeman Gosden

Further reading: Heim, Chris. "Riding the Waves: The Rise of Black Radio in Chicago," *Chicago Tribune Sunday Magazine* (February 12, 1989); Newman, Mark. *Entrepreneurs of Profit and Pride: From Black Appeal to Radio Soul* (1988).

Paul Cornell

Real Estate Developer

born: August 5, 1822
White Creek, New York
died: March 3, 1904
Chicago, Illinois

In the 1840s a young lawyer named Paul Cornell came to Chicago from the East. He arrived with a suit of clothes, a pack of business cards, $1.50 in his pocket, and a heart full of hope. Despite his youth—he was only twenty-five years old—he had a shrewd and far-reaching mind. As soon as he was able, he began to acquire property south of the city limits. Eventually he became one of the largest suburban real estate developers in Chicagoland, but today he is best known as the person who laid out the streets and parks of the community he called Hyde Park.

In the early days, Hyde Park was a series of oak ridges running across an open prairie, a low-lying area frequently under water. Cottage Grove was a dirt road. At the southeast corner of 63rd Street and Cottage Grove Avenue stood a barn where horses were kept. The main roads were Lake and Stony Island Avenues, but during or after a rain storm, travelers were forced to use Vincennes Avenue.

Born in upstate New York, Cornell moved with his family to Adams County, Illinois, shortly after his father died. When he was old enough, he decided to study law. In 1847 he was admitted to the Illinois bar and moved to Chicago. On his first night in town, however, his entire savings were stolen from his hotel room. Fortunately, a sympathetic attorney came to his rescue, providing the young man with both a loan and a position in a Chicago law firm.

While working in the law office of Skinner and Hoyne, Cornell met Senator Stephen Douglas who reportedly encouraged him to save all his money and invest it in land situated between the city limits and the Calumet area. Intrigued by this counsel, Cornell rode on horseback to the site and became convinced that a viable community could be built there.

By 1853 Paul Cornell had accumulated enough capital to buy three hundred acres of land from 51st to 55th Streets, which he subdivided and sold to private investors. Although sparsely populated, Cornell assured the community's existence by selling sixty acres of land at its southern edge to the Illinois Central Railroad, with the provision that the railroad make six stops a day at the 53rd Street station. He also created an anchor in the community by building the Hyde Park Hotel. The little community thus became a haven for weary Chicagoans who sought peace and tranquility and wished to get away from the city for a few days. In an effort to attract new residents, Cornell advertised the area as "beautifully situated on high ground interspersed with groves, on the lake shore six miles from Chicago."

In 1861 the residents petitioned the Illinois General Assembly to create the separate township of Hyde Park. About that time the townspeople erected their first public institutions: the First Presbyterian Church of Hyde Park in 1860, a public grammar school a few years later, and a high school in 1870.

After the Civil War, Cornell lobbied in Springfield for the creation of the South Park Commission, an agency that would purchase land and develop a public park system for the area. He hired renowned landscape architect Frederick Law Olmsted to create Jackson and Washington Parks and the Midway Plaisance and thus transform the marshy land into an attractive green belt. Although a lack of capital and the Chicago Fire of 1871 slowed the area's development, the broad boulevards and extensive parks became major selling points in the growth of Hyde Park.

In 1889 Hyde Park was annexed to the city of Chicago. The following year Chicago was chosen as the site of a world's fair, to be held in 1893, to celebrate the four hundredth anniverary of Columbus's journey to America. The influential architect and city planner, Daniel H. Burnham, suggested that nearby Jackson Park would be the perfect location to host such an event. In 1892 the University of Chicago opened, and by the time Cornell died, Hyde Park was clearly no longer a sparsely settled village.

Cornell was a charter member of the South Park Commission and served on it for more than thirteen years. He also acted as the township's first supervisor. Later, he purchased land further south and developed the community of Grand Crossing, which was originally called Cornell.

Cornell, often called the father of Hyde Park, died in Chicago in March of 1904. The elite suburb that he founded developed into one of the city's most prestigious and important neighborhoods with quality housing, schools, shopping, and the much respected University of Chicago.

See also: Daniel H. Burnham, Stephen A. Douglas, John Wellborn Root

Further reading: Block, Jean F. *Hyde Park Houses: An Informal History, 1856–1910* (1978); Holt, Glen E. and Dominic A. Pacyga. *Chicago: A Historical Guide to the Neighborhoods, The Loop and South Side* (1979); Pacyga, Dominic A. and Ellen Skerrett. *Chicago: City of Neighborhoods* (1986).

Charles Correll & Freeman Gosden

Radio Entertainers

born: February 2, 1890
Peoria, Illinois
died: September 26, 1972
Chicago, Illinois

born: May 5, 1899
Richmond, Virginia
died: December 10, 1982
Los Angeles, California

Two of the most popular and durable names in radio history were "Amos" and "Andy." Freeman F. Gosden as Amos and Charles J. Correll as Andy entertained America for over thirty years until changing values and the advent of the Civil Rights movement forced them off the airwaves.

Charles James Correll was born in Peoria, Illinois. After graduating from Peoria High School, Correll worked as a stenographer for the state superintendent of public instruction. Later, he learned the bricklaying trade. But Correll had a creative side, too. He tinkered on the piano and participated in local amateur theater productions.

Freeman Fisher Gosden attended school in Richmond, Virginia, and Atlanta, Georgia, and then sold tobacco products and later automobiles. During World War I he served as a Navy radio operator.

Gosden met Correll while he was working for a firm that staged amateur theater productions. They became fast friends and began traveling together for several years, putting on amateur shows.

In 1924 the duo began singing on radio station WEBH that broadcasted from the Edgewater Beach Hotel in Chicago. The following year they joined the staff of WGN radio. Within two years they starred in their own radio show as two stereotypical African-American characters named "Sam" and "Henry."

Despite the success of the show, the pair decided to switch stations, jumping to WMAQ in 1928, and they changed the names of their characters to the more euphonious, "Amos" and "Andy."

Gosden portrayed Amos Jones, the lazy but good-natured partner who was always making promises he couldn't keep, while Correll was the shrewd and mischievous Andy Brown. As co-owners of the Fresh-Air Taxicab, they ruled over a motley assortment of characters—most of them played by Gosden and Correll—including the Kingfish, Lightnin', and Madame Queen.

On August 19, 1929, "Amos 'n Andy" aired nationally on NBC. By 1930 the show was running six nights a week with Gosden writing most of the scripts. It was said that during the 1930s the program was so popular that the country came to a halt for fifteen minutes every night. "Amos 'n Andy" was on the air continuously, five nights a week, from 1929 until the spring of 1943, when it became a weekly half-hour show. It continued on radio until 1960. In 1948 CBS bought the rights to the characters from Correll and Gosden for a reported $2.5 million.

The pair appeared in blackface in two movies, *Check and Double Check* (1930) and *The Big Broadcast* (1936).

In the late 1940s Correll and Gosden searched the country for African-American actors to play the title roles in the television version, rather than portraying the characters themselves. "The truth is," said Correll, "we don't look believable in blackface. We look like something out of burlesque or a minstrel show." More than eight hundred African-American actors were auditioned, according to a report in the *Chicago Tribune*. The TV show, which premiered in 1951, was the first network series with an all-black cast: Spencer Williams played Andy, Alvin Childress played Amos, and Tim Moore played Kingfish.

During its radio heyday, few African-Americans actually protested the show. "Amos 'n Andy" was, according to at least one veteran radio executive, possibly more popular among blacks than among whites. Scattered complaints did occur, of course, especially among black professionals who attacked the program as a stereotypical depiction of African-American life. As early as 1931 the *Pittsburgh Courier* petitioned the FCC to cancel "Amos 'n Andy." The show continued, however.

In 1951, the National Association for the Advancement of Colored People (NAACP) charged that the television series portrayed African-Americans "in a stereotyped and derogatory way." Correll and Gosden, who produced the program, denied the accusations. Rather, they insisted, they were merely satirizing human nature. Nevertheless mounting protests during the mid-sixties forced the withdrawal of the television show from syndication.

In 1972 Correll died in Chicago of cardiorespiratory problems at the age of eighty-two. Gosden died in Los Angeles in 1982. He was eighty-three.

See also: Jack L. Cooper

Further reading: Ely, Melvin Patrick. *The Adventures of Amos 'n' Andy: A Social History of an American Phenomenon* (1991); MacDonald, J. Fred. *Don't Touch That Dial: Radio Programming in American Life from 1920 to 1960* (1979); Newman, Mark. *Entrepreneurs of Profit and Pride: From Black Appeal to Radio Soul* (1988).

John Coughlin

Politician

born: August 15, 1860
Chicago, Illinois
died: November 8, 1938
Chicago, Illinois

Along with his partner, Michael "Hinky Dink" Kenna, "Bathhouse John" Coughlin held the aldermanic seat of the corrupt 1st Ward for over forty-five years. Through bribery, chicanery, and a shrewd understanding of Chicago politics, Coughlin maintained control.

Photograph reprinted with permission from the *Chicago Sun-Times*.

John Coughlin was Irish on both sides. His father hailed from County Roscommon, his mother from County Limerick. He grew up in an area east of the Chicago River between Adams and Monroe Streets known as Connelly's Patch. His father made a respectable living as the proprietor of a small grocery store, but like many Chicagoans, he lost everything in the Chicago Fire of 1871. Coughlin attended classes at the Jones School at Harrison and Federal Streets. After hours, he labored as an assistant to the school janitor. He left Jones at age thirteen and spent two years at the Christian Brothers' Industrial School. At fifteen he had had enough of schooling and was ready to go to work.

An amiable and easy-going lad, Coughlin took any job that came his way—as a delivery boy and then clerk in his father's store. He was ecstatic when his brother Joe got him a job as a rubber in a Turkish bathhouse on Clark Street. Here young Coughlin got his first glimpse of the trappings of power and the men who ran the city. He was duly impressed. He rubbed down politicians, prize fighters, merchants, and underworld figures, and he hoped that one day he would join their prominent ranks. "I formed my philosophy while watching and studying the types of people who patronized the bathhouses," he would later say. "I watched and learned never to quarrel, never to feud. I had the best schooling a young feller could have."

One year later Coughlin got a job in the finest bathhouse in the city, located in the Palmer House, and met more of the city's movers and shakers. Through such connections, he was able to open his own establishment in 1882. A few months later, he opened another and earned the nickname, "Bathhouse John."

The rough and tumble world of Chicago politics appealed to the young businessman. He became a member of the 1st Ward Democratic Club and then became a precinct captain. Coughlin was a natural-born politician. He felt at home in the company of these brash men and enjoyed the privileges and status that political office brought. Most importantly, he knew when to shut his mouth and play along, and in Chicago politics that virtually guaranteed success.

He wore the clothing of a young man on the rise—loud colors, silk bowler hat, frock coat, and mauve gloves. But Coughlin wanted more. Dissatisfied with being on the periphery of politics, he longed to see it from the inside. He got his wish on April 5, 1892, when he was elected alderman of the 1st Ward. The 1st Ward was the richest and most notorious of the city's wards since it contained the central business district and the extremely lucrative red-light district. Never one to rock the boat, Coughlin voted as he was told by fellow city council members on important city ordinances.

But the winds of Chicago politics frequently change course. Shortly after his election, Coughlin found himself at odds with the mayor. Carter Harrison (I) had just been reelected for the fifth time. A practical man, Harrison had chosen to distance himself from the underworld element ("I am for the people. I will not have anything to do with the bummers," he insisted). Coughlin, who made the mistake of supporting the incumbent Mayor Hempstead Washburne during the campaign, was conveniently cast aside. Powerless and friendless, the hapless alderman turned to Michael "Hinky Dink" Kenna for help. Kenna was a taciturn saloonkeeper who kept to himself and spoke only when necessary, but he knew Chicago politics inside and out. All Coughlin had to do, advised Kenna, was stay out of trouble and warm up to Harrison. Harrison would eventually come around.

It worked. Coughlin soon found himself in Harrison's good graces again. Kenna was elected alderman in 1897, and with Kenna by his side—for twenty-six years, they ruled as aldermen of the 1st Ward—Coughlin made inroads into the lucrative underworld trade then thriving in the Levee, the city's sprawling red-light district. Protection money from gamblers, saloonkeepers, brothels, and gaming houses helped to line the pockets of Coughlin and Kenna and the ward organization.

Despite the money that was flooding into the area, the 1st Ward was always hard pressed for cash. Coughlin and Kenna devised an ingenious solution one day in Hinky Dink's saloon. Why not stage a lavish ball to bring revenue into the coffers of the Democratic ward organizaton? Why not indeed? And so began a colorful Chicago tradition with the first ball taking place on Christmas of 1896.

For ten years the notorious 1st Ward balls were examples of Chicago at its most sinful. Truth be told, the city had never seen anything quite like it. The highlight of a typical 1st Ward ball, the moment that everyone waited for, was the arrival of "Bathhouse John" himself—dressed in lavender trousers, pink gloves, yellow pumps, and silk top hat—leading the grand march at the stroke of midnight. While reformers recoiled in horror at the sight of pimps, burglars, and prostitutes mingling with police officers, politicians, and businessmen, historians tell us that Bathhouse John and Hinky Dink counted the proceeds and laughed all the way to the bank.

The days of the 1st Ward balls were soon to end, however. Public outrage and reformers like George E. Cole, president of the Municipal Voters' League, a watchdog organization, and Arthur Burrage Farwell, president of the Chicago Law and Order League, made sure of it. The last 1st Ward ball was held in 1910. The Everleigh Club, the Levee's most famous brothel, was shut down on October 24, 1911, by orders of Mayor Herrison. After constant raiding by the police, the Levee was finally shut down altogether in 1912.

With Coughlin and Kenna's influence waning in the 1920s, a new, more dangerous element gained control of the 1st Ward—gangsters with names like Colosimo and Torrio were taking over. Even Coughlin's self-proclaimed status as "Chicago's poet alderman" came under attack when newsman Jack Lait revealed that *Tribune* reporter Jack Kelley, not Coughlin, wrote all his poetry.

Coughlin spent his last years in city hall as a pawn for the bosses of the underworld. Kenna and Coughlin became mere puppets of Al Capone. Most of Coughlin's colleagues from the old days were gone, and the new breed expressed little interest in his incoherent ramblings. For months he lay sick and feeble in the Lexington Hotel. He died on November 8, 1938, with debts from his lavish spending habits totaling $56,000.

See also: Al Capone, Carter Harrison I, Carter Harrison II, Michael Kenna

Further reading: Kogan, Herman and Lloyd Wendt. *Lords of the Levee: The Story of Bathhouse John and Hinky Dink* (1943).

Richard J. Daley

Politician

born: May 15, 1902
Chicago, Illinois
died: December 20, 1976
Chicago, Illinois

Richard Joseph Daley ran Chicago for twenty-one years, from 1955 to 1976— longer than any other mayor in Chicago history. Indeed, many Chicagoans knew no other mayor. By forging a multi- ethnic coalition that consisted of the working class, middle class, white ethnics, and African-Americans, Daley was able to control city hall for over two decades. Daley never coveted any higher office, never made any great fortune. He was simply the mayor.

Photograph reprinted with permission from the *Chicago Sun-Times*.

Daley grew up in the ethnically diverse neighborhood of Bridgeport, the son of an Irish-American metalworker/union activist father and a suffragette mother. Born at 3602 South Lowe Avenue, he was baptized at Nativity of Our Lord Catholic Church at 37th Street and Union Avenue. He attended a Catholic high school, De LaSalle Institute, at 35th Street and Wabash Avenue and later found work in the nearby stockyards while attending law school at night. In 1933 he graduated from DePaul University, becoming the first member of his family to earn a college degree. A life-long resident of Bridgeport, Daley continued to reside in the brick bungalow at 3536 South Lowe—one block away from his place of birth—even after winning the mayor's seat.

At twenty-one, Daley became a precinct captain and, a bit later, a clerk in the city council. In 1927 he served as clerk-secretary to 11th Ward alderman Joseph P. McDonough after which he held a variety of positions in local government—secretary to the county treasurer, deputy county comptroller, and ward committeeman. In 1936 Daley, a Democrat, was elected to the Illinois legislature as a write-in Republican when the state representative, David Shanahan, died. After resuming office, however, Daley returned to the Democratic fold. Two years later, he won a seat in the state senate.

In 1946 Daley lost in his bid to become county sheriff—his only defeat—but recuperated sufficiently to be appointed deputy comptroller of Cook County. Three years later, he was named director of the Illinois Department of Finance by Governor Adlai E. Stevenson. In 1950 he was chosen Cook County clerk, and in 1953 he became chairman of the Cook County Democratic Central Committee—a position with considerable clout.

In 1955 Daley was nominated for mayor of Chicago. He challenged and defeated the incumbent, Martin H. Kennelly, in the Democratic primary and then faced the Republican nominee, Robert E. Merriam, son of educator and politician, Charles E. Merriam. Daley defeated his opponent 708,222 to 581,255. At age fifty-three, the native of Bridgeport had won his first mayoral election.

Daley inherited a political machine. He consolidated his power and extended his party influence to the state and national levels. His enthusiastic support of John F. Kennedy for president in 1960 helped elect the New Englander to the White House. Daley became known as a kingmaker. He was reelected in 1959, 1963, 1967, and 1971.

Daley's longevity was due in no small measure to his ability to compromise. During his years in office, he initiated a massive program of public works, including the construction of O'Hare International Airport, the development of the expressway system, and the launching of extensive urban renewal projects in the Hyde Park-Kenwood, Near North, and Near West Side neighborhoods. He made sure the streets were cleaned and repaired and the garbage collected.

In 1968 Chicago and other American cities experienced ugly race riots following the assassination of Dr. Martin Luther King, Jr., in Memphis. The intensity of the violence prompted Daley to issue his now infamous "shoot to kill" order. During the Democratic convention in August of the same year, the city again was the scene of violent demonstrations, this time between police and anti–Vietnam War demonstrators. Despite criticism from the press, newspaper polls revealed that public opinion supported Daley's hardnosed crackdown.

In 1974 Daley suffered two strokes, yet recovered. During the 1975 reelection campaign, he beat liberal alderman William Singer and black state senator Richard Newhouse in the primaries before easily defeating Republican challenger John J. Hoellen in the general election, winning an unprecedented sixth term in office. Although it proved to be his highest margin of victory—75 percent—it was based on one of the lowest voter turnouts in the city's history.

The various Daley administrations saw their share of scandals over the years, including the notorious Summerdale police scandal of 1960—police officers from the Summerdale district were charged with being part of an extensive burglary ring—but none ever touched Daley personally.

Not known as a great orator, Daley frequently misspoke, often to devastatingly funny effect. Consider these choice Daley malapropisms: "We must rise to ever higher and higher platitudes of achievement;" or "They have vilified me," he said, referring to yet another run-in with the press, "they have crucified me, yes, they have even criticized me;" and perhaps his most famous remark, "Gentlemen, get the thing straight, once and for all: the policeman isn't there to create disorder, the policeman is there to preserve disorder."

The quote, however, that best sums up Daley's philosophy was a deceptively simple yet exceedingly wise statement he made in 1955: "As a leader of the Democratic Party of Cook County I pledge to continue a policy based on the principle that good government is good politics—and good politics is good government."

Daley suffered a fatal heart attack while in his doctor's office on December 20, 1976. He was seventy-four.

See also: Anton J. Cermak, Julius J. Hoffman, Edward J. Kelly, Ralph Metcalfe, Harold Washington

Further reading: Allswang, John M. "Richard J. Daley: America's Last Boss" in *The Mayors: The Chicago Political Tradition*, Paul M. Green and Melvin G. Holli, eds.(1987); Gleason, Bill. *Daley of Chicago: The Man, the Mayor, and the Limits of Conventional Politics* (1970); Kennedy, Eugene. *Himself! The Life and Times of Mayor Richard J. Daley* (1978); O'Connor, Len. *Mayor Daley and His City* (1975); O'Connor, Len. *Requiem: The Decline and Demise of Mayor Daley and His Era* (1977); Rakove, Milton. *Don't Make No Waves—Don't Back No Losers: An Insider's Analysis of the Daley Machine* (1975); Royko, Mike. *Boss: Richard J. Daley of Chicago* (1971).

Arnold Damen

Priest

born: March 15, 1815
Leur, Holland
died: January 1, 1889
Omaha, Nebraska

Arnold Damen pioneered Catholic education in the frontier town of Chicago. He was the founding father of Holy Family parish, often referred to as the parish on the prairie and the first Jesuit parish in Chicago.

The seventh of nine chidren, the Dutch-born Damen was the son of John Damen, a prosperous builder. As a young boy, Damen leaned toward a life in the priesthood. He became determined to follow the path of God after hearing the words of Father Peter DeSmet, a missionary to the Native American community, and Damen offered himself as a candidate for Jesuit missions to America. The forthright and hard-working Damen was accepted.

Damen trained at the village of Florissant, some fifteen miles from St. Louis, Missouri. He was ordained in 1844 at the age of twenty-nine. After three years assisting in parish work, Damen was appointed the first pastor of St. Francis Xavier's Church in St. Louis, where he stayed for ten years.

Damen, a fellow clergyman noted, was "gifted with uncommon eloquence." He drew crowds to his sermons and became known throughout St. Louis and the state of Missouri. As his reputation spread, Damen was invited to conduct a series of sermons in Chicago. At the request of Bishop Anthony O'Regan, he conducted a mission in Chicago in August of 1856 with three other Jesuits, Isidore Boudreaux, Benedict Masselis, and Michael Corbett. O'Regan invited them to stay and to establish a parish and an educational system. They preferred, however, to form a new parish altogether rather than merely take over Holy Name Church at State and Superior Streets.

Damen acquired property near the intersection of Blue Island Avenue and 12th Street (later called Roosevelt Road) in May of 1857 and began building a frame church, Holy Family, at 11th and May Streets—the only Catholic church on the West Side

and, indeed, one of the few structures in the neighborhood. Many Jesuits criticized Damen's decision to settle in such a remote location.

Nevertheless, the church was dedicated by Bishop James Duggan on July 12, 1857. The early parishioners were hard-working folk—mostly Irish but also Bohemian and German—who labored in the nearby railroad yards or along the Chicago River, loading and unloading boats or working as mechanics, blacksmiths, bricklayers, and carpenters.

The cornerstone of the present church was laid on August 23, 1857, and was dedicated on August 26, 1860. It was—and still is—a handsome church, said to be the third largest church in the country at that time. The interior was designed by the respected Chicago architect John Van Osdel. The *Chicago Tribune* called it "certainly one of the finest edifices of its class in the United States."

Damen, who was said to know everyone in the parish by name, then went about establishing a comprehensive school system in the parish—the Holy Family Free School for Girls in 1857 and, in the same year, the Holy Family Free School for Boys. In 1860 the Religious of the Sacred Heart order opened a parochial school at Taylor and Lyle Streets.

In 1867 Father Damen invited the Sisters of Charity of the Blessed Virgin Mary from Dubuque, Iowa, to teach at the Holy Family parish. That summer they opened two schools, St. Aloysius and St. Stanislaus. On September 5, 1870, St. Ignatius College, forerunner of Loyola University, opened on West Roosevelt Road with Father Damen acting as the school's first president. The school miraculously survived the Chicago Fire of 1871. While the fire raged outside, Father Damen, it is said, made a promise at the shrine of Our Lady of

Perpetual Help to keep seven lighted candles burning on the altar if the school and church were spared.

Damen served as president of the college until 1872 while retaining his title as pastor of the Holy Family parish. Damen established parochial schools in the frontier town and tried to instill in his congregation a love of the written word. More important, he resolved to preach and bring the word of the Gospel to the poor. Damen was such a dominant force in the community that Holy Family began to be known as simply "Damen's church" and the parish as "Damen's parish."

In 1877 Damen was appointed superior of the missions, headquartered at St. Ignatius College. Two years later, he was appointed pastor of Sacred Heart Church. By the following year, a new four-story brick school had been completed. By 1890 Holy Family parish had become the largest English-speaking parish in the country.

In 1888 Damen was sent to Creighton College in Omaha, Nebraska. On June 4, 1888, while preaching in Evanston, Wyoming, he suffered a stroke. His condition deteriorated during the following months, and he died in Omaha on New Year's Day 1889. He was seventy-four.

In 1927 Robey Street was renamed Damen Avenue in honor of the clergyman.

Dwindling enrollment and financial hardship had taken such a heavy toll upon Holy Family that the Jesuit owners had reluctantly decided to demolish the structure unless one million dollars in cash was raised by the December 31, 1990 deadline. Racing against the clock, the Holy Family Preservation Society mounted a whirlwind eleventh hour appeal.

People from throughout the city and, indeed, the country responded generously and Holy Family Church was saved from the wrecking ball.

The work that Father Damen began so many years ago on the Illinois prairie continues.

See also: Jacques Marquette [appendix], George Mundelein, James Quigley

Further reading: Conroy, Joseph P. *Arnold Damen, S.J.: A Chapter in the Making of Chicago* (1930); Garraghan, Gilbert J., S.J. *The Jesuits of the Middle United States.* 3 vols. (1984); Koenig, Rev. Msgr. Harry C., S.T.D. *A History of the Parishes of the Archdiocese of Chicago.* 2 vols. (1980); Lane, George A. and Algimantas Kezys. *Chicago Churches and Synagogues: An Architectural Pilgrimage* (1981).

Clarence Darrow

Lawyer

born: April 18, 1857
Kinsman, Ohio
died: March 13, 1938
Chicago, Illinois

Clarence Seward Darrow, a magnificent orator and lifelong dissenter, defended unpopular causes and handled the most sensational trials of his day. A celebrity lawyer during a time when the profession was populated by faceless figures in sterile courtrooms, Darrow befriended the poor, the weak, the powerless, the disenfranchised, and the forgotten.

Photograph courtesy of Charles H. Kerr Publishing Company.

Born in northeastern Ohio, Darrow came from a family of free thinkers. His father was an agnostic and an ardent abolitionist as well as the village cabinetmaker, furniture dealer, and undertaker. Darrow studied at Allegheny College and at the University of Michigan Law School. Admitted to the bar in 1878, he practiced law in northeastern Ohio. Several years of small town law convinced him to move to a bigger city.

In 1888, Darrow arrived in Chicago, where he met a fellow liberal thinker and judge, John Peter Altgeld. Darrow had greatly admired Altgeld's impassioned critique, *Our Penal Machinery and Its Victims,* which urged prison reform. The two men became fast friends and eventual business associates. Later Darrow formed a partnership with the lawyer/poet, Edgar Lee Masters.

In 1890 Darrow was appointed assistant corporation counsel for the city. He resigned to become general counsel for the Chicago and Northwestern Railway and then left in 1895 to defend Eugene Debs in the Pullman strike trial. The trial was a turning point in Darrow's career. "The decision to defend Debs led me away from the world of wealth to that of wretchedness and misery," he wrote later. "For making it I have no regrets."

In 1902 Darrow was elected to the Illinois House on the Public Ownership ticket, an independent party that advocated public ownership of the city's streetcar lines. He served one term. By this time Darrow had gained a national reputation as a labor lawyer. He represented miners in the anthracite (coal) strike of 1902 in Pennsylvania and, in 1907, successfully defended William D. Haywood, who was accused of the murder of former Idaho governor Frank Steunenberg. In 1911 he defended the McNamara brothers, two terrorists accused of bombing the *Los Angeles Times* building in a labor dispute that ultimately killed twenty innocent workers. Darrow once again emerged victorious but, in the process, he himself was accused of jury tampering. Although acquitted, the experience devastated him so that it took some time for the famed attorney to get back on his feet again. He returned to Chicago in 1913, in his words, "pretty near done."

Darrow's biggest case came in 1924. Nathan Leopold and Richard Loeb were teenage sons of prominent Chicagoans who kidnapped and murdered fourteen-year-old Bobby Franks for "kicks." Loeb, seventeen, had long wanted to commit the "perfect crime" and persuaded his friend, Leopold, to assist. While the public clamored for the death penalty, Darrow pleaded for mercy. In the end, he won. On September 10, 1924, the court sentenced the defendants to life imprisonment.

Another sensational case was the infamous Scopes "monkey trial." In 1925 a twenty-four-year-old Tennessee schoolteacher, John T. Scopes, was indicted and charged with a misdemeanor for teaching Charles Darwin's theory of evolution in a public school. The Scopes trial tested the constitutionality of a new "anti-evolution" law that had just passed the Tennessee general assembly. Broadcast over WGN radio, the landmark case mesmerized Chicago and, indeed, the rest of the country. In one corner stood the "infidel" Darrow on the side of science and free speech; on the other the true believer, William Jennings Bryan, a former statesman and a great orator in his own right. The case was later dismissed by a Tennessee court on a technicality.

Early in his career, Darrow opposed the principle of capital punishment. He tried unsuccessfully, for example, to stop the execution of Eugene Prendergast, who was convicted of the assassination of Chicago mayor Carter Harrison I in 1893. Darrow sincerely believed that poverty caused crime and other forms of anti-social behavior. "If everybody had a minimum wage of $50 a day," he said back in 1932, "there would be no crime." Punishment, as such, he deemed an ineffectual way of handling transgressions.

Darrow wrote many novels and essays. Among his books are *An Eye for an Eye* (1905); *Crime, Its Cause and Treatment* (1925); and his autobiography, *The Story of My Life* (1932).

Darrow died of heart disease in March of 1938 at his home at 1537 East 60th Street, overlooking the bridge over the Jackson Park lagoon. He was eighty years old. Funeral services were held in the Bond Chapel on the University of Chicago campus, and his ashes were scattered in the lagoon. On May 1, 1957, the bridge was dedicated the Clarence Darrow Bridge. Every year a wreath-laying ceremony is held commemorating the life of the celebrated lawyer.

Such a larger-than-life figure couldn't help but attract the attention of Hollywood producers and screenwriters. Several actors, including Spencer Tracy, portrayed Darrow on the big screen. Henry Fonda played the lawyer on the stage in a popular one-man show during the 1970s.

See also: John Peter Altgeld, Eugene Debs, Henry Demarest Lloyd, Edgar Lee Masters

Further reading: Darrow, Clarence. *The Story of My Life* (1932); Stone, Irving. *Clarence Darrow for the Defense* (1941); Tierney, Kevin. *Darrow: A Biography* (1979); Weinberg, Arthur, ed. *Attorney for the Damned: Clarence Darrow in the Courtroom* (1957); Weinberg, Arthur and Lila. *Clarence Darrow: A Sentimental Rebel* (1980).

Charles Gates Dawes

Politician

born: August 27, 1865
Marietta, Ohio
died: April 23, 1951
Evanston, Illinois

Charles Gates Dawes served as comptroller of the currency during the McKinley administration and as vice-president of the United States under Calvin Coolidge from 1925 to 1929. But more than this, Dawes was a lawyer, banker, diplomat, soldier, statesman, and philanthropist, something of a Renaissance man, and an avowed patriot who scorned convention and despised pomposity in all its forms.

Among his other achievements, Dawes served as brigadier general during World War I; was the first Director of the Budget in 1921; developed the Dawes Plan, for which he was awarded the Nobel Peace Prize in 1925; served as ambassador to Great Britain from 1929 to 1932; and acted as the finance chairman of the 1933 Chicago World's Fair.

Dawes came from a long line of military men. The son of a Civil War general, he was a descendant of William Dawes, who made the famous midnight ride with Paul Revere to warn the Americans of the British advance. Dawes spent his boyhood in the river town of Marietta, Ohio, and at age nineteen he received a bachelor of arts degree from Marietta College. He then attended the Cincinnati Law School, was admitted to the Ohio bar, and moved to Lincoln, Nebraska, to set up a law practice.

In 1894 he left the legal profession and entered the natural gas supply business, first in La Crosse, Wisconsin, and then in Evanston, Illinois. Two years later he entered politics and campaigned for presidential hopeful William McKinley. His business acumen did not go unnoticed, for when McKinley won the election he appointed Dawes, at age thirty-one, comptroller of the currency.

In 1902 Dawes made his first try for elected office, running for the Republican nomination for the Illinois Senate, but he was decisively beaten. His political curiosity satisfied, he returned to banking and established the Central Trust Company.

During World War I, Dawes joined the army, earned the rank of major in the Corps of Engineers, and was given the responsibility of purchasing supplies for the American Expeditionary Force in Europe. In this capacity he was especially good at

cutting through government bureacracy. Later he was appointed brigadier general under General John J. Pershing.

In 1923 he authored the Dawes Plan, an ambitious attempt to rebuild Europe and to collect German reparations. For this he was awarded the Nobel Peace Prize in 1925, sharing it with Sir Austen Chamberlain, British foreign secretary.

After returning to the United States, Dawes was appointed the first director of the budget under President Warren G. Harding. His career improved considerably in 1924 when Calvin Coolidge chose him as his vice-presidential running mate. Dawes spent most of his time on this campaign trail attacking the Ku Klux Klan.

In 1929 President Herbert Hoover made Dawes ambassador to Great Britain. As ambassador, he caused a minor diplomatic row when he refused to wear knee breeches at the Court of St. James.

Dawes retired from public life in 1932 and returned to Chicago to help his brother Rufus organize the Century of Progress exhibition. He was then appointed the first chairman of the Reconstruction Finance Corporation, which attempted to restore financial stability in Europe. He resigned when he discovered that the Central Trust Company he had founded was encountering financial difficulties.

Always an outspoken statesman, the old soldier opposed American involvement in World War II.

Dawes wrote eight books on banking and government, including *The Banking System in the United States, Journal of the Great War,* and *First Year of the Budget.* His personal fortune, derived from banking and public utilities, was reportedly one of Chicago's largest.

Dawes married Carol Blymyer in 1888. In 1912 their only son, Rufus, drowned off Lake Geneva, Illinois. In 1913 Dawes built a $100,000 hotel for the homeless at 12 South Peoria Street in Chicago as a memorial to his son.

Dawes lived in a twenty-eight-room mansion at 225 Greenwood Street in Evanston from 1909 until his death in 1951. The mansion is now maintained by the Evanston Historical Society and was declared a National Historic Landmark in December of 1976. It is open to the public.

Further reading: Timmons, Bascom N. *Portrait of an American: Charles G. Dawes* (1953).

Eugene Debs

Labor Activist

born: November 5, 1855
Terre Haute, Indiana
died: October 20, 1926
Elmhurst, Illinois

Eugene Victor Debs, the foremost leader of the American socialist movement, began his public life as a Democrat. He earned the socialist party's nomination for president on five occasions and traveled the country speaking on many controversial subjects: women's rights, equality for blacks, birth control, and child labor. An outspoken foe of capitalism, Debs spent his entire life fighting against what he considered the tyranny of corporations, who judged employees solely in terms of their profit value.

Photograph courtesy of Charles H. Kerr Publishing Company.

Debs came from a close-knit French family who had settled in the largely French community of Terre Haute, Indiana. He quit school at fourteen to work for the railroad, scraping paint and grease from locomotives. Laid off during the recession of 1873, he tried to find work in Evansville, Indiana, but when he did not succeed there, he went to St. Louis where he was hired as a locomotive fireman.

The death of a friend in a locomotive accident and the prodding of his mother, who feared for his safety, convinced Debs to abandon railroading in 1874. He returned to Terre Haute and took a job as a loader at a wholesale grocery company.

In 1875 Debs joined his first labor union, the Brotherhood of Locomotive Firemen. He was elected city clerk of Terre Haute, and in 1884 he won a seat in the Indiana House of Representatives. During his term there he supported various civil rights measures, including a bill to abolish race discrimination and one that extended suffrage to women. Both bills were defeated. Not willing to compromise his ideals, he decided not to seek reelection.

In 1893 Debs was one of the founders of the American Railway Union (ARU), and he later became its president. "Labor," he said, "can organize, it can unify, it can consolidate its forces. This done, it can demand and command."

A devastating war broke out between capital and labor in 1893–94. There were many skirmishes across the land, but the eyes of the nation were focused on Illinois. The battle was fought in the company town of Pullman, with Eugene Debs acting as the ARU's field commander. For this reason, the Pullman boycott of 1894 was nicknamed "The Debs Rebellion."

Pullman was portrayed by the popular press as a "model" community run by a benevolent and just manager. In reality, George Pullman was hardly the kind figure he was made out to be. In 1893 a severe economic depression gripped the nation. In order to maintain the company goal of a 6 percent profit Pullman dismissed workers and cut their wages but refused to lower their rents. The workers grew angrier and more resentful. Meanwhile, Pullman remained in his plush Prairie Avenue mansion, unyielding and implacable in his resolve to weather the storm.

In May of 1894 the workers voted to strike despite an injunction forbidding it. Pullman was adamant. He refused to talk with the ARU. In retaliation, Debs ordered the ARU's 150,000 members not to handle any Pullman cars or equipment but cautioned them to avoid violence. Debs's defiance landed him in the McHenry County Jail in Woodstock, Illinois, under the charge that he had conspired to obstruct the mails. It would not be the last time he served a jail sentence. The strike ended in July, and, for the moment, Pullman emerged victorious.

For a brief period in his life, Debs supported the Populist party (a pro-farmer, pro-worker party popular in the 1890s), but finding it an inadequate answer to the inequities of American society, he abandoned capitalism altogether and converted to socialism. On June 10, 1898, the Social Democracy of America party met in Chicago. Its manifesto called for the public ownership of all industries controlled by monopolies and trusts, the public ownership of all railroads, national insurance for workers against accidents and unemployment, and the replacement of war with international arbitration.

And several years later—on June 27, 1905—a new industrial union was formed, also in Chicago. The members, who included Debs, William Haywood, Lucy Parsons, and "Mother" Jones, called themselves the Industrial Workers of the World (IWW).

Despite Deb's leadership, the Socialist party in America was in trouble from the start. Its direction was unclear, its goals wavered, and the radical ideology that occasionally surfaced clashed with that of the more conservative members.

On June 16, 1918, at the Ohio Socialists' state convention in Canton, Ohio, Debs delivered a speech urging workers to oppose the war effort. A government reporter in the audience zealously wrote down the labor leader's every word and gesture. Debs was arrested on June 30, 1918, and indicted for violation of the Espionage Act. The trial began in Cleveland that September. The jury deliberated for six hours and found him guilty.

Despite Debs's confinement in an Atlanta penitentiary, the members of the National Socialist Convention in New York renominated him for a fifth term as president of the union. As time went on, more and more petitions for Debs's release arrived on the desk of President Woodrow Wilson. Many feared that the feeble sixty-five-year-old man might die in prison. Wilson, however, denied parole. It wasn't until Warren G. Harding took office that the labor leader was freed, on Christmas Day in 1921. He had spent almost three years in jail.

After his release, despite rheumatism, kidney trouble, and heart problems, Debs continued to speak and write on behalf of socialism. In September of 1926 he checked into the Lindlahr Sanitarium in west suburban Elmhurst, Illinois, hoping to regain his health. But his condition deteriorated and by mid-October he lapsed into a coma. The man who abhorred poverty, had an abiding faith in the sanctity of human fellowship, and served as an inspiring role model for a generation of labor leaders died on October 20, 1926. He was eulogized from Chicago to Moscow.

See also: John Peter Altgeld, Clarence Darrow, William "Big Bill" Haywood [appendix], Henry Demarest Lloyd, Lucy and Albert Parsons

Further reading: Brommel, Bernard J. *Eugene V. Debs: Spokesman for Labor and Socialism* (1978); Carwardine, William H. *The Pullman Strike* (1973); Ginger, Ray. *The Bending Cross: A Biography of Eugene Victor Debs* (1949); Ginger, Ray. *Altgeld's America: The Lincoln Ideal Versus Changing Realities* (1958).

Oscar De Priest

Politician

born: March 9, 1871
Florence, Alabama
died: May 12, 1951
Chicago, Illinois

Oscar Stanton De Priest was a popular figure in Chicago's African-American community and one of its most powerful politicians. A Republican, De Priest became the first black alderman in Chicago, the first black Cook County commissioner, and the first African-American elected to Congress from a northern state. This latter victory proved a landmark in the history of the black community, inspiring other African-Americans across the country to follow his example.

Photograph courtesy of the *Chicago Defender.*

Born in rural Alabama, De Priest received his education in the Salinas, Kansas, public school system. At the age of seventeen he ran away with two friends to Dayton, Ohio. He eventually settled in Chicago in the 1890s where he found work as a house painter. He entered politics as a candidate for county commissioner in the early 1900s and served two terms on the county board before being defeated for reelection in 1908.

For many years the city's white power structure thwarted the ambitions of black politicians. White bosses such as Martin Madden and George Harding ruled over predominantly black wards. As black people became more vociferous, however, and began demanding representation in their neighborhoods, the Republican organization could no longer ignore them. Succumbing to this pressure, party leaders nominated De Priest for alderman of the the 2nd Ward in 1915. He won the election.

In 1916 De Priest garnered tremendous support from the black community when he introduced a civil rights ordinance in the Chicago City Council. It was a valiant try but clearly ahead of its time, for it was loudly ridiculed and soundly defeated. Black politicians still bowed to the wishes of the white bosses rather than serve the needs of their own people. In this regard, De Priest was a typical politician. Indeed, his critics found his voting record particularly deficient. The Municipal Voters' League, a watchdog group whose aim was to rid the city council of corrupt aldermen, censured De Priest and charged that he voted against virtually every reform bill that came his way. "No alderman in Chicago's history (has) piled up a more notorious record in so short a time," they said, and they described him as "a colored politician who for years has been used by white politicians to line up colored votes; has considerable force and ability, but is thoroughly self-seeking."

Controversy followed De Priest in 1917 when he was indicted for accepting payoffs from gamblers and for bribing police officers. The embattled alderman insisted that the alleged payoffs were, in fact, campaign contributions and charged that he was the victim of racism. Thanks to the brilliant defense of his lawyer, Clarence Darrow, De Priest was acquitted, but his reputation was severely damaged. He decided to sit out the 1917 aldermanic race. The next year, though, he was ready to make a comeback.

Party leaders, however, wanted no part of his plan, and they chose to support another African-American, Robert R. Jackson. Despite De Priest's popularity with black voters, who still considered him a hero and their friend, Jackson won by a narrow margin. In a bold move that presaged the tactics of a later generation of black politicians, De Priest formed an independent party—the People's Movement, which preached racial pride and solidarity—and ran against Jackson in the general election. He still failed to win.

De Priest maintained a low profile until 1928 when he successfully gained the congressional seat from the 1st District. As congressman, he tentatively championed civil rights. He fought against Jim Crowism and sought to enact a national anti-lynching law. De Priest was reelected to Congress in 1930 and 1932. In 1934, however, he was defeated by the Democratic candidate, Arthur W.

Mitchell. De Priest continued to serve as Republican committeeman and regained his aldermanic seat in 1943, this time in the 3rd Ward, but lost it again in 1947.

In January of 1951 De Priest was knocked down by a Chicago Motor Coach bus while crossing an intersection near his home. He died several months later in Provident Hospital. He was buried in Graceland Cemetery.

See also: Ralph Metcalfe, William Hale Thompson, Harold Washington

Further reading: Drake, St. Clair and Horace R. Cayton. *Black Metropolis: A Study of Negro Life in a Northern City* (1962); Gosnell, Harold F. *Negro Politicians: The Rise of Negro Politics in Chicago* (1935); Spear, Allan H. *Black Chicago: The Making of a Negro Ghetto, 1890–1920* (1967); Travis, Dempsey J. *An Autobiography of Black Politics* (1987).

William E. Dever

Politician

born: March 13, 1862
Woburn, Massachusetts
died: September 3, 1929
Chicago, Illinois

William Emmett Dever was a good man, a highly respected man. Of that, there was no doubt. And when he became mayor of Chicago in 1923, he had nothing but the people's best wishes. Encouraged by this sincere display of good will and support, he set about putting Chicago on course. He sponsored massive public works, revitalized public services, and fought an unrelenting battle to rid the city of bootleggers. What's more, his administration had no hint of scandal—a remarkable achievement for a city that took peculiar pride in its flaws. These accomplishments made Dever a subject of admiration throughout the world, and in his own country it earned him the accolade of America's best mayor. From coast to coast he became known as the man who

"cleaned up" Chicago. Yet despite these considerable accomplishments, he only served one term—from 1923 to 1927—losing his bid for reelection to his nemesis, William Hale Thompson. To this day Dever is probably the least remembered of Chicago's twentieth-century mayors.

Dever was educated in the Woburn, Massachusetts, public school system. At fourteen, after one year of high school, he entered the family tannery. After five years working for his father he moved to Boston and then spent two years on the road. On a business trip to Olean, New York, he met Kate Conway, whom he later married, and the two settled in Boston. One day Kate noticed a newspaper clipping claiming that Chicago tanners could make good money—as much as $24 per week.

The Devers arrived in Chicago in 1887, and William began work at a tannery on Goose Island while going to law school at night. Following his graduation from the Chicago College of Law in 1890, he began his own law practice. He later attended discussion groups at the Chicago Commons settlement house. Its president, Graham Taylor, liked the young man and tried to persuade him to run for alderman. Dever gently refused the offer, but after much prodding, he finally agreed. He lost the election in 1900 but ran again two years later and was elected alderman from the 17th Ward.

Dever soon earned a reputation as one of the city council's most hard-working and well-respected members. He built parks, installed public baths, and improved the streets of his ward. In 1910 he was elected judge of the Superior Court of Cook County and was reelected in 1916 and 1922.

Dever enjoyed his status as a judge. In 1911 he and his family moved into a new apartment at 708 West Buena Avenue in what was then fashionable

Uptown. Four years later he purchased a brick three-flat at 5901 North Kenmore Avenue in Edgewater.

With the exception of the fraud trial of former Illinois Senator, William Lorimer, most of the cases Dever handled were routine and hardly newsworthy. In 1916, while still a sitting trial judge, Dever was appointed to the Appellate Court for the 1st District, an influential position, where he heard appeals from lower court decisions.

In early 1903 George Brennan, chairman of the Democratic party, chose Dever as the mayoral candidate with the best chance to defeat the incumbent, William Hale Thompson, in the upcoming campaign.

With his impeccable credentials and liberal tendencies, Dever became the darling of reformers and independents. "Chicago needs a mayor who has the courage to say 'no' and say it to all his best friends," Clarence Darrow declared. Unable to withstand the pressure, Thompson eventually withdrew from the race, and Dever, backed by the full force of the Democratic party, easily defeated the Republican candidate, Arthur C. Lueder.

Dever's first days in office were jovial and imbued with a great spirit. He wanted to be remembered, he said, as the mayor who did "something big, something worthwhile" for the city. He wasted no time in assembling a strong cabinet—Francis X. Busch, dean of the DePaul University Law School, was named corporation counsel, and social reformer Mary McDowell was appointed welfare commissioner. He filled the school board with his own appointees, a largely progressive group; and he chose a new police chief, Morgan A. Collins, who had a reputation as an honest cop and who promised to bring discipline and integrity back to the department.

Dever's term was full of public works accomplishments. Under his leadership Wacker Drive was completed; the northern section of Ogden Avenue extended; Ashland and Western Avenues widened; Union Station opened; the Chicago River straightened; the South Water Street market improved; and the city's first airport, Municipal Airport (later renamed Midway) was built. A major disappointment was his failure to solve the city's public transportation problem. Dever fought for municipal ownership of the city's bus and rapid transit lines, at that time privately owned, but his measures were overwhelmingly defeated in a public referendum.

Dever devoted a large part of his time to combating the bootleggers and gangsters who threatened to take over the city. Although he described himself as "wet," he made it his business to enforce the Prohibition laws and thereby unwittingly caused his own downfall. "It's the law. What else can I do but enforce it?" he explained in an address delivered to the Chicago Bar Association.

Dever's initial attempts to crush the bootleggers met with success. The media labeled it "The Great Beer War." It made the mayor something of a national celebrity. The police raided saloons and nightclubs, shut down breweries, suppressed the bootlegging trade, and revoked thousands of licenses. The people supported his efforts, and, for a time, crime subsided.

But the truce was short-lived. By 1925 Chicago was in the middle of a full-fledged gang war. Not only were crime statistics on the rise, but the crimes were more vicious and daring than ever. Chicagoans who opened their newspapers in the morning were greeted with reports of shoot-outs on downtown streets in broad daylight, of robberies at elegant hotels, and of murders of public officials. Dever's political career was one of the casualities.

The last two years of his term were spent trying to stem the tide of gangster violence. Still, the violence escalated. Although Dever admitted in 1926 before Senate hearings on Prohibition that "the great experiment" was a "tremendous mistake," he still believed he had no choice but to try to enforce the law.

Democratic Party leaders and prominent citizens persuaded Dever to run against William Thompson for a second term. Out of a sense of duty, he agreed. "Big Bill," forever the street fighter in time with the pulse of the voters, promised to return Chicago to its "wide open" status.

Dever lost by 83,000 votes, and the nation, unfamiliar with Chicago's brand of politics, was understandably stunned. Dever, for one, was glad to leave. "I have always felt that being mayor was a four-year job," he said. "Any man faithfully performing the duties of the office must be prepared to serve only a single term."

Dever accepted the position of vice-president of the Bank of America but was forced to leave due to illness. He died of cancer in 1929 only two years after leaving office.

See also: Al Capone, Mary McDowell, William Hale Thompson

Further reading: Green, Paul M. and Melvin G. Holli, eds. *The Mayors: The Chicago Political Tradition* (1987); Holli, Melvin G. and Peter d'A. Jones, eds. *The Biographical Dictionary of American Mayors, 1820–1980: Big City Mayors* (1981); Rex, Frederick F. *The Mayors of the City of Chicago* (1934); Schmidt, John R. *"The Mayor Who Cleaned Up Chicago": A Political Biography of William E. Dever* (1989).

R. R. Donnelley

Publisher

born: November 15, 1836
Hamilton, Ontario
died: April 8, 1899
Chicago, Illinois

Richard Robert Donnelley, one of the city's first commercial printers, aspired to be the best in his profession. The "Donnelley way" required that one devote the proper time, energy, and talent necessary in order to do a good job. Donnelley dedicated both his personal and business life to these principles.

Donnelley was apprenticed to a printer in his native town of Hamilton, Ontario. He was offered a partnership in a shop while still a teenager. In 1857 he decided to relocate to New Orleans, and he eventually became a partner in a shop owned by the *True Delta* newspaper. When the Civil War erupted, however, he returned to Canada, where he and his partner, Joseph Lawson, established a successful printing business.

In October of 1864 Donnelley accepted an offer from Chicago publishers, Edward Goodman and Leroy Church, to join them. The firm of Church, Goodman, and Donnelley, located at 108–110 Dearborn Street, soon became one of the major publishing houses in the Midwest, producing some twenty-three weekly, monthly, and quarterly publications. In 1870 the company was renamed the Lakeside Publishing and Printing Company.

Plans were made to erect a Gothic structure to house the thriving company. The double impact of the Chicago Fire of 1871 and the Panic of 1873, however, forced the business to close. Donnelley, like countless other Chicagoans, lost everything.

A determined Donnelley traveled to New York, in search of financing. Due to his strong character and impeccable reputation, he was able to secure enough credit to rebuild. By 1873 the company was back on its feet again and a new building—the Lakeside Building—consisting of lithographers, mapmakers, engravers, binders, and manufacturing equipment, was constructed.

In 1886 the company decided to diversify by publishing its first directory for the Chicago Telephone Company, the predecessor of Illinois Bell (Ten years earlier, Alexander Graham Bell had applied for a patent on new invention he called the telephone). Their first directory was 244 pages and included 6 pages of advertisements, 88 pages of Chicago listings, 25 pages of suburban listings, and 108 pages of classified listings.

Branching out into fiction, the firm established the Lakeside Publishing and Printing Company and operated a successful business producing inexpensive paperbacks. This was a significant accomplishment since Donnelley made good literature accessible to the general public, including the works of major American and European writers. In 1903, after Donnelley's death, the first volume of the Lakeside Classics, Benjamin Franklin's autobiography, was published.

Donnelley believed printing and publishing to be two separate functions. In 1880 he formed a subsidiary, the Chicago Directory Company, to handle the publishing side of the business. In 1882 the printing firm was named R. R. Donnelley and Sons Company and continued to grow. The company printed circulars and catalogs for many of the city's big department stores, including Montgomery Ward. In 1897 the firm moved into larger headquarters at the Lakeside Press Building, designed by noted architect Howard Van Doren Shaw, at Polk Street and Plymouth Court.

Donnelley died in 1899. The presidency of R. R. Donnelley and Sons, the printing branch, fell to his son, Thomas Elliott Donnelley. Another son, Reuben Hamilton, joined the publishing end of the business as a clerk in 1882 and eventually took it over.

In 1908 Thomas established the Apprentice School of the Lakeside Press, a comprehensive seven-year training program for aspiring printers. The first class of twenty-four apprentices graduated in 1915.

In 1916 the publishing firm changed its name to the Reuben H. Donnelley Corporation, and it eventually became the largest publisher of telephone directories in the country. Today the two separate companies are R. H. Donnelley, a subsidiary of Dun and Bradstreet, which publishes the Donnelley directories; and R. R. Donnelley and Sons, which prints, among other things, the Donnelley directories, the Sears catalog, and the *Chicago Tribune Sunday Magazine*.

In 1929 a new plant, also designed by Howard Van Doren Shaw, was completed at 22nd Street and Calumet Avenue.

See also: Howard Van Doren Shaw

Stephen A. Douglas

Politician

born: April 23, 1813
Brandon, Vermont
died: June 3, 1861
Chicago, Illinois

Stephen Arnold Douglas was Chicago's first politician to make a name for himself on the national scene. Although small in size, Douglas possessed a great spirit. Like many diminutive men, he made up in personality what he lacked in stature. For several years, he was considered the country's foremost statesman. With his magnificent speaking voice and forceful personality, Douglas earned the nickname "the Little Giant."

Douglas spent his boyhood years on a Vermont farm. His father had died when Douglas was still an infant. At fifteen, he was apprenticed to a cabinet maker. After his mother remarried, the family moved to Canandaigua, New York, where he enrolled at the local academy. He then studied law in the office of one of the town's leading attorneys. Working his way westward, Douglas settled in Jacksonville, Illinois, in 1833 and was admitted to the Illinois bar that same year.

Douglas held a succession of prestigious positions throughout his career—lawyer, member of the Illinois legislature, state prosecutor, land office commissioner, secretary of state of Illinois, and judge of the Illinois Supreme Court. He rapidly ascended the ladder of success and prominence. He became a congressman at age thirty and a senator at thirty-four.

A firm believer in "manifest destiny," Douglas strongly supported western expansion. He encouraged the federal government to acquire California and to annex Texas during the Mexican-American War (1846–1848). He also urged the construction of a transcontinental railroad that would link Chicago to the West.

Douglas pushed through Congress the Kansas-Nebraska Act of 1854, a controversial piece of legislation that repealed the Missouri Compromise of 1820, which had set boundaries between slave states and free territories. Douglas, a devout states' rights advocate, dubbed the new law "popular sovereignty." Douglas felt that by allowing freedom of choice he could avert tragedy. It was a costly error from which his career would never fully recover.

During his campaign for reelection to the U.S. Senate, Douglas faced a formidable challenger by the name of Abraham Lincoln. Lincoln, a member of the new Republican party, favored keeping slavery out of the territories. Seven Lincoln-Douglas debates were scheduled during the summer of 1858, including one at Ottawa, Illinois, where more than ten thousand people came to witness the confrontation of the two politicians. At stake was not only the future of both men's careers but also the future of an entire country. The major issue during the debates was the concept of popular sovereignty. Although Lincoln won the popular vote during the general election, Douglas emerged triumphant when the Democratic state legislature voted to return him to Washington.

By today's standards, Douglas harbored blatantly racist views. "This is a white man's government made by white men, for white men and their descendants," he once said. The slavery issue tore the country apart and split the Democratic party. In 1860 Douglas won the Democratic nomination for president but lost to Lincoln in the general election.

Douglas had always considered himself a patriot. Although he disagreed with Lincoln over the issue of slavery during the campaign, he could not turn his back against the government when Lincoln was finally elected. When war was declared in 1861, Douglas rallied behind the new president and encouraged his followers to do the same.

Douglas, who lived in Chicago during the last fourteen years of his life, invested heavily in Chicago real estate, especially along the lakefront and in the Lake Calumet area. He also established the Illinois Central railroad. In 1852 he bought seventy acres between 31st and 35th Streets west of the IC tracks. Two years later he built his home, which he called Oakenwald, near Cottage Grove Avenue and 35th Street. Douglas also made donations and was one of the incorporators of the original University of Chicago, which opened in 1860 at 34th Street and Cottage Grove Avenue but closed due to financial difficulties in 1886. In 1892 another University of Chicago opened—it had no ties to the old school—in Hyde Park.

Douglas died in Chicago of typhoid fever in 1861 at age forty-eight.

In 1861 a federal prison camp was established between 31st Street, Cottage Grove Avenue, 33rd Street, and Forest Avenue (now Giles Avenue) on land owned by Douglas and was named Camp Douglas in honor of the late senator. The camp, which had earned a notorious reputation due to overcrowding and unsanitary conditions, closed in late 1865.

Around the turn of the century the Douglas neighborhood had evolved into a thriving African-American commercial and entertainment center. Black-owned businesses as well as scores of nightclubs proliferated along 35th and South State Streets. Since the depression the area has drastically deteriorated. Nevertheless, a number of late-nineteenth century homes still exist, primarily between 31st and 35th Streets and along Calumet, Giles, and Prairie Avenues, which comprises the Douglas Historic District.

At the eastern end of 35th Street between Lake Park Avenue and the Illinois Central railroad tracks stands a memorial to Douglas. Perched atop a 104-foot column is a statue of the man they called the "Little Giant." The sculpture, completed by Leonard Wells Volk in 1881, is visible from the IC and from nearby Lake Shore Drive and is a popular destination stop for Civil War and Chicago history buffs.

Further reading: Carr, Clark E. *Stephen A. Douglas: His Life, Public Services, Speeches and Patriotism* (1909); Johannsen, Robert W. *Stephen A. Douglas* (1973).

Theodore Dreiser

Novelist

born: August 27, 1871
Terre Haute, Indiana
died: December 28, 1945
Los Angeles, California

Herman Theodore Dreiser was a novelist of the realist school whose best work contained a biting and bitter condemnation of the hollowness of the American dream. Obsessed with the "brittle cruelty" of life, Dreiser didn't shy away from harsh realities. His novels were vilified and denounced as obscene and immoral, and several were banned. Despite this reception, Dreiser remained a singular literary voice, widely imitated and grudgingly admired even by his fiercest critics. By the time of his death in 1945, he was considered one of the most influential American novelists of the twentieth century.

Photograph courtesy of the Theodore Dreiser Collection, Special Collections Department, Van Pelt/District Library at the University of Pennsylvania.

Dreiser spent most of his boyhood in Warsaw, Indiana, the twelfth child in a family of thirteen. His first taste of big city life came in the 1880s when his mother and the other children—his father stayed in Indiana—moved to Chicago, living in a six-room apartment at Madison Street and Throop Avenue. The family decided to return to Indiana after only a short time. Determined to stay in Chicago, though only a teenager, Dreiser held a succession of odd jobs: dishwasher, cook, boxcar tracer, and stockboy.

The generosity of a former teacher allowed Dreiser to enroll at Indiana University. One year later he dropped out and returned to Chicago, convinced that journalism was the only profession in which he could shine. He tried his hand at reporting at the *Chicago Daily Globe* and then moved to the *St. Louis Globe-Democrat* where, in addition to his regular duties, he reviewed as many as three plays per evening. On one occasion, he was scheduled to attend three different performances but, unexpectedly, was told to cover a holdup. Even so, he wrote glowing reviews, mostly culled from press agency releases. The next morning he awoke to the ghastly news that none of the troupes had performed that night due to a delayed train. Too embarrassed to face his editor, he left an apologetic note, gathered his belongings, and kept a low profile until he joined the second-rate morning newspaper, the *Republic*. When he eventually left St. Louis, he landed a job on the *Pittsburgh Dispatch*.

Although still a young man in his early twenties, Dreiser feared that time was running out. In 1894 he moved to New York where he joined the staff of the *World* newspaper. His reporting skills hadn't improved—he was still careless with facts—and he quit before he was fired.

After an unsuccessful attempt to publish a music magazine with his brother Paul, Dreiser left New York to stay with a friend, Arthur Henry, in Maumee, Ohio. Henry, city editor of the *Toledo Blade* was working on a novel at the time, and, according to Dreiser's biographer W. A. Swanberg, encouraged Dreiser to do the same. "Finally I took out a piece of yellow paper and to please him wrote down a title at random—*Sister Carrie*," Dreiser later recalled. He had no plot, no characters—just a name.

Sister Carrie provoked violent reactions. Condemned for its frank portrayal of sex, it is credited with bringing the American novel into the twentieth century. It told the tale of Carrie Meeber, a young country girl who moves to Chicago, sets up house with a married man, and becomes a prominent actress. Dreiser never apologized for Carrie's behavior nor did he punish her, as required of "respectable" fiction of the day. His publisher, Doubleday, Page and Company, initially tried to be released from its contractual obligations. After Dreiser threatened to file a lawsuit, however, the company agreed to print a nominal number of books—only one thousand copies.

Early reviews were disappointing; most critics called the book immoral and unrelentingly downbeat. A few, however, praised Dreiser for his courage and some even suggested greatness. In September of 1901 *Sister Carrie* was published in Britain to generally favorable reviews. In 1907 a tiny New York publisher, B. W. Dodge and Company, reissued the book. This time the reception was considerably better. The *World*, Dreiser's old paper, called it a book of "uncommon quality," and the *San Francisco Call* referred to it as "a work of genius."

After *Sister Carrie* was first published Dreiser continued jumping from job to job—assisant feature editor of the *New York Daily News,* editor of *Smith's* magazine, and editor of *Broadway* magazine. Following the successful reissue of *Sister Carrie,* Dreiser was offered a high-salary position as editor-in-chief at the prestigious Butterick Publishing Company, which published women's magazines.

Dreiser's second novel, *Jennie Gerhardt* (1911), received mostly positive reviews. Literary critic Floyd Dell called it a great book, and H. L. Mencken compared it favorably with the works of Tolstoy, Zola, and Conrad.

Dreiser then turned his pen to the turbulent career of Chicago traction tycoon, Charles Tyson Yerkes. In 1912 he returned to Chicago to research the career of Yerkes. The result was the Frank Cowperwood trilogy, which consisted of *The Titan* (1912); *The Financier,* (1914); and *The Stoic* (1947). Dreiser depicted Cowperwood as a ruthless robber baron who turned self-gratification and the relentless pursuit of power into a career.

Dreiser's most successful novel was *An American Tragedy* (1925), which explored American society's insatiable thirst for wealth and pleasure. Like his earlier novels, it reflected Dreiser's continual fascination with class and status. Based on a true story, it recounted the tale of a vacuous young man, Clyde Griffiths, who leaves his working-class girlfriend, Roberta Alden, for a wealthy woman after Alden becomes pregnant with his child. He plots to murder her by taking her to a deserted lake and staging an accident but is unable to follow through. The boat somehow

overturns, however, and the young woman drowns. Though he maintains he is innocent, Griffiths is sentenced to die in the electric chair. *An American Tragedy* was an unqualified success and was hailed as one of the greatest novels of the twentieth century.

The film *A Place in the Sun* (1951), starring Montgomery Clift, Elizabeth Taylor, and Shelley Winters, was based on Dreiser's classic.

Dreiser's literary output during the last twenty years of his life was minimal. Just prior to his death, he resumed writing and completed two novels, *The Bulwark* and *The Stoic* (the final novel of the Frank Cowperwood trilogy). His other works include several one-act plays: *The Blue Sphere, In the Dark, Laughing Gas, The Spring Recital,* and *The Light in the Window.*

Dreiser died in Los Angeles in 1945 of a heart attack at age seventy-four.

See also: Floyd Dell [appendix], James T. Farrell, Charles Tyson Yerkes

Further reading: Elias, Robert H. *Theodore Dreiser: Apostle of Nature* (1949); Kramer, Dale. *Chicago Renaissance: The Literary Life of the Midwest, 1900–1930* (1966); Lingeman, Richard. *Theodore Dreiser: At the Gates of the City 1871–1907* (1986); Lingeman, Richard. *Theodore Dreiser: An American Journey 1908–1945* (1990); Pizer, Donald. *The Novels of Theodore Dreiser: A Critical Study* (1976); Swanberg, W. A. *Dreiser* (1965).

Finley Peter Dunne

Humorist/Journalist

born: July 10, 1867
Chicago, Illinois
died: April 24, 1936
New York, New York

In Martin Dooley, the fictitious barkeep of a working-class Bridgeport saloon, Finley Peter Dunne created a Chicago character who won instant acceptance in his hometown and renown nationwide. At the peak of his popularity in pre–World War I America, Dunne was hailed as an Irish-American Mark Twain and one of the great humorists of his day.

Dunne was born and raised in St. Patrick's parish on the Near West Side of Chicago. His father owned a small lumberyard, and his relatives were active in Democratic ward politics and included a number of prominent Chicago priests. After graduating from West Division High School, young Pete—he added Finley, his mother's maiden name, after her death—entered the newspaper business at age sixteen as a copy boy at the *Chicago Telegram*. Later he was promoted to police reporter. His knowledge of the city and his skill as a journalist allowed him to advance quickly. He left the *Telegram* to join the *Chicago Daily News* where, among his general assignment and editorial duties, he covered the sports beat. (Dunne is credited with coining the term *southpaw* to refer to a left-handed baseball pitcher). In 1888 he became political reporter on the *Times* and was quickly promoted to city editor—at twenty-two the youngest in Chicago. From there he jumped to the *Daily Tribune* and, in 1892, he joined the staff of the *Chicago Evening Post* as an editorial page editor.

In October 1893, Dunne began writing in Irish dialect for the *Evening Post*. Literary historian Charles Fanning calls Dunne's great creation, Martin Dooley, bartender/philosopher from the South Side neighborhood of Bridgeport, the first dialect voice of genius in American literature. From 1893 to 1898 these weekly columns created a full picture of Irish-American working-class urban life. The portraits of laborers, streetcar drivers, and mill workers contain memorable dignity and depth. Sage, satirist, social critic, philosopher, and thinker, Mr. Dooley was immensely popular. Readers identified with his resourcefulness, his quick wit, and his ordinary common sense. Modeled after a real life Chicago bartender, Mr. Dooley tended bar in a mythical Irish tavern along Archer Road, or as he referred to it, the "Archey Road."

Through Mr. Dooley, Dunne examined the customs, habits, and attitudes of a working-class Chicago neighborhood and explored other themes too—the great Irish potato famine of the 1840s, the plight of the immigrant, the fight for Irish independence, the struggle of the Irish to attain respectability in America, and the pains of assimilation. But Dunne was not only concerned with Irish subjects. He also addressed other themes such as social reform, the Pullman strike, and Chicago politics.

Dunne's satirical columns on the Spanish-American War in 1898 were widely reprinted and ushered in the second phase of his career. In 1900 he moved to New York City and his columns became nationally syndicated. The wise old sage of Bridgeport was quoted across breakfast tables throughout America, so that by World War I Dunne was the most famous columnist in the country.

Dunne wrote approximately seven hundred Mr. Dooley columns. He died in his New York apartment in the Delmonico Hotel in 1936 after a long illness. By that time, Dunne had fallen into relative obscurity. The fictitious Mr. Dooley, however, was still fondly remembered. Today, Dunne and his famous character are the subject of several new books and academic conferences.

Dunne's first anthology *Mr. Dooley in Peace and War* (1898) was followed by *What Dooley Says* (1899); *Mr. Dooley in the Hearts of His Countrymen* (1899); *Mr. Dooley's Philosophy* (1900); *Mr. Dooley's Opinions* (1901); *Observations by Mr. Dooley* (1902); *Dissertations by Mr. Dooley* (1906); *Mr. Dooley Says* (1910); *Mr. Dooley on Making a Will and Other Necessary Evils* (1919); and *Mr. Dooley At His Best* (1936).

See also: George Ade, Eugene Field, Ring Lardner

Further reading: DeMuth, Jerry. *Small Town Chicago: The Comic Perspective of Finley Peter Dunne, George Ade, Ring Lardner* (1980); Ellis, Elmer. *Mr. Dooley's America: A Life of Finley Peter Dunne* (1941); Fanning, Charles, ed. *Mr. Dooley and the Chicago Irish: An Anthology* (1976); Fanning, Charles. *Finley Peter Dunne and Mr. Dooley: The Chicago Years* (1978); Fanning, Charles. "The Literary Dimension," in *The Irish in Chicago*, Lawrence McCaffrey et al, eds. (1987); Schaff, Barbara C. *Mr. Dooley's Chicago* (1977).

Jean Baptiste Pointe du Sable

Pioneer

born: circa 1745
San Marc, Haiti
died: August 28, 1818
(according to some sources:
August 29, 1818)
St. Charles, Missouri

Jean Baptiste Pointe du Sable, credited with being the first permanent resident of Chicago, also started the city's first commercial enterprise: a trading post on the Chicago River.

Photograph courtesy of DuSable Museum of African-American History.

Of French and African-American ancestry, du Sable attended Catholic school in France. In 1764 du Sable and his boyhood friend, Jacques Clemorgan, left Haiti on the sloop, *Suzanne*, and traveled to New Orleans to begin a new life. The following year the pair, accompanied by a Potawatomi Indian named Choctaw, began the six hundred–mile journey up the Mississippi River to St. Louis.

Du Sable had a deep and abiding respect for Native Americans. At times he acted as peacemaker between various warring tribes. The Potawatomis "adopted" du Sable as one of their own and allowed the Haitian to marry a young Potawatomi named Catherine, cousin of their chief, Pokagon. As a result du Sable's trade with the Indians flourished.

Du Sable traveled up the Mississippi, Illinois, and Des Plaines rivers into the Chicago River where he established a trading post as early as 1772, according to some accounts, near what is now Pioneer Court. The post consisted of a bakehouse, a smokehouse, a poultry house, a dairy, a workshop, a barn and two stables. The first child to be born in Chicago was reportedly born at his trading post. The city's first recorded marriage occurred there as did the first election. It also housed the city's first court and first post office.

With the assistance of his Indian friends, du Sable created a haven on the prairie wilderness. He set aside tracts of land and grew wheat, corn, hay, and alfalfa, and raised dairy and beef cattle, which allowed him to supply meat and dairy products to clients in Detroit. He constructed dairy and cattle barns, a milk house, a blacksmith shop, a poultry house, and a grist mill.

Du Sable was described by one British officer as "a handsome Negro, well-educated, and settled at Eschecagou." (The name of the settlement, *Eschecagou* or *Checagou,* came from an Indian word commonly thought to mean "wild onions.") In late 1778 he was arrested by the British, charged with harboring French sympathies, and taken as prisoner to Fort Michilimackinac in present-day Michigan. Du Sable demanded his freedom and was finally released in the spring of 1779.

Following the Revolutionary War, the newly formed American government claimed the Great Lakes as a part of the United States, referring to it as the Northwest Territory. Scores of land-hungry Americans began to settle on the once desolate plain. In 1800 du Sable sold his property to Jean Lalime, a French-Canadian trapper. A short time later, John Kinzie purchased it.

In 1805 du Sable made his last visit to the place he knew as Eschecagou, but he barely recognized it. Fort Dearborn had been founded two years earlier on the south bank of the Chicago River, and a new generation of pioneers had transformed the once sleepy settlement into a bustling town.

Du Sable moved to Peoria where he stayed for ten years before eventually settling with his granddaughter and her husband in St. Charles, Missouri. He died there in 1818.

Since founding the Du Sable Museum of African-American History in 1961, director Margaret Burroughs has been a tireless campaigner on behalf of the Haitian's achievements. It is primarily due to her efforts that Jean Baptiste Pointe du Sable is now generally considered Chicago's first permanent settler.

See also: Gurdon S. Hubbard, John Kinzie, Jacques Marquette [appendix]

Further reading: Cortesi, Lawrence. *Jean du Sable, Father of Chicago* (1972).

Elmer E. Ellsworth

Army Officer

born: April 11, 1837
Malta, New York
died: May 24, 1861
Alexandria, Virginia

Colonel Elmer Ephraim Ellsworth was Chicago's first war hero: the first Union officer killed in the Civil War. As the leader of Chicago's Zouave Cadets, Ellsworth offered an ideal, romantic portrait of war that today may appear naive and sentimental. For a time though, Ellsworth and his Zouaves epitomized the nation's best qualities— patriotism, self-sacrifice, and unswerving loyalty. Songs were composed about them, and Zouave dolls, dressed in tiny scarlet trousers, flooded the market.

Ellsworth moved to Chicago in 1854 when a young New Englander, Arthur F. Devereux, offered him a position as a clerk in his patent-soliciting business. "My life has been a constant struggle between duty and inclination," he wrote to a friend. Chronic health problems prevented him from attending West Point. Although disappointed, he pursued the study of law, living very frugally in order to save money for his education.

Ellsworth had always dreamed of military glory. In 1859 he was hired as a drill master for volunteer regiments in Chicago. Ironically, he was too poor to join these companies, which consisted mostly of young men of high social standing and some wealth. Their uniforms were expensive, and they staged lavish balls, and participated in parades and elaborate drills for the entertainment of the public.

The dashing, handsome Col. Ellsworth wanted to be a nineteenth-century King Arthur. When perusing European magazines, he came across the colorful uniforms of the French Zouaves, named after a mountain tribe in Algeria. The French adopted this tribe's system of warfare and thus distinguished themselves during the Crimean War. Ellsworth obtained a copy of a Zouave drill manual from his fencing master, Dr. Charles A. De Villers, who had served as a surgeon in a French Zouave regiment.

The Zouave drill required top physical fitness, precision, and skill. The soldiers were taught to load and fire on the run, when lying down, and when kneeling. They learned how to bayonet effectively. And although some people dismissed their training as nothing more than "idle and foolish recreation," Ellsworth disciplined his troops unsparingly, four hours every evening, except Sunday, in

order to make them combat-ready. Later, many Zouaves distinguished themselves in the Civil War as a result of this training.

Word of this exciting new unit and their handsome leader circulated within Chicago's military circles. Their uniforms, too, became the subject of conversation: beaded blue jackets, red vests, collarless blue shirts, gold-trimmed jackets, yellow sashes, baggy scarlet trousers, and blue caps. Colorful though they were, these uniforms were hardly made for combat duty. Eventually the uniforms were discarded altogether and the soldiers ordered to don regular Union army clothing.

Ellsworth's cadets won the drill championship of the United States and Canada in 1860. That same year Ellsworth published *Manual of Arms for Light Infantry*, arranged for U.S. Zouave Cadets. Following the Zouave's successful national tour, Ellsworth came to the attention of Abraham Lincoln, then a prominent lawyer. Lincoln, impressed with Ellsworth's integrity, invited the young man to join his law firm in Springfield, Illinois, but the outbreak of war the following year ended Ellsworth's brief legal career.

In 1861 Ellsworth was appointed adjutant and inspector general of militia for the United States Army. He later quit as drill master to train Illinois troops, but later still he returned to his native New York where he trained the New York Zouaves.

In May of 1861 Ellsworth and his men traveled to Alexandria, Virginia. When he saw a Confederate flag waving atop the Marshall House hotel, he turned to his men and cried, "Boys, we must have that down before we return." This simple act of patriotism cost him his life. He was fatally wounded by the hotel's manager, James W. Jackson. Jackson was in turn slain by Ellsworth's troops.

Chicago was "profoundly agitated" upon learning of Ellsworth's death, according to an editorial in the *Chicago Tribune*. "No man has been watched by our citizens with warmer interest than Col. Ellsworth."

See also: James Mulligan, Philip Sheridan

Further reading: Randall, Ruth Painter. *Colonel Elmer Ellsworth: A Biography of Lincoln's Friend and First Hero of the Civil War* (1960).

Ada Everleigh & Minna Everleigh

Madames

born: February 15, 1866
near Louisville, Kentucky
died: January 5, 1960
Roanoke, Virginia

born: July 13, 1878
near Louisville, Kentucky
died: September 16, 1948
New York, New York

For over a decade Minna and Ada Everleigh were the proprietors of the most celebrated brothel in America, a fifty-room mansion at 2131–33 South Dearborn Street.

The Everleigh sisters (their original family name was reported to be Lester) enjoyed an aristocratic upbringing. Their father was a wealthy Kentucky lawyer who spared no expense in providing his daughters with a proper education, which included finishing school.

Married life held little interest for Ada and Minna. After acting in several repertory companies in Washington, D.C., they opened their first brothel in Omaha, during the Trans-Mississippi Exposition. After the exposition closed in 1899, they headed for Chicago.

The Everleigh Club opened its doors on February 1, 1900, without any advance publicity or advertisements. It was as elegant as any first-class hotel. Culture was very important to the sisters, as was maintaining a refined atmosphere. There was a library lined with rare books, an art gallery, a dining room, oil paintings, silk curtains, mahogany staircases, gilded bathtubs, and gold-plated spittoons. There was a waiting list to work at the Everleigh Club. According to historian Charles Washburn, in order to be hired, a girl needed to be in perfect health, possess a pretty face and figure, and look good in evening clothes. The girls were also given daily drills in proper behavior. "Be polite, patient, and forget what you are here for," Minna directed. "Remember the Everleigh Club has no time for the rough element, the clerk on a holiday, or a man without a checkbook. Your youth and beauty are all you have. Preserve it. Stay respectable by all means."

There were fourteen sound-proof rooms (or parlors), each with its own name: Moorish, Gold, Silver, Copper, Red, Rose, Green, Blue, Oriental, Japanese, Egyptian, Chinese, Music, and Ballroom according to Washburn. To gain admittance, a prospective guest had to produce a letter of recommendation, an engraved card, or a formal introduction. The prices were not cheap: $12 bought a bottle of champagne, $50 an evening with dinner.

In October of 1909 the English evangelist, Gipsy Smith, led a parade into the heart of the Levee, the city's red-light district. The Levee, prepared for the invasion, was on its best behavior. The blinds were drawn, the lights dimmed. Not even the sound of a tinkling piano could be heard. Smith and his cadre of reformers knelt outside the infamous Everleigh Club and prayed and prayed. After the marchers departed, the Levee resumed its old character. The doors of the Everleigh Club opened, the lights went on, and the music spilled out into the streets. It was reportedly the busiest night the district had ever had.

In 1910 a vice commission, consisting of some of the most respected names in town including Julius Rosenwald, the Rev. Frank W. Gunsaulus, and Graham Taylor, was appointed by Mayor Fred A. Busse to probe Chicago's escalating vice problem. The commission concluded that "the problem will remain just as long as the public conscience is dead to the issue or is indifferent to its solution. The law is only as powerful as the public opinion which supports it."

Disregarding the vice commission's study, *The Social Evil in Chicago,* the sisters published a brochure advertising the finer points of the Everleigh Club. It fell into the hands of Mayor Carter Harrison II. Incensed, Harrison issued an order to close the club on October 24, 1911. Segregated vice was no longer regarded as an appropriate solution to the problem of prostitution, and politicians, bowing to public pressure, could no longer afford to look the other way.

The sisters knew the end was in sight. "Well, boys, we've had good times, haven't we," said a bejeweled Minna to the men of the press. "You have all been darlings. You've played square. And we thank you sincerely."

At one o'clock on the morning of October 25, 1911, the order came down. "Nothing we can do about it," uttered a police officer.

Within a week the Everleigh sisters had boarded the Twentieth Century Limited at Union Station and headed with their $1 million in savings for sunny Italy. They returned to Chicago six months later with hopes of reopening their old club. But it was not to be.

Minna died in 1948 in New York's Park West Hospital. Ada lived a quiet life until the age of ninety-three. She was buried next to her beloved sister near Roanoke, Virginia. The building that housed the notorious Everleigh Club was demolished in 1933.

See also: John Coughlin, Carter Harrison II, Michael Kenna

Further reading: Asbury, Herbert. *Gem of the Prairie: An Informal History of the Chicago Underworld* (1942); Kogan, Herman and Lloyd Wendt. *Lords of the Levee: The Story of Bathhouse John and Hinky Dink* (1943); Washburn, Charles. *Come Into My Parlor: A Biography of the Aristocratic Everleigh Sisters of Chicago* (1936).

James T. Farrell

Novelist

born: February 27, 1904
Chicago, Illinois
died: August 22, 1979
New York, New York

James Thomas Farrell was a novelist, critic, essayist, short story writer, poet, and journalist as well as a first-rate social historian whose powerful novels captured the frustration, humiliation, and anger of a generation of working-class Irish-Americans.

Photograph reprinted with permission from the *Chicago Sun-Times.*

One of fifteen children born to James Francis Farrell and Mary Daly, James Thomas was raised by his maternal grandmother when his father could not afford to feed yet another hungry mouth. Young Farrell worked as a clerk for the American Realty Express Company, as a cigar store clerk and as a service station attendant before enrolling at the University of Chicago in 1927. He dropped out two years later to devote all of his energy to writing. His first novel, *Young Lonigan* (1932), was a brutally frank depiction of an Irish-American youth in Chicago's Washington Park neighborhood. It sold millions of copies and brought Farrell an early fame.

The Lonigan trilogy—which also included *The Young Manhood of Studs Lonigan* (1934) and *Judgment Day* (1935)—made a tremendous impact on the literary world. Farrell's sympathetic but scrupulous portrayal of the life of ordinary people set his novels apart from proletarian literature of the thirties, and he exerted a profound influence on generations of American writers from Norman Mailer and Kurt Vonnegut, Jr., to Tom Wolfe and Bette Howland.

Farrell's output was significant. He wrote twenty-five novels, seventeen collections of short stories, and many books of non-fiction. The Studs Lonigan series, however, overshadowed everything else he created. "Writing is my life and 'Studs' is part of my life as a writer," he once said, "but I do resent having other works compared with *Studs Lonigan*. I don't think of myself as a pole vaulter who must break my own record with each book.... To examine life, and to explore the nature of experience, is my aim."

The critical tide is now turning and Farrell's other novels are beginning to receive the attention they deserve, including Farrell's largely autobiographical novels beginning with *A World I Never Made* (1936). The O'Neill-O'Flaherty novels, which follow Danny O'Neill from the South Side of Chicago to New York literary circles, include: *No Star Is Lost* (1938); *Father and Son* (1940); *My Days of Anger* (1943); and *The Face of Time* (1953).

An outspoken man with strong leftist views, Farrell served as chairman of the American Committee for Cultural Freedom from 1954 to 1956, but his early repudiation of Stalinism earned him the enmity of prominent literary critics and intellectuals.

The Death of Nora Ryan, the last novel published in Farrell's lifetime, appeared in 1978. The following year, NBC-TV aired a critically acclaimed three-part series based on the Lonigan trilogy. Several other books remained in manuscript form, one of which, *Sam Holman,* was published in 1983.

Farrell was the first American novelist to put Irish ethnic life into a coherent urban context. Not only did he examine the thoughts, aspirations, and values of working and middle-class Irish-Americans in the half century between 1900 and 1950, but he depicted in stunning detail the neighborhoods in which they lived. Throughout his long literary career, Farrell's constant aim was "to write so that life may speak for itself." His novels did precisely that.

Other novels include *Tommy Gallagher's Crusade* (1939), *Ellen Rogers* (1941), *Bernard Clare* (1946), *The Road Between* (1949), *Yet Other Waters* (1952), *This Man and This Woman* (1951), *A Brand New Life* (1972), *The Dunne Family* (1976), and the

Eddie Ryan series of novels, including *The Silence of History* (1963), *What Time Collects* (1964), *Lonely Future* (1966), and *When Time Was Born* (1967).

Farrell died of a heart attack in his Manhattan apartment on August 22, 1979. He is buried in the Farrell family plot in Calvary Cemetery in Evanston.

See also: Jack Conroy, Theodore Dreiser, Finley Peter Dunne

Further reading: Branch, Edgar Marquess. *James T. Farrell,* (1963); Fanning, Charles. "The Literary Dimension" in *The Irish in Chicago,* Lawrence McCaffrey et al, eds. (1987); Fanning, Charles and Ellen Skerrett. "James T. Farrell and Washington Park: The Novel as Social History" *Chicago History* (Summer 1979).

Edna Ferber

Novelist

born: August 15, 1887
Kalamazoo, Michigan
died: April 16, 1968
New York, New York

*Popular novelist and short story writer, Edna Ferber launched her literary career in Chicago. Her most popular novel, **So Big,** had a Chicago setting as did many of her early short stories, including "The Gray Old Dog," "Home Girl," and "Mother Knows Best."*

Ferber was the daughter of a Hungarian immigrant, Jacob Charles Ferber, and a second-generation German, Julia Neumann, and was raised in the Jewish faith. After high school, Ferber made $3 a week as a reporter for the *Appleton* (Wisconsin) *Daily Crescent* but was fired from the job by an editor who did not like having a woman on his staff. Ferber, who later got a post with the *Milwaukee Journal,* had taken up fiction writing for therapeutic reasons after suffering a nervous breakdown. She met with some success, and a number of her short stories were published in various magazines.

Ferber arrived in Chicago in 1910 and found work as a reporter on the *Chicago Tribune.* Pounding away on a $17 used typewriter, Ferber sat down and wrote, in 1911, her first novel, *Dawn O'Hara,* based on her newspaper experience in Milwaukee. It was rejected so many times that she gave up and threw it into the furnace. Fortunately, her mother rescued it from the flames.

In 1917 she wrote *Fanny Herself* about a young woman who comes to Chicago to work in a mail-order firm. By the mid-1920s, Ferber had settled in New York and had become a successful playwright. She collaborated with George S. Kaufman on *The Royal Family* (1927); *Dinner at Eight* (1932); *Stage Door* (1936); *The Land is Bright* (1951); and *Bravo!* (1949).

In 1924, her next novel, *So Big,* returned to Chicago themes. Set on a truck farm in South Holland, just south of the city, *So Big* earned her the Pulitzer Prize for fiction (she was the first Jew to win the highly coveted award) and catapulted her to national attention. The novel, a classic of American literature, soon became required reading on high school and college campuses. Ferber was surprised as anyone at the book's monumental success. "Not only did I not plan to write a bestseller," she confessed, "but I thought I had written the world's worst seller. I didn't think anyone would ever read it." *So Big* is still considered an American classic.

Among her other novels were *Showboat* (1926), which captured theatrical life on the Mississippi and was adapted into a successful musical by Jerome Kern and Oscar Hammerstein; *Cimarron* (1930) about the early days of Oklahoma; *Come and Get It* (1935), which was set in the lumber camps of Wisconsin and Michigan; and *Great Son* (1944), which was set in the Pacific Northwest. In addition were the novels *Saratoga Trunk* (1941), *Giant* (1952), and *Ice Palace* (1958). Many of her books were turned into movies, including *Giant,* which starred Elizabeth Taylor, Rock Hudson, and, in his last role, James Dean.

Other Ferber works included *Cheerful—By Request* (1918); *The Girls* (1921); *Gigolo* (1922); *American Beauty* (1931); and *They Brought Their Women* (1931).

Ferber died in her Park Avenue home in New York City in 1968 at the age of eighty.

Enrico Fermi

Physicist

born: September 29, 1901
Rome, Italy
died: November 28, 1954
Chicago, Illinois

The nuclear age began in 1942 in a converted squash court beneath the stands of Stagg Field on the campus of the University of Chicago. Its unlikely hero was a quiet, soft-spoken Italian immigrant named Enrico Fermi.

The son of an Italian railroad official, Fermi studied at the University of Pisa from 1918 to 1922. Later on he attended the universities of Leyden and Gottingden in Holland. He was appointed professor of theoretical physics at the University of Rome in 1927.

In 1934 in his laboratory at the University of Rome, he studied the effects of bombarding atoms with negatively charged neutrons. Using simple equipment, Fermi and his team decided to experiment further by bombarding all the elements of the periodic table. Four years later Fermi received the Nobel prize for successfully splitting the uranium atom.

Fermi traveled with his family to Sweden to receive the award but later decided not to return to Italy because of the rise of fascism there. First he went to London, then, in 1939, he accepted an offer to join the faculty of Columbia University as a professor of physics, where he continued his pioneering atomic research.

In 1942 he was transferred from Columbia to the University of Chicago and placed in charge of constructing the world's first atomic bomb—code name: the Manhattan Project. Fermi and his team of scientists worked diligently in secrecy until December 2, 1942, when they achieved the first controlled nuclear reaction.

Because of the urgency of the situation, there was no time to build a proper lab. Instead, a makeshift reactor, molded in the shape of a giant beehive and consisting of graphite blocks interspersed with chunks of uranium, was constructed. To control the reaction, rods of cadmium were inserted into the pile. When the rods were removed, a chain reaction took place and fission resulted.

On that cold December day, Fermi and other members of his team stood on a balcony at one end of the squash court, opposite the reactor. A three-person "suicide squad" suspended a bucket of boron solution over the pile should the heat become intolerable. On the squash court floor, another scientist handled the master control rod.

At 3:20 p.m. Fermi ordered the rod removed. After a tense moment and several adjustments, he matter-of-factly announced, "The reaction is self-sustaining." The time was 3:25 p.m. The world would never be the same again.

In 1944 the federal government moved Fermi and other scientists associated with the Manhattan Project to Los Alamos, New Mexico, in total secrecy and under false names (Fermi's new name was Eugen Farmer). On July 16, 1945, the years of hard work reached fruition when the first atomic bomb was exploded in a test at Alamogordo Air Base. Three weeks later, the United States dropped atomic bombs on Hiroshima and Nagasaki, forcing a Japanese surrender.

It is uncertain how Fermi felt about the mass destruction caused by the atomic bomb. He tended to keep his opinions to himself. Laura Fermi once remarked that her husband believed that nothing was served "by trying to halt the progress of science." Further, he asserted, "Whatever the future holds for mankind, however unpleasant it may be, we must accept it, for knowledge is always better than ignorance."

In December of 1945 Fermi returned to the University of Chicago as a professor in the Institute of Nuclear Physics where he remained until he died of cancer in 1954. He was only fifty-three years old. There is no concrete evidence that the cancer was caused by exposure to radiation. *Nuclear Energy,* a sculpture by Henry Moore, now marks the spot where Fermi and his team of scientists conducted their famous experiment.

"His needs were few," recalled friend and fellow scientist Dr. Herbert Anderson at a memorial service shortly after Fermi's death. All he needed were "chalk, a blackboard, and an eager student."

Further reading: deLatil, Pierre. *Enrico Fermi: The Man and His Theories* (1964); Fermi, Laura. *Atoms in the Family—My Life with Enrico Fermi* (1954); Segre, Emilio. *Enrico Fermi, Physicist* (1970).

Eugene Field

Journalist/Poet

born: September 2, 1850
St. Louis, Missouri
died: November 4, 1895
Chicago, Illinois

"I am a Yankee by pedigree and education but I was born in that ineffably uninteresting city of St. Louis," wrote Eugene Field. Poet and merry prankster, Field wrote the "Sharps and Flats" column in the **Chicago Daily News** *for over a dozen years. He was the first of the so-called literary journalists of Chicago—including George Ade, Finley Peter Dunne, and Ring Lardner—to achieve national recognition. Field presented two faces to the world—the gentle man who wrote children's poetry and the worldly journalist who professed a penchant for drink.*

Both of Field's parents hailed from Vermont. When his mother died in 1857, a cousin took care of him and acted as his foster mother. His love of practical jokes got him expelled from three schools—Williams College, Knox College, and the State University of Missouri. Field began his journalism career at the *St. Louis Evening Journal* in 1872. Three years later he joined the *St. Joseph* (Missouri) *Gazette.* He returned to St. Louis to assume an editorship on the *Times-Journal.* He then joined the staff of the *Kansas City Times* but left in 1881 to become managing editor of the *Denver Tribune* at age thirty-one. At the *Tribune* he initiated a popular column, "Odds and Ends," for which he was the principal contributor.

In 1883 Field accepted an offer from Melville E. Stone to join the staff of the *Chicago Daily News.* His column debuted on August 15, 1883, under the banner of "Current Gossip." Two weeks later the title was changed to "Sharps and Flats." It was a wide-ranging column and, according to historian Alson J. Smith in *Chicago's Left Bank,* it was the first daily newspaper column in the country. Field commented upon politics, the arts, and sports. He didn't care much about facts and figures but about anecdotes and the idiosyncrasies of human nature. The whimsical side of life appealed to him.

Field developed a curious ritual when he was ready to begin his day's work. "Getting ready to write" is how his editor, Charles H. Dennis, described it. He seldom arrived at the office before 11 a.m. and never wrote down a single word until 3 p.m but always managed to finish his column by 6 p.m. He spent the hours between 11 and 3 socializing, gossiping, and chatting among his colleagues. After finally entering his office, he would discard his coat, take off his shoes, don a pair of comfortable slippers, and roll up his trousers above his

ankles. Then he would sit down, place his feet on the desk, and cross his legs. Only then would he begin writing.

Although Field did not complain, historian Kenny J. Williams maintains that the columnist was heavily censored by his editor, John Ballantyne, who deleted any copy that was too critical of the moneyed establishment. The unspoken rule was that Field could gently ridicule but could not overtly criticize.

At the same time he was earning a living as a columnist, Field began to write children's verse and compose poetry, mostly of a sentimental nature. Although his poetry is largely forgotten today, there was something about it—its innocence and cheerfulness perhaps—that appealed to nineteenth-century American tastes. Field may have been a newspaperman but it was his poetry that made him famous.

A devout bibliophile, Field and a circle of literary friends often met at the Saints' and Sinners' rare book corner of McClurg's Bookstore at Wabash Avenue and Monroe Street to discuss books and literature.

During his last years, Field, in ill health, wrote his column from home. His son delivered it to the office each day.

Field wished to be recognized as a serious writer of fiction, but instead he became one of the best-loved columnists and poets of his day. Kenny J. Williams calls him the first Chicago journalist to receive national fame. Field died in his sleep due to heart failure in November of 1895. He was forty-five.

Among his books of verse and poetry were *Denver Tribune Primer* (1882), *Culture's Garland* (1887), *Little Book of Western Verse* (1889), *A Little Book of Profitable Tales* (1890), *Second Book of Verse* (1893), and *Echoes from the Sabine Farm* (translations of Horace) (1893).

In 1922 a statue dedicated to Field was unveiled in Lincoln Park Zoo. The sculpture by Edward McCartan, which is east of the Small Mammal House, depicts the figure of an angel dropping flowers over two sleeping children. Verses from two of Field's most popular children's poems, "Wynken, Blynken, and Nod" and "Sugar Plum Tree," were carved in the granite.

For many years Field lived at 4240 North Clarendon Avenue on the North Side. He was buried in Graceland Cemetery. In 1926 his remains—with the consent of the Field family—were removed to the Church of the Holy Comforter in Kenilworth, Illinois.

See also: George Ade, Finley Peter Dunne, Ring Lardner, Victor Lawson, Melville E. Stone

Further reading: Smith, Alson J. *Chicago's Left Bank* (1953); Thompson, Slason. *Eugene Field: A Study in Heredity and Contradictions.* 2 vols. (1901); Williams, Kenny J. *Prairie Voices: A Literary History of Chicago from the Frontier to 1893* (1980).

Marshall Field

Merchant

born: September 18, 1834
Conway, Massachusetts
died: January 16, 1906
Chicago, Illinois

Mandel Brothers, The Fair Store, Carson, Pirie, Scott—all were, and the latter still is a big Chicago department store. But none quite matched the grandeur and dignity of Marshall Field and Company. Like Potter Palmer and John G. Shedd, Marshall Field was a Yankee who made good in Chicago. The quiet-mannered Field reminded his employees, "Always remember, we are the servants of the public." The company motto? "Give the lady what she wants."

Marshall Field was working for a dry goods store in Pittsfield, Massachusetts, when talk of a rough and ready town, a thriving center of commerce on the Midwestern prairie, captured his imagination. Field had saved some money, and by 1855 he was ready to leave Massachusetts to seek his fortune out west.

Field arrived in Chicago in 1856 and soon found work at the wholesale firm of Cooley, Wadsworth and Company as a clerk. His employer, John Farwell, observed, "He had a merchant's instinct . . . and he never lost it." Field worked hard and lived frugally, devoting all of his time to learning the business. He soon rose to be a junior partner and was placed in charge of sales and credit. Within a year he was offered a full partnership and the new firm of Farwell, Field and Company was formed. Potter Palmer, founder of the company and in ill health at the time, sold his retail and wholesale business to the new firm. Thus Field, Palmer and Leiter was born: Settling on State Street, Field encouraged other retail businesses to open there also.

On October 12, 1868, Field's grand new store at State and Washington opened to a huge throng who gathered eagerly outside its doors. Field wanted to please his new clientele, and so he guaranteed their money back if customers were not entirely satisfied. Furthermore, Field introduced free delivery service and opened a bargain basement store. Most of all, he carefully nurtured an irresistible atmosphere. Women, especially, enjoyed the attentiveness and respect of the well-mannered and efficient store clerks.

Field and his partner, Levi Leiter, soon clashed over policy matters, and in 1879 Field bought Leiter out. In 1881 Field, Palmer and Leiter became Marshall Field and Company.

In 1887 the wholesale division moved into a new building designed by Boston architect H. H. Richardson. A massive Romanesque structure, it filled the entire city block bounded by Adams, Quincy, Wells, and Franklin Streets. It was demolished in 1930.

Field reportedly attracted the most aggressive men in the retail business. John G. Shedd, a New Hampshire farm boy, rose through the organization to become president of the company. Another important figure was the quick-tongued, ambitious Harry Gordon Selfridge, who started with the company in 1879 as a stock boy in the wholesale house. It was Selfridge's idea to open a restaurant in the store. At first Field objected. "This is a dry-goods store," he said, "we don't feed people here." Then he reconsidered, and in April 1890 a tearoom was opened. As manager of the retail division, Selfridge is credited with transforming Marshall Field and Company from a dry goods store into the full-fledged department store that we know today. Selfridge later founded the famous department store in London that bears his name.

A generous benefactor, Field donated money to the University of Chicago to be used toward an athletic field. For years the students referred to it simply as "Marshall Field" until it was renamed Stagg Field, in honor of the great University of Chicago football coach. The Field Museum of Natural History was founded in 1893 during the World's Columbian Exposition by a $1 million gift from Field. Initially located in the old Palace of Fine Arts building in Jackson Park, it was moved to its present site at Roosevelt Road and Lake Shore Drive in 1921.

On January 16, 1906, the merchant prince fell, a victim of pneumonia. A bell rang through the State Street store at the news of his death, and the shades were drawn. On the day of his funeral, all the stores along State Street closed, out of respect to his memory. Field was buried in Graceland Cemetery.

With the death of Marshall Field IV in 1965 at the age of forty-nine, the Field family relinquished control of the company with the sale of its last remaining stock. In 1982 BAT Industries, a London tobacco conglomerate, acquired the company, and in April 1990, the Minneapolis-based Dayton Hudson Corporation took over.

See also: Potter Palmer, John G. Shedd

Further reading: Wendt, Lloyd and Herman Kogan. *Give the Lady What She Wants! The Story of Marshall Field and Co.* (1952).

John Fischetti

Cartoonist

born: September 27, 1916
Brooklyn, New York
died: November 18, 1980
Chicago, Illinois

Pulitzer-prize winning cartoonist John Fischetti was considered by many in his profession to be one of the best editorial cartoonists in the country.

Giovanni Fischetti knew by the time he was twelve that he wanted to be a newspaper cartoonist. Born in Brooklyn to an Italian immigrant family, Fischetti ran away from home at sixteen. He hopped freight trains, toiled as a cabin boy on a ship bound for South America, and mopped hallways. In 1919 he returned home to study commercial art at the Pratt Institute in Brooklyn.

Fischetti's first cartooning job was with Walt Disney's studio on the West Coast animating Mickey Mouse. While there, he picked up several assignments on the *Los Angeles Times*. Later, Fischetti moved to San Francisco and then Chicago where he freelanced for *Coronet* and *Esquire* magazines.

In 1941 the *Chicago Sun* hired Fischetti as an editorial cartoonist, but the outbreak of World War II cut short his career plans. From 1942 to 1946 he served in the army, and worked for *Stars and Stripes* in Paris. When he returned to the United States, he joined the *New York Herald Tribune* as an editorial cartoonist. From 1951 to 1961 he was a syndicated editorial cartoonist but returned to Chicago in 1966 to join the *Chicago Daily News*. He won the Pulitzer prize two years later for general excellence in cartooning. When the *Daily News* ceased publication in 1978 Fischetti moved to the *Chicago Sun-Times*.

Fischetti was a pioneer of what he referred to as the "new look" cartoons. He drew wide horizontal cartoons, a departure from the more vertical styles of traditional cartooning, and satirized everything from fads and fashions to contemporary mores and values. He reserved his most acerbic bite, however, for politics and politicians, whom he described as the "linchpin of most of the social ills."

Fischetti often created his best work under deadline pressure. One of his most critically acclaimed—and poignant cartoons—depicted the figure of a weeping Abraham Lincoln on the floor of the Lincoln Memorial on the day of John F. Kennedy's assassination. Another was his drawing of an African-American man, bound with chains labeled "white racism," and accompanied by the caption: "Why don't they lift themselves up by their own bootstraps like we do?"

In 1973 Fischetti published his autobiography *Zinga Zanga Za!*, which was profusely illustrated with 150 of his cartoons.

Fischetti suffered heart attacks in 1972 and 1973 and underwent triple bypass surgery in 1979. He died in November of 1980 at age sixty-four after collapsing in his Near North Side home.

In 1980 a John Fischetti Scholarship Dinner was established in his name. Proceeds from the annual event, held each November, go toward a scholarship fund for outstanding Columbia College journalism students.

See also: John T. McCutcheon

Further reading: Fischetti, John. *Zinga Zanga Za!* (1973).

Morris Fishbein

Physician

born: July 22, 1889
St. Louis, Missouri
died: September 27, 1976
Chicago, Illinois

For many years Dr. Morris Fishbein was the most influential person in American medicine. As editor of the **Journal of the American Medical Association** *for almost forty years, Fishbein helped the American Medical Association (AMA) grow into a powerful organization that still greatly affects both medical practices and health legislation.*

Photograph reprinted with permission from the *Chicago Sun-Times.*

Fishbein's father, Benjamin, a glassware merchant, wanted his son to become a rabbi, but young Morris had other ideas. He received a bachelor's degree from the University of Chicago in 1910 and an M.D. in 1912 from Rush Medical College.

Fishbein began his clinical career in Durand Hospital at the McCormick Institute for Infectious Diseases located at 637 South Wood Street as a house physician in 1912. In 1913 he became assistant to Dr. George H. Simmons, editor of the *Journal of the American Medical Association.* He held that post until 1924 when he was promoted to editor.

Fishbein turned the journal into one of the most influential and well-read medical publications. In its pages he attacked quacks, promoted good medical practices, and disparaged socialized medicine—including subsidized medicine for the poor and the elderly—as a threat to professional standards, a position that he would later retract. By 1965 he supported medicare and other federal health programs as necessary aspects of health care. "As conditions change we must adapt to the changes," he explained. "When conditions become so severe they can no longer be handled by private initiative government must step in."

In addition Fishbein founded a lay magazine, *Hygeia,* and established the American Medical Association's public relations department. In 1921 he became *Time* magazine's first medical editor. From 1924 to 1950 he edited the *Journal of the American Medical Association,* founded the weekly, *Medical World News,* and wrote a popular syndicated medical column. From 1958 to 1967 he acted as editor of *World-Wide Abstracts of General Medicine.* He was also president of the Chicago Medical Society and president of the Chicago Heart Association.

In 1950 Fishbein retired but continued his work as a medical editor with Encyclopedia Britannica. During a speech to the graduating class of the Chicago Medical College in 1965, Fishbein said the old-time physician who made house calls was dead. "The modern doctor must combine the tactfulness of a diplomat, the eloquence of a lawyer, the impartiality of a judge, the decision of a general, the frankness of a witness, and the astuteness of a man on trial for his life with the precision of a mathematician, the imagination of an artist, the altruism of a philanthropist and the tenacity of a pawnbroker."

In 1969 Fishbein published his autobiography, *Morris Fishbein, M. D., An Autobiography.* Among his forty books are: *Do you Want to Become a Doctor?* (1939), *History of the American Medical Association* (1947), and *The Handy Home Medical Advisor and Concise Medical Encyclopedia* (1953).

In 1970 a new professorship for the teaching of history of science and medicine was established at the University of Chicago in his name. In 1975 Fishbein was honored by Jackson Park Hospital and the medical division of the State of Israel Bonds for his contributions to medicine and the economic development of the Jewish state.

Fishbein, who lived at 5454 South Shore Drive, died in Jackson Park Hospital in 1976. He was eighty-seven.

See also: Frank Billings

Fahey Flynn

Television News Broadcaster

born: August 6, 1916
Escanaba, Michigan
died: August 8, 1983
Chicago, Illinois

His trademarks—the bow tie, the jaunty "Howwww do you do, ladies and gentlemen"—branded Fahey Flynn as a newsman of the old school. For more than thirty years, Chicagoans invited Flynn into their living rooms. Said one admiring colleague at a 1981 testimonial dinner in his honor, "Can you imagine any station manager today hiring a man who is 5-foot-5-inches high, overweight, with a leprechaun face, wearing a bow-tie and bearing his unlikely name?" Perhaps not, but by the end of the seventies, Fahey Flynn had become a local broadcasting institution.

Photograph courtesy of WLS-TV.

The son of a railroad man, the broadcaster's unusual name was a combination of the surname of his father, Flynn, and of his mother, Fahey.

Flynn was a graduate student in economics at the University of Wisconsin during the late 1930s when he found part-time work at radio stations in Fond du Lac and Madison. He then joined WEMP radio in Milwaukee as a $60-a-week announcer and broadcasted the minor league Milwaukee Brewers baseball games. Flynn eventually earned a bachelor's degree in history and English from the University of Wisconsin-Oshkosh.

In 1941 Flynn auditioned for a broadcasting job at WBBM radio in Chicago—and got it. After a tour of duty in the Navy during World War II, Flynn resumed his radio career. In 1948 he won several radio journalism awards for his series, "Report Uncensored," an exposé on conditions at a delinquent boys school in St. Charles, Illinois. Two years later, he won more acclaim for his program on race relations, "The Quiet Answer."

On March 3, 1953, Flynn made his television debut on Channel 2, sporting one of his favorite polka dot bow ties. A new Chicago tradition was born. For a decade, Flynn teamed up with meteorologist, P. J. Hoff, an affable sort who drew cartoons to illustrate the weather, on the 10 p.m. WBBM newscast.

Flynn won six Chicago Emmy awards including, in 1958, the first Chicago Emmy award for newscasting. He also received an Emmy for "Outstanding Spot Coverage" during the May 1979 crash of American Airlines flight 191 at O'Hare International Airport. In 1980 he was honored as the Chicago Variety Club's "Man of the Year."

Flynn left Channel 2, WBBM-TV, in 1968 when the general manager, in an effort to upgrade the newscast's image, forced him to wear regular ties. Flynn bolted to rival, Channel 7, WLS-TV, and was replaced at Channel 2 by a young, personable newsman named Bill Kurtis. He, too, became a local broadcasting tradition.

At Channel 7, Flynn along with co-anchor Joel Daly and meteorologist John Coleman launched a new format called "Eyewitness News." Although some critics disparagingly referred to it as "Happy Talk," Chicagoans found the friendly repartee and the apparently genuine camaraderie among the newscasters refreshing. The ratings soared. Flynn and company were credited, along with others, for leading Channel 7's Eyewitness News to the top of the ratings for virtually all of the 1970s.

Flynn died of complications from internal hemorrhaging at Northwestern Memorial Hospital in Chicago. He was sixty-seven.

Flynn was praised for his professionalism, his integrity, and his grace under pressure. Said friend and colleague, Joel Daly, at the funeral mass, "In our peculiar world of prima donnas, Fahey Flynn was one of a kind. A man of tact, a man of sensitivity for whom rank had no particular privileges."

See also: Frazier Thomas

Bob Fosse

Choreographer/ Film Director

born: June 23, 1927
Chicago, Illinois
died: September 23, 1987
Washington, D.C.

A hard-driving, fiercely competitive song-and-dance man, Robert Louis Fosse was one of the most widely acclaimed choreographers of the Broadway stage as well as a respected motion picture director. Although his theatrical work usually consisted of upbeat and energetic musicals, his movies—especially **Lenny, All That Jazz, Cabaret,** *and* **Star 80**—*traveled down darker paths.*

The son of a salesman who moonlighted as a vaudeville singer, Fosse received his first dance lesson at age nine above a drugstore at Ashland and Montrose Avenues in Chicago. Though fond of baseball, Fosse's idol was not an athlete but a dancer, Fred Astaire.

By the time he was thirteen, Fosse had formed his first nightclub act and began performing in clubs around the Midwest. He did stints as a teenage hoofer in Chicago burlesque houses and nightclubs. "I got $10 a night, six nights a week, and that makes you a very interesting figure in high school," said Fosse who attended Amundsen High School on the city's North Side and performed in the school's variety shows.

While serving in the Navy during World War II, Fosse appeared in several productions that toured the Pacific. Upon his discharge, he teamed up with Mary Ann Niles, his first wife, in several road-show productions. In 1953 Fosse left for Hollywood and appeared in several films, including *Kiss Me Kate,* with Howard Keel and Kathryn Grayson. *Kiss Me Kate* was the first film in which Fosse's own choreography appeared. He was allowed to stage his own dance numbers, but Gower Champion, the film's choreographer, was given credit. Fosse later admitted that he began doing his own choreography out of self-defense, because there weren't enough good choreographers to go around. His aim was to blend dancing and dialogue so that "you can't tell where one stops."

In 1954 Fosse headed for Broadway where he choreographed *Pajama Game* (for which he won his first Tony) and *Damn Yankees.* Other shows followed—*New Girl in Town* with Gwen Verdon and then *Redhead* and *Sweet Charity,* which he both choreographed and directed. *Sweet Charity* was a Broadway smash. Its songs included such showstoppers as "Big Spender" and "If My Friends Could See Me Now." Fosse also choreographed *Little Me* and *How to Succeed in Business without Really Trying.* Among these successes, he only suffered one flop, *Pleasures and Palaces,* about the unlikely pairing of Catherine the Great and John Paul Jones.

Fosse's debut as a movie director in 1968 was far from promising. Critics panned *Sweet Charity,* starring Shirley MacLaine as the prostitute with a heart of gold, as being downbeat and confusing. Critics praised Fosse's choreography but criticized his "choppy" direction. The 1987 Broadway revival of *Sweet Charity,* however, was a hit and was considered the definitive production.

Everything came together with Fosse's next film, the Oscar-winning *Cabaret* (1972), starring Liza Minnelli as an American singer in a cabaret in Berlin during the waning days of the Weimar republic and Joel Grey as the sneering master of ceremonies. By allowing the songs to comment on the action and foreshadow the lives of the characters, *Cabaret* breathed new life into a moribund art form and, in the process, broke every rule in the movie musical tradition. Innovative, brash, and unsentimental, *Cabaret* was called the first "adult" musical. The scenes inside the Kit Kat Klub captured Fosse's choreography at its most provocative with its finger-snapping rhythm, deliberately jerky movements, and a sensual, almost vulgar, earthiness.

In 1973 Fosse won every major award in the entertainment industry. In addition to his Oscar for *Cabaret,* he brought home a Tony for *Pippin* and an Emmy for "Liza with a Z."

Fosse's next film, *Lenny* (1974), starred Dustin Hoffman as the acid-tongued comedian Lenny Bruce. Though flawed and uneven, it was further evidence of the director's fascination with the underside of American society.

The largely autobiographical *All That Jazz* (1979) was a thinly veiled account of Fosse's near fatal heart attack, which occurred in 1974 while he was rehearsing a Broadway musical, *Chicago,* and editing the movie, *Lenny.* Roy Scheider played the overworked song-and-dance man with great aplomb. *All That Jazz* received nine Oscar nominations and won four awards.

Fosse's last movie, *Star 80* (1983), was a harrowing account of the murder of Playboy model, Dorothy Stratten, by her jealous husband. A box office failure, it nevertheless received generally positive reviews for its unflinching examination of the dark side of human nature.

Despite his cinematic success, Fosse always felt more at home on the stage than he did with movies. His most popular efforts include: *Chicago* (1975), a musical ode to the city of his birth; *Pippin(1972),* a sort of medieval coming-of-age tale and—at five years—Fosse's longest-running show and one for which he won Tonys for best director and best choreographer; and *Dancin'* (1978), a joyous celebration of the Broadway musical and its hardworking chorus line, for which he won a Tony for best choreographer.

In 1986 Fosse directed his last Broadway show, *Big Deal.* Set in the Chicago of his youth, the show used popular songs of the thirties and forties. Although Fosse won another Tony for best choreography, it was ultimately both a critical and commercial flop and closed after only seventy performances.

Fosse suffered a fatal heart attack at George Washington University Hospital in Washington, D.C., minutes after the opening of the revival of *Sweet Charity* in 1987.

Work, he had always maintained, was his way of attaining a piece of immortality. It was both his saving grace and his downfall.

See also: Vincente Minnelli [appendix]

Further reading: Grubb, Kevin Boyd. *Razzle Dazzle: The Life and Work of Bob Fosse* (1989).

Bud Freeman

Musician

born: April 13, 1906
Chicago, Illinois
died: March 15, 1991
Chicago, Illinois

As a member of the legendary Austin High Gang, tenor saxophonist Lawrence "Bud" Freeman played a crucial role in the development of what came to be known as the Chicago style of jazz, a style modeled after the great African-American jazz musicians but marked by a fluent and strong rhythmic beat. Freeman, one of the most influential figures in Chicago jazz history, continued to perform until he was well into his eighties.

Photograph courtesy of Joe Segal.

Freeman, the son of a Jewish garment cutter and a French-Canadian woman, grew up in the Austin community on the Far West Side. While attending Austin High School he befriended several young men who would form the nucleus of the seminal Austin High Gang.

The Austin High Gang consisted of Freeman on saxophone, Jimmy McPartland on cornet, Dick McPartland on guitar, Jim Lannigan on bass, Frank Teschemacher on alto sax and clarinet, Dave North on piano, and Dave Tough on drums. Occasionally a reserved young man from the Maxwell Street neighborhood—Benny Goodman—would sit in with the gang. Most of the boys were already taking violin and piano lessons. Freeman, who didn't play an instrument but had grown up surrounded by music in his home, took saxophone lessons from McPartland's father.

In his autobiography Freeman recalls the times he and his friends would spend at the Spoon and Straw soda parlor in Oak Park, listening to records on the jukebox by the New Orleans Rhythm Kings. "We were so excited by that first record that we decided that afternoon to become jazz musicians and form our own band," noted Freeman. Freeman would travel to the Lincoln Gardens on the South Side to hear cornetist Joe "King" Oliver's Creole Jazz Band and an unknown trumpeter named Louis Armstrong. Another favorite was Bix Beiderbecke, the trumpet genius from Iowa who lived in Chicago for a brief period and performed in North Side clubs.

In 1924 Freeman made his professional debut playing with Dave Tough in a Sheboygan, Wisconsin, roadhouse. Back in Chicago, the gang rehearsed together and honed their skills by playing at parties and dances. In December of 1927 Freeman, Teschemacher, Jimmy

McPartland, Lannigan, pianist Joe Sullivan, guitarist Eddie Condon, and drummer Gene Krupa, went into the studio and recorded several classic examples of Chicago jazz: "Liza," "Nobody's Sweetheart Now," "China Boy," and "Sugar." Although influenced by Armstrong and Beiderbecke as well as contemporary French composers, Freeman by this time had developed a distinctive style that incorporated the rythmic swing of the great jazz masters and the complex harmonies of classical music, yet was marked by a mellow and lyrical tone.

Freeman continued to perform with local dance/jazz bands until 1928, when he joined Ben Pollack in New York. In 1935 he formed the Windy City Five with Bunny Berigan, Claude Thornhill, Eddie Condon, Grachan Moncur, and Cozy Cole. The following year he teamed up with Jimmy and Tommy Dorsey but left in 1937 to join Benny Goodman's band. It was not a pleasant experience, recalls Freeman, who refers to it as "the biggest mistake of my life. Benny liked to do all the playing, as well as he should have. There wasn't much for me to do there, and he was very difficult to work for." He stayed only one year.

In 1943 he was drafted and sent to the Aleutian Islands where army brass took advantage of his talent and made him the leader of the military band. After the war he returned to New York to resume his career. During the next few decades, Freeman lived a nomadic existence, spending a large portion of his time playing clubs and concerts across the U.S., in Canada, and in Europe.

In the late sixties Freeman formed the World's Greatest Jazz Band, a ten-piece outfit based in New York. WGJB performed at the best nightclubs in the country. A noted Anglophile, Freeman moved to London in 1974. He stayed there for six years.

After a prolonged absence from the city, Freeman returned to Chicago in 1980 to perform at the Chicago Jazz Festival. At this point he fell in love with his hometown all over again and decided to stay.

Freeman recorded with many bands during his long career. Some titles include *Bud Freeman and His Orchestra* (1928), *Bud Freeman and His Windy City Five* (1935), *Bud Freeman Trio* and *Bud Freeman and His Gang* (1938), *Bud Freeman and His Summa Cum Laude Orchestra* (1939), and *Bud Freeman and His Famous Chicagoans* (1940). *The Compleat Bud Freeman*, an anthology of career highlights, was released in the early seventies.

Freeman denied inventing the Chicago school of jazz—he always gave Armstrong and Oliver their proper due. "Our own contribution," he recalled several years ago in the *Chicago Tribune*, "was really to popularize the tenor saxophone in a band setting."

Freeman died of cancer a month before his eighty-fifth birthday at the Warren Barr Pavilion nursing home at 66 West Oak Street.

See also: Louis Armstrong, Benny Goodman, Earl Hines, Gene Krupa, Mezz Mezzrow, Joe "King" Oliver

Further reading: Clarke, Donald. *The Penguin Encyclopedia of Popular Music* (1989); Freeman, Bud, as told to Robert Wolf. *Crazeology: The Autobiography of a Chicago Jazzman* (1989); Travis, Dempsey J. *An Autobiography of Black Jazz* (1983).

Henry Blake Fuller

Novelist

born: January 9, 1857
Chicago, Illinois
died: July 28, 1929
Chicago, Illinois

A distinguished Chicago blueblood, Henry Blake Fuller's elegant, graceful writing style epitomized the short-lived genteel tradition of Chicago literature that was prominent during the late nineteenth century.

Photograph courtesy of the University of Chicago Archives.

Fuller was born near Van Buren and LaSalle Streets on the future site of the LaSalle Street railroad station. With the exception of one year spent at the Allison Classical Academy on the shores of Lake Oconomowoc, Wisconsin, Fuller received his entire education in Chicago's public schools. After graduating from South Division High School, Fuller held a quick succession of clerical jobs—clerk in a kitchenware shop on State Street, messenger for the Bank of Illinois, and bookkeeper for the Home National Bank—before he left Chicago to spend one year in Europe.

Upon his return from Europe, Fuller began writing a fantasy romance, *The Chevalier of Pensieri-Vani*, (1891). Written in an office on Lake Street, Fuller's first novel was an episodic work set in the Italy of his imagination. It didn't attract much reader interest—few Fuller novels did, esoteric as they were—but it was appreciated by a small segment of the literary set.

The Cliff-Dwellers (1893), Fuller's second novel—and his first set in Chicago—received virtually unanimous acclaim. *The Cliff-Dwellers* (the name refers to the skyscraper office of its main characters) has often been identified as the first important American urban novel. It not only was one of the first credible portraits of the business world in American literature it was also one of the first to use Chicago as a fictional setting. "The Cliff-Dwellers" is also the name of the prestigious social club, founded in 1907 by Fuller and fellow writer Hamlin Garland, that has its headquarters on the ninth floor of Orchestra Hall—although that situation may soon change. In May 1990 the Chicago Symphony Orchestra notified the club that it will have to find new quarters when its lease expires in April 1992.

Fuller's second Chicago novel *With the Procession* (1895) received even more glowing reviews than *The Cliff-Dwellers*. Generally considered his most mature work, *With the Procession* chronicles Chicago's progress from isolated fort to bustling metropolis. *Under the Skylight*, a collection of short stories that contained descriptions of Chicago's artistic life, including a thinly veiled portrait of Hamlin Garland, was published in 1901. Fuller devoted the next two decades to writing primarily short stories, essays, and one-act fantasy plays.

During the last year of his life, Fuller experienced an energetic burst of creativity. Within a seven-month period he managed to complete two novels—*Gardens of This World* and *Not on the Screen*—and began work on a third. *Gardens of This World* returned to the romantic fantasy genre of his first novel while *Not on the Screen* satirized Chicago's fledgling motion picture industry.

In addition, Fuller wrote a column of literary criticism for the *New York Evening Post* and was on the management staff of *Poetry* magazine. He was also a frequent contributor to *The New Republic.*

His other novels include *On the Stairs* (1918) and *Bertram Cope's Year* (1919). The University of Chicago featured prominently in the latter.

Although not generally well known even among students of American literature, Fuller was an important figure on the Chicago literary scene. Theodore Dreiser placed Fuller in the "vanguard of the New Realism," and later, such Midwestern writers as Thornton Wilder and Glenway Wescott acknowledged their debt to him. By the time of his death in 1929, his novels of manners were considered typical examples of nineteenth-century writing.

A painfully shy man who devoted most of his life to his work, Fuller felt comfortable around only a few close friends, though even they were expected to maintain a respectable distance. Fuller did, however, develop a good working relationship with Harriet Monroe, publisher of *Poetry* magazine. He was a member of its publication advisory committee for three years.

After the death of his mother in 1907, Fuller lived in a succession of rooming houses in Hyde Park. When he died of heart disease in 1929 at the age of seventy-two, he was living at a friend's home at 5411 South Harper Avenue.

See also: Theodore Dreiser, Hamlin Garland, Harriet Monroe, Lorado Taft

Further reading: Bowron, Bernard R., Jr. *Henry B. Fuller of Chicago: The Ordeal of a Genteel Realist in Ungenteel America* (1974); Griffin, Constance. *Henry Blake Fuller: A Critical Biography* (1939); Regnery, Henry. *The Cliff Dwellers: The History of a Chicago Cultural Institution* (1990).

Mary Garden

Opera Singer

born: February 20, 1877
Aberdeen, Scotland
died: January 4, 1967
Aberdeen, Scotland

Mary Garden dominated Chicago opera for more than twenty years. Candid, temperamental, and always entertaining, she retired at the peak of her career in the early 1930s. "I began at the top. I stayed at the top and I quit at the top," said the unpredictable diva.

Born in Aberdeen, Scotland, Garden emigrated with her family to the United States, settling first in Chicopee, Massachusetts, and later in Hartford, Connecticut. The family moved to Chicago in 1888. At age sixteen Garden appeared in an amateur production of Gilbert and Sullivan's *Trial By Jury*. The wife of a local merchant heard her singing in a suburban church choir and, smitten with her voice, offered to pay for her to be trained in Paris.

Garden arrived in Paris in 1897 and made her professional debut three years later at the Opera Comique. As luck would have it, she was sitting in the audience when the star of the show fell ill. She went onstage in the third act of Charpentier's *Louise* and enraptured the audience and continued to do so for one hundred successive nights. She filled houses in Brussels, London, New York, Boston, and, eventually, Chicago.

Although Garden put Chicago opera on the map, the first opera performed in the city was Bellini's *La Sonnambula* on July 29, 1850, at John Rice's theater on West Randolph Street. In the 1860s a young distiller from Massachusetts, Uranus H. Crosby, built a combined opera house, art gallery, and office building at Washington and State Streets.

By 1909 the city had matured sufficiently to support its own resident company, the Chicago Grand Opera. Financed partly by Harold F. McCormick, head of the International Harvester Company, and Charles Gates Dawes, vice-president of the United States, the new company launched its inaugural season on November 3, 1910, at the Auditorium Theater with a production of *Aida* . Two days later Mary Garden made her Chicago debut in *Pelléas et Mélisande.*

During her first year, Garden performed her most controversial role, *Salome*, in the opera of the same name by Richard Strauss. *Salome* was condemned from pulpit to editorial desk. Garden's sensual performance offended the sensitivity of a significant portion of the opera-going public, notes Ronald L. Davis in *Opera in Chicago,* and prompted Arthur Burrage Farwell, president of the Chicago Law and Order League, to protest to the chief of police, Leroy T. Steward. Although *Salome* played to two sold-out houses, the third show was canceled, apparently in a concerted effort to save the reputation of the fledgling company.

Despite the support of the opera-going public, the Chicago Grand Opera ended the 1913–14 season with a $250,000 deficit, notes Davis. The outbreak of World War I further aggravated its fragile economic situation and the company was forced to declare bankruptcy. In the spring of 1915 a new company emerged, the Chicago Opera Association, with McCormick retaining his title of president.

In 1921 Garden became general director of the association, the first woman to head an opera company. Her tenure, a tempestuous one, lasted only one year. She brought in high priced contemporary stars—a move that almost bankrupted the company—waged feuds and carried on artistic squabbles with members. By the end of the year, her confrontational management style led to the resignation of her business executive, her artistic director, and many singers. Tired of the daily battle, she agreed to step down. "I am an artist and my place is with the artists," she explained.

Despite the $1 million deficit, critics agreed that Garden delivered her promise of going "out in a blaze of glory." The *Tribune* confessed, "There is no question but that the operatic season this year has been more brilliant than ever before."

In 1922 the Chicago Opera Association was reorganized into the Chicago Civic Opera. Unlike the older company, which was financed through the generosity of a handful of wealthy patrons, the new organization, led by business magnate Samuel Insull, was bankrolled by contributors who pledged to pay a specific amount over a five-year period. Garden continued to perform with the new company and continued to be a crowd pleaser.

Garden gave her Chicago farewell performance on January 24, 1931, in *Le Jongleur de Notre Dame* at the Civic Opera House, which had opened two years earlier. When the curtain fell, she gathered her belongings and left, without saying goodbye to anyone. From Paris she cabled a succinct message: "My career in America is done."

After she retired, Garden visited Chicago frequently. She performed in an occasional vaudeville show in the city—something that she had always wanted to do and, in 1935, she taught a course in opera at the Chicago Musical College.

Garden was a free spirit who did what she wanted—damn the consequences—and lived where she wanted. When it came to choosing between marriage or career, there was never any doubt which side would win. "I always put it in the scales and weighed it against art. It was always the same," she confessed. "Down went the gentlemen and up went art." After all, she reasoned, "If you have a great career, why do you want a man trailing you?"

Garden made her last public appearance in Chicago in January 1954 as a guest on WGN-AM radio while on a lecture tour of the United States. Although she professed to love America, she said she wished to live and die a Scot. Garden spent the last twenty-five years of her life in her native Aberdeen and died in January 1967, seven weeks short of her ninetieth birthday.

See also: **Charles Gates Dawes, Samuel Insull, Ruth Page**

Further reading: Brubaker, Robert L. "130 Years of Opera in Chicago," *Chicago History* (Fall 1979); Davis, Ronald L. *Opera in Chicago* (1966); Garden, Mary and Louis Biancolli. *Mary Garden's Story* (1951); Moore, Edward C. *Forty Years of Opera in Chicago* (1930).

Hamlin Garland

Novelist

born: September 14, 1860
West Salem, Wisconsin
died: March 4, 1940
Hollywood, California

A pioneering novelist of American fiction, Hamlin Garland settled in Chicago at the time of the 1893 World's Columbian Exposition and became a major figure in the Chicago Literary Renaissance movement.

Photograph courtesy of the Chicago Historical Society.

Garland was born on a farm near West Salem, Wisconsin, in 1860. When he was eight, he and his family traveled across the Mississippi River into Winneshick County, Iowa. As a youngster, he worked on his father's farm in the summer and attended Cedar Valley Seminary in the winter. In 1882 Garland moved to the East Coast but returned to the Midwest a year later and settled in McPherson County, North Dakota. After spending a year on the wind-swept Dakota prairie, he again headed back east. In 1899 he married Zuleme Taft, sister of the Chicago sculptor, Lorado Taft.

Garland's initial touch of fame came with the publication of *The Moccasin Ranch*, the first of his Mississippi Valley stories. At that time he was teaching private classes in English and American literature in Boston. As a member of the Boston literary circle, he came into contact with some of the leading figures in American arts, letters, and public life, including Oliver Wendell Holmes, William Dean Howells, Edward Everett Hale, and Edwin Booth.

In 1887 he made a return visit to the Midwest from which emerged a series of sketches, *Main Traveled Roads.* The following year he published his first novel, *A Spoil of Office.* In 1893 he decided to settle in Chicago where he wrote a dozen novels in addition to a biography of Gen. Ulysses S. Grant.

Rose of Dutcher's Coolly (1895), considered by many critics to be his best novel, focuses on a rural Wisconsin girl who decides to pursue a poetry career in Chicago. He also wrote a largely autobiographical Midwestern trilogy: *A Son of the Middle Border, A Daughter of the Middle Border,* and *Trailmakers of the Middle Border.*

In 1907 Garland approached several prominent friends, including novelist Henry Blake Fuller, sculptor Lorado Taft, and publisher Ralph Clarkson, about establishing a prestigious social club for the city's literary elite, comparable to the Players Club in New York. At Garland's suggestion, they named it the Cliff-Dwellers Club which was also the title of Fuller's 1893 novel. (Historian Emmett Dedmon argues that the name derives from the cliff-dwelling Indians of the American Southwest, not from Fuller's novel.)

On November 6, 1907, Garland, Fuller, Taft, bookseller Francis Browne, and painter Ralph Clarkson organized the prestigious social club and made their headquarters on the ninth floor of Orchestra Hall, 220 South Michigan Avenue. The club continues to meet there although that status may change—the club's lease expires in April of 1992. The landlord, the Chicago Symphony Orchestra, has publicly announced that it does not intend to renew the lease, as the organization is strapped for space.

In 1930 Garland moved to Hollywood where he he lived across the street from film director, Cecil B. DeMille. While in the movie capital, Garland worked on half a dozen books including one that probed psychic phenomena.

In his later years, critics sometimes referred to Garland as the dean of American letters. Writes literary historian Kenny J. Williams: "Mr. Garland's stories, though very powerful, are inexpressibly sad. They deal with the horror of hard work. His characters toil and droop and languish on the treadmill of fate."

Garland died in his Hollywood house at age seventy-nine due to a cerebral hemorrhage while completing the final chapters of his book, *The Fortunate Exile*, which described his ten years in California.

See also: Henry Blake Fuller, Lorado Taft

Further reading: Holloway, Jean. *Hamlin Garland* (1960); Williams, Kenny J. *Prairie Voices: A Literary History of Chicago from the Frontier to 1893* (1980).

Dave Garroway

Broadcaster

born: July 13, 1913
Schenectady, New York
died: July 21, 1982
Swarthmore, Pennsylvania

Although he lived in Chicago for less than a decade, David Cunningham Garroway was the most distinguished representative of the so-called "Chicago school of television," which was known for its easygoing, informal approach to entertaining and was practiced by Fran Allison, Burr Tillstrom, Studs Terkel, and others. Garroway made his first splash in broadcasting on Chicago radio where his wry sense of humor attracted a loyal following. In 1952 he launched NBC's durable talk-and-news program, "The Today Show." With his bow tie, horn-rim glasses, and mild manner, Garroway won over the national audience too.

Photograph reprinted with permission from the *Chicago Sun-Times*.

Garroway was born in New York State, the son of a mechanical engineer. The family later settled in St. Louis. In 1935 he graduated from Washington University with a bachelor's degree in English. He had a brief career as a piston ring salesman before realizing that selling was not his strong suit. He then studied at Harvard University's business school for a short time.

In 1937 Garroway found work as a page at NBC for $16 a week. Although he fared poorly in the network's radio announcing class, he was hired as an announcer at station KDKA in Pittsburgh the following year.

He served in the Navy during World War II and taught at a school for radio technicians in Hawaii. Discharged in 1945 he came to Chicago as a staff announcer at station WMAQ, broadcast from the Merchandise Mart. In January 1946 he made his radio debut with "The 11:60 Club," a late-night program that featured jazz and Garroway's distinctive nocturnal musings. In between records, Garroway dispensed advice and comments and uttered wise and witty observations. "The rapport he established with his audiences was nearly mystical," wrote Chicago columnist Bob Wiedrich in 1982. "You felt you had a friend behind the microphone who understood and identified with the loneliness of night people. He was an iconoclast of sorts. But most of all he lifted your spirits ."

In April of 1949 Garroway hosted an original variety show based in Chicago called "Garroway at Large." The show departed from the usual television format. Instead of painted backdrops Garroway's set featured a threadbare studio with a stagehand's ladder as the only prop. Soon his charm and intelligence earned him a national reputation.

The success of the show led the top brass in New York to hire him as the host of the "Today" show. During the 1953–54 season he also hosted his own variety program on NBC, "The Dave Garroway Show." Later he was featured on NBC's "Wide, Wide World."

The accidental death of his wife from an overdose of sleeping pills led to Garroway's premature retirement in 1961. A decade or so later, Garroway attempted a comeback, "The CBS Newcomers," a one-hour summer replacement variety show. But no one seemed interested in the former talk show host.

"It was the most exciting rut in the world," said Garroway about his stint on the "Today" show, "but you lived one kind of a life, and it made you think that you knew what was going on, but you really didn't."

Garroway committed suicide in his Philadelphia suburban home in 1982 after suffering complications from open-heart surgery. He was sixty-nine.

The career of Dave Garroway and others of the "Chicago School" are highlighted at the Museum of Broadcasting Communications at 800 South Wells Street.

See also: Fran Allison, Burr Tillstrom

Maurice Goldblatt

Merchant/Philanthropist

born: circa 1892
Poland
died: July 17, 1984
Chicago, Illinois

Maurice Goldblatt maintained two careers in his life: cofounder of one of the biggest department stores in Chicago history—and one of Chicago's most successful Jewish businessmen—and chairman of the University of Chicago Cancer Research Foundation. Polish-born Jews, the Goldblatt brothers served Eastern European immigrants in Chicago much as they had in the old country.

Goldblatt came to Chicago from Poland in 1905 and found work in a Milwaukee Avenue dry goods store. In 1914 the Goldblatt brothers—twenty-one-year old Maurice and his nineteen-year-old brother Nathan—opened their first retail store in a wooden bungalow at 1617 W. Chicago Avenue with $1,000 capital. Later their younger brother, Louis, ran errands while the youngest, seven-year-old Joey, rang the cash register. By 1934 they operated a chain of seven stores and adopted the slogan:"America's Fastest Growing Department Stores." The company incorporated in 1928.

Goldblatt's flourished during the Depression by offering essential goods at low prices. Business was so good that in 1937 the firm opened its flagship store at 333 South State Street.

In 1944 Nathan died of cancer. Maurice had been extremely close to his younger sibling. Grief-stricken, Maurice decided to devote the rest of his life to raising funds for cancer and heart disease research. In 1948 Nathan's widow, Frances, founded the Nathan Goldblatt Society for Cancer Research, which became affiliated with the University of Chicago. Maurice initially donated $1 million to the university's Nathan Goldblatt Memorial Hospital for Cancer Research.

In the late 1940s, Goldblatt served on the board of the National Heart Advisory Council—one of the few lay-people to do so—and in 1950, he was appointed to the National Advisory Cancer Council.

Goldblatt retired in 1946 as chief executive officer of the company but continued as chairman into the 1960s. At one time, the chain operated forty-seven stores that accounted for 15 percent of the Chicago retail market.

Falling on hard times, Goldblatt Brothers closed the firm's flagship store on State Street in 1981 and filed for bankruptcy. Family squabbles were allegedly commonplace and, according to newspaper accounts, may have actually contributed to the company's decline. In addition, the introduction of discount chain stores such as K-Mart and Venture also cut considerably into the firm's profits.

In 1982 the administration of Mayor Jane Byrne purchased the vacant Goldblatt building on South State Street for conversion into a new central library. Byrne's successor, Harold Washington, decided not to renovate the Goldblatt building but to erect instead a new library building at the corner of State and Van Buren Streets. Finally in 1989 the city and DePaul University announced plans to buy the Goldblatt Building and transform it into a part of the university's downtown campus.

In 1978 Goldblatt's had hired several outsiders with merchandising ability to rescue the firm from certain financial ruin. When a change in management proved insufficient, Goldblatt's returned to its original no-frills policy and, in a remarkable comeback, reopened six stores in March of 1982. Rather than carrying furniture and major appliances, the new Goldblatt's concentrated on brand name apparel, small appliances, and housewares. Today eleven Goldblatt's stores operate in the Chicago area.

"We always knew we would make it," Lionel Goldblatt, company chairman and nephew to Maurice, told a *Chicago Tribune* reporter in 1989.

Maurice Goldblatt died at the University of Chicago's Bernard Mitchell Hospital from a heart attack in July of 1984. He was ninety-two.

See also: Marshall Field, Richard Sears, Aaron Montgomery Ward, William A. Wieboldt

Benny Goodman

Musician

born: May 30, 1909
Chicago, Illinois
died: June 12, 1986
New York, New York

Swing was the music of a generation between the Depression and World War II, and Benjamin David Goodman, the "King of Swing," was its monarch. Goodman, a high school dropout from the Maxwell Street ghetto, changed the course of popular music. He did not invent swing—a danceable type of big-band jazz that reached the height of its popularity during the pre–World War II era—but he was the one who developed it into a great and popular art form.

Photograph reprinted with permission from the *Chicago Sun-Times*.

Goodman's parents, David Goodman and Dora Rezinsky, were Russian immigrants who had met and married in Baltimore but moved to the Maxwell Street area of Chicago in 1902. His father was a tailor. "Pop would get up before any of us, about six o'clock, make the fire and fix breakfast for us. We started to drink coffee as soon as we were weaned, because milk for so many kids cost more than he could afford," recalled Goodman in his autobiography, *The Kingdom of Swing*. The family moved frequently from cramped apartment to cramped apartment.

Young Benny received music lessons at Kehelah Jacob Synagogue, near his home at 1125 Francisco Avenue. Later, he joined the Hull-House band and played John Philip Sousa marches. Goodman, too, took private lessons from Franz Schoepp, a brilliant clarinet teacher who also coached members of the Chicago Symphony.

Eventually Goodman was asked to join what would later be called the "Austin High Gang," a group of musicians, including saxman Bud Freeman. The members of the group attended Austin High School on the West Side except for Goodman, who was a student at Harrison High School. Recalls Freeman, "He was no more than thirteen years of age. He played the clarinet so beautifully—it was not to be believed. He was a very pleasant little guy, who hadn't the faintest idea of the extraordinary talent he possessed."

Goodman's talents were in demand. He began performing polkas and waltzes and popular tunes with small dance bands at high schools and colleges and at local dances. Later he would play at cabarets, in dance halls, and at nightclubs such as the Green Mill Gardens (now called the Green Mill Lounge) at Broadway and Lawrence. By the time Goodman was fourteen he was so busy that he decided to drop out of school.

The music Goodman loved, the music he truly wanted to play, was the new phenomenon that was sweeping the country. Jazz was everywhere, and to Goodman it was the only music that mattered. Thursday was "Jazz Night" at Balaban and Katz's Central Park Theater, and Benny's brother, Charlie, persuaded the manager to let his talented sibling play clarinet there. The manager liked Benny so much that he hired Goodman as a fill-in.

The young clarinetist quickly built a reputation as one of the best musicians in Chicago. In 1925 he joined the Midway Gardens Orchestra. A large indoor/outdoor dance hall at Cottage Grove Avenue and 60th Street designed by Frank Lloyd Wright in 1913, the Midway Gardens was inspired by European beer gardens and offered extravagant food, drink, and entertainment.

Later that year bandleader Ben Pollack wired Goodman and invited him to come to California. After a successful tour, the band returned to Chicago in early 1926 and played in some of the city's top clubs.

When not performing with Pollack, Goodman found work as a freelance musician. In 1934 he felt confident enough to form his own band. The Goodman Band made its debut at the Roosevelt Hotel in New York one year later. The manager, despite an enthusiastic response from the audience, was not impressed with this "new" sound, which, with its uptempo beat and soaring rhythms, was a sharp departure from the romantic balladry and slick pop tunes then in vogue. Gradually the press began referring to this sophisticated and exciting style of dance music as "swing," and young people quickly embraced it as their own.

One of the historic moments in jazz was the Benny Goodman Orchestra concert at Carnegie Hall in January 1938. Although the hall was filled to capacity, the reaction of the New York press—mostly classical music critics—was lukewarm, at best. Goodman's ground-breaking performance represented a turning point in the history of popular music, however. Jazz, once dismissed as primitive music, was now becoming accepted in "polite society."

Goodman was not the easiest man to get along with. Admitted Bud Freeman, who left Tommy Dorsey in 1937 to join Goodman, "Working for Benny was the most miserable experience of my life." Historian James Lincoln Collier describes Goodman as "self-absorbed, moody, irritable." A perfectionist, he hired and fired musicians so rapidly that it was virtually impossible to keep track of the comings and goings. Although a great improviser and technically proficient on his instrument, Goodman relied on outside arrangers—people like Fletcher Henderson, Dean Kincaide, Benny Carter, and Lyle "Spud" Murphy. Henderson wrote some of Goodman's most important tunes, including "King Porter Stomp" and "Sometimes I'm Happy."

No matter how far he traveled, no matter how famous he became, Goodman never forgot his roots. In 1945, he donated $5,000 to the Hull-House music school and, as late as 1976, performed a charity concert there.

Goodman, who made his first record in Chicago in 1926 on the Victor label, was credited with being the first white musician to utilize black talent. Pianist Teddy Wilson played with Goodman as did drummer Lionel Hampton, among others. Indeed, over the years, Goodman's constantly changing personnel featured some of the greatest names in jazz—black or white—including Gene Krupa, Harry James, Georgie Auld, and singers Helen Forrest and Peggy Lee.

Swing fell on hard times after World War II, the victim of both changing economics and changing tastes in music. A new generation of teenagers rejected the big band sound in favor of solo singers such as Frank Sinatra and Eddie Fisher, and hard-core jazz fans turned their ears to a brash new music—bebop—that was emerging from the nightclubs of Harlem. Swing, notes Collier, was perceived as old-fashioned, commercial dance music.

Yet Goodman continued to perform. Throughout the forties, fifties, and into the sixties he put together various bands to play at special events, including a tour of the Soviet Union in 1962. In the late 1960s Goodman performed classical music concerts, featuring the works of Brahms, Mozart, and Copland, and he recorded a number of classical pieces.

In 1955 a biographical film of Goodman's life and music, *The Benny Goodman Story*, starring Steve Allen was released.

Goodman continued to play big band music until 1986 and had even scheduled a West Coast concert tour for that year, but he never made it. The old man of jazz, by this time he was a veritable American institution, died of a heart attack in the study of his New York apartment on June 12, 1986.

See also: **Louis Armstrong, Bud Freeman, Earl Hines, Gene Krupa, Mezz Mezzrow, Joe "King" Oliver**

Further reading: Berkow, Ira. *Maxwell Street: Survival in a Bazaar* (1977); Collier, James Lincoln. *Benny Goodman and the Swing Era* (1989); Connor, D. Russell. *Benny Goodman: Listen to His Legacy* (1988); Dance, Stanley. *The World of Swing* (1979); Freeman, Bud, as told to Robert Wolf. *Crazeology: The Autobiography of a Chicago Jazzman* (1989); Goodman, Benny and Irving Kolodin. *The Kingdom of Swing* (1939).

Steve Goodman

Musician

born: July 25, 1948
Chicago, Illinois
died: September 20, 1984
Seattle, Washington

*One of Chicago's best-loved singer/
songwriters, Steve Goodman's vibrant
stage personality and gently satiric lyrics
earned him a loyal following on the
Chicago folk circuit during the late
1960s and early 1970s. Along with
John Prine and Bonnie Koloc, Goodman helped put Chicago on the folk
music map.*

Goodman grew up listening to rock
and roll, Chicago blues, Hank Williams, and Woody Guthrie. He spent
his formative years on the North Side
and in Evanston and attended high
school at Roosevelt and Maine East.
By the time he graduated, he was
composing his own songs. In 1971 he
played a gig with Kris Kristofferson
at the Quiet Knight at 959 West
Belmont Avenue. In the audience
sat Paul Anka, who was so impressed
that he brought Goodman to New
York for some recording sessions.
Goodman then signed a deal with
Buddah Records.

His self-titled debut album, produced
by Kristofferson, featured contemporary folk material. Although it received generally positive reviews, it
didn't do well commercially, prompting Buddah to drop Goodman from
the label. He jumped to Asylum
Records but again failed to attract a
substantial following. Frustrated by
the lack of response, he formed his
own label, Red Pajamas.

Goodman began playing at the popular Wells Street hangout, the Earl of
Old Town, in 1967, while working as
a clerk in the Park Ridge post office
and attending Lake Forest College.
Within two years, he was able to support himself with club dates and
jingle work.

Goodman's most popular song, "City
of New Orleans," was a top twenty hit
for Arlo Guthrie in 1972. Many of his
best efforts had Chicago themes such
as "Daley's Gone," "Go Cubs Go," "A
Dying Cub Fan's Last Request," and
"Lincoln Park Pirates," a tongue-in-
cheek indictment of a local towing
company. A Lincoln Avenue bar,
Somebody Else's Troubles, was named
after a Goodman song.

Goodman was stricken with leukemia
in 1969, but he kept his illness a
secret until publicity forced him to

go public when he missed a Harry
Chapin memorial concert in 1982.
"The reason that I had kept a low
profile about it for so long was that
I didn't want any favors, didn't want
to have to explain my special set of
circumstances. I couldn't see drag-
ging it around as part of my press
kit," he explained in 1983.

Goodman and his wife moved to Seal
Beach, California, in 1980. The
singer died at the University of Washington hospital in Seattle in 1984 at
age thirty-six.

Goodman's albums include: *Steve
Goodman, Jessie's Jig & Other Favorites,
Words We Can Dance To, Say It In Private, High and Outside, Hot Spot, Artistic Hair, Affordable Art,* and *Santa Ana
Winds.* He also produced fellow Chicagoan John Prine's critically acclaimed album, *Bruised Orange* and
had a minor hit with "The Dutch-
man," composed with Chicago
singer/songwriter Michael Smith.

Said fellow musician Corky Siegel
following Goodman's death, "The
Steve on stage is the same as the
Steve off stage. Steve had a philosophy that life is too important to take
too seriously."

Goodman was a musician's musician.
Although widespread commercial
success eluded him—he only had a
handful of minor hits—he was held
in high esteem by his fellow musicians both in Chicago and across the
country.

"He was truly a great musician," said
singer Bonnie Raitt, "and he loved to
play for anyone, anywhere, any time."
On January 26, 1985, friends of the
singer—including John Prine, Bonnie Koloc, David Bromberg, Arlo
Guthrie, Bonnie Raitt, Jethro Burns,
and Richie Havens—gathered at the
Arie Crown Theater to perform a
five-hour tribute. The proceeds of

the show were donated to leukemia research. A live double album was released in December 1985 on Goodman's Red Pajamas label.

Further reading: Clarke, Donald, ed. *The Penguin Encyclopedia of Popular Music* (1989).

Harold "Red" Grange

Football Player

born: June 13, 1903
Forksville, Pennsylvania
died: January 28, 1991
Lake Wales, Florida

Football legend Harold "Red" Grange, nicknamed the "Galloping Ghost" by sportswriter Grantland Rice, put the University of Illinois on the map. What's more, Grange—football's first superstar—helped turn professional football into a big business. Combining the grace of a gymnast with the speed of a runner, Grange was often called the best player to ever play the sport.

Photograph courtesy of the Chicago Historical Society.

The son of a Wheaton lumber dealer, Grange was born in a small Pennsylvania town. His mother died when he was five, and his father decided, several months later, to move the family to Wheaton, a suburb of Chicago. The red-haired Grange was a natural athlete. Known around town as the "Wheaton Ice Man," he worked his way through college by delivering blocks of ice every summer to customers. He enrolled at the University of Illinois at Champaign-Urbana but had no desire to play football—at slightly under six feet tall and not quite 170 pounds he felt he was too small. Nevertheless he was accepted on the freshman squad, and he did well. He also found time to join the basketball and track teams.

On October 18, 1924, the Illinois-Michigan game catapulted Grange's name across the nation's sports pages as Illinois routed the undefeated and highly favored Michigan team 39 to 14. Grange scored four touchdowns in twelve minutes—all in the first quarter. In total he gained 402 yards, carried 21 times, and completed 6 passes for 64 yards.

College football was enjoying its glory days during the twenties and Grange was its star player. The halfback's fleetness of foot captured on grainy newsreels inspired imaginations in motion picture theaters across the country. Thousands of football fans flocked to university stadiums— crowds of 60,000 or more were not uncommon on some of the larger campuses—to watch their heroes in action. College athletes epitomized the purity and goodness of amateur sports. "Football," declared Grange's coach Bob Zuppke, "isn't meant to be played for money."

Professional football, on the other hand, was floundering. What the game needed in order to survive was a big name to attract more customers to the stadiums. It's often been said that "Red" Grange made professional football respectable.

Grange played his final game as a college athlete on November 21, 1925, when Illinois defeated Ohio State 14 to 9. One day later, after much secret negotiation, Chicago Bears coach George Halas signed Grange to an unprecedented $25,000 contract. Grange's decision upset not only his father but also his college coach and his legions of fans, who were aghast that the darling of the collegiate gridiron would deign to play "commercialized football." Grange was accused of selling out when in fact, as he later admitted, he had a simpler and more compelling motive: He needed the money.

Some 36,000 Chicago fans—attendance at Bears games usually averaged 5,000 and was rarely more than 12,000—got their first glimpse of the "Galloping Ghost" several days later on Thanksgiving Day when the Bears played the Chicago Cardinals at Wrigley Field. It wasn't a very impressive debut. Grange gained only thirty-six yards in a 0-0 tie. Three days later, however, he redeemed himself when he gained 140 yards and led the Bears to a 14 to 13 victory over the Columbus Tigers.

Grange agreed to participate in a sixteen-game postseason barnstorming cross-country tour to promote professional football. By that time Grange was attracting crowds wherever he played. Advertisements encouraged fans to come out to "See Red Grange with the Chicago Bears."

Promoters, taking advantage of the moment, made a small fortune by selling Red Grange dolls, sweaters, caps, and ginger ale to eager fans.

Due to Grange's unprecedented popularity, Grange's agent, C. C. Pyle, asked Halas for a five-figure salary and one-third ownership of the team. Halas balked at what he considered an outrageous request. Pyle countered by establishing in 1926 the nine-team American Football League (AFL), rival to the National Football League (NFL).

Grange initially played with the AFL's short-lived local franchise, the Chicago Bulls (no relationship to the current basketball team of the same name). But even Grange's formidable presence couldn't keep the team afloat. He then signed with the New York Yankees football club, also of the AFL. By the end of the 1926 season, the AFL had collapsed due to a lack of interest and the Yankees were allowed to join the NFL. The next time Chicagoans—more than 30,000 of them—saw the Galloping Ghost in person was at Wrigley Field in a Yankee uniform. During the game, which the Bears won 12 to 0, he suffered a debilitating knee injury and spent the 1928 season on the injured list.

When the Yankee franchise folded in 1929, Halas invited Grange to return to the Bears lineup at his old position of running back and when that proved too strenuous he switched to defensive back. Grange retired in 1934, although he made his last appearance with the Bears during an exhibition game in January of 1935. In the fall of that year Grange turned down an offer from Halas to become head coach, instead choosing the less stressful position of assistant coach. He retired from football altogether in 1937.

Grange's gridiron exploits thrilled the crowds and turned the then fledgling sport of professional football into big business. Grange was inducted into the Pro Football Hall of Fame in 1963. In addition to his football career, Grange tried his hand at other ventures, including managing a nightclub on Sheridan Road, managing sales of a bottling company, selling insurance, and broadcasting for radio and television for ten years. Grange also appeared in several movies: *The Galloping Ghost, One Minute to Play,* and *The Racing Romeo.*

A modest man, Grange tended to downplay his fame. "If you have the football and eleven guys are after you, if you're smart, you'll run," he once said with characteristic good humor.

Grange died of complications from pneumonia in a Florida hospital. He was eighty-seven.

See also: George Halas, Bronko Nagurski, Amos Alonzo Stagg

Further reading: Vass, George. *George Halas and the Chicago Bears* (1971).

Samuel E. Gross

Real Estate Developer

born: November 11, 1843
near Dauphin, Pennsylvania
died: October 24, 1913
Battle Creek, Michigan

Master builder Samuel Eberly Gross billed himself as "The World's Greatest Real Estate Promoter." Gross is credited with building twenty-one suburbs, constructing over ten thousand houses, and selling more than forty thousand lots. His most distinguished project, the Alta Vista Terrace block in Wrigleyville, is a landmark Chicago district.

Gross moved with his parents from Pennsylvania to Illinois in the mid-1840s. When the Civil War started in 1861, he joined the 41st Illinois Volunteer Infantry, but he was forced to leave because of his youth.

After the war, Gross moved to Chicago, then in its infancy but holding great promise. He graduated from Union College of Law in 1866 and was admitted to the Illinois bar the same year. While still practicing law, Gross opened a real estate office and purchased empty lots of land with the intention of transforming them into livable communities.

Gross managed to accumulate a fortune selling lots of land and homes to middle-class buyers and working-class immigrants. By the end of the 1890s the realtor was said to be worth an estimated $3 to $5 million. Among the neighborhoods and communities he developed are Grossdale, an area west of the city limits in what is now Brookfield, Illinois; Gross Park on the North Side, bounded by Addison Street and Belmont, Western, and Ashland Avenues; Brookdale, west of the Illinois Central railroad tracks between 69th and 71st Streets; the southern suburb of Calumet Heights, Illinois; the Lakeview neighborhood around Wellington and Southport Avenues; McKinley Park, an area on the South Side near Hoyne Avenue and 34th Street; and the Back of the Yards, between 45th and 47th Streets and from Laflin to Ashland Avenue. This development included Gross Avenue, now known as McDowell Avenue.

Around the turn of the century, construction began on what has become his most enduring legacy—Alta Vista Terrace—from property that he purchased east of the Chicago, Milwaukee, Saint Paul, and Pacific railroad tracks. Modeled after a street in the Mayfair section of London, Alta Vista Terrace is a charming and elegant example of late Victorian architecture within hailing distance of Wrigley Field. Forty brick row houses line the one-block stretch between Grace and Byron Streets.

Often called the "street of forty doors," Alta Vista Terrace is a marvel of architectural symmetry. A replica of every house is duplicated on the other side of the street. The mostly two-story townhouses feature such exquisite details as Gothic doorways, Ionic and Doric columns, coachlights, and bay windows. Alta Vista Terrace was designated a landmark district by the Commission on Chicago Historical and Architectural Landmarks in 1971.

In addition to his thriving real estate ventures, Gross was also a playwright. In the 1870s he wrote a play, *The Merchant Prince of Cornville*, a comedy of manners that featured a character with a large nose. Gross's play created quite a stir in late nineteenth-century Chicago when he charged that Edmond Rostand's French comedy *Cyrano de Bergerac* (1897), based on the life of the seventeenth-century French poet, dramatist, and soldier, plagiarized *The Merchant Prince*. In 1902 a Chicago judge ruled that Gross was indeed the true author and that the popular French play was "clear and unmistakable piracy." Maintaining his innocence from his country estate in France, Rostand argued that "there are big noses everywhere in the world." Despite the ruling, Rostand's play is the one that is remembered, and Gross's play has been completely forgotten.

Gross died in 1913 in Battle Creek, Michigan, at the age of sixty-nine.

See also: Arthur Rubloff

Further reading: Cahan, Richard. *Landmark Neighborhoods in Chicago* (1981); Pacyga, Dominic A. and Ellen Skerrett. *Chicago: City of Neighborhoods* (1986).

George Halas

Football Coach

born: February 2, 1895
Chicago, Illinois
died: October 31, 1983
Chicago, Illinois

One of the grand old men of sports, George Stanley Halas, or "Papa Bear," as he was called, revolutionized football. He founded and coached the Chicago Bears to National Football League (NFL) championships in 1933, 1941, 1946, and 1963 against the New York Giants; and in 1940 and 1943 against the Washington Redskins. He helped create the National Football League, and he became the NFL's "winningest" coach, earning a league record of 326 wins, 151 losses, and 31 ties.

Photograph courtesy of the Chicago Bears.

George Halas was the youngest son of a Bohemian tailor who owned his own shop around 18th Street and Ashland Avenue in the heart of Chicago's Pilsen neighborhood. Halas's life was one of good fortune and good timing.

An avid athlete, Halas excelled at both baseball and basketball at Crane Technical High School. At the University of Illinois he joined the football team and graduated in 1918 with a civil engineering degree. During World War I he served one year in the Navy, was stationed at the Great Lakes Naval Training Station, and played on the Great Lakes football team. The team was good enough to earn an appearance at the 1919 Rose Bowl against the Mare Island (California) Marines. Halas was named the most valuable player.

In 1919 Halas joined the New York Yankees as a promising outfielder. His baseball career was cut short, however, when he suffered a hip injury, causing him to miss many games. He played the remainder of the season for a Saint Paul, Minnesota, minor league team, then returned to Chicago and got a job in the engineering department of the Chicago, Burlington, and Quincy Railroad.

Halas then played professional football, during the 1919–20 season for the Hammond Pros, at a time when football attracted few fans. In 1920 A. E. Staley, president of a Decatur-based corn products company, hired him to organize the Decatur Staleys, a semipro football team.

In the same year, Halas became one of the founders of the American Professional Football Association (APFA). The group's first meeting took place in the automobile showroom of Ralph Hay, owner of the Canton Bulldogs, in Canton, Ohio.

Hard times hit A. E. Staley in 1921. Looking for ways to save money, the company was forced to abandon its football team. Staley suggested that Halas move to Chicago, and he offered to provide the young coach with $5,000 in start-up costs. He had only one request, that Halas call the team the Chicago Staleys for one season. Halas promised he would and moved north. In 1922 he renamed the team the Chicago Bears, in a playful nod to the Chicago Cubs. The team's orange and blue colors he took from his alma mater, the University of Illinois. In the same year, the APFA changed its name, at Halas's suggestion, to the National Football League (NFL).

Professional football, however, failed to win many converts until the arrival of Harold "Red" Grange in 1925, the halfback whose gridiron feats earned him the nickname the "Galloping Ghost." Grange turned the game around entirely, drawing unprecedented crowds into the stadiums and creating a palpable excitement on the playing field and in the stands.

One of Halas's greatest coaching moments, of which there were many, occurred during the 1940 championship game when the Bears routed the Washington Redskins with a 73-0 victory.

From 1942 to 1946, Halas served in the naval reserves and was awarded the Bronze Star. After the war he resumed his coaching position with the Bears, stepped down in 1955, and returned three years later. He retired as head coach on May 27, 1968.

In 1963 Halas was chosen to be a charter member of the Football Hall of Fame. In 1974 general manager Jim Finks took over day-to-day operations of the Bears while Halas retained the title of chairman of the board. Halas assumed the Bears' presidency in 1979. After witnessing too many miserable seasons, with Jim Dooley as coach from 1968 to 1972, Abe Gibron from 1972 to 1974, Jack Pardee from 1974 to 1978, and Neill Armstrong from 1978 to 1982, Halas hired Mike Ditka as head coach in 1982.

Some of the Bears' finest athletes played during the Halas years. In addition to "Red" Grange, there were quarterbacks Sid Luckman, Johnny Lujack, and Jim McMahon; kicker George Blanda; fullback Bronko Nagurski; center Clyde "Bulldog" Turner; linebackers Bill George and Dick Butkis; tight end Mike Ditka; halfbacks John "Paddy" Driscoll and George McAfee; wide receiver Johnny Morris; and running backs Willie Galimore, Gale Sayers, and Walter Payton.

More than anything else, Halas was considered an innovator. He insisted, for example, that no player could be signed until he completed college. In the 1930s he pushed through rule changes that allowed for more forward passing. In 1940 he introduced the T-formation, the basis of all contemporary football offensive tactics, that opened up the game. He recommended that throwing the football from behind the line of scrimmage be legalized. Furthermore, the Chicago Bears was the first team to film and study their games, the first to hire their own band, the first to publish a team newspaper, and the first to practice every day.

Halas died in his North Side apartment in October 1983 at age eighty-eight.

See also: Harold "Red" Grange, Bronko Nagurski

Further reading: Halas, George S. with Gwen Morgan and Arthur Veysey. *Halas: An Autobiography* (1986); Vass, George. *George Halas and the Chicago Bears* (1971).

Margaret Haley

Labor Activist

born: November 15, 1861
Joliet, Illinois
died: January 5, 1939
Chicago, Illinois

Margaret Haley grew up to be the leader of one of the country's most militant unions—the Chicago Teachers Federation—fighting the good fight to improve public education.

Raised on an Illinois farm, Haley was the eldest daughter of a family of eight. Her mother was a native of Ireland and her father an Irish-American who came to Chicago to work on the Illinois and Michigan Canal. When she was ten, her father moved the family to Channahon to operate a stone quarry. Haley attended a convent school in Morris. At sixteen she began teaching at a country school near Minooka and then taught in Joliet before moving to Chicago to teach in 1882. Eventually Haley secured a job at the Hendricks School near the Union Stockyards. Later, she studied under Francis W. Parker, principal of the Cook County Normal School and one of the country's most progressive educators.

In 1900 Haley was elected district vice-president of the Chicago Teachers' Federation, an organization founded in 1897. She acted as the business representative until her death. The CTF's objective was "to raise the standard of the teaching profession." CTF contributed greatly to the progressive reform movement then enveloping the city, and, through it, Haley campaigned vigorously for tax reform, municipal ownership, teacher benefits, an elected school board, and women's suffrage.

In 1902 members of the CTF voted to affiliate with the Chicago Federation of Labor. Many viewed this decision with alarm, calling it a "radical departure." Three years later, Haley welcomed the election to city hall of Edward Dunne, whom she considered a friend of labor. With Haley acting as Dunne's "silent" advisor, the mayor appointed one of the most progressive school boards in Chicago history, consisting of an unprecedented number of women, reformers, and civic leaders. Controversy followed Dunne's choices, however, especially among business interests. Tensions eased somewhat in 1909 with the appointment of Ella Flagg

Young as superintendent of the Chicago public schools. But by 1915 things had turned ugly again as the new mayor, the indomitable William Hale Thompson, assailed the policies of both Haley and the CTF.

More trouble mounted with the appointment of William McAndrew in 1924 as superintendent. McAndrew's decisions, which included abolishing the advisory teachers' councils, proved immediately unpopular among teachers and drew fire from the CTF.

In May of 1916 the American Federation of Teachers was formed and the CTF chartered as Local #1 with Haley designated as the CTF's national organizer. The following year, however, the CTF withdrew from the AFT after the Illinois Supreme Court granted the Chicago School Board the power to hire or dismiss a teacher at will and for no cause. One day later, however, the Illinois governor, Frank Lowden, signed the Otis Law, which affected only the City of Chicago and which gave Chicago teachers the security of tenure. In 1937 a new organization was formed, the Chicago Teachers' Union, but the CTF refused to join.

The CTF, which consisted entirely of women grade school teachers, clashed with various high school unions, including the Chicago Federation of Men Teachers and the Federation of Women High School Teachers. Haley favored granting the same standard wage for all teachers, regardless of grade level or sex, notes historian Robert L. Reid. Since high school salaries were substantially higher than grade school wages, Haley found little support outside the CTF.

The CTF continued until 1968 when factionalism and bitter labor disputes led to its dissolution. The Chicago Teachers Union (CTU), a combination of two high school federations and the Elementary Teachers' Union, remains a potent presence on the current labor scene.

Haley began her autobiography with the words, "I never wanted to fight." But a fighter she was—her enemies called her a "lady labor slugger"— until the day she died of heart disease in January 1939 at age seventy-seven.

Through her vigorous leadership, Haley improved teacher salaries and benefits, provided job security, and helped raise the standard of the teaching profession.

See also: Francis W. Parker, William Hale Thompson, Ella Flagg Young

Further reading: Reid, Robert L, ed. *Battleground: The Autobiography of Margaret A. Haley* (1982).

Fred Hampton

Political Activist

born: August 30, 1948
Chicago, Illinois
died: December 4, 1969
Chicago, Illinois

Described by his admirers as a cross between Malcolm X and Dr. Martin Luther King, Jr., and by his detractors as a dangerous revolutionary, Fred Hampton lived a brief life that ended tragically in violence. Chairman of the Illinois Black Panther Party, Hampton was killed in a police raid on party headquarters at a West Side apartment in 1969.

Photograph reprinted with permission from the *Chicago Sun-Times*.

Born in Chicago but raised in west suburban Maywood, Illinois, Hampton attended Proviso East High School. During his years there he became a spokesman for African-American youth—black enrollment at the school in the midsixties was approximately 30 percent—and led protests against the school administration, demanding that African-American children be assured equal treatment. Hampton served as president of the youth council of the Maywood branch of the National Association for the Advancement of Colored People (NAACP). Under his leadership, says writer Dempsey Travis, membership rose from forty to over five hundred members.

In June 1967 Hampton and several other young African-Americans protested to Maywood officials of the lack of a swimming pool in their neighborhood (blacks were not allowed to use the whites-only pool). Hampton led a peaceful march to city hall, averting what may have turned into a violent confrontation. Even so police arrested him and charged him with mob action. He was acquitted.

Hampton's transformation from suburban teenager to civil rights activist was a relatively rapid one. In June 1968 Hampton, Bobby Rush, Jewell Cook, and Billy Brook founded the Illinois branch of the Black Panthers. Under Hampton's leadership, the organization grew to over one thousand members during a twelve-month period.

The Black Panther Party was founded by Huey Newton and Bobby Seale in Oakland, California, on October 15, 1966. Their ten-point program demanded "social change by direct action, including force, if necessary, to restructure the 'system' to permit blacks to control their own status." In March 1968, J. Edgar Hoover,

director of the FBI, called the Panthers "the single most dangerous threat to the internal security of the United States."

But the Panthers did not only talk about revolution at the point of a gun. They also sponsored programs to help African-American communities across the country. In the spring of 1969, the Chicago Panthers, led by Hampton, took a cue from their brethren on the West Coast, and sponsored a free breakfast program at the Better Boys Foundation on South Pulaski Avenue. By the end of May, reports writer Dempsey Travis, the program had been expanded to the Marcy-Newberry Association at 16th Street and Homan Avenue, the Peoples' Church at 201 South Ashland Avenue, the Precious Blood Church at Congress Street and Western Avenue, and St. Dominic's Church at 357 West Locust Street in the Cabrini-Green housing project. In addition, the Chicago branch organized the Peoples' Medical Center at 3850 West 16th Street, which was affiliated with Mount Sinai Hospital.

On December 4, 1969, Hampton, 21, and Mark Clark, 22, died of gunshot wounds suffered during a police raid, orchestrated by then Cook County State's Attorney, Edward V. Hanrahan, on Panther headquarters at 2337 West Monroe Street. Four other occupants of the apartment were wounded. Black Panther members maintained that police murdered Hampton and Clark.

An FBI investigation revealed that the police, who had a warrant to search for illegal weapons, fired over ninety shots. The occupants, on the other hand, fired only one.

In 1982 the Cook County Board, after a year of negotiation between government attorneys and the plaintiffs, approved a $1.85 million settlement, which called for the federal

government, Cook County, and the City of Chicago, to each pay $616,333 in damages. The settlement, believed to be the largest in a civil rights suit, concurred that there was a conspiracy to destroy the Black Panther Party. The suit, originally filed in 1970 and dismissed in 1977 by U. S. District Court judge, Joseph Sam Perry, accused law enforcement officials with violating the civil rights of Black Panther members.

The Black Panther Party disbanded in the midseventies. In an example of how times change, former Black Panther Bobby Rush was elected alderman of the 2nd Ward in 1983.

See also: Julius J. Hoffman

Further reading: Peck, Abe. *Uncovering the Sixties: The Life & Times of the Underground Press* (1985); Rice, Jon F. *Up on Madison, Down on 75th: A History of the Illinois Black Panther Party* (1983); Travis, Dempsey J. *An Autobiography of Black Chicago* (1981).

Lorraine Hansberry

Playwright

born: May 19, 1930
Chicago, Illinois
died: January 12, 1965
New York, New York

"I was born on the South Side of Chicago. I was born black and female. I was born in a depression after one world war and came into adolescence in another." So begins Lorraine Hansberry's autobiographical play, **To Be Young, Gifted and Black.**

Photograph reprinted with permission from the *Chicago Sun-Times.*

Lorraine Vivian Hansberry enjoyed a middle-class upbringing. Her father was a United States marshal and later a successful real estate broker and banker. Even so, he frequently was required to fight battles against city codes that enforced racial segregation.

Born at 5330 South Calumet Avenue, Hansberry moved with her family when she was eight into the predominantly white Washington Park neighborhood. In 1938, when Illinois courts evicted the family from their home on the grounds of racial housing codes, Hansberry's father appealed to the federal courts. Two years later the U.S. Supreme Court ruled in Hansberry's favor, prohibiting the practice of racially restrictive housing ordinances.

Lorraine attended the Betsy Ross Elementary School at 61st Street and Wabash Avenue. From there she went to Englewood High School. At that time she wanted, she said, to be a journalist. After graduation she studied painting at the Art Institute of Chicago and attended classes at the University of Wisconsin and at the University of Guadalajara, in Ajijic, Mexico. She moved to New York at the end of her sophomore year, in 1950, where she met her future husband, Robert Nemiroff, on a New York University picket line, and the following year she joined the staff of *Freedom* magazine, a political journal published by actor Paul Robeson.

Although she had no training in theater aside from a few courses in set designing and theater history at the University of Wisconsin, Hansberry began writing plays soon after her marriage. In 1956 she wrote a three-act play, *A Raisin in the Sun.* Inspired by the Langston Hughes poem of the same name, *A Raisin in the Sun* incorporated elements from the author's own life. It tells the story of a poor black family on Chicago's South Side and their attempt to escape from the ghetto by purchasing a home in an all-white neighborhood.

A Raisin in the Sun made its Chicago debut in February 1959 during a tryout run at the Blackstone Theater. The cast included Sidney Poitier, Ruby Dee, Diana Sands, Glynn Turner, Ivan Dixon, and Louis Gossett, artists who would later make names for themselves in television and film. *Chicago Tribune* theater critic Claudia Cassidy called the work "a remarkable play" performed by a "gifted" cast. "More important to Chicago," she wrote, "is that it has the fresh impact of something urgently on its way." *Raisin* won universal acclaim when it opened on Broadway the following month. *A Raisin in the Sun* became the first play by a black woman to be produced on Broadway, and Hansberry became the youngest American playwright—and the first African-American—to win the New York Drama Critics Circle Award for best play. It was an outstanding achievement. In 1961 Poitier starred in the successful film adaptation and, in 1973, a musical version, *Raisin,* won a Tony Award for best musical.

Hansberry's second play, *The Sign in Sidney Brustein's Window,* about the social awakening of a young Jewish intellectual in Greenwich Village, was not as successful and met with mixed reviews. Hansberry, too, was criticized among her peers for daring to write from the perspective of a white male.

Hansberry died from cancer in January 1965. She was only thirty-four.

Her last effort, *To Be Young, Gifted and Black: The World of Lorraine Hansberry,* was a distillation of her work—from a novel, letters, and plays—newly scripted and presented by her husband as a fitting memorial to her life and work. *To Be Young, Gifted and Black* premiered in New York on January 2, 1969, at the Cherry Lane Theatre.

Among her works published posthumously was *Les Blancs*, about the making of an African-American revolutionary and several shorter plays, *The Drinking Gourd*, about slavery during the 1850s, and *What Use Are Flowers?*, a modern-day fable.

In recent years, there has been a renewed interest in Hansberry's work. A revival of *A Raisin in the Sun* ran at the Goodman Theatre in 1983 and a new biography of the playwright's life and work was published in 1991.

Actor Douglas Turner Ward, who appeared in the original Broadway production of *A Raisin in the Sun,* called Hansberry a "pioneer" and further stated, "She broke new ground. She created new possibilities. Her impact and influence upon her own generation and succeeding ones are historic."

Further reading: Carter, Steven R. *Hansberry's Drama: Commitment Amid Complexity* (1991); Cheney, Anne. *Lorraine Hansberry* (1984).

William Rainey Harper

Educator

born: July 26, 1856
New Concord, Ohio
died: January 10, 1906
Chicago, Illinois

William Rainey Harper was one of the cofounders and the first president of the University of Chicago. A gregarious man with a magnetic personality, he dominated the university like few others, expanding its influence beyond its Hyde Park campus and, in the spirit of unity, building a foundation based upon service to the community, to the city, and, by extension, to the world.

Born in Ohio of Scots-Irish stock, Harper was a precocious youngster. He entered Muskingum College at the age of ten and graduated at fourteen. He worked in his father's dry goods store for a short time before enrolling at Yale as a graduate student in philology at seventeen. He received his Ph.D. in 1875 before he reached his nineteenth birthday. In the same year he married the daughter of the president of the college.

Harper then became the principal of Masonic College in Macon, Tennessee. The following year he moved to Granville, Ohio, as a tutor in the preparatory department at Denison University, which ultimately became Granville Academy. Recognizing Harper's prodigious talents as an administrator, the new institution then made the young scholar principal. In 1879 he accepted a position teaching Hebrew at the Baptist Union Theological Seminary in Chicago, which had relocated from Douglas Park to Morgan Park, on the Southwest Side, two years earlier. Harper founded two scholarly journals, the *Hebrew Student* and *Hebraica*, and established the American Institute of Hebrew. In 1886 Harper decided to teach at Yale as professor of Semitic languages in the graduate department and as instructor in the Divinity School.

Harper had grandiose visions of founding a great institution of higher learning, preferably in the Midwest. He persuaded several wealthy figures of the feasibility of his plan. In 1890 merchant Marshall Field donated a plot of land east of Ellis Avenue and north of 57th Street to the new venture while entrepreneur/philanthropist John D. Rockefeller provided the initial $600,000 to get the project off the ground. Field, businessman Martin Ryerson, and other prominent Chicagoans contributed additional money.

In September of 1890 Harper was elected president of the new University of Chicago. An older university of the same name had stood at Cottage Grove and 34th Street since 1861, until it declared itself bankrupt in 1886. The new university was incorporated on September 10, 1890.

The university opened its doors on October 1, 1892. The success of Harper's university was built on the principle of service. Harper established a university press in order to spread the university's beliefs and philosophy throughout the world. Men and women, Harper agreed, should be admitted to the university on an equal footing. Further, Harper required all first-year students to pass an entrance examination. The university itself consisted of four undergraduate colleges, a nonprofessional graduate school, and schools of divinity, law, medicine, engineering, pedagogy, fine arts, and music. The University Extension was modeled after Cambridge University and consisted of lectures given outside the university proper, evening courses, correspondence courses, special courses, and a library extension. Harper divided the university year into four quarters of twelve weeks, each followed by a one-week break. Each quarter, in turn, was divided into two terms of six weeks each. Instruction was thus offered throughout most of the year, allowing for greater freedom and flexibility for both the students and the staff.

Harper recruited the brightest and the best by offering good wages and the promise of freedom of expression to any and all prospective teachers. He would not take no for an answer. His perseverance paid off. Harper persuaded some of the best minds available to participate in his bold experiment in the heartland, including Albert A. Michelson, physics professor; Albion W. Small, head of sociology; Thorstein B. Veblen,

assistant professor of political economy; Amos Alonzo Stagg, physical education teacher and coach of the Maroons football team; John Dewey, philosopher and educator; novelist Robert Herrick from the Massachusetts Institute of Technology; poet William Vaughn Moody; James Henry Breasted, the first teacher of Egyptology in the nation and the founder of the Oriental Institute; Emil G. Hirsch, Old Testament scholar; and Robert Francis Harper, the president's brother and famed Assyriologist. In addition, the University of Chicago founded the country's first university press, and it was one of the first institutions of higher learning to introduce graduate programs in such areas as business management, sociology, and social work.

Harper wrote many books, including *The Trend in Higher Education, The Priestly Element in the Old Testament, The Structure of the Text of the Book of Hosea, The Commentary on Amos and Hosea,* and *The Prophetic Element in the Old Testament.*

Harper died of cancer in 1906 at the age of forty-nine. He died before he had achieved his greatest goal—to establish a medical school at the university—yet his legacy and his memory live on. He, no doubt, would be pleased to learn that the school he founded and the medical center, founded in 1898, continue to be among the very best in the nation and, indeed, the world.

See also: Frank Billings, Marshall Field, Robert Herrick, Emil G. Hirsch, Robert Maynard Hutchins, Albert A. Michelson, Amos Alonzo Stagg, Thorstein B. Veblen [appendix]

Further reading: Goodspeed, Thomas Wakefield. *The Story of the University of Chicago, 1890–1925* (1925); Storr, Richard J. *Harper's University: The Beginnings* (1966).

Carter Henry Harrison I

Politician

born: February 15, 1825
(according to some sources:
February 25, 1825)
Fayette County, Kentucky
died: October 28, 1893
Chicago, Illinois

A brilliant orator, "Our Carter" (a nickname referring to the close relationship between the mayor and the citizenry) served four consecutive terms as mayor of Chicago from 1879 to 1887 and won an unprecedented fifth term in 1893. A pragmatist, Carter Henry Harrison defended the right of anarchists to stage meetings as long as they were peaceful, and he tolerated segregated vice. Outgoing, genial, charming, Harrison was a friend of the people. Despite his upper-class background, he was able to win the support of the common laborer, the burgeoning immigrant population, and the business class. Harrison was a Chicago booster from the moment he set foot in the city in 1855.

Harrison's father died when he was eight months old. Young Carter received most of his early education from his mother and from Kentucky country schools. He graduated from Yale in 1845 and then transferred to the law school of Transylvania University in Lexington, Kentucky. He then spent two years traveling abroad in Europe, Asia, and Egypt.

In 1855 Harrison came to Chicago where he made his fortune in real estate during the land boom. In 1871 he entered politics and was elected a member of the first board of commissioners of Cook County. He held this post until December of 1874 when he won the seat for the 2nd District in the United States House of Representatives. Reelected two years later, he declined the nomination in 1878.

In 1879 Harrison won his first term as mayor of Chicago and was reelected in 1881, 1883, and 1885. He sat out the 1887 election. That summer he quenched his passion for travel by setting off on a world tour. In 1889 he rejected the mayoral nomination, but two years later he agreed to run against Democrat Dewitt C. Cregier. He lost that bid. Determined, he ran as an independent, but lost again— this time to the Republican, Hempstead Washburne.

Carter Harrison was a larger-than-life figure as he galloped up and down the city streets on his horse. The mayor's "live and let live" philosophy allowed saloons, brothels, and gambling houses to carry on business unimpeded by city hall and the police department. Harrison thought these "institutions" were just as important in their own way as churches,

and he regarded gambling and prostitution as unfortunate but necessary evils. As long as the voters agreed with his laissez-faire thinking, it served him well.

In the latter half of 1891, Harrison bought the *Chicago Times* newspaper, primarily as an organ from which he could launch his still considerable political ambitions. More than anything, Harrison wanted to be the mayor during the World's Columbian Exposition of 1893. He ran in a bitterly contested battle against Republican Samuel W. Allerton, and emerged triumphant, enjoying the biggest margin of his colorful career. Although most of the daily papers dismissed him as the ally of gangsters and thugs, he still exuded great personal appeal and was well-liked by the ordinary citizens.

The Mayor Harrison of 1893 proved vastly different from the Mayor Harrison of years past. Displaying a new face to the public, he disavowed any connection with the city's underworld. Yet he was always a practical man. When the reformers were in the spotlight, Harrison turned reformer; and when the public no longer demanded reform, Harrison turned the other cheek.

The opening of the World's Columbian Exposition in May of 1893 found the mayor in a jubilant mood. Visitors from throughout the country— indeed, the world—descended upon the city. At the closing of the fair in October of 1893, Harrison made a confident speech before a convention of mayors. That night he returned to his Ashland Avenue mansion. When the doorbell rang, he opened the door and started to speak; an intruder drew a revolver and fired. Harrison fell, mortally wounded. Patrick Eugene Prendergast, a disappointed office seeker, was charged with the murder and was eventually convicted and hanged.

Instead of celebrating Chicago's future, the World's Fair ended on a somber note as a mournful city buried its beloved mayor.

See also: John Coughlin, Carter Harrison II, Michael Kenna

Further reading: Johnson, Claudius O. *Carter Henry Harrison I: Political Leader* (1928); Kogan, Herman and Lloyd Wendt. *Lords of the Levee: The Story of Bathhouse John and Hinky Dink* (1943); Rex, Frederick F. *The Mayors of the City of Chicago* (1934).

Carter Henry Harrison II

Politician

born: April 23, 1860
Chicago, Illinois
died: December 25, 1953
Chicago, Illinois

Like his father before him, Carter Henry Harrison II was a pragmatist and a natural politician. He also served five terms as mayor of Chicago. Yet his contributions have been sorely neglected, even ignored. His considerable achievements—he established playgrounds in slum neighborhoods, developed the outer harbor, and extended city services—have been eclipsed by the towering figure of his famous parent.

Carter Harrison II received his early schooling in Germany in the duchy of Saxe-Altenburg (a European education was highly valued among Chicago's elite). After his mother's death in 1876, he returned to Chicago and enrolled at St. Ignatius College, now Loyola University. He then earned a law degree from Yale. In 1888 he entered the real estate business with his brother, William Preston Harrison. For several years the brothers operated the *Chicago Times*, which their father had bought in 1891. It did not fare well, and they sold it at a loss.

Harrison served four consecutive two-year mayoral terms (from 1897 to 1905) and one four-year term (from 1911 to 1915). The 1897 campaign revolved around such emotional reform issues as the suppression of vice, the municipal ownership of public utilities, and the operation of an honest, efficient government. Harrison, tearing a page from his father's book of political etiquette, did not believe in legislating public morality; he advocated instead the populist concept of "personal liberty."

Harrison attracted a broad constituency, from laborers to immigrants, and he was equally at home, notes historian Edward R. Kantowicz, "in a poker game with party hacks or at a reception on the Gold Coast." Unlike his father, however, Harrison earned a reputation as somewhat of a reformer and thus attracted a modicum of middle-class support.

One of the biggest issues confronting the Harrison administration was the thorny and complex traction drama—the dispute over municipal ownership of public transportation—with the indomitable Charles Tyson Yerkes of Philadelphia playing the role of villain. In 1881 Yerkes arrived in Chicago and began purchasing streetcar lines. His goal was to buy all the lines in the city and reap the

substantial rewards from such a monopoly. A series of bills were introduced in the state senate extending Yerkes's franchise for fifty years. It failed. Yerkes tried again and goaded a pliable representative to introduce a bill—the Allen Bill—that authorized city councils to grant the franchises. It passed the Illinois Senate. However, through the valiant efforts of Mayor Harrison it was defeated in the Chicago City Council in 1898.

But the traction problem was far from over. There was widespread discontent with streetcars. Invariably they were overcrowded and usually late. The public demanded action, but the city, insisted the mayor, did not have the necessary funds to finance a takeover of the streetcars.

In 1905 Harrison, for health reasons, retired from politics and moved to California. Edward F. Dunne campaigned on the promise of immediate ownership by the city and won, but he, too, failed to settle the traction dispute. Two years later, the city council and the streetcar companies finally came to terms. Streetcar operators agreed to upgrade their cars and, in return, gave the city the option to buy at any time.

In 1911 Harrison resumed his political career with a narrow primary victory over ex-mayor Dunne. In the general election he faced the Republican challenger, the professor turned alderman, Charles E. Merriam. Harrison won—barely.

The narrow margin indicated that all was not well. Harrison's last term was marred by partisan infighting and an ugly maneuvering for power, much of it due to the behind-the-scene machinations of the corrupt Democratic boss, Roger A. Sullivan. Harrison's most dramatic act occurred during his waning days in office in 1911 when he shut down the infamous Everleigh Club.

In 1915 Harrison lost the Democratic primary to a Sullivan loyalist, Robert A. Sweitzer. Sweitzer, in turn, was defeated in the general election by the Republican, William Hale Thompson.

During World War I, Harrison served as a captain with the American Red Cross in France. There were rumors that he would run for a seat in the United States Senate in 1927, but he did not. In 1933 he was appointed Collector of Internal Revenue for the Northern District of Illinois.

Harrison didn't run for elected office after WWI, and he resigned as Internal Revenue Collector in 1944. In 1947 he served as the chair of the Citizens of Greater Chicago Committee, which supported the mayoral candidacy of Martin Kennelly.

Harrison died at the age of ninety-three, on Christmas Day, 1953.

See also: John Peter Altgeld, John Coughlin, Ada and Minna Everleigh, Michael Kenna, Charles E. Merriam, Charles Tyson Yerkes

Further reading: Harrison, Carter H., II. *Stormy Years: The Autobiography of Carter H. Harrison, Five Times Mayor of Chicago* (1935); Harrison, Carter H., II. *Growing Up with Chicago* (1944); Kantowicz, Edward R. "Carter H. Harrison II: The Politics of Balance" in *The Mayors: The Chicago Political Tradition*, Paul M. Green and Melvin G. Holli, eds. (1987); Kogan, Herman and Lloyd Wendt. *Lords of the Levee: The Story of Bathhouse John and Hinky Dink* (1943); Rex, Frederick F. *The Mayors of the City of Chicago* (1933).

Ben Hecht

Journalist/Playwright

born: February 28, 1893
New York, New York
died: April 18, 1964
New York, New York

Ben Hecht led the kind of life that legends are made of. During his multifaceted career, Hecht produced about seventy screenplays, twenty-six books, twenty plays, and hundreds of short stories and magazine articles. He is best remembered today for his vivid portrayal of wisecracking, cynical Chicago journalists in the play **The Front Page***, which he coauthored with Charles MacArthur.*

Born in New York of Russian-Jewish immigrants, Hecht moved with his family to Chicago when he was six and, in 1903, settled in Racine, Wisconsin. After high school Hecht moved in with his aunt and uncle in Chicago. He soon got a job on the *Chicago Daily Journal* as a picture chaser—a dubious start, perhaps, but one that gave him plenty of opportunity to display his ingenuity. His chief function was to secure photographs, by whatever means necessary, of noteworthy people who had fallen on bad times. According to biographer William MacAdams, Hecht did everything within—and outside of—the law to please his editors. He used fire escapes, crawled through open windows, posed as a gas meter inspector, and broke into locked houses. Hecht quickly earned a reputation as the best picture thief in the business.

Hecht's editors were so impressed that they sent him off to cover news stories. Not sure how to gather the facts, Hecht did what many inventive news reporters of that era reportedly did— he made them up. As he gained more experience on the street, however, he turned into an ace reporter and covered several major stories, including the Dayton flood of 1913 and the founding of President Theodore Roosevelt's Bull Moose Party.

But Hecht had other ambitions. In 1913 he met Kenneth Sawyer Goodman, an aspiring dramatist and the son of a lumber millionaire. Goodman and Hecht collaborated on several one-act plays. *The Wonder Hat*, a collection of their plays, was published when Hecht was nineteen.

In 1914 Hecht secured a job at the *Chicago Daily News*. Editor Henry Justin Smith reigned over an impressive group of novelists and poets who disguised themselves as reporters. Smith, recalled Hecht, "loved our paper with an interest that ignored circulation and saw it as a daily novel written by a wild but willing bunch of Balzacs."

Hecht was the unofficial king of Chicago's literary world. His biting wit and devastatingly scathing tongue held forth at Schlogl's, the august downtown tavern that was home to a host of *Daily News* staffers and other literary types. The leading figure on Chicago's bohemian circuit, Hecht made fast friends with others in the close-knit circle—Carl Sandburg, Sherwood Anderson, Ring Lardner, and Margaret Anderson, among many others—and was a frequent visitor to the notorious Dill Pickle Club. With fellow bohemian, Maxwell Bodenheim, he founded the Players' Workshop, an alternative theater on the South Side.

In 1923 Hecht and Bodenheim teamed up again to publish the *Chicago Literary Times*, an insolent biweekly newspaper that poked irreverent fun at posers, politicians, writers, artists, society types, hangers-on, and just about anyone and everyone that the pair deemed worthy enough to hold up to ridicule.

Writing newspaper stories and one-act plays or publishing saucy journals did not wholly satisfy the ambitious journalist. Hecht soon joined the other top literary talent who wrote for the silver screen, which included William Faulkner, George S. Kaufman, and Ring Lardner. Although he criticized the banality of the Hollywood machine, he was very much in demand. Among his many screenplays are *Scarface* (1930), *Wuthering Heights* (1939), *Gunga Din* (1939) *Spellbound* (1945), *Notorious* (1946), and *A Farewell to Arms* (1957), as well as scores of uncredited films including *The Prisoner of Zenda* (1937), *A Star is Born* (1937), *Angels with Dirty Faces* (1938), *Gone with the Wind* (1939), *His Girl Friday* (1940),

and *A Walk on the Wild Side* (1962). Hecht won Academy Awards for two scripts, *Underworld* (1927) and *The Scoundrel* (1934), which he also directed.

A prolific wordsmith, Hecht reportedly once wrote a screenplay in one night and dictated a novel in thirty-six hours. "I think it's better to keep writing than to labor over every word, trying to make it a gem," he once said.

Hecht's best known work is *The Front Page*, the hit play he coauthored with Charles MacArthur in 1928, set in the rough-and-tumble world of Chicago journalism. There have been several motion picture versions of the play, including *His Girl Friday* (1940) starring Cary Grant, Rosalind Russell, and Ralph Bellamy; *The Front Page* (1974) starring Jack Lemmon and Walter Matthau; and *Switching Channels* (1988) starring Burt Reynolds, Kathleen Turner, and Christopher Reeve. Another play, *Twentieth Century*, was made into a movie in 1934.

Though politically neutral for most of his life, Hecht helped raise money for the establishment of a Jewish state in what was then British-owned Palestine and what is now Israel, when the horrors of the Nazi concentration camps became known. The author's outspoken support of Zionism—the movement supporting the establishment and maintenance of a Jewish homeland—and his criticism of British policy in Palestine resulted in his movies being banned in Britain for four years.

In 1954 Hecht's massive 950-page autobiography, *A Child of the Century*, was published by Simon and Schuster. From 1958 to 1959 Hecht hosted his own talk show on a local New York City television station. In 1969 *Gaily, Gaily*, the colorful memoirs of Hecht's days as a cub reporter

originally published in 1963, was turned into a motion picture directed by Norman Jewison and starring Beau Bridges as the young Hecht.

Hecht's novels include *Erik Dorn* (1921), *Gargoyles* (1922) and *Count Bruga* (1926), among many others. In 1921 an anthology of his Chicago newspaper articles, *1001 Nights in Chicago*, was published. In addition to *The Front Page* and *Twentieth Century*, his plays include *The Egoist* and *Fun To Be Free*.

One of his last plays, a gangland musical called *Chicago*, was never produced. His last book, *Letters from Bohemia*, a collection of letters, was published posthumously in 1964.

Hecht suffered a heart attack in April of 1964 in his New York apartment.

See also: Margaret C. Anderson [appendix], Sherwood Anderson, Kenneth Sawyer Goodman [appendix], Ring Lardner, Charles MacArthur [appendix], Carl Sandburg

Further reading: Fetherling, Doug. *The Five Lives of Ben Hecht* (1977); Hecht, Ben. *Child of the Century: An Autobiography* (1954); Hecht, Ben. *Gaily, Gaily: The Memoirs of a Cub Reporter in Chicago* (1963); MacAdams, William. *Ben Hecht: The Man Behind the Legend* (1990).

Robert Herrick

Novelist

born: April 26, 1868
Cambridge, Massachusetts
died: December 23, 1938
St. Thomas, Virgin Islands

Novelist and university professor Robert Herrick, a transplanted New Englander from Massachusetts, had a love/hate relationship with Chicago, his adopted city. Repelled by what he considered Chicago's physical ugliness, he was also attracted by its crude emotional vitality. He lived and taught in Chicago for thirty years and set many of his novels here. Herrick was a realist in the tradition of William Dean Howells and Henry James; he wrote what he saw.

Photograph courtesy of the University of Chicago Archives.

A graduate of Harvard University, Herrick accepted an offer in 1893 from William Rainey Harper to teach in the English department of the new University of Chicago. In the early years, Herrick moved from one Hyde Park apartment to another.

Herrick was a member of the so-called Chicago school of writing, which referred not so much to a particular style as to an obsession with the city, its history, its mores, and its environment. Others in this category include Theodore Dreiser, Henry Blake Fuller, Sherwood Anderson, and Floyd Dell, as well as such individual works as Frank Norris's *The Pit* and Upton Sinclair's *The Jungle.* "Its members cannot be identified with a literary or philosophical creed, a program of reform, or even a particular physical community," writes Blake Nevius in *Robert Herrick: The Development of a Novelist.* "If they are united at all it is is their common acknowledgement that the Chicago of their day provided the best example for the realist of the emerging urban and industrial civilization."

Most of Herrick's novels critiqued American culture and condemned greed and the mad rush to make more money. The typical Herrick hero, often wrestling with inner demons, struggles to maintain moral responsibility in a corrupt, materialistic society. Herrick felt that, of all American cities, Chicago best symbolized the dangers of unchecked capitalism. *The Gospel of Freedom* (1898), about the love between a woman and a Chicago businessman, made liberal use of Chicago locations. It was generally well received except among members of the local press, who objected to the author's harsh treatment of the city. *The Web of Life* (1900) told the story of a young doctor who rejects a lucrative practice to serve the poor on the far South Side and becomes disillusioned by the poverty and class hatred he finds

there. In *The Common Lot* (1904) a Chicago architect enters into a partnership with a shady contractor to erect jerry-built structures. He suffers pangs of guilt when fire destroys one of his buildings, a hastily constructed hotel, and results in a tragic loss of life.

The Memoirs of an American Citizen (1905), considered by many critics to be Herrick's best novel, chronicles the ascent and decline of a successful meatpacker who rises to the top of his profession through bribery and corruption. Set against the backdrop of the Union Stockyards and the Packingtown neighborhood, the book incorporates historical events and actual places into its narrative, including the Haymarket Affair, the World's Columbian Exposition, and the Pullman strike.

Chimes (1926), largely autobiographical, follows the founding of an innovative university—clearly modeled after the University of Chicago—through its first three decades.

In December 1923 Herrick resigned from the University of Chicago in order to devote his time exclusively to writing. During the last years of his life, Herrick made a drastic change. He abandoned writing altogether to enter public service. In January 1935 he accepted the position of Government Secretary of the Virgin Islands. He died there at the age of seventy.

Herrick's works have not aged particularly well. Although praised by his contemporaries, his reputation has fallen considerably in comparison to Dreiser, Anderson, Hemingway, and Farrell.

Among his other novels are *A Life for a Life* (1910), *The Healer* (1911), *His Great Adventure* (1913), *Clark's Field* (1914), *Homely Lilla* (1923), and *The End of Desire* (1932).

See also: Sherwood Anderson, Floyd Dell [appendix], Theodore Dreiser, James T. Farrell, Henry Blake Fuller, William Rainey Harper, Ernest Hemingway [appendix]

Further reading: Nevius, Blake. *Robert Herrick: The Development of a Novelist* (1962).

John Hertz

Entrepreneur

born: April 10, 1879
Ruttka, Austria
died: October 8, 1961
Los Angeles, California

Transportation king John D. Hertz gave Chicago its first organized taxicab service and founded the Hertz rental car agency.

Photograph courtesy of The Hertz Corporation.

The Austrian-born Hertz was brought to the United States by his parents when he was five years old. The family settled on Chicago's West Side where young Hertz attended public school. He quit in the sixth grade to find work to help support his family.

Hertz began his career selling newspapers on Chicago streets and then became a $6 per week wagon driver. Later he found work as a copy boy at the old *Chicago Morning News*, which later changed its name to the *Chicago Record*. Eventually Hertz was promoted to sports reporter and later to assistant sports editor, but he lost the job when the paper merged with another.

An athlete himself, Hertz took boxing lessons at a gym on North Clark Street. Because of the anti-Semitism at that time, he decided to use the name Dan Donnelly. As Donnelly, he won championships in amateur tournaments at the Chicago Athletic Association. Later he fought under his own name and managed Benny Yanger, a contender for both lightweight and middleweight titles. Hertz also operated weekly boxing shows at the Star Theater on Clark Street.

A friend convinced Hertz that the future lay in automobiles, and, indeed, few other inventions in history have so profoundly affected patterns of human life. Hertz couldn't even drive, but in 1904 he began selling cars. He was so successful that several years later he became a partner in an automobile agency. Much of the company's business involved trade-ins, or used cars. In a moment of inspiration, Hertz decided, in 1907, to turn the secondhand vehicles into taxicabs. At that time, taxicabs were the province of the rich—ordinary citizens couldn't afford to pay the extravagantly high fares. Hertz responded by slashing prices and, to further lure customers, he boasted that he could have a cab at a particular destination within ten minutes.

Hertz provided a service and, thus, demanded high standards from his employees. He insisted that his drivers be well-dressed, polite, and personable, and maintain a clean car.

The taxicab, notes historians Gorman Gilbert and Robert E. Samuels, "represented a new, faster, more convenient form of personal urban transportation." Mass transportation suffered as the automobile and taxicab industries expanded.

The development of the taxi industry paralleled the popularity of the automobile and, in turn, affected public transportation. At the turn of the century over four thousand automobiles were manufactured in the U.S. A decade later the number rose to 181,000, and four years later it jumped to over 548,000. By 1930 the American automobile industry produced five million cars annually.

With seven limousine cars, Hertz established the Yellow Cab service in 1915. When the public complained that the fares were too high, he introduced smaller models at cheaper rates and he painted his cars yellow for easy identification. By 1940, he had a fleet of forty and was able to build his own manufacturing plant. The company prospered and eventually expanded into bus and truck manufacturing.

Hertz entered the car rental business in 1923 when he purchased a rental firm from a local salesman named Walter Jacobs. The following year he established the Yellow Drive-It-Yourself Company and began promoting a spacious automobile, called the "Ambassador," as a rental car. The idea floundered—customers apparently didn't want to be seen driving an obviously rented vehicle (the "Ambassador" was larger than most cars). In 1925 he sold both the manufacturing branch and the rental arm of the

company to General Motors. Four years later Hertz sold the Yellow Cab Company to the Parmalee System, which, in turn, was bought by Checker Motors. In 1953 GM sold Yellow Drive-It-Yourself to Hertz's Omnibus Corporation, which then changed its name to Hertz Rent-A-Car.

Hertz held many positions in the business world: director of the First National Bank of Chicago, director of Keeshin Transcontinental Freight Lines, and director of Paramount Pictures Corporation. In addition, he was an active partner in the investment firm of Lehman Brothers for more than twenty-seven years.

Hertz served in various capacities during both world wars, as a civilian expert with the Motor Transport Division of the U.S. Army in World War I and as assistant in charge of motor vehicles to Undersecretary of War Robert Patterson in World War II, for which he received the Presidential Medal of Merit.

In addition to his business interests Hertz was a successful breeder of horses. In 1928 his horse, the Reigh Count, won the Kentucky Derby. Another of his horses, Count Fleet, won the Derby in 1943.

In 1955 Hertz retired as chairman of the boards of the Hertz Corporation. Two years later he and his wife, Fannie, founded the Fannie and John Hertz Engineering Scholarship Foundation, which provided cash scholarships to needy and deserving engineering students.

Hertz died in October 1961 in California at age eighty-two.

For many years, the Chicago-based Yellow Cab and Checker Cab—two of the largest taxicab fleets in the world—monopolized the taxi industry in Chicago. In 1963 a city ordinance granted 80 percent of the city's

4,600 cab licenses to Yellow Cab Company and Checker Cab Company. Twenty-five years later the city council finally broke the stranglehold by proposing an ordinance that added five hundred new licenses, called medallions, per year for three years.

See also: **Charles Tyson Yerkes**

Further reading: Gilbert, Gorman and Robert E. Samuels. *The Taxicab: An Urban Transportation Survivor* (1982); Mayer, Harold M. and Richard C. Wade. *Chicago: Growth of a Metropolis* (1969).

Earl Hines

Musician

born: December 28, 1903
Duquesne, Pennsylvania
died: April 22, 1983
Oakland, California

Earl "Fatha" Hines was one of the most influential pianists in jazz. As a bandleader, he launched the careers of such famous musicians as Dizzy Gillespie, Charlie Parker, Billy Eckstine, and Sarah Vaughan. As a musician, he revolutionized the role of the jazz piano during the 1920s by making it an important and integral component of jazz ensemble performance. A brassy pianist, he played the piano like a trumpet—rhythm with his left hand, melody with his right. "No musician has exerted more influence over the course of piano jazz history," noted critic Dick Hadlock.

Photograph reprinted with permission from the *Chicago Sun-Times.*

Although it was an African-American music, jazz did not receive widespread acceptance until white musicians (the first jazz recordings were made by a white group, the Original Dixieland Jazz Band, in 1917) brought it to the forefront. During the twenties and thirties, white musicians such as Benny Goodman, Artie Shaw, and Tommy and Jimmy Dorsey transformed jazz into America's popular music. Meanwhile, African-American artists had obscure careers or, like Hines, played to predominantly white audiences in elegant clubs for a mere pittance.

Hines's love of music was nurtured from an early age. His father played the trumpet, his mother the pipe organ. Born in a suburb of Pittsburgh, the classically-trained Hines started piano lessons at the age of nine. He quit high school and began accompanying singer Lois Deppe, who soon moved to Chicago and encouraged the young pianist to accompany her.

Hines's first Chicago gig was in 1923 at the Elite Club at 3030 South State Street. He landed a job with the Carroll Dickerson Orchestra, and it was there that he met a young man from Louisiana named Louis Armstrong. In 1926 the band played the Sunset Cafe at 315 East 35th Street. When Dickerson left, Armstrong took over and launched a new jumpy sound that became known as the Chicago style of jazz. Many young white pupils, including Benny Goodman, Gene Krupa, Tommy and Jimmy Dorsey, Dave Tough, Muggsy Spanier, Bud Freeman, and Bix Beiderbecke, came to learn a lesson or two from the jazz masters.

In December of 1927, Armstrong, Hines, and drummer Zutty Singleton rented their own space at Warwick Hall at 543 East 47th Street and began performing, with other musicians, as Louis Armstrong's Hot Six.

It was a short-lived venture, and Hines was soon back in the clubs. He became a featured soloist with clarinetist Jimmy Noone's quintet at the Apex Club on 35th Street between South Prairie and South Calumet Avenues. In 1928 he went into the studio and recorded with Armstrong under the name of the Hot Five. In the same year, he made a number of classic recordings with Noone as well as several solo piano records.

By the end of 1928, Hines formed his own unit, and it became the house band at the Grand Terrace, originally at 3955 South Parkway (now King Drive) and later at the southwest corner of 35th Street and South Calumet Avenue, where he remained for more than a decade. Nightly broadcasts from the Terrace gave the pianist a national reputation. Like many Chicago nightclubs in the 1920s, the Grand Terrace was owned by the Capone syndicate.

In 1940 Hines turned down an offer to join Benny Goodman's orchestra, opting, instead, to form another outfit. This was to be no ordinary band. By 1941 the Hines lineup boasted some of the most formidable talent in the history of jazz, including singer Billy Eckstine, who doubled on trumpet, trombonist Benny Green, trumpeter Dizzy Gillespie, and pianist and second vocalist Sarah Vaughan. Although the group stayed together for almost a year, they never cut a record because of the American Federation of Musicians' recording ban of 1942, when James C. Petrillo, president of the AFM, ordered union members not to record.

Hines joined Louis Armstrong's All-Stars in 1948, but he left in 1951 to play with his own group at the Hangover Club in San Francisco. In 1957 he toured Europe with trombonist Jack Teagarden.

Hines died of a heart attack in Oakland, California, in 1983.

"If 'genius' is a word that still has meaning," offered music critic Larry Kart a few days after the musician's death, "Earl Hines was just that—a man whose music not only tested the rules but left us in doubt as to whether there are any rules, other than the ones his inspiration managed to create."

Hines toured and recorded extensively with groups and as a solo act throughout the sixties and seventies. Among his recordings are *Quintessential Recording Session* (1970), *Quintessential Continued* (1973), and *An Evening with Earl Hines* (1973). Hines also recorded tributes to Louis Armstrong, Hoagy Camichael, Duke Ellington, Cole Porter, and George Gershwin. Hines most famous compositions are "Rosetta," "My Monday Date," "Piano Man," "57 Varieties," and his biggest hit, "Boogie Woogie on the St. Louis Blues."

See also: Louis Armstrong, Bud Freeman, Benny Goodman, Gene Krupa, James C. Petrillo

Further reading: Dance, Stanley. *The World of Earl Hines* (1977); Shapiro, Nat and Nat Hentoff, eds. *The Jazz Makers: Essays on the Greats of Jazz* (1957); Travis, Dempsey J. *An Autobiography of Black Jazz* (1983).

Emil G. Hirsch

Rabbi

born: May 22, 1851
Luxembourg
died: January 7, 1923
Chicago, Illinois

One of the foremost Jewish scholars of his day, Emil Gustav Hirsch articulated his unorthodox views as rabbi of the Chicago Sinai Congregation at 46th Street and Grand Boulevard (now King Drive) for over forty years. Reformed Jews, said Dr. Hirsch, must work to rebuild their faith and continually question the fundamental ethic of their foundation.

Photograph courtesy of the Asher Library—Spertus College.

Born in Luxembourg and educated in Germany, Hirsch came to the United States as a teenager and attended the Episcopal Academy of Philadelphia. Later he enrolled at the University of Pennsylvania, where he received his degree in 1872, and then spent four years of study in Berlin and Leipzig. He became a rabbi in 1877 and was assigned to a synagogue in Baltimore. One year later he was transferred to the Adath Israel Congregation in Louisville, Kentucky, and in 1880 he came to the Sinai Congregation in Chicago.

As a Reformed Jew, Hirsch held unconventional views. He believed that the Sabbath need not be celebrated only on Saturday, and to the consternation of many, he established Sunday morning services for those who could not attend on Saturday. He held that the Scripture need not be treated as a museum piece but was, in fact, a living document, open to interpretation.

Always outspoken, Hirsch suggested that a settlement house be built on the South Side for the sons of millionaires since, he felt, they were often more ignorant than the poor. He criticized wealthy Jews for being more concerned about showing off their jewelry than helping those less fortunate than themselves.

Hirsch was radical in other ways, too. At a time when women were segregated in Jewish synagogues, he invited two women—Jane Addams and Hannah G. Solomon, founder of the National Council of Jewish Women— to speak before the temple congregation. He also lectured on the need for workers' compensation and factory safety legislation.

He founded the *Reform Advocate*, a weekly newspaper that gave him a national platform for his opinions.

"He was not a Zionist," insisted his son, David Hirsch. "He felt Judaism was a universal religion and that its mission was everywhere."

"He was a master in the knowledge of comparative religions and in higher criticism, and he likewise knew the highest teachings of the morals of Judaism. He was especially a prophet in this industrial age. He stressed the ethical obligations of religion to do justice, love mercy, and walk humbly with God," observed Dr. Stephen S. Wise, rabbi of the Jewish Free Synagogue in New York, following Dr. Hirsch's death in 1923.

In addition to his religious duties, Hirsch served as president of the board of the Chicago Public Library and as a member of the board of commissioners of the Public Charities of Illinois. Later he became professor of Semitic languages and literature at the University of Chicago in 1892, the first American rabbi to teach at a secular institution of higher learning. In addition, he was a lecturer at Johns Hopkins University in 1902.

The Chicago Sinai Congregation, now located at 5350 South Shore Drive, is one of the best known Jewish congregations in the city. Hirsch High School, built in 1925 at 77th Street and Ingleside Avenue, was named in the rabbi's honor.

"He was the greatest Jewish preacher of his generation, a mighty and un-afraid prophet of truth," said Wise.

Further reading: Hirsch, David E. *Rabbi Emil G. Hirsch: The Reform Advocate* (1968).

Julius J. Hoffman

Judge

born: July 7, 1895
Chicago, Illinois
died: July 1, 1983
Chicago, Illinois

Julius J. Hoffman, nicknamed "Julius the Just," gained national attention as the cantankerous judge who presided over the raucous Chicago Seven conspiracy trial in 1969.

Photograph courtesy of the *Chicago Daily Law Bulletin.*

Educated in Chicago public schools, Hoffman attended the Lewis Institute and Northwestern University. He was admitted to the Illinois bar in 1915. Hoffman worked as an associate and partner in the law firm of White and Hawxhurst until 1936, when he became general counsel for the Brunswick-Balke-Collender Company. In 1944 he joined Markheim, Hoffman, Hungerford and Sollo and remained there until 1947, when he was elected a judge of the Superior Court of Cook County for a six-year term. During this period, Hoffman also served on the faculty of the Northwestern University Law School. In 1953 President Dwight D. Eisenhower named Hoffman to the United States District Court in Chicago.

Hoffman presided over a number of important trials. Some of his most noteworthy cases include the prosecution of the promoters of krebiozen, a controversial anticancer drug; the desegregation suit against the South Holland school district; the tax evasion trial of mobster Tony Accardo; and the deportation suit against alleged Nazi war criminal Frank Walus. The United States Court of Appeals overturned Hoffman's guilty ruling on the latter case and ordered a new trial.

But the most notorious case of Hoffman's long career belonged to the Conspiracy Seven trial. In 1969 five of the Chicago Seven—Rennie Davis, David Dellinger, Tom Hayden, Abbie Hoffman, and Jerry Rubin—were convicted of conspiracy to cross state lines with the intent to incite riots during the 1968 Democratic Convention held in Chicago. A reporter once described the tense atmosphere inside the courtroom as "unruliness disturbed by only occasional bouts of decorum."

The trial of the Chicago Seven reflected the sometimes frenzied, always tense atmosphere of the time as the U.S. was embroiled in war in Vietnam and thousands of antiwar demonstrators took to the streets in protest. The original eight defendants were David Dellinger, Rennie Davis, Tom Hayden, Abbie Hoffman, Jerry Rubin, Lee Weiner, John Froines, and Bobby Seale. The government claimed that the defendants conspired together to encourage people from throughout the United States to come to Chicago to protest during the Democratic Convention in August of 1968 with the intent to confront the Chicago Police Department and other symbols of authority in order to create riot conditions. Hoffman and Rubin disrupted proceedings during the one-hundred-day trial with frequent interruptions of name calling and mocked the legal system by donning judicial robes. Witnesses included everyone from poet Allen Ginsberg to novelist Norman Mailer. Judge Hoffman cited a total of 175 contempt of court charges against the defendants and their lawyers, which included such violations as commenting aloud without permission, laughing, applauding, and blowing a kiss to the jury. Hoffman's attempts to control the court often turned to extremes as when he ordered Black Panther leader Bobby Seale gagged and bound and tied to his chair when Seale refused to obey an order to keep silent. Seale was later separated from the other defendants and charged with contempt of court.

The court sentenced Dellinger, Davis, Hayden, Hoffman, and Rubin to five years in prison and fined each $5,000. The appeals court later overturned the convictions. "The demeanor of the judge and the prosecutors," noted one judicial opinion, "would require reversal even if errors did not." Tom Hayden later insisted that the entire youthful generation of the sixties was on trial. "Our crime was our identity," he wrote in *Trial.* "The charges against

us made no sense. Our crime was that we were beginning to live a new and contagious life style without official authorization. We were tried for being out of control."

In 1982 the Executive Committee of the United States District Court ordered that the then eighty-six-year-old jurist be assigned no new cases, citing as evidence his age and frequent complaints that he had been acting increasingly erratic and abusive on the bench. Despite the censure, Hoffman continued to hear cases as senior U. S. District Court judge until his death in July of 1983.

Hoffman was active in philanthropic and charitable affairs and served as vice-chairman of the Hospital Building Fund of the Jewish Federation of Chicago. He was also a member of the Chicago Sinai Congregation.

Hoffman died of natural causes at the age of eighty-seven at his home at 179 East Lake Shore Drive.

Further reading: Hayden, Tom. *Trial* (1970); Levine, Mark L., George C. McNamee, and Daniel Greenberg, eds. *The Tales of Hoffman* (1970); Peck, Abe. *Uncovering the Sixties: The Life & Times of the Underground Press* (1985).

Henry Horner

Politician

born: November 30, 1878
Chicago, Illinois
died: October 6, 1940
Winnetka, Illinois

Judge of the Probate Court of Cook County since 1914, Henry Horner made history in 1932 when he was elected Illinois's first Jewish governor. In addition to attracting a broad constituency, Horner managed to unite the usually fractured Jewish vote, which had historically been torn between the desires of the more established German Jews and the recently arrived Eastern European Jews.

Horner's father, Solomon Levy, was brought to Kentucky from Bavaria in 1850 by his uncle. Settling in Chicago in 1870, he married Dilah Horner one year later. In 1878 Dilah gave birth to their third son, Henry, in their South Michigan Avenue apartment. By this time, though, the marriage was strained. Dilah filed for divorce, accusing her husband of physical cruelty. Hannah Horner, Dilah's mother, offered housing for her daughter and two of the children—the father received the custody of the eldest son—under one condition: that Dilah and the children's names be changed to Horner.

Henry attended the Chicago Manual Training School on the South Side. Then he enrolled at Kent College of Law at night and worked as a law clerk by day.

Horner received his first taste of Chicago politics on the streets of the 1st Ward where his uncle Isaac worked for aldermen Michael Kenna and John Coughlin. When still a law student, Horner campaigned in 1897 for Carter Harrison II, further advancing his political education. Two years later he was admitted to the Illinois bar and began a lucrative law practice, specializing in real estate and probate law. Early in his career Horner realized the value of establishing relationships with important civic and political leaders. He joined, for example, the prestigious Standard Club—his maternal grandfather, Henry Horner I, had been one of its charter members. By the turn of the century Horner was a well-respected young man appreciated by both the diverse Jewish community and the regular Democratic machine.

In 1907 Horner was appointed attorney for the Cook County Board of Assessors and, in 1914, was elected judge of the Probate Court of Cook County, wining each contest by progressively wider margins. In 1930,

notes his biographer, Thomas Littlewood, Horner received more votes than anyone else on the county ticket. Horner earned an excellent reputation as an honest and meticulous judge and a man of irreproachable integrity.

Such a loyal and reliable vote-getter did not go unnoticed. In 1932 the Democratic party endorsed Horner for governor. A great compromiser, Horner enjoyed broad support, appealing to Democrats, Republicans, independents, reformers, Jews, and gentiles. He won by, at that time, the largest majority in Illinois history, aided considerably by the monolithic support of the Jewish electorate.

In 1933 the new governor clashed over control of the licensing of city saloons with the new mayor of Chicago, Edward J. Kelly, who was appointed chief executive by the city council following the murder of Mayor Anton Cermak in Miami. Kelly fought for local jurisdiction while Horner insisted that the state should manage the operations. The relationship between the two leaders deteriorated as Kelly increasingly felt threatened by Horner's stubborn independence. Despite the refusal of Kelly to endorse Horner for reelection, the governor managed to pull off a stunning upset during the 1936 Democratic primaries, defeating Kelly's choice, Chicago Health Commissioner Herman C. Bundesen, by a substantial margin. In the November general election, Horner easily beat the Republican candidate C. Wayland Brooks, carrying the city alone by over 300,000 votes. Once again the Jewish community came to the aid of their favorite son.

In 1938 Horner, stricken with cerebral thrombosis (a blood clot of the brain), decided not to seek reelection for governor in 1940. A financial scandal among his staff exacerbated his weakened condition. Horner died of cardiovascular disease and inflammation of the kidneys at age sixty-one in October of 1940.

Horner contributed his time and money to various charities and causes. He acted as president of the Young Men's Jewish Charities and served as chairman of the social service committee of Michael Reese Hospital. The bachelor governor, who was extremely fond of children, personally conducted a tour of the state capital whenever his friends' children visited.

The worth of Horner's administration cannot be measured in legislation alone. At his funeral, Rabbi Louis L. Mann hailed the fallen politician as "a martyr to the cause of good government." His greatest strength, writes biographer Littlewood, was his character. He will be remembered not for what he did but for who he was. Said poet Carl Sandburg upon his death, "He was the real goods. In the realm of politics there have been too few like him. He collaborated with men who were purchasable without becoming purchasable himself. He had thoroughgoing integrity. He got to high places without selling his soul."

See also: John Coughlin, Carter Harrison II, Edward J. Kelly, Michael Kenna

Further reading: Bregstone, Philip P. *Chicago and Its Jews: A Cultural History* (1933); Littlewood, Thomas B. *Horner of Illinois* (1969); Mazur, Edward. "Jewish Chicago: From Diversity to Community," in *Ethnic Chicago,* Melvin G. Holli and Peter d'A. Jones, eds. (1984).

Gurdon S. Hubbard

Pioneer

born: August 22, 1802
Windsor, Vermont
died: September 14, 1886
Chicago, Illinois

Fur trader, merchant, and statesman, Gurdon Saltonstall Hubbard was one of the greatest of the pioneers of early Chicago. He arrived when Chicago was but a remote village in the middle of the vast Midwest. When he died more than sixty years later, it had grown into an exciting and prosperous city. The city's first meatpacker and banker, he was also instrumental in the building of the Illinois and Michigan Canal. In addition, he reportedly wrote the city's first insurance policy, bought the first Chicago fire engine, built the first brick hotel in Chicago, and was a founder of the Board of Trade.

Of Yankee stock, Hubbard attended the Windsor school in Vermont at age six. Financial difficulties compelled his parents to send him to live with a relative in Bridgewater, Massachusetts. Finally, deep in debt, his father fled with the family to Montreal to avoid his creditors.

In 1816 Hubbard apprenticed at a Montreal hardware store that supplied goods and equipment to fur traders. He ran errands, unpacked crates, delivered goods along the waterfront, and helped with the bookkeeping. And, when the day's work was done, he read. His favorite subject was the French exploration in North America.

In early 1818 he left Montreal for the Indian territory with French-Canadian traders. At age sixteen Hubbard was a trading post clerk for the American Fur Company owned by the famous trapper, John Jacob Astor. After a summer in Mackinac, Michigan, he came to Chicago in late 1818. Eventually he established a successful fur trade from Danville to Chicago. It was called "Hubbard's trail."

In 1824 Hubbard was appointed superintendent of the Illinois River trading posts of the American Fur Company, at the present-day location of Mackinac Island, where he came into regular contact with various Indian tribes—the Potawatomis, Winnebagos, and Chippewas, among others—and learned to respect and appreciate Indian ways and traditions. The Indians, in return, admired the young man's honesty and his great physical strength. They called him Papamatabe, the Swift Walker. Contemporary newspaper accounts reported that he could walk as much as seventy miles in one day. Three years later Hubbard became owner of an American Fur Company franchise.

Representing Vermilion county, Hubbard introduced in the state legislature a bill creating what would later become the Illinois and Michigan Canal. The canal formed a link between the Great Lakes and the Mississippi River and thus opened up northern Illinois for future commercial development. After much debate and delay, the bill finally passed through both houses in January of 1836. Hubbard was appointed one of the commissioners of the I&M Canal Commission.

In 1834 Hubbard settled in Chicago permanently, becoming one of the village's first trustees. He purchased a log cabin on Lake Michigan from Billy Caldwell, the half-Potawatomie, half-Irish Indian chief. Often called Chicago's most "useful" citizen, Hubbard engaged in many productive activities. He built a warehouse and packing plant, which was dubbed "Hubbard's Folly" due to its tremendous size. He established a shipping line, organized an insurance agency, and speculated heavily in real estate. He was also a partner in Chicago's first hotel, the Lake House, at Rush and Kinzie Streets.

In 1860 Hubbard was elected alderman of the 7th Ward. In the same year tragedy struck when his passenger ship, the *Lady Elgin*, was rammed by a schooner, the *Augusta*, off the Winnetka shore, resulting in 297 deaths. Two years later another of his ships, the *Superior*, went down in a storm.

Hubbard lost most of his possessions in the Chicago Fire of 1871. Near bankruptcy, he—like the city itself—began the painful and arduous process toward recovery.

In May of 1883, Hubbard became critically ill. The following year excruciating pain resulted in the removal of his left eye. "True to his Indian training he resolutely refused an anesthetic," wrote his nephew, Henry R. Hamilton. "He simply lay down without a murmur or tremor and let doctors cut out his eye." In 1885 his other eye was removed.

When he died at the age of eighty-four in September of 1886, the local press referred to him in glowing terms as the city's "oldest settler." He was buried in Graceland Cemetery.

Hubbard's career became synonomous with the growth of Chicago. When he settled in Chicago in 1834, the little village had a population of under two hundred inhabitants. By the time of his death in 1886 the town had blossomed into a booming metropolis of three quarters of a million people. In his massive three-volume history of Chicago, A. T. Andreas sums up Hubbard's accomplishments best. "He held nearly every office of trust that his fellow citizens could thrust upon him. It may be said here that he never violated any trust bestowed."

See also: Jean Baptiste Pointe du Sable, John Kinzie

Further reading: Andreas, A. T. *History of Chicago from the Earliest Period to the Present Time.* 3 vols. (1884–86); Poole, Ernest. *Giants Gone: Men Who Made Chicago* (1943); Wendt, Lloyd. *"Swift Walker": An Informal Biography of Gurdon Saltonstall Hubbard* (1986).

Robert Maynard Hutchins

Educator

born: January 17, 1899
Brooklyn, New York
died: May 14, 1977
Santa Barbara, California

Charming, erudite, debonair. Scholar, philosopher, reformer. Robert Maynard Hutchins was all this and more. At thirty he became president of the University of Chicago—the youngest head of a major American university. Called the most celebrated intellectual of his time, Hutchins was also chairman of Encyclopedia Britannica and editor of the Great Books series. Admirers praised him as the "boy wonder" of academe, while critics fumed that he was nothing more than an arrogant, trouble-making Yankee iconoclast. Clearly, Robert Maynard Hutchins, the renegade scholar, ran resolutely against established academic practices.

Photograph courtesy of the University of Chicago Archives.

Hutchins's father, a minister, imbued his son with a firm appreciation of the Protestant ethic. He enrolled Robert at Oberlin Theological Seminary in Ohio in 1915. During World War I, Robert enlisted in the Army ambulance service, and in June of 1918 he was assigned to Genoa as part of the American Expeditionary Force with the Italian army.

After the war Hutchins resumed his education, receiving both a bachelor's degree in 1921 and a law degree in 1925 from Yale and graduated magna cum laude in 1925. Hutchins then joined the Yale faculty, and within two years he attained the rank of associate professor. In 1927 he was appointed dean of the Yale Law School. And finally, on April 25, 1929, the University of Chicago chose the thirty-year-old Hutchins as its president.

Hutchins acted with bold strokes. He preached cultural literacy before it was fashionable to do so. Hutchins insisted, however, that his programs were merely continuations of the late William Rainey Harper's original vision. It was Harper, the champion of liberal arts and the university's first president, said Hutchins, who urged that "an essential element in the education of every man . . . is a study of the great heritage we have received from the past."

Hutchins revamped the entire curriculum and divided the university into an undergraduate college with separate graduate schools. What's more, he stressed the importance of a liberal education and unilaterally opposed vocational training at the university level, instituting instead an undergraduate curriculum based upon the Great Books program, which studied the great classics of Western civilization. Mandatory class attendance was abolished—rather, students had to pass comprehensive examinations.

Hutchins was more concerned with what a student knew than with how many A's or B's he or she accumulated.

Hutchins humanized the study of law. He introduced psychology, history, economics, political theory, and philosophy into the law curriculum in order to "produce educated lawyers and not merely lawyers who know the rules and how to manipulate them," he said.

In 1939 Hutchins abolished intercollegiate football at the University of Chicago, insisting that the school could no longer effectively compete with the big, public universities—during the final season, Chicago lost miserably to such opponents as Harvard (61-0) and Michigan (85-0). Not exactly a surprising decision, considering Hutchins's Puritan past and his belief, according to his biographer, that enjoyment was a form of indolence. "There is no doubt on the whole that football has been a major handicap to education in the United States," he said. Understandably, Hutchins's controversial decision caused great dissension on campus. Years later, in 1969, varsity football returned to the Midway. In 1976 Chicago joined the Midwest Conference but left in 1986 to join the University Athletic Association.

In 1943 the University of Chicago obtained control of the Encyclopedia Britannica, and Hutchins was appointed chairman of Britannica's board of editors. He took a leave of absence from the university to work in Britannica's adult education program and served as director of the encyclopedia from 1947 to 1974.

In 1947 Hutchins and Mortimer Adler introduced the "Great Books of the Western World" courses. Hutchins believed studying the classics prepared one for "the good life," and that in order to consider oneself educated, a person must be aware of

these works. He insisted, however, should anyone dare to brand him an elitist, that the course be made available to everyone. In 1952 he became editor-in-chief of the Great Books of the Western World.

In 1945 Hutchins became chancellor of the University of Chicago. He left the university in 1951, however, to become an associate director of the Ford Foundation. From 1954 to 1974 he served as chief executive officer of the Fund for the Republic, a civil rights organization that supported efforts to safeguard the freedom of the press, brought religious and racial discrimination to the attention of the American public, and attacked the abuses of McCarthyism, among other things.

In 1959 Hutchins organized the Center for the Study of Democratic Institutions, a California-based think tank. He retired in 1974 but returned when an effective successor could not be found. In 1975 the headquarters of the institute moved from Santa Barbara, California, to Chicago.

Shortly after Hutchins left the university, administration officials—many of whom did not subscribe to Hutchins's expansive, liberal arts approach to education—began to dismantle his programs so that by 1949 the Hutchins legacy had all but disappeared. Only three programs in the United States, notes *Chicago Tribune* feature writer and university alumnus, Ron Grossman, continue along the Great Books model—St. John's College in Annapolis, Maryland, and Santa Fe, New Mexico; Shimer College in Waukegan, Illinois; and Thomas Aquinas College in Santa Paula, California.

Robert Maynard Hutchins, the most celebrated educator of his generation, died in 1977 at the age of seventy-eight in Santa Barbara, California.

Among Hutchins's many books are *The Higher Learning in America* (1936), *The Conflict in Education* (1953), *Some Observations on American Education* (1956), *Education for Freedom* (1963), and *Education: the Learning Society* (1968)

"Education," Hutchins once said, "is not a substitute for experience. It is preparation for it."

See also: William Rainey Harper

Further reading: Ashmore, Harry S. *Unseasonable Truths: The Life of Robert Maynard Hutchins* (1989).

J. Allen Hynek

Astronomer

born: May 1, 1910
Chicago, Illinois
died: April 27, 1986
Scottsdale, Arizona

*Joseph Allen Hynek was the leading authority on UFOs in the country and the director, from 1948 to 1969, of the Air Force's Project Blue Book, a government-sponsored program that gathered, analyzed, and studied information about UFOs. Hynek was credited with coining the term "close encounter" to refer to an actual meeting with an extraterrestrial. Director Steven Spielberg borrowed this term for the title of his 1977 blockbuster movie, **Close Encounters of the Third Kind**. Dr. Hynek adopted strict scientific principles for the* study of UFOs, *bringing a semblance of respectability to what many of his colleagues considered the dubious science of ufology.*

Photograph reprinted with permission from the *Chicago Sun-Times.*

Born in Chicago to Czech parents, Hynek attended public schools in Chicago. After graduating from Crane High School, Hynek enrolled at the University of Chicago, where he received his Ph.D. in 1935. The following year he accepted a position of assistant professor in the Department of Physics and Astronomy at Ohio State University in Columbus, Ohio. From 1946 to 1955 he was the director of the McMillin Observatory, at Ohio State, and from 1956 to 1960 he was the associate director of the Smithsonian Astrophysics Observatory in Cambridge, Massachusetts.

In 1960 Hynek returned to the Chicago area to assume the chairmanship of the Department of Astronomy at Northwestern University. Five years later he became the director of Northwestern's Lindheimer Astronomical Research Center.

In September 1947 the Air Force—under the code name Project Blue Book, with headquarters at the Wright-Patterson Air Force Base in Dayton, Ohio—asked Hynek to evaluate UFO sightings. Hynek took the assignment seriously. Rather than dismissing UFOs as figments of overworked imaginations, he discovered, to his complete surprise, that there were many more questions than answers. Although most reports could be explained as aircraft sightings or the result of atmospheric conditions, there were others that could not be so easily identified. But in December 1969, after two decades of investigation with no solid evidence, Secretary of the Air Force Robert C. Seamans officially terminated Project Blue Book based on the recommendation of Dr. E. U. Condon, a scientist who served as director of an air force–sponsored study group at the University of Colorado.

In 1975 Hynek founded the Center for UFO Studies in Evanston, Illinois. The center, a nonprofit organization that functioned as a clearinghouse for UFO reports, received the cooperation of municipal police departments as well as the support of scientists from a dozen American universities. In 1981, due to a lack of funds, Hynek was forced to shut down his office and moved the center into his Evanston home at 2623 Ridge Avenue. Hynek continually sought research funds from the National Science Foundation, NASA, and private foundations. Most requests, however, were met with a snicker and not-so-polite suggestions to try elsewhere.

Despite Hynek's impeccable reputation as a highly respected scholar, not everyone in the scientific community approved of his work. In 1975 scientist Carl Sagan, interviewed in the *Chicago Tribune*, referred to the study of UFOs as "a nonscience. It's entirely anecdotal. You have to have data other than hearsay for anything to be scientific." Even some members of Hynek's staff questioned his activities. In 1982 Rudolph H. Weingartner, dean of Northwestern's College of Arts and Sciences, stressed in a letter to a member of the university relations staff that "the Lindheimer Observatory has nothing to do with UFOs and never did. Hynek's UFO Center has always been a *non*-Northwestern affair. There are many who think that what he's up to has nothing to do with research."

Hynek's work perhaps received the greatest boost in 1977 when motion picture director Steven Spielberg addressed the subject of UFOs in *Close Encounters of the Third Kind*. Dr.

Hynek not only acted as consultant but also made a brief cameo appearance during the film's climactic "encounter" scene.

Hynek retired from his teaching position at Northwestern in 1978, although he continued as professor emeritus until he moved his headquarters from Evanston to Scottsdale, Arizona, in 1984. He died in Scottsdale of a brain tumor in May of 1986. He was seventy-five.

Hynek authored several books including *Astrophysics* (1951), *Challenge of the Universe* (1962), and *The UFO Experience: A Scientific Inquiry* (1972).

Samuel Insull

Entrepreneur

born: November 11, 1859
London, England
died: July 16, 1938
Paris, France

Samuel Insull was one of the most powerful businessmen in the country during the 1920s. For many years people idolized him as the embodiment of the great American success story. Here was a poor young Englishman who started with nothing and made a fortune through hard work, intelligence, and perseverance. At its height, the Insull empire included Commonwealth Edison, Peoples Gas, the elevated railways of Chicago, and the interurban lines connecting Chicago with its suburbs.

Insull possessed a boundless energy and a burning ambition to achieve respectability. A quick study, he had an inquisitive, agile mind. If he didn't know something, he would learn it and would memorize whatever he read.

Insull began his career as an office boy in an English auction firm. Although he did well—and indeed was even promoted to clerical supervisor—he was unceremoniously fired one day when an important client insisted that his son have Insull's position. Crushed by this rejection, Insull answered an ad for a secretary to an American banker. He was hired.

Several years earlier, Insull had read about a young American inventor named Thomas Edison. Edison became Insull's hero. And as it turned out, his new employer was not, in fact, a banker but Edison's European representative.

In 1881 Insull arrived in the United States as Thomas Edison's private secretary. He traveled across the country promoting Edison's inventions and quadrupling his sales.

In 1892 the Chicago Edison Company began looking for a new president. The directors asked Insull if he could recommend anyone. Insull thought it improper to mention himself. His mother, who was visiting at the time, had no such qualms and persuaded her son to offer his services. He did, and the directors accepted his offer.

At that time electricity was thought of as a luxury item. Insull reasoned that everyone should have electricity, and he promoted the somewhat radical idea that lower prices would create bigger sales and thus yield greater profits.

Chicago Edison grew and so did Insull's reputation. In 1889 he became vice-president of the Edison General Electric Company, and three years later he was named president. In 1907 Commonwealth Edison Company was formed. In 1913 Insull assumed the chairmanship of the Peoples Gas, Light, and Coke Company.

Between 1911 and 1914, according to his biographer, Insull became Chicago's leading traction magnate and began to acquire and modernize the interurban railroads that connected Chicago and the suburbs.

Insull was a practical man. A happy environment makes for happy employees, he reasoned. He treated his workers fairly, but he demanded respect and loyalty. In return he gave them many fringe benefits: in addition to pension, disability compensation, medical care, and life insurance, he added such niceties as athletic teams and savings and loan plans. Furthermore, employees were urged to become stockholders. Insull had a highly sophisticted social conscience, and he subtly encouraged all of his employees to participate in some form of community service activity.

Insull attended the opera regularly. Offended by opera's elitist image, he sought ways to bring it to the people. When Harold and Edith Rockefeller McCormick chose to step down as the major patrons of the Chicago Opera Company in 1922, he saw his opportunity. Insull decided to build a new home for the opera along the Chicago River at Wacker and Madison. He hired the august architectural firm of Graham, Anderson, Probst, and White to design a combination opera house and office building. Construction began in January of 1928 and was completed during the dark weeks following the stock market crash of 1929.

Insull's business interests fell apart as a result of the crash. He tried to buy up his own stock, but debt engulfed his holding companies, and scores of small investors—including many of his employees—lost everything. Exhausted and embarrassed, Insull fled temporarily to the safe refuge of Europe in order to avoid prosecution. In his absence, he was charged with fraudulent use of the mails and accused of violating the Bankruptcy Act. Insull insisted he would return but only when a fair trial was possible. He admitted no wrongdoing and felt his decisions were more a matter of taking care of business than any malevolent act.

Insull was forced to return to Chicago in 1934 to face the court. He was tried three times for fraud, violation of federal bankruptcy laws, and embezzlement, but he was acquitted on all three counts.

Insull died of a heart attack in the summer of 1938, while waiting to board a Paris subway train.

See also: Carter Harrison II, Charles Tyson Yerkes

Further reading: McDonald, Forrest. *Insull* (1962).

Mahalia Jackson

Singer

born: October 26, 1911
New Orleans, Louisiana
died: January 27, 1972
Evergreen Park, Illinois

Mahalia Jackson popularized gospel music in the 1950s and 1960s, spreading its warmth and joy around the world. She sang at humble storefront churches as well as on the stages of the world's premier concert halls. Although her recordings sold millions of copies, and she performed for kings, queens, prime ministers, and presidents, including singing the national anthem at John F. Kennedy's inauguration, she remained a sincere person, genuinely surprised, and even touched, by the depth of her success. "I love singing. Period," she once said.

Photograph reprinted with permission from the *Chicago Sun-Times*.

Born in a three-room shack in New Orleans in 1911, Mahalia Jackson was the granddaughter of a slave. Her father was a combination stevedore, barber, and minister. Several of his sisters performed in vaudeville routines, but his children were only allowed to listen to religious music.

As a youth, Mahalia joined her father's church choir. She dropped out of school after eighth grade to work as a servant. When she was sixteen, she left New Orleans for Chicago where she worked as a hotel maid, a private servant, and a packer in a factory. One day her aunt took her to a service at the Greater Salem Baptist Church at 215 West 71st Street. She sang "Hand Me Down My Silver Trumpet, Gabriel," and the pastor was so impressed that he asked the young girl to join the church's choir as a soloist.

Jackson saved enough money to study at beauty school, and she opened a small beauty shop, "Mahalia's Beauty Salon," at 3252 South Indiana Avenue. Later she invested in real estate and opened a flower shop. She made her professional singing debut at the Olivet Baptist Church, at 31st Street and Grand Boulevard, in 1928. She then joined the Johnson Gospel Singers, which toured storefront churches. Although Jackson cut her first record for Decca in 1937, she didn't gain national recognition until the release of Rev. W. Herbert Brewster's "Move On Up A Little Higher" on the Apollo label in 1947, the first gospel record to sell a million copies. Her follow-up, "Even Me, Lord," fared equally well so that by 1949 she had closed her beauty shop to pursue singing full-time. Around this time gospel music was finally becoming accepted as a legitimate part of church services—further proof that gospel had finally arrived.

Jackson made her first appearance in New York's Carnegie Hall in 1950 to a sold-out crowd. "Think of it, me—a washwoman—standing there singing where such persons as Lily Pons and Caruso stood. I've never gotten over it," she once recalled in a newspaper interview. Four years later she hosted her own radio show, "Mahalia," on Sunday evenings and signed a record contract with Columbia. In the 1960s she became involved in the civil rights movement and performed at many demonstrations.

Listeners were often overwhelmed by the power and raw honesty of Jackson's singing, falling to their knees and weeping. She sang songs about the black experience and about being black in white America. Jackson combined the soulful singing of Bessie Smith with Baptist hymns and spirituals.

After suffering a heart attack in 1964, Jackson's health continued to deteriorate. She died in 1972 at the age of sixty in Evergreen Park, Illinois. She is buried in a suburb of New Orleans.

Her recordings include *The World's Greatest Gospel Singer, Right Out of the Church, The Great Mahalia Jackson,* and *America's Greatest Hymns*—all on Columbia—and *I Sing Because I'm Happy* on Folkways.

Mahalia Jackson had two dreams that remained unfulfilled at the time of her death—to establish a church, and to found a school of African-American music. A musical based on her life, *Mahalia,* opened on Broadway in 1984.

See also: Nat "King" Cole, Sam Cooke

Further reading: Goreau, Laurraine. *Just Mahalia, Baby* (1975); Jackson, Mahalia and E. M. Wylie. *Movin' On Up: the Mahalia Jackson Story* (1966).

William Le Baron Jenney

Architect

born: September 25, 1832
Fairhaven, Massachusetts
died: June 15, 1907
Los Angeles, California

Called the "father of the skyscraper," William Le Baron Jenney designed such pioneering buildings as the Leiter Building, the Fair department store, the Manhattan Building, the Sears Building at State and Van Buren, the Montgomery Ward Building at State and Adams, and the Home Insurance Building, the world's first skyscraper. Virtually every major Chicago architect worked in Jenney's architectural firm, including Louis Sullivan, Daniel H. Burnham, William Holabird, Martin Roche, and Howard Van Doren Shaw.

Shortly after turning eighteen, Jenney traveled to California by way of clipper ship to join in the Gold Rush. Finding no easy fortune, he spent some time in the Philippines. Upon his return to the United States, he attended Harvard University and in 1853 enrolled as an engineering student at the Ecole Centrale des Arts et Manufactures in Paris where he shared rooms with English writer George du Maurier and American painter James Whistler.

In 1857 Jenney was appointed a chief engineer on the Isthmus of Tehuantepec, Mexico. During the Civil War, he was assigned to the staff of Gen. Ulysses S. Grant and then served under Gen. William T. Sherman. Jenney acted as the chief engineer of the 15th Corps at the battle of Vicksburg and later served as the army's chief engineer. He attained the rank of major in March of 1865 and resigned in May of 1866. In the late 1860s, he and his wife, Elizabeth H. Cobb, settled in Riverside, Illinois, a suburb laid out by noted landscape architects Frederick Law Olmsted and Calvert Vaux.

Jenney developed steel-frame construction, which replaced the burdensome masonry-bearing wall of architecture made famous by the Monadnock Building. In the steel-frame method, the exterior wall was reduced to a curtain supported by interior framing, a technological breakthrough that made possible the development of the modern skyscraper. Architectural critic Carl W. Condit called it "the first adequate solution to the problem of large-scale urban construction." He claimed further that skeletal construction "completed the most radical transformation in the structural art since the development of the Gothic system of construction in the twelfth century." Jenney's innovative method was quickly adopted across the country.

Jenney's twelve-story Home Insurance building, constructed in 1884–1885 at the northeast corner of La Salle and Adams Streets, is credited with being the world's first skyscraper, and it was reportedly the first structure to use steel as a building material. Unfortunately, this landmark was razed in 1931.

Jenney entered into several partnerships during his career. In February of 1891 he formed a partnership with William B. Mundie. Later E. C. Jensen joined and the firm was known as Jenney, Mundie and Jensen.

Jenney was elected Fellow of the American Institute of Architects in 1872 and also served as president of the Illinois chapter of the AIA. He retired in 1905 and moved to California, where he died in 1907. His body was returned to Chicago, and his ashes were scattered next to his wife's grave in Graceland Cemetery.

See also: Daniel H. Burnham, William Holabird [appendix], Howard Van Doren Shaw, Louis Sullivan

Further reading: Condit, Carl W. *The Chicago School of Architecture: A History of Commercial and Public Building in the Chicago Area, 1875–1925* (1964).

Jack Johnson

Boxer

born: March 31, 1878
Galveston, Texas
died: June 10, 1946
Raleigh, North Carolina

John Arthur Johnson was not only the first black heavyweight champion of the world, he was also one of the greatest fighters in the history of boxing.

Photograph courtesy of Charles H. Kerr Publishing.

Johnson quit school in Galveston, Texas, after the fifth grade. Endowed with lightning speed, he learned to box at a neighborhood gym. He traveled the country on freight trains and was frequently arrested for vagrancy.

Back in Galveston, a local boxer offered the princely sum of $5 to anyone who could stay on his feet in the ring with him for four rounds. Johnson accepted the challenge and defeated his astonished foe handily. Shortly afterwards Johnson was offered a match at the Galveston Athletic Club. After a few more semiprofessional bouts, he rode the trains again and made his way to St. Louis, then to Florida, and finally to Chicago where he got a job as a sparring partner for the West Indian welterweight, Joe Walcott.

He then went to California where he found work as a sparring partner with "Kid" Carter. He began winning match after match, always against black men. His earnings grew, but he spent his money as quickly as he made it. A natural showman, Johnson also performed on the vaudeville stage demonstrating basic boxing movements, warbling a few songs, dancing, and playing the harmonica and bass fiddle.

In 1905 Johnson fought a white boxer, Marvin Hart, in San Francisco. Although observers agreed that Johnson was the clear winner, the referee thought otherwise and gave the decision to Hart. This devastating loss set Johnson's goal of attaining a championship back several years.

Johnson continued to win, however. His victory over another white boxer, Tommy Burns, on December 26, 1908, in Sydney, Australia, led to pandemonium. Blacks celebrated as angry whites took to the streets. But rather than pronouncing Johnson the new title holder, the crown reverted back to former heavyweight champ James J. Jeffries. Johnson beat Jeffries on July 4, 1910, in Reno, Nevada, and he was finally declared the undisputed heavyweight champion of the world.

Johnson lived well out of the ring, wearing impeccably tailored suits and driving fancy cars. The boxer chose to keep company with white, usually blond women, many of whom were prostitutes. Three of Johnson's four marriages were to white women. This didn't go over well with the boxing establishment nor with the general public who preferred their heroes to be monogamous and to maintain the color line.

Johnson flouted conventional morality. His flamboyant life-style was criticized not only by whites but also by conservative blacks, who found his conduct deeply offensive. Johnson's notoriety inspired the state legislatures of Wisconsin, Iowa, Kansas, Minnesota, New Jersey, Michigan, and New York to introduce bills outlawing interracial marriages.

The bulk of the African-American community, however, still felt a source of pride in Johnson's achievements—if not his exploits. Significantly, the *Chicago Defender*, the city's black newspaper, staunchly supported Johnson.

In 1911 Johnson opened his own cafe, the Cafe de Champion, at 42 West 31st Street, just south of Chicago's red-light district. Then a series of personal tragedies ensued. Johnson's second wife committed suicide, and one of his employees, Adah Banks, shot the boxer in the foot during a dispute over the attentions of a young white girl, Lucille Cameron. Cameron worked as bookkeeper and secretary at Johnson's cafe. Her mother, who resented her daughter's independent spirit, accused Johnson of abducting her. "Jack Johnson," she insisted, "has hypnotic powers, and he has exercised them on my little girl." But Lucille refused to cooperate. Responding to public pressure, the city council passed a resolution denouncing Johnson and urged the revocation of his cafe license. The state of Illinois closed the cafe down shortly thereafter. After the tumult subsided, Jack Johnson and Lucille Cameron were married.

In 1912 Johnson was convicted of violating the Mann Act, which prohibited the transportation of women across state lines for immoral purposes. Johnson allegedly sent money to Belle Schreiber, a former prostitute at the infamous Everleigh Club, so she could return to Chicago from Pittsburgh. Convicted and sentenced to one year and a day in the Joliet penitentiary, he jumped bail and sailed for France.

His flight caused a sensation, and Johnson became the world's most famous fugitive. He resumed his fighting career abroad. In 1915 he fought Jess Willard in Cuba. Willard won by a knockout in the 26th round. Johnson later claimed that he had thrown the fight but then repudiated that story.

For the next four or five years Johnson lived the life of a hobo, moving from country to country. He traveled to Barcelona and talked of starting an advertising agency and then made his debut as a professional matador in July 1916. In 1919 he moved to Mexico where he planned to open a saloon and promote prize fights. Unable to bear the thought of spending the rest of his life in exile, Johnson returned to the United States, surrendering to federal agents in San Diego on July 20, 1920. He was ordered to serve out his term at Leavenworth, Kansas.

After his release ten months later, Johnson returned to the vaudeville circuit, although with less success. In his mid-forties, he reentered the ring, fighting Homer Smith in Montreal, and won in ten rounds. In his later years he appeared at exhibition bouts, but his chief source of income was as a circus attraction. In 1936 he made his operatic debut in a cameo role as a captured general in *Aida* at New York's Hippodrome.

Johnson died in an automobile accident near Raleigh, North Carolina, in 1946. His body was returned to Chicago and buried in Graceland Cemetery.

In 1968 Johnson's colorful life was dramatized in Howard Sackler's popular Broadway play, *The Great White Hope*, starring James Earl Jones in the role of Jack Jefferson, a persecuted black heavyweight champion modeled after Johnson. Jones won the 1969 Tony for best actor. The following year, Jones received an Oscar nomination for his performance in the film version.

Johnson was inducted into boxing's Hall of Fame in 1954.

Further reading: Farr, Finis. *Black Champion: The Life and Times of Jack Johnson* (1964); Johnson, Jack. *Jack Johnson Is A Dandy, An Autobiography* [published posthumously] (1969).

John Jones

Politician

born: circa 1816
Greene County, North Carolina
died: May 27, 1879
Chicago, Illinois

The most eminent African-American of his day, John Jones was reportedly the first black person to hold elected office in Cook County and in the state of Illinois. Jones began his career as a tailor and eventually gained prominence as a civil rights leader and abolitionist in early Chicago.

Photograph courtesy of the *Chicago Defender.*

Jones was born in North Carolina, the son of a freed slave woman and a German man named Bromfield. Jones learned the craft of tailoring from a Mississippian named Richard Clere. He married Mary Richardson in Alton, Illinois, before moving to Chicago in 1845 with a total savings of $3.50. The couple rented a one-room cottage at the corner of Madison and Wells, and Jones opened a small tailor shop a few blocks away. Jones, who taught himself to read and write, prospered making clothes for wealthy white Chicagoans.

Jones often entertained fellow abolitionists, such as Allan Pinkerton, John Brown, and Frederick Douglass, in his home. His shop functioned as one of the stops along the underground railroad, that secret network of farmers, merchants, and clergy, among others, who shepherded thousands of slaves to safety in the North.

By 1871 Jones earned the distinction of being the wealthiest African-American in the Midwest and one of the most affluent in the country. The Chicago Fire, however, reduced his income considerably, although he continued to enjoy a comfortable standard of living.

Jones waged an effective campaign against Illinois's notorious "Black Laws," which deprived African-Americans of the right to testify in courts and forbade them to purchase property. Moreover, an Illinois law prohibited free blacks from settling in the state. In response, Jones wrote a sixteen-page pamphlet in 1864 entitled *The Black Laws of Illinois and a Few Reasons Why They Should Be Repealed.* He made speeches and lobbied the state legislature until these statutes were finally revoked in 1865.

In 1872 Jones was elected to a three-year term to the Cook County Board of Commissioners, winning with significant white support. He was defeated three years later, however.

Jones died in 1879 after a long illness. He was buried in Graceland Cemetery in Chicago.

See also: Allan Pinkerton

Further reading: Bontemps, Arna and Jack Conroy. *Anyplace But Here* (1966); Gosnell, Harold F. *Negro Politicians: The Rise of Negro Politics in Chicago* (1935); Logan, Rayford W. and Michael R. Winston, eds. *Dictionary of American Negro Biography* (1982); Siebert, Wilbur Henry. *The Underground Railroad from Slavery to Freedom* (1967); Spear, Allan H. *Black Chicago: The Making of a Negro Ghetto, 1890–1920* (1967); Travis, Dempsey J. *An Autobiography of Black Chicago* (1981).

Florence Kelley

Social reformer

born: September 12, 1859
Philadelphia, Pennsylvania
died: February 17, 1932
Philadelphia, Pennsylvania

Florence Kelley led the struggle for the passage of pioneering social and labor laws, helped women organize unions, coordinated the campaign to abolish child labor law, and fought to secure minimum wage laws in the United States. Labeled a political radical by her enemies, Kelley was a combative intellectual who used her talents in order to remedy social ills. She especially focused her reform efforts on helping women and children. Although she lived in Chicago only eight years, Kelley left an indelible imprint on the city and its institutions.

Kelley came from a prominent Philadelphia family of Quakers. Her father, a judge and a congressman, was also one of the founders of the Republican party in Pennsylvania. A sickly child, Kelley devoured the English and American classics of literature that lined her father's library shelves. She studied at Cornell University at a time when very few women attended college. Denied permission to enter the School of Law at the University of Pennsylvania, Kelley instead established an evening school for working women in Philadelphia. Later she studied in Leipzig, but again not allowed to graduate, she enrolled at the Law School of Zurich, where exposure to Marxist theory led her to become an ardent socialist and prompted her in 1886 to translate into English Friedrich Engels' *The Condition of the Working-Class in England in 1844.*

After marrying a young Polish-Russian Jewish physician, Lazare Wischnewetsky, the couple moved to New York in 1886 with their infant son. Another son and a daughter were born soon after. Several years later, she divorced her husband and moved with her three children to Chicago, determined to meet Jane Addams and visit the famous house on Halsted Street.

Kelley arrived at Hull-House "on a snowy morning between Christmas 1891 and New Year's 1892 . . . a little before breakfast time," she recalled. Addams put her to work as head of the Hull-House Bureau of Labor, a placement service for young girls.

She stayed for seven years. In her first year at the settlement house, Kelley canvassed the area and was appalled to find the neighborhood surrounded by unventilated, foul-smelling sweatshops and dimly lit, drab tenements. "Shops over sheds or stables, in basements or on upper floors of tenement houses," she wrote, "are not fit working places for men, women, and children."

From this study emerged *Hull-House Papers and Maps*, a devastating piece of investigative reporting that exposed the horrors of the sweatshops to the general public. Her work resulted in the passage of the first factory law in Illinois, which prohibited employment of children under the age of fourteen in the factories. On July 12, 1893, Governor John Peter Altgeld appointed her Chief Factory Inspector, with a staff of twelve. Around this time she registered at the Northwestern University Law School. She graduated in 1894 and was admitted to the Illinois bar. She chose never to practice law, however.

Kelley left Chicago in 1899 to become the general secretary of the National Consumers League in New York, which, under her leadership, became the single most important lobbying group in the nation for social and labor reform. In 1909 she presented the minimum wage idea at the league's annual meeting. By 1913 it had become a national issue. It wasn't until 1938, however, that Congress passed the Fair Labor Standards Act, which established both a national minimum wage and an eight-hour day. Vice-president of the National Woman Suffrage Association for many years, Kelley also served on many important national organizations, including the U. S. Children's Bureau, the National Child Labor Committee, and the General Federation of Women's Clubs.

Because of her belief in socialism, Kelley was the subject of various FBI probes. She died in 1932 at the age of seventy-two before seeing many of her ideals come to fruition. Concepts that once seemed radical—such as the minimum wage and the eight-hour day—are now taken for granted. Through Kelley's pioneering efforts, the dehumanizing effects of industrial capitalism were alleviated.

See also: Grace Abbott, Jane Addams, John Peter Altgeld, Alice Hamilton [appendix], Henry Demarest Lloyd, Ellen Gates Starr [appendix]

Further reading: Addams, Jane. *Twenty Years at Hull-House* (1910); Blumberg, Dorothy Rose. *Florence Kelley: The Making of a Social Pioneer* (1966); Buhle, Mari Jo. *Women and American Socialism* (1979); Carson, Mina. *Settlement Folk: Social Thought and the American Settlement Movement 1885–1930* (1990); Davis, Allen F. and Mary Lynn McCree, eds. *Eighty Years at Hull-House* (1969); Goldmark, Josephine. *Impatient Crusader: Florence Kelley's Life Story* (1953); Preston, William Jr. *Aliens and Dissenters: Federal Suppression of Radicals, 1903–1933* (1963); Sklar, Kathryn Kish, ed. *The Autobiography of Florence Kelley: Notes of Sixty Years* (1986).

Edward J. Kelly

Politician

born: May 1, 1876
Chicago, Illinois
died: October 20, 1950
Chicago, Illinois

Edward Joseph Kelly served as mayor of Chicago for fourteen years, and with Pat Nash, his righthand man, he ran the most powerful political machine in the nation. Stubborn and outspoken with a fierce Irish temper, Kelly was a popular mayor, and with his plush accommodations on the Gold Coast and his elegant wardrobe, he looked and acted the part.

Photograph reprinted with permission from the *Chicago Sun-Times.*

Kelly dropped out of school in the fifth grade to work full-time. At the age of eighteen, this second generation Irishman from Bridgeport got a job with the Chicago Sanitary District where he worked for thirty-nine years. He started humbly enough, chopping down trees on canal banks, but he eventually rose to the post of chief engineer.

Kelly also served as president of the South Park Board. Many major civic improvements occurred during his term: the beautification of Grant Park; the construction of the Shedd Aquarium, the Adler Planetarium, Buckingham Fountain, and Soldier Field; and the renovation of the Museum of Science and Industry. Although situated on the periphery of Chicago politics, Kelly counted a number of influential and high-ranking politicians among his friends, including 28th Ward alderman Patrick A. Nash.

When Mayor Anton J. Cermak was killed by an assassin's bullet in 1933, Cook County Democratic Chairman Nash chose Kelly, an old friend, as the perfect successor. Kelly had never held elected office before. Nash viewed this as an advantage. The new mayor would have executive ability without any political liabilities.

Kelly's administration benefited enormously from New Deal programs. According to historian Michael F. Funchion, "Federal funds allowed the city to build [the State Street] subway and new highways, improve roads and sewage systems, enlarge its airport and construct ten housing projects." Most importantly, Kelly sought early in his term to trim the city's bloated budget, starting with the public schools. The troubled school system was especially hard hit by the Depression. For months teachers did not receive any pay. There was even talk of closing down the schools. Determined to keep them open, Kelly instead embarked on a program of severe belt tightening. He removed all physical education and home economics courses from elementary schools, increased teacher workloads, shortened the school year by one month, slashed teacher's salaries by almost 25 percent, and closed all special schools and departments. Kelly insisted that such drastic action was unfortunate but, short of closing the schools altogether, was necessary.

Kelly turned the city into a smooth, efficiently run machine and was reelected in 1935 in a landslide. Such efficiency, however, came at a high price. Money was needed to run the city, to provide the services, and to maintain the quality of life. For this, according to historian Roger Biles, Kelly and the Democratic machine turned to the seemingly unlimited resources of organized crime. According to some estimates, the city received approximately twenty million dollars a year in illegal revenue, much of it from gambling. Another source of financial assistance came from the Roosevelt White House. Roosevelt not only admired Kelly's political astuteness, he also enjoyed his company and invited him to luncheons and social gatherings.

Kelly lured a large share of black voters away from the Republican party. He ceased the police harrassment of black gambling operations that was so prevalent during Cermak's term in office, and, according to Funchion, "he appointed some blacks to influential positions in city government, and he dispensed patronage jobs to them in greater numbers than any previous Chicago mayor." Kelly's courting of the black vote was not simply politics. He took

several unpopular stands, such as advocating school integration and open housing, which angered many white voters. "The time is not far away when we shall forget the color of a man's skin and see him only in the light of intelligence of his mind and soul," he said.

Kelly was reelected in 1939 and 1943, but the death of his friend and colleague, Pat Nash, in 1943 came as a devastating blow. The affable Nash had acted as a peacemaker. Without his diplomatic skills, dissension ran unchecked in the city council. Kelly's fierce temper and occasional high-handedness further exacerbated matters.

A series of scandals, erratic garbage collection and street cleaning, police corruption, and high taxes brought down the once popular mayor, but Biles suggests that it was Kelly's stubborn commitment to open housing (a housing situation in which people of all races and creeds live in the neighborhoods of their choice), that galvanized the city's ethnics against him and guaranteed his political demise.

Top Democrats, unhappy with Kelly's choice of candidates for the 1946 election, chose former 24th Ward alderman Jacob Arvey as the new party leader. They convinced Kelly to resign in favor of another Bridgeport Irishman, Martin J. Kennelly.

When Kennelly won the mayoral election, Kelly retired from public life, content to play the role of elder statesman. In 1950, during a routine examination in his doctor's office, Kelly suffered a fatal heart attack. He was buried in Calvary Cemetery in Evanston.

Kelly expanded the power and influence of the Democratic machine, attracting into its fold groups that had been ignored or taken for granted

by earlier administrations. Kelly laid the foundation for the broad-based support and success of the Daley administration.

See also: Jacob Arvey, Anton J. Cermak, Richard J. Daley

Further reading: Biles, Roger. *Big City Boss in Depression and War: Mayor Edward J. Kelly of Chicago* (1984); Funchion, Michael F. "Political and Nationalist Dimensions" in *The Irish in Chicago,* Lawrence McCaffrey et al, eds. (1987); Levine, Edward M. *The Irish and Irish Politicians* (1966).

Michael Kenna

Politician

born: August 20, 1857
Chicago, Illinois
died: October 19, 1946
Chicago, Illinois

For more than four decades Michael "Hinky Dink" Kenna, the tight-lipped Democratic boss of the 1st Ward, controlled the purse strings of a segregated area of brothels and saloons just south of the Loop known as the Levee. His aldermanic partner in vice, John "Bathhouse" Coughlin, may have received most of the attention, but Kenna quietly ran the show.

Photograph reprinted with permission from the *Chicago Sun-Times.*

Michael Kenna was born in a frame shack at the edge of an Irish neighborhood, commonly referred to as Connelly's Patch (sometimes Conley's Patch), that ran from 12th to 16th Streets and from Michigan Avenue to the lake. He left school at the age of ten and began hawking newspapers on State Street, running errands for saloonkeepers, and striking up friendships with madames and hostesses. Already quite an aggressive entrepreneur, he purchased a newsstand at Monroe and Dearborn Streets at age twelve.

Kenna was a loner who thirsted for adventure. In 1880 he made his way to Leadville, Colorado, which had earned a reputation as wild and untamed. Carrying a letter of recommendation from *Chicago Tribune* publisher Joseph Medill, Kenna landed a position as circulation manager of the *Lake County Reveille.* He stayed in Leadville for two years, but the continual violence—shootings and street brawls were commonplace—persuaded him to return to Chicago.

Back in town, he opened a saloon, the Workingmen's Exchange, at Clark and Van Buren Streets, and became something of a political operator, working quietly behind the scenes and making his presence felt. He dutifully supported John Coughlin for alderman of the 1st Ward. With the twilight of Mike McDonald, Chicago's first underworld kingpin, Kenna saw his opportunity. All he needed was a friend in the city council; Coughlin was his man.

It was a strange match—the brash, loud, outspoken Coughlin and the morose, distant, and somber Kenna. Kenna was a devout teetotaler and was regarded as an exemplary husband, while Coughlin, although no philanderer, did enjoy an occasional nip from the bottle. Despite their differences both men seemed to need each other. Kenna laid the groundwork for a political organization that would be built on graft, corruption, and thievery, whose membership included a network of pimps, gamblers, saloonkeepers, and brothel owners. In return for protection against police raids, Kenna demanded their loyalty, and most importantly, their votes. Kenna also gained the votes of the 1st Ward homeless and residents of boarding houses. It was a foolproof plan, and it worked beautifully.

Kenna soon itched for a seat of his own in the city council. He lost in 1895, but his next attempt was more successful. He trounced the Republican incumbent of the 1st Ward, Francis "Paddy" Gleason in 1897.

Kenna's saloon at Clark and Van Buren Streets was the real seat of 1st Ward politics. Here he would hang out with "the boys," conducting business and plotting schemes. Upstairs was a boarding house that was always full—it reportedly could hold as many as three hundred men. On one side of Kenna's barroom stood a table heaped with free food, which his customers consumed appreciatively. The "free lunch" bought a lot of votes in its day. As Prohibition loomed ahead, however, Kenna's famous saloon was shut down and transformed into a combination candy, sandwich, and cigar store.

When an ordinance was passed providing for one alderman per ward in 1923, Kenna agreed to step down and left John "Bathhouse" Coughlin to take care of business. He did, however, retain his title of Democratic ward committeeman, and he continued to wield his power until Coughlin's death in 1938, although in a diminished capacity, for as early as the mid-twenties a violent pall characterized 1st Ward politics as people like Johnny Torrio and Al Capone began to take over.

With his partner gone, Kenna was persuaded, although over eighty, to run for Coughlin's old seat in 1939. Kenna ran and won. For a while he dutifully attended sessions at city hall until, one day, he stopped coming altogether. In his place, he sent his secretary.

Kenna retired from active political life in 1943 and spent the last years of his life in seclusion in various downtown hotels. He died at the age of eighty-nine in the Blackstone Hotel.

See also: Mathias "Paddy" Bauler, Al Capone, John Coughlin, Ada and Minna Everleigh, Carter Harrison I, Carter Harrison II

Further reading: Kogan, Herman and Lloyd Wendt. *Lords of the Levee : The Story of Bathhouse John and Hinky Dink* (1943).

Charles H. Kerr

Publisher

born: April 23, 1860
LaGrange, Georgia
died: June 1, 1944
Los Angeles, California

Charles Hope Kerr published socialist and labor books, novels, magazines, and pamphlets in Chicago, a city that by the late nineteenth century had earned the reputation as the center of leftist publishing in the English-speaking world. Today the company he founded in 1886 is the oldest labor publishing house in the United States.

Photograph courtesy of Charles H. Kerr Publishing Company.

Kerr was the son of Congregational liberals. His father, Alexander Kerr, was born in Scotland but immigrated with his family to Illinois in 1838. After graduating from Beloit College, Wisconsin, in 1855, Kerr found work as a schoolteacher in LaGrange, Georgia, seventy miles from Atlanta. Following the outbreak of the Civil War, Kerr, a dedicated abolitionist, his wife, and his infant son, Charles, fled along the Underground Railroad, a secret network that carried runaway slaves and sympathizers to safety in the North. In 1871 the elder Kerr accepted a position as chairman of the classics department at the University of Wisconsin at Madison. Charles grew up in Rockford, Illinois, and Madison, Wisconsin, and graduated from the University of Wisconsin at Madison in 1881 with a degree in Romance languages. He then settled in Chicago.

Kerr began his career as a clerk in the independent publishing firm of James Colegrove, which specialized in Unitarian books and tracts and published *Unity*, a socialist magazine. In 1883 Kerr began working on the magazine. When the Colegrove company dissolved in 1886, Kerr established his own firm, Charles H. Kerr and Company and took over *Unity*. Growing disillusioned, he left the magazine in 1893 to become the publisher of a radical Unitarian magazine, *New Occasions*.

In 1894 Kerr published *The Pullman Strike*, Rev. William H. Carwardine's classic inside account of the Pullman strike and its devastating effect on both the town and the labor movement.

In 1899 Kerr allied himself with the burgeoning socialist movement, joining the Chicago branch of the Socialist Party of America in 1901. Around this time, the Kerr Company began billing itself as a "Socialist Cooperative Publishing House." Kerr helped establish a socialist school, Ruskin College (named after a workingmen's college in Oxford, England) in Glen Ellyn, Illinois. In 1900 Kerr launched a new monthly, the *International Socialist Review*. The *Review*, promised Kerr, sought "to counteract the sentimental Utopianism that has so long characterized the American movement." The concept of utopianism, which took its name from the title of Thomas More's futuristic novel *Utopia*, refers to the belief that humankind can learn to live in an ideal state. The *Review* soon became the leading socialist journal in the country. The *Review's* top-flight contributors included Eugene Debs, Elizabeth Gurley Flynn, Mary Harris "Mother" Jones, folksinger Joe Hill, Helen Keller, John Reed, and its most prominent names, Jack London and Carl Sandburg.

In 1899 Kerr began publishing his "pocket library of socialism," including Clarence Darrow's *Realism in Literature and Art*, Jack London's *The Scab*, and Upton Sinclair's *Our Bourgeois Literature: The Reason and the Remedy*. The company also published the works of Mother Jones, Mary E. Marcy, and William "Big Bill" Haywood and issued the English-language edition of Karl Marx's *Das Kapital* as well as the writings of Lenin, Trotsky, and Irish labor leader James Connolly.

Yet Kerr didn't just publish socialist tracts. The company also released alternative titles, including books on animal rights, the first book in the United States on the Baha'i faith, and a fair number of utopian, science-fiction, and fantasy novels.

Impatient with the methodical and overly cautious tactics of the socialist agenda, Kerr turned his support to the Industrial Workers of the World, who like him, vehemently opposed America's participation in World War I. Such so-called treasonous talk prompted the postmaster general to refuse to send the *International Socialist Review* through the mails in adherence to the Espionage Act, which forbade any materials inciting "treason, insurrection, or forcible resistance to any law of the United States." It was censorship at its most effective and it, for all intents and purposes, shut down the magazine.

Growing increasingly frustrated with the conservatism of the socialist movement, Kerr left Chicago and the company he founded, in 1928. That year Scots-born John Keracher, head of the Proletarian party, assumed control of the company. Kerr retired to Los Angeles where he died in June of 1944 at age eighty-four.

In 1986 the Charles H. Kerr Company celebrated its centennial, publishing eleven new titles, including *The Haymarket Scrapbook*. From its headquarters at 1740 West Greenleaf Avenue in Rogers Park, the company continues to reissue old radical classics and publish new works.

See also: John Peter Altgeld, Clarence Darrow, Eugene Debs, William "Big Bill" Haywood [appendix], Henry Demarest Lloyd, Mary E. Marcy [appendix], Lucy and Albert Parsons, Allan Pinkerton, George Pullman, Carl Sandburg

Further reading: Maass, Alan. "The Little Red Book House," *Chicago Reader* (October 17, 1986); Roediger, Dave and Franklin Rosemont, eds. *Haymarket Scrapbook* (1986); Ruff, Allen M. "Socialist Publishing in Illinois: Charles H. Kerr & Company of Chicago, 1886–1928," *Illinois Historical Journal* (Spring 1986).

John Kinzie

Pioneer

born: circa 1763
Quebec
died: January 6, 1828
Chicago, Illinois

Often called the "Father of Chicago," John Kinzie was Chicago's first permanent white settler. A trader by profession, he was a man respected both by his fellow whites and by the Indians.

Born in Quebec, Kinzie was the son of John McKenzie (also spelled McKinzie), a British army surgeon. Shortly after John's birth, his parents moved to Detroit, where his father died. As a young boy, Kinzie ran away and made his way back to Quebec, where he became an apprentice to a silversmith. He roamed the forests and developed a friendly relationship with the Indians, trapping and trading and producing buckles and bracelets. He mastered their language and earned a reputation among them as fair and trustworthy.

Kinzie established business connections in Sandusky and Maumee, Ohio, and as far west as St. Joseph, Michigan, and he later became an Indian trader in Detroit.

Kinzie arrived in Chicago in 1804 and almost immediately established friendly relations with the native population. Indeed, the Kinzie family became the outpost's leading citizens. Jacqueline Peterson in *Ethnic Chicago* refers to Kinzie as "unquestionably the most powerful man" in Chicago from 1804 to 1812.

Kinzie sold supplies to the soldiers at Fort Dearborn and bought furs from the Indians, but squabbles among the traders did occur. Kinzie was on bad terms, for example, with the Indian interpreter Jean Lalime. During a confrontation in April of 1812, Lalime reportedly shot Kinzie in the shoulder. Kinzie retaliated by fatally stabbing Lalime. One theory is that Lalime attacked Kinzie in a fit of jealousy over the trader's success. Another argued that Kinzie was the aggressor. Whatever the truth, an inquiry was held and Kinzie was acquitted.

On August 9, 1812, instructions from Detroit reached Capt. Nathan Heald, the commander at Fort Dearborn, to evacuate the garrison, which had come under threat of a possible Indian attack, and to proceed to Fort Wayne, Indiana. Kinzie argued against evacuation, maintaining that it was safer to remain in the fort rather than risk journeying through hostile Indian territory. Capt. William Wells, a noted Indian scout, arrived with twenty-seven Miami Indians as escorts for the journey.

Concerned for his family's safety, Kinzie placed his wife and four children on a boat. He, however, accompanied Capt. Wells and the rest of the party headed for Fort Wayne. On August 15, 1812, one of the most tragic episodes in Chicago history occurred. Five hundred Indians—mostly Potawatomi—attacked the procession less than two miles from the fort and near what is now 1600 South Indiana Avenue. Twenty-six soldiers (according to some sources, twenty-eight), including Wells, twelve children, and two women were slain.

Theories as to the reason for the attack vary. Historian Allan Eckert argues that the Indians attacked for military purposes. The War of 1812 had just begun, and the Indians were allies of the British; Fort Dearborn was an important, strategically located base and, therefore, an obvious military target.

After the fighting, Kinzie's wife, Eleanor, returned to her house with the children and hid under feather mattresses. When Kinzie returned, unharmed, the Indians threatened to kill him until Billy Caldwell—the half-Potawatomi and half-Irish chief—interceded. After the fighting subsided, Kinzie and his family fled by boat to the safety of Detroit.

Kinzie returned to Chicago in 1816 and resumed his Indian business, partly on his own and partly as an employee of the American Fur Company. He never regained his former status, however. Kinzie died in Chicago in January of 1828 at age sixty-five.

Subsequent generations of Kinzies exerted considerable influence in the city so that by 1832, notes historian Peterson, "Kinzie was once again the foremost name in Chicago."

See also: Jean Baptiste Pointe du Sable, Gurdon S. Hubbard

Further reading: Andreas, A. T. *History of Chicago from the Earliest Period to the Present Time.* 3 vols. (1884–86); Currey, Josiah Seymour. *The Story of Old Fort Dearborn* (1912); Eckert, Allan. *Gateway to Empire* (1982); Kinzie, Juliette A. *Wau Bun, the "Early Days" of the Northwest* (1901); Peterson, Jacqueline. "The Founding Fathers: The Absorption of French-Indian Chicago 1816–1837" in *Ethnic Chicago*, Melvin G. Holli and Peter d'A. Jones, eds. (1984); Pierce, Bessie Louise. *A History of Chicago.* 3 vols. (1937–57); Quaife, Milo. *Chicago and the Old Northwest, 1673–1835* (1913).

James L. Kraft

Entrepreneur

born: December 11, 1874
Fort Erie, Ontario
died: February 16, 1953
Chicago, Illinois

James Lewis Kraft, a Canadian immigrant, revolutionized the packaging and merchandising of cheese and cheese products. He experimented until the Kraft company produced an item that had longer shelf life, a more uniform flavor, and a taste that appealed to millions of consumers.

The son of Minerva and George Franklin Kraft, Kraft attended school in Ontario. At age sixteen he left home to earn money for his financially strapped family, peddling eggs in hotels and retail shops across the border in Buffalo, New York. In Buffalo he attended a business class, walking the twelve miles from the school to his home in Ontario.

When he was eighteen, Kraft found work at a grocery shop in Fort Erie and saved enough money to establish his own ice business. It collapsed, however. Then he invested in a Buffalo cheese company and moved to Chicago in 1903 to manage the regional branch. When his partners phased him out, Kraft, with only $65 capital to his name, rented a wagon and a horse named Paddy and bought a supply of cheese from a wholesaler and resold it. By the end of the first year, Kraft was $3,000 in debt. "In those days people didn't care very much for cheese," Kraft said in 1931. "Our national per capita consumption was less than one pound a year. And that was easy to understand for American-made cheese of that day was an uncertain commodity. You bought it in chunks—and no chunk was ever like another." Kraft continued working as a cheese retailer and the business slowly began to prosper.

In 1909 the business was incorporated as J. L. Kraft and Brothers Company. In 1916 Kraft acquired a patent to make a pasteurized processed cheese, a product that could be shipped long distances without spoilage. During World War I, the United States government ordered more than six million tons of Kraft cheese to feed its hungry, war-weary soldiers on the front. The cheese business boomed, and in 1911 Kraft became an American citizen.

In 1924 the first Kraft test kitchen was established. Four years later, the company merged with the Phenix Corporation, which included Philadelphia Brand cream cheese. By the end of 1929, the company owned more than fifty subsidiaries with operations in Canada, Australia, England, and Germany. In 1930 Kraft became a subsidiary of National Dairy Products Corporation, and Kraft became chairman of the board in 1943. Two years later, the company name became Kraft Foods Company. In 1986 Dart and Kraft, a multinational food, consumer, and commercial products company, split into two companies— Kraft and Premark International, and in 1988 Kraft became a subsidiary of Philip Morris Companies.

Kraft produced a diverse line of products. The company introduced Miracle Whip salad dressing in 1933, Kraft macaroni and cheese dinners in 1936, and Parkay margarine in 1937. The firm also manufactured caramels, marshmallows, and ice cream toppings.

Kraft used innovative advertising methods to sell his products. He was among the first businessmen to advertise in consumer journals, for example, and an early promoter of full-color advertisements in national magazines such as *Ladies Home Journal* and *Good Housekeeping*. In 1933 the company entered show biz when it sponsored a two-hour musical and variety radio program, the "Kraft Musical Revue," which eventually became "Kraft Music Hall." In 1948 the "Kraft Television Theatre" premiered on the NBC television network.

A devout Baptist and an active member of the North Shore Baptist Church at 5244 North Lakewood Avenue, Kraft was the president and treasurer of the International Council of Religious Education and chairman of the organization committee of the Council's Crusade for Christian Education.

Over the years Kraft accumulated an impressive collection of carved Chinese jade pieces. In the process, he became quite an expert on the subject and wrote a book about it, *Adventure in Jade*, in 1947.

Kraft died at the age of seventy-eight in Chicago in February of 1953.

In 1972 the Kraft corporate office moved to northwest suburban Glenview, Illinois.

Further reading: Heise, Kenan and Michael Edgerton. *Chicago: Center for Enterprise.* 2 vols. (1982).

Ray Kroc

Entrepreneur

born: October 5, 1902
Chicago, Illinois
died: January 14, 1984
La Jolla, California

Ray Albert Kroc, a high school dropout and former paper cup salesman, sold billions of hamburgers in over thirty countries in his lifetime and, in so doing, helped change the eating habits of the American public. "McDonald's is not a restaurant. It's a hamburger business. It's a religion," he used to say. The secret of success, suggested Kroc, is not intelligence, education, or even talent, but self-discipline. McDonald's, the world's largest restaurant chain, operates approximately twelve thousand outlets in fifty-two countries.

Photograph reprinted with permission from the *Chicago Sun-Times*.

Kroc always considered himself a regular guy. "I've never liked codfish aristocrats or society," he said. Once described as the service sector's equivalent of Henry Ford, Kroc was the son of a real estate agent. He dropped out of Oak Park-River Forest High School when he was fifteen and served with the Red Cross Ambulance Corps in France during World War I. Fellow Chicagoan and friend, Walt Disney, was in the same unit.

A music lover, Kroc spent a brief time playing jazz piano professionally. When he was nineteen, he joined the vaudeville circuit with his partner, Harry Sosnick. It was a short-lived but lucrative relationship, bringing in $150 a week. At the age of twenty, Kroc turned away from the arts, married, and got a respectable job selling paper cups. It didn't last long. He soon quit and got a job as musical director of Chicago radio station WGES. He then moved to Florida to sell real estate and lost everything. "I was stone broke. I didn't have an overcoat, a topcoat, or a pair of gloves," he recalled.

In 1926 Kroc returned to Chicago and went back to selling cups for the Lily Tulip Cup Company.

In the late 1930s, Kroc had become the sole distributor of a soda fountain machine, called Multimixer, that was able to mix five milkshakes simultaneously. A short-order restaurant in San Bernardino, California, owned by Dick and Mac McDonald, had purchased eight of Kroc's machines—an unusually high number. Curious about this, Kroc decided to visit the restaurant. He was impressed with what he saw. "They had people standing in line, clamoring for more," he recalled.

Kroc tried to talk the brothers into opening a chain of hamburger stands so he could supply them with his milkshake makers. They balked at the suggestion but agreed to allow Kroc to franchise the restaurant and their small chain of hamburger stands for 0.5 percent of the gross.

On April 15, 1955, Kroc opened the first McDonald's franchise at 400 Lee Street in Des Plaines, Illinois. It was a tiny red-and-white tiled building without seats or bathrooms. In those days hamburgers sold for 15 cents and french fries for 10 cents.

In 1961 Kroc founded the McDonald Corporation and bought out the McDonald brothers for $2.7 million. The first year the company grossed $6 million. By 1969 it had leapfrogged to $266 million. In 1962 Hamburger University, the McDonald's training school, was opened in Elk Grove Village, Illinois.

Kroc's populist policies made the Oakbrook-based McDonald's Corporation one of the most progressive businesses in the country. His door, he insisted, was always open. "He liked being treated like one of the boys," said Fred Turner, a McDonald's corporate executive.

McDonald's changed the leisure habits of the average American by making eating out inexpensive, fast, and enjoyable. Kroc did not invent the fast-food business—there were other fast-food franchises in the mid-fifties such as Burger King, Kentucky Fried Chicken, and Chicken Delight, already in existence—but McDonald's did dominate the industry to such an extent that the Golden Arches has become an integral part of American popular culture. "Slightly more than half of the U.S. population lives within a three-minute drive to a McDonald's unit," notes John F. Love in his book *McDonald's Behind the Arches*. By insisting upon uniform standards of cleanliness, quality, and quick service,

Kroc revolutionized the food industry. With few exceptions—such as an upscale McDonald's in lower Manhattan that aggressively caters to an adult clientele—a McDonald's restaurant in Portland, Maine, is virtually indistinguishable from a McDonald's restaurant in Portland, Oregon.

In 1974 Kroc bought the San Diego Padres, after his attempt to buy the Chicago Cubs, his favorite baseball team, failed. Kroc was a controversial owner. Tempestuous and hot-tempered, he scolded his players over the public address system on opening day of his first home game for "putting on a lousy show . . . [with] the most stupid baseball playing I've ever seen." He later apologized.

In 1976 Kroc bought the San Diego Mariners hockey team but sold them one year later.

Kroc donated generously to charities through the Kroc Foundation. He received the Horatio Alger award in 1972. One of the charitable programs that Kroc helped found is the Ronald McDonald House, which provides free or low-cost lodging at a nearby hospital for families with children requiring extended care. There are 116 Ronald McDonald Houses in the U.S. and 24 abroad. The first Ronald McDonald House opened in Philadelphia in 1974. There are two in Chicago—622 West Deming Place on the North Side, which opened in 1977, and 5736 South Drexel Avenue on the South Side, which opened in 1986.

Since the early seventies McDonald's has successfully exported its brand of Americana overseas. Today the golden arches are a familiar sight at more than 3,000 outlets throughout the world, from Vancouver to London, Sydney to Tokyo, and Paris to Moscow.

Kroc died in his La Jolla, California, home at the age of eighty-one in 1984. Only seven weeks after his death, the original McDonald's in Des Plaines—too small to accommodate seating or the requisite drive-through window—was shut down. A new and bigger McDonald's was built directly across the street.

"I can tell you I have never worked a day in my life," Kroc said in 1973. "Work is something you hate to do. To do what you love is not work."

See also: Ike Sewell [appendix]

Further reading: Kroc, Ray with Robert Anderson. *Grinding It Out: The Making of McDonald's* (1977); Love, John F. *McDonald's Behind the Arches* (1986).

Gene Krupa

Musician

born: June 15, 1909
Chicago, Illinois
died: October 16, 1973
Yonkers, New York

A pioneering jazz drummer, Gene Krupa, epitomized the Chicago style of jazz with his relentless beat and showy stage personality. Krupa's frenetic drumming never failed to stir the audience.

Photograph courtesy of the Chicago Historical Society.

Of German and Polish extraction, Krupa grew up on the South Side around 88th Street and Commercial Avenue. One night in 1925 his older sister took him to meet drummer Roy C. Knapp, a studio musician and highly respected music teacher, at the Capitol Theater at 7941 South Halsted Street. Krupa wanted to learn timpani "but I talked him into studying drums," recalled Knapp years later. Krupa studied with Knapp for several years.

"Chicago was a real training ground," Krupa noted. "Great drummers like Baby Dodds, George Wettling, Zutty Singleton, Tubby Hall, and Davey Tough were playing all around at clubs like the Sunset or the Grand Terrace or Kelly's Stables."

Krupa was particularly influenced by Dave Tough. Ironically, after Tough left for Europe, Krupa was asked to join the legendary Austin High Gang (a group of jazz musicians who attended Austin High School on the West Side and modeled their intense style of playing after Louis Armstrong and Joe "King" Oliver) even though he attended a different school, Bowen High on the South Side.

In December of 1927 Krupa, along with Frank Teschemacher, Jimmy McPartland, Bud Freeman, Joe Sullivan, Jim Lannigan, and Eddie Condon, recorded four tunes— "Liza," "Nobody's Sweetheart," "China Boy," and "Sugar"—that are considered the epitome of what came to be called the Chicago style of jazz, an energetic, highly rhythmic music that, in the jargon of the day, could really "swing."

In 1929 Krupa moved to New York to work with trumpet player and bandleader Red Nichols and then began to gig and record with the likes of Benny Goodman and Bix Beiderbecke. In 1936 Krupa appeared with Goodman, pianist Teddy

Wilson, and vibraphone player Lionel Hampton at the Congress Hotel in what is considered the first performance by a racially integrated group in a downtown Chicago hotel. "We didn't worry about what would happen," Krupa confided to jazz critic Harriet Choice in 1973. "A guy was either a good musician or a bad one, and we just got out there and played." Krupa formed his own outfit in 1938. Backed by singer Anita O'Day and trumpeter Roy Eldridge, Krupa's group became one of the most popular swing bands of its day.

In 1943 Krupa was arrested and sentenced to ninety days in San Quentin for contributing to the delinquency of a minor. Accounts of the episode vary. According to newspaper reports, Krupa had sent his valet, still a minor, to fetch his marijuana cigarettes. Another account asserts that Krupa, tipped off by a friend of an imminent police search, warned his valet to dispose of any marijuana. Instead the valet retained possession of what he had found. Others say it was a set-up, that Krupa had refused to pay off crooked cops. Whatever the exact circumstances, the incident damaged Krupa's career, soiled his reputation among his fans, and caused severe financial strain. Benny Goodman extended his full support and Krupa, uncertain of the long-term effect of the episode on his career, accepted Goodman's gracious offer to rejoin the band. After touring with Goodman and later with Tommy Dorsey's orchestra, Krupa formed his own big band in 1944. He led several combos sporadically throughout the fifties.

In 1960 Krupa suffered a heart attack but continued to play throughout the sixties and early seventies. In 1959 a Hollywood film was made of his life, *The Gene Krupa Story*, starring Sal Mineo in the title role.

To borrow a jazz term, Krupa was a "hot" drummer. Krupa's aggressive style evolved from the music of New Orleans marching bands, especially the drumming of Zutty Singleton and Warren "Baby" Dodds, musicians who had moved to Chicago and played in South Side clubs. Music historian Donald Clarke calls him the "original model" of today's rock drummer. Krupa's hair-flying, arms flailing, gum-chewing performances made a tremendous impact on audiences. Some critics felt that his showy style—booming bass and noisy snares—was too overbearing and complained that his loud and frenzied drumming tended to drown out other instruments. He is credited, however, with focusing public attention on the drum as a solo instrument. Benny Goodman himself once called Krupa "without doubt" his favorite drummer.

Krupa died from leukemia in 1973. He was sixty-four. Several days after his death his body was flown back to Chicago where a high mass was held at the Immaculate Conception Church, 2944 East 88th Street in his old neighborhood. He was buried at the family plot in Holy Cross Cemetery in Calumet City, Illinois.

See also: Bud Freeman, Benny Goodman

Further reading: Charters, Samuel B. and Leonard Kunstadt. *Jazz: A History of the New York Scene* (1981); Clarke, Donald. *The Penguin Encyclopedia of Popular Music* (1989); Collier, James Lincoln. *Benny Goodman and the Swing Era* (1989).

Kenesaw Mountain Landis

Judge/ Baseball Commissioner

born: November 20, 1866
Millville, Ohio
died: November 25, 1944
Chicago, Illinois

Some thought he was baseball's worst commissioner, others thought he was the best. Whatever the opinion, Judge Kenesaw Mountain Landis couldn't be ignored. Baseball commissioner from 1921 until his death in 1944, Landis was called a bully, a buffoon, a flamboyant publicity seeker, and a man in love with his own name and reputation. No one could deny, however, that he was baseball's greatest fan.

Landis was born of Swiss and German ancestry on an Ohio farm. His father, Dr. Abraham Landis, had served as a surgeon in the Union Army and named his newborn son after the Battle of Kennesaw Mountain (the second 'n' was dropped in his son's name), which took place in northwestern Georgia on June 27, 1864.

The Landis family moved to Indiana when Kenesaw was eight. As a young man he got a job on a local newspaper and also played amateur and semipro baseball. A self-starter and intrigued by the legal profession, he taught himself the new art of shorthand and secured a position as an official court reporter for the Cass County Circuit Court. He enrolled in the YMCA Law School of Cincinnati, completed his degree at the Union Law School in Chicago in 1891, and was admitted to the Illinois bar in the same year. The eager lawyer opened his own practice shortly thereafter.

Landis received a big career boost in 1892 when he was chosen as secretary to Judge Walter Q. Gresham, then secretary of state in the administration of President Grover Cleveland. He returned to Chicago after Gresham died in 1895 and resumed his law practice.

Landis always expressed an interest in politics. He managed the unsuccessful gubernatorial campaign of Frank O. Lowden in 1904. Even though Lowden didn't win, Landis's work attracted the attention of Theodore Roosevelt. In 1905 Roosevelt appointed the thirty-eight-year-old Landis to the United States District Court for the Northern District of Illinois.

As judge, he often stood squarely on the side of conservatism—albeit a conservatism tempered with his own idiosyncratic streaks of defiance. He advocated firing squads for German spies caught in America. He sentenced Wobbly (a nickname for

Industrial Workers of the World, the influential labor organization founded in Chicago in 1905) William "Big Bill" Haywood to twenty years in prison for condemning the nation's war effort during World War I, but then he angered the business community by fining the Standard Oil Company a whopping $29,240,000 in 1907 for violations in a freight-rebate case. This decision was later reversed by the Supreme Court.

Landis earned a reputation as an outspoken magistrate whose outrageous behavior on the bench raised eyebrows among the more sedate members of the profession. He blurted out whatever came into his head. Indeed, his courtroom etiquette was far from what was considered proper. When an elderly offender protested that his sentence was too severe by saying "I'm a sick man. I can't do five years." Landis, with little sympathy, rebutted, "Well, you can try, can't you?"

The shocking circumstances surrounding the 1919 "Black Sox" scandal resulted in efforts to "clean up" the game and to renew public confidence in the national sport. Landis was elected baseball's first commissioner in 1920—he took office in 1921— to serve a period of seven years. He refused to relinquish his judgeship, but when threatened with impeachment for holding both the position of federal judge and the position of baseball commissioner, he resigned from the bench.

From the start, Landis was a controversial figure. He banned the eight White Sox players associated with the "Black Sox" scandal from baseball, even though they had been acquitted in a court of law. "Regardless of the verdict of juries, no player that throws a ball game . . . will ever play professional baseball!" declared an angry Landis. He made many enemies and received many threats, but he remained fearless. "I have no yellow streak," he boasted.

Throughout his tenure, he remained a devout baseball fan. Two days before the World Series of 1944, Landis entered St. Luke's Hospital for a general check-up. He was too ill to attend the game, the first World Series he had missed since taking office in 1921. A little more than a week after he was reelected to his final seven-year term, Landis died.

See also: Charles A. Comiskey

Further reading: Spink, J. G. Taylor. *Judge Landis and Twenty-Five Years of Baseball* (1947).

Ring Lardner

Humorist/Journalist

born: March 6, 1885
Niles, Michigan
died: September 25, 1933
East Hampton, New York

A prolific sports writer, Ringgold Wilmer Lardner wrote darkly sardonic stories in the American vernacular. He had a good ear for the way his fellow citizens talked. He composed usually in the first person and adopted the idiom of the common folk, accurately reflecting the dialect of everyday speech. In the words of one writer, Lardner made "a literary style out of bad English." His baseball stories won him a national following and along with George Ade and Finley Peter Dunne, he ranks as one of Chicago's great humorists.

Lardner received a wealthy upbringing in Niles, Michigan, five miles north of the Indiana border. After graduating from high school, Ring (he never went by Ringgold) held a series of inconsequential jobs. His father, concerned that young Lardner would become an incorrigible roustabout, sent him off to the Armour Institute of Technology in Chicago to study mechanical engineering.

Lardner displayed no talent for nor any interest in engineering, and he returned to Niles in 1905, landing a job as a sportswriter for the *South Bend Times*. Lardner covered baseball during its infancy, when the game wasn't very respectable, populated as it was, claims biographer Jonathan Yardley, by crude, unsophisticated men who drank too much but had the good fortune to be able to throw, catch, or hit a ball. To Lardner and thousands of other young men and boys of his generation—as Yardley points out, there were very few women in the ballpark stands in those days—the players were heroes just the same.

When Lardner entered journalism, sports writing was a dull, usually anonymous occupation (he received no by line during his early years with the *South Bend Times*). He injected life into the characters and portrayed the game he loved so dearly as "clean, honorable, ordered, subtle, intricate, beautiful, somehow natural," according to Yardley.

Lardner's peripatetic career in journalism included many stops in many towns on many papers. He worked briefly in Chicago for the *Inter-Ocean* and the *Examiner* before coming to the *Chicago Tribune*, in 1909. In December of 1910 he joined *Sporting News* in St. Louis as editor, then jumped to the *Boston American* as baseball correspondent in February of 1911 before returning to Chicago and accepting a desk job on the *Chicago American*. He became a baseball reporter for the *Chicago Examiner* in 1912, and finally, from 1913 to 1919, he wrote the sports column for the *Chicago Tribune*, "In the Wake of the News," that made him famous.

Lardner was only twenty-eight when he took over "In the Wake of the News" column from the late Hugh E. Keough. It was a popular feature of the paper, and Lardner did his best to live up to his predecessor's high standards. During the first four years, he turned out a column seven days a week.

In 1914 a series of letters from "Jack Keefe," a fictitious pitcher for the Chicago White Sox, was published in the *Saturday Evening Post*. The series later appeared in *You Know Me, Al* in 1916. The book was so popular that Lardner followed it up with more collections, *Treat 'Em Rough* in 1918 and *The Real Dope* in 1919.

Disillusioned with baseball after the "Black Sox" scandal of 1919, Lardner wrote a devilishly wicked parody of the song "I'm Forever Blowing Bubbles."

I'm forever throwing ball games
Pretty ball games in the air
I come from Chi
I hardly try—
Just go to bat and fade and die.

In 1919 Lardner left the *Tribune* and moved to the East Coast and settled in Greenwich, Connecticut. He began writing the nationally syndicated "Ring Lardner's Weekly Letter." He enjoyed tremendous freedom to write about whatever he wanted—his family, his travels, life among the rich and famous, politics—but he almost never wrote about sports. In 1922, however, he agreed to work on a comic strip version of *You Know Me, Al* for the Bell Syndicate in New York.

Even after moving to New York, Lardner often wrote variations of the Chicago characters and situations that had made him famous. Instead of satirizing big city mores, however, he mocked the hypocrisy of small town America.

In 1928, Lardner wrote a four-times-a-week column for the *New York Morning Telegraph* called "Ring's Side." By this time, though, he was physically and psychologically spent, and the heavy drinking he had done most of his life was beginning to show. The magic was gone and the strain proved too much. Even so, in 1931, Lardner accepted another offer, this time from the Bell Syndicate and the Chicago Tribune–New York Daily News Syndicate, to write a one hundred–word essay six times a week, "Night Letter from Ring Lardner," for a then princely $750 per week. The first installment appeared February 1, 1931, and the last one, only two months later, on April 24. His last major writing assignment was as a radio critic for the *New Yorker*.

Lardner's best-known short story is "Champion," about an ambitious boxer who alienates his family and friends on his way to the top. *Champion* was made into a movie in 1949 starring Kirk Douglas as boxer Midge Kelly. Lardner's other works of fiction include: *Gullible's Travels* (1917); *Own Your Own Home* (1919); *The Big Town* (1921); *How To Write Short Stories* (1924); *What of It?* (1925) and *The Love Nest and Other Stories* (1926). He collaborated with George M. Cohan on the play *Elmer the Great* (1928), and with George S. Kaufman, on the play *June Moon* (1929).

For many years, Lardner alternated between heavy drinking and abstinence. His health declined. He contracted tuberculosis and on September 25, 1933, he suffered a fatal heart attack at age forty-eight.

See also: George Ade, Finley Peter Dunne

Further reading: DeMuth, Jerry. *Small Town Chicago: The Comic Perspective of Finley Peter Dunne, George Ade, Ring Lardner* (1980); Elder, Donald. *Ring Lardner* (1956); Lardner, Ring. *The Best Short Stories of Ring Lardner* (1988); Yardley, Jonathan. *Ring: A Biography of Ring Lardner* (1977).

Victor Lawson

Publisher

born: September 9, 1850
Chicago, Illinois
died: August 19, 1925
Chicago, Illinois

*Along with Melville E. Stone, Victor Fremont Lawson founded the **Chicago Daily News** and was the founder of the Associated Press. Under his leadership, the **Daily News** became the most prominent evening newspaper in the United States.*

Victor Lawson was the son of a frugal Norwegian immigrant, Iver Larson Bo, who joined a Norwegian community that had settled in the Fox River Valley of Illinois and changed his name to Lawson. Within two years, young Iver moved to Chicago, opened a small clothing store, and began investing in real estate.

Lawson was born in his parents' home on Superior Street on September 9, 1850. His first job was in the circulation department of the *Chicago Journal*. He attended Phillips Academy in Andover, Massachusetts, and then enrolled at Harvard University. Although a hard-working and bright student, Lawson suffered from poor eyesight and ill health. Several trips to Minnesota for hunting and fishing improved his condition tremendously.

In 1866 Iver Lawson and a fellow Norwegian, John Anderson, founded the *Skandinaven* newspaper. When his father died, Victor Lawson returned to Chicago and became the publisher of the paper—the only daily newspaper in the Norwegian language in the United States. In 1876 Lawson purchased shares in the *Chicago Daily News*, which had been established a year earlier with $5,000 from English publisher Percy R. Meggy.

Lawson assumed the title of publisher in August of 1876 and teamed up with his partner, Melville E. Stone, a high school classmate. Stone handled the editorial chores while Lawson took care of business matters. The *Daily News*, promised Stone, would carry "pure news only." By the end of the 1870s, the *Daily News* had established itself as the leading newspaper in the city and remained so until the turn of the century. The list of illustrious names who worked under Lawson was considerable. It includes Eugene Field, George Ade, John T. McCutcheon, James Weber Linn, and Harold L. Ickes.

Lawson was notoriously tight when it came to paying his reporters but could also be extremely generous, as when he offered free lectures and language courses to immigrants and sponsored special health-care programs for the city's poor children. Children held a special place in his heart. He built a "Newsboys' Hall" overlooking Calhoun Place, on Wells Street near Madison and Washington Streets, that contained a stage, a clubroom, a gymnasium, a restaurant, and a drill hall where the members of the *Daily News* Newsboys' Band practiced. Among the street urchins who got their start hawking Lawson's paper were Michael "Hinky Dink" Kenna and James C. Petrillo of the Musicians Union.

Lawson was a pioneer in many ways. He was the first publisher to print a paper's circulation figures. He introduced the idea of using children as news hawkers, a policy that reformers eventually campaigned against. Lawson's was the first paper to run full-page ads, the first to utilize the new Mergenthaler linotype machine, and the first to publish a daily newspaper column in the country— Eugene Field's "Sharps and Flats."

A deeply religious man, Lawson forbade liquor advertisements in the paper, yet he employed staffers who were known to partake of the bottle frequently. Hiring competent reporters to cover the news, especially foreign news, was Lawson's overriding concern. He trained his correspondents thoroughly before they ventured overseas. Lawson didn't neglect the arts either. After World War I he introduced an innovative book section and hired Henry B. Sell as its editor.

In 1890 Lawson established the Chicago City Press Association, a forerunner of the City News Bureau, a local news-gathering operation that supplied material to Chicago newspapers. He served as president of the Associated Press—originally established in 1848 by seven newspapers in New York as the New York Associated Press—from 1894 to 1900 and as a member of the board of directors from 1893 to 1925.

In addition to his newspaper duties, Lawson was also prominent in civic affairs and served as a member of the Chicago Commission on Race Relations in 1920.

Lawson died in 1925 of a heart attack. His memory is commemorated by sculptor Lorado Taft's imposing figure of a medieval knight, entitled *The Crusader*, in Graceland Cemetery.

Lawson was universally admired for his integrity, his forthrightness, and for the highly developed social conscience he brought to journalism. Fellow journalist Ben Hecht called Lawson "the fairest mind American journalism has produced."

See also: George Ade, William Bross, Eugene Field, Henry Demarest Lloyd, John T. McCutcheon, Melville E. Stone.

Further reading: Dennis, Charles H. *Victor Lawson: His Time and His Work* (1935).

Meyer Levin

Novelist

born: October 7, 1905
(other sources say October 8, 1905)
Chicago, Illinois
died: July 9, 1981
Jerusalem, Israel

*Much of Meyer Levin's fiction revolved around Jewish-American themes or was based on historical incidents from Chicago's past. **The Old Bunch** (1937) was Levin's first attempt to portray Jewish-American life and culture. **Citizens** is set during the violent clash that occurred between police and workers at the Republic Steel plant in 1937, and **Compulsion** is a fictionalized account of the infamous Leopold-Loeb murder case.*

Born near Maxwell Street, Meyer Levin was the son of Jewish immigrants. He loved to read, and as a youngster he would check out books from the Jewish People's Institute on nearby Taylor Street. His first story, about a Jewish boy who tries to hide his humble Maxwell Street origins from his gentile girlfriend, was published when he was fifteen in a magazine called *Ten Story Book*. At sixteen, he entered the University of Chicago and graduated two years later. Levin started his career as a reporter with the *Chicago Daily News* in 1924. He had sent a sketch of a short story to his idol, and *Daily News* staffer, Ben Hecht, who replied with a terse but encouraging, "You can write." That was all Levin needed. "In those days," recalled Levin in his autobiography, "one didn't apply for a newspaper job in order to become a journalist. One applied in order to become an author."

Levin's most compelling childhood memory was of "fear and shame at being a Jew." Racine Avenue, where he grew up, was the dividing line between Jews and Italians. The Italian children would bully and taunt the bookish Levin. These experiences were so traumatic that for many years, Levin confessed in his autobiography, he hid his Jewish heritage.

His early novels—*Reporter* in 1929 and *Frankie and Johnny* in 1930—deliberately avoided Jewish themes altogether. Yet his early short stories were primarily concerned with Jewish subjects. "Molasses Tide" is a portrait of Jews along Roosevelt Road. In "Chewing Gum," he wrote about an old Jewish immigrant who peddles gum for a living. "A Seder" returns to a theme popular with Jewish authors at that time: the alienation between Old World Jews and the younger, secular generation of Americanized

Jews. In 1931 Levin wrote his first novel with a Jewish theme, *Yehudah*, based on his six-month experience on a kibbutz in Haifa in 1927.

Although he visited Palestine three times as a young man, it wasn't until he served as a war correspondent during World War II for the Jewish Telegraphic Agency and the Overseas News Agency that he was able to fully accept and come to terms with his Jewish identity. Only then was he able "to recover my feeling of free and full identification as a Jew. For through my war experiences I came to recognize the . . . indestructability of the Jewish quality," he explained in his autobiography, *In Search*. At that point confronting and writing about his Jewishness almost became an obsession. In 1947 he worked with the Jewish underground to illegally transport Jewish emigrants to Palestine, the future state of Israel. These Israeli themes cropped up years later in two novels about Zionist pioneers, *The Settlers* (1972) and *The Harvest* (1978).

In 1956 Levin wrote his best-selling book, *Compulsion*, based on the true story of Richard Loeb and Nathan Leopold, sons of wealthy German Jews, who kidnapped and killed fourteen-year-old Bobby Franks, a neighbor's son, for "kicks." The book zoomed up the best-seller charts, and the heretofore obscure Levin found himself "a celebrity, an authority."

Levin's works were frequently the subject of lawsuits. In 1964 Leopold, after serving a thirty-three year prison sentence, sued Levin and fifty-six other defendants, including publisher Simon and Schuster and film producer, Darryl F. Zanuck, for $1,405,000 in damages, on the grounds that the book and the subsequent movie version of *Compulsion* invaded his privacy. Leopold ultimately lost.

In 1954 Levin became embroiled in another ugly legal battle involving the play based on the diary of concentration camp victim Anne Frank. Levin had discovered the diary while on assignment in Europe and translated it into English. Originally, Otto Frank, Anne's father, agreed that Levin would write a Broadway play based on the diary. In 1954 Levin sued Frank and two Broadway producers, Kermit Bloomgarden and Cheryl Crawford, for fraud and plagiarism. Levin had already written the play only to be told by Bloomgarden that his effort was "unstageworthy." When Crawford reportedly hired two non-Jewish writers to complete the stage adaptation, Levin became convinced that the work was rejected because it was, in his words, "too Jewish." According to biographer Steven J. Rubin, the stage adaptation was almost identical to Levin's original. "The main difference between the two versions was that they left out the Jewish character and concentrated on the schmaltz," said Levin who was later awarded $50,000 in damages.

During his later years, Levin divided his time between New York and Israel. He died in Jerusalem in 1981 at the age of seventy-five.

Levin wrote over twenty books, including two autobiographies, *In Search* (1950) and *The Obsession* (1973). His last novel, *The Architect* (1981), loosely based on the life of Frank Lloyd Wright, featured a cast of prominent Chicago historical figures, including Dankmar Adler, Louis Sullivan, Clarence Darrow, Jane Addams, Theodore Dreiser, and Harriet Monroe.

Further reading: Berkow, Ira. *Maxwell Street: Survival in a Bazaar* (1977); Rubin, Steven J. *Meyer Levin* (1982).

Vachel Lindsay

Poet

born: November 10, 1879
Springfield, Illinois
died: December 5, 1931
Springfield, Illinois

Although hailing from downstate Illinois, Nicholas Vachel Lindsay studied in Chicago, was a considerable presence on the local literary scene for several years, and became the first member of the so-called poetry revivalists to become famous. Lindsay attempted to reform American poetry. Poet Edgar Lee Masters described him as a latter-day Johnny Appleseed, planting the seeds of literary mysticism with whoever would listen and dreaming of rescuing America—through the spoken word—from the clutches of the commercialism that it had so wholeheartedly embraced. Lindsay was given many epithets: ascetic, visionary, mystic, and puritan. In him dwelt the soaring and restless spirit of a Walt Whitman or William Blake.

Photograph courtesy of University of Chicago Archives.

Lindsay was born in Springfield, Illinois, in 1879, the son of a country doctor. Lindsay was especially close to his mother. A fragile child, he avoided the rough and tumble boys' games in favor of reciting stories. The Lindsays were devout Christians, followers of Alexander Campbell, who had established a religious society in 1812 called the Disciples of Christ. Dr. Lindsay was an elder of Springfield's First Christian Church, and Vachel's mother taught the adult Sunday School class.

Lindsay was encouraged to follow in his father's footsteps. As a dutiful son, he enrolled at Hiram College, a Campbellite institution in Ohio, but he did miserably in all his medical courses.

Lindsay's attitude brightened when he was accepted as a student at the Art Institute of Chicago. He wished to become an illustrator or a cartoonist although he had a natural talent for writing and kept a diary of his activities and thoughts. Lindsay arrived in Chicago on January 2, 1901, and rented an apartment on South Paulina Street. He registered for night classes and subsisted on a diet of milk and pastries. Lindsay detested alcohol, didn't smoke, and believed in pursuing a chaste life. Indeed, his greatest vice was his weakness for sweets.

Lindsay attended church regularly and began reading the poems of the English mystic poet William Blake. He then moved to Kenwood Avenue and 50th Street on the South Side, found a job in the toy department at Marshall Field's sorting boxes, and began to write poetry.

From 1904 to 1905 he moved to New York City and continued his art studies at the New York School of Art, and also lectured against alcohol and other vices. The Chicago-based *Poetry* magazine virtually launched Lindsay's career when it published

"General William Booth Enters Into Heaven," an arresting tribute to the founder of the Salvation Army. It was also the title of his first poetry book, published in 1913. Critics hailed Lindsay as a major new figure on the poetry scene and praised his work as a masterpiece. William Dean Howells called it "this fine brave poem that makes the heart leap." "It is perhaps the most remarkable poem of a decade," said another.

The highly rhythmic musical quality of his work contained elements of ragtime, evangelical hymns, and marching bands. Popular or cult heroes were the subjects of many of his poems—Abraham Lincoln, William Jennings Bryan, Ralph Waldo Emerson, and Charles Darwin.

In 1912 Lindsay took to the road, a Christ-like figure traversing the countryside, and lived the life of the vagabond, preaching his gospel of peace and beauty. His pockets were empty. Beggary, he insisted, was "the noblest occupation of man." In return for money, lodging, and a meal, he exchanged booklets and recited poetry. He made his first national lecturing tour in 1920 and began to attract a devoted and large following. That same year he became the first American poet invited to recite at Oxford.

Strongly attached to his mother—she died in 1922—and, according to Edgar Lee Masters, "not attractive to women," Lindsay did not wed until May of 1925, when, at forty-five, he married Elizabeth Conner. They had two children and resided in Spokane, Washington, until 1929 when they returned to Springfield. In December of 1931, exhausted and debt-ridden from family obligations and the renovation of his home, he committed suicide as his wife and children slept.

Lindsay was a true visionary, a misunderstood troubadour trapped in the wrong century.

Some of Lindsay's other important poems include "The Congo," "Bryan, Bryan, Bryan, Bryan," "Abraham Lincoln Walks at Midnight," "The Santa Fe Trail," and "The Eagle That Is Forgotten," the last a tribute to John Peter Altgeld.

See also: Edgar Lee Masters, Harriet Monroe

Further reading: Kramer, Dale. *Chicago Renaissance: The Literary Life of the Midwest 1900–1930* (1966); Masters, Edgar Lee. *Vachel Lindsay: A Poet in America* (1935).

Mary Livermore

Suffragette/Social Reformer

born: December 19, 1820
Boston, Massachusetts
died: May 23, 1905
Melrose, Massachusetts

Mary Ashton Rice Livermore was involved in many reform movements during the nineteenth century from suffrage to temperance to the abolition of slavery. And like other reformers of her day, she turned her back on a life of comfort to seek ways to better the human race.

Photograph courtesy of the Chicago Historical Society.

Mary Rice grew up in Boston and attended public school there. As a teenager she enrolled in the Female Seminary, considered one of the best in New England, in Charleston, Massachusetts, where she taught after graduating. In 1845 she married Daniel Parker Livermore, a Universalist minister.

The couple moved to Chicago in 1857. Livermore contributed her time to various charitable groups such as the Chicago Home of the Friendless. In addition, she co-founded the Home for Aged Women and the Hospital for Women and Children. She and her husband also edited a Unitarian periodical called the *New Covenant*. She became convinced that the key to social reform—the way to improve the status of women in particular and society in general— was to support women's suffrage.

Along with Jane Hoge, Livermore became associate manager of the Chicago branch of the United States Sanitary Commission during the Civil War, a volunteer organization run by civilians. The organization inspected camps, raised money, and stored and dispatched supplies to Union soldiers. According to historians J. Christopher Schnell and Jeanne Madeline Weimann, during the Battle of Vicksburg, Livermore carried over three thousand supply boxes down the Mississippi River.

As casualties mounted and additional food and supplies were desperately needed, the commission became strapped for cash. In the autumn of 1863, Livermore and Hoge came up with the idea of sponsoring the Great Northwestern Sanitary Fair as a fundraising venture. War mementos and souvenirs were sold to the highest bidder, a series of dinners were served—prepared by an all-volunteer staff—and in the evenings guests attended concerts, pantomimes, and lectures. It was a great success, bringing in an estimated $86,000, and it became the prototype for similar fairs around the country in New York, Philadelphia, Cleveland, Pittsburgh, and St. Louis.

Livermore next turned her attention to the woman's suffrage movement and organized the first suffrage convention in Chicago in 1868—speakers included such famous suffragettes as Elizabeth Cady Stanton and Susan B. Anthony. She was elected president of the Illinois Woman's Suffrage Association. In 1869 she founded the city's first woman's suffrage publication, *The Agitator*. The following year it merged with the Boston-based *Woman's Journal*. Livermore then moved, in 1870, to the Boston suburb of Melrose to take over the editorial duties of the journal and became active in the suffragist movement in Massachusetts.

In 1872 she joined the lecture circuit, promoting the education of women and challenging the liquor laws.

Livermore wrote two autobiographies, *My Story of the War: A Woman's Narrative of Four Years' Personal Experience*, in 1888 and *The Story of My Life, or, The Sunshine and Shadow of Seventy Years*, in 1897. Along with Frances Willard, president of the Woman's Temperance Union, she edited *A Woman of the Century*, a biographical dictionary of prominent women, that appeared in 1893.

Livermore died at her home in Melrose of bronchitis and a heart condition at age eighty-four.

A *Chicago Tribune* editorial of May 24, 1905, said, "During all her long life her influence and her ability to its utmost were used quietly, persistently

and effectively, for the advancement of the individual and national life, and for the betterment of woman's condition."

See also: Frances E. Willard [appendix]

Further reading: Livermore, Mary A. *My Story of the War: A Woman's Narrative of Four Years' Personal Experience* (1888); Livermore, Mary A. *The Story of My Life, or, The Sunshine and Shadow of Seventy Years* (1897); Schnell, J. Christopher. "Mary Livermore and the Great Northwestern Fair," *Chicago History* (Spring 1975); Weimann, Jeanne Madeline. *The Fair Women* (1981).

Henry Demarest Lloyd

Social Reformer/Journalist

born: May 1, 1847
New York, New York
died: September 28, 1903
Chicago, Illinois

The first of the great journalistic muckrakers, Henry Demarest Lloyd spent a lifetime trying to right society's evils. He advocated the principle of direct democracy—the belief that people should be able to manage their own community affairs as much as possible—and believed in the oneness of the human race.

Photograph courtesy of Charles H. Kerr Publishing Company.

Born in New York City, Lloyd was the son of a Calvinist minister of the Dutch Reformed Church. He graduated from Columbia College in 1867 and later from the Columbia Law School. In 1869 he was admitted to the New York bar. Active in the local reform movement, he campaigned against New York's corrupt political machine boss, William Tweed. He contributed articles to the *New York Post* and edited two monthlies, *People's Pictorial Tax-Payer* and *Free-Trader*.

In 1872 Lloyd moved to Chicago to join the staff of the *Chicago Tribune,* as financial and literary editor, where he conducted numerous investigations into corporate misdoings. He directed his most vehement criticism toward monopolies, especially the Standard Oil Company, which he described as "the greatest, wisest, meanest monopoly in history."

In 1873 Lloyd married Jessie Bross, daughter of *Chicago Tribune* publisher William Bross. Five years later, the couple settled in the village of Wilmette, north of Chicago.

In 1885 Lloyd left the *Tribune* to pursue his reform agenda further. He wrote several books on labor problems, including *Wealth Against Commonwealth* (1894), a defiant denunciation of the Standard Oil Company. His brand of adversarial politics was too militant for many, and he was defeated in his bid for the United States Congress in 1888 and 1894.

Lloyd stood by his convictions—no matter how unpopular the cause. During the hysteria that came in the wake of the Haymarket Affair of 1886, he asked Gov. John Peter Altgeld to grant executive clemency to the Haymarket martyrs. This led his father-in-law to prevent both Lloyd and his wife from inheriting *Tribune* stock. Lloyd supported Eugene Debs during the Pullman strike of 1894 and was on the side of the anthracite miners in Pennsylvania during the coal strike of 1902.

Lloyd experimented in unconventional living arrangements. Various generations of his family lived in his Wayside mansion in Wilmette along with honored guests. At various times, these guests included Jane Addams, Eugene Debs, Florence Kelley, and Booker T. Washington. Young factory workers and other toilers of labor were also welcome in the Lloyd residence.

Lloyd was a leading force in Wilmette community life. He was village treasurer in 1886 and served as a member of the school and village boards. The Wayside mansion still stands at Lloyd Place and Sheridan Road. A statue, designed by Charles Haag in 1914, commemorates Lloyd's life and achievements.

During his later years, Lloyd traveled extensively in England, Ireland, Switzerland, and New Zealand, where he studied different methods used to cope with labor problems. From these travels emerged two books: *Labour Copartnership* (1898) and *A Country Without Strikes* (1900).

Lloyd succumbed to pneumonia in 1903 while campaigning for public ownership of public transportation in Chicago.

See also: Jane Addams, John Peter Altgeld, William Bross, Eugene Debs

Further reading: Destler, Chester McArthur. *Henry Demarest Lloyd and the Empire of Reform* (1963); Ebner, Michael H. *Creating Chicago's North Shore: A Suburban History* (1988); Thomas, John L. *Alternative America: Henry George, Edward Bellamy, Henry Demarest Lloyd and the Adversary Tradition* (1983).

Vito Marzullo

Politician

born: September 10, 1897
Senerchia, Italy
died: March 5, 1990
Chicago, Illinois

Vito Marzullo, the Italian immigrant who became the undisputed dean of the city council for over thirty years, epitomized Chicago politics of the old school where "who you knew" was more important than "what you knew." And sometimes it seemed that Marzullo ran the 25th Ward on the Near West Side as if it was his own personal fiefdom and the residents his subjects. Yet the garrulous Marzullo was more of a benevolent monarch than a ruthless despot.

Photograph reprinted with permission from the *Chicago Sun-Times.*

Young Vito came to the United States from Italy in 1910 with his family. After receiving only a fourth-grade education, he trained as a machinist at the Lewis Institute, then located at Madison Street and Damen Avenue. His initial attempt to enter politics was not enouraging—he was defeated in his effort to become a Democratic precinct captain. His first political job was as a clerk in the county treasurer's office.

In 1939 Marzullo was elected to the Illinois state legislature, while, at the same time, holding the position of ward superintendent in the Department of Streets and Sanitation. In 1953 he won his first term as alderman of the 25th Ward. He also served as Democratic ward committeeman in the 25th Ward from 1956 until 1984.

Imbued with a fierce independent streak, Marzullo frequently defied the organization. Although a long-time admirer of Richard J. Daley, Marzullo broke with the mayor when he refused to back the Democratic presidential hopeful, George S. McGovern in 1972. He supported the Republican candidate, Richard M. Nixon, instead. "I'd rather drop dead (than support McGovern)," he offered as an explanation. He went his own way again in 1983 when he backed Republican mayoral candidate Bernard Epton over the Democratic choice, Harold Washington. Why the party switch again? "He says he don't want no Machine," said Marzullo, referring to the late mayor's reform agenda.

In 1983 Marzullo stepped down as the 25th Ward's Democratic committeeman. Two years later the federal court redrew the map of his ward, to reflect the change in population makeup to a largely African-American and Latino base. Marzullo decided to retire. "The intellectuals, the millionaires, the obstructionists,

they messed it up," he grumbled. "They redrew my ward and they used cats and dogs and mouses and counted them as people."

They say you only live once, but Marzullo had the rare experience of reading about his own death in the morning paper. In April of 1989, he read his obituary over a bowl of corn flakes in the pages of the *Chicago Tribune.* Momentarily stunned, the politician merely complained later that the premature report of his demise "ruined" his breakfast.

Marzullo came out on top in more than twenty-three elections, most of them unopposed. "Nineteen times nobody filed against me, even for public nuisance!" said Marzullo, according to author Milton Rakove. He survived so long in the notoriously treacherous world of politics because he knew how to play the game, and, most importantly, he knew how to please the people that mattered the most—his constituency. Marzullo was aided by an army of precinct captains—foot soldiers, he called them—who functioned as his eyes and ears on the street. These public servants would canvass the neighborhood, listening to the needs and complaints of the residents—which ranged from providing free legal service to repairing broken street lights—then report back to their boss.

Considered a genuine relic of old-style Chicago politics, Marzullo was often asked to speak at prestigious universities around the country about clout, vice, and other infamous Windy City peculiarities. Some of his words of wisdom include: "Those who know the least speak the most." "Do good and forget; do bad and remember."

Marzullo died of pneumonia at Rush Presbyterian-St. Luke's Hospital in 1990 at the age of ninety-two. He was buried in Mount Carmel Cemetery in Hillside, Illinois.

See also: Richard J. Daley

Further reading: Fremon, David K. *Chicago Politics Ward by Ward* (1988); Rakove, Milton. *Don't Make No Waves—Don't Back No Losers: An Insider's Analysis of the Daley Machine* (1975); Rakove, Milton. *We Don't Want Nobody Nobody Sent: An Oral History of the Daley Years* (1979).

Edgar Lee Masters

Poet

born: August 23, 1869
Garnett, Kansas
died: March 5, 1950
Philadelphia, Pennsylvania

Edgar Lee Masters was one of the leading figures of the Chicago Renaissance literary movement of the early twentieth century. For over twenty years, Masters toiled in literary obscurity. It wasn't until the publication of **Spoon River** *that Masters received any recognition.* **Spoon River Anthology** *became the single most widely read book of American poetry in its day, and with its plain, straightforward verse, it influenced the direction of modern poetry.*

Born in Kansas, Masters moved with his family to Lewistown, Illinois, as a young child. He studied the great works of English literature—Emerson, Dickens, Scott, Thackeray, Byron, and Shakespeare. When he was old enough, he secured a position on the local newspaper and occasionally submitted poetry. His father thought he should receive a proper education and encouraged him to pursue a "respectable" calling. Masters enrolled at Knox College in Galesburg, Illinois, to study law, was admitted to the Illinois bar in 1891, and moved to Chicago in 1892.

Masters found a room in a boarding house two blocks away from the Levee, Chicago's infamous red-light district. He got a job with the Edison Company as a bill collector and sometime lawyer. In 1893 Masters found work at a downtown law firm. According to literary historian Dale Kramer in *Chicago Renaissance*, Masters was terrible in the courtroom—he was a poor speaker with no flair for the dramatic—but he did prepare excellent drafts, briefs, and contracts.

After working long hours at the office, Masters went home and continued to toil late into the night on his own writing. In his spare time he wrote political essays for the *Chicago Chronicle* and organized and acted as president of the Jefferson Club, a social club that sponsored banquets in honor of the charismatic Democratic leader, William Jennings Bryan.

In 1903 Clarence Darrow invited Masters to join his firm. The two men had known each other for several years. Masters managed the office and handled the civil litigation cases. Although his salary increased considerably, he took no pleasure in his legal career. He concentrated further on his writing.

In 1914 Masters published poetry in *Reedy's Mirror*, a St. Louis literary paper under the pseudonym of Webster Ford (he felt that using his real name might damage the firm's credibility). The poems consisted of monologues by the deceased residents of a fictitious Illinois town called Spoon River. "Spoon River" explored the restrictions and desperation of small town life. Published in book form in 1915 as the *Spoon River Anthology*, it caused a literary sensation. By 1940 it had been published in seventy editions and translated into several languages. Masters's literary reputation rests largely on *Spoon River*.

Eventually Masters moved to New York. Although a prolific writer, none of his other works were as successful. They include *Domesday Book* (1920), *The New Spoon River* (1924), and *The Sangamon* (1942). Masters also was an accomplished biographer. His biography *Vachel Lindsay: A Poet in America*, was awarded the Mark Twain Medal in 1935. He also wrote biographies of Mark Twain, Abraham Lincoln, and Walt Whitman. In 1936 he published his autobiography, *Across Spoon River*.

By 1943 Masters, in poor health as a result of pneumonia and malnutrition, was living alone in New York's Chelsea Hotel. Although reports circulated that he was broke, Masters always denied being poor. Upon learning of Masters's fate, members of Manhattan's literary circle were both acutely embarrassed and startled that one of their own was living under such dire conditions. As a result, the Academy of American Poets awarded Masters a $5,000 fellowship.

Masters died at the age of eighty in a Philadelphia convalescent home in 1950.

See also: Clarence Darrow, Vachel Lindsay, Harriet Monroe

Further reading: Kramer, Dale. *Chicago Renaissance: The Literary Life of the Midwest 1900–1930* (1966); Masters, Edgar Lee. *Across Spoon River* (1936); Yatron, Michael. *America's Literary Revolt* (1959).

Oscar F. Mayer

Businessman

born: March 29, 1859
Kaesingen, Germany
died: March 11, 1955
Chicago, Illinois

*Oscar F. Mayer founded and acted as chairman of the board of Oscar Mayer and Company, the giant meatpacking firm. Today his name is virtually synonomous with the word **hotdog**.*

The Mayers were an old Bavarian family of ministers and foresters. Mayer's father died in 1870, forcing the young Oscar to leave school to support the family. He left his home in Bavaria to travel to Munich to work for a cousin, John M. Schroll, who owned a grocery store. The business failed, and Schroll decided to move with his family to America in 1873. Oscar asked his mother's permission to accompany his cousin. She agreed. They originally settled in Detroit where Mayer, then fourteen, found work at a butcher shop.

In 1876 the young immigrants moved to Chicago. Mayer got a job as an apprentice at the Armour meat-packing company while Schroll opened a drug store on North Avenue near Larrabee Street. Mayer then found work in Kohlhammer's meat market on Clark Street, which served the wealthy Gold Coast neighborhood, learning the retail meat business. He stayed for three years.

In 1880 Mayer wrote home to his brother Gottfried suggesting that he study sausage-making in Nuremburg and then come to Chicago. Gottfried agreed and he and another brother, Max, emigrated to the U.S.

In 1883 Mayer and his brothers rented Kolling Meat Market, a small butcher and sausage-making shop in a predominantly German neighborhood on Sedgwick Street on the North Side. The shop, which he called Oscar Mayer and Brothers Company, specialized in home-made sausages and weiners.

The business prospered and Mayer built a two-story building several blocks away at 1241 North Sedgwick Street. On the first floor he established his business. The second floor he used as living quarters for his family—by this time he had a wife and infant son—and his two brothers. Gottfried managed the production department and Max ran the bookkeeping department.

In 1883 Mayer founded Oscar Mayer and Company. The combination of masterful salesmanship and excellent products dictated success. Company salesmen traveled throughout the city and suburbs by horse and wagon making deliveries. By the turn of the century, the company employed forty-three workers, which included, according to one veteran, "five wagon salesmen, one pig-head-and-feet cleaner and cooker, and two stablemen."

Mayer began to add new products and experiment with innovative marketing techniques. In 1924 packaged sliced bacon appeared on the market. By 1928 fifteen varieties of sausages were being sold, and by 1929 Oscar Mayer became the first company to adopt brand identification. Every fourth weiner was wrapped in a yellow paper ring, which carried the company name and an official U. S. government inspection stamp.

In 1936 the company introduced Little Oscar. For many Chicagoans, Little Oscar—the little person who dressed in white, wore an oversize chef's hat, and traveled across the country in the Weinermobile—came to personalize Oscar Mayer and Company. Later a cartoon image of Little Oscar appeared in television commercials, in newspaper advertisements, and on billboards. The Weinermobile continues to make appearances throughout the U.S.

In 1919 the company relocated its national headquarters to Madison, Wisconsin, while retaining its Chicago plant at 1241 North Sedgwick Street. Although Mayer maintained an active interest in the company, he had no problem delegating authority. From 1928 to 1955 he served as chairman of the board.

Mayer, who lived at 5727 North Sheridan Road for over forty years, died in 1955 at the age of ninety-five after a brief illness. Upon his death, his son, Oscar G. Mayer, was elected chairman of the board while Oscar G. Mayer, Jr., the founder's grandson, became president.

Aloysius A. Mazewski

Community Organizer

born: January 5, 1916
North Chicago, Illinois
died: August 3, 1988
Portage, Wisconsin

Aloysius A. Mazewski was one of the most influential figures in the Polish-American community for over thirty years. As president of both the Polish National Alliance and the Polish American Congress, his clout spread far beyond Chicago's borders. Mazewski was the voice of Polonia in Washington, D. C., and he had the ear of every president from Lyndon Johnson to Ronald Reagan on matters concerning the Polish-American community.

Photograph reprinted with permission from the *Chicago Sun-Times.*

Mazewski's father came to the United States at the age of fourteen. Aloysius was born in the suburb of North Chicago but lived at 5805 West Cullom Avenue in Portage Park on the Northwest Side for most of his life. He attended Lane Technical High School, where he was president of the Polish Students' Club and organized Polish-American activities.

After graduating from DePaul University Law School, Mazewski served as an Army administrator during World War II. He left the service in 1946 with the rank of major, became active in ward politics, and started a successful law practice. In September 1967 Mazewski was elected president of the Polish National Alliance (P.N.A.) and the following year he became president of the Polish American Congress (P.A.C.).

The P.N.A. is a fraternal insurance organization founded in Philadelphia in 1880. Its aims were several but none were more important than to lay the "proper foundation for the construction of institutions dedicated to the material and moral advancement of the Polish immigration in America." These institutions consisted of Polish settlement houses, schools, educational facilities, shelters, and businesses in the Polish community. By the end of 1880, the alliance established its headquarters in Chicago. In its early years, the P.N.A. moved from rented office to rented office—338 South Clark Street, 26 West Washington Street, 60 West Noble Street, 112 West Division Street, and 547 West Noble Street—until it built its first permanent office at 1404 West Division Street in 1896.

Polish fraternal groups were first organized in America during the 1860s to provide burial insurance and illness benefits for Polish immigrants.

Eventually they acquired more of a patriotic flavor. The P.N.A., in particular, staunchly advocated Polish independence and promoted ethnic pride.

Mazewski modernized the P.N.A.'s antiquated insurance program by offering a variety of plans to meet the needs of its diverse membership. In June of 1977 the P.N.A. moved into its spacious new quarters at 6100 North Cicero Avenue on the far Northwest Side.

Mazewski was a tireless campaigner for human rights in Poland and was an early supporter of that country's Solidarity movement. In 1981 the alliance, under his leadership, organized a food drive for Poland at a time when the country was experiencing severe food shortages. The Polish American Congress Charitable Foundation, which he founded, raised $150 million for Poland during the Solidarity strikes of 1980.

In 1970 Mazewski became the first Polish-American special delegate to the United Nations General Assembly. Among his other accomplishments, he was a member of the International Human Rights Conference in Madrid in 1980, and he served on the Federal Ethnic Studies Commission, which helped create the Ethnic Heritage Studies Act of 1972. In 1980 he was named to the United States Holocaust Commission. Along with Illinois Congressman Frank Annunzio, Mazewski was responsible for the passage of the Polish Veterans' Act of 1976, which provided medical benefits to Polish war veterans living in the United States who fought on the Allied side during World War II.

Mazewski suffered a fatal heart attack in 1988 at the age of seventy-two while playing golf near his summer cottage in Wisconsin. An estimated ten thousand mourners filed through St. Hyacinth Catholic Church at 3636 West Wolfram Street as he lay in state for two days.

Further reading: Greene, Victor. *For God and Country: The Rise of Polish and Lithuanian Ethnic Consciousness in America* (1975); Holli, Melvin G. and Peter d'A. Jones, eds. *Ethnic Chicago* (1984); Kantowicz, Edward. *Polish American Politics in Chicago* (1972); Pienkos, Donald E. *P.N.A.: Centennial History of the Polish National Alliance of the United States of North America* (1984).

Cyrus H. McCormick

Entrepreneur

born: February 15, 1809
Rockbridge County, Virginia
died: May 13, 1884
Chicago, Illinois

Cyrus Hall McCormick revolutionized farming and played an important role in the industrialization of Chicago. Before the invention of the horse-drawn McCormick reaper, farming consisted of crude tools and primitive techniques. Afterwards, neither farming nor McCormick would ever be the same. McCormick became a household word throughout the world.

McCormick received little formal education. His father, Robert McCormick, was also an inventor and had tried to invent his own reaper years earlier. Where he failed, his son succeeded. With the help of Jo Anderson, a slave, the twenty-two-year-old McCormick built his reaper in six weeks in the smithy of his father's farm in Virginia. Unknown to McCormick, there were forty-seven other patents for reapers at the time.

Although McCormick is credited with inventing the reaper in 1831, it was not marketed until the early 1840s. He obtained a patent in 1834. The first sales did not occur, however, until 1840 when he sold his invention for $100. For several years he kept the reaper off the market while he made additional improvements and even waged several legal battles over patent violations. One of the lawyers who represented him in court was Abraham Lincoln from Springfield, Illinois.

The first McCormick reaper could reportedly harvest as much as ten acres of wheat per day—a vast improvement over the two acres that a farm laborer could harvest. McCormick's reaper liberated the farmer from the land and was the first step on the road to farm mechanization.

McCormick scouted locations for a manufacturing plant. In 1847 he chose Chicago, formed a partnership with businessman Charles M. Gray, bought land on the North Branch of the Chicago River, and built a factory there. His brothers, along with Leander J. and William Sanderson, joined him, and together they began the mass production of the original reaper. In the first year McCormick's factory produced 500 machines. At the time of the Chicago Fire of 1871, production had grown to 10,000 reapers. By the turn of the century, 214,000 reapers were produced annually in the McCormick works, which by that time had relocated to the corner of Blue Island and Western Avenues. McCormick traveled around the world promoting his invention and expanding his network of dealers. One of his important innovations in marketing was the extension of liberal credit to the farmer.

In his later years, McCormick contributed funds to what became the McCormick Theological Seminary. In 1859 he started the *Chicago Times* newspaper, the leading antiwar paper in the North. Indeed, McCormick, the Virginian, was a vocal advocate of the "Copperheads," Northerners sympathetic to the Southern cause. McCormick became active in Democratic politics in Illinois and ran unsuccessfully for Congress in 1864.

McCormick, who was happiest when working, uttered his last words in May of 1884 in his brownstone mansion at 675 North Rush Street. According to Chicago folklore they were, appropriately enough, "Work, work!"

After McCormick's death his wife, Nettie Fowler McCormick, took over the business. In 1902 the firm merged with the Deering Harvester Company to form the International Harvester Company.

See also: Robert R. McCormick, Joseph Medill, John S. Wright

Further reading: Cassin, Herbert N. *Cyrus Hall McCormick* (1909).

Robert R. McCormick

Publisher

born: July 30, 1880
Chicago, Illinois
died: April 1, 1955
Wheaton, Illinois

*Robert Rutherford McCormick bore a famous name and came from an old established family, but with his aristocratic bearing and his penchant for English clothing, the eccentric McCormick was hardly a typical Midwesterner. For over forty-five years as editor and publisher of the **Chicago Tribune**, he determined all **Tribune** policy and ran the paper the way he saw fit. It was his paper. In effect, it was his life, too.*

Solemn, reserved, and aloof, Robert R. McCormick boasted an impressive pedigree. He was the son of Katherine Medill and Robert S. McCormick, the grandson of Joseph Medill and the nephew of Cyrus H. McCormick. He attended the prestigious Ludgrove School in Middlesex, England, for three years and then enrolled at Groton Preparatory School in Massachusetts. After graduating from Yale in 1903, he entered the Northwestern University Law School and was admitted to the bar in 1908.

After law school McCormick entered into a short-lived partnership with his Northwestern classmate Samuel E. Thomason before turning to politics. From 1904 to 1906 he held the Republican aldermanic seat from Chicago's 21st Ward on the far South Side. In late 1905 he became president of the board of trustees of the Chicago Sanitary District. Torn between politics and journalism, McCormick ultimately chose the latter, declining the Republican nomination to the United States Congress in 1912.

When *Tribune* editor Robert W. Patterson died suddenly in 1910, McCormick became coeditor of the paper with his cousin, and Robert's son, Joseph Medill Patterson. McCormick handled the business side, while Patterson concentrated on the editorial functions. In 1911 McCormick became president of the Tribune Company.

In 1915 McCormick served as a war correspondent in Europe, and one year later he became a major in the First Cavalry of the Illinois National Guard. From 1917 to 1918 he acted as an artillery officer with the American Expeditionary Force in France. He left with the rank of colonel. It was a title that he grew to cherish. Some people downplay their military past; McCormick emphasized it and became known as "the Colonel."

In 1921 McCormick became one of the founders of the Medill School of Journalism at Northwestern University. Four years later he became the sole editor and publisher of the *Tribune,* while his cousin Joe became editor of the *New York Daily News.*

In 1922, in honor of the *Tribune's* 75th anniversary, McCormick announced a $100,000 world competition for the design of a new office tower. Raymond Hood, a little known architect from New York, won the honors.

In 1924 McCormick purchased radio station WGN (the call letters refer to the *Tribune's* then self-proclaimed title of the "World's Greatest Newspaper"). In 1939 he began broadcasting his own weekly radio show, "Chicago Theatre of the Air," where he talked at length about whatever was on his mind. These weekly ramblings amounted to an oral history of his life. He reminisced about incidents from his past or discussed his personal heroes—from General Douglas MacArthur to Sir Walter Scott to Thomas Jefferson.

Unlike other newspaper editors, McCormick had no problem with delegating authority. "The task of the editor cannot be handled by one man, no matter how remarkable he might be," he admitted. But he still had definite ideas as to what made a great newspaper. The paper, he said, must answer to the needs, hopes, and fears of its readers. "When the editor is sympathetic with the interests of every honest person, from ditch-digger to multimillionaire, his paper will be truly great."

McCormick held some strong opinions and was not afraid to express them. He staunchly advocated freedom of the press, considered himself a friend of big business, and supported nationalism. As an isolationist, he opposed the United States' entry into both World Wars, he denounced labor unions, he criticized the New Deal policies of President Franklin D. Roosevelt, and he condemned the progressive stance of social reformer Jane Addams.

The *Tribune* circulation soared during his tenure from 200,000 when he first arrived to almost 900,000 at his death. He expanded the Tribune Company holdings, buying paper mills and forests in Canada, shipping companies, radio and television stations, and publishing houses. He was also chairman of the board of the *New York Daily News,* which he and Patterson had founded in 1919. In 1951 he assumed the position of editor and publisher of the *Washington Times-Herald.* Several years later it was sold to the *Washington Post.*

In 1953 McCormick caught pneumonia, which was complicated by cirrhosis of the liver and circulatory problems. Two years later he died in his sleep at his Wheaton estate of Cantigny, the former home of his grandfather Joseph Medill. McCormick was seventy-four.

See also: Victor Lawson, Cyrus H. McCormick, Joseph Medill

Further reading: Morgan, Gwen and Arthur Veysey. *Poor Little Rich Boy (and how he made good)* (1985); Tebbel, John W. *An American Dynasty: The Story of the McCormicks, Medills and Pattersons* (1947); Waldrop, Frank C. *McCormick of Chicago: An Unconventional Portrait of a Controversial Figure* (1966); Wendt, Lloyd. *Chicago Tribune: The Rise of a Great American Newspaper* (1979).

John T. McCutcheon

Cartoonist

born: May 6, 1870
near South Raub, Indiana
died: June 10, 1949
Lake Forest, Illinois

*John Tinney McCutcheon, war correspondent, author, and dean of American cartoonists, turned his memories of a Hoosier boyhood and a talent for drawing into some of the best-loved and most warmly remembered cartoons in American journalism. McCutcheon, whose work reflected his own good humor and tolerance of human foibles, is perhaps best known for the charming "Injun Summer" cartoon, which debuted in the **Chicago Tribune** in 1907. Combining whimsy with unabashed sentimentality, McCutcheon's magic pen transformed shocks of corn into Indian teepees. It was but one of the highlights of his long and distinguished career.*

Ironically, McCutcheon had no desire to become a cartoonist. "He wanted to be an illustrator," once recalled his good friend and colleague, George Ade. "He was a realist and simply wanted to picture people as he saw them. Later he found that people liked some of his quaint cartoons, and he began developing them slowly, by adding such features as the little dog in the corner, the little boy in another."

McCutcheon spent his early years on the family farm in Indiana and then moved with his family to Lafayette, Indiana, when he was six. He attended Purdue University where he met fellow Hoosier George Ade. After graduating in 1889, McCutcheon moved to Chicago and got a job in the art department of the morning edition of the *Chicago News* (which became the *Chicago Record* and later the *Chicago Record-Herald*). Ade joined McCutcheon in Chicago. They proved to be an enthusiastic team. Ade provided the stories and McCutcheon illustrated them. For three years, they roomed together in a tiny, furnished apartment near Michigan Avenue.

McCutcheon created his first political cartoons during the 1896 presidential campaign, which pitted William Jennings Bryan against William McKinley.

McCutcheon began his long career with the *Chicago Tribune* on July 1, 1903. Following the death of Pope Leo XIII a few weeks later, McCutcheon created what many consider to be one of his finest cartoons. Bearing no caption, it consisted of a globe wrapped in a black bow. The public reaction was immediate. Profoundly moved by the cartoon's powerful simplicity, it was reproduced by newspapers and magazines all over the world.

McCutcheon filed his cartoons and dispatches from far, out-of-the-way places. He witnessed the Battle of Manila Bay during the Spanish-American War, toured China and Japan in 1899, and journeyed to South Africa at the turn of the century to cover the Boer War. His other adventures include big-game hunting with Teddy Roosevelt in 1909, covering the Mexican Revolution in 1914, and serving as a war correspondent in Europe from 1915 to 1916.

McCutcheon's kindness and humor endeared him to millions. Perhaps because he understood human frailties so well, his brand of political satire was never vicious. Instead, he gently poked fun at world leaders from Pancho Villa to Teddy Roosevelt.

McCutcheon deliberately tugged at his readers' heartstrings. "Mail Call," a cartoon published during the height of World War II, depicted a soldier, head in hands, sitting dejectedly on the steps of an army barracks because he didn't receive a letter from home.

His cartoons were collected in several anthologies: *Cartoons by McCutcheon* (1903); *Bird Center Cartoons* (1904); *The Mysterious Stranger and Other Cartoons* (1905); *Congressman Pumphrey, the People's Friend* (1907); *In Africa* (1910); *T. R. In Cartoons* (1910); *Dawson '11—Fortune Hunter* (1912); *The Restless Age* (1919); *An Heir At Large* (1922); and *Crossed Wires and The Master of the World* (1928).

In addition to illustrating George Ade's *Chicago Stories*, McCutcheon also illustrated Ade's *Artie, Pink Marsh, Doc Horne, Fables in Slang,* and *More Fables in Slang.*

In 1917 McCutcheon married Evelyn Wells Shaw, daughter of architect Howard Van Doren Shaw. He won a Pulitzer prize in 1932 for the 1931 cartoon, "A Wise Economist Asks a

Question," about the victims of bank failures during the Depression, and he retired from newspaper work in 1945. He died four years later in his Lake Forest home.

See also: George Ade, John Fischetti

Further reading: McCutcheon, John T. *Drawn From Memory, Containing Many of the Author's Famous Cartoons and Sketches* (1950).

Mary McDowell

Social Reformer

born: November 30, 1854
Cincinnati, Ohio
died: October 14, 1936
Chicago, Illinois

Mary McDowell was a pioneering social reformer. As founder of the University of Chicago settlement house, she attempted to break down ethnic barriers in order to promote a universal brother- and sisterhood. It didn't always work, and she made some enemies along the way, but to the vast number of residents of the South Side community she became a familiar and cherished friend. "I've always been interested in unpopular causes," she once said.

Born in Cincinnati, Ohio, Mary McDowell entered the field of social work at the age of twenty. She came to Chicago to study at Hull-House and began working as an associate of Jane Addams. Addams recommended McDowell to head the University of Chicago settlement house (later renamed in her honor). McDowell was also one of the founders of the Northwestern University Settlement.

During the spring of 1893, graduate students at the University of Chicago canvassed an area north of the stockyards, a neighborhood consisting largely of immigrants. The University of Chicago settlement house was established in 1894 by the philanthropic committee of the Christian Union of the university and incorporated with its own board of directors in 1898. McDowell was named head resident. The first house was in a small flat near 47th Street and Ashland Avenue.

The settlement grew slowly. McDowell opened a kindergarten for area children. In 1896 four flats and an adjacent shop were rented to accommodate clubs, classrooms, lectures, and concerts. The following year, McDowell purchased four lots on Gross Avenue (later changed to McDowell Avenue).

The settlement house served the needs of the changing community and adopted a good-neighbor policy. McDowell became affectionately known as the "Settlement Lady." As the organization developed and its reputation grew, prominent citizens from outside the neighborhood visited: Thomas G. Masaryk, the first president of Czechoslovakia; Sen. Medill McCormick; educator Booker T. Washington; and author Upton Sinclair, who was in town gathering information for his novel *The Jungle*.

The settlement house provided many essential services. Immigrants received English lessons and classes in nutrition and hygiene. In addition, they had access to a public bathhouse, neighborhood playgrounds, and vocational schools.

McDowell was a doer. She frequently harassed the local alderman to "clean up the neighborhood" and made trips abroad to study methods of garbage disposal. In 1914 she became the Progressive party's candidate for county commissioner. In 1923 Mayor William E. Dever appointed her public welfare commissioner.

McDowell was also quite vocal on other matters, including the passage of legislation insuring an eight-hour work day. The economic plight of women especially concerned her. McDowell founded the Woman's City Club and was the first president of the Illinois Woman's Trade Union League. After the 1919 race riots in Chicago, she organized the first interracial committee of women. She also acted as executive of the Chicago branch of the NAACP (National Association for the Advancement of Colored People) and was a member of the Chicago Urban League's executive committee.

Moreover, McDowell was a member of the Illinois Equal Suffrage Association, and she later became chairman of the National League of Women Voters' committee on International Cooperation to Prevent War. She also served as director of the Chicago Immigrants' Protective League.

"We believe that God hath made of one blood all nations of men, and that we are His children, brothers and sisters of all," McDowell wrote.

McDowell died in October of 1936 at the age of eighty-one in the home of her brother at 5345 South Ellis Avenue.

In 1967 the Mary McDowell Settlement House merged with the Chicago Commons Association. Today the Chicago Commons, a social service agency, operates seven community centers throughout the city: 5021 South Laflin Avenue; 645 North Wolcott Avenue; 1335 West 51st Street; 1258 West 51st Street; 125 North Hoyne Avenue; 915 North Wolcott Avenue; and 1441 North Cleveland Avenue. In addition, the Commons each year sponsors a summer camp in Three Oaks, Michigan, and offers gang prevention programs at 1913 West Division Street and at 1551 West Madison Street.

See also: Jane Addams, William Rainey Harper, Graham Taylor

Further reading: Carson, Mina. *Settlement Folk: Social Thought and the American Settlement Movement 1885–1930* (1990); Slayton, Robert A. *Back of the Yards: The Making of a Local Democracy* (1986); Wilson, Howard Eugene. *Mary McDowell, Neighbor.* (1928).

Joseph Medill

Publisher/Politician

born: April 6, 1823
Saint John, New Brunswick, Canada
died: March 16, 1899
San Antonio, Texas

Joseph Meharry Medill was a pioneer in the development of modern journalism. His paper, the **Chicago Tribune**, *reflected, for better or worse, the man himself. Persistent, opinionated, and determined, Medill played a crucial role in the growth of the Republican party in Illinois and served as mayor of Chicago (from 1871 to 1873) during two of the most chaotic years of the city's history.*

Medill was born to a family of ship-builders in the Canadian maritime province of New Brunswick. His parents had emigrated from Ulster in 1819. The family moved to Stark County, Ohio, when Joseph was nine. He later studied law in Massillon, Ohio, and was admitted to the Ohio bar in 1846. He formed a partnership with George McIlvaine but later decided to change careers to enter the more exciting world of journalism. With his three younger brothers, he purchased the *Coshocton* (Ohio) *Whig* which he renamed the *Republican*. After moving to Cleveland in 1851 he established the *Daily Forest City* and renamed it the *Cleveland Leader*.

In 1855 Medill and an associate, Dr. Charles Ray of Galena, Illinois, purchased an interest in the *Chicago Tribune*, with Medill assuming the title of business manager and managing editor. From the beginning the *Tribune* was a controversial paper. In 1859 Medill advocated the nomination of Abraham Lincoln for president. Some historians contend that without the *Tribune's* vociferous support, Lincoln would never have received the nomination, much less the presidency. During the Civil War the Republican *Tribune* competed against Cyrus McCormick's equally strident antiwar paper, the *Chicago Times*, battling for the hearts and minds of the city's readers. Ironically, the two families came to a mutual understanding when Medill's daughter married McCormick's nephew and a newspaper dynasty was born.

Medill was a man of strong opinions. He detested gambling. An avowed teetotaler, he staunchly supported the temperance movement. The somber and aloof Medill also harbored some rather unusual and con-tradictory beliefs. An outspoken abolitionist and one of the first journalists to oppose slavery, he was also blatantly racist and anti-Catholic. He held little sympathy for the unemployed and, according to historian David L. Protess, especially loathed strikers whom he called the "scum and filth of the city." Indeed, in one particulary cruel editorial, he proposed placing "a little strychnine or arsenic" in their food.

In 1869 Medill was elected to the Illinois constitutional convention. Shortly after the Great Fire of 1871, he was elected mayor of Chicago on a platform that called for strict fire-proofing regulations. He was an effective administrator. He convinced the Illinois legislature to grant the mayoral office more power; supervised the rebuilding of the city; established Chicago's first public library; and reformed the police and fire departments. During his first year in office he rescued the city from virtual bankruptcy through frugal and sound management practices. Succumbing to pressure from Protestant ministers, Medill enforced the Sunday closing laws that shut down taverns on the Sabbath. He never recovered politically from this very unpopular decision.

In ill-health and exasperated by the daily grind of city government, Medill asked the city council for a leave of absence for the remainder of his term. He designated Alderman Lester L. Bond of the 10th Ward as acting mayor. He toured Europe, regained his strength, and returned to Chicago in 1874, not as mayor but as editor-in-chief of the *Tribune*. As editor, he promoted business interests and criticized the burgeoning labor movement. During the days leading up to the Spanish-American War, Medill published defiantly jingoistic editorials.

Medill died in San Antonio, Texas, in 1899 at the age of seventy-five.

That same year Medill's son-in-law, Robert W. Patterson, assumed the position of editor-in-chief at the *Tribune* and when Patterson died in 1910 his son, Robert R. McCormick, took over. On October 19, 1925, the Tribune Company authorized funding for the Medill School of Journalism at Northwestern University—the school had existed since 1921—in honor of Medill's considerable contribution to the world of journalism.

See also: William Bross, Robert R. McCormick, Wilbur F. Storey

Further reading: Protess, David L. "Joseph Medill: Chicago's First Modern Mayor" in *The Mayors: The Chicago Political Tradition,* Paul M. Green and Melvin G. Holli, eds. (1987); Rex, Frederick F. *The Mayors of the City of Chicago* (1934); Wendt, Lloyd. *Chicago Tribune: The Rise of a Great American Newspaper* (1979).

Charles E. Merriam

Educator/Politician

born: November 15, 1874
Hopkinton, Iowa
died: January 8, 1953
Rockville, Maryland

Charles E. Merriam was one of the foremost economists in the United States. As an alderman, he strived to adapt scientific principles to the tumultuous world of Chicago politics. As political science professor at the University of Chicago, he taught a liberal, some would say radical, brand of political theory to generations of college students.

Merriam received his education in the Iowa public school system, at Lenox College, and at the University of Iowa. He received his doctorate degree in political science from Columbia University in 1900. He also studied at the universities of Paris and Berlin.

Merriam came to Chicago in 1900 to join the faculty of the University of Chicago. Eleven years later he became chairman of the political science department. In 1909 he turned theory into practice when he was elected alderman from the 7th Ward on the far South Side, which extended from 71st Street on the south to 51st on the north, State Street on the west and Lake Michigan on the east. In 1911 he ran as the Republican candidate for mayor, but he was narrowly defeated by Carter Harrison II. In 1912 he was reelected to his aldermanic seat and remained in office until 1917. Two years later, in 1919, he opposed William Hale Thompson in the Republican primary of the mayoral election, but again he was defeated.

Merriam was the darling of the city's reform element. He called for the streamlining of local government, advocated an end to political patronage, and suggested improvements in the civil service system. Moreover, he urged the consolidation of the police, health, fire, water, drainage, recreational, and judicial services of both city and county governments. Merriam was at his most unorthodox when he endorsed independent statehood or "city-state" status for Chicago.

As a leading member of the Chicago Charter Convention during the first decade of this century, Merriam called for the adoption of a special city charter, reiterated the necessity of controlling local finances through tax collection, and recommended a municipal court system to replace the antiquated justice of the peace courts. Further, Merriam maintained that Chicago had the right to manage its own affairs without first seeking approval from Springfield.

During World War I, Merriam served as a captain in the United States Army Signal Corps. He traveled to Italy in 1918 as a member of the American Commission on Public Information for which the Italian government decorated him with the rank of Commander of the Order of the Royal Crown of Italy.

Merriam served as vice-chairman of President Herbert Hoover's Commission on Social Trends, and he was appointed a member of President Franklin Roosevelt's National Planning Board. He was instrumental in the planning of Roosevelt's monumental social security program, and he helped organize the Social Science Research Council, a national clearing house. He was elected president of that council in 1924. In that same year he assumed the presidency of the American Political Science Association.

A prolific writer, among his many books are *A History of American Political Theories* (1903), *American Political Ideas* (1920), *New Aspects of Politics* (1925), *Chicago: A More Intimate View of Urban Politics* (1929), *The Role of Politics in Social Change* (1936), *The New Democracy and the New Despotism* (1939), and *Systematic Politics* (1945).

Merriam, who lived at 6041 South University Avenue, retired from the faculty of the University of Chicago in 1940. In March of 1952 he suffered a stroke. He died in January 1953 in Rockville, Maryland. Two years later, his son Robert Merriam ran for mayor but was defeated by Richard J. Daley.

See also: Richard J. Daley, Carter Harrison II, William Hale Thompson

Further reading: Karl, Barry D. *Charles E. Merriam and the Study of Politics* (1974).

Ralph Metcalfe

Politician

born: May 30, 1910
Atlanta, Georgia
died: October 10, 1978
Chicago, Illinois

Ralph H. Metcalfe, a former Olympic track star, rose through the ranks of the Cook County Democratic organization to emerge as a powerful alderman and congressman in the African-American community. For most of his political life, he was a solid and silent member of Richard J. Daley's team until late in his career when Metcalfe asserted his independence and broke with the mayor. The Daley camp branded Metcalfe a turncoat but, in the eyes of the African-American community, he was a hero.

Photograph reprinted with permission from the *Chicago Sun-Times.*

Born in Atlanta, Georgia, Metcalfe moved with his family to Chicago, where he grew up at 3409 South Calumet Avenue and attended the public schools. He became a track star at Tilden Technical High School. At Marquette University in Milwaukee, Wisconsin, Metcalfe became captain of the college track team and emerged as a national collegiate champion in the 100- and 220-yard dashes. A member of the United States Olympic track team in 1932 and 1936, Metcalfe won silver medals both times, finishing second to Jesse Owens and sharing a gold medal in the 400-meter relay in 1936. During World War II Metcalfe served in the army as a lieutenant.

After the war Metcalfe returned to Chicago and entered politics. In 1949 he became the first African-American appointed to the Illinois State Athletic Commission and served as an administrative assistant to the Board of Examiners under Mayor Martin Kennelly.

Metcalfe was a protégé of United States representative William L. Dawson, a powerful black politician who ran his South Side district with an iron fist. With Dawson's backing, Metcalfe replaced State Senator C. C. Wimbish in 1952 as Democratic committeeman of the 3rd Ward. In 1955 Metcalfe supported Richard J. Daley's bid for mayor and won his first term as alderman of the 3rd Ward. When Dawson retired in 1970, Daley supported Metcalfe's bid to take over Dawson's 1st Congressional District seat. Metcalfe won reelection three times.

In 1969 Metcalfe became the first African-American elected to the post of president pro tempore of the city council. As a member of the Black Congressional Congress, Metcalfe grew increasingly critical of the Daley administration. When several close friends complained of police harassment, he openly advocated police reform. Finally in 1972, Metcalfe broke rank with Daley over the sensitive issue of police brutality.

In 1974 influential members of the African-American community formed a committee to elect an African-American mayor. When Daley made clear that he would run again, however, Metcalfe dropped his candidacy—he didn't think he had a chance—and instead endorsed independent hopeful, Alderman William S. Singer. Metcalfe received a great deal of criticism for supporting Singer, a white man, over the only black candidate, State Senator Richard Newhouse. Metcalfe countered that his decision was a matter of politics not of race. He did not agree with Newhouse on several important issues, he explained, including Newhouse's lack of support for the Equal Rights Amendment (ERA).

In 1976 Daley and the Democratic party refused to support Metcalfe for reelection. Instead, Daley chose aide Erwin France to challenge Metcalfe in the Democratic primary for Congress. Metcalfe won easily. It was the first time in Chicago history, declares historian Dempsey Travis, that any politician—black or white—had defeated the machine in a congressional primary or general election.

Metcalfe founded the Ralph H. Metcalfe Youth Foundation, which sponsored health, athletic, and educational programs in the African-American community. A popular figure among his constituency, he never lost his base of support even in 1972 when he was investigated by the IRS concerning allegations that he took zoning bribes while he was a member of the city council. The charges were later dropped.

Metcalfe died of a heart attack in his third floor apartment at 4530 South Michigan Avenue in 1978. He was sixty-eight.

In 1981 the West Pullman–Nansen Area School located at 12339 South Normal Avenue was renamed in his honor.

See also: Richard J. Daley, Harold Washington

Further reading: Travis, Dempsey J. *An Autobiography of Black Chicago* (1981); Travis, Dempsey J. *An Autobiography of Black Politics* (1987).

Mezz Mezzrow

Musician

born: November 9, 1899
Chicago, Illinois
died: August 5, 1972
Paris, France

*Clarinetist and saxman, Milton Mesirow founded one of the first interracial jazz bands. Mezzrow, a young white Jewish boy from a wealthy Chicago family, found sustenance in African-American culture. He survived prison and drug addiction to become an important figure in local, national, and international jazz circles. To some he was a sycophant and hanger-on and a mediocre musician at best, others saw in him a touch of genius. "If you want to play real jazz," he wrote in his autobiography, **Really the Blues**, "go live close to the Negro, see through his eyes, laugh and cry with him, soak up his spirit."*

A high-strung kid with a great deal of nervous energy, Mezzrow turned to crime out of boredom. "Don't get the idea I was born a criminal," he wrote in his autobiography. "My family was as respectable as Sunday morning, loaded with doctors, lawyers, dentists, and pharmacists, and they all worked hard to make a solid citizen out of me. They almost did it, too." "The law," wrote Mezzrow, "didn't catch up with me until I was sixteen years old."

Mezzrow first picked up a musical instrument, the saxophone, at the Pontiac Reformatory in Michigan while serving a jail sentence for stealing a car. Following his release in 1917, he played clubs in and around Chicago.

Mezzrow turned professional in 1923 and played occasionally with members of the famous Austin High gang of the 1920s, including Bud Freeman, Jimmy McPartland, Gene Krupa, and Frank Teschemacher. He also played with Irving Rothschild in 1925 and Husk O'Hare's Wolverines in 1926.

In 1928 Mezzrow recorded with the Jungle Kings and the Chicago Rhythm Kings and in the same year served as the leader of the short-lived Purple Grackle Orchestra.

As many Chicago musicians did, Mezzrow moved to New York in 1928 to further his career, subbing for Gil Rodin in Ben Pollack's Band. In October of 1928, according to jazz writer John Chilton, he recorded with Eddie Condon. The following March he sailed for Europe and led his own band in Paris. By April of 1929 he was back in New York. He later worked as a freelance musician in New York during the 1930s and 1940s.

In 1937 his interracial band, the Disciples of Swing, played the Harlem Uproar House and the Savoy Ballroom. During the early 1940s he worked with fellow Chicagoan Art Hodes. Later, Mezzrow formed his own record company, King Jazz. In the late 1940s and early 1950s he toured Europe before settling again in Paris, where he worked as a self-proclaimed entrepreneur and jazz promoter, organizing touring bands. During the 1950s he formed several all-star bands, which featured such top-notch musicians as Lee Collins, Zutty Singleton, and Buck Clayton.

Mezzrow is known not so much because of his music—which most critics find lacking in both execution and substance—but due to his sensational autobiography, *Really the Blues*, which he co-wrote with Bernard Wolfe in 1946. *Really the Blues* met with great literary success. Despite the recognition the book brought to Mezzrow, the achievement for which he truly deserves a place in the annals of jazz is the many important recording sessions with the great masters that he organized, especially those with clarinetist/saxophonist Sidney Bechet and trumpeter Tommy Ladnier.

Mezzrow set his own rules and lived life the way he saw fit. Tenor saxophonist Bud Freeman, who used to visit Mezzrow in his cramped Rogers Park apartment, recalls in his autobiography that Mezzrow "was the first white man I ever knew to move to Harlem and marry a black woman and have a child by a black. I had to love that about him because we lived in a time when prejudice was unbelievable. Mezz . . . knew things about the black people, their way of thinking and their music, that very few white people did." Mezzrow adopted black music and culture to such an extent that, according to coauthor Bernard Wolfe, he believed he actually was black.

Mezzrow continued to make appearances at festivals in Europe during the 1960s. During his last years, however, he rarely performed in public. Like many of the African-Americans he idolized, Mezzrow died in Paris, in self-exile, in 1972.

See also: Bud Freeman, Benny Goodman, Gene Krupa

Further reading: Chilton, John. *Who's Who of Jazz: Storyville to Swing Street* (1978); Freeman, Bud, as told to Robert Wolf. *Crazeology: The Autobiography of a Chicago Jazzman* (1989); Kernfeld, Barry, ed. *The New Grove Dictionary of Jazz.* vol. 2 (1988); Mezzrow, Mezz and Bernard Wolfe. *Really the Blues* (1972).

Albert A. Michelson

Physicist

born: December 19, 1852
Strelno, Prussia
(now Strzelno, Poland)
died: May 9, 1931
Pasadena, California

Albert Abraham Michelson is regarded as one of the great minds of the twentieth century. He strove for absolute accuracy in his pioneering experiments to determine the speed of light, and this work, which he completed at the University of Chicago, paved the way for Einstein's theory of relativity.

Albert's mother, Rosalie Pruzlubsk, the daughter of a physician, married Samuel Michelson, proprietor of a dry goods store in Prussia. The family immigrated to the United States when Michelson was two. He grew up in Virginia City, Nevada, and in San Francisco. He graduated from the United States Naval Academy in Annapolis, Maryland, in 1873. After two years of duty, Michelson returned to the academy to teach chemistry and physics. In 1878, while an instructor at Annapolis, he conducted preliminary experiments measuring the speed of light—the most precise measurements at that time—using a makeshift instrument that he constructed himself. In 1881 he resigned from the Navy to concentrate further on his own scientific work.

In 1883 Michelson became professor of physics at Case School of Applied Science (now Case Western Reserve University). Six years later he moved to Clark University in Ohio. In 1892 he was appointed head of the physics department at the recently established University of Chicago.

When he arrived in Chicago, Michelson was already a famous man. He continued to devote a large part of his research to measuring the speed of light. In 1880 he had invented the interferometer, a highly sensitive instrument that measured light rays and determined distances that even the most powerful telescope couldn't determine. In 1887 Michelson and Edward W. Morley ran two beams of light against each other from opposite directions and proved that the speed of light is a constant. At that time the scientific community was grappling with the problems of measuring absolute motion (as opposed to relative motion). The concept of "ether" (an elastic medium in space through which motion occurs) helped to resolve certain fundamental theoretical difficulties of electricity and magnetism. Michelson and

Morley demonstrated the absence of ether. The results of Michelson and Morley's experiments were not explained by classical Newtonian physics, and, therefore, formed the foundation of Albert Einstein's theory of relativity.

In 1920, by using the interferometer, Michelson was able to measure the diameter of the star Betelgeuse, which allowed scientists to obtain a more accurate picture of the size of the universe. In 1927, after flashing light beams from Mount Wilson to another nearby peak, he calculated the speed of light at 186,284 miles per second. He spent his last years producing a more precise figure.

In 1907 Michelson was the first American to be awarded the Nobel Prize for Physics, for his work in meteorology and spectroscopy, which he had studied in Lake Geneva, Wisconsin. Michelson was appointed head of the physics department at the University of Chicago in 1892 and remained on the faculty until he announced his retirement in 1930. In 1925 Michelson became the first Distinguished Service Professor at the University of Chicago.

He wrote several books, including *Velocity of Light* (1902); *Light Waves and Their Uses* (1903); and *Studies in Optics* (1927).

Michelson was one of the most respected scientists in the world. Among the universities that awarded him honorary degrees were Cambridge, Yale, Princeton, Leipzig, McGill, Western Reserve, and Pennsylvania. He died in Pasadena, California in 1931. He was seventy-eight.

See also: William Rainey Harper

Further reading: Livingston, Dorothy Michelson. *The Master of Light: A Biography of Albert A. Michelson* (1973).

Ludwig Mies van der Rohe

Architect

born: March 27, 1886
Aachen, Germany
died: August 19, 1969
Chicago, Illinois

One of the founding fathers of modern architecture, Ludwig Mies van der Rohe's designs were deceptively simple. To critics his work was cold, austere, and sterile; to admirers, it was bold, breathtaking, and innovative. Eventually, Mies van der Rohe came to epitomize modern architecture. By the time of his death, every major city in the Western world, wrote noted art critic Franz Schulze, bore Mies van der Rohe's indelible stamp.

Photograph reprinted with permission from the *Chicago Sun-Times*.

Born Ludwig Mies in the German city of Aachen (in 1921, he added his mother's name, Rohe, with "van der" as the connecting bridge), Mies studied at a local trades school. He worked as an architectural draftsman until he moved to Berlin in 1905, where he was apprenticed to a furniture designer. At twenty-one, he designed the residence of a prominent client, which brought him to the attention of Germany's premier architect, Peter Behrens. After working with Behrens for three years, Mies established his own practice.

Fascinated by the aesthetic possibilities of glass, Mies was one of the first architects to design glass skyscrapers. By the early 1920s he had become a leading figure of modern architecture. In 1927 Mies, Walter Gropius, Behrens, and others constructed a housing estate, the Weissenhof settlement, on a hill overlooking the city of Stuttgart. The settlement, designed as a contemporary living space for the urban dweller, shocked the architectural establishment from their complacency. Weissenhof was such a radical departure from historic architectural norms—consisting as it did of low, box-like structures—that though designed with the ordinary citizen in mind it soon became the favored living quarters of journalists, actors, and intellectuals. Mies's stock rose even higher. It wasn't until 1929, however, with the completion of the German Pavilion at the Barcelona International Exposition—critics referred to it as Mies's European masterpiece—that the architect finally emerged as a world-class artist.

In 1930 Mies was appointed director of the Bauhaus, the influential German school of design. Yet three short years later, Mies shut down the school as Hitler and Nazism spread throughout the country.

In 1936 Mies received a letter from John A. Holabird of the Chicago architectural firm of Holabird and Root. Holabird headed a search committee to locate a director of the architecture school at the Armour Institute of Technology (now the Illinois Institute of Technology). Mies expressed interest. In 1938, with conditions in Germany rapidly deteriorating, he accepted the offer. He stayed for twenty years. The following year the administration asked him to draw up a master plan for the school's one-hundred-acre campus.

Mies's spare, functional glass towers changed the Chicago landscape. Whereas the skyscrapers of the late nineteenth to early twentieth century used traditional materials such as stone and brick decorated with classical columns and motifs, Mies preferred a simpler, angular design with little or no ornamentation. Some critics would later condemn Miesian architecture for its sterility and lack of humanity. Mies, however, argued that architecture should mirror its particular culture and milieu. Thus his work, in large part, reflected the twentieth-century obsession with technology and industry.

Some of his most important buildings in Chicago include the Promontory Apartments at 5530 South Shore Drive (1949); the twin apartment buildings at 860-880 North Lake Shore Drive, among the first glass-and-steel highrises in the world (1952); Crown Hall on the Illinois Institute of Technology campus on South State Street between 31st and 35th Streets (1956); and the Federal Center at Jackson, Dearborn, Adams, and Clark Streets (1965). The last building he designed was the fifty-two-story IBM building, completed in 1971. Among his famous international commissions are: the New National Gallery in Berlin (1967) and the Dominion Centre in Toronto (1969).

In 1944 Mies became an American citizen. Although a man of means in his later years, he never lived a luxurious lifestyle. His apartment at 200 East Pearson Street was simply furnished. He reportedly preferred to live there rather than in a building that he designed for he feared that tenants might complain to him personally, notes Schulze.

In 1958 Mies retired from IIT. During the last decade of his life, arthritis confined him to a wheelchair, but he kept working. In 1966 he contracted cancer of the esophagus and died three years later from pneumonia at the age of eighty-three. His body was cremated and his ashes buried in Graceland Cemetery in Chicago near the graves of two other prominent Chicago architects, Daniel H. Burnham and Louis Sullivan.

Following Mies's death, there was a pronounced movement away from modernism. Postmodernists such as Michael Graves, Philip Johnson, and Thomas Beebe bemoaned the numbing sameness of highrise boxes that dotted the urban skylines. In recent years, though, Mies's accomplishments have been reevaluated and his stature as one of the great architects of the twentieth century seems secure.

After his death such Miesian disciples as Joseph Fujikawa, Dirk Lohan, and Helmut Jahn carried on his legacy as did the firms of C. F. Murphy and Associates and the prolific Skidmore, Owings and Merrill. Several prominent examples of Miesian-influenced architecture include the Richard J. Daley Center at Washington and Dearborn Streets (1965); the CNA Tower at Jackson Boulevard and Wabash Avenue (1972); the Sears Tower at Adams and Franklin Streets (1974); Illinois Center at North Michigan Avenue and East Randolph Drive (1975); and the Federal Building at 77 West Jackson Boulevard, which is presently under construction and which complements Mies's Federal Center a few blocks north.

In 1986 several museums, including the Illinois Institute of Technology and the Art Institute of Chicago, sponsored major exhibitions of his life and work in honor of the centennial of his birth.

See also: Daniel H. Burnham, Louis Sullivan, Frank Lloyd Wright

Further reading: Molloy, Mary Alice. *Chicago Since the Sears Tower: A Guide to New Downtown Buildings* (1990); Saliga, Pauline A., ed. *The Sky's the Limit, A Century of Chicago Skyscrapers* (1990); Schulze, Franz. *Mies van der Rohe: A Critical Biography* (1985).

Harriet Monroe

Poet/Publisher

born: December 23, 1860
Chicago, Illinois
died: September 26, 1936
Arequipa, Peru

*Poet, journalist, essayist, Harriet Monroe is best remembered as the guiding spirit behind **Poetry**, the magazine that she founded in 1912. Not only did **Poetry** form the heart and soul of the Chicago Literary Renaissance, it was the only magazine in the U.S. at that time devoted exclusively to poetry.*

Harriet's father, Henry Monroe, a lawyer, arrived in Chicago in 1852. Harriet was born in 1860 in the family's rented house at 12th Street and Wabash. A lonely child, Harriet found solace in the books that lined her father's library. According to historian Geoffrey Johnson she was unusually sensitive, and even at ten years old she had considered suicide to relieve her from her inner demons. Social historian Dale Kramer wrote that Monroe's emotional attachments were toward "the arts and to countries and to mountains. Harriet dedicated herself to a poet's life."

In 1877 Monroe enrolled at Visitation Convent, a genteel girls' boarding school in Georgetown. Most of her classmates were there to learn how to become perfect wives. Monroe had other ideas. After graduation, she began planning her future. As she states in her autobiography, she wanted her life to have a purpose, to accomplish a great good, for "to die without leaving some memorable record" was, in her mind, a great tragedy. "My career was to be rich and all-embracing."

Monroe supported herself with freelance articles, lectures, and teaching. At two different periods in her life, she served as the art critic for the *Chicago Tribune*.

In 1891 she convinced members of the World's Columbian Exposition committee that a poem commemorating the fair was not only appropriate but essential. The committee commissioned Monroe, at her suggestion, and she submitted her first draft in May of 1893.

Influential committee members rejected the poem, which honored the United States and its heroes, as too long and too staid. Even so, Monroe insisted on her fee of $1,000. After much heated discussion, the poem was used. In December of 1894 Monroe became embroiled in a legal battle when the *New York World* published "Columbian Ode" without her permission. In a bold, precedent-setting move, she sued for infringement of copyright and was awarded $5,000 in punitive damages.

Monroe continued to write sporadically for the *Tribune* as well as published literary and travel essays in the *Atlantic, The Century*, and *London's Fortnightly Review*. She also supplemented her income with teaching and lecturing. In 1910 she took off on one of her frequent journeys, traveling across Siberia from Moscow en route to visit her sister in Peking. After much thought, she returned to Chicago in 1911, determined to create a market for poetry. "The poets needed a magazine, an organ of their own, and I would start one for them!" she declared.

It was a bold move. No magazine of its kind existed in the United States. With the financial help of Hobart C. Chatfield-Taylor, a wealthy Chicago socialite, Monroe pushed ahead with her plans. She was able to convince one hundred prominent people to pledge $50 a year for five years toward the fledgling magazine. The list of contributors included a veritable Who's Who of Chicago's elite: Potter Palmer, businessman Martin Ryerson, George Pullman, businessman John Glessner, Daniel H. Burnham, Samuel Insull, Charles L. Hutchinson, president of the Art Institute; Edith Rockefeller McCormick; Charles H. Swift; Rev. F. W. Gunsaulus, president of the Armour Institute of Technology; Herman H. Kohlsaat, editor of the *Chicago Record-Herald*; Victor Lawson, editor and publisher of the *Chicago Daily News*; Howard Van Doren Shaw; Clarence Darrow; and Harriet Moody, widow of the poet William

Vaughn Moody. Next, she began recruiting poets, gambling on the young and untried. One of those poets was Ezra Pound, a self-imposed American exile, who had become the literary sensation of London and Paris.

Pound was instrumental in the success of Monroe's new magazine, which she simply called *Poetry*. He introduced the work of William Butler Yeats, Robert Frost, Richard Aldington, James Joyce, Ford Madox Ford, D. H. Lawrence, William Carlos Williams, and an American student of philosophy at Oxford, Thomas Stearns Eliot. It was Pound who sent Monroe a copy of Eliot's "The Love Song of J. Alfred Prufrock."

Back in Chicago, Harriet worked diligently on the day-to-day chores of putting out a magazine. Among her editorial assistants were Chatfield-Taylor, Edith Wyatt, and Henry Blake Fuller. The first issue was published on September 23, 1912, and included an essay by Monroe, a poem by William Vaughn Moody, and contributions from Pound and others.

Poetry became the talk of the literary set. The city's poets and authors—including Carl Sandburg, Vachel Lindsay, and Edgar Lee Masters—stopped by the magazine headquarters on 543 North Cass Street (now Wabash Avenue). Monroe herself became a close friend and confidant to the city's literary folk and distinguished guests—Glenway Wescott, Marianne Moore, Robert Graves, Malcolm Cowley, Eunice Tietjens, and many others. She published the early works of Lindsay and Masters. The local press was generally supportive of the magazine, and Chicago newspapers, including the *Tribune* and the *Friday Literary Review*, were generous in their praise.

Monroe's collected verse, *Chosen Poems*, was published in 1935. She also wrote a biography of her famous brother-in-law (he was married to her sister, Dora), architect John Wellborn Root. She began to write her autobiography when she was invited in 1936 to represent Chicago for a convention of P.E.N. (International Association of Poets, Playwrights, Editors, Essayists, and Novelists) in Buenos Aires. Taking advantage of the South American locale, she decided to take a side trip to Chile and Peru. The journey proved too strenuous for her—she was seventy-five—and she died on September 26, 1936, in the Peruvian village of Arequipa and was buried there.

See also: Henry Blake Fuller, Vachel Lindsay, Edgar Lee Masters, William Vaughn Moody [appendix], John Wellborn Root, Carl Sandburg

Further reading: Johnson, Geoffrey. "Little Captain of the Ragged, the Mad Army of Poets," *Chicago Reader* (September 6, 1985); Kramer, Dale. *Chicago Renaissance: The Literary Life of the Midwest, 1900–1903* (1966); Monroe, Harriet. *A Poet's Life: Seventy Years in a Changing World* (1938); Smith, Alson J. *Chicago's Left Bank* (1953); Williams, Ellen. *Harriet Monroe and the Poetry Renaissance: The First Ten Years of Poetry, 1912–22* (1977).

Dwight L. Moody

Evangelist

born: February 5, 1837
Northfield, Massachusetts
died: December 22, 1899
Northfield, Massachusetts

Although not ordained, Dwight Lyman Moody was an influential evangelist whose wildly successful campaigns predated a later generation of preachers from Billy Graham to Jimmy Swaggart. Not so much concerned with social sins—smoking, card playing, drinking, gambling—Moody chose to emphasize the spiritual well-being of his congregation. "Character," he once said, "is what a man is in the dark."

The sixth child of Edwin and Betsy Holton Moody, Dwight attended school in Northfield, Massachusetts, until he was thirteen and then moved to Boston at seventeen to work in his uncle's shoe store. His employment, however, was on the condition that he attend the Mount Vernon Congregational Church. Moody began attending Sunday school classes at the church, taught by Edward Kimball. In April of 1855 Kimball converted Moody to evangelical Christianity. The following year Moody moved to Chicago and found work as a shoe salesman. He spent more time, however, with pursuits more spiritual than selling shoes.

Moody started a Sunday school for slum children in 1858 at Chicago Avenue and Wells Street. Then he moved the Sunday school to an abandoned saloon on the north side of the Chicago River in a section of town called "Little Hell." With attendance overflowing capacity, he used the upstairs room in North Market Hall on Hubbard Street for his school, and he reportedly recruited students by pulling orphans off the street. In February of 1864 he opened the Illinois Street Church. When this was destroyed in the Chicago Fire in 1871, he rebuilt the church and called it the North Side Tabernacle. The name was changed again to the Chicago Avenue Church, located at Chicago Avenue and LaSalle Street, predecessor of today's structure at LaSalle Street and North Avenue.

Moody was a familiar figure on Chicago streets. He went about the business of selling God to thousands of apathetic Chicagoans. He ventured into saloons and brothels, accosted thief, liar, and beggar, and demanded to know if they were Christian. If not, he would ask why not. "Come to my church. Be saved!"

Journalists called him "Brother Moody." Others, less kind, dismissed him as "Crazy Moody."

During the Civil War, Moody conducted missionary services among the Union soldiers at Camp Douglas on the South Side. When the war ended he became president of the Chicago branch of the Young Men's Christian Association (YMCA). From 1873 to 1875 he embarked with organist Ira D. Sankey on tours through Scotland, England, and Ireland, where he spread the expansive spirit of evangelism.

He returned to the United States a famous man. Deciding to leave Chicago, he returned to his hometown to establish the Northfield School for Girls and, several years later, the Northfield School for Boys. He made another successful tour of Great Britain from 1881 to 1883 and a final one from 1891 to 1892.

During his prolonged absence from the city, Moody's work was continued by Emma Dryer, a teacher at Illinois State Normal University, whom he first met in 1870. In 1886 he returned to Chicago to deliver a lecture calling for the establishment of a permanent ministry training school. The following year the Chicago Evangelization Society was organized, and on September 26, 1889, the Chicago Bible Institute, a coeducational missionary school, officially opened. The goal of the organization was "to educate, direct, and maintain Christian workers as Bible readers, teachers, and evangelists."

Moody purportedly reached more people than any church-sanctioned clergyman. He achieved this by preaching a simple brand of Christianity that millions of ordinary folk found immensely appealing. Contemporary accounts describe Moody's campaigns as the spiritual equivalent of business conventions.

With singer Sankey, Moody published several popular collections of hymns, including *Sacred Songs and Solos* (1873) and *Gospel Hymns* (1875-1891). Although Sankey wrote only a handful of hymns himself (and the tone-deaf Moody didn't write any), he is credited with popularizing the gospel hymn among the white community.

The growth of the Chicago Bible Institute coincided with Chicago's rapid escalation as a great commercial center. Moody's aggressive recruiting methods as well as his insistence on a quality teaching staff helped transform his humble Sunday school into a top-notch institution. Indeed, throughout its long history, the Moody Bible Institute (the Chicago Bible Institute was renamed the Moody Bible Institute of Chicago after Moody's death) has enjoyed a stellar reputation as a world-class evangelical training center. The institute combines theological education with Biblical training and offers programs leading to B.A., B.S., and M.A. degrees. Over one hundred years after its founding, the school continues to spread the Word.

In December of 1899 Moody died in his native Massachusetts of a heart attack at the age of sixty-two. The Moody Church, dedicated in 1925 at North Avenue and LaSalle Street, serves as a memorial to this remarkable evangelist.

See also: Jenkin Lloyd Jones [appendix], David Swing, Billy Sunday

Further reading: Curtis, Richard K. *They Called Him Mister Moody* (1962); Getz, Gene A. *MBI: The Story of the Moody Bible Institute* (1969); Moody, Paul D. *My Father: An Intimate Portrait of Dwight Moody* (1938); Pollock, John C. *Moody: A Biographical Portrait of the Pacesetter in Modern Mass Evangelism* (1963); Reid, Daniel G., ed. *Dictionary of Christianity in America* (1990).

Archibald J. Motley, Jr.

Painter

born: October 7, 1891
New Orleans, Louisiana
died: January 16, 1981
Chicago, Illinois

Archibald John Motley, Jr., the brother of novelist Willard Motley, was the first American painter who devoted his career exclusively to African-American subject matter and one of the first successful black artists in this century. Motley's candid depictions attempted to portray African-American life as accurately as possible.

Photograph courtesy of the Chicago Historical Society.

Born in New Orleans, Motley moved to Chicago with his family in 1894. Motley's upbringing—his father, a Pullman porter, played an important role in the founding of the Brotherhood of Sleeping Car Porters; and Motley's mother was a schoolteacher—instilled a strong sense of pride in his African heritage.

Motley was the only male in his Englewood High School art class. Through his position as a railroad porter, Motley's father met Rev. Frank W. Gunsaulus, president of the Armour Institute of Technology. Gunsaulus offered Motley a full scholarship to study architecture at the Armour Institute. Flattered but determined to become a painter, Motley turned him down. Gunsaulus, impressed by the young man's persistence, then offered to pay for one year of study at the Art Institute. Motley agreed, and he enrolled in 1914. Four years later he graduated with honors, "one of the few Chicago blacks," says Elaine D. Woodall in *Chicago History,* "to have completed the full four-year course."

Unable to secure employment as a commercial artist at advertising agencies because of his race, Motley found work as a dining car waiter, a steamfitter in the Union Stockyards, and a plumber, while continuing to paint in the evenings. In 1920, at the urging of friends, he submitted *Portrait of My Mother* to the Art Institute for its Annual Exhibition by Artists of Chicago and the Vicinity. During the next few years *Portrait* and four other works were accepted. This recognition was a major turning point in Motley's career.

In 1928 Motley's paintings were exhibited at the New Gallery in New York. Motley was one of the first African-American artists to have a solo exhibition at a commercial gallery. Woodall refers to this exhibition as "the unrivaled hit of the season."

The following year Motley won a Guggenheim fellowship to study art in Paris for one year. That same year he became one of twelve African-Americans to receive a Harmon Foundation award for his painting *Octaroon Girl.*

The Harmon Foundation, founded by a wealthy white businessman named William E. Harmon, was a philanthropic organization that mounted traveling exhibitions of African-American art from 1928 to 1933 (although it no longer sponsored shows, the organization itself continued to exist until 1967). The foundation's exhibitions revealed an aspect of African-American life that few white Americans knew existed.

Motley portrayed contemporary African-American life in all its forms. He painted African-Americans at play in dance halls, in pool halls, and at family picnics and other family gatherings; he painted aristocrats and criminals; and occasionally, he depicted historical scenes. Portraiture was his forte. *Portrait of My Mother,* which Woodall calls one of the first realistic portrayals of an African-American by an African-American, is considered a landmark in African-American art.

Motley's frank representation of black life offended certain members of the African-American community. One of the most outspoken critics was William Farrow, president of the Chicago Arts League, an African-American arts organization. Farrow objected to Motley's depiction of what Farrow considered "low life" situations—cabarets and dance halls—and which Farrow believed only reinforced negative stereotypes of the race.

Motley returned to the U.S. from Paris as the country faced the economic hardship of the Depression.

Private funding for the arts consequently withered, and Motley, like
other artists, could only find work
through the government-sponsored
arts programs. From 1935 to 1939
Motley worked for the mural division
of the Illinois Federal Arts Project. In
1935 he taught as artist-in-residence
at Howard University in Washington, D. C.

Among Motley's major pieces are *A
Mulattress* (1924), *Mending Socks* (1924),
Syncopation (1924), *Black Belt* (1934), *Dans
la rue, Paris* (1929), *Blues* (1929), *Playing
Poker* (1930), *Picnic* (1936), *The Liar*
(1936), and *Gettin' Religion* (1948).

Motley's work, among the work of
other African-American artists, was
featured in August 1990 in "Against
the Odds: African-American Artists
and the Harmon Foundation," at the
Chicago Public Library Cultural Center. In October of 1991 the Chicago
Historical Society will sponsor "The
Art of Archibald J. Motley, Jr.," a
major retrospective of his career.

Motley did not consider himself an
"African-American artist"—he found
that expression too limiting—but
rather an American painter of African-American art. It is ironic then
that he is remembered as one of the
first members of his race to achieve
success in the art world.

Motley painted only sporadically
during the last thirty years of his life.
He lived at 350 West 60th Street for
many years, but later moved to 1809
North Lincoln Park West, where he
died at the age of eighty-nine.

"I feel my work is peculiarly American, a sincere personal expression of
the age, and I hope a contribution to
society," he said. "The Negro is part
of America and the Negro is part of
our great American art."

See also: Willard Motley

Further reading: Low, W. Augustus
and Virgil A. Clift. *Encyclopedia of
Black Americans* (1981); Ploski, Harry
A. and James Williams, eds. *The Negro
Almanac: A Reference Work on the Afri-
can American* (1989); Reynolds, Gary
A. and Beryl J. Wright. *Against the
Odds: African-American Artists and the
Harmon Foundation* (1989); Woodall,
Elaine D. *Archibald J. Motley, Jr.: Ameri-
can Artist of the Afro-American People,
1891–1928* (1977); Woodall, Elaine
D. "Looking Backwards: Archibald J.
Motley and the Art Institute of Chi-
cago, 1914–1930," *Chicago History*
(Spring 1979).

Willard Motley

Novelist

born: July 14, 1912
Chicago, Illinois
died: March 4, 1965
Mexico City, Mexico

A disciple of the realism school of writing, Willard Motley wrote about the dark side of urban life. Although African-American, his books were populated with characters named Romano and Kosinski who lived out their sad, empty lives on Chicago's desolate streets and back alleys.

Photograph reprinted with permission from the *Chicago Sun-Times*.

The Motleys were the only African-American family in the all-white Englewood neighborhood on Chicago's South Side. With the notable exception of the race riots that swept through the South Side in the summer of 1919, Motley's youth was mostly free from racial strife.

Motley decided at an early age to be a writer. His literary career began in 1922 when he wrote a children's column for the *Chicago Defender*. After graduating from Englewood High School in 1929, he searched for work, but with the country in the middle of the Depression he gave up the struggle and instead decided to take advantage of the free time and bicycled to New York. This and other trips formed the raw material for much of his fiction.

Upon his return to Chicago, Motley held a series of blue-collar jobs that allowed him to observe life through the eyes of society's working poor directly. He was an order filler for the Rock Island railroad, a dishwasher, a short order cook, a waiter, and a janitor.

In 1937 he gathered his meager savings, bought an old car, and headed for the West Coast. He traveled extensively in California, Colorado, and the Pacific Northwest.

In 1940 he submitted a story to the *New Anvil*, a leftist publication edited by Jack Conroy and Nelson Algren. Although the piece was rejected, Conroy and Algren invited Motley to come down to their offices to talk. They introduced Motley to the Chicago literary scene.

Motley then found work with the WPA Writers Project, conducting interviews and gathering case histories. His beat was the West Side

slums, where he talked to as many people as he could from police officers to social workers to judges and lawyers.

In the early 1940s Motley sold his first short stories to *Commonweal* magazine. In 1941 he moved to a converted sweatshop on Maxwell Street and conducted extensive research on the West Madison Street skid row area. He prowled the streets and alleys, the bars and juke joints, diners and flophouses, gospel missions and run-down hotels, always asking questions and jotting down observations in his notebook.

His first novel, *Knock On Any Door* (1947), centered around a young Italian-American named Nick Romano, a former altar boy turned cop killer who was executed in the electric chair. His motto: "Live fast, die young, and make a good-looking corpse." Motley spent eight years researching and writing the book. With a draft at 2,100 pages and 600,000 words, it was a monumental first effort. After extensive editing, however, Motley emerged with a bestseller on his hands. It was later made into a movie starring John Derek as Romano and Humphrey Bogart as his lawyer.

Motley's next novel, *We Fished All Night* (1951), was set in postwar Chicago and told the tale of three veterans and their rise to the top of local politics. Motley made extensive use of Chicago locations, from the Gold Coast to Bughouse Square, Soldier Field to Riverview Park.

Let No Man Write My Epitaph (1958) was set on skid row and continued the story of the Romano family, focusing on Nick Romano, Jr., the illegitimate son of the lead character from *Knock On Any Door*. Although reviews were mixed, the book did attract the attention of Hollywood, and in 1960 it was turned into a movie starring James Darren and Shelley Winters.

From 1944 to 1945 Motley worked on a three-act play, *You Lovely People*, about the bohemians of Chicago's Near North Side. It was never completed. He moved to Mexico in September of 1951 and died in a Mexico City clinic from gangrene in 1965. He was only fifty-two.

At the time of his death Motley was working on another book, *My House Is Your House* (he also considered calling it *Tourist Town*), about an influx of visitors into a small Mexican village. It was edited and retitled *Let Noon Be Fair* and was published posthumously in 1966.

Race was never a central issue in Motley's work. Unlike Richard Wright who chronicled the African-American experience exclusively, Motley wrote mostly about ethnic whites. Nelson Algren once called Motley a white writer. "He wrote about white people for white people," he insisted. Neither Motley nor his brother, painter Archibald J. Motley, Jr., wanted to be considered "African-American" artists. Not until he was older did Motley address racial concerns, and that was primarily in the form of newspaper articles and essays.

See also: Robert S. Abbott, Nelson Algren, James T. Farrell, Archibald J. Motley, Jr., Richard Wright

Further reading: Klinkowitz, Jerome. *The Diaries of Willard Motley* (1978); Ploski, Harry A. and James Williams, eds. *The Negro Almanac: A Reference Work on the African-American* (1989).

Elijah Muhammad

Religious and Community Leader

born: October 10, 1897
(according to some sources:
October 7, 1897)
near Sandersville, Georgia
died: February 25, 1975
Chicago, Illinois

Elijah Muhammad—born Elijah Poole—was a day laborer who rose to become the millionaire leader of the Nation of Islam, also known as the Black Muslims, with national headquarters located on the South Side of Chicago. Muhammad promulgated the philosophy of black help and black self-determination with the ultimate goal of black nationhood. As spiritual leader of the Black Muslim movement, he was one of the most powerful religious figures of twentieth-century America.

Photograph reprinted with permission from the *Chicago Sun-Times*.

Poole's father was a former slave and Baptist preacher in rural Georgia. As a boy, Elijah worked as a sawmill helper and field hand. He attended school through the fifth grade and left home at sixteen. He moved to Atlanta where he married and then moved with his wife and children to Detroit in 1923. He worked at odd jobs in Detroit and for a brief spell was a Baptist minister.

In 1931 Elijah met Wallace Fard (or Wali Farad), a former Detroit silk peddler and leader of a small religious sect. "I recognized him," Muhammad later recalled, "to be the person the Bible predicted would come 2,000 years after Jesus' death." Fard denounced Christianity as the white man's way of keeping blacks enslaved. Poole converted, abandoned his "slave" name, adopted a Muslim name, and became Fard's chief assistant. Fard had already founded Temple No. 1 of the Nation of Islam in 1931 in Detroit. Under Fard's direction, Temple No. 2 was established in Chicago in 1934. Fard mysteriously disappeared that same year and Muhammad assumed the leadership role. When his succession was disputed, Muhammad moved the base of operations from Detroit to Chicago, organized his own movement, and deified Fard as the incarnation of Allah.

Muhammad frequently clashed with both local and national authorities. In 1934 Muhammad was arrested on charges of contributing to the delinquency of a minor because he refused to enter his son into the Detroit public school system, preferring to enroll him in a Muslim parochial school instead. During World War II he was convicted of evading selective service and accused of supporting the enemy (Muhammad supported Japan because it was a nonwhite country). Although he forbade participation in the American armed forces it wasn't because he abhorred violence but because he didn't want his followers to participate in "Caucasian wars." Muhammad served a four-year sentence in a Michigan federal prison but continued to act as leader of the Black Muslims from his cell.

One of his best-known converts was heavyweight boxing champion Cassius Clay, who later changed his name to Muhammad Ali. Ali refused to serve in the armed forces in 1967 on the ground that he was a practicing Muslim minister. For this act he was stripped of his boxing title, although the U.S. Supreme Court overturned his draft evasion conviction in 1971. Ali's well-publicized conversion brought the organization to the attention of the American public and gave it a legitimacy that it had not previously had.

In the mainstream press, Muhammad was criticized for being anti-white. The Black Muslims, in contrast to the civil rights movement, which called for integration, sought a complete break from the "white devils" who controlled the country. Furthermore, Muhammad made other demands: freedom for all Black Muslim prisoners, an end to police brutality, equal employment opportunity for blacks, exemption from taxation, the banning of interracial marriages, and total racial unity and religious conformity.

In 1974 the Muslim leader softened his criticism of the white power structure, exhorting his followers to "stop putting the blame on the slave owner. You have only yourself to blame."

The Black Muslim financial empire was built on a network of black-owned businesses across the country, which included clothing stores, restaurants, farms, banks, grocery stores, import businesses, and food processing plants. As the Black Muslim membership grew, so did conflicts within the movement itself. In 1972 reports of a power struggle emerged when four people were killed in Baton Rouge, Louisiana. Probably the most controversial incident during Muhammad's years in power occurred when one of his protégés, Malcolm X (born Malcolm Little), who had started his own nationalist movement, was assassinated in New York in 1965.

The father of eight children, Muhammad reportedly fathered an additional thirteen out of wedlock. In 1982 circuit court judge Henry Budzinski ruled in favor of three of Muhammad's illegitimate children and five of his legitimate to recover assets previously given to the sect.

Muhammad died in February of 1975 at the age of seventy-seven in Chicago's Mercy Hospital. At the time of his death he was living in a large Middle Eastern–style mansion at 4847 South Woodlawn Avenue. He was buried in Mount Glenwood Cemetery in Glenwood, Illinois, twenty-five miles south of Chicago.

Following the death of his father, Wallace D. Muhammad (he later changed his first name to Warith) took over the Nation of Islam and shortly thereafter repudiated his father's separatist teachings and embraced orthodox Islam. "We believe that Jews, Christians, and Muslims share an affinity. We believe in one and the same God. We represent one humanity," the younger Muhammad said. In 1980 he changed the name of the organization from the World Community of Al-Islam in the West to the simpler American Muslim Mission with its local headquarters at 4855 South Woodlawn Avenue.

In 1978 Louis Farrakhan, a former calypso singer from Boston who became a Black Muslim in 1955, revived the Nation of Islam and, with a core of several thousand followers, established an office in a former funeral parlor at 734 West 79th Street. Despite talk of a possible reconciliation between the two organizations, Farrakhan continues to carry on Muhammad's black nationalist legacy.

Further reading: Black, Edwin. "Louis Farrakhan—would you buy a toothpaste from this man?" *Chicago Reader* (April 11, 1986); Lincoln, C. Eric. *The Black Muslims in America* (1961).

James Mulligan

Army Officer

born: June 25, 1830
Utica, New York
died: July 26, 1864
Kernstown, Virginia

James Adelbert Mulligan commanded one of Chicago's most celebrated units during the Civil War. Not only did he emerge as a local hero, he also won recognition throughout the North.

Born in New York State, Mulligan came to Chicago with his Irish immigrant parents when he was six years old. After graduating from St. Mary of the Lake University in 1850, he accompanied John L. Stevens, a noted traveler of the day, to South America. Upon returning to Chicago, Mulligan worked in the law office of Arnold, Larned and Lay. In 1854 he edited a Catholic weekly, the *Western Tablet.* The following year he was admitted to the Illinois bar.

When the Shields' Guards, an Irish military group, was formed in 1854, Mulligan was chosen to be its first lieutenant. Later he became secretary and then captain. In 1857, President James Buchanan appointed him to a clerkship in the Interior Department in Washington, D.C. Mulligan then returned to Chicago and formed a partnership with lawyer Henry S. Fitch, United States Attorney for the Chicago District.

After the fall of Fort Sumter, South Carolina, to Confederate forces in April of 1861, Mulligan placed an ad in a local newspaper exhorting all men of Irish extraction to fight "for the honor of the Old Land and for the defense of the New." Several Irish military units already existed in Chicago, including the Montgomery Guards and the Emmet Guards. There was some fear among native politicians that the solidly Democratic Irish would refuse to support the Union cause and the Republican president. Their concern was unjustified. According to historian A. T. Andreas, 325 men signed up within an hour and a half. By the end of the week, the number had grown to more than 1,000. Mulligan was elected colonel of the new unit, which earned the nickname of "Mulligan's Brigade."

By this time, however, Illinois had already met its military quota. Despite the setback, the brigade voted to remain together and continue to drill and prepare for battle. A determined Col. Mulligan traveled to Washington and persuaded the War Department in May of 1861 to accept his regiment into the Union Army. On June 5, 1861, notes historian Bessie Louise Pierce, Mulligan's Irish Brigade became the first independent Illinois regiment. Its official name was the 23rd Illinois Infantry.

Upon Mulligan's return to Chicago, the preparation for war began in earnest. The company obtained permission to use the grounds of Kane's Brewery on West Polk Street between Blue Island and Archer Avenues and renamed it "Fontenoy Barracks."

The newly formed regiment was ordered to report to St. Louis, Missouri, to be equipped with artillery. By the end of August of 1861, the brigade, stationed in Lexington, Missouri, was given the task of holding the city against an attack by Confederate General Sterling Price. After continuous fighting, the city fell in late September. The brigade suffered severe casualties—over one hundred men died—and the lack of water and ammunition made matters worse. Among the many wounded was Mulligan himself who, at the insistence of his commanding officer, reluctantly surrendered. He was later released in exchange for a captured Confederate officer. The battle-scarred Irishman, who received a Congressional citation for his efforts, returned to Chicago to a hero's welcome. He then traveled to Washington to ask President Lincoln to resurrect the Irish Brigade.

In December of 1861 Major General George McClellan ordered the brigade restored with company headquarters based at Camp Douglas on the South Side. The regiment patrolled the camp until June of 1862.

The Mulligan battery was then attached to the Illinois Light Artillery and saw action in Virginia in the Shenandoah Valley campaigns before being ordered to Annapolis, Maryland. In July of 1863 Mulligan was placed in command of all federal troops at Hancock, Maryland. At Petersburg, Virginia, he established Fort Mulligan.

In April of 1864 the 23rd Illinois Infantry returned to Chicago to recoup. Its weary soldiers, reduced from eight hundred to three hundred, prepared themselves for another long campaign. Returning to Virginia, the brigade formed a part of the 1st Infantry Division, again under Mulligan, and was ordered to occupy Leetown.

On July 24, 1864, at the Battle of Kernstown, Virginia, Mulligan was mortally wounded. As he fell off his horse, he saw the colors of the Irish Brigade waving above him. "Lay me down," he reportedly told his men, "and save the flag." He was carried to a nearby farmhouse and died two days later. His body was returned to Chicago and was buried in Calvary Cemetery, Evanston.

See also: Elmer E. Ellsworth, Philip Sheridan

Further reading: Andreas, A. T. *History of Chicago from the Earliest Period to the Present Time.* 3 vols. (1884–86); Pierce, Bessie Louise. *A History of Chicago.* 3 vols. (1937–57).

George Mundelein

Priest

born: July 2, 1872
New York, New York
died: October 2, 1939
Mundelein, Illinois

In 1916, at the remarkably young age of forty-three, George William Mundelein became archbishop of Chicago. During his twenty-four years in office, Mundelein emerged as an influential figure in both national and international church affairs.

One of nine children, Mundelein was a third-generation German-American. His maternal grandfather fought for the Union at Fort Sumter during the Civil War. Mundelein grew up poor on the streets of New York. He received his education at the Christian Brothers' De La Salle Institute, and at seventeen he graduated with a bachelor of arts degree from Manhattan College. Around this time he chose to enter the priesthood and won a scholarship to begin his ecclesiastical studies at St. Vincent's Seminary in Latrobe, Pennsylvania. An energetic and bright student, Mundelein earned an outstanding academic record before he went on to study further in Rome.

After he was ordained in 1895, Mundelein returned to Brooklyn where he became assistant secretary to the bishop. On weekends he served a Lithuanian congregation. Two years later he was made chancellor of the Brooklyn diocese. In 1906 Mundelein became the nation's youngest monsignor, and three years later, its youngest auxiliary bishop.

When James Quigley, Archbishop of Chicago, died in 1915, Mundelein was chosen to succeed him. He was installed as archbishop on February 9, 1916. Unlike his congenial predecessor, Mundelein projected a harsher, more business-like image. He would tolerate no insubordination.

Mundelein was a thorough and efficient administrator, and his term was one of the most productive in Chicago ecclesiastical history. He authorized the construction of over two hundred new churches, according to historian Edward R. Kantowicz. In addition, several important institutions were erected during his term: Quigley Preparatory Seminary in 1918 (originally established in 1905 by Archbishop Quigley as Cathedral College preparatory school); Rosary

College in west suburban River Forest in 1922; and Mundelein College, a women's commuter college, in 1930. In 1918 he purchased land in Area, Illinois, forty-five miles northwest of Chicago, and founded a seminary—St. Mary of the Lake—whose goal was to train priests for the Chicago diocese. The town was later renamed Mundelein in his honor. Furthermore, the archbishop devoted a good share of his time and efforts to philanthropic activities. He created the Associated Catholic Charities, founded homes for wayward boys and girls, and established the Big Brother organization.

Mundelein advocated a strong central authority. Not surprisingly, his methodical approach to management did not always win converts. Indeed, some fellow clergy criticized him for running the archdiocese like a "German meat market."

Mundelein tried to "Americanize" the Catholic Church by emphasizing cultural homogeneity and downplaying cultural pluralism. To this end, he directed that English be used as the chief language of instruction in parochial schools and that a uniform curriculum be implemented throughout. In essence, he sought to mold a peculiarly American brand of Catholicism. He didn't, for example, believe in "hyphenated" Americans, since he thought divided loyalty among the citizenry would only diminish national identity. People, he once said in a *Chicago Tribune* interview, could not serve two nations simultaneously. While he recognized the existence of national parishes—that is, parishes dominated by a particular ethnic group—he attempted to restrict the creation of new ones.

On March 24, 1924, Mundelein became cardinal. Two years later, he and Chicago hosted the International Eucharistic Congress, the first ever held in the United States. A resounding success, the event attracted millions of Roman Catholics from around the world.

Mundelein counted Franklin Delano Roosevelt among his many influential friends. He fermently supported the president's New Deal policies, and Roosevelt, in turn, reciprocated by appointing Catholics to high-ranking positions in his administration.

The cardinal died in October of 1939 at the age of sixty-seven in his home at St. Mary of the Lake Seminary in Mundelein, Illinois.

See also: Arnold Damen, James Quigley

Further reading: Kantowicz, Edward R. *Corporation Sole: Cardinal Mundelein and Chicago Catholicism* (1983); Shanabruch, Charles. *Chicago's Catholics: The Evolution of an American Identity* (1981).

Paul Muni

Actor

born: September 22, 1895
Lemberg, Austria
died: August 25, 1967
Santa Barbara, California

Actor of a thousand faces, Paul Muni was one of the most respected thespians of his generation. From Al Capone to Louis Pasteur to Emile Zola to Benito Juarez, Muni didn't just play a part, he lived it.

Born in Austria but brought to the U.S. as a child, Muni Weisenfreund got his start on the stage of the Yiddish theater. Muni came from a theatrical family, which settled in New York, then Cleveland, and finally in Chicago. Muni originally had ambitions of becoming a violinist. When his parents needed an actor to play the role of an old man and no one else was available, they turned to their young son.

His parents owned their own theater, the Weisenfreund Theater, on 12th Street near Halsted. Here in the back rooms and dusty stages of the Maxwell Street neighborhood, Muni quickly mastered the tricks of the trade, playing a wide range of roles.

Muni moved to Philadelphia where he joined a burlesque company and then signed up with Molly Picon's troupe in Boston. In 1918 he joined the Yiddish Art Theater Company in New York and toured the country. He made his Broadway debut in *We Americans* in 1926 at the age of thirty-one. The following year Muni landed the role of the gangster in *Four Walls*, which led to a major part in *The Dybbuk* in London.

In 1928 Muni arrived in Hollywood. It proved to be a humbling experience for him. Twentieth Century Fox changed his name to the more manageable, Paul Muni. And when he was signed up to appear in *The Valiant* in 1929, his film debut, studio officials were not impressed. "Who hired that actor?" one executive asked. "He has no sex appeal. Girls won't be interested in him." Surprisingly, his role in *The Valiant* earned him his first Academy Award nomination for best actor. Muni's second film, *Seven Faces* (1929), flopped, but the actor made a comeback with two back-to-back successes—both in 1932—*Scarface* and *I Am A Fugitive From A Chain Gang*. The latter earned him his second best actor nomination.

Muni won his first Oscar for his performance as the French scientist in *The Story of Louis Pasteur* (1936). In the following year, *The Life of Emile Zola*, won the best picture award, and Muni garnered his fourth nomination. In 1956 he won a Tony for *Inherit the Wind*.

Muni took his profession seriously. He labored for months on a characterization—he spent six months alone preparing for the role of Emile Zola before even going in front of the camera—and he thoroughly researched his roles. A proudly defiant actor, Muni refused to be typecast and even refused to sign any long-term contracts. He simply would not compromise when it came to quality, even if it meant rejecting a role that he felt was not right for him. In 1940 he canceled an $800,000 contract in a gangster movie because he didn't like his part. The movie was *High Sierra* and the actor who replaced him was Humphrey Bogart. "The movies," he said in an interview with the *Chicago Tribune*, "are, really, no place for an actor. Everyone in a studio must, of necessity, be dependent on everyone else. On the stage, I am on my own—entirely dependent on myself."

A private man who had no interest in the Hollywood life-style, Muni once stated that he openly disdained applause "because no actor should come out of his role to take bows." He disapproved, too, of the star system and refused to bow to its pressures. Unlike most screen actors, he would not make more than two films a year, which allowed him to accept stage work.

In 1959 Muni appeared in *The Last Angry Man* and received his fifth, and last, Oscar nomination. His health deteriorated and he died from a heart attack in his Santa Barbara home in 1967. He was seventy-one.

Some of Muni's other movies include: *The Good Earth* (1937), *Juarez* (1939), *Hudson's Bay* (1940), *A Song To Remember* (1944), and *Angel On My Shoulder* (1946).

See also: Dina Halpern [appendix]

Further reading: Berkow, Ira. *Maxwell Street: Survival in a Bazaar* (1977); Lawrence, Jerome. *Actor: The Life and Times of Paul Muni* (1974).

Bronko Nagurski

Football Player

born: November 3, 1908
Rainy River, Ontario
died: January 7, 1990
International Falls, Minnesota

Maybe it's the name that sounds bigger than life. At six-foot-two and 235 pounds, Bronko Nagurski was often called the strongest man to play the game of football. He was also the sport's most versatile player—he was able to play most positions. The highlight of his football career came during his years with the Chicago Bears. More than any other player, Nagurski's exploits on the field and his aggressive playing style earned the Bears's the nickname of "Monsters of the Midway."

Photograph reprinted with permission from the *Chicago Sun-Times.*

Nagurski's hulking frame looked intimidating both on and off the gridiron. "I assure you that you will not see a more remarkable physical specimen anywhere," Bears coach, George Halas, once observed. Indeed, Nagurski's brute strength is the stuff of sports legends—how he knocked over burly linebacker after burly linebacker as if they were human bowling pins and how he scrambled forty-five yards for a touchdown, sent two linebackers reeling in opposite directions, ran over a halfback, and straight-armed the safety before careening off the goalposts and smashing into a brick wall.

Born in Ontario, Bronislaw Nagurski was raised across the border in International Falls, Minnesota. He played every position on his high school football team. Minnesota coach Clarence Spears recruited him after seeing the strapping lad plowing a field—without a horse. Nagurksi enrolled at the University of Minnesota in 1926 and became the star of the team, playing tackle on both defense and offense. In 1929 he became the only player in college football history to be named All-American in two positions—tackle and fullback.

In 1930 Nagurski joined the Chicago Bears of the National Football League at those positions and turned the team into a contender. He played with the Bears until age twenty-nine, when arthritis forced him to retire. During his nine seasons with the Bears, Nagurski gained more than 4,031 yards running in 872 carries and earned 19 touchdowns, according to newspaper accounts. He made all-Pro three times and led the Bears in rushing in 1933 and again in 1936. He is eighth on the club's all-time rushing list.

In 1943, with so many young men away at war, Nagurksi was persuaded to come back to play one final season with his old team as tackle. During the NFL title game on December 26 against the Washington Redskins at Wrigley Field—then the Bears's home—he agreed to run with the ball. In the last quarter he scored the last touchdown of his career, an easy three-yard romp to the goal line. The Bears won 41-21.

Nagurski retired permanently from football in 1943 and devoted his time to farming. For a brief period he was the backfield coach at UCLA. In 1945 he turned to professional wrestling, which he had first tried in 1933. In 1939 he won the National Wrestling Alliance championship.

He retired from the wrestling mat in 1960 to become a wrestling referee. Three years later he became a charter member of the Pro Football Hall of Fame.

Nagurski shied away from publicity of any kind. He operated a gas station in International Falls up until 1968. Occasionally he would grant an interview, as in 1985 when his old team battled for the Super Bowl championship, but generally he preferred to stay out of the limelight.

Most of Nagurski's football career took place during the height of the Depression. Unlike today's players, where multimillion dollar contracts have become the norm, Nagurski reportedly never earned more than $5,000 a year.

Nagurski died of natural causes in January of 1990 at Falls Memorial Hospital in International Falls, Minnesota. He was eighty-one.

See also: Harold "Red" Grange, George Halas

Further reading: Vass, George. *George Halas and the Chicago Bears* (1971).

Agnes Nestor

Labor Activist

born: June 24, 1880
Grand Rapids, Michigan
died: December 28, 1948
Chicago, Illinois

Agnes Nestor rose from lowly worker in a glove factory to a position of power in the Glove Workers Union to the presidency of the Chicago Women's Trade Union League (WTUL) at a time when there were few women labor leaders. She sought better working conditions for working women and championed women's suffrage.

Photograph reprinted with permission from the *Chicago Sun-Times.*

Born in Michigan, Nestor came to Chicago when still a teenager and found work at the Eisendrath Glove Factory as a glove-maker. By the time she was in her early twenties, she had developed into a quietly effective labor activist. In 1902 Nestor led a successful ten-day strike against the factory. Among her demands were an end to rental of machinery and payment for supplies from the employees' pockets and the formation of a union shop. The same year she became president of the Local 2 of the International Glove Workers Union (IGWU). In 1904 Nestor joined the Chicago Women's Trade Union League (WTUL). The purpose of the league was to organize all women workers throughout the country in an effort to secure better working conditions, reduce working hours, and win a decent living wage. In 1906 Nestor was elected secretary-treasurer of the IGWU. She served in that capacity until 1913.

In 1909 Nestor and fellow labor activist Elizabeth Maloney introduced a bill in the Illinois legislature that attempted to reduce the number of working hours for women in the state. Opposition to the bill was fierce. Merchants, manufacturers, and small business vigorously fought for its defeat. In 1909 the Illinois Ten Hour Day law was passed, which reduced the number of working hours for women from twelve to ten. On several occasions, the league attempted to pass the Eight Hour Day law through the Illinois legislature. Not until 1937—twenty-seven years after it was introduced—did that bill finally succeed.

Following the resignation of Margaret Dreier Robins, Nestor was elected president of the Chicago WTUL in 1913. President Woodrow Wilson, impressed with her accomplishments and determination, appointed her a member of a national commission to investigate vocational education. In the autumn of 1915 Nestor was elected president of the International Glove Workers Union.

During World War I she was a member of the Council of National Defense and was the only woman on the Advisory Council to the Secretary of Labor. She was also the American labor representative to conferences in Britain, France, and Austria. In addition, she served as director of the National Women's Trade Union League of America and was a member of the World's Fair Commission.

In 1930 Nestor was appointed the only woman member of the Commission on Unemployment and Relief, a group launched to raise millions for the city's jobless poor. The commission conducted surveys in order to discover the number of unemployed people who were not on relief. It was replaced, in February 1932, by the Illinois Emergency Relief Commission. At the same time, the Chicago WTUL established its own Unemployment Relief Committee to deal with the special problems of unemployed women members of the league.

In 1942 Nestor authored *Brief History of the International Glove Workers Union of America*. In 1948 she wrote her autobiography, *Woman's Labor Leader*.

Nestor broke barriers and set new ground. Not only did she and the union improve working conditions for countless working women, she also served as a role model for many young girls. During her lifetime, Nestor witnessed a dramatic change in the number of women employed in the workforce. Following World War II, women entered fields that were traditionally not open to them. "In my mother's day," she recalls in her autobiography, "less than two million women were employed in the industry. In 1897, when I first went to work, there were five million women employed in industry. Today, there are twenty-odd million working women, and industry is constantly looking to hire more."

The *Chicago Journal* called her "the biggest little woman in Chicago." Upon her death in December of 1948, the labor press remarked that "the woman who works has lost her best friend."

See also: Jane Addams, Margaret Haley, Florence Kelley, Mary McDowell, Ellen Gates Starr [appendix]

Further reading: Nestor, Agnes. *Woman's Labor Leader* (1954); Sochen, June. *Movers and Shakers: American Women Thinkers and Activists, 1900–1970* (1973).

William Butler Ogden

Politician/Entrepreneur

born: June 15, 1805
Walton, New York
died: August 3, 1877
Fordham Heights, New York

An early Chicago booster, William Butler Ogden was Chicago's first mayor (1837–1838) and helped to write the city charter. "I was born close to a saw-mill, was early left an orphan, graduated from a long schoolhouse and at 14 fancied I could do anything I turned my hand to," he once wrote. Ogden was a popular and influential figure in Chicago's salad days.

Ogden planned to study law but the sudden death of his father forced him to take over the family business—his father was a real estate developer—when still a teenager. Although Ogden enjoyed a successful career in real estate, he felt that politics was the nobler profession. In 1834 he was elected to the New York legislature. The following year he moved to Chicago to try to salvage an investment of his brother-in-law. In 1835 Chicago was still a frontier village of swamp and prairie, not a very encouraging sight for a transplanted Easterner. Despite the bleak setting, Ogden had great faith in the future of the town and decided to stay. Within several years, Ogden had made a fortune in real estate, becoming one of the richest men in the city.

The Panic of 1837, which plunged the country into a recession, brought Ogden his share of hard times, but he managed to weather the storm. In 1837 he was elected Chicago's first mayor. The population of the village at that time was slightly over 4,000 people. As mayor, Ogden is credited with keeping the city solvent and, by refusing to panic, preventing it from falling deeper into debt. By the early 1840s, Chicago was back on its feet again.

After completing his one-year term as mayor, Ogden was ready to serve the city in other ways. In 1840 he was elected alderman of the 6th Ward and, in 1847, alderman of the 9th Ward.

The railroad brought phenomenal growth to the city and virtually guaranteed it a promising and vital future. Ogden, more than anyone, understood this. The rails brought the world to Chicago and Chicago to the world. In 1848 Ogden introduced the first railroad to the city, the Galena and Chicago Union Railroad, which linked the prosperous mining town of Galena in western Illinois with the then small town of Chicago.

Due to its central location and proximity to water transport, Chicago quickly became the railroad capital of the country and a great commercial center.

Unhappy with management policy, Ogden quit the Galena and Chicago Union and founded another railway, the Chicago and North Western Railroad, which later acquired the Galena and Chicago Union line. From 1859 to 1868 he served as president of the Chicago and North Western. In 1862 he was elected the first president of the Union Pacific. Less than a year into his term, he left.

In 1857 Ogden became one of the founders of the Chicago Dock and Canal Company, which he and two associates, Van H. Higgins and Stanley H. Fleetwood, established to develop an industrial area on the north bank of the Chicago River. Today this area at McClurg Court and Illinois Street, called the Ogden Slip, is the home to North Pier Terminal. Once a busy industrial and shipping center, North Pier has recently undergone a massive renovation and reopened in 1988 as a commercial and retail complex. Ogden was also the first president of Rush Medical College and president of the board of trustees of the University of Chicago.

Above all these other activities, Ogden was a builder. He was instrumental in the construction of nearly one hundred miles of city streets, erected the first swinging bridge over the Chicago River, and donated land for churches and schools.

Although a life-long Democrat, Ogden opposed slavery and felt compelled to switch to the Republican party. In 1860 he ran for the Illinois Senate. Two years later, he bolted from the party as a result of a dispute with President Lincoln over the

Emancipation Proclamation—he reportedly felt the proclamation was premature. Ogden then retired from politics altogether.

Ogden purchased property in Fordham Heights, New York, in 1866. He died there in 1877.

The Ogden School at 24 West Walton Street, part of the Chicago public school system, is built on the former site of his brother's home. The current building was constructed in 1953. A quotation from one of Ogden's favorite poets, Sir Walter Scott, is carved on the wall: "Breathes there the man with soul so dead, who never to himself hath said, this is my own, my native land."

Further reading: Casey, Robert J. and W. A. S. Douglas. *Pioneer Railroad: The Story of the Chicago and North Western System* (1948); Rex, Frederick F. *The Mayors of the City of Chicago (1934).*

Joe "King" Oliver

Musician

born: May 11, 1885
New Orleans, Louisiana
died: April 8, 1938
(according to other sources:
April 10, 1938)
Savannah, Georgia

Joseph "King" Oliver, an early exponent of jazz, spread New Orleans–style jazz to Chicago and inspired a young musician, Louis Armstrong, to take it into altogether new directions. Oliver's Creole Jazz Band, write Walter C. Allen and Brian A. L. Rust in **King Joe Oliver,** *"set an accepted standard of ensemble improvisation which has seldom been equalled."*

Oliver joined a brass band as a youngster in New Orleans. He earned his nickname during a gig at the Adabie Cabaret where his brilliant cornet playing upstaged his colleagues.

When Storyville, the sprawling New Orleans red-light district, was shut down in November 1917 by orders of the U.S. Navy, scores of jazz musicians fled north to the wide-open city of Chicago, hoping to re-create a little bit of Louisiana on the shores of Lake Michigan. Oliver found gigs at the Dreamland Cafe at 35th and State Streets and the notorious Pekin Cabaret, a gangland favorite, on State near 27th Street, among many other clubs.

In January of 1920, Oliver formed his own band at the Dreamland. After spending some time in California, Oliver returned to Chicago in 1922 to open at the Lincoln Gardens at 459 East 31st Street under the name of King Oliver's Creole Jazz Band. In mid-1922 he decided to add a second cornet to the band and sent a telegram to Louis Armstrong, a young protégé of his from New Orleans, and asked him to come to Chicago. Armstrong wasted no time. The band toured the Midwest on a series of one-night stands, playing to enthusiastic crowds. In 1923 they made their first recording on the Gennett label. Successive record deals followed on Okeh, Paramount, and Columbia. Other members of this seminal Chicago band included Honore Dutrey on trombone, Johnny Dodds on clarinet, Lil Hardin on piano, and Baby Dodds on drums.

Soon after the studio sessions, Armstrong left to pursue his own career. Meanwhile Oliver found work at the Plantation Cafe before spending several years in New York. He returned to Chicago in 1928. In early

1931 Oliver went back into the studio. These Brunswick and Vocalion sessions were Oliver's last known recordings.

Dental trouble in the early thirties forced Oliver to cut back on gigs. In 1937 he moved to Savannah, Georgia. The following year he died there of a cerebral hemorrhage at age fifty-two.

Oliver composed many jazz standards, including "Dipper Mouth," "West End Blues," "Snag It," "Dixieland Blues," "High Society," and "Doctor Jazz."

Jazz critics often refer to Oliver's Creole Jazz Band as the epitome of New Orleans–style jazz and consider Oliver an early musical pioneer. Music writer Donald Clarke has called Oliver "one of the founding fathers of American music."

See also: Louis Armstrong

Further reading: Allen, Walter C. and Brian A. L. Rust. *King Joe Oliver* (1955); Clarke, Donald. *The Penguin Encyclopedia of Popular Music* (1989); Travis, Dempsey J. *An Autobiography of Black Jazz* (1983).

Francis O'Neill

Musician/Police Officer

born: August 25, 1849
Tralibane, Ireland
died: January 28, 1936
Chicago, Illinois

Chief of the Chicago police department from 1901 to 1905, Francis J. O'Neill is best remembered as a great authority on traditional Irish folk music. He wrote seven books on the subject and rescued old tunes from certain oblivion. O'Neill preserved traditional Irish music for future generations. To this day, O'Neill's collections remain the definitive reference source for musicians, scholars, and students of Irish folklore.

O'Neill learned to love the music of his native Cork from his neighbors, which included a lively group of psalm singers, flutists, and pipers, who gathered in the home of his grandfather.

O'Neill left home at sixteen to become a cabin boy, sailed to Australia, to the Black Sea, and around Cape Horn, and survived a shipwreck in the Pacific. After a brief sojourn in San Francisco, he worked as a shepherd, a schoolteacher, and a railway clerk at various places throughout the country before settling in Chicago in 1873. He found work with the Chicago and Alton Railroad as a laborer in a freight house. Unhappy with the long hours and low pay, he sought a more challenging profession. Like many Irishman before and since, he joined the police department, and there he remained for thirty-two years, until his retirement in 1905. One month after joining, O'Neill was shot in the back by a burglar. He survived the attack and moved up through the ranks, becoming a sergeant in 1887 and a lieutenant in 1890. In 1894 he was promoted to captain and assigned in charge of the 8th district, which included the Union Stockyards. In July of that year he was credited with helping to quell potentially violent strikes at the yards. In 1901 Mayor Carter Harrison II appointed O'Neill chief of police. By that time, O'Neill had become one of the best and most popular officers on the force.

An accomplished flute player, O'Neill went wherever there was hope of finding a tune. And in perhaps the most unusual kind of patronage in the city's history, he made it a practice to hire as many Irish musicians to the force as possible. Even when he was chief of police, he would not let the duties of his office interrupt his search for the music. One day when no one could find

O'Neill, rumors began circulating that he had been assassinated. In a near panic, a contingent of officers was dispatched to locate the missing police chief. After searching unsuccessfully, a policeman who knew O'Neill's love for music suggested a visit to the Brighton Park neighborhood where a fiddler friend of O'Neill's lived. When the officers arrived they found the two musicians in the living room, the chief with his flute and the friend with his fiddle.

On his travels to discover Irish music in the city, O'Neill was often accompanied by Sergeant James O'Neill (no relation), who wrote down the tunes (O'Neill could not read music). O'Neill collected tunes from local Irish immigrants as well as from noted Irish musicians who passed through town.

By 1903 O'Neill had spent close to three decades collecting tunes, sifting through material, and discoursing with musicians. That year he published, at his own expense, *O'Neill's Music of Ireland*, a monumental work that contained 1,850 pieces of music, including dance tunes, airs, and compositions by the famous blind Irish harper, Turlough O'Carolan. In 1905 he resigned from the police force to devote the rest of his life to the study of Irish music, collecting lyrics and compiling tunes. More volumes followed: *The Dance Music of Ireland* (1907), *Irish Folk Music: A Fascinating Hobby* (1910), and *Irish Minstrels and Musicians* (1913), among others.

In 1934 O'Neill contributed arrangements to *The Pageant of the Celt*, a musical dramatization of Irish history, which was staged at Soldier Field.

Two years later O'Neill died in his home at 5448 South Drexel Boulevard from a heart ailment. He was eighty-six.

In recent years there has been a revival of interest in traditional Irish music both in Ireland and in the United States. Musicians from the Chieftains to the Pogues to Chicago's own champion button accordionist Jimmy Keane and fiddler Liz Carroll owe a large debt to the work of Francis J. O'Neill.

See also: John McGreevy [appendix], Terence Teahan

Further reading: Ffrench, Charles, ed. *Biographical History of the American Irish in Chicago* (1897); Krassen, Miles and Larry McCullough. Liner notes to *Irish Traditional Instrumental Music from Chicago, Volume II* (1978); McCullough, Lawrence E. *Irish Music in Chicago: An Ethnomusicological Study*. Diss. (1978).

James O'Reilly

Actor/Director

born: January 11, 1927
Chicago, Illinois
died: May 19, 1990
Naperville, Illinois

James O'Reilly left an indelible mark on Chicago theater as both an actor and as a director. He served as artistic director for two of the leading off-Loop theater companies in town—the Court Theatre in Hyde Park from 1964 to 1970 and the Body Politic Theatre in Lincoln Park, from 1980 to 1986—and he gave some of the most powerful and heartfelt performances ever to grace a Chicago stage.

Photograph reprinted with permission from the *Chicago Sun-Times*.

A Chicago native, O'Reilly was raised in the Norwood Park neighborhood on the far Northwest Side and spent his freshman year at Taft High School. When still a teenager he moved with his father to Texas and finished high school in a small town near Brownsville. After his father's death in the early 1940s, O'Reilly returned to Chicago and enrolled at Loyola University to study chemistry. A brief stint in the army toward the end of World War II interrupted his studies, but after the war he returned to Chicago and resumed his education at Loyola. At the same time he worked at the *Chicago Daily News,* first on the loading dock and later in the mailroom. Despite his success in the theater, O'Reilly worked in the *Daily News* mailroom well into the early seventies.

O'Reilly caught the acting bug at Loyola. In those days local theater consisted of little more than stock companies, community groups, suburban theater, and college productions. Although there were several attempts to create a uniquely Chicago theatrical community in the fifties, it wasn't until the late sixties and early seventies that contemporary off-Loop professional theater really blossomed.

O'Reilly continued to live two lives. By day he worked in the *Daily News* mailroom; in the evening he pursued his love of the theater, acting and directing in as many productions as he could handle. In 1964 he became artistic director of the Court Theatre in Hyde Park.

After three decades in Chicago theater, O'Reilly felt he was ready for a change. In 1970 he resigned from the Court Theatre, left the city, and spent several years as director of the Meadowbrook Theater in Michigan and at the Cohoes Music Hall in upstate New York. By the time he returned in the mid-seventies,

Chicago was in the middle of a theatrical renaissance. Young fledgling companies with names like Steppenwolf and Wisdom Bridge were making the city an exciting place to work.

O'Reilly started all over again. He began to find work as a freelance actor and director. He returned to his old home, the Court Theatre, and appeared in such plays as George Bernard Shaw's *Mrs. Warren's Profession*, Henrik Ibsen's *A Doll's House*, and most successfully, in Sean O'Casey's classic, *Juno and the Paycock*, as the blustery Capt. Jack Boyle.

In 1979 O'Reilly directed two short plays by South African playwright Athol Fugard at a new theater company, the financially struggling Body Politic Theatre. The theater was, at that time, searching for a new artistic director. O'Reilly offered his services and was immediately accepted.

Under O'Reilly's leadership, the Body Politic presented fresh interpretations of Shakespearean classics as well as vibrant productions of contemporary Irish and English drama. The Body Politic quickly earned a reputation as the premier presenter of finely crafted Anglo/Irish drama in the city.

O'Reilly developed and nurtured an ensemble company. He is credited with turning the Body Politic around—both financially and artistically. It was he who suggested that the Body Politic pool resources and share space with the adjacent Victory Gardens Theater to cut costs. Now such arrangements are common.

O'Reilly portrayed a wide range of characters. Among his more notable performances: Hugh, the old schoolmaster, in Brian Friel's *Translations* in 1982, which he also directed; the worldly barkeep in John Millington Synge's *Playboy of the Western World* in

1983; the aging actor in *The Dresser* in 1983; the cynical civil servant in Hugh Leonard's *A Life* in 1984; Shylock in Shakespeare's *The Merchant of Venice* in 1984; and the weary London police inspector in *The Rat and the Skull* in 1985. In the same year O'Reilly directed Bob Gibson's *The Courtship of Carl Sandburg* at the Northlight Theater in Evanston and the Apollo Theater in Chicago, for which he received popular and critical acclaim.

O'Reilly made his last appearance on a Chicago stage in 1989 in *King Lear*. Meanwhile he continued to teach theater classes at Loyola University and Northern Illinois University in Dekalb, Illinois. O'Reilly also appeared in several motion pictures, including *Class* and *The Killing Floor*.

In May 1990 O'Reilly collapsed at a friend's house and died shortly afterward at Edward Hospital in Naperville, Illinois. At the time of his death, he was planning to direct and act in three plays, including an adaptation of *Macbeth* for the Pendragon Theatre Company in Lakeside, Michigan.

See also: Kenneth Sawyer Goodman [appendix]

Further reading: Special Collections Department of the Chicago Public Library. *Resetting the Stage: Theater Beyond the Loop 1960—1990* (1990).

Ruth Page

Dancer/Choreographer

born: March 22, 1899
Indianapolis, Indiana
died: April 7, 1991
Chicago, Illinois

*Ruth Page was a pioneer of American dance, and for more than seven decades she was a formidable presence on the Chicago dance scene. At a time when the best dance was almost exclusively associated with foreign countries, Page departed from tradition and dared to choreograph ballets with peculiarly American themes. She worked with virtually every Chicago opera company at one time or another. Further she is credited with creating a new art form, opera into ballet, a repertoire that included **La Traviata**, **Carmen**, and **The Barber of Seville**.*

Photograph courtesy of the Chicago Historical Society.

Page was the daughter of a prominent Indianapolis family. Her father was a surgeon and her mother was a professional pianist and one of the founders of the Indianapolis Symphony Orchestra. Page decided at the age of five to be a dancer when her mother took her to see the famous Russian ballerina Anna Pavlova, in Indianapolis.

As a teenager Page took summer ballet classes in Chicago with Anna Pavlova's company. Then, still a teenager, she joined the company, accompanied by her mother, and toured Latin America. Upon returning to the United States, she attended a girls' boarding school in New York and studied ballet with the Belgian dancer Adolph Bolm.

In 1914 Page became a soloist for the Metropolitan Opera ballet in New York. Several years later, in 1919, she made her Chicago debut with the Chicago Grand Opera Company in a production of Bolm's *The Birthday of the Infanta*, based on a story by Oscar Wilde. She continued as a member of the Bolm's Ballet Intime company for several years.

In 1924 Page became the principal ballerina of the Chicago Allied Arts, an experimental group, and choreographed *Oak Street Beach*, which was inspired by the Chicago beach of the same name. The following year she became the first American dancer to perform with Sergei Diaghilev's *Ballets Russes*. She returned to Chicago in 1926 to become the premier dancer of the Ravinia Opera Company in Highland Park, Illinois. From 1934 to 1937 she served as the chief dancer and ballet director of the Chicago Opera Company.

Page was determined to build an indigenous dance repertoire in a country with little or no dance roots. She earned a reputation for creating unconventional ballet. *Americans in Paris* featured tap dancing. *Hear Ye! Hear Ye!*, with music by noted American composer Aaron Copland, was set during a murder trial. *La Guiablesse*, based on a legend from Martinique, was performed at the Century of Progress Exposition in 1933 in Chicago with a virtually all-black cast, including Talley Beatty and Katherine Dunham, then an anthropology student at the University of Chicago.

In 1938 Page and Bentley Stone established the Page-Stone Ballet Company and spent several years touring across the U.S. and in Latin America. That year they presented their celebrated production of *Frankie and Johnny,* a ballet based on the American folk ballad. It has since become a modern ballet classic.

Page believed that opera, with its broad emotions and intense passions, could be successfully translated into the language of dance. In 1939 she transformed the opera *Carmen* by Bizet into the ballet *Guns and Castanets,* and set it in the Spanish Civil War of the thirties. Other examples of opera into ballet include *Camille,* a dance version of Verdi's *La Traviata* and *Revenge,* based on Verdi's *Il Trovatore.*

Despite her periodic absences from the city, Page continued to exert considerable influence on the Chicago dance scene. From 1942 to 1943 and again in 1945 she served as ballet director and premiere dancer with the Chicago Opera Company. In 1954 she became ballet director of the Chicago Lyric Opera and two years later she became ballet director

and choreographer with the Chicago Opera Ballet, which attracted such international guest artists as Maria Tallchief and Mia Slavenska.

Throughout her long career Page never relinquished her dream of establishing a resident, professional ballet company in the city. In 1974 she formed Ballet Chicago. But even her indomitable presence was not enough. The troupe folded four years later due to lack of funding, inadequate community support, and insufficient theater space.

From 1962 until her death Page served as director and choreographer for the annual *Nutcracker* production at the Arie Crown Theatre in McCormick Place. It has since grown into a cherished Christmas tradition.

In 1970 Page founded the Ruth Page Foundation and School of Dance in a former Moose lodge at 1016 North Dearborn Parkway. The school continues to offer classes in dance to adults and children and also houses the Chicago Repertory Dance Ensemble, one of the leading modern dance troupes in the city.

Outspoken and always entertaining, Page was quick to offer an opinion on most subjects: from theater critics ("The professional critic, he is a strange beast, and we would probably be better off if he were banished from the theater."); to architects ("Sometimes I think I would like to line up all the architects who have designed theaters in this country and shoot them."); to Chicago itself ("I have learned from long experience that Chicago is the most difficult city in the world to get things going in. Chicagoans are timid and don't trust their own taste, and they must be sure that what they are getting has been approved every place else before they can accept it.").

In 1986 the Chicago Dance Arts Coalition, an arts organization and professional association for dance founded in 1981, presented the first Ruth Page Awards for excellence in dance. In 1989 Delaware Place between Dearborn and Clark was renamed Ruth Page Place.

Page died of heart failure in April of 1991 at her North Lake Shore Drive apartment. She was ninety-two.

See also: Mary Garden, Joseph Holmes [appendix]

Further reading: Davis, Ronald L. *Opera in Chicago* (1966); Martin, John. *Ruth Page: An Intimate Biography* (1977); Page, Ruth. *Page to Page.* Edited by Andrew Mark Wentick. (1978).

Bertha Honore Palmer

Philanthropist

born: May 22, 1849
Louisville, Kentucky
died: May 5, 1918
Sarasota, Florida

For many years, Bertha Honore Palmer held the title of the nation's hostess. Overseas, she became an unofficial goodwill ambassador for the United States. At home, she entertained politicians, labor leaders, and ordinary folk. Like another wealthy socialite, Louise DeKoven Bowen, Honore used her riches to relieve the suffering that existed all around her.

Bertha Honore led a charmed life. She was the daughter of a prominent family from the West Side. Her father, real estate developer Henry M. Honore, brought his family to Chicago from Louisville, Kentucky, in 1855. Bertha attended the best schools—St. Xavier's Academy and the Dearborn Seminary.

In August of 1870 Honore, at the age of twenty-one, married Potter Palmer, a diligent, somber-faced Yankee from Massachusetts, who was twenty-three years her senior.

The Great Chicago Fire of 1871 destroyed the couples' considerable fortunes. Their magnificent buildings burned to the ground; the Grand Pacific Hotel, the Sherman House, Crosby's Opera House, and the Palmer House all were reduced to rubble and ash.

Potter Palmer was not only determined to build a bigger and better hotel, he was also determined to erect a luxurious mansion far away from the Prairie Avenue district where the elite of the city lived. In 1882 he commissioned Henry Ives Cobb and Charles S. Frost to design a three-story castle on three thousand feet of marshland, which later became Lake Shore Drive. The castle contained a great hall, an eighty-foot tower, marble mosaic floors, and a grand oak staircase.

The Palmer castle ushered in a new era in Chicago hospitality. Here, in this fantastic testament to Chicago's burgeoning strength as an industrial capital, Bertha Palmer entertained princes, statesmen, politicians, actors, labor leaders, artists, opera stars, and even presidents. She also welcomed factory girls and millinery workers to her home—the Woman's Trade Union met there, for example. She

became an avid collector of American and French Impressionist paintings and was considered somewhat of a trendsetter in her day. Palmer never backed away from a cause that she believed in. She championed the rights of working women and lobbied for the improvement of the status of women, including the "novel" notion of equal pay for equal work. It was neither "unfeminine nor monstrous" to compete with men, she believed. Palmer spoke frequently about social abuses, poor wages, and the inadequate educational opportunities for women.

Palmer was also a leading figure on the women's club scene, belonging to both the Fortnightly Club and the Chicago Woman's Club. She helped push for protective legislation and supported the causes of women reformers, including Jane Addams, Mary McDowell, and Louise DeKoven Bowen. She was also a familiar sight at Hull-House. Moreover, she was vice-president of the Civic Federation, a group of prominent Chicagoans who organized to fight vice and corruption.

In 1893 Chicago hosted the World's Columbian Exposition, which Palmer saw as a great opportunity to advance women's rights. In addition to proposing the general plan of the interior of the Women's Building, she also played hostess to many of the distinguished visitors who came from around the world.

Her husband, Potter, died on May 4, 1902, at age seventy-five. Shaken but determined to carry on, Bertha moved to Sarasota, Florida, in 1910 at age sixty-one. She farmed and tended to her new estate until she died of cancer in 1918. She was buried in a mausoleum at Graceland Cemetery next to her husband and close to her parents and brothers.

See also: Jane Addams, Louise DeKoven Bowen, Potter Palmer

Further reading: Ross, Ishbel. *Silhouette in Diamonds: The Life of Mrs. Potter Palmer* (1960).

Potter Palmer

Merchant

born: May 20, 1826
Potter's Hollow, New York
died: May 4, 1902
Chicago, Illinois

A quiet, self-educated man, Potter Palmer revolutionized merchandising in Chicago—some would say throughout the country—thus, earning the title of the first merchant prince of Chicago.

Palmer's grandparents were Quakers who moved to New York from the whaling town of New Bedford, Massachusetts. At eighteen, Palmer obtained a job at a general store in Durham, New York, as a clerk. In 1847 he opened his own dry goods store in Oneida and later opened one in Lockport, New York.

Searching for a larger market, he moved to Chicago in 1852 and opened a dry goods store, P. Palmer and Company, on Lake Street. His little shop grew, and sales steadily increased. A shrewd businessman, Palmer invested in vast amounts of real estate, which contributed greatly to his growing wealth.

In 1856 Palmer hired a hard-working assistant from Massachusetts named Marshall Field. The New Englander believed personable service and quality goods equaled success. Palmer watched him closely. Within a few months, Palmer promoted Field to head salesman.

In 1867 an exhausted Palmer, weary of the retail business, retired and left the business to his partners, Marshall Field and Levi Z. Leiter. He then proceeded to buy property along State Street. After persuading the city council to widen the street, he made plans to erect an opulent hotel that would lure customers away from Lake Street, at that time the retail center of the city. Further he agreed to build his former colleagues—then operating under the name of Field, Leiter and Company—a spanking new store at State and Washington Streets. The elegant six-story structure opened in October of 1868.

The first Palmer House, designed by Chicago's pioneer architect, John Van Osdel, opened on September 26, 1870, at the corner of State and Quincy Streets only to perish in the Great Chicago Fire in October 1871. Rather than giving up, the fire only served to goad Palmer into even more furious activity. He built a bigger and better Palmer House a few blocks north at State and Monroe Streets. This postfire Palmer House claimed to be the world's first fireproof hotel and the first equipped with electricity, telephones, and elevators. It was demolished in 1925 to make way for the present Palmer House.

The city's elite lived along elegant Prairie Avenue on the near South Side. Marshall Field had settled there as did George Pullman and businessman John Glessner. Palmer, breaking from tradition, decided to build an extravagant mansion on Lake Shore Drive between Banks and Schiller Streets. It was a prophetic move—the area was little more than a marshy wilderness.

Palmer purchased the land and hired a pair of famous architects, Henry Ives Cobb and Charles S. Frost, to build him a new home at 1350 North Lake Shore Drive. Made of Ohio limestone and Wisconsin granite, the pseudo-Gothic Palmer castle ultimately cost more than one million dollars—an unbelievably vast sum in those days. Some of the city's most splendid balls and dances were held in the ballroom of the massive mansion, hosted by his gracious wife, Bertha Palmer. Soon, like-minded affluent Chicagoans abandoned Prairie Avenue to follow the State Street merchant to the North Side. By the turn of the century so many affluent families had moved to Lake Shore Drive and adjacent streets that the area soon earned the sobriquet of the "Gold Coast." Sadly, Palmer's castle became yet another victim of the wrecker's ball when it was demolished in 1950 to make way for a highrise apartment building.

As a retailer, Palmer introduced many innovations. He allowed customers to examine merchandise in their homes and then return it if they were not satisfied or to exchange it, after it was bought, for other items. He advertised heavily. Above all, Palmer treated his customers—no matter what their economic status— with courtesy and respect. Potter Palmer based his successful career on pleasing his patrons. It was a lesson that others emulated, most notably, his protégé Marshall Field.

Palmer died in Chicago in May of 1902, several weeks shy of his seventy-sixth birthday.

In recent years the central shopping district has shifted from State Street to Michigan Avenue as many of the big department stores such as Goldblatt's, Sears, and Montgomery Ward went out of business. Despite these changes, the Palmer House remains a Loop landmark. One of the last great downtown hotels, the Palmer House continues to invite guests from around the world to come to its State and Monroe address.

See also: Marshall Field, Bertha Honore Palmer, Richard Sears, Aaron Montgomery Ward

Further reading: Heise, Kenan and Michael Edgerton. *Chicago Center for Enterprise.* 2 vols. (1982); Mayer, Harold M. and Richard C. Wade. *Chicago: Growth of a Metropolis.* (1969); Wendt, Lloyd and Herman Kogan. *Give the Lady What She Wants! The Story of Marshall Field and Co.* (1952).

Francis W. Parker

Educator

born: October 9, 1837
Bedford, New Hampshire
died: March 2, 1902
Pass Christian, Mississippi

Called "the father of progressive education," Francis Wayland Parker founded the Chicago Institute, which eventually merged with the University of Chicago, and earned a reputation as an indefatigible advocate of progressive teaching methods.

Photograph courtesy of the Francis W. Parker School.

The son of a cabinet maker, Parker was orphaned when still a small child and raised by a farmer. At age thirteen he enrolled at Mt. Vernon Academy in New Hampshire, and at sixteen he began to teach. Parker taught in several New Hampshire schools until 1853 when he was appointed principal of a one-room frontier school in Carrollton, Illinois. He remained there until the outbreak of the Civil War.

Parker then returned to New Hampshire and joined the 4th New Hampshire Volunteers as a lieutenant. Soon thereafter he was promoted to colonel and was taken prisoner by Confederate troops and incarcerated in a military camp in Greensburg, North Carolina.

After the war, Parker resumed his teaching career. In 1869 he was appointed principal of the Dayton, Ohio, school system. Following his wife's death in 1871, Parker resumed his own education, studying in Germany and observing the teaching methods of such progressive pioneers as Friedrich Froebel and J. N. Pestalozzi. In 1875 he was appointed superintendent of schools in Quincy, Massachusetts.

Parker began experimenting with new methods of teaching. Influenced by the principles of E. A. Sheldon, he broke all the traditional rules. At that time, students learned by the rote method. They memorized facts and figures and regurgitated the statistics at the appropriate time. Parker's method was different. He demanded that his pupils actually think for themselves, and learn to gain enough confidence to express themselves. Each child, he argued, was a unique individual and each child learned at his or her own rate. He advocated a curriculum that emphasized observation, recommended field trips,

and preached that the moral development of a child was just as important—perhaps more—as the act of learning.

Parker came to Chicago in 1883 and was appointed principal of the Cook County Normal School, a training school for elementary and high school teachers, then located in the village of Englewood, Illinois. Englewood was annexed to Chicago in 1889 and the renamed Chicago Normal School was incorporated under the aegis of the Chicago Board of Education in 1896. Much criticism was directed at Parker's controversial ideas. He resigned in 1899 to head an experimental school—the Chicago Institute—devoted to unconventional teaching methods. The institute consisted of a training school for teachers, a kindergarten, an elementary school, and another school—the Francis W. Parker School—located on the North Side near Lincoln Park. In 1901 the Chicago Institute was incorporated into the University of Chicago as the School of Education. John Dewey became the director after Parker's death. Dewey resigned in 1904 to accept a position at Columbia University. The Parker school, a private institution, continues to serve the Lincoln Park community and, through its extensive adult education evening classes, the greater Chicago area. Parker alumni include actress Celeste Holm, cinematographer Haskell Wexler, and playwright/director David Mamet.

Truth be told, Parker was a bit of a tyrant. "He roared, he growled, he stormed, he banged . . . he scared the wits out of students, and he terrified teachers," wrote one of his supporters, union leader Margaret Haley. But, as Haley also admitted, he proved to be an inspiring role model.

Among his books are *Talks on Pedagogics* (1894) and *Talks on Teaching* (1896).

Complaining of illness, Parker spent February of 1902 in Mississippi at the advice of his doctor. He died the following month at the age of sixty-four.

See also: John Dewey [appendix], Margaret Haley, William Rainey Harper, Ella Flagg Young

Further reading: Campbell, Jack K. *Colonel Francis W. Parker: The Children's Crusader* (1967); Heffron, Ida Cassa. *Francis Wayland Parker: An Interpretative Biography* (1934).

Albert Parsons & Lucy Parsons

Labor Activists

born: circa 1848
Montgomery, Alabama
died: November 11, 1887
Chicago, Illinois

born: circa March 1853
Johnson County, Texas
died: March 7, 1942
Chicago, Illinois

*Lucy Ella and Albert R. Parsons were influential leaders in the Chicago labor movement of the late nineteenth century. An eloquent and fiery orator, Lucy marched and protested in the name of economic freedom and spoke frequently about labor unrest, anarchism, industrial unionism, women's rights, and civil rights. Albert, an apprentice printer, served in the Confederate Army during the Civil War. After the war he edited the **Waco** (Texas) **Spectator** and from 1869 to 1871 he worked as assistant assessor for the Internal Revenue Service. He is best remembered as one of the Haymarket Eight.*

Photographs courtesy of Charles H. Kerr Publishing Company.

Lucy's personal background is rather sketchy. Born Lucy Gathings, she was thought to be a former slave of mixed African-American, Indian, and Mexican ancestry. She married Albert Parsons in 1872. The couple settled in Chicago in late 1873 at a time when the city was in great economic and social turmoil. Albert joined the Social Democratic Party of North America and cofounded the first Knights of Labor Assembly in Chicago. He also ran for alderman of the 15th Ward on the North Side. At that time, the Parsons lived near Larrabee Street and North Avenue.

City officials viewed both Lucy and Albert Parsons with nervous suspicion. In 1878 Albert founded the Trades and Labor Assembly of Chicago and was elected secretary of the Chicago Eight Hour League. He edited two radical publications, the *Socialist* and, with Lizzie Swank, the *Alarm*, the publication of the International Working People's Association.

Lucy was every bit as radical as her husband. A major foe of capitalism, she compared the American businessman with members of the European aristocracy, believing that wage workers were not much higher on the social scale than slaves, and she advocated nothing less than the destruction of the existing ruling class. Parsons championed the establishment of a fair and equitable society based upon the principle of cooperation rather than competition and promoted equal rights for all, regardless of sex or race. Parsons argued that the social evils of society are a result of economic injustice and, thus, concluded that the abolition of capitalism would produce racial and sexual equality.

A clash between workers and police at the McCormick Harvesting Machine Company on May 3, 1886, led to a protest meeting on Desplaines Street near Haymarket Square the following evening. Albert was one of the speakers who addressed the crowd that rain-soaked night. Mayor Carter Harrison I also attended the meeting but returned to his Ashland Avenue mansion, certain that all was well. Before retiring for the evening he stopped at the Desplaines Street police station and told Captain John Bonfield to send his officers home. For reasons still unclear, Bonfield defied the mayor's wishes, marched to Haymarket Square, and ordered the crowd to disperse.

In the tumult that followed, an unidentified figure hurled a bomb. Albert and Lucy Parsons who, by this time, had walked to nearby Zepf's Hall at 630 West Lake Street to escape the rain, heard the commotion

outside. When the uproar subsided, Lucy returned home and Albert stayed at a friend's house in Geneva, Illinois.

At the insistence of Lucy who feared for his safety, Albert fled to Waukesha, Wisconsin, to escape possible prosecution. He surrendered several weeks later on June 21, 1886. On August 20, the jury returned a guilty verdict against eight men for the murder of police officer Mathias Degan and conspiracy to start a police riot—George Engel, Samuel Fielden, Adolph Fischer, Louis Lingg, Oscar Neebe, Parsons, Michael Schwab, and August Spies. Ultimately, seven (Louis Lingg died in prison under mysterious circumstances), including Albert, were sentenced to death. Lucy crisscrossed the country proclaiming her husband's innocence and explaining the wretched conditions that led to the Haymarket Riot and the rise of the eight-hour-day movement. During her crusade, she spoke to an estimated 200,000 people in some 16 states. Her efforts were not enough. Four of the Haymarket Eight—Parsons, Spies, Fischer, and Engel—were executed at noon on November 11, 1887, a day that came to be known around the world as "Black Friday." Two days later, the funeral procession began at the house of August Spies, one of the Haymarket martyrs, at 2132 West Potomac Avenue in Wicker Park. The procession traveled south along Milwaukee Avenue and down Wells Street to the Grand Central railroad station. The bodies were then taken by train to Waldheim Cemetery in Forest Park, Illinois— the only cemetery willing to accept their remains.

On June 26, 1893, Governor John Peter Altgeld pardoned the surviving defendants—Oscar Neebe, Samuel Fielden, and Michael Schwab. Lucy carried on. In 1891, she and Lizzie Holmes edited *Freedom, A Revolutionary Anarchist-Communist Monthly* and from 1905 to 1906, Parsons

edited *The Liberator*. She became involved in Eugene Debs' Social Democratic party and was a seminal figure in the founding of the Industrial Workers of the World.

Parsons was a featured speaker at various anarchist forums in Chicago and was known to drop in at the city's foremost bohemian hangout, the Dill Pickle Club on the Near North Side. As late as the 1930s, she traveled and lectured across the country in defense of free speech and fair working conditions. In 1889, she wrote a biography of her late husband, *The Life of Albert R. Parsons, with Brief History of the Labor Movement in America*.

In March of 1942, Parsons and a companion died when her wood stove caught fire at her home at 3130 North Troy Street. She was buried next to the grave of the Haymarket Martyrs in Waldheim Cemetery.

The identity of the bomb thrower that caused the Haymarket riot remains a mystery. Novelist Frank Harris in his fictional account of the Haymarket Affair, *The Bomb,* claimed it may have been Rudolph Schnaubelt, Michael Schwab's brother-in-law.

See also: John Peter Altgeld, Eugene Debs, William "Big Bill" Haywood [appendix], Carter Harrison I, Ben Reitman

Further reading: Adelman, William J. *Haymarket Revisited* (1976); Ashbaugh, Carolyn. *Lucy Parsons, American Revolutionary* (1976); Calmer, Alan. *Labor Agitator: The Story of Albert R. Parsons* (1937); Foner, Philip, ed. *Autobiographies of the Haymarket Martyrs* (1976); Harris, Frank. *The Bomb* (1963); Parsons, Lucy E. *The Life of Albert R. Parsons, with Brief History of the Labor Movement in America* (1889); Roediger, Dave and Franklin Rosemont, eds. *Haymarket Scrapbook* (1986).

James C. Petrillo

Labor Activist

born: March 16, 1892
Chicago, Illinois
died: October 23, 1984
Chicago, Illinois

James Caesar Petrillo, president of both the American Federation of Musicians and the Chicago local of the AFM, was one of the most powerful and controversial labor leaders of his day. His rough, combative, and often confrontational style earned him the nickname "Little Caesar." Although extreme in his tactics, no one doubted his sincerity or questioned his honesty. It was understood he merely wanted the best for "his boys."

Photograph courtesy of Charles H. Kerr Publishing Company.

The son of an immigrant Italian sewer cleaner, Petrillo grew up in the Little Italy neighborhood around the vicinity of Halsted and Taylor Streets. He had a difficult time in school. Indeed, he felt a perverse pride in revealing that it took him eight years to get as far as the third grade. "I was in the third grade three times. Finally, after the third year, they told me, 'You're impossible. Get out of here.' And I did. It was the best thing that ever happened to me."

He quit school and hit the streets, picking up any kind of work he could find. He ran an elevator, sold newspapers, and drove a horse and cart. At Hull-House, Jane Addams instilled in him a love of the cornet—he looked like a musician, she said. At fourteen, he formed his own four-piece band, playing at picnics and at Polish and Italian weddings. He secured his first union job as a $10 a week sergeant-at-arms of the American Musicians Union (AMU). His duty was to maintain order in the union hall. In 1914 at age twenty-two, he was elected president of the AMU. In 1917, however, he lost the position. "They threw me out," he said. "They said I was too rough—the way I talked and hollered."

In retaliation he jumped to the rival Chicago Federation of Musicians Local 10 of the American Federation of Musicians (AFM). In 1919 he was elected vice-president of Local 10, and in 1922 he became president, a post that he retained for forty years.

In the early days, the union struggled to stay on its feet, but when the mob began intimidating the musicians and actually threatened to take over, Petrillo held firm. With each year, his power and influence increased. In 1931 he became vice-president of the national AFM.

Working conditions for Chicago musicians were never easy. Many changes occurred in the entertainment field during the first few decades of the twentieth century. The decline of vaudeville and burlesque and the gradual disappearance of live music in the theater adversely affected the employment opportunities of musicians. What's more, technological advances, what Petrillo called "canned music," threatened the livelihood of the live performer. In *The Musicians and Petrillo*, Robert D. Leiter estimates that two thousand musicians were employed in Chicago theaters during the silent film era, providing music accompaniment to the images on the screen. The introduction of sound drastically curtailed the need for live musicians, forcing them to find other means of support. Many couldn't. The number of unemployed musicians during the thirties skyrocketed. In order to provide them with work, Petrillo initiated a series of concerts in Grant Park during the Depression. The performances ran from 1935 through 1943 under the joint sponsorship of the union local and the Park District.

In 1940 Petrillo was elected national president of the AFM. One of the first things that he did upon assuming office was to require radio stations to pay musicians who performed on radio programs. (Previously they had played for the free publicity.) Although Petrillo ultimately prevailed, radio stations surreptitiously circumvented the measure by substituting phonographic records and thus misleading the public into believing that what they were hearing were live performances.

On August 1, 1942, Petrillo directly confronted the problem of recorded music when he forbade the 133,000 union membership to record or use electrical transcriptions or any other mechanical means of reproducing music. This drastic action effectively ended any recording for twenty-seven months.

In June 1944 the War Labor Board ordered the union to end the ban. Petrillo refused. Even the personal request of President Franklin D. Roosevelt couldn't change his mind. Two federal court suits, a War Labor Board hearing, and a Senate investigation followed, yet Petrillo remained intractable. In actuality Petrillo permitted the recording industry to produce records but only for enjoyment in the home and for armed forces use. Consequently many young musicians who were just coming into their own at that time—such as Earl Hines, Billy Eckstine, and Woody Herman—were denied the opportunity to record during this crucial stage in their career. Records were still being released, however. Manufacturers, aware of Petrillo's intention, simply released reissues or relied on their backlogs in order to survive. When the controversy finally ended in November 1944, record companies agreed to pay royalties to the union treasury for every record produced, to be placed into a special Music Performance Trust Fund for unemployed musicians. Petrillo and the union had achieved a major victory. Even so, four years later, Petrillo announced a second ban, which did not have as much of an impact.

In 1948 Petrillo resigned from the presidency of the AFM although he retained his hold on the local chapter until 1962 when, in one of the biggest upsets in local union history, dissident members defeated his bid for reelection of the presidency of Local 10 by a margin of less than one hundred votes.

In 1964 Petrillo accepted the chairmanship of a newly created civil rights department within the union. At that time, over thirty cities had dual musician locals—one black and one white. Although Petrillo traveled across the country until 1971, ostensibly promoting the integration of the segregated music unions, several

historians have recently questioned his sincerity. Petrillo, insists Clark D. Halker, a musician and former history professor at North Central College in Naperville, Illinois, did virtually nothing to end discrimination against African-Americans in local unions. The musicians had to do it themselves.

The controversial labor leader died of cancer in October of 1984 in St. Joseph Hospital. He was ninety-two.

See also: Jane Addams, Earl Hines

Further reading: Halker, Clark D. "Banding Together," *Chicago History* (September 1989); Leiter, Robert D. *The Musicians and Petrillo* (1953).

Allan Pinkerton

Detective

born: August 25, 1819
Glasgow, Scotland
died: July 1, 1884
Chicago, Illinois

The motto of the Pinkerton Detective Agency was "The eye that never sleeps." Diligent sleuth, romantic loner, loyal patriot—those were the images of the Pinkerton detective that founder Allan Pinkerton so carefully nurtured and presented to the world. Pinkertons scoured the country in search of outlaws, robbers, and thieves, and the Pinkerton name became known and feared throughout the land.

The son of a Glasgow police sergeant, Pinkerton was a cooper by trade. As a young man, he joined the Chartists, a working-class movement that was sweeping across Britain, demanding rights for the common laborer. In order to avoid being sent to a penal colony for his radical activities, Pinkerton and his wife immigrated to America in 1842. He spent his first year in Chicago, working at Lill's Brewery, then opened a cooper's shop in the Scottish settlement of Dundee, forty miles west of the city, where he made barrels and casks. Pinkerton was introduced to detective work by accident when he came across the hideout of a gang of counterfeiters and helped capture them. He was elected deputy sheriff of Kane County in the late 1840s. An avowed abolitionist, he converted his shop into one of the stops on the underground railroad.

In 1850 Pinkerton opened his own detective agency, the Pinkerton National Detective Agency. Its original purpose was to help runaway slaves escape to Canada but quickly Pinkerton's one-man operation began to pursue small-time crooks who passed bogus checks. At the same time, Pinkerton also acted as a special agent for the post office, investigating mail robberies and verifying the honesty of employees. He returned to Chicago in the early 1850s, was appointed a deputy sheriff of Cook County in 1852, and, by 1860, had became prominent in abolitionist circles.

Pinkerton's detective agency supplied a much-needed service—protection of the citizenry. Organized law enforcement was slow to get off the ground in many U.S. cities. Chicagoans, like other Americans who were distrustful of authority, feared a centralized police system. Instead, private citizens maintained their own vigil against crime. In the evening night watchmen patrolled the streets.

Such an overtaxed system was woefully inadequate to meet the security needs of the growing metropolis, however.

Despite his working-class origins, Pinkerton felt little sympathy toward unions. Strikes were, he thought, unnecessary evils, and unions nothing more than hotbeds of anarchy. Pinkerton agents infiltrated labor unions and passed on whatever they learned to the employers. "Between 1933 and 1935," writes Pinkerton historian Frank T. Morn, "the agency had 1,228 operatives . . . in practically every union in the country." Pinkerton firmly believed that workers who applied the Protestant ethic of hard work and perseverance would be amply rewarded in the end.

Pinkerton's reputation spread far beyond the boundaries of Chicago. During the Civil War, President Abraham Lincoln chose Pinkerton to run the United States Secret Service for the Union Army. Two of his chief functions were to investigate Union spies and to gather information behind Confederate lines. In addition, he investigated various plots against the government, including an alleged assassination attempt against Lincoln in Baltimore in 1861.

In the early days of the firm, Pinkerton would go undercover himself, often donning various disguises and rounding up some of the country's most notorious outlaws, including the infamous Reno brothers of Indiana.

Pinkerton undercover agents were almost as famous as the criminals they sought. Frank Dimaio, for example, pursued Butch Cassidy and the Sundance Kid's "Hole in the Wall" Gang, successfully tracing them all the way to Argentina. Another Pinkerton in the 1890s was Tom Horn, a gunman, army scout, and former Indian fighter. Detective

writer Dashiel Hammett was a Pinkerton from 1913 to 1918, and for a brief time in the twenties he worked on the Fatty Arbuckle case in Hollywood. One of the most determined Pinkertons was Charles Siringo. Siringo, who had used sheriff Pat Garrett's name as a reference while applying for the job and whose first assignment was to prevent jury tampering during the Haymarket trial in 1887, also spent some time pursuing Butch Cassidy and his gang. Indeed, he claimed to having logged twenty-five thousand miles in search of the elusive outlaws.

Probably the most celebrated detective on staff was James McParlan (sometimes spelled McParland) who infiltrated the Pennsylvania coal mines in the late 1800s and was largely responsible for the crushing of the Irish labor organization, the Molly Maguires. In 1970, a movie based on McParlan's exploits, called *The Molly Maguires*, starring Sean Connery, with Richard Harris as McParlan, was released.

Pinkerton complained that dime novels, lurid and sensational as they were with simple-minded plots and cardboard characters, demeaned his profession. As early as 1871 he considered writing stories, based on actual Pinkerton cases, to combat the frivolous image of the detective. His first book, *The Expressman and the Detective,* in 1875 was a great success, selling a brisk fifteen thousand copies within sixty days of its publication, notes Frank T. Morn. Between 1874 and 1884 Pinkerton published— although he did not actually write them—sixteen detective books, including *The Molly Maguires and the Detectives* (1877), *Strikers, Communists, Tramps and Detectives* (1878), *The Spy of the Rebellion* (1883), and *Thirty Years a Detective* (1884).

After Pinkerton suffered a slight stroke in 1869, his two sons, William and Robert, assumed control of the agency. Pinkerton died in July of 1884 in Chicago. He was buried in Graceland Cemetery. The Pinkerton Detective Agency, now called Pinkerton Investigations and based in Hillside, Illinois, with national headquarters in Van Nuys, California, is still in business, although Pinkerton agents today are more likely to track down fraudulent insurance claims than bank robbers.

Further reading: Flinn, John J. *History of the Chicago Police from the Settlement of the Community to the Present Time* (1887); Horan, James D. *The Pinkertons: The Detective Dynasty That Made History* (1967); Lindberg, Richard. *To Serve and Collect: Chicago Politics and Police Corruption from the Lager Beer Riot to the Summerdale Scandal* (1991); Morn, Frank T. *The Eye That Never Sleeps: A History of the Pinkerton National Detective Agency* (1982); Poole, Ernest. *Giants Gone: Men Who Made Chicago* (1943).

George Pullman

Industrial

born: March 3, 1831
Brocton, New York
died: October 19, 1897
Chicago, Illinois

George Mortimer Pullman revolutionized rail travel. Prior to the invention of the Pullman sleeping car, passengers had to endure interminable, uncomfortable, and oftentimes unbearable rail journeys. A practical businessman, Pullman founded the company town of Pullman on the shore of Lake Calumet so that his employees could work and live in a peaceful setting, far removed from the corrupting influences of urban living or labor strife. Visitors came from all over the world to see it. Pullman, however, was hardly a benevolent boss, and the community he created was hardly a workers' paradise.

One of ten children, Pullman left school at fourteen to become a sales clerk and apprentice cabinet maker. In the early 1850s he moved to Rochester, New York, where he invented an innovative system of raising entire city blocks from their muddy foundation to a higher street level by placing thousands of giant jackscrews under the buildings and, with the help of a few hundred able-bodied men, turning the screws. In 1855 Pullman moved to Chicago and continued the lucrative business of street raising. A busy downtown hotel, the Tremont, located at the corner of Lake and Dearborn Streets, was slowly falling into a quagmire of mud. Pullman insisted he could raise it without breaking a window or even disturbing a single guest. And in 1858, he did just that.

For a while Pullman had been considering the idea of building railroad cars with sleeping facilities. In 1858 he contracted with the Chicago and Alton Railroad to design sleeping berths. Passengers loved the comfortable new arrangements, but the railroads were skeptical. Pullman had made the car one foot wider and two and one half feet higher than the usual standards. If the railroads wished to use his sleeping cars they would have to widen their bridges and station platforms. Some called the new invention "Pullman's Folly."

Impatient and tired of waiting for a reply, Pullman moved to Colorado in 1859 to seek his fortune among the gold mines. He devoted most of his time, though, to improving the sleeping car's design. He returned to Chicago in 1865 and introduced the first Pullman car: the Pioneer. In 1867, he founded the Pullman Palace Car Company and completed the first combination sleeping and dining car, followed by the first dining car one year later. Shortly thereafter, he opened his first manufacturing plant in Palmyra, New York, then moved it to Detroit and added additional plants in St. Louis, Missouri; Elmira, New York; Wilmington, Delaware; and San Francisco.

In 1880 the Pullman Company bought four thousand acres on the western shore of Lake Calumet, ten miles south of Chicago, and established Pullman, Illinois. By creating a controlled environment, he thought the town of Pullman would be an effective means of reducing labor unrest. Historian William C. Adelman suggests that the industrialist modeled the community of Pullman after the northern England town of Saltaire.

Pullman hired a twenty-six-year-old architect from New York, Solomon S. Beman, to design the community, the nation's first planned industrial town. Most of the residential units, which were to be inhabited by skilled workers, consisted of row houses, but there were also apartments and some single family homes. Unskilled workers, though, lived in shabby tenements or in wooden shanties. The town had its own newspaper, church, schools, and hospital. The Hotel Florence, named in honor of Pullman's daughter, faced the park. A miniature lake was created, and schooling was free through the eighth grade. The Arcade, a sort of precursor to today's shopping malls, contained a theater, a library, a post office, a YMCA, a bank, and approximately thirty shops.

Despite this apparent concern for his employees, Pullman was, above all, a businessman; and the company town of Pullman was in the business of making money. During the depression of 1893, company profits fell drastically. Pullman announced layoffs, reduced hours, and slashed wages, yet rents remained the same.

In 1894 the workers went on strike in one of the ugliest clashes between capital and labor in Chicago, and indeed, labor history. They were soon joined by Eugene Debs's American Railway Union, which then boycotted Pullman cars, against the initial advice of Debs, who sought arbitration. When Pullman refused to compromise, Debs endorsed the strike.

By the end of June, the strike reached national proportions as workers refused to handle Pullman cars and the country's railroads screeched to a halt. In response, President Grover Cleveland dispatched troops from nearby Fort Sheridan to the town to restore order and to have Debs arrested. The strike ended in July and the Pullman plant reopened in early August. Pullman made no concessions.

A man who had never known want, Pullman had little in common with his employees and either could not or would not sympathize with their plight. His policies—wage reductions while maintaining high rents—created a community populated by angry, bitter people. "We are born in a Pullman house, fed from the Pullman shop, taught in the Pullman school, catechized in the Pullman church, and when we die we shall be buried in the Pullman cemetery and go to the Pullman hell," observed one resident.

Although Pullman emerged victorious, his victory rang hollow for he died in 1897 a bitter man, despised by labor and criticized by members of his own family who disagreed with his cavalier treatment of Pullman employees. He was buried in Graceland Cemetery under tons of asphalt, safe from the wrath of angry workers.

The town of Pullman was annexed to Chicago in 1889 despite Pullman's objections. In 1908 the Illinois Supreme Court ordered the company to sell its property. The South Pullman District between 111th and 115th Streets and Cottage Grove and Langley Avenues was designated a national landmark in 1971 and a Chicago landmark on October 16, 1972.

In 1991 playwright Jeffrey Sweet's play *American Enterprise*, a theatrical portrait of Pullman's life and times, enjoyed a successful run at the Organic Theater in Chicago.

See also: John Peter Altgeld, Clarence Darrow, Eugene Debs

Further reading: Adelman, William C. *Touring Pullman* (1972); Buder, Stanley. *Pullman: An Experiment in Industrial Order and Community Planning, 1880–1930* (1967); Carwardine, William H. *The Pullman Strike* (1973); Harding, Carroll Rede. *George M. Pullman 1831–1897 and the Pullman Company* (1951); Pacyga, Dominic A. and Ellen Skerrett. *Chicago: City of Neighborhoods* (1986).

James Quigley

Priest

✝

born: October 15, 1854
Ontario
died: July 10, 1915
Rochester, New York

As the city's second archbishop, James Edward Quigley sought to bring together the city's multiethnic Catholics. Quigley believed that Catholicism did not end when the church door swung closed. Rather, he felt, notes historian Charles Shanabruch, "that Catholicism must extend to all aspects of life." Quigley encouraged the establishment of national parishes within the Chicago archdiocese as the best possible way of maintaining church ties with the city's burgeoning immigrant population. Quigley respected the uniqueness of all nationalities.

Born in Canada of Irish immigrant parents, Quigley moved with his family to Lima, New York, before settling in Rochester. When he was ten, the Quigleys moved again, this time to Buffalo. Here he studied with the Christian Brothers at St. Joseph's College, graduating in 1872. When he was still a teenager Quigley was accepted at West Point. His mother, however, had hoped that her eldest son would join the priesthood. Bowing to her wishes, Quigley enrolled at the Vincentian seminary of Our Lady of the Angels in Buffalo and then continued his studies at the University of Innsbruck in Austria. In 1879 he earned a doctor of theology degree from the College of the Propaganda in Rome.

Ordained shortly after, Quigley was assigned to a parish in Attica, New York. In 1884 he was chosen as rector of the Buffalo cathedral and, in February of 1897, Quigley was consecrated bishop of Buffalo.

In December of 1902 Quigley was chosen to succeed the late Patrick Feehan, Chicago's first archbishop, as head of the Chicago diocese. The new archbishop arrived in the city in March of the following year. In his first speech to his constituency he proclaimed, "I shall seek the counsel of others and in the multitude of counsel may find the right, but I must decide for myself. Whatever I do, I shall do in justice and charity. Having done it, I will be ready to bear the consequences, if I shall make a mistake."

Quigley's twelve-year term as archbishop of Chicago was a fruitful one. He built parochial schools, organized Catholic charities, and encouraged the Jesuits to establish what would later become Loyola University and the Vincentians to organize DePaul University. In 1904 he founded Cathedral College, a Catholic preparatory school for boys. Continuing the policy of his predecessor, Quigley formed national parishes to appeal to the city's various immigrant groups. Quigley, however, was especially interested in reaching the poor and the disadvantaged, to make the Church less intimidating, and to make it a regular part of the daily life of his parishioners. The Church under Quigley, asserts historian Shanabruch, attempted to answer the spiritual—as well as social and financial—needs of its diverse flock.

Archbishop Quigley died unexpectedly on July 10, 1915, at the age of sixty in his brother's home in Rochester, New York. His body was returned to Chicago, and he was buried in Mount Carmel cemetery in Hillside, Illinois.

See also: Arnold Damen, George Mundelein

Further reading: Koenig, Rev. Msgr. Harry C., S.T.D. *A History of the Parishes of the Archdiocese of Chicago.* 2 vols. (1980); Shanabruch, Charles. *Chicago's Catholics: The Evolution of an American Identity* (1981).

Ben Reitman

Social Activist/Physician

born: circa 1879
St. Paul, Minnesota
died: November 17, 1942
Chicago, Illinois

Outlandish in dress and shocking in behavior, Ben Reitman was one of the most colorful figures in Chicago. But he wasn't all flash. Reitman contributed significantly to the social welfare of the poor and the homeless. Nicknamed the "King of the Hoboes," Reitman served as the director of the peripatetic Hobo College where the city's drifters, misfits, and malcontents gathered. As a young boy he succumbed to the excitement of a life on the road. It was a deeply ingrained habit that he would never outgrow.

Photograph reprinted with permission from the *Chicago Sun-Times.*

Reitman's father, an itinerant peddler who moved to New York from Russia, abandoned his wife and two sons. For several months the family lived in Cleveland before moving to Chicago and settling in the red-light district on South Clark Street, shuttling in and out of cheap rooming houses. Some of Ben's earliest acquaintances were hookers, thieves, and bums. An inquisitive boy who loved adventure, he hopped the freight cars and quickly mastered the art of panhandling. Reitman made his mark all over the world. He worked for Buffalo Bill's Wild West show in Paris, was mistakenly arrested on a murder charge in Ireland, and was in San Francisco when the devastating quake of 1906 struck.

Reitman secured a job at the Polyclinic Laboratory in 1898 in Chicago, where he was encouraged to study medicine. A kindly doctor, Dr. Leo Loeb, offered to pay his tuition at the College of Physicians and Surgeons. Reitman gratefully accepted and, despite his lack of a formal education, enrolled at the college.

In July of 1901, he married May Schwartz, who was, according to Reitman's biographer Roger A. Bruns, an emotionally troubled student at the Chicago Musical College. During their European honeymoon, Reitman deserted his then pregnant wife—he could not handle the responsibility, suggests Bruns—and returned to Chicago in time to enroll for his sophomore year at the College of Physicians and Surgeons. He graduated in 1904, obtained a license, and opened an office at 39th Street and Cottage Grove Avenue.

In 1915 Reitman founded the Hobo College at 1118 West Madison Street. "The word hobo should be a badge of honor, like the name of any profession," declared Reitman. "We seek to make it so." Funded through the generosity of merchants and

benefactors, the college attracted assorted denizens of skid row and visiting hoboes. The most notable benefactor was James Eads How, a wealthy eccentric from St. Louis who financed several hobo colleges across the country.

The college, which changed locations almost yearly, presented lectures, debates, and discussions on almost any subject—economics, health, religion, philosophy, as well as more practical matters such as the ins and outs of the vagrancy laws. The college once presented a course in panhandling "from the viewpoint of a scientist." It offered short courses in law, public speaking, and English composition in addition to amateur plays, debates, open forums, and musical programs.

Reitman's college attracted top-notch guest lecturers—professors from local universities, physicians, psychologists, lawyers, and reformers. Regular speakers included "Prof" Paddy Carroll who lectured on "How To Live Without Eating" and "Yellow Kid" Weil, king of the con men. Several hobo speakers delivered lectures at University of Chicago sociology classes. The university and the Hobo College also held debates, and there were a few instances where the hoboes actually bested the allegedly superior Hyde Parkers—much to the chagrin and embarrassment of the university students.

Reitman always made an effort to drop by the infamous Dill Pickle Club, Chicago's premier bohemian hangout. He delivered speeches, lined up speakers, and chaired meetings.

Reitman and his lover, the radical Emma Goldman, gained national notoriety when they publicly advocated birth control, which had become a national issue by 1915. Reitman and Goldman circulated pamphlets in major cities across the country, including Chicago. In October of that year they were arrested in Portland, Oregon, for distributing the pamphlets, which, according to local law, violated an obscenity ordinance, and were fined $100 each. Later, Reitman was arrested in New York on the same charge and was sentenced—and served—sixty days in the workhouse. In Cleveland he was sentenced—and again served—six months and received a $1,000 fine. He was acquitted of charges in Rochester.

Despite the notoriety that surrounded Reitman, Dr. John Dill Robertson, commissioner of the city's Health Department, hired him in 1917 to work among Chicago's hobo population. Reitman did much to eradicate the spread of sexually transmitted diseases. He established the first municipal disease clinic in Chicago at the Iroquois Hospital that year. Later he inaugurated similar programs at the Cook County Jail and the Chicago House of Corrections before establishing his own organization, the Chicago Society for the Prevention of Venereal Disease. In 1937 the Chicago Syphilis Project hired Reitman to study vice and prostitution in the city's sprawling slums and especially in the areas around North Clark and West Van Buren Streets, along West Madison Street, and on South State Street between 31st and 35th Streets. During the project's first two years, notes Bruns, Reitman submitted over three hundred reports. Further, he gave talks on the subject at YMCAs, labor organizations, and churches.

In 1932 Reitman wrote *The Second Oldest Profession*, a study of prostitution. In 1937 he published a second book, *Sister of the Road: The Autobiography of Box-Car Bertha*, which was made into a movie in 1972, starring Barbara Hershey and David Carradine and directed by Martin Scorsese.

In October of 1939 Reitman suffered a stroke. Three years later he succumbed to a fatal heart attack at the age of sixty-three in his home at 6826 South Bishop Street in Chicago. He was buried in Waldheim Cemetery in Forest Park, Illinois.

See also: Albert and Lucy Parsons

Further reading: Bruns, Roger A. *The Damndest Radical: The Life and World of Ben Reitman, Chicago's Celebrated Social Reformer, Hobo King, and Whorehouse Physician* (1987); Walljasper, Jay. "Those Vagabond Days." *Chicago Tribune Sunday Magazine* (August 15, 1982).

George F. Root

Composer/Music Publisher

born: August 20, 1820
Sheffield, Massachusetts
died: August 6, 1895
Bailey's Island, Maine

*One of the most popular songwriters during the Civil War era was a frail-looking gentleman named George Frederick Root whose most famous song, "The Battle Cry of Freedom," became the Union rallying cry, rivaling Julia Ward Howe's "Battle Hymn of the Republic," and propelled him to national fame. "There was no song," wrote **Chicago Tribune** music critic George Upton, "that equaled 'The Battle Cry' in popularity and patriotic inspiration."*

The first child of Sarah Flint and Frederick Ferdinand Root, George Frederick came from a musical family. In 1826 they moved to Willow Farm in North Reading, Massachusetts. Later, Root studied flute and voice at the Boston Academy of Music Chorus. After finishing school he accepted a position as a music teacher at Jacob Abbott's School for Young Ladies in New York. He also taught music at Rutgers Female Institute in New Jersey. In 1859 Root went to Paris to continue his studies in piano and singing. Years earlier, in 1851, he had written his first cantata, *The Flower Queen; or The Coronation of the Rose*.

In 1852, inspired by the success of Stephen Foster, Root began experimenting with popular compositions. Still not certain of public reaction, he published his first song, "Hazel Dell," under the pseudonym G. Friedrich Wurzel. Much to his happy surprise, it became a great success. Despite this good fortune he continued his association with "serious" music. In January of 1853 he taught sacred music at the Union Theological Seminary in New York and, in the same year, helped establish the first Normal Musical Institute also in New York City.

In 1858 George's brother, Ebenezer Towner Root, and Chauncey Marvin Cady formed the music publishing firm of Root and Cady in Chicago at 95 Clark Street. George joined the company two years later and settled in Hyde Park at Cornell and Lake Park Avenues. Root and Cady quickly became one of the city's leading sheet music publishing firms.

The attack on Fort Sumter on April 12, 1861, inspired Root's first war song, "The First Gun Is Fired! May God Protect the Right!" A quick three days later it was published. The American sheet music industry capitalized on the outbreak of war. Topical and patriotic songs were in great demand by the public and sold briskly.

The inspiration for "The Battle Cry of Freedom," probably Root's best-loved composition, came one day in 1862 when President Lincoln had issued a second call for Northern troops. "We must rally for the Union," Root agreed. The next morning, he wrote these words at his desk:

Yes, we'll rally round the flag,
boys, we'll rally once again.
Shouting the battle cry of Freedom;

We'll rally from the hillside,
We'll gather from the plain,
Shouting the battle cry of Freedom

As he finished writing the song, Jules and Frank Lumbard, two of Chicago's best singers of war songs at the time, walked into his office asking if he had any new material to sing. A war meeting was to be held outside the courthouse and the brothers needed something stirring to appease the crowd. Root handed them the manuscript of "The Battle Cry of Freedom." The crowd loved it and joined in the singing of the chorus.

Before long the North was singing along to Root's song; recruiting figures skyrocketed. Root, it was said, had accomplished more with one song than a battalion of general's enlistment speeches could ever do. And the song boosted morale in the Union trenches, too. A young soldier wrote: "The tune put as much spirit and cheer into the army as a splendid victory. Day and night you could hear it by every campfire and in every tent."

Root wrote many other war songs, including "Just Before the Battle, Mother" (1864), "Tramp, Tramp, Tramp" (1864), and "The Vacant Chair" (1862). Root's most popular sentimental ballad was "Rosalie, the Prairie Flower," published in 1855. He also wrote gospel hymns. Popular evangelists Dwight Moody and Ira Sankey frequently used Root's compositions in their services. The firm also published music books and issued a monthly magazine, *The Song Messenger of the Northwest*.

Like many Chicagoans, Root lost much of his wealth in the Chicago Fire of 1871 when his office was destroyed. In 1872, the University of Chicago awarded him the degree of Doctor of Music.

In 1891, Root penned his autobiography, *The Story of a Musical Life*. He died at his summer home in Maine in August of 1895. He was seventy-four.

See also: Dwight L. Moody

Further reading: Crawford, Richard. *The Civil War Songbook* (1977); Epstein, Dena J. *Music Publishing in Chicago before 1871: The Firm of Root & Cady* (1969); Silber, Irwin, ed. *Songs of the Civil War* (1960); Spaeth, Sigmund. *History of Popular Music in America* (1948).

John Wellborn Root

Architect

born: January 10, 1850
Lumpkin, Georgia
died: January 15, 1891
Chicago, Illinois

With the possible exception of Dankmar Adler and Louis Sullivan, the partnership of Daniel H. Burnham and John Wellborn Root constituted the most important architectural affiliation in the city. Architecture, Root felt, must reflect its age and environment. "Now, in America, we are free of artistic traditions," he once wrote. "A new spirit of beauty is being developed and perfected, and even now its first achievements are beginning to delight us. This is old things made over; it is new. It springs out of the past, but it is not tied to it; it studies the traditions, but it is not enslaved by them."

Root came from proud Southern stock. His family fled from their native Georgia when Gen. William T. Sherman's army ransacked the town during the Civil War. Root spent nearly two years abroad near Liverpool, England, where he studied music and architecture. He returned to the United States and entered New York University and graduated with a civil engineering degree in 1869. For a short time, he worked in New York as a draftsman under James Renwick, the architect who designed St. Patrick's Cathedral. In 1871 Root moved to Chicago to take a job as a draftsman at the firm of Carter, Drake and Wight. It was here that he first met Daniel H. Burnham, another young man on the rise in the city's architectural world.

In 1873 Burnham and Root established their own company. After struggling for several years, they made a name for themselves as an innovative firm that welcomed challenge and diversity. Their first important work was in 1874 when they were commissioned to design the Prairie Avenue house of John B. Sherman, nicknamed "the father of the Stockyards." Important commercial assignments followed—the Montauk Building at 64 West Monroe Street (1882); the Rookery at 209 South Lasalle Street (1886); St. Gabriel's Church at 4501 South Lowe (1888); and the Monadnock Building at 53 West Jackson Boulevard (1891). The Montauk, which was demolished in 1902, revolutionized building construction. The base of the Montauk rested on what Root called a "floating raft," a slab of concrete reinforced with steel rails, which helped distribute weight throughout the structure.

Even more significant was the Monadnock. Generally considered Root's masterwork, it was nothing less than a pioneering feat that broke completely with traditional styles of architecture and used the most advanced design techniques then known. Six-foot thick walls at the base supported a sixteen-story building, which indicated that it was not possible to erect a structure taller than the Monadnock using traditional masonry construction. Taller buildings required the skeleton construction method. Robert D. Andrews, president of the Boston Architectural Club, applauded Root's "prodigious courage" and called the building an achievement that he found "unsurpassed in the architectural history of our country."

In 1892 the firm designed the twenty-two story Masonic Temple at the northeast corner of State and Randolph Streets, at that time the tallest building in the world. One of Root's last major works was for the headquarters of the Women's Christian Temperance Union (1892) at the southwest corner of LaSalle and Monroe Streets. Known as the Woman's Temple, it was demolished in 1926.

Root was a popular figure in Chicago. His standing in the artistic community grew when he married the sister of *Poetry* magazine founder, Harriet Monroe. Poet and drama critic, Harriet Monroe was also an able biographer. She wrote a well-received study of her brother-in-law in 1896.

The famed Chicago school of architecture celebrated American design. Although several of the Chicago school architects, including Louis Sullivan, were trained in Europe, they looked to America for inspiration and found their most distinctive identity in the form of the skyscraper. Root, in particular, had no desire to slavishly emulate old models. "He wished to offer to the older nations," notes Monroe, "a proof of new forces, new ideals, not yet developed and completed, but full of power and prophetic of charm."

Root served on the planning commission for the World's Columbian Exposition of 1893. It was he who recommended the area around Jackson Park as the best possible site. At first it seemed a curious choice. A semi-wild patch of marshland, Root pronounced it perfect for his vision of "a Venetian effect of palaces and lagoons against the lake's beautiful open spaces." He drew a plan that called for a classically influenced structure, the Court of Honor, to be situated around a basin that contrasted with a series of modern buildings fronting the lagoons. Root envisioned a shimmering city of many colors, shades, and hues that reflected the innovative Chicago school and expressed the vibrant architecture of the American heartland.

Root's conception of an exuberant, playful, modern American exposition was never realized. On the blustery evening of January 11, 1891, he escorted several guests to their carriage from his Astor Street home. The next day he contracted pneumonia. He died January 15 at the age of forty-one.

See also: Daniel H. Burnham, Harriet Monroe, Louis Sullivan

Further reading: Badger, R. Reid. *The Great American Fair: The World's Columbian Exposition and American Culture* (1979); Burg, David F. *Chicago's White City of 1893* (1976); Condit, Carl W. *The Chicago School of Architecture: A History of Commercial and Public Buildings in the Chicago Area, 1875–1925* (1964); Condit, Carl W. *The Rise of the Skyscraper* (1952); Hoffman, Donald. *The Architecture of John Wellborn Root* (1973); Monroe, Harriet. *John Wellborn Root, A Study of His Life and Work* (1966).

Julius Rosenwald

Entrepreneur/Philanthropist

born: August 12, 1862
Springfield, Illinois
died: January 6, 1932
Chicago, Illinois

Imaginative businessman and generous philanthropist, Julius Rosenwald derived his greatest enjoyment from helping others. "Charity is the one pleasure that never wears out," he said. He founded the Museum of Science and Industry, contributed considerably to African-American and Jewish charities, and, as president of Sears, Roebuck and Company, ran one of the biggest mail-order firms in the country. He was, in the words of his biographer, Morris R. Werner, a "practical humanitarian."

Photograph reprinted with permission from the *Chicago Sun-Times*.

Rosenwald's father, Samuel, emigrated from Germany in the 1850s and settled in Springfield, Illinois, where he established himself as a leading clothing merchant. Rosenwald attended public schools in Springfield. In 1879 he moved to New York to work in his uncle's clothing firm, Hammerslough Brothers, as a stock boy for $5 a week. In 1884 he and his brother, Morris, started their own store, J. Rosenwald and Brothers. One year later, he settled in Chicago, and with his cousin, Julius E. Weil, he established Rosenwald and Weil, a clothing outfit, in the Farwell Block at 185 Market Street (now Wacker Drive). Among his customers was the fledgling firm of Sears, Roebuck and Company. Rosenwald and his brother-in-law, Aaron Nusbaum, bought shares in the company. In 1895 Rosenwald advanced to vice-president. Richard Sears retired in late 1908 partly due to ill health and partly due to minor business differences with Rosenwald. There were no hard feelings, however, and the two men parted amicably. According to company historian, Lorin Sorenson, Rosenwald became president of Sears in 1908 and chairman of the board in 1924.

Under Rosenwald's innovative and progressive management, the company experienced phenomenal growth. He improved the quality of goods and services, insisted on accurate catalog descriptions, established a laboratory to set and maintain standards, and developed an efficient and fast system of processing orders. When he initiated the innovative money-back guarantee, sales skyrocketed. Further, he opened retail stores and established mail-order branches throughout the country. In February of 1925, the first retail outlet opened in a corner of Sears's mail order plant at Homan Avenue and Arthington Street. Eight months later, the first Sears retail department store opened in Evansville, Indiana.

Establishing better working conditions for his employees was a priority to Rosenwald. He introduced generous health benefits, offered paid vacations, and built athletic fields and tennis courts for the enjoyment of his employees.

As business thrived and his personal fortune grew, Rosenwald felt obligated to share his good fortune with society. "I really felt ashamed to have so much money," he confessed in his later years. Rosenwald abhorred waste and extravagance and believed that "unselfish effort" gave his life purpose. Prior to his death, he provided over $60 million to civic causes. In 1917 he established the Julius Rosenwald Foundation and made sizable contributions to the building of YMCAs and YWCAs, including a YMCA for African-Americans on Wabash Avenue.

In the beginning, Sears catered primarily to farmers and isolated homesteaders who had little or no access to affordable goods. Within a matter of years, the firm expanded its customer base to include an increasing number of urban dwellers.

Rosenwald was touched by the autobiography of Booker T. Washington and came to believe African-Americans and Jews had much in common. Both, he believed, suffered greatly from years of discrimination. He helped build more than 5,300 public schools for African-Americans in the South. In addition, he subsidized the construction of recreational and residential centers for African-Americans in over two dozen

Northern communities and contributed several million dollars to black universities, including Howard, Fisk, and Dillard.

Rosenwald also was concerned for the welfare of the Jewish community. In 1908 he donated $75,000 toward the construction of the Chicago Hebrew Institute, a cultural and educational center on Taylor Street; he served as president of the Associated Jewish Charities of Chicago; and he contributed to various other Jewish charities.

In Chicago, Rosenwald acquired a tract of land between 46th and 47th Streets and Michigan and Wabash Avenues to provide low-income housing facilities for some of the city's African-Americans. The Michigan Boulevard Garden Apartments at 4638 South Michigan Avenue was completed in 1929 and, unlike today's public housing units, included a mixture of professionals and working-class tenants.

Impressed with industrial museums in Munich and Vienna, Rosenwald promoted the idea of one in Chicago and, indeed, actually purchased material for the museum exhibits. He did not live long enough to see his work completed. The Museum of Science and Industry opened more than a year after Rosenwald's death.

In later years, Rosenwald suffered from bone disease and a weak heart. Despite his poor health, he never officially retired. He did, however, reduce his workload. In May of 1929 Augusta, Rosenwald's wife of thirty-nine years, died. He remarried on January 8, 1930. Two years later he died in his sleep on January 6, 1932. He was buried in Rosehill Cemetery beside the graves of his mother and his first wife.

The advent of the automobile brought drastic changes to the mail-order business. As patrons became less and less dependent on the Sears catalog, more retail stores were opened. Anticipating the popularity of the automobile, Rosenwald's successor, Robert E. Wood, who became president in 1928, introduced a policy to locate retail stores in the suburbs where there was plenty of free parking.

See also: Richard Sears, Aaron Montgomery Ward

Further reading: Bregstone, Philip P. *Chicago and Its Jews: A Cultural History* (1933); Harris, Leon. *Merchant Princes: An Intimate History of Jewish Families Who Built Great Department Stores* (1979); Jeuck, John E. and Boris Emmet. *Catalogues and Counters: A History of Sears, Roebuck & Co.* (1950); Katz, Donald R. *The Big Store: Inside the Crisis & Revolution at Sears* (1987); Kogan, Herman. *A Continuing Marvel, The Story of the Museum of Science and Industry* (1973); Sorensen, Lorin. *Sears, Roebuck and Co. 100th Anniversary 1886–1986* (1985); Werner, Morris R. *Julius Rosenwald, The Life of a Practical Humanitarian* (1939).

Barney Ross

Boxer

born: December 23, 1909
New York, New York
died: January 18, 1967
Chicago, Illinois

Barnet David Rasofsky, the Maxwell Street boy who held boxing's lightweight, junior welterweight, and welterweight crowns during the 1930s, was a graduate of the school of hard knocks. Yet the easy-going Ross took whatever life dished out to him in stride. Ross is considered one of the top ten welterweights in boxing history.

Photograph reprinted with permission from the *Chicago Sun-Times.*

Though born in New York, Ross and his family moved to Chicago when he was an infant. His father, a Russian Jewish immigrant, opened a grocery store in the Maxwell Street neighborhood. Barney was a sickly child, suffering from a lung ailment and arthritis. In 1924 tragedy struck when his father was killed in his store on Jefferson Street during a robbery attempt.

Ross quit school at fourteen and began hanging out with a rough crowd, joined a gang, and even ran errands for Al Capone. He learned how to take and throw punches. "You had to," he said later. "The Jews and Italians (on the Near West Side) were always at war. Many a night I would come home cut and bruised and get another licking at home for fighting."

During the Depression, Chicago produced many Jewish boxers, including welterweight champ Jackie Fields and heavyweight contender King Levinsky, a former fish peddler also from Maxwell Street. Ross, a street fighter in his own right, thought maybe he, too, had the makings of a boxer. He began working out in gyms and, with an eye toward turning professional, changed his name to the more American-sounding "Ross."

At eighteen, he fought amateur bouts. In 1929 he won both the Chicago and Intercity Golden Gloves featherweight championships. He turned pro, he once said, because he wanted to earn enough money to get his two younger brothers out of the orphanage, in which they were placed when Ross's mother moved to Connecticut to take care of her late husband's blind mother.

In 1933 Ross beat Tony Canzoneri in a ten-round decision at the Chicago Stadium to win both the lightweight and junior welterweight titles. He won a rematch later that year. In

1934 Ross captured the welterweight championship in New York against Jimmy McLarnin. He lost the title but regained it in 1935. Ross remained unbeaten until 1938 when he lost by decision to Henry Armstrong.

After eighty-two bouts with no knockouts, Ross retired from the ring. For a time, he operated a cocktail lounge in Chicago. When World War II broke out, he joined the Marines and saw action at Guadalcanal where he was hit by shrapnel and contracted malaria. During the battle, he was credited with killing twenty-two Japanese soldiers. Promoted to corporal and then sergeant, he was awarded the Silver Star for his acts of gallantry.

Ross's injuries required extensive hospitalization. To relieve the pain, doctors injected him with morphine. He became addicted.

On September 11, 1946, Ross confessed he was a drug addict and entered the United States public health hospital in Lexington, Kentucky. At one point, he estimated he had spent $250,000 on his habit. His wife, Catherine, then divorced him.

Ross persevered, kicked the habit, and remarried his wife. A movie was made about his drug problems, *Monkey On My Back,* without Ross's consent. Ross later filed suit against the producers of the film, asking for $5 million in damages, and claiming that the movie's advertisements ruined his reputation. He lectured frequently and traveled across the country talking about the evils of narcotics.

In 1947 Ross became the secretary-treasurer in charge of labor relations for the Eureka Shipbuilding corporation in Newburgh, New York. The following year, he joined the George Washington legion, an organization of American volunteers recruited to fight for the Jewish state in Palestine.

With Martin Abramson, Ross wrote his autobiography, *No Man Stands Alone*, in 1957.

In January of 1967, Ross died at age fifty-seven of throat cancer in his Lake Shore Drive apartment.

Further reading: Berkow, Ira. *Maxwell Street: Survival in a Bazaar* (1977); Ross, Barney with Martin Abramson. *No Man Stands Alone: The True Story of Barney Ross* (1957).

Arthur Rubloff

Real Estate Developer

born: June 25, 1902
Duluth, Minnesota
died: May 24, 1986
Chicago, Illinois

One of the leading real estate figures of the Midwest, Arthur Rubloff coined the term "Magnificent Mile" and helped to develop North Michigan Avenue, among other projects.

Photograph reprinted with permission from the *Chicago Sun-Times*.

Born in Minnesota, the son of a Russian Jewish immigrant, Rubloff dropped out of grade school and left home to find work as a galley boy on a Great Lakes ore boat. He then spent several years in a Cincinnati furniture store and picked up a few other odd jobs until he moved to Chicago in 1917, where his father had set up a clothing factory. A year after his arrival, his father's plant burned down. The tragedy effectively put the elder Rubloff out of business. Good fortune surfaced, however, when Arthur met a Chicago realtor who, impressed with the young man's vigor, persuaded him to enter the realty business. In 1921, Rubloff joined Robert White and Company, where he stayed until 1930, when he left to establish his own firm, Arthur Rubloff and Company.

Like that other famous Chicagoan, Daniel H. Burnham, Rubloff dreamed big. In 1945 he conceived the idea of Evergreen Plaza on the South Side, one of the first enclosed malls in the country. "It took nine years to get off the ground and I almost went broke because the concept was so new that it was very difficult to generate interest," he recalled.

In 1947 Rubloff, together with John Root of the architectural firm of Holabird and Root, unveiled a $200 million plan for the development of upper Michigan Avenue from the Chicago River to Oak Street that promised to turn the boulevard to the "most modern mile in the world." Initially the idea met with a cool reception. "I'd spent $50,000 preparing the plans and I was called all kinds of names," recalled Rubloff. "Some people thought I was trying to steal the town." Despite this initial trouble the North Michigan Avenue Association ultimately gave their approval to the proposal. By 1949 the association sponsored the planting of trees along the street; property owners and retailers echoed their support.

Rubloff was instrumental in the development and revitalization of other Chicago neighborhoods such as Old Town and Sandburg Village. Sandburg Village, built on the former site of a housing project, was completed in 1966 and attracted to the area thousands of predominantly young, white men and women. He also promoted a plan to renovate 14.5 acres in the North Loop. Mayor Richard J. Daley expressed interest in the idea but succeeding administrations—especially Michael J. Bilandic and Jane Bryne—rejected the plan as too costly and outmoded.

Rubloff, whose worth was estimated at $100 million when he died in 1986, donated $6 million to the Art Institute in 1984, reportedly the largest single contribution made to the institution. Substantial gifts were also given to Northwestern University, the University of Chicago, Michael Reese Hospital, the Lincoln Park Zoo, and the Chicago Historical Society as well as the United Negro College Fund, Lewis University, Hull-House, and the United Way.

Rubloff was a master at blowing his own horn. He took hyperbole to new heights. "I did North Michigan Avenue's Magnificent Mile. I built Sandburg Village. Saved the Near North Side, that's what I did. Everyone was against it," he once remarked to a local writer.

Rubloff's critics, however, were not quite as generous. Many contended that such projects would have eventually been developed—with or without his help. As far back as 1913, the Bowes Realty Company, a successful brokerage firm, began to buy and sell property along the street from the Michigan Avenue Bridge to Chicago Avenue and leased space to a number of elegant shops, which started a trend that continues to this day. Frederic Bowes, the president of the firm, reportedly convinced property owners not to allow "undesirable" businesses—such as gas stations and saloons—to locate there.

It was Rubloff, however, who aggressively promoted the beautification of North Michigan Avenue and envisioned the thoroughfare as Chicago's showpiece, comparable to Fifth Avenue in New York or the Champs Elysées in Paris. Nelson Forrest, executive director of the Greater North Michigan Avenue Association, called Rubloff a "promotional pioneer. He sparked the momentum for the area to become a private-enterprise development."

Rubloff died in his Lake Shore Drive highrise in May of 1986 at the age of eighty-three.

At the time of his death Rubloff was affiliated with Arthur Rubloff and Company in an advisory role only.

See also: Richard J. Daley

Carl Sandburg

Poet

born: January 6, 1878
Galesburg, Illinois
died: July 22, 1967
Flat Rock, North Carolina

Carl August Sandburg was a quintessentially American poet and one of the most loved poets of the twentieth century. But Sandburg was more than just a poet. He was also a crusading journalist, a teller of children's tales, a historian of Lincoln, an idealistic socialist, and a traveling troubador who sang and collected the folk songs of his native land.

Sandburg was the son of Swedish immigrants, August and Clara Johnson, who had settled in Galesburg, Illinois. According to literary historian Dale Kramer, his father, a blacksmith, changed the family name to Sandburg before Carl was born. Called Charley as a youth, Sandburg started to work at fourteen, driving a milk wagon. Then he held a series of jobs: dishwasher, porter at a barber shop, potato digger, window washer, and manual laborer in the harvest fields.

During the Spanish-American War of 1898, Sandburg enlisted in Company C Sixth Infantry Regiment of the Illinois Volunteers in the Army and served eight months in Puerto Rico. Upon his return to Illinois, he enrolled at Lombard College in Galesburg. In 1899 he applied to West Point, but he failed to pass the entrance exam. At Lombard, he edited the college monthly, served as a correspondent for a Galesburg newspaper, and captained the basketball team. He printed his first book of poetry there, *In Reckless Ecstasy* (1904), using a printing press owned by his former professor.

Sandburg dropped out of college in 1902 and continued his habit of working at whatever came his way. For a period of time he sold stereoscopic photographs. In 1907 he settled in Milwaukee, where he became a socialist organizer and later an advertising manager for a department store. He also recruited members for the Social Democratic party and worked on several Milwaukee newspapers until the city's socialist mayor, Emil Seidel, asked him to serve as his secretary. Sandburg accepted and stayed there for two years.

In 1908 Sandburg married Lillian Steichen, sister of the noted photographer, Edward Steichen. In 1912 the couple moved to Chicago, where Sandburg had friends, and settled down into the second-floor apartment of a frame house at 4646 North Hermitage Avenue in the Ravenswood neighborhood. Sandburg then decided to try his hand at journalism, which he felt offered more job opportunities. He began working on the *Chicago World,* and later switched to an experimental tabloid, *Day-Book,* at 500 South Peoria Street, that accepted no advertising. In 1917 Sandburg joined the *Chicago Daily News,* where he covered the labor beat. Later he reviewed movies. Sandburg remained on the staff until 1927.

Sandburg had poetry published as early as 1904 in obscure journals, but it wasn't until his work appeared in *Poetry* magazine in 1914 that his career took off. Poems like "Fog," or his most famous, "Chicago," attracted the most attention. His free verse, liberally scattered with slang and street-corner colloquialisms, caught the literary world off guard and ushered in a new era of what some critics referred to as poetic modernism. Two years later his collection of poetry, *Chicago Poems,* received mostly favorable reviews. Some of his other poetry volumes include *Cornhuskers* (1918), *Smoke and Steel* (1920), and *Slabs of the Sunburnt West* (1922).

Sandburg proved to be an astute and compassionate reporter. In 1919 he wrote *The Chicago Race Riots,* a penetrating analysis of the riots that ravaged the city's Black Belt during the hot summer of that year.

Sandburg was also a biographer. The last volume of his monumental six-volume biography of Lincoln (1939), *Abraham Lincoln: The War Years,* earned him the Pulitzer Prize for history in 1940.

In 1936 he compiled *The People, Yes,* a history of the common folk told in poetry. Sandburg preserved songs that otherwise may have been lost, collecting material from people "who sing because they must," he wrote. He scoured the country with his guitar in hand, collecting and singing the songs of the cowboy, the hobo, and the railroad worker. Collections of his songs include *The American Songbag* (1927) and *New American Songbag* (1951). He also wrote several children's books including *Rootabaga Stories* (1922) and *Potato Face* (1930). His last works include *Remembrance Rock* (1948), a novel—his first—that begins at Plymouth Rock and continues through World War II; *Complete Poems* (1950), which won him a second Pulitzer Prize in 1951; the autobiographical *Always the Young Stranger* (1952), a reminisence of his youth in Galesburg; and *Honey and Salt* (1962).

In 1962 Governor Otto Kerner, Jr., designated Sandburg the poet laureate of Illinois. In 1985 contemporary folksinger Bob Gibson produced a musical play, *The Courtship of Carl Sandburg,* that incorporated the writer's letters, poetry, children's tales, and stories.

Sandburg was a rarity—a critically acclaimed poet who also appealed to a broad audience. Called one of America's natural resources, he was often compared to another American icon, Mark Twain.

Sandburg died at his North Carolina home in July of 1967 at the age of eighty-nine.

Several schools in the Chicago area are named in his honor—Carl Sandburg Middle School in Mundelein, Carl Sandburg High School in Orland Park, and Carl Sandburg Junior High School in Elmhurst.

See also: Floyd Dell [appendix], Eugene Field, Ben Hecht, Harriet Monroe

Further reading: Golden, Harry. *Carl Sandburg* (1961); Kramer, Dale. *Chicago Renaissance: The Literary Life of the Midwest, 1900–1930* (1966); Sandburg, Carl. *Chicago Race Riots, July 1919* (1919); Smith, Alson J. *Chicago's Left Bank* (1953).

Abe Saperstein

Basketball Coach

born: July 4, 1902
London, England
died: March 15, 1966
Chicago, Illinois

That truly American sports institution, the Harlem Globetrotters, was founded by a native of London's Whitechapel district, Abe Saperstein. For nearly forty years, he led his team to glory in countries all over the world while such gifted athletes as Meadowlark Lemon, Goose Tatum, and Wilt Chamberlain provided hilarious comedy routines and displayed breathtaking ball-handling techniques. Saperstein championed the value of African-American athletes long before it was fashionable to do so.

Photograph reprinted with permission from the *Chicago Sun-Times*.

Saperstein moved to Chicago from England with his family as a youngster. He attended Lakeview High School on the North Side and later the University of Illinois. Although small in stature—he was an inch or so under five feet—Saperstein excelled in sports. When he realized he was too short to make the college basketball squad, he decided to try his hand at coaching.

Saperstein began his coaching career at Welles Park at Western and Montrose Avenues. Then he began coaching the Armour Post American Legion team. Saperstein recruited African-American players from the South Side to play at the Boys' Brotherhood Republic (BBR), a Jewish youth center founded in the Maxwell Street neighborhood. In 1927 he was hired to coach an African-American semipro team in Chicago, the Giles Post American Legion Quintet. The following year the team played twice a week at the Savoy Ballroom. After the engagement at the Savoy ended, several of the players, who were having so much fun, vowed to continue to play.

Saperstein had wanted a colorful, descriptive name for his team, something catchy and easy to remember. Since they were a traveling unit, he coined the term "Globetrotters," and since they were all an all-black outfit, he referred to them as the "Harlem" Globetrotters. In those days the team consisted of only five or six players, though sometimes Saperstein himself donned a uniform. The number of players increased as the team grew in popularity. Saperstein did virtually everything. In addition to his coaching duties, he acted as the team chauffeur—driving his players from town to town in a Model T Ford—booked and arranged play dates, and scouted. The Globetrotters played anybody, anywhere. Sometimes it was

for a straight guarantee up front, other times for a percentage of the box office.

Occasionally they played two games a night. Saperstein suggested that the players relieve the tension of life on the road by doing tricks with the ball—rolling it up and down their arm, for example. At first they balked at such a suggestion, believing it would demean the game they loved so well. Finally, one day in Newton, Iowa, they decided to give the coach's idea a workout. They spun the ball on their fingers and drop-kicked it through the hoop. The crowd, after they got over the novelty of the impromptu performance, roared with delight. Under Abe Saperstein, the Globetrotters became the world's most watched—and most watchable—basketball team and their exploits were reported in the pages of the daily press.

In the summer of 1961 Saperstein founded the American Basketball League with eight teams—including the Chicago entry, the Chicago Majors—after being denied a franchise in the rival National Basketball Association. He also served as commissioner of the ill-fated league. Saperstein's name, however, attracted more attention than any of his players. Basketball posters advertised "Abe Saperstein's Chicago Majors." Taking advantage of his fame and his association with the Harlem Globetrotters, Saperstein began featuring entertainment such as bicycle acts, ping-pong champions, and jazz bands during halftime. Even the Globetrotters made an occasional appearance. Yet the crowds didn't come. By December of 1962, the team had folded.

Saperstein died of a heart attack in 1966 at Weiss Memorial Hospital in Chicago. He was sixty-three.

Wrote *Chicago Tribune* sports columnist Dave Condon, following the coach's death, "Abe Saperstein adopted the United States and did more for his nation than most other men in sports. Abe Saperstein reduced the globe to the size of a basketball. From behind the Iron Curtain to the tip of South America, he displayed America's Negro athlete with a dignity that was the best advertisement that democracy ever knew."

Saperstein was inducted into the National Basketball Hall of Fame in 1971. Today a new generation of Harlem Globetrotters continue to entertain both here and abroad. The Globetrotters are currently owned by International Broadcasting Corporation with offices in Hollywood, California.

Further reading: Waldman, Frank. *Famous American Athletes of Today* (1951).

Richard W. Sears

Merchant

born: December 7, 1863
Stewartville, Minnesota
died: September 28, 1914
Waukesha, Wisconsin

Richard Warren Sears was an affable Minnesota farmboy with a knack for business who founded the "Cheapest Supply House on Earth." The mail order firm of Sears, Roebuck and Company prospered due to high quality goods and personal service. The firm that he cofounded is one of the largest department store chains in the country, and the Sears name is one of the most recognizable in Chicago.

Photograph courtesy of Sears, Roebuck and Company.

Sears began his career at the Minneapolis and St. Louis Railway as a station agent in North Redwood, Minnesota. In 1886 he received an offer from manufacturers to sell a shipment of pocket watches that had been refused by a local merchant and left at the station. At the bargain rate Sears was offering, the watches sold quickly. This first flush of success convinced him that there was more money to be made in the big city.

He left the railway in 1886 and established his own firm, the R. W. Sears Watch Company, in Minneapolis.

The following year he set up headquarters in Chicago near Dearborn and Randolph Streets, which at that time was experiencing rapid growth and offered ample business opportunities, and placed a small ad in the *Chicago Daily News* for a watchmaker. He hired a young Hoosier named Alvah Roebuck, who had been working for a Hammond, Indiana, jeweler, to repair the watches. In 1888 Sears opened a branch office in Toronto and issued his first mail-order catalog. In 1889, tired of the mail-order business, he sold his interest to Roebuck and moved to Iowa where he entered banking. Rural life, he discovered, was not to his liking, so in 1892 he resumed his business relationship with Roebuck, and started another mail-order venture. In 1893 the firm changed its name to Sears, Roebuck and Company and rented a large building on West Van Buren Street. By this time, Sears had begun adding other merchandise to the catalog, from silverware to revolvers.

Sears was always on the lookout for new products to sell. Gradually he began adding more merchandise—baby carriages, bicycles, even ready-to-assemble houses. Occasionally, he got carried away, advertising items that he didn't yet have in stock, but this oversight had more to do with his good-natured enthusiasm than any deliberate attempt to cheat his customers, according to historian Lorin Sorenson. On the contrary, Sears promised quality goods at inexpensive prices, and he delivered. For those who still remained skeptical, he boldly offered the revolutionary "Send no money" policy—goods were payable on inspection. It was risky but it worked. "All but a small fraction," notes Sorenson, "paid promptly and most sent in new orders." Despite stiff competition from an already established mail-order firm, Montgomery Ward and Company, sales zoomed.

The company's chief selling point was the bulky Sears, Roebuck and Company catalog. Sears, who did most of the writing, composed homespun passages in a folksy, familiar manner that appealed to his predominantly rural readers. By 1894 the book had grown to a hefty five hundred pages and was as much a part of the American household as the Bible, according to Sorenson.

With sales booming, construction began in January 1905 on a larger plant at Homan and Arthington Streets on the West Side. When completed in 1906, the nine-story building contained its own printing plant, dining halls, and landscaped parks.

In 1895 Roebuck left the firm. Julius Rosenwald, who ran a clothing factory and supplied suits to the firm, bought shares in the company and became vice-president.

In November of 1908 Sears resigned over a dispute with Rosenwald regarding company policy. Sears wanted to offer discounts and promote popular items to encourage sales. Rosenwald recommended waiting until the economy, which had taken a slight downturn, improved.

Sears chose to retire to his Wisconsin farm in early 1909. The parting of ways, however, was amicable. Rosenwald then succeeded Sears as president.

Sears died on September 28, 1914, in Waukesha, Wisconsin, at the age of fifty. He left behind an estate worth $25 million and a name that is still one of the most widely recognized in the retail business.

The world's tallest building, the Sears Tower, at Franklin and Adams Streets, built in 1974, honors the founder of the firm. In 1989 Sears, Roebuck and Company announced that it planned to move its headquarters from downtown Chicago to northwest suburban Hoffman Estates.

See also: Julius Rosenwald, Aaron Montgomery Ward

Further reading: Jeuck, John E. and Boris Emmet. *Catalogues and Counters: A History of Sears, Roebuck & Co.* (1950); Katz, Donald R. *The Big Store: Inside the Crisis & Revolution at Sears* (1987); Sorenson, Lorin. *Sears, Roebuck and Co., 100th Anniversary 1886–1986* (1985).

Howard Van Doren Shaw

Architect

born: May 7, 1869
Chicago, Illinois
died: May 7, 1926
Baltimore, Maryland

Howard Van Doren Shaw was the preferred architect of Chicago's commercial and industrial elite. The Ryersons, the Swifts, and the Donnelleys all turned to him to design their substantial homes. According to biographer Thomas Tallmadge, Shaw was "probably the most highly regarded architect in the sphere of domestic, ecclesiastical, and non-commercial architecture in the Middle West."

Photograph courtesy of the Chicago Historical Society.

A Midwesterner taught at Ivy League schools, Howard Van Doren Shaw belonged to the privileged class. He attended the Harvard School, a private prep school in Chicago and, in 1890, graduated from Yale University. Three years later he received his degree from the Massachusetts Institute of Technology. Shaw then traveled extensively in Europe.

Shaw returned to Chicago and apprenticed under William Le Baron Jenney, the designer of the world's first skyscraper. After a year or two, Shaw set up his own practice in the attic of his father's home on South Calumet Avenue. In 1895 he moved into an office downtown.

Shaw's architecture was not Midwestern in the sense that the Prairie school style of Frank Lloyd Wright was Midwestern. Rather the eclectic Shaw borrowed freely from a variety of sources and was greatly influenced, in particular, by the English Arts and Crafts movement of the nineteenth century. Many of his private homes feature that movement's characteristic high-gabled and half-timbered look. Although he preferred English-based designs, Shaw also adopted French and Italian elements when it suited his purpose.

Shaw was a zealous worker. His wife noted that "he wished to do every detail himself." Even at his most successful, his staff never consisted of more than twenty members.

Shaw, who moved to north suburban Lake Forest in 1897, designed homes along the North Shore for Chicago's wealthy industrial and commercial elite who desired suburban retreats far removed from the bustle of the city and who, like Shaw, admired the classicism of European architecture. Shaw's greatest achievement was Market Square, the architectural showpiece of Lake Forest, often called the first planned suburban shopping center in America. Constructed between 1912 and 1916, Market Square consisted of a group of two-story buildings surrounding a square that "invoked the setting of a Tudor market town with elements borrowed from Flanders and northern Germany of the fifteenth and sixteenth centuries," notes historian Michael H. Ebner.

Shaw was made a fellow of the American Institute of Architects in 1907. In 1926 the federal government appointed him a member of a small architectural committee to design and build war memorials in Europe—a memorial chapel at Flanders Field in Belgium, and a naval war monument at Brest, France. In the same year, Shaw received the Gold Medal of the American Institute of Architects.

Among his most important commercial works are the Second Presbyterian Church at 1936 South Michigan Avenue, which he remodeled extensively in 1901 after a fire gutted the building the previous year; the Lakeside Press Building at 731 South Plymouth Court (1897), his first nonresidential design; the Mentor Building at the corner of Monroe and State Streets (1906); the now demolished Nyberg Automobile Works, 2435–37 South Michigan Avenue (1907), the heart of what was then "Automobile Row"; R. R. Donnelley and Sons Company building at 350 East 22nd Street (1912); the Fourth Presbyterian Church at 125 East Chestnut Street (1912); the Quadrangle Club at the University of Chicago (1921); and the Goodman Memorial Theatre (1925), his last work.

In addition to many large single-family homes in the Hyde Park and Kenwood neighborhoods, Shaw also designed a number of highrises, including the nine-story 1130 North Lake Shore Drive building (1910), the first luxury apartment building in the city constructed in the Tudor style. Shaw was the designer and one of the owners as well as a resident.

Ragdale, Shaw's Lake Forest estate completed in 1898, is a writer's retreat today and the only artists' colony in the Midwest that operates throughout the year. Shaw borrowed the name from a Tudor house that he had seen one summer in England. It suggested, he thought, a kind of "cultivated shabbiness."

Shaw died in 1926 in a sanitarium in Baltimore of pernicious anemia on his fifty-seventh birthday. He was buried in Graceland Cemetery.

See also: Daniel H. Burnham, R. R. Donnelley, William Le Baron Jenney, John Wellborn Root, Frank Lloyd Wright

Further reading: Block, Jean F. *Hyde Park Houses: An Informal History, 1856–1910* (1978); Condit, Carl W. *The Chicago School of Architecture: A History of Commercial and Public Building in the Chicago Area, 1875–1925* (1964); Dart, Susan. *Evelyn Shaw McCutcheon and Ragdale* (1980); Eaton, Leonard K. *Two Chicago Architects and Their Clients: Frank Lloyd Wright and Howard Van Doren Shaw* (1969); Ebner, Michael H. *Creating Chicago's North Shore: A Suburban History* (1988); Hayes, Alice and Susan Moon. *Ragdale: A History and Guide* (1990); Saliga, Pauline A., ed. *The Sky's the Limit, A Century of Chicago Skyscrapers* (1990).

John G. Shedd

Entrepreneur/Philanthropist

born: July 20, 1850
Alstead, New Hampshire
died: October 22, 1926
Chicago, Illinois

Financier, merchant, philanthropist, John Graves Shedd was the millionaire chairman of the board of Marshall Field and Company. During his term as president, over nineteen thousand men and women were in his employ, prompting him to boast that "the sun never sets on Marshall Field's." Despite his importance in the business world, Shedd is best known today as the man who financed the great aquarium that bears his name.

Born on a farm in New Hampshire, Shedd was the youngest son of a family of eight. When not quite seventeen, the ambitious lad announced he was "going to find something better than farming." Poorly educated by today's standards—his entire schooling consisted of nothing more than attending country schools "off and on during winters"—Shedd found work at several grocery and dry goods stores in Vermont and New Hampshire.

Feeling restrained by small-town life, Shedd decided to start over again in the West. He arrived in Chicago after the great fire of 1871, determined to work for "the biggest store in town." Within a year he was offered a job as a $10-a-week stockroom clerk at Field and Leiter's store. The hard-working Shedd caught Marshall Field's attention. He rose quickly through the ranks from stockboy to salesman to department head to merchandise manager. In 1893 he was made a partner, and finally, in 1901, a vice-president. When Field died in 1906, Shedd succeeded him to the presidency.

Shedd celebrated his success by moving from his brick home in the South Lawndale neighborhood to a newly built twenty-two room Gothic mansion at 4515 South Drexel Boulevard in Kenwood, one of Chicago's most fashionable neighborhoods during the 1890s.

Throughout his life Shedd stressed character building as the road to a long and successful career. At the dedication of the YMCA Hotel, Shedd said: "Anything that stands for right living and right thinking—for purity and truth—is just as necessary to the development of character in the young as sunlight and pure air are to the development of plant life. In building character, I place plain straightforward truthfulness first."

Like fellow businessman Julius Rosenwald, Shedd gave generously to various causes and groups. Among his gifts were $125,000 to the YMCA, $50,000 to the Art Institute, and $50,000 to the YWCA.

In 1922 Shedd retired from the presidency of Field's to become chairman of the board of directors. Even so, he maintained a full and busy schedule.

For many years, the South Park Board had contemplated building an aquarium that would add significantly to Chicago's stature as a world-class city. Shedd made an offer to assist in its financing during a meeting at the architectural offices of Graham, Anderson, Probst, and White in 1924. As a gift to the city of Chicago, Shedd donated $3 million to the board for the construction of the world's first and largest aquarium in Grant Park, located just east of the Field Museum. Construction began in the autumn of 1927. The doors opened to the public on June 1, 1930.

Shedd died in 1926 due to complications from appendicitis at the age of seventy-six.

On April 27, 1991, a new $43 million Oceanarium opened at the Shedd Aquarium. The Oceanarium was the first addition to the aquarium since it opened in 1930. The 170,000-square-foot pavilion re-creates a Pacific Northwest rain forest and houses aquatic mammals and birds, including beluga whales, white-sided dolphins, seals, sea otters, and penguins.

See also: Marshall Field, Potter Palmer, Julius Rosenwald

Further reading: Wendt, Lloyd and Herman Kogan. *Give the Lady What She Wants! The Story of Marshall Field and Co.* (1952).

Philip Sheridan

Army General

born: March 6, 1831
Albany, New York
died: Nonquitt, Massachusetts
August 5, 1888

Philip Henry Sheridan, for whom Sheridan Road and Fort Sheridan are named, was one of the most competent generals in the Civil War, respected by both northern and southern forces. A great tactitian, he was also a great leader of men and earned the reputation as the Union army's best cavalry soldier.

The third of six children of John and Mary Sheridan, Irish immigrants from County Cavan, Sheridan grew up in Somerset, Ohio. As a teenager he found employment in a country store. In 1848, he entered West Point. His graduation was delayed until 1853 due to an altercation with a cadet officer who the hotheaded Sheridan attempted to attack with a bayonet.

Sheridan earned a reputation as a brave and fearless leader in battle, known to rout the enemy when other, less daring commanders would choose to stand back. His courageous—some would say foolhardy—derring-do won the admiration of no less than the laconic General Ulysses S. Grant. "No man ever had such a faculty of finding things out as Sheridan," wrote Grant. So impressed was the general that he made Sheridan commander of the cavalry of the Army of the Potomac during the Civil War.

Sheridan was involved in several key Civil War battles, including Chickamauga, Chattanooga, Wilderness, Spotsylvania Courthouse, and participated in the Richmond raid against General J. E. B. Stuart. In1864 he was placed in command of the Union army at Shenandoah. On the morning of October 19, he heard the roar of cannon fire and turned a near disaster into victory when he rallied his confused troops and successfully routed the army of General Jubal A. Early. Sheridan's famous ride from Winchester to Cedar Creek, Virginia, resulted in his promotion to major general of the regular army.

After the war, Sheridan was appointed as military governor of Louisiana and Texas. In the winter of 1868–69, he participated in raids against the Cheyenne Indians, spent a year in Europe during the Franco-Prussian War, and then returned to the United States in 1871 to settle in

Chicago, where he was placed in charge of Army headquarters. As founder and first president of the Washington Park Club, which opened in 1884 at 61st Street and South Park Avenue, Sheridan cut a dashing figure on the city's social scene. Not only was he a fine dancer, according to contemporary newspaper accounts, but his charm was especially popular with the ladies.

Soon after Sheridan's arrival in 1871, the Great Chicago Fire erupted. Reacting quickly, Sheridan ordered buildings on South Wabash Avenue near Congress Street blown up to check the fire from spreading further south—a tactic that saved lives and property. The city was placed under martial law and federal troops were brought in to preserve order. Sheridan dispatched to Mayor Roswell B. Mason this optimistic report, "I am happy to state that no case of outbreak of disorder has been reported. No authenticated case of incendiarism has reached me and the people of the city are calm, quiet and well-disposed."

In 1884 Sheridan succeeded General William T. Sherman as commander in chief of the army, and in 1888 Congress granted him the rank of full general.

In May of 1886, the city's business community became alarmed when violence erupted during the tragic Haymarket Affair. The Commercial Club of Chicago and the Board of Trade pledged to sell the six-hundred-acre tract of land along the Lake Michigan shoreline nearly thirty miles north of the city for $10 if the government agreed to construct a fort on the site. On March 3, 1887, the government consented. One year later General Sheridan visited the site, then called Fort Highwood. When Sheridan died in 1888, the fort was renamed in his honor.

Sheridan died in Nonquitt, Massachusetts, in August of 1888 at age fifty-seven, three days after completing his memoirs.

On July 16, 1924, General Sheridan's daughter, Mary Sheridan, unveiled a bronze statue of her father at the intersection of Belmont Avenue and Sheridan Road as an estimated 100,000 people looked on. The piece, designed by the noted Belgian sculptor Gutzon Borglum, captured the general in a characteristically energetic pose—mounted on a horse and ready for battle as he rode through the Shenandoah Valley.

See also: Elmer E. Ellsworth, James Mulligan

Further reading: Ebner, Michael H. *Creating Chicago's North Shore: A Suburban History* (1988); O'Connor, Richard. *Sheridan the Inevitable* (1953).

John M. Smyth

Merchant/Politician

born: July 5, 1843
off Newfoundland
died: November 4, 1909
Chicago, Illinois

Pioneer Chicago furniture dealer John M. Smyth was one of the city's most influential businessmen. The furniture company that he founded in 1867 continues to be a familiar name.

Born at sea off the banks of Newfoundland in 1843, Smyth came to Chicago with his parents, Irish immigrants Michael and Bridget, in 1848 after having originally settled in Montreal.

At thirteen Smyth found work at a printing office to help support his recently widowed mother and sibling. He held other jobs too—news carrier, clerk, and advertising salesman for several Chicago newspapers. Using $250 of his savings, Smyth formed a partnership with Thomas Mitchell and, in 1867, opened a small furniture store at 92 West Madison Street. Within a year he bought Mitchell out.

The first Smyth furniture store was a modest effort. A mere secondhand shop, it nevertheless upheld policies that were, for that time, revolutionary. For one thing, Smyth generously offered credit to newlyweds and to all those who had lost everything in the Chicago Fire.

A rapid population growth, access to raw materials, and an increased demand for comfortable domestic furniture helped to make Chicago the furniture capital of the United States by the turn of the century. In 1895, notes historian Sharon Darling, there were 276 furniture manufacturing companies in the city that employed over 28,000 workers.

Taking advantage of Chicago's booming market, Smyth was able to move to larger headquarters at 12 North Michigan Avenue in 1880. Unfortunately, that building suffered a ruinous fire in April of 1891. Seven months later, he was ready to start over again, erecting an eight-story building on the same site.

Smyth was also actively involved in local politics. A lifelong Republican, he served as a Chicago alderman from 1878 to 1882. He managed various political campaigns on the county and national levels. In 1892 Mayor Hempstead Washburne appointed him to the library board, but he resigned three years later. He was chairman of the Republican County Central Committee for several years, and he was considered by many to be an exemplary mayoral candidate. Smyth, although flattered, declined.

Smyth succumbed to pneumonia in Chicago at the age of sixty-six in November of 1909.

Today the corporate offices of John M. Smyth Company—and its chain of Homemakers outlets—are located at 1013 Butterfield Road in Downers Grove, Illinois.

In 1983 the Smyth Company closed seven of its furniture stores due to escalating operating costs. Other retailers that specialized in furniture and furniture-related accessories, such as Colby's and Pier 1 Imports, helped fill the void. In probably the most ambitious event to hit the Chicago furniture industry in many years, Crate and Barrel opened their flagship store at 646 North Michigan Avenue in September of 1990.

Further reading: Darling, Sharon. *Chicago Furniture Art, Craft, & Industry 1833–1983* (1984).

Albert G. Spalding

Baseball Player/Manager

born: September 2, 1850
Byron, Illinois
died: September 9, 1915
Point Loma, California

As one of its founding fathers, Albert Goodwill Spalding contributed greatly to the rise of baseball as an American institution, and more importantly, notes historian Peter Levine, "as respectable entertainment for the urban middle class." Spalding cofounded the National League, managed and owned the Chicago White Stockings (which later became the Chicago Cubs), and founded a successful sporting goods business that still bears his name. Sports, he said, builds character. It was Spalding who molded baseball into the game we know today.

Born to Harriet and James Spalding in 1850 in the farming town of Byron, Illinois, Spalding's happy family life was shattered when his father died at forty-six. His mother sent her grieving son to school in the neighboring town of Rockford. There, miserable and lonely, young Spalding fell in love with the game of baseball. Baseball instilled in the forlorn youth a confidence and self-assurance that he had never experienced before.

In 1865 members of Rockford's business community asked Spalding to join their new baseball club, the Forest City, as a pitcher. The new team played in various regional tournaments, including one held against the highly respected Washington Nationals, then billed as the best team in the country. In one of the great moments of the young athlete's life, Spalding's team edged the mighty Nationals 29-23. Impressed by the victory and by Spalding's pitching arm, the Chicago Excelsiors asked him to join their team. He accepted the offer and moved to Chicago in September of 1867.

In 1871 Spalding signed with the Boston Red Stockings. He led his team to a second-place finish that year and to four consecutive league championships between 1872 and 1875. Spalding became a local hero.

In the summer of 1875, president William A. Hulbert signed Spalding to the Chicago White Stockings as captain, manager, and pitcher. It was a fortuitous event both for Spalding and for the team because he managed to turn the White Stockings into the sport's most successful club, and at the same time he transformed what once was a lowly sport into a respectable pastime for all of middle America. Furthermore, he was instrumental, with Hulbert, in establishing a new professional league, the National League of Professional Baseball Clubs in 1876.

In their quest for middle-class respectability, managers like Spalding, Adrian Anson, and Charles A. Comiskey went to great lengths to impress upon their players the importance of good moral behavior and used whatever means necessary—admonishments, fines, even dismissal—to curb their excesses. Spalding banned Sunday ball, for example, in order not to offend churchgoers, and he built comfortable and attractive ballparks throughout the city.

Spalding led the team's inaugural 1876 season in the new league all the way to the pennant. After the 1877 season, however, he retired from active play, serving instead as the team's secretary. When Hulbert died in 1882, Spalding became club president and owner.

Under Spalding, the White Stockings grew in popularity. In 1895 the team played at the Congress Street Grounds on the West Side in "an attractive middle-class neighborhood," writes historian Steven A. Reiss in *City Games*. In 1891 Spalding moved the team to the 35th Street Grounds and several years later to the West Side Park near 12th and Taylor Streets.

Spalding's White Stockings dominated baseball for the next ten years, winning pennant titles in 1882, 1885, and 1886. Leading the team to victory after victory was first baseman Adrian "Cap" Anson. Other outstanding athletes during those golden years included third baseman Ned Williamson, shortstop Tommy Burns,

second baseman Fred Pfeffer, catcher Frank Flint, and the great right fielder, Mike "King" Kelly. Yet baseball players, observes Reiss, still had "little social prestige—baseball players were placed on the same unfavorable social level as actors and prize fighters." It wasn't until after the turn of the century when club owners began to charge higher admission prices and increase players' salaries that the game began to attract an appreciable middle-class clientele. Further, the growth of cities created an interest in recreational activity. Spalding and others tapped into this growing segment of the population. The rise in mass transit also allowed increased access to public sporting events, so by 1920 baseball, for these and other reasons, had become the national pastime.

Meanwhile, capitalizing on his reputation and good name and clearly sensing the palpable interest that the sport was inciting across the country, Spalding opened a sporting goods store in Chicago in 1876. In addition to the usual bats and balls, Spalding provided a full line of sporting goods equipment. Business boomed.

In the 1880s Spalding published the National League's official play book, the annual *Spalding's Official Baseball Guide*, and in 1892 he formed a separate division within the sporting goods firm, the American Sport Publishing Company. Always looking for additional ways to advertise his wares, he provided the National League teams with baseballs—all bearing, of course, the Spalding insignia. In order to cash in on the bicycle craze then sweeping the country, Spalding began, in 1894, to manufacture his own line of bicycles. In addition, he organized baseball tours around the world.

In September of 1915 Spalding suffered a minor stroke. Shortly thereafter he succumbed to another, more devastating, attack and died at the age of sixty-five.

Baseball, Spalding declared, served as a good training ground for life beyond the diamond. Spalding not only shaped the leisure activities of America in the late nineteenth century, he also, concludes historian Levine, helped turn—through his roles as athlete, manager, publisher, and promoter—a simple sandlot game into a national sport and a much beloved national pastime.

In 1939 the Baseball Hall of Fame inducted Spalding posthumously into its membership.

See also: Adrian Anson, Charles A. Comiskey

Further reading: Bartlett, Arthur Charles. *Baseball and Mr. Spalding* (1951); Coombs, Sam and Bob West, eds. *America's National Game* (1991); Levine, Peter. *A. G. Spalding and the Rise of Baseball: The Promise of American Sport* (1985); Names, Larry D. *Bury My Heart at Wrigley Field: The History of the Chicago Cubs—When the Cubs Were the White Sox* (1990); Reiss, Steven A. *City Games: The Evolution of American Urban Society and the Rise of Sports* (1989).

Amos Alonzo Stagg

Football Coach

born: August 16, 1862
West Orange, New Jersey
died: March 17, 1965
Stockton, California

The career of Amos Alonzo Stagg paralleled the development of intercollegiate football. As the coach at the University of Chicago, he gave the city six Big Ten conference titles and five unbeaten seasons. He contributed greatly to the strategy of football. But more than this, he viewed sports as a great moral force and football, in particular, as the greatest of character builders. Thus he fought vigorously against the professionalizing of sports. Stagg felt that athletes should play sports not for profit but for enjoyment.

Stagg's father, a cobbler, always worked to better himself and passed this ethic down to his son. Stagg toiled his way through high school tending furnaces, lawns, and gardens. Since the nearest high school was several miles away in Orange, New Jersey, he was forced to pay a nonresident tuition. Determined to complete his education, Stagg didn't finish high school until he was twenty-one. He spent one year at Phillips-Exeter Academy in New Hampshire and lived a miserable existence in dire poverty.

Stagg entered Yale in the fall of 1884, the star player of their baseball team, where he pitched five successive championships. He was called the greatest pitcher of his day and received many offers from professional baseball teams while still a student. He turned them all down in order to finish school and because he preferred what he considered the honesty of the college game, where he felt the sport remained pure, unscathed by the influence of money. In 1888 Stagg received his bachelor's degree. He then studied for two more years at Divinity School with the intent of becoming a preacher. There was, however, one major stumbling block: he was a terrible public speaker. "I sized myself up and decided I wasn't cut out to be a pulpit man. My goal, though, remained the same—to guide and train youth."

In 1890 Stagg accepted a coaching job with the YMCA College in Springfield, Massachusetts. Two years later he met with William Rainey Harper, one of his professors at Yale, at the Murray Hill Hotel in New York. Harper told Stagg that millionaire John D. Rockefeller was building a university in Chicago that would be unlike any college institution in the country. He encouraged Stagg to come aboard and offered him the position of director of the athletic department. Stagg was the first coach to be given academic status. Like many coaches at that time, Stagg also played on the team.

Stagg insisted that a stadium be built for his players. Marshall Field, the wealthy merchant, donated ten acres of land in an area just north of the campus. Initially called Marshall Field, the stadium was renamed Stagg Field in the late 1890s.

Stagg pioneered many changes during his forty-year-plus career. One of the most important was the forward pass, which allowed the ball to be moved up and down the field more quickly—previously football had been primarily a running game. President Theodore Roosevelt had expressed alarm at the number of football casualties. Coaches at that time employed a dangerous blocking technique called the *flying wedge* in which the players formed a V-shape phalanx around their team's ball carrier, locked arms, and moved down the field, protecting the ball carrier by beating back the opposing team's tacklers. During the 1905 college season alone, three athletes died on the playing field and almost ninety sustained serious injuries. Concerned critics of the game recommended rule changes. Stagg agreed. He helped organize the National Collegiate Athletic Association and served on the National Football Rules Committee. He also advocated the forward pass. Its full acceptance from collegiate football officials changed the essential character of the game. Since more points could be scored faster, it allowed for a more exciting game.

In addition, Stagg created the game's first tackling dummy; introduced knee pads, the huddle, and the short punt formation; and pioneered the T-formation, the fake pass, and the onside kick. He was the first to award varsity letters to deserving athletes and the first to use numbers on football player jerseys for the convenience of both spectators and the press.

In 1932, at age seventy, Stagg was forced to retire due to the university's mandatory retirement clause. As a way of making amends, the administration offered the coach a post in the public relations department at a higher salary. Stagg refused and, instead, accepted the head coaching position the next season at the College of the Pacific in Stockton, California. He stayed for fourteen years, resigning in December of 1946 to join his son, the director of athletics, at Susquehanna University in Selinsgrove, Pennsylvania. In 1953 he became advisory head coach at Stockton Junior College in California.

In 1927 Stagg wrote *Touchdown*, his memoirs. A five-time member of the Olympic committee—he coached the 400- and 800-meter runs and the 1600-meter relay in the 1924 Olympics in Paris—Stagg was the only man elected to the Football Hall of Fame as both a player and a coach. At age eighty-one he was named coach of the year at the College of the Pacific.

When he turned ninety-five, Stagg admitted that age was finally beginning to catch up with him. "I slipped a little. I stopped running," he said. By the time he retired at age ninety-eight, he was suffering from Parkinson's disease. Stagg, the "grand old man of the Midway" died in 1965 at a Stockton, California, nursing home at age one hundred and two.

At the end of the 1939 season, the University of Chicago dropped intercollegiate football altogether at the insistence of university president Robert Maynard Hutchins, who felt that team sports distracted students from the business of learning. Years later, in May of 1969, varsity football returned to the Hyde Park campus. In 1966 Stagg Field was demolished. A new 1,500-seat Stagg Field, located at East 56th Street and Cottage Grove Avenue, replaced the original stadium that had stood at East 57th Street and Ellis Avenue—the site of the world's first controlled nuclear reaction on December 2, 1942.

See also: Marshall Field, Harold "Red" Grange, William Rainey Harper, George Halas, Robert Maynard Hutchins, Knute Rockne [appendix]

Further reading: Goodspeed, Thomas Wakefield. *The Story of the University of Chicago, 1890–1925* (1925); Lucia, Ellis. *Mr. Football, Amos Alonzo Stagg* (1970); Stagg, Amos Alonzo, as told to Wesley Winans Stout. *Touchdown* (1927); Storr, Richard J. *Harper's University, The Beginnings* (1966).

Melville E. Stone

Editor

born: August 22, 1848
Hudson, Illinois
died: February 15, 1929
New York, New York

*Melville Elijah Stone opposed the "yellow journalism" that was so prevalent in the newspaper business during his lifetime. He thought newspapers could be objective and fair and didn't need to resort to sensationalism. During his tenure as editor, the **Chicago Daily News** grew. He had a sense of what the people wanted, and he delivered it. A man of high integrity, he insisted that the newspaper not only be entertaining but also informative and, most of all, reliable. He wanted a paper that rivaled the **Chicago Tribune**. Uncertain of his own talents, Stone surrounded himself with one of the finest staffs of any American newspaper.*

The son of a Methodist minister, Stone and his family lived in several Illinois towns, including Dekalb and Naperville, before settling in Chicago in 1860. While still a student at Chicago High School, he did some reporting for the *Chicago Tribune*. In 1868 he became the sole proprietor of a promising iron foundry and machine shop, the Lake Shore Iron Works at 371–77 Illinois Street, but lost everything in the Chicago Fire of 1871. After the loss, Stone turned once again to journalism. He became managing editor of the *Republican*, which soon changed its name to the *Chicago Inter-Ocean* for which he served as city editor. The *Inter-Ocean's* motto, which history later showed to be a dubious one, proclaimed: "Republican in everything, independent in nothing."

In June of 1873 Stone jumped to the *Evening Mail*, which later merged with the *Chicago Evening Post*, where he rose to the position of managing editor. Stone then quit and moved east to Washington, D. C., and became a correspondent for several New York and St. Louis newspapers. He returned to Chicago in 1875 with the idea of launching an independent paper. He was able to do so with reporter William E. Dougherty and a wealthy Englishman, Percy Meggy, who provided the necessary $5,000 cash. Together, they started the *Chicago Daily News*, the city's first penny newspaper. The following year Victor Lawson bought Meggy and Dougherty's shares. Stone handled the editorial duties and Lawson the business functions.

With Stone's consent, Lawson took over as publisher in 1876. Lawson owned the building where the newspaper was published and was the editor-publisher of the *Daily Scandinaven* located on the ground floor.

The *News's* biggest rival was the afternoon paper, the *Evening Post*, run by Jim and Dave McMullen. It was a bitter rivalry. The *Daily News* claimed that the *Post* was stealing their material, and Stone devised a mischievously clever scheme to prove it. One day the *News* published a dispatch allegedly from a Belgrade, Yugoslavia, correspondent who reported that the Serbs were starving, "Er us siht la Etsll iws nel lum cmeht," followed by the alleged translation. Sure enough, it appeared in the next edition of the *Post*—verbatim. The cryptic message simply read, "The McMullens will steal this sure"—spelled backward. From then on, the circulation of the maverick *News* zoomed and the *Post*, the laughing stock of the city, nose-dived. In a final coup, the *Daily News* purchased the *Evening Post* in 1878. In 1881 Stone and Lawson started a morning newspaper, the *Chicago Morning News*.

Stone made a conscious effort to recruit the best writers in the business. He hired John Ballantyne, formerly of the *Chicago Herald*, as managing editor and Slason Thompson as chief editorial writer. Borrowing a practice from the august *London Times*, he had on call a score of scholars who were able to file reports whenever necessary. He also brought on board some of the finest columnists and cartoonists to grace the page of a daily newspaper—including John T. McCutcheon, George Ade, and Eugene Field.

Despite his considerable success in the journalism field, Stone felt woefully inadequate to his position of editor. An editor, he maintained, of a major American newspaper should be worldly and well educated. "I had a staff of unequalled capacity," he wrote in his autobiography, *Fifty Years a Journalist*. "But I alone was unequipped. I was prematurely prominent." In 1888 Stone decided to leave the *Daily News* and sold his interest to Lawson. To avoid competition Lawson agreed to pay Stone $10,000 a year for ten years to stay out of the newspaper business in Chicago. Stone traveled in Europe and returned to Chicago several years later to become vice-president and eventually president of the Globe National Bank. He held that position until the bank merged with the Continental Bank in 1898.

In 1893 Stone assumed the management of the Chicago office of the Associated Press (AP) of Illinois. Under his leadership, the AP earned a reputation as an astute observer of the international scene. Various special interest groups, however, asserted that the AP, which dispatched correspondents all over the globe, held a monopoly on the news and insisted that the operation was not as objective as it claimed. Trade unionists, for example, appeared before a congressional inquiry and denounced the AP as "unfriendly to their cause." When the wire service reported the death of Pope Leo XIII in 1903, several Methodist ministers accused Stone of being Catholic or at least of harboring Vatican sympathies. The monopoly issue was finally resolved in 1918 when the U.S. Supreme Court declared that news is a commodity "of such high public need that any one dealing in it was charged with a public duty to furnish it to any one demanding it and ready to pay the price."

Stone retired from the AP in 1921 and moved to New York City. He died there in 1929 at the age of eighty. Dwindling circulation caused the *Chicago Daily News* to cease publication on March 4, 1978.

See also: George Ade, Eugene Field, Victor Lawson, Robert R. McCormick, John T. McCutcheon, Joseph Medill, Wilbur F. Storey

Further reading: Dennis, Charles H. *Victor Lawson: His Time and His Work* (1935); Stone, Melville E. *Fifty Years a Journalist* (1921).

Wilbur F. Storey

Editor/Publisher

born: December 18, 1819
Salisbury, Vermont
died: October 27, 1884
Chicago, Illinois

*As the unorthodox and controversial editor of the **Chicago Times**, Wilbur Fisk Storey earned the dubious title of the father of sensational journalism years before William Randolph Hearst arrived on the scene. He was many things during his life—most of them negative. Though a chauvinist, nationalist, and unabashed racist, Storey knew what made the news, and he transformed the lowly **Times** into a newspaper of national importance. He did his job exceedingly well—at one point the **Chicago Times** enjoyed the largest circulation of a daily in Chicago. Perhaps the paper's motto, "to print the news and raise hell!" best sums up both Storey's life and profession.*

Storey was born on a farm near Salibury, Vermont. When he was ten, his father moved to Middlebury. Two years later, young Storey learned the printer's trade in the offices of the *Middlebury Free Press.* In 1836 he went to New York and secured a position as a compositor on the *Journal of Commerce.* With ambitions of becoming a journalist, Storey moved to LaPorte, Indiana, where he founded the *LaPorte Herald.* He also established newspapers in Mishawauka, Indiana, and Jackson, Michigan. In 1854 he purchased an interest in the *Detroit Free Press.*

In 1861 Storey settled in Chicago and purchased the *Chicago Times* from Cyrus H. McCormick. Storey's lurid sheet printed tales of murder, robbery, and scandal. Many of the reports consisted of bold-faced lies and wild fabrications. Anything and everything was grist for the mill. The paper found a ready market.

Storey was constantly being sued—in one period, twenty-one libel suits and three criminal indictments were leveled against the *Times.* And, in a highly publicized incident, Storey was soundly horsewhipped in public by Lydia Thompson, a burlesque performer, in February 1870, when the editor dared to publish an editorial casting doubt on her morals. "You dirty old scoundrel," she cried out in indignation. Storey pressed charges and appeared in court the next day. Thompson was fined $100, but the judge suspended the fine.

A firm believer in state rights, Storey originally opposed the nomination of Abraham Lincoln for president. Once Lincoln won, however, and war was declared, he supported the new administration's attempt to save the union. Like many citizens, he saw no contradiction in supporting the war while opposing abolition. After the issuance of the Emancipation

Proclamation in 1862, everything changed. Storey believed the president had gone too far. He would back Lincoln as long as the Illinoisan made no effort to free the slaves. An unabashed racist, Storey firmly believed that neither the African-American, the Asian-American—indeed any non-Caucasian—had a place in the American nation. He venomously attacked all who were not of Anglo-Saxon stock and even advocated returning the black people to Africa. While he admitted that slavery was "a great evil," he felt an even greater danger lay in allowing slaves to remain in the country. But at the same time, he defended the natural and civil rights of the American Indian, whom he called the "original Americans."

The most feared editor of his day, Storey didn't care whom he offended. His enemies were legion—temperance reformers, abolitionists, Republicans, fellow editors, and even Union generals. On June 2, 1863, Gen. Ambrose Burnside charged Storey with sedition and issued an order to suppress the newspaper. Federal troops swooped down in the largely Democratic city of Chicago, taking possession of the *Times* office. In turn, a mob of pro-Storey demonstrators threatened to burn down the rival and pro-Republican paper, the *Chicago Tribune.* On June 5, President Lincoln revoked the order and the *Times* resumed publication.

By 1871 the *Chicago Times* was the premier newspaper in the Midwest. The building that housed the paper was destroyed during the Chicago Fire. At first devastated, Storey vowed to return. He rented a shack at 105 West Randolph Street and on October 18, 1871—ten days after the fire had raged through the city—the *Times* was back in business.

But Storey was not just any rabble-rousing publisher. Despite the controversy he inspired, he was a pioneer in the field of journalism. According to his biographer, Justin E. Walsh, Storey introduced the first Sunday newspaper in the Midwest devoted to "entertainment" journalism, and he refined the craft of newspaper feature writing.

In 1863 Storey had contracted paresis, a partial paralysis brought on by syphilis. As his emotional and mental state deteriorated, Storey's behavior became even more erratic and unpredictable until he finally descended into periods of madness, fluctuating back and forth between incoherency and lucidness.

Despite his illness, in 1876, Storey established the short-lived *Chicago Evening Telegraph,* an afternoon newspaper. But the interest and readership simply wasn't sufficient to sustain its survival beyond a brief three months. The following year he formed an overseas branch of the *Times*—the first foreign office of a Midwestern newspaper in Europe.

In May of 1882 a stroke—his third—left Storey totally paralyzed. He died two years later and was buried in Rosehill cemetery. In 1876 Storey, who supervised every detail of his inflammatory paper, had said: "I don't wish to perpetuate my newspaper. I am the paper! I wish it to die with me so that the world may know I was the *Times!*"

Ultimately Storey received his wish. Without Storey, the paper had lost its spirit. In 1891 Carter Harrison I—then considering to run for mayor again—purchased the *Times* and established it as a Democratic mouthpiece. On March 3, 1895, the publication that Storey founded died. Erratic circulation persuaded the Harrison family to sell the paper to Herman H. Kohlsaat who merged it with his own daily, the *Chicago Herald,* and renamed it the *Times-Herald.*

Further reading: Walsh, Justin E. *To Print the News and Raise Hell: A Biography of Wilbur F. Storey* (1968).

Louis Sullivan

Architect

born: September 3, 1856
Boston, Massachusetts
died: April 14, 1924
Chicago, Illinois

Chief theorist of the Chicago school of architecture, Louis Henri Sullivan was called the greatest architect of his day. Indeed many consider him the father of modern architecture. Along with Daniel H. Burnham, John Wellborn Root, and Frank Lloyd Wright, he epitomized the famed Chicago school and promulgated the theory that architecture should respond to the particular milieu of a period and not slavishly copy European models. "Form follows function," he declared. It was a characteristically simple statement and it became the basis for the Chicago style and, indeed, the foundation for all contemporary design.

Sullivan trained at the Massachusetts Institute of Technology from 1872 to 1873 and attended the Ecole des Beaux-Arts in Paris from 1874 to 1875. He then settled in Chicago, where his parents had lived since 1869, and began working for various Chicago architects, including William Le Baron Jenney, who is credited with building the first skyscraper.

In 1881 Sullivan joined forces with Dankmar Adler and formed a partnership two years later. Adler was a brilliant engineer while Sullivan was an unsurpassed designer. Their firm gained international recognition with the completion of the architecturally significant Auditorium Theater at Michigan Avenue and Congress Parkway, which was dedicated with much fanfare on December 9, 1889. A young apprentice by the name of Frank Lloyd Wright was the one who had turned Sullivan's rough sketches into blueprints. The Auditorium took three-and-one-half years to complete and cost $3.2 million—the most expensive building in the city at that time. Many called the Auditorium the finest structure in the city—perhaps even the country.

Sullivan and Adler were famous. They turned away from residential assignments, which had been their bread and butter, to concentrate on commercial work, including the Getty Tomb in Graceland Cemetery (1890); Holy Trinity Cathedral at 1121 North Leavitt Street (1900); and the Schlesinger and Mayer Store—now Carson, Pirie, Scott and Company—at State and Madison Streets (1904). In 1885 Sullivan helped organize the Illinois State Association of Architects.

The World's Columbian Exposition of 1893 was supposed to showcase the best of Chicago architecture. Instead, fair director Daniel H. Burnham, who took over following the death of his partner John Wellborn Root in

1891, transformed the exposition into a celebration of the Beaux-Arts style, a classical form based on European models. Sullivan referred to the fair as "an appalling calamity" in *The Autobiography of an Idea.* "The damage wrought by the world's Fair," he wrote, "will last for half a century." The firm of Adler and Sullivan contributed one of the few departures from the classical motif—their Transportation Building.

In 1895 Adler quit the partnership over a misunderstanding with Sullivan. Sullivan, alone at the helm and in the middle of an economic recession, experienced severe financial difficulties. What's more, he refused to compromise his architectural vision. Clients either had to agree to his terms or he wouldn't work with them at all. As a result, business floundered. Finally, in 1909, he was forced to sell everything he owned—even his most cherished possessions which included, according to biographer Robert Twombly, his jade collection and his copy of Walt Whitman's *Leaves of Grass*—to make ends meet.

By 1910 Sullivan was suffering from insomnia and exhibited suicidal tendencies brought on by poverty and constant worry. Although he designed a number of buildings in his last years, none were major, and he never regained his former stature. Conditions became so bad that in 1917 he considered accepting a civil service position with the government. His last project, in 1922, was the Krause Music Store facade on Lincoln Avenue.

Some other notable Sullivan and Adler and Sullivan works in Chicago include: the Standard Club (1887); the Martin Ryerson tomb in Graceland Cemetery (1887); and the James Charnley residence at 1365 North Astor Street (1891), which featured the work of Frank Lloyd Wright.

Sullivan was devoted to modernism, especially in the form of the skyscraper. His far-thinking designs were not fully appreciated in his lifetime. He believed in a purely American brand of architecture based on forms that reflected its time period. Yet his work, as many critics have pointed out, was not merely lines and drawings. Rather he succeeded in finding a warm poetic touch—with such ornamental flourishes as rounded arches, terra cotta panels, and floral decoration—in the steel, brick, and mortar. Indeed, Sullivan left behind an indelible personal legacy in architecture, the most public of arts.

Shortly after completing *The Autobiography of an Idea* in 1924, Sullivan died of kidney and heart trouble in the back room of a run-down Chicago hotel at age sixty-seven. The dean of American architects died a poor man with few possessions and little capital. He was buried next to his parents in Graceland Cemetery.

Sullivan is hardly forgotten today, however. A renewed appreciation of his special genius exists among contemporary critics and architects who see in his heartland vision the democratic spirit of America.

See also: Daniel H. Burnham, William Le Baron Jenney, John Wellborn Root, Frank Lloyd Wright

Further reading: Duncan, Hugh Dalziel. *Culture and Democracy: The Struggle for Form in Society and Architecture in Chicago and the Middle West during the Life and Times of Louis H. Sullivan* (1989); O'Gorman, James F. *Three American Architects: Richardson, Sullivan, and Wright, 1865–1915* (1991); Siry, Joseph. *Carson Pirie Scott, Louis Sullivan and the Chicago Department Store* (1988); Sullivan, Louis H. *The Autobiography of an Idea* (1924); Twombly, Robert C. *Louis Sullivan, His Life and Work* (1986).

Billy Sunday

Evangelist

✝

born: November 19, 1862
Ames, Iowa
died: November 6, 1935
Chicago, Illinois

By denouncing scientists, radicals, and liberals and cloaking his xenophobic, narrow-minded speeches under the mantle of patriotism, the flamboyant preacher William Ashley Sunday gained an enormous following, especially in rural America, during the late nineteenth and early twentieth centuries. A former baseball player from the cornfields of Iowa, Sunday venerated hard work and clean living. His sermons, peppered with common slang and everyday speech, combined the euphoria of frontier camp meetings with the cautious morality of small-town life. Sunday touched a raw nerve. Battered by economic recessions, strikes, and political corruption, the nation looked for easy answers to its woes. Sunday supplied the cure—an old-fashioned return to the "good old days" of God-fearing,

Christian morality. Sunday, a master manipulator, told his followers, which included a large segment of the American public, what they wanted to hear. During his prime years, between 1896 and 1918, Billy Sunday was the most popular preacher on the evangelist circuit.

Sunday's father was the son of German immigrants—Sonntag ("Sunday" in German) was the original family name. He died of pneumonia one month after his son was born. Sunday endured a poverty-ridden childhood. After high school, he held a series of casual jobs. He was working as an undertaker's assistant when Adrian Anson, manager of the Chicago White Stockings baseball team, discovered him. Sunday, it seems, was an extremely fast runner and his speed-demon feet led him to a career in baseball. He joined the White Stockings in 1883. Sunday played professional baseball for a total of eight years for teams in Chicago, Pittsburgh, and Philadelphia. His lightning speed proved an asset—he stole ninety-five bases in one season—but he was no hitter. Still, he was a dedicated athlete and Anson rewarded his hard work by making him business manager of the team.

In 1886 Sunday underwent a religious conversion. While sitting with his teammates outside a tavern in Chicago, he began listening to an evangelist group from the Pacific Garden Mission who were singing gospel hymns. He returned many times until one night he "publicly accepted Christ as [his] Saviour." He was ordained in the Presbyterian Church in 1903.

In 1891 Sunday began working with the Young Men's Christian Association and then served as an assistant to evangelist J. Wilbur Chapman, described by fellow preacher Dwight Moody as "the greatest evangelist in the country." Sunday started to preach on his own in 1896, meeting in churches and tents and eventually graduating to the much larger tabernacles—makeshift wooden structures that could shelter thousands of people—in the major cities. His enthusiastic style, unassuming folksiness, and sheer magnetic personality were a hit from the start. In 1900 he hired a popular white gospel singer, Fred Fischer, to sing such crowd-pleasing hymns as "In the Sweet Bye and Bye" and "We Will Gather By the River."

As his popularity grew, Sunday's demands increased. He insisted, according to historian William G. McLoughlin, Jr., that no preaching take place by local ministers and all regular church services be discontinued while he was in town. The ministers, cognizant of his popularity, invariably complied. He had no need to fear competition, however. For many years, it seemed that he had none. He drew thousands upon thousands to his revival meetings and sensationalized a style of preaching that predated the likes of Billy Graham, Jimmy Swaggart, and Jim Bakker. Entertaining and controversial, Sunday used whatever it took to persuade customers to fill his increasingly large tabernacles. And, in tune with public attitudes, he denounced the abuse of wealth, attacked the consumption of liquor, and vilified the sinful wickedness of America's big cities, encouraging his followers to return to simpler times. Further, he castigated birth control advocates as "the devil's mouthpiece" and warned decent young ladies to avoid movies that were "too suggestive." Smokers and drinkers, saloon keepers and immigrants, the hobo and the unemployed, the nonconformist and the rebel, the atheist and the sinner—none of these people had a place in Sunday's pantheon. Indeed, he easily dismissed them as pawns of Satan.

During his later years, Sunday was the subject of numerous scandals (his eldest son, George, committed suicide in 1933) and lawsuits. The times had changed—the youth of the "Roaring Twenties" expressed little interest in evangelical reform—but Sunday refused to change with it. Further, the twenties witnessed a rapid growth among more moderate Catholics and mainline Protestants in urban settings. Sunday lost touch with the public and, more and more, began to symbolize the beliefs and values of an older, nineteenth-century America.

In 1935, at his brother-in-law's house in Chicago, Sunday suffered a heart attack—his third—that proved to be fatal. He was buried in Forest Lawn Cemetery in Chicago.

See also: Adrian Anson, Jenkin Lloyd Jones [appendix], Dwight L. Moody, David Swing

Further reading: Brown, Elijah. *The Real Billy Sunday* (1914); Ellis, W. T. *Billy Sunday: The Man and His Message* (1936); McLoughlin, William G., Jr. *Billy Sunday Was His Real Name* (1955).

Gustavus F. Swift

Industrialist

born: June 24, 1839
Sandwich, Massachusetts
died: March 29, 1903
Chicago, Illinois

Gustavus Franklin Swift, founder of Swift and Company, was one of the great figures of the business world in nineteenth-century Chicago. Like many leaders in the business of that era, he exhibited initiative, self-reliance, and a burning ambition. "He talked little and accomplished much and let the results talk for him," said newspaper accounts.

A native of New England, Swift was brought up on a farm, the ninth child of a family of twelve, and educated in the local public schools. At fourteen, he joined his brother in the meat business. In 1859 he opened a butcher shop in the village of Eastham, Massachusetts, with $20 in capital from his father. With this, he bought a heifer, which he slaughtered and dressed and sold. Already an astute businessman, he began experimenting with different packaging methods to make the products look attractive. He opened meat businesses in several Massachusetts towns, traveling in meat wagons to market directly to the customers, but the buying and selling of cattle became his most profitable venture.

In 1872 Swift formed a partnership with James A. Hathaway in Boston and later expanded the business to Albany and then to Buffalo, New York. Sensing that the real center of the cattle market lay in the Midwest, Swift decided to move his base to Chicago in 1875. In the same year, another cattleman, Philip Danforth Armour, had also settled in the city.

Swift acted as a cattle buyer before he turned to meat packing. In order to avoid paying freight costs, he conceived the idea of slaughtering the cattle in Chicago and shipping the dressed beef—instead of live cattle—to Eastern cities. Some, not convinced of the viability of such a method, called him "that crazy man Swift." Uncertain, too, was Hathaway, who sold his share of the business. Meanwhile, Swift introduced a refrigerator car to prevent meat from spoiling while in transit and sent his first refrigerated shipment to Boston in 1877. It quickly became the accepted mode of transporting highly perishable goods.

As early as 1861, Chicago had earned the unofficial title "Porkopolis" of the Midwest. With the opening of the

Union Stock Yard in December 1865, the business of buying, selling, and distributing livestock took place in one location. Railroads delivered the animals to Chicago while more and more packing facilities were built and plants were enlarged. As the industry grew, so did the city, until by the end of the 1870s, reports historian Louise Carroll Wade, more than seventy livestock firms were doing business in Chicago.

When Swift moved his base of operations to Chicago in 1875, the city was primarily known for its pork curing and packing. Although he didn't invent the refrigerated car—it was a gradual process—he is credited with being the first packer to fully understand its significance. The quick acceptance of refrigerated transportation in the 1880s not only allowed the packing houses to operate year round, it also made possible a tremendous increase in chilled beef shipments.

Other meat packers followed suit. Faced with stiff competition, Swift transformed the beef by-products into such highly profitable items as margarine, glue, soap, and fertilizer. In 1885 Swift and Company incorporated with branch packing houses established in Kansas City, Omaha, and St. Louis. He also opened offices in Britain and the Far East.

Swift, like most meatpackers of his day, felt he had the right to hire and dismiss whomever he pleased and conduct business as he saw fit. Wade points out that he hired nonunion workers from as far away as Baltimore, Philadelphia, and New York to break strikes. Many of these strikebreakers were Polish, Bohemian, and German immigrants as well as African-Americans from the South.

Swift was concerned with every detail of the business and expected his workers to be also. He did not tolerate any mistakes. Swift believed in

awarding good work not with words but with a raise in pay and greater responsibility. Although a wealthy man, he cared little for money or the extravagances that it could bring. He had two chief interests in life besides his business—his family and his church.

Swift and his wife attended services regularly at the Union Avenue Methodist Church. Meetings of the church's board of trustees frequently met in the living room of his home on South Emerald Avenue, which was just three blocks away. Swift was such a fixture at the institution that it came to be known as "Swift's Church." Today the Union Avenue Methodist Church continues to conduct services at 4345 South Union Avenue.

By the time Swift died in 1903 at age sixty-three, Swift and Company employed over twenty thousand workers and sales had grown to $200 million. After his death, the company expanded beyond its meatpacking base into the processing of poultry, dairy products, and such specialty items as Brown 'N Serve sausage, butterball turkeys, and Hostess Ham. Esmark, a Chicago-based holding company founded in 1973, divested Swift Independent Packing Company in 1980 and established in its place Swift Fresh Meat Company. In 1984 Esmark was sold to Beatrice Companies.

See also: Philip Danforth Armour

Further reading: Goodspeed, Thomas Wakefield. *Gustavus Franklin Swift, 1839–1903.* Vol 1 (n.d.); Swift, Louis F. with Arthur Van Vlissingen, Jr. *The Yankee of the Yards: The Biography of Gustavus Franklin Swift* (1927); Wade, Louise Carroll. *Chicago's Pride: The Stockyards, Packingtown, and Environs in the Nineteenth Century* (1987).

David Swing

Minister

born: August 18, 1830
Cincinnati, Ohio
died: October 3, 1894
Chicago, Illinois

David Swing was a controversial yet popular figure in the Chicago religious community for almost three decades and one of the most famous preachers of his generation. Like another outspoken minister, Preston Bradley, Swing challenged established Church doctrine.

Swing studied classical literature at Miami University in Oxford, Ohio. After graduating in 1852, he decided to study theology at the Old School Seminary in Cincinnati. Only one year later, he was offered—and accepted—a position to teach Greek and Latin at his alma mater. He taught there for twelve years. At the same time, he began to preach in the area and soon accepted other preaching assignments at churches throughout southern Ohio. In 1866 he agreed to become pastor at the Westminster Presbyterian Church in Chicago.

A forceful and articulate speaker, Swing quickly began to attract a large and devoted following. His sermons were published weekly in local newspapers. In 1871 the Westminster Presbyterian Church and the North Presbyterian Church united to form the Fourth Presbyterian Church at Grand and Wabash Avenues. Shortly after the merger, however, the church was destroyed in the Chicago Fire. The congregation met temporarily in the Standard Hall at 13th Street and Michigan Avenue but the hall's small size necessitated a move to the larger space of the McVicker Theatre on West Madison Street. The congregation finally moved into their new, permanent home at Rush and Superior Streets in January of 1874.

Swing was an unconventional minister during a time when a wave of religious skepticism was sweeping the country. The Presbyterian Church, in particular, had come under attack in some quarters for failing to address the spiritual needs of its congregations. Swing, one of the most vociferous critics, attempted to personalize the Church, to update Church teachings, and to make the Church relevant to the daily lives of his congregation. In

1873 Swing became chief writer for the *Alliance,* a nondenominational weekly with a liberal bent. The publication helped spread the preacher's beliefs.

Not everyone agreed with Swing's brand of liberal Presbyterianism, however. In 1874 Rev. Dr. Francis L. Patton, editor of the *Interior,* a Presbyterian journal, accused Swing of teaching heresy and filed charges against him before the Chicago Presbytery. Swing, Patton insisted, had failed to faithfully teach the essence of the Gospel in his role as Presbyterian minister and had advocated doctrines contrary to Presbyterian theory.

The trial, held in the lecture room of the First Presbyterian Church at Indiana Avenue and 21st Street, held the city's attention for weeks and even gained national exposure. Swing was ultimately acquitted of all charges. Nevertheless Patton promised to appeal to the Synod of Northern Illinois, the governing Church body. Despite support from his congregation and the ministry of the Fourth Presbyterian, who requested that he continue his work, Swing chose to resign rather than endure the ordeal again and in order to avoid any further damage to the reputation of the Church.

Friends of Rev. Swing decided to contribute $1,000 each for three years to establish a new, independent church. The Central Church opened in 1879 at the corner of State and Randolph Streets. Swing preached there until his death in October of 1894 in his Lake Shore Drive home. He was sixty-four.

The Fourth Presbyterian Church, located at Michigan Avenue and Chestnut Street since 1914, continues to serve the citizens of Chicago—from Gold Coast residents to the working poor—through service and ministry. The church's outreach programs, counseling centers, and tutoring classes, guarantee that its considerable influence stretches far beyond its North Michigan Avenue location. Further, the eloquent tradition begun by Rev. Swing has been maintained by succeeding generations of preachers from Harrison Ray Anderson, pastor from 1928 to 1961, and Elam Davies, pastor from 1961 to 1984, to John M. Buchanan, the current pastor.

The other church so strongly identified with Rev. Swing—the Central Church—still exists and is currently located at 18 South Michigan Avenue.

See also: Preston Bradley, Jenkin Lloyd Jones [appendix], Dwight L. Moody, Billy Sunday

Further reading: Scroggs, Marilee Munger. *A Light in the City: The Fourth Presbyterian Church of Chicago* (1990).

Lorado Taft

Sculptor

born: April 29, 1860
Elmwood, Illinois
died: October 30, 1936
Chicago, Illinois

*Lorado Zadoc Taft was the first Chicago sculptor to receive widespread recognition. Several of his works, including **Fountain of Time** in Washington Park, are scattered throughout the city. Taft, it was said, attempted to create work that hinted of eternity. "I cannot think of art as a mere adornment of life—a frill on human existence—but as life itself," he once said.*

Born in Elmwood, Illinois, Taft and his family moved to Champaign in 1871, where Lorado's father secured a position teaching geology at the University of Illinois. Taft graduated from the University of Illinois in 1879 and studied sculpture at the Ecole des Beaux-Arts in Paris for three years. In 1886 he opened a studio in Chicago and from 1886 to 1907 taught at the Art Institute. In 1919 Taft returned to the University of Illinois as a nonresident professor of art.

In 1906 Taft moved from the Loop to a brick coach house at 60th Street and Ellis Avenue in Hyde Park and founded Midway Studios, an artists' colony where ideas were exchanged and visions realized. Taft enjoyed playing the role of mentor. He furnished emotional sustenance, provided housing, and found work for his budding artists. In 1929 the studio was moved one block away to 6016 South Ingleside Avenue.

With a few friends, Taft established another artists' colony at Eagle's Nest in western Illinois in the late 1890s as a summer refuge for novelists, architects, musicians, and poets, including Henry Blake Fuller, Hamlin Garland, and Harriet Monroe as well as such prominent visitors as physicist Albert A. Michelson and cartoonist John T. McCutcheon.

Taft first came to prominence with his statuary sculptor for the Horticulture Building at the World's Exposition in 1893. In 1911 he achieved even greater recognition with his magnificent sculpture of the Indian chief, Black Hawk, in Oregon, Illinois.

Examples of Taft's finest sculpture are scattered throughout Chicago. Outside the Art Institute is *The Fountain of the Great Lakes* (1913) while inside stands *The Solitude of the Soul* (1911); *Seated Woman with Children* is in the Belden Triangle (1915); *Pastoral* and

Idyll (both 1913) in the Garfield Park Conservatory; and two impressive portraits are in Graceland Cemetery—*Eternal Silence: Dexter Graves Monument* (1909) and *The Crusader: Victor Lawson Monument* (1931).

By far his most acclaimed work is the massive *Fountain of Time* at the west end of the Midway Plaisance in Washington Park near the University of Chicago. Dedicated in 1922, its weathered patina still manages to convey both a sad beauty and a haunting timelessness. Based on a poem, "The Paradox of Time," by Austin Dobson ("Time goes, you say? Ah, no,/Alas, time stays; we go"), Taft envisioned a teeming wave of humanity—men, women, and children—rushing toward an invisible goal in the figure of Father Time. *Fountain of Time* took fourteen years to complete.

Fountain of Time was part of Taft's grand scheme to turn the Midway Plaisance into a sculpture park. A canal would run down the center, flanked on both sides by statuary of the world's great thinkers. At the east end of the mile-long parkway, Taft planned to construct a companion piece, *Fountain of Creation*, based on the Greek myth of Deucalion and his wife, Pyrrha. Taft devoted many years to this project but, due to a lack of funds, it remained a dream unfulfilled.

Another vision that never came to fruition was his plan for a "dream museum," a hall of sculpture consisting of chronically arranged miniature plaster models of the great sculpture of civilization.

Taft wrote articles, lectured extensively, served on fine arts commissions, and wrote several books including *The History of American Sculpture* (1903) and *Modern Tendencies in Sculpture* (1921). A staunch classicist, he attacked modern art as a capricious flight of fancy, unable to withstand the test of time. Taft loved discussing art, but he did more than just talk. He actually demonstrated the artistic process to his students, by using modeling clay.

In October of 1936 Taft suffered a stroke in his Ingleside studio. He died at age seventy-six.

In 1946 his widow, Ada Bartlett Taft, wrote a biography of her husband, *Lorado Taft: Sculptor and Citizen.*

Further reading: Bach, Ira J. and Mary Lackritz Gray. *A Guide to Chicago's Public Sculpture* (1983); Duis, Perry R. and Glen E. Holt. "Escape to Eagle's Nest," *Chicago History* (September 1982); Reynolds, Patrick. "'Fra Lorado,' Chicago's Master Sculptor," *Chicago History* (Summer 1985); Riedy, James L. *Chicago Sculpture* (1981); Taft, Ada Bartlett. *Lorado Taft: Sculptor and Citizen* (1946); Weller, Allen. *Lorado in Paris: The Letters of Lorado Taft, 1880–1885* (1985).

Graham Taylor

Social Reformer

born: May 2, 1851
Schenectady, New York
died: September 26, 1938
Ravinia, Illinois

As founder of the Chicago Commons settlement house, Graham Taylor promoted understanding between different classes, races, and faiths through championing social Christianity. Taylor believed that the power of the Word could quell, if not resolve, society's ills. Taylor stands with Jane Addams and Mary McDowell as one of Chicago's great social pioneers.

Taylor came from a long line of ministers of the Dutch Reformed Church. His father, William Taylor, moved to Philadelphia shortly after Graham's birth in 1851 and remarried when Graham's mother died. The family worshiped together daily. To young Graham, Sunday was "the gladdest time of the week . . . because in the afternoon and early evening play and merriment mingled with instruction, story-telling, vesper hymns, and dear home-companionship." In 1866 he enrolled at Rutgers College in New Jersey to study theology. Disturbed by the harshness and severity of the Dutch Reformed Church—he remembered the pulpit as an ominous place presided over by stern-faced preachers—Taylor found solace in the gentle faith of his father, but he credited his Sunday school teacher with teaching him "what religion had to do with life"—that the Church could have a positive impact on the daily activities of the community.

In 1873 Taylor, while still a theology student at the Reformed Theological Seminary in New Brunswick, New Jersey, accepted an invitation to preach at the Dutch Reformed Church in Hopewell, New York. Shortly thereafter, he was ordained on July 1, 1873. In 1880 the Fourth Congregational Church in Hartford, Connecticut, hired Taylor as their new pastor. Eight years later he was appointed to the faculty of the Hartford Theological Seminary, and his reputation grew.

In 1892 Taylor agreed to head the Department of Christian Sociology at the Chicago Theological Seminary. There he advocated a brand of social Christianity that emphasized the natural kinship of the human family. This kinship was possible for everyone to attain, said the social reformer, by applying Christian principles to everyday life. Taylor was a popular and influential lecturer.

Taylor was also a frequent visitor to Jane Addams's Hull-House, the legendary settlement house on the Near West Side. He felt that Chicago needed "a multiplication of Hull-House all over the city."

In 1894 Taylor established the Chicago Commons settlement house, which was modeled very closely after Hull-House, and moved his family into a dilapidated brick dwelling on the West Side at the corner of Union Street and Milwaukee Avenue. The Commons was located in a working-class neighborhood populated by mostly German, Scandinavian, and Irish immigrants.

The Chicago Commons offered classes, operated a nursery school, sponsored social clubs, and arranged picnics in the park and outings at country camps. It promoted cultural activities, too, in the form of a library, music lessons, concerts, and theater. From October to June, the Commons presented weekly lectures on everything from child labor to "Tolstoy and the Russian Peasant." Guest speakers there included Clarence Darrow, Emma Goldman, and Lucy Parsons.

From 1896 to 1905, Taylor published a small magazine, the *Commons,* which later merged with *Charities* and, in 1909, became a bimonthly called the *Survey.* The magazine contained news and activities of the Commons and enjoyed a national and foreign readership. Taylor wrote a weekly column for the *Chicago Daily News* from 1902 until 1938.

From 1903 to 1906, Taylor taught at the Chicago Theological Seminary and lectured at the University of Chicago's department of sociology and anthropology. In 1908 Taylor established the Chicago School of Civics and Philanthropy, which was absorbed by the University of Chicago in 1920 and became the

School of Social Service Administration (SSA). Although Taylor was not on the faculty, the curriculum continued to reflect his influence. In 1923 the SSA attained status as a fully-fledged graduate school within the university.

Although not a trailblazer in the manner of Jane Addams, Taylor was a devoted and energetic spokesman for the Social Gospel Movement, a movement that applied the teachings of Jesus to an urban setting and whose followers included Addams, Mary McDowell, Henry Demarest Lloyd, and John Dewey. Taylor never intended for the Chicago Commons to replace the influence of the church as some theologians had suggested. Rather, he felt the Commons and other settlement houses could supplement and support the work of the ministries.

Taylor died quietly in his sleep in September of 1938 at his home in Ravinia. He was eighty-seven.

In 1913 Taylor authored *Religion in Social Action.* In 1930 he completed his autobiography, *Pioneering on Social Frontiers,* and in 1936 he wrote about his settlement house experiences in *Chicago Commons through Forty Years.*

Today the Chicago Commons Association operates seven community centers in Chicago and a summer camp in Three Oaks, Michigan.

See also: Jane Addams, John Dewey [appendix], Henry Demarest Lloyd, Mary McDowell, Dwight L. Moody, David Swing

Further reading: Carson, Mina. *Settlement Folk: Social Thought and the American Settlement Movement 1885–1930* (1990); Taylor, Graham. *Pioneering on Social Frontiers* (1930); Taylor, Graham. *Chicago Commons Through Forty Years* (1936); Wade, Louise Carroll. *Graham Taylor, Pioneer for Social Justice 1851–1938* (1964).

Terence Teahan

Musician

born: August 17, 1905
Castleisland, Ireland
died: April 19, 1989
Chicago, Illinois

Terence P. Teahan, or "Cuz," as he was affectionately called, was one of the last great links between indigenous Irish music and Irish-American music. A gifted musician and a natural story-teller, Teahan contributed greatly to the city's rich Irish-American musical heritage.

Photograph by Tom Kastle.

A native of County Kerry, Teahan used to listen to music at the local ceilidhs (informal dances) or at the homes of the area's fiddle, flute, and concertina players. He began to play the concertina when he was a small boy and studied for two years under the legendary fiddler, Padraig O'Keeffe. Teahan didn't pick up the instrument again until nearly thirty years later when he had immigrated to the United States, yet a large portion of his repertoire consisted of tunes learned under the great master. "There was no radio or television or even records to distract you then," explained Teahan. "When you heard a tune at a dance, there was nothing in the world to knock it out of your head unless maybe the birds or the wind. Once you had a tune, you had it."

Teahan initially came to Chicago in 1928 and found work with Sears, Roebuck and Company and Western Electric. He went back home to Ireland in 1931 for several years, then returned to Chicago in 1933. In 1936 the Illinois Central Railroad hired Teahan as a laborer in its freight yards. He stayed at the railroad until his retirement in 1970.

Despite his rich musical background, Teahan didn't perform for many years. However, he did enjoy attending dances at Gaelic Park, then located at 47th Street and California Avenue. In 1940 an acquaintance entered his name for an amateur contest on the "Morris B. Sachs Radio Hour." Borrowing a battered accordion, Teahan performed "Miss McLeod's Reel" and beat the competition hands down.

Teahan played at dances, taverns, and dancing schools, at weddings, benefits, and various Irish community functions around Chicago and the Midwest. He earned a reputation as a patient and generous teacher and as a wonderful storyteller. He was always there to encourage or offer a kindly word of advice to younger musicians.

Teahan was not only a collector—and discoverer—of old Irish tunes, he was also a prolific composer as well. He penned Irish polkas, slides, jigs, horn-pipes, and reels. With Josh Dunson he coauthored the book *The Road to Glountane*, a collection of original compositions and poetry.

A great preservationist of Kerry music, Teahan composed many tunes in the Kerry style—generally known for its strong rhythmic quality—and in the grand Irish tradition, named them for family members, friends, and occasionally for acquaintances. He was also known to compose a nod to himself ("Cuz from Castleisland") or his native soil ("The Road to Glountane" refers to the road he took to get to his home in Castleisland). Like virtually all traditional Irish musicians, Teahan owed a considerable debt to the great collector of Irish tunes Francis O'Neill, and Teahan included in his repertoire many tunes that O'Neill had collected decades earlier.

Teahan's recordings include *Old Time Music in America* (Topic), *Irish Music in Chicago* (Rounder), and the self-produced cassette *On the Hill of Memory*. His compositions have been recorded by some of the best talent on the Irish music scene today, including the Chieftains, the Dahills, and Chicago's Liz Carroll.

Teahan died in April of 1989 at the age of eighty-three.

See also: John McGreevy [appendix], Francis O'Neill

Further reading: Krassen, Miles and Larry McCullough. Liner notes to *Irish Traditional Instrumental Music from Chicago, Volume II* (1978); Teahan, Terence and Josh Dunson. *The Road to Glountane* (1980).

Frazier Thomas

Television Entertainer

born: June 3, 1918
Rushville, Indiana
died: April 3, 1985
Chicago, Illinois

For thirty years Frazier Thomas hosted children's programs on WGN television. Generations of Chicago-area youngsters grew up watching the big, gentle man and the beloved puppet character he created, Garfield Goose.

Photograph courtesy of WGN-TV.

Thomas worked as a summer replacement and later as a staff announcer on radio station WLW in Cincinnati. In the late 1940s he appeared on Cincinnati's WLW-TV, an experimental television station where he began developing the character of a goose named Garfield.

Although the name *Garfield* was formed from the first three numbers of WLW's telephone exchange, the idea of making the character a goose was inspired by an incident from Thomas's childhood. A Catholic church that stood across the street from his house held many bazaars and church socials. On one occasion the nuns used a goose puppet to exchange prizes for a nickel. Thomas, in turn, remembered the goose when he needed a gimmick to give birthday prizes away on a Cincinnati children's show.

When he came to WBBM-TV in Chicago in 1952, Thomas built the show around the Garfield character and developed it further with the help of Ivan Hill, a Chicago advertising executive. "Hill was an amateur psychologist," noted Thomas in 1959. "Together we would outline and build the goose's character, taking great care to make his reactions as normal as possible." Two years later, Thomas moved to WGN, taking the goose with him.

Thomas, an ex-magician, wrote, produced, and hosted *Garfield Goose and Friends.* Garfield was the mad goose who referred to himself as "king of the United States" while Thomas, the sane host, acted as the "prime minister" dressed, appropriately, in a military uniform. Telecast Monday through Friday after school, it also featured Beauregard Burnsides III, sort of a canine Sherlock Holmes, who diligently tracked down the elusive Romberg Rabbitt.

"Actually a goose is ideal for a puppet character, if you know geese," Thomas said in a newspaper article in 1957. "A goose will take over a farm. Get a couple of geese on a farm and they run the place. It's only natural for Gar to think he's king of the United States."

Thomas once described Garfield as "rather human." Although he couldn't talk, he did display distinctly human tendencies. "He's boastful, selfish and sometimes even greedy and stubborn," said Thomas. "Giving emotions to a goose helps a youngster to see his own mistakes. Seeing a goose goof may help a youngster understand his own world better."

Garfield Goose wasn't the only program that Thomas produced. He also started *Family Classics* in the early 1960s, which presented movies suitable for the entire family. He himself screened and, when necessary, edited the films. "The matter of what is in good taste and what is not is a very personal thing; it differs from family to family," he once explained. "I know I can't possibly please everyone, but at the same time I try to keep every film I show within the boundaries of good taste as I see it."

The avuncular Thomas never talked down to his audience. Perhaps this quality accounted for his phenomenal success and longevity. *Garfield Goose* was not so much a pioneering show as an extremely popular one. There was an especially strong connection between Thomas and the audience. "Children like to pretend," he said, "but there is a limit to what they'll accept. We knew they wouldn't believe a goose could talk, but it was just barely conceivable a goose could be trained to punch typewriter keys with his beak."

In 1976 *Garfield Goose* show went off the air and was incorporated into a segment of WGN-TV's long running *Bozo's Circus.* When Thomas succeeded

Ned Locke as host and circus master of the popular children's program, the Garfield Goose character was included in the show. The segment was discontinued in 1981 when *Bozo's Circus* changed its format. Garfield Goose made his last appearance on Chicago television in January 1981.

Thomas died in April of 1985 in Ravenswood Hospital at the age of sixty-six.

See also: Fran Allison, Burr Tillstrom

Theodore Thomas

Conductor

born: October 11, 1835
Esens, Germany
died: January 4, 1905
Chicago, Illinois

Christian Friedrich Theodor Thomas, founder and conductor of the Chicago Symphony Orchestra, brought symphonic music to the general public. He turned the Chicago Symphony into one of the best orchestras in the world and helped to raise the musical tastes of the rough-hewn city on the prairie.

Thomas was trained by his father, also a musician. He made his violin debut in Germany at the age of ten. In 1845 his family immigrated to the United States and settled in New York City. At fourteen, Thomas went on his own as a violinist and toured the South. For the next several years he performed solo and with various orchestras in New York. In 1854 he met pianist William Mason, the son of a prominent Boston composer. Mason invited Thomas to join a new chamber group. The Mason-Thomas ensemble performed a popular series of concerts in New York. By the end of the decade, Thomas was guest conducting the house orchestra at the Academy of Music, a theater in New York City that presented various companies. The following year he became its regular conductor.

In 1864 Thomas founded the New York–based Theodore Thomas Orchestra. In 1866 he was appointed musical director of the Brooklyn Philharmonic. Two years later the Theodore Thomas Orchestra began a series of evening concerts at the Central Park Gardens, a popular restaurant and open-air beer garden. The concerts attracted a large and loyal following. The next year Thomas, encouraged by the audience response, decided the time was right to tour the country.

In 1876 Thomas was invited to become conductor of the New York Philharmonic. In 1878 he accepted the position of musical director at the newly established Cincinnati College of Music, while still associated with the Brooklyn and New York orchestras.

In 1891 Thomas accepted an offer to take over the Chicago Symphony—originally called the Chicago Orchestra. Until 1913 the organization was referred to as the Theodore Thomas Orchestra. Prior to the construction of Orchestra Hall in 1904, concerts were held in the Auditorium Theater.

Thomas had yearned to settle down in one location and conduct his own permanent orchestra. Chicago, with its gruff image and large ethnic working-class population, offered the conductor his greatest challenge. Although early programs were criticized for being too long and too highbrow, the city eventually warmed to the stern perfectionist. Thomas did his best to reach out to the citizenry, and he frequently arranged a series of concerts for the city's working-class population. The first of a series of three "workingmen's" or "people's" concerts was held in the Auditorium Theater on January 20, 1893, notes historian Philo Adams Otis. The audience, according to contemporary *Chicago Tribune* accounts, listened intently. Thomas encouraged the city's industrialists to take a break from their money-making ventures to attend concerts.

Shortly after settling in Chicago, Thomas was asked to be the musical director of the World's Columbian Exposition of 1893. He found the experience rather disappointing—Chicagoans flocked to the free early afternoon concerts, which featured lighter fare, but avoided the more serious evening performances. Still, the exposition did showcase the considerable talents of the members of Thomas's orchestra as well as thirty musicians from other American and international cities.

During his early years with the Chicago Orchestra, Thomas toured regularly, mostly to Midwestern cities, but he also made forays into the South and to the West Coast.

Thomas was a risk-taker. To get people into the seats, he presented Beethoven and Wagner, but once he knew the audience was his, he experimented with more adventuresome programming such as the Chicago premiere of Antonin Dvorak's *Symphony from the New World* and Richard Strauss's *Death and Transformation*. There were so few qualified musicians in Chicago during the 1890s, however, that Thomas had to import players from New York—quite a difficult task, since many musicians were reluctant to move to a city with such a sparse cultural life.

Furthermore, Thomas was unhappy with the massive size of the Auditorium Theater—it took more than excellent acoustics to fill the empty seats, he noted. At a seating capacity of over 4,800, it was much too large for symphony concerts. What's more, Thomas grew weary of the constant abuse heaped on him by the local press who criticized his programming for not including more American composers. Under such conditions, the short-tempered Thomas threatened to resign.

A fund-raising campaign launched to finance the construction of a new—and smaller—home for the orchestra helped to change his mind. Music lovers from throughout the city contributed a total of $750,000 toward the structure. On December 14, 1904, Orchestra Hall—a few blocks north of the Auditorium Theater—was dedicated in a program that featured Handel, Beethoven, Wagner, and Strauss.

Unfortunately, Thomas didn't have the opportunity to enjoy his new home. Three weeks after the dedication ceremonies, which he had conducted, he died of pneumonia in his home at 43 East Bellevue Place. He was succeeded by his former assistant, thirty-two-year-old Frederick Stock.

Thomas, the most celebrated American conductor of the late nineteenth century, laid the foundation for the current Chicago Symphony Orchestra. The CSO began to develop an international reputation under Budapest-born Fritz Reiner who conducted from 1953 to 1963. Fellow Hungarian Sir Georg Solti has continued the grand tradition since his appointment in 1969.

The CSO's 1990–91 season was historically significant for two reasons—the 100th anniversary of the CSO and the farewell appearance of Solti. The future now lies with Solti's forty-seven-year-old successor Daniel Barenboim.

Further reading: Hofmeister, Rudolph A. *The Germans of Chicago* (1976); Otis, Philo Adams. *The Chicago Symphony Orchestra, Its Organization, Growth and Development 1891–1924* (1924); Schabas, Ezra. *Theodore Thomas, America's Conductor and Builder of Orchestras, 1835–1905* (1989); Upton, George P., ed. *Theodore Thomas: A Musical Autobiography* (1964).

Mary Harris Thompson

Physician

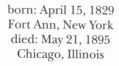

born: April 15, 1829
Fort Ann, New York
died: May 21, 1895
Chicago, Illinois

In 1865 Dr. Mary Harris Thompson founded the Chicago Hospital for Women and Children at 49 Rush Street as a haven for indigent and pregnant women, Civil War widows, and orphans, who would otherwise be forced to rely on the run-down and overcrowded Cook County Hospital. Mary Thompson is credited with being Chicago's first woman surgeon. She worked passionately to change society's attitude toward women in medicine. Her goal was to create a hospital solely staffed by women to minister to the welfare of women and children.

Born in New York State of English parents, Mary Thompson grew up on a farm and received her education at a country school. Her parents then sent her to Fort Edward Institute at Fort Edward, New York, and later to West Poultney School in Vermont. An instructor at West Poultney, who was impressed with Mary's intelligence, persuaded her to attend the New England Female Medical College in Boston. At first she studied to become a teacher of physiology, anatomy, and hygiene, but she changed her mind and decided to become a physician. After one year at the New York Infirmary for Women and Children, she returned to Boston to graduate and chose to seek the road virtually no woman—or at least, very few women—had dared travel.

Thompson began practicing medicine in Chicago in July of 1863 at the age of thirty-four. Despite her competence, she had to endure many frustrating years in the medical profession. She was not allowed to perform surgery, for example, without a male surgeon present.

In 1865 she rented a large frame house at Rush and Indiana Streets and began taking care of indigent women and children as patients. Thompson's hospital had fourteen beds. In 1866 the hospital moved to 212 Ohio Street, and four years later to a large wooden structure at 402 North State Street.

According to the accepted wisdom of the time, women were "mentally unsuited" to practice medicine. It was considered "unladylike" behavior and those who harbored such ambitions were viewed with suspicion. Thompson established her own hospital not only because she was unwelcome in Chicago medical schools but also because she particularly wished to help women and children—especially Civil War widows and their offspring—in need of medical treatment.

In 1865 Thompson approached Dr. William Heath Byford, an influential staff member of the Chicago Medical College, requesting that women be allowed to attend lectures at the college. While managing the Chicago Hospital for Women and Children, Thompson had applied to several Chicago medical schools in order to further her education, but was rejected. Dr. Byford supported her proposal.

In 1869 Thompson was selected as one of four women admitted to the Chicago Medical College during its one-year experiment to admit women. Thompson graduated at the end of that year although some faculty members continued to question the wisdom of granting a degree to a woman. Consequently the program was discontinued the following year.

In 1870 Byford suggested the establishment of a separate college—the Woman's Hospital Medical College—that would prepare women for a career in the medical profession. Thompson was hired as a teacher. Lectures were held at the Chicago Hospital for Women and Children. Declining enrollment, however, convinced committee members to reorganize in 1877. Thompson, for reasons unclear, refused to accept a position on the faculty.

The Chicago Hospital for Women and Children and the college were destroyed during the Great Chicago Fire of 1871. Several temporary homes were utilized until 1885 when a new hospital was constructed at Paulina and Adams Streets at a cost of $64,000. The Relief and Aid Society, a charitable organization, helped raise much of the funding.

Thompson's hospital pioneered a number of medical firsts, many after the founder herself died. In 1871 the Chicago Hospital for Women and Children established the first women's medical college in the Midwest. The hospital established Chicago's first nursing school in 1874; installed the Midwest's first cancer detection clinic in 1943; and established the first mental hygiene clinic for working women in 1946.

The Chicago Hospital for Women and Children was managed and staffed by women; men began to be admitted as patients in the 1890s. Among the women physicians on its staff were Drs. Lucy Waite, Frances Dickinson, Marie J. Mergler, Sara Hackett Stevenson, and Julia H. Smith, who was the first woman to be admitted to the American Medical Association.

Thompson died in May of 1895. By that time she was a well-respected physician, known throughout the country, whose achievements helped rid opposition to women in the medical profession. In 1892 Northwestern University made the Woman's Hospital Medical College a department of the university. Financial difficulties led to its closing in 1902.

On June 27, 1895, the Board of Trustees voted to change the name of the Chicago Hospital for Women and Children to the Mary Thompson Hospital. It operated at 140 North Ashland Avenue from 1928 until 1988, when economic problems forced it to close.

Further reading: Bonner, Thomas Neville. *Medicine in Chicago 1850–1950, A Chapter in the Social and Scientific Development of a City* (1957); Lucas, Carter. *History of Medicine and Surgery and Physicians and Surgeons of Chicago* (1922).

William Hale Thompson

Politician

born: May 14, 1867
Boston, Massachusetts
died: March 19, 1944
Chicago, Illinois

Few political careers in Chicago have been as controversial, as colorful, and as flamboyantly outrageous as that of William Hale Thompson. He has been called a buffoon, a charlatan, a rogue, and many other less-than-flattering titles. Despite these epithets, there's no denying his considerable popularity— he was elected mayor of Chicago three times—and his rough charm. There was something irresistibly appealing about Thompson. Though he made his share of empty and asinine campaign promises ("If I am elected mayor, I will protect the fair womanhood of Chicago!"), he usually spoke his mind—even if it

was from both sides of his mouth—and kept the city entertained for a good many years. Thompson was a great showman but an abysmal statesman.

Contrary to his low-brow, man-on-the-street image, William Hale Thompson was, in fact, a child of wealth. His father, a real estate developer, brought the family to Chicago when "Big Bill" was an infant. As a young man, Thompson worked out West, as a brakeman for the Union Pacific Railroad and as a cook on a cattle ranch in New Mexico, in a stab at independence. After his father's death in 1891, he returned to Chicago to take over the family business.

Thompson joined the Chicago Athletic Club and within a year became captain of the water polo team as well as captain of the Chicago Athletic Association football team. A big, handsome young man, he was considered prime political property. "The worst you can say of him is that he's stupid," said an insider.

In 1900 Thompson entered politics as the Republican aldermanic candidate from the 2nd Ward and defeated the Democratic incumbent, candy manufacturer Charles F. Gunther. From 1902 to 1904 Thompson was a member of the county board. In 1915 he won the mayoral seat for the first time. Three years later he made an unsuccessful attempt against Representative Medill McCormick for a seat in the U. S. Senate. In 1919, he was re-elected mayor.

Thompson enjoyed a tight relationship with Chicago's gangsters. Al Capone and Johnny Torrio reportedly contributed large sums of money toward his campaign war chest, and he paid back the favor. Thompson, of course, denied that he and the Capone element were in cahoots. Thus, when Judge John H. Lyle accused him of bowing to the orders of thugs and criminals, Thompson blew up. "I don't care about name-calling, but he has attacked my integrity and I'd like to knock this loony judge down, kick him in the face and kick hell out of him!"

In 1917 the United States declared war on Germany, but Thompson would have none of it. Partly to appease the half-million people of German descent in the city, the mayor vociferously opposed America's entry into the war under the jingoistic banner of "America First." Critics dubbed him "Kaiser Bill."

By 1923, however, Thompson's scandal-racked administration had lost all credibility. Thompson, who at one time had high hopes of climbing to the presidency, knew he couldn't even win back the mayor's chair. He decided to sit out the 1923 election. Anti-Thompson factions in the Republican party nominated instead the perfectly respectable postmaster, Arthur C. Lueder. Lueder, in turn, lost to reform candidate, William E. Dever.

From his early days in politics, Thompson had always attracted a considerable African-American vote. He openly courted the black constituency, attended civic functions, rallies, and funerals on the South Side, and appointed black politicians like Edward Wright and Archibald Carey to high positions in city government. Consequently, Thompson was hailed as a loyal friend in the African-American community. However, one of the worst race riots in Chicago history occurred during his term in 1919. Thompson stood idly by for several days, refusing to summon the state militia—although state troops did eventually play a major role in quelling white violence—while the South Side burned.

Thompson's 1927 campaign against Dever was one of the wildest in Chicago mayoral history. Dever had shut down countless taverns during his term in office in obedience to Prohibition laws. Thompson promised to reopen them and to return the city to the wide-open town status of the old days. "When I'm elected we will not only reopen places these people have closed, but we'll open 10,000 new ones." His campaign strategy worked and he was elected for the third time.

During this, his final term, Thompson lost control of the city to the mob. Racketeering became the biggest business in Chicago. When critics blasted Thompson for his close ties with crime figures, he simply ignored them, instead introducing bogus issues. One such issue was his quest to oust school superintendent William McAndrew—who had been appointed by Dever. Thompson accused McAndrew of being a pawn of the British government, promising to rid the schools of any subversive British influence, and, if necessary, to "punch King George in the snoot." As Chicagoans shook their head in dismay, the rest of the country barely stifled a disbelieving laugh.

Thompson's most enduring legacy is that of "Big Bill the Builder." During the Thompson years, several major beautification projects got off the ground, including the construction of playlots and bridges as well as the improvement of city streets and sewers.

In 1931, his career on the ropes again, Thompson won the Republican mayoral nomination, but was overwhelmingly defeated by Anton J. Cermak. Undaunted, he sought a fourth term. He couldn't muster the votes.

In 1936 Thompson stubbornly returned to politics by forming the short-lived Union Progressive party

to run for governor. He was ignominiously defeated by Henry Horner. In 1939 he threw his hat into the Republican mayoral primary ring one last time against Dwight H. Green. He lost again. Green was defeated by incumbent mayor Edward J. Kelly in the general election.

In February of 1944, Thompson caught a bad cold and lapsed into a coma. He died in his suite at the Blackstone Hotel at age seventy-six on March 19.

See also: Al Capone, Anton J. Cermak, William E. Dever, Edward J. Kelly

Further reading: Bukowski, Douglas. "Big Bill Thompson: The 'Model' Politician," in *The Mayors: The Chicago Political Tradition*, Green, Paul M. and Melvin G. Holli, eds. (1987); Peterson, Virgil W. *Barbarians In Our Midst: A History of Chicago Crime and Politics* (1952); Rex, Frederick F. *The Mayors of the City of Chicago* (1934); Wendt, Lloyd and Herman Kogan. *Big Bill of Chicago* (1953).

Burr Tillstrom

Television Entertainer

born: October 13, 1917
Chicago, Illinois
died: December 6, 1985
Palm Springs, California

From 1947 to 1957 "Kukla, Fran, & Ollie" reigned as one of the most popular children's programs on television. It was unscripted and spontaneous television at its best. Created by Burr Tillstrom, the hand puppets of KFO were as human—perhaps more so—as any fictional character. Along with Dave Garroway and Studs Terkel, Tillstrom and his Kuklapolitans epitomized the best of the Chicago school of television of the late fifties, which consisted of locally produced shows noted for their low key, no-frills approach to programming.

Photograph reprinted with permission from the *Chicago Sun-Times.*

A generation of kids grew up watching the antics of KFO. Hal Boyle, an Associated Press columnist, once said that the Kuklapolitans had done more for Chicago than Mrs. O'Leary's cow. Tillstrom's opinion of his achievements was more humble. His creativity and his life were fueled by one key ingredient—humor. "Being able to laugh at yourself is the only thing that will save the world," he once remarked. "It has to start with you."

A native North Sider, Burr Tillstrom attended Senn High School. In 1935 he worked for a puppet theater under the auspices of the WPA at the Chicago Park District. He gave up a partial scholarship in puppetry at the University of Chicago to work at it for a living. When he attended the first American Puppet Festival in Detroit in 1936, he was further convinced that he had made the right decision. "I went back to basic cloth construction that I knew, and I made a clown. I used to stuff him in my oversize pocket." For six months Tillstrom's new creation had no name, until he went backstage one night to the dressing room of a ballerina, Tamara Toumanova, who was appearing at the Auditorium Theater. As she pulled the puppet from his pocket, Toumanova exclaimed, "Ah, Kukla!" a term of endearment in Russian and Greek for doll. The name stuck and, to Tillstrom's wonder and delight, a star was born.

"Kukla, Fran & Ollie" premiered on Chicago television in 1947 on WBKB before moving to the NBC network. The human element of the show was Fran Allison. In 1952, NBC curtailed the highly respected show to fifteen minutes a day and then trimmed it further to a half-hour Sunday broadcast. KFO then moved to ABC, where it remained on the air until 1957.

With nothing more than his hands, his imagination, and his remarkable voice, Tillstrom created a diverse set of most believable characters. There was Kukla, the wistful everyman with the sad eyes and bulbous nose; Ollie, the sharp-witted, one-toothed dragon; the garrulous Madame Oglepuss, whom Tillstrom created because of his fondness "for buxom babes who sing in opera;" and the bluntly honest Beulah Witch who never hesitated to speak her mind. Other tightly drawn personalities included Col. Cracky, Fletcher Rabbit, Mercedes, Clara Coo Coo, and Cecil Bill.

"The puppeteer's world is different from any other," explained Tillstrom. "You can express things that happen only in the imagination. You can make up and tell stories, fairy tales that nobody else can touch, and you can poke fun without being cruel."

In addition to the KFO show, Tillstrom did some solo work, appearing regularly on "That Was the Week That Was." One segment of this, a "hand ballet" that represented a couple separated by the Berlin Wall, earned him an Emmy.

Tillstrom returned to Chicago in 1967 when the Kuklapolitans joined Channel 32 (WFLD-TV) as "news commentators." They appeared three times a week and gently poked fun at current events. "No matter how bad the shape of the world," said Tillstrom, "I think humor can save us all."

At the height of the KFO's popularity—from 1948 to 1957—the cast received fifteen thousand letters a day, and the monthly, *Kuklapolitan Courier,* enjoyed a circulation of twenty-two thousand. In 1954

Oliver J. Dragon, himself, made his debut at the Lyric Opera House with the Boston Pops Orchestra for the Midwest performance of *St. George and the Dragon,* written by Tillstrom and KFO music director, Jack Fascinato. A generation later, in 1970, the Kuklapolitans briefly resurfaced on public television.

Tillstrom won three Emmys and two Peabody awards during his career. He died in December of 1985 at the age of sixty-eight in Palm Springs, California.

See also: Fran Allison, Dave Garroway

Bill Veeck

Baseball Club Owner

born: February 9, 1914
Hinsdale, Illinois
died: January 2, 1986
Chicago, Illinois

William Louis Veeck, Jr., was one of the most controversial sports figures in the business; to this outgoing, wisecracking, maverick promoter, baseball was entertainment. Some argued that by injecting humor into the game—such as sending a midget to the plate—he demeaned the sport. Others credited him with saving the game, insisting that his cartoon-like antics actually helped boost attendance figures. Bill Veeck, often described as the "Barnum of baseball," was one of a kind.

Photograph courtesy of the Chicago White Sox.

Bill Veeck was the son of William Veeck, a Chicago sportswriter who later became president of the Chicago Cubs. Veeck grew up in Hinsdale and attended Hinsdale High School before transferring to Phillips Academy in Andover, Massachusetts, for a brief eight weeks. He finally ended up at the Ranch School in Los Alamos, New Mexico.

When his father died in 1933, Veeck dropped out of Kenyon College in Ohio to work for the Chicago Cubs, toiling at various positions. By the early 1940s he had advanced to treasurer. More than anything else, Veeck wanted to own a baseball club, but with Philip K. Wrigley firmly ensconced at the top, that didn't seem likely with the Cubs.

In 1941 Veeck and Charley Grimm purchased the Milwaukee Brewers, a Cub farm team in the American Association, transforming the once-lowly team from last place to winners of three consecutive American Association pennants.

Veeck enjoyed turning losing teams into winners. In 1945 he sold his interest in the Milwaukee Brewers, and the following year he became part owner of the Cleveland Indians of the American League. At thirty-two he had earned the title of the youngest chief executive in baseball and by 1948 his team had won the World Series. In 1951 Veeck bought the St. Louis Browns of the American League, but the results were something less than spectacular. He left after two disappointing seasons.

Many club owners didn't like Veeck's unconventional tactics. When he signed the American League's first African-American player, Larry Doby, to the Cleveland Indians in 1947, he reportedly received thousands of hate letters in the mail. The following year he signed the legendary African-American pitcher, Satchel Paige, to the Cleveland Indians. In Milwaukee during World War II, he introduced early morning baseball for the night-shift workers, and he even served coffee and donuts. On one occasion, in 1949, he drove a hearse around the baseball diamond to indicate the death of his team's pennant chances. In 1960 he introduced an exploding scoreboard at Comiskey Park that went off whenever a White Sox player hit a home run.

The most notorious incident of Veeck's career occurred in August of 1951 in St. Louis when he signed Eddie Gaedel—at three feet seven inches and sixty-five pounds—and sent him to pinch hit in the second game of a double header. The fans loved it, but the top brass didn't. The next day Will Harridge, president of the American League, barred Gaedel from baseball, a move that Veeck called discriminatory against "little people."

In 1959 Veeck bought the Chicago White Sox. With Veeck in charge, the team won its first American League pennant in forty years. The glory days, however, did not last long. In ill health, Veeck left the Sox in 1961 and, in obedience to his doctor's orders, he slowed down, took it easy, and lived a leisurely life in Easton, Maryland. From 1968 to 1970 he served as president of Suffolk Downs racetrack near Boston.

In 1975 Veeck learned that the White Sox were about to be sold and the club moved to Toronto or Seattle. He feverishly put together enough money to make a bid to keep the team in Chicago. Although he met the financial obligations, Veeck's offer was turned down due to his reputation as a showman with questionable judgment. Detroit Tigers owner, John Fetzer, intervened and convinced the league that in all

fairness to Veeck another vote should be taken. This time his bid was accepted. Veeck, however, had not changed his ways. In 1977, strapped for cash and in dire need of good people, he came upon the novel idea of "renting" a player for a short-term lease. The free agent system, which gave athletes the right to negotiate with other teams for the most lucrative contract, had priced quality players out of his range.

Veeck signed thirteen ballplayers each to a one-year contract, including such power hitters as Richie Zisk, Oscar Gamble, and Eric Soderholm. The "Go-Go Sox" or the "South Side Hit Men," as they were invariably called, hit home run after home run—a total of one hundred and ninety two, in fact. They didn't win a pennant that year, but they did create a lot of excitement in the city, especially on the South Side.

In 1979 a Veeck gimmick—the Disco Demolition—turned into a disaster. He had offered reduced admission to anyone who brought a disco record into the stadium. The records, part of the anti-disco movement that was particularly strong that year, were then collected and destroyed. But despite personal appeals from Veeck himself, the fans went wild, burning the records and running onto the field. It was one of the most embarrassing moments in Veeck's professional career. He had had enough of baseball, and, it seems, baseball had had enough of him.

In 1980 Veeck attempted to sell the team to Edward DeBartolo, Sr., a multimillionaire and Ohio business-man with racetrack holdings, when baseball commissioner Bowie Kuhn thwarted the deal. Veeck then sold the team in early 1981 to the current owners, Jerry Reinsdorf and Eddie Einhorn. When Einhorn publicly slighted Veeck's management ability,

the offended Veeck switched his allegiance to Wrigley Field. He did not attend a game at Comiskey Park for five years.

Veeck wrote four books, including *Veeck—as in Wreck: The Autobiography of Bill Veeck*. For a short time he served as president of Samuel and Veeck, a Cleveland public relations firm.

In October of 1984 Veeck underwent surgery to remove a malignant lung tumor. He died in January of 1986 at the age of seventy-one.

During a memorial service held two days after his death, eight hundred fans, family, and friends gathered at St. Thomas the Apostle Church at 5472 South Kimbark Avenue in Hyde Park to honor his life and celebrate his spirit. Rev. Thomas Fitz-gerald delivered a moving and eloquent eulogy to the uncommon man with the common touch. "You are a prince in all the good senses of the word," he stated. "A prince without pretensions."

See also: Adrian Anson, Charles A. Comiskey, William Wrigley, Jr.

Further reading: Eskenazi, Gerald. *Bill Veeck: A Baseball Legend* (1987); Veeck, Bill with Ed Lynn. *Veeck—as in Wreck: The Autobiography of Bill Veeck* (1962).

Charles H. Wacker

Entrepreneur/Civic Leader

born: August 29, 1856
Chicago, Illinois
died: October 31, 1929
Lake Geneva, Illinois

Charles H. Wacker made his fortune in the beer brewing business, but he is best remembered as a prominent civic leader who led the movement to beautify Chicago. He was largely responsible for the two-level thoroughfare along the Chicago River that bears his name.

The son of German immigrants, Wacker attended public school in Chicago and at the Lake Forest Academy. He studied music in Stuttgart, Germany, and attended lectures at the University of Geneva in Switzerland.

Wacker began his career as an office boy in the grain commodities firm of Moeller and Company. In 1880 he formed a partnership with his father to establish F. Wacker and Son, a malting business. In 1882 he joined the firm of Wacker and Birk Brewing and Malting Company as secretary and treasurer, with his father as president. In 1884 his father died and Charles became president.

In 1888 Wacker was nominated for treasurer of the state of Illinois, but he chose to avoid public office. In 1893 he served as one of the principal stockholders and directors of the World's Columbian Exposition, which celebrated the four hundredth anniversary of Columbus's journey to America and announced to the world Chicago's arrival as a great city.

Buoyed by the success of the exposition, architect Daniel H. Burnham developed a method to adapt the fair's sense of beauty and harmony to the city. In 1907 he persuaded two influential citizens' groups, the Commercial Club and the Merchants Club, to raise the necessary money to fund his vision. Inspired by the broad boulevards and grand parks of Paris, Burnham's Chicago Plan, among other things, called for the beautification of the lakefront, the expansion of the park system, and the widening of major north-and-south arteries into the city's downtown district. As chairman of the Chicago Plan, Wacker promoted and helped achieve Burnham's vision. The Commercial Club published Burnham's *Plan of Chicago*, coauthored with Edward Bennett, in 1909.

The city adopted the Chicago Plan in 1910. Wacker recommended removing, to relieve traffic congestion, the South Water Street market—the city's major produce district—from the south branch of the Chicago River and replace it with a modern, double-decker thoroughfare.

James Simpson, president of Marshall Field and Company, was one of the first prominent citizens to recommend that South Water Street be changed to Wacker Drive and the market be moved. The proposal was introduced in the city council in 1924. "Every village which has a town pump has a Water Street," noted Alderman A. A. McCormick. "I urge you to give this great new improvement a name that will mean something. I want to see Mr. Wacker honored while he is still alive." The city council passed the ordinance with only one dissenting vote. The South Water market was relocated to the Southwest Side two years later in 1926.

The construction of Wacker Drive and the opening of the North Michigan Avenue bridge in 1920 changed the essential character of Michigan Avenue north of the river. By making the area more accessible to the Loop, it assured the future of the boulevard and its adjacent streets as an important commercial and retail district.

Wacker was president of the Chicago Relief and Aid Society, president of the United Charities of Chicago, and a director of the Chicago chapter of the American Red Cross. In addition to his many civic interests, Wacker exerted a strong influence on German-American activities in the city. He was treasurer of the German Opera House Company, a director of the German Old People's Home, and was a member of several German singing societies. A long-time resident of the North Side, Wacker lived at 2340 North Commonwealth Avenue. His boyhood home at 1838 North Lincoln Park West is still standing.

Wacker died in October of 1929 in his Lake Geneva home. He was seventy-three.

See also: Daniel H. Burnham

Further reading: Condit, Carl W. *Chicago 1910–29: Building, Planning, and Urban Technology* (1973); Pacyga, Dominic A. and Ellen Skerrett. *Chicago: City of Neighborhoods* (1986).

Charles Walgreen

Entrepreneur

born: October 9, 1873
Rio, Illinois
died: December 11, 1939
Chicago, Illinois

Charles Rudolph Walgreen turned the corner pharmacy into a multimillion dollar business and, in the process, popularized the drug store soda fountain and lunch counter.

Born a few miles outside of Galesburg, Illinois, Walgreen was the son of immigrant Swedes. In 1887 Charles moved with his family to Dixon, Illinois. He enrolled at Dixon Business College for one year and then found a job as a bookkeeper in the town's largest general store. He left that position to do piecework at the Henderson Shoe Factory.

Although apprehensive about waiting on the public, Walgreen reluctantly took a job as a $4-a-week apprentice at a neighborhood drug store. When the town was hit by a severe snowstorm, Walgreen was ordered by the owner, David S. Horton, to shovel the snow off the sidewalk. Unfortunately, he became so engrossed with a conversation with several friends who had dropped by that he simply forgot. Needless to say, his boss was not pleased and young Walgreen left on a bad note. It proved an important move because he then decided to leave Dixon altogether. He borrowed $20 from his sister and caught the train to Chicago.

Walgreen held jobs in a number of downtown, North Side, and South Side pharmacies. In 1897 he passed the Illinois State Board of Pharmacy. During the Spanish-American War, Walgreen enlisted in the Illinois National Guard and was shipped off to Cuba. He saw no action but was assigned to handle the pharmaceutical chores at Siboney Hospital.

Using savings borrowed from his father, Walgreen purchased his first store at 4134 South Cottage Grove Avenue in 1901. The store was typical of small drug stores at that time, both in design and merchandise. It sold such products as tooth powder, soaps, vegetable tonics, perfumes, pills, and tablets. Determined to make his establishment stand out from the crowd, Walgreen devised an ingenious system for attracting neighborhood customers. Whenever a customer telephoned for nonprescription items, he would repeat the caller's name and address and the articles ordered loudly and clearly so his assistant, standing nearby, could wrap and collect the items and deliver the order to the caller's home before the caller hung up. It was great public relations and it worked. Word got out that Walgreen's was a good place to do business. In 1909 he opened his second store at Cottage Grove Avenue and 39th Street.

Walgreen devoted more and more time to the appearance of his stores. He displayed attractive products in the windows while, inside, customers were charmed by the pleasant aroma of toiletries and perfume bottles. An important part of Walgreen's success was the soda fountain, always popular with customers. As soon as the first hint of winter arrived, however, business plummeted so badly that Walgreen was forced to shut down the fountain from mid-October to mid-May.

Alarmed at the loss of clientele, Walgreen began introducing sandwiches, desserts, and hot fare. Curiously, Walgreen worried that the heady mixture of food and toiletries would clash and, perhaps, offend some of his more sensitive customers. "For a long time Dad wouldn't sell toasted sandwiches," admitted his son, Charles R. Walgreen, Jr., in 1959 to the *Chicago Tribune*, "because he thought the odor would interfere with the sale of perfume."

In 1921 Walgreen opened a store in the Venetian Building at 17 East Washington Street in the heart of the busy downtown retail district and only two blocks from Sargent's, the city's oldest pharmacy. This bold move deviated sharply from the previous and successful practice of locating outlets in densely populated residential neighborhoods.

In 1922 a Walgreen's employee, Ivar Coulson, made history when he added a few scoops of vanilla ice cream to the company's watery malted drinks of milk, chocolate syrup, and malt powder. Then he added a generous dollop of whipped cream and capped it with a bright red cherry. Before long, eager customers were lining up three and four deep for a taste of Walgreen's double-rich chocolate malted milk.

By 1916 Walgreen's consisted of nine stores and by the mid-twenties, more than sixty. There were ninety-two stores in the Chicago area alone by 1926 in addition to outlets in Hammond and Gary, Indiana; Milwaukee, Wisconsin; and Joliet, Illinois. The company's first store in New York opened the following year. In 1931 there were 446 stores separated into 18 divisions and stretching from Minneapolis to Houston. By the time Walgreen retired in 1934, there were more than five hundred stores across the country.

Through successful marketing techniques, aggressive promotion, and knowledgable service, Walgreen's developed from a neighborhood store into the nation's largest drugstore chain.

In 1949 the company moved from its South Side headquarters into new corporate offices at 4300 West Peterson Avenue. In 1975 Walgreen's relocated to the northern suburb of Deerfield, Illinois.

On September 6, 1984, Walgreen's celebrated the opening of its one-thousandth store. The following year the firm was chosen by Dun's *Business Month* as one of the nation's five best-run companies.

For years Walgreen lived in a mansion at 116th Street and Longwood Drive in the Morgan Park neighborhood on the South Side. In 1946 the house became part of the Cenacle retreat house. It is now part of the Mercy Mission, a girls' school.

Walgreen died of cancer two weeks before Christmas in 1939 at the age of sixty-six.

See also: Marshall Field, Potter Palmer

Further reading: Kogan, Herman and Rick. *Pharmacist to the Nation: A History of Walgreen Co.* (1989); Walgreen, Myrtle R. and Marguerite Harmon Bro. *Never a Dull Day.* (1963).

Aaron Montgomery Ward

Merchant

born: February 17, 1844
Chatham, New Jersey
died: December 7, 1913
Highland Park, Illinois

Aaron Montgomery Ward was a self-made man who established the world's first mail-order business and later one of the largest department stores in Chicago. More significant, though, was his determination to maintain and expand Chicago's frontyard. For this reason, Ward earned the title "watchdog of the lakefront."

Though born in New Jersey, Ward attended grade school in Niles, Michigan. At eleven he started working in a barrel factory, at fourteen in a brickyard. He worked for various dry goods firms in St. Louis, Missouri, and St. Joseph, Michigan, until coming to Chicago after the Civil War, where he found work as a clerk at Field, Palmer, and Leiter. He stayed for several years before becoming a traveling salesman who sold goods to general stores. It proved a valuable experience.

Ward observed the ways of rural life. Farmers, he soon learned, often exchanged news and indulged in a little gossip at the country store. He heard the farmers' complaints that prices were too high and selections too limited. Ward had a novel idea. Why not sell directly to the farmers via the mail? No one had ever done it before, but he felt it was worth the risk. By avoiding the cost of a middleman, he would be able to save money which, in turn, he could pass along to the customers in the form of lower prices.

In 1872 Ward opened a small mail-order dry goods business on North Clark Street and, within two years, issued his first catalog. His enlightened policies—a return of goods was allowed—virtually ensured success. The business expanded and the catalog grew. By 1890 the company moved into a building at the corner of Michigan and Madison which, says historian Nina Baker, became "the showplace of Michigan Avenue." Chicagoans flocked downtown to see its six steam elevators and gleaming marble lobby. In 1899 the structure was enlarged with the addition of a tower, capped by the "Spirit of Progress," a weathervane in the form of a seventeen-foot statue of a young girl that came to symbolize the company. In 1908 a new home was built at

Chicago and Larrabee Avenues. By World War I, Montgomery Ward and Company had established itself as an American institution.

Ward bought property on Michigan Avenue. From his office he could see Grant Park, which in those days was used primarily as a dumping ground, littered, as it was, with squatters' shacks, railroad sheds, freight cars, and assorted debris. Incensed, Ward waged a one-man campaign to protect the lakefront from commercial development.

Increasingly, Ward devoted less and less time to his business, although he still acted as president of the company. His utmost priority was maintaining an unobstructed lakefront by keeping Grant Park between Randolph and 11th Streets clear of structures. Ward often took matters into his own hands—literally. If he saw someone lugging debris into the lakefront area, he would send his lawyers down to the scene immediately.

Eventually Ward took his battle against developers to save the lakefront into the courts—at his own expense and frequently requesting court injunctions—in an effort to preserve the park for the people of Chicago. Many citizens, however, did not agree with his methods or honor his quest. In a rare interview Ward told a newspaper reporter, "I think there is not another man in Chicago who would have spent the money I have spent in this fight. . . . I fought for the poor people of Chicago—not the millionaires."

In 1897 the Supreme Court declared that no building with the exception of the Art Institute could be erected on the strip of property between Michigan Avenue and the lake.

Ward retired in 1901. In 1907 he bequeathed $8 million toward the construction of what would later become the Field Museum of Natural

History. Following his death, Ward's wife endowed $9 million to Northwestern University for the establishment of a medical and a dental school.

Ward died in 1913 of pneumonia in Highland Park, Illinois. He was buried in Rosehill Cemetery.

Unlike its chief competitor, Sears, Roebuck and Company, Ward's was slow to enter the retail market. Management opened retail outlets initially in small to mid-sized cities. It was not until much later that the company felt confident to compete with the large department stores in the big cities. Ward's State Street store, for example, did not open until 1957.

See also: Marshall Field, Potter Palmer, Richard W. Sears

Further reading: Baker, Nina. *Big Catalogue: The Life of Aaron Montgomery Ward* (1956); Boorstin, Daniel J. "A. Montgomery Ward's Mail-Order Business," *Chicago History* (Spring/Summer 1983); Latham, Frank B. *1872–1972 A Century of Serving Customers: The Story of Montgomery Ward* (1972); Wille, Lois. *Forever Open, Clear and Free: The Historic Struggle for Chicago's Lakefront* (1972).

Harold Washington

Politician

born: April 15, 1922
Chicago, Illinois
died: November 25, 1987
Chicago, Illinois

The election of Harold Washington as Chicago's first black mayor in 1983 united the disparate elements of the black population into a collective whole. From ghetto street children to middle-class professionals, Washington's appeal was monolithic and cut across economic and social lines. Within the African-American community—and indeed, even outside it—Washington was a genuine folk hero.

Photograph reprinted with permission from the *Chicago Sun-Times*.

Washington was born in Cook County Hospital in 1922, the fourth child of Roy and Bertha Washington. He once described his father, a lawyer and minister, as his "one and only hero in life." Roy Washington attended law school at night and worked full time in the Union Stockyards, and he instilled in his inquisitive son a love of learning. Young Harold started reading before he was four years old. Washington spent his formative years at a number of South Side addresses in the heart of the Black Belt: 3936 South Grand Boulevard (now King Drive), across the street from the famous Grand Terrace nightclub; 3936 South Parkway; 4507 South Vincennes Avenue; 4444 South Indiana Avenue; and 111 East 44th Street. After graduating from DuSable High School, Washington joined the Civilian Conservation Corps for six months. In 1940 he got a job in the freezer department of Wilson and Company, the meatpackers, and two years later he enlisted in the army.

Upon returning to Chicago, Washington enrolled at Roosevelt College, a new institution that boasted open enrollment for blacks. In 1948 Washington was unanimously elected president of his class. In 1952 he graduated from Northwestern University Law School. He was admitted to the Illinois bar the following year.

Washington learned about politics from his father, a former precinct captain. In 1954 he joined the 3rd Ward democratic organization as corporation counsel. The new ward committeeman, Ralph Metcalfe, gave Washington a chance to revive an organization called the Young Democrats, whose purpose was to attract young professionals into machine politics. Within a few months Washington developed the Young Democrats into the largest minority political organization in town.

In 1964 Washington was elected to the Illinois House of Representatives. During those years he straddled the fence on several key issues, trying to step gingerly between independent action and party loyalty. He sponsored or cosponsored bills that forbade realtors, banks, and savings and loan associations from discrimination on the basis of race, creed, or color. In 1969, one year after the assassination of Dr. Martin Luther King, Jr., in Memphis, Washington introduced legislation to celebrate the fallen civil right leader's birthday in Illinois. Gov. Dan Walker finally signed the bill into law in 1973.

The rise of the civil rights movement in the 1960s, coupled with years of benign neglect under the regular Democratic organization—white leaders took black voters for granted—led to anger and resentment in the African-American community. For the first time, black independent candidates thought the unthinkable—that a black candidate, under proper circumstances, could actually defeat the machine.

The African-American community faced its first test when Mayor Richard J. Daley died on December 20, 1976. Alderman Wilson Frost, an African-American ally of Daley and president pro tempore of the city council, declared that he was—adhering to the chain of command—the acting mayor of the city. But Daley supporters refused to accept Frost. Instead they locked the door to the late mayor's city hall office and installed guards outside to discourage intruders. When the city council convened the next day, the members elected a white alderman, Michael J. Bilandic, of the 11th Ward, by a lopsided vote of 45-2. Outraged at the treatment of Frost, the Committee for a Black Mayor—which included Rev. Jesse Jackson, Metcalfe, and Cecil Partee—assembled a list of potential candidates. Among those

considered were Roland Burris, Erwin France, Frost, Jackson, Metcalfe, Washington, and Partee. After serious deliberation, the committee made their choice: Harold Washington.

During the special mayoral election held in April of 1977, Washington only received 11 percent of the vote—African-Americans didn't support him because they didn't think he could win a general election, and whites simply didn't know who he was. Washington realized that his candidacy was little more than a symbolic protest against the policies of city hall rather than a serious attempt to win the mayor's seat. That attempt would have to wait for another day; meanwhile, the seeds of discontent had been assiduously planted.

The black community pulled further and further away from the regular Democratic organization. When Washington was slated for a vacant state senate seat in 1977, he won easily. In 1980 he defeated incumbent Bennett Stewart—long considered a yes man in the black community—for U.S. representative from the 1st Congressional District. He was reelected to a second term in 1982.

By 1983, straw polls indicated that the African-American community was ready to run a candidate for mayor again. Washington, who enjoyed his work in Congress and didn't think the time was right, reluctantly agreed to run. He defeated incumbent mayor Jane Byrne and state's attorney Richard M. Daley in the Democratic primary. But faced with the prospect of supporting a black candidate for mayor, many white Democrats bolted the party and voted for Bernard Epton, a white Republican. In addition, Washington's conviction of failure to file his federal income tax forms for four years—he served thirty-six days in Cook County Jail in 1972—made more than a few voters

uneasy. Nevertheless, in April of 1983, Harold Washington did what many thought was the impossible. He became the first African-American mayor in Chicago history.

Washington's first term in office was marred by intraparty squabbles over such issues as maintaining city services to promoting affirmative action programs. The mayor's forces—the Washington 21—consisted of sixteen blacks and five whites, while the opposition—the Vrdolyak 29—consisted of twenty-eight whites, led by 10th Ward alderman Edward Vrdolyak, and one Latino. Nicknamed "Council Wars" by Chicago comic Aaron Freeman, the struggle in the city council chambers severely compromised Washington's ability to govern. Even two years into his term, the Vrydolak 29 refused to confirm Washington's nominees for various boards and committees.

In December of 1982, U.S. District Judge Thomas R. McMillen ordered the city to draw a new map, creating new ward boundaries that would accommodate four additional wards—two black and two Latino. In May of 1984 the 7th U.S. Court of Appeals ruled that McMillen did not go far enough and ordered the redrawing of boundaries to properly reflect the black and Latino majorities to five wards. In December of 1985, Judge Charles R. Norgle of the U.S. District Court ordered that a special election be held in March of 1986. This election broke the stalemate, and Washington gained control of the city council.

In 1987 Washington ran for reelection. While not as vicious or racially hostile as the campaign four years earlier, the election did have its share of troubling racial overtones, augmented by a disconcerting amount of party switching.

But Washington didn't have much time to enjoy his second term. In November of 1987 he was stricken with a massive heart attack while working in his office.

The body of the late mayor lay in state in the rotunda of city hall. Thousands of mourners waited outside in the rain to offer their last respects and thousands more packed into Christ Universal Temple, at 11901 South Ashland Avenue, for the funeral service on Monday, November 30. The funeral procession then weaved through South Side neighborhoods en route to the burial site in Oak Woods Cemetery, 1035 East 67th Street. From 119th Street to Vincennes Avenue, 71st Street to Cottage Grove Avenue, people waved, wept, and offered a silent prayer.

Washington served four years and seven months in office. During that time he savored many victories and endured many defeats. Among his triumphs: four years of a balanced budget; the institution of the city's first Ethics Ordinance; collective bargaining in city hiring; construction of a central library, currently near completion at State and Van Buren Streets and named in his honor; a renewed commitment to the neighborhoods; and an increased representation of women and minorities in city government.

Yet there was much left to be done—the Chicago Housing Authority and school reform were also on the Washington agenda. Despite a spate of biographies published following his death, the final word has yet to be written on the late mayor. Historians will be debating his accomplishments—and the exact meaning of the Washington legacy—for a long time to come.

See also: Richard J. Daley, Ralph Metcalfe

Further reading: Grimshaw, William J. "Harold Washington: The Enigma of the Black Political Tradition" in *The Mayors: The Chicago Political Tradition,* Green, Paul M. and Melvin G. Holli, eds. (1987); Holli, Melvin and Paul M. Green. *The Making of a Mayor, Chicago 1983: Harold Washington* (1983); Levinsohn, Florence H. *Harold Washington: A Political Biography* (1983); Miller, Alton. *Harold Washington: The Mayor, The Man* (1989); Travis, Dempsey J. *An Autobiography of Black Politics* (1987); Travis, Dempsey J. *Harold—The People's Mayor: An Authorized Biography of Mayor Harold Washington* (1989).

Muddy Waters

Musician

born: April 4, 1915
Rolling Fork, Mississippi
died: April 30, 1983
Westmont, Illinois

When Muddy Waters added an electric guitar to the Mississippi Delta blues, he created a musical revolution whose reverberations are still being felt. An entire generation of young, white musicians from the Rolling Stones to Rod Stewart found inspiration in his raw, unpolished sounds.

Photograph by Ray Flerlage.

A sharecropper's son, McKinley Morganfield began playing harmonica and singing at family gatherings when he was still a young boy. He didn't take up guitar until he was seventeen. Early musical influences included such seminal bluesmen as Son House and Robert Johnson. According to musical legend, he received his famous sobriquet because he liked to play in a muddy creek near his home.

In the early 1940s folklorists Alan Lomax and John Work traveled through the South making field recordings of traditional music for the Library of Congress. Waters was working on the plantation of Col. William Stovall near Clarksdale, Mississippi, when the two researchers captured his raw blues on tape.

In 1943 Waters settled in Chicago, joining the thousands of other African-Americans who moved to the great cities of the North in search of a better life. But unlike his fellow migrants, Waters had every intention of becoming a professional musician.

Postwar Chicago had an active club scene, especially along South 43rd Street. Sonny Boy Williamson I, Lonnie Johnson, Roosevelt Sykes, Big Maceo, Tampa Red, Memphis Minnie, and "Big" Bill Broonzy attracted a substantial following, and older players like Arthur "Big Boy" Crudup, Sunnyland Slim (Albert Luandrew), and Robert Nighthawk (Robert McCollum) performed late into the night. Waters got a job during the day in the shipping department of a paper factory, loading and unloading trucks. In the evening, he played house parties around town. At first Waters stayed with friends at 3652 South Calumet Avenue. Then he lived with a cousin at 1857 West 13th Street on the West Side before

finding his own place a few houses down at 1851 West 13th Street. He lived at 4339 South Lake Park Avenue during the fifties and sixties.

Broonzy took the young Mississippian under his wing, while Sunnyland Slim arranged a recording session with Chess's Aristocrat label. In April of 1948 Waters recorded "Rollin' Stone," "I Can't Be Satisfied," and "I Feel Like Going Home." He also made other connections, hooking up with Eddie Boyd, Blue Smitty, and Jimmy Rogers. In the fifties, he had several R&B hits including "Hoochie Coochie Man," "Mannish Boy," and "Got My Mojo Working." He worked with such notable musicians as Junior Wells, Buddy Guy, Otis Spann, James Cotton, Willie Dixon, Hubert Sumlin, Earl Hooker, and Big Walter Horton. The brash sound of Waters's brand of urban blues ensured that the music would thrive in Chicago's loud and raucous clubs.

White musicians discovered blues in the late 1950s and early 1960s. In Chicago, Paul Butterfield and Mike Bloomfield began playing the blues, influenced partly by English musicians who had picked it up and partly by an older generation of black bluesmen. This blues revival revived the careers of many bluesmen, including Muddy Waters. Waters made extensive tours of Europe, and in 1960 he appeared at the Newport Jazz Festival. He became an "overnight sensation" when he opened for the Rolling Stones.

"I always wanted to be great. I always wanted to be known cross-country, not like an ordinary person who just lives and dies," Waters said in 1981.

The bluesman died in 1983 in his Westmont, Illinois, home. He was sixty-eight. In 1984 a musical biography, *Muddy Waters: The Hoochie Coochie Man,* by Jimmy Tillman and Jackie Taylor enjoyed a successful run at the Jane Addams Center.

In August of 1985 the Chicago City Council named the stretch of South 43rd Street between Oakenwald Avenue and State Street Muddy Waters Drive.

See also: "Big" Bill Broonzy, Leonard Chess, Sonny Boy Williamson I [appendix], Howlin' Wolf

Further reading: Charters, Samuel B. *The Bluesmen* (1967); Guralnick, Peter. *Feel Like Going Home: Portraits in Blues and Rock 'n Roll* (1981); Keil, Charles. *Urban Blues* (1966); Palmer, Robert. *Deep Blues* (1981); Rowe, Mike. *Chicago Breakdown* (1975); Shaw, Arnold. *Honkers and Shouters: The Golden Years of Rhythm and Blues* (1978).

Johnny Weissmuller

Swimmer/Actor

born: June 2, 1904
Windber, Pennsylvania
died: January 20, 1984
Acapulco, Mexico

Sportswriters often called Peter John Weissmuller the greatest swimmer of the twentieth century. During his career, Weissmuller set sixty-seven world records and won five Olympic gold medals. On the screen, he became internationally known as the man who played "Tarzan" and "Jungle Jim."

Photograph reprinted with permission from the *Chicago Sun-Times.*

Shortly after Weissmuller was born in 1904 in Pennsylvania, his Austrian parents moved to Chicago. Weissmuller grew up on the North Side and lived at 1921 North Cleveland Avenue. He was an altar boy at St. Michael Church, 458 West Eugenie Street. When he contracted polio at age nine, doctors recommended swimming as therapy. At fifteen, Weissmuller attracted the attention of Bill Bachrach, swimming coach at the Illinois Athletic Club (IAC). Scouting for good swimmers one day, Bachrach saw the lithe Weissmuller with friends at Lake Michigan. Impressed, he invited him to swim a few laps in the IAC pool. Bachrach wasted no time in signing him up as a member and began offering him swimming lessons. The relationship apparently worked, for Bachrach became Weissmuller's coach, mentor, and friend. In August of 1921 Weissmuller won the 50- and 220-yard national championships.

At the 1924 Olympics in Paris, Weissmuller set world records in the 100- and 400-meter freestyle events, and four years later, at the Olympic games in Amsterdam, he won the 100-meter race. Weissmuller retired from swimming in 1929. By that time he held every world freestyle record.

In 1930 Weissmuller was working out at a Hollywood Athletic Club pool when he was seen by novelist Cyril Hume, who at the time was working on a screenplay adaptation of Edgar Rice Burrough's *Tarzan.* Weissmuller passed the screen test and a movie career was born. "I went to the back lot at MGM. They gave me a G-string and said, 'Can you climb a tree? Can you pick up that girl?' I could do all that," Weissmuller once recalled.

Although not the first, Weissmuller was the screen's most popular *Tarzan.* He made a dozen *Tarzan* movies during a seventeen-year period beginning with *Tarzan the Ape Man* in 1935

and ending with *Tarzan and the Mermaids* in 1948. Since the actor's lines amounted to little more than "Me Tarzan, you Jane," acting in front of the camera was hardly a challenge. The economic rewards were large, but he grew weary of portraying the monosyllabic, chest-beating, tree-climbing ape man. "I've been wearing animal skin scanties too long," he explained. Instead, he turned, in 1948, to another woodland character, "Jungle Jim," only this time he was allowed to wear clothes. He made a number of "Jungle Jim" movies during the forties and fifties, including *Jungle Jim* (1948) and *Jungle Jim in the Forbidden Land* (1952) until "Jungle Jim" moved to television in 1958.

When his television career subsided in 1968, Weissmuller promoted health food stores and cocktail lounges. In the early 1960s he returned to the Chicago area as vice-president of public relations for the General Pool Corporation in Addison, Illinois.

In 1950 the Associated Press rated Weissmuller the greatest swimmer of the last half century.

In October of 1983 Weissmuller was inducted into the U.S. Olympic Hall of Fame.

Weissmuller, who had a history of heart trouble, suffered a series of strokes in 1977. An invalid since 1979, Weissmuller died in Acapulco, Mexico, in 1984 at age seventy-nine. He was buried there. A memorial mass was held several days later at St. Michael Church, the Weissmuller family church.

See also: Edgar Rice Burroughs

Further reading: Weissmuller, Johnny. *Water, World and Weissmuller* (1964).

Ida B. Wells

Social Reformer

born: July 16, 1862
Holly Springs, Mississippi
died: March 25, 1931
Chicago, Illinois

A proud and courageous woman, Ida B. Wells fought against discrimination of all guises and demanded equal justice for African-Americans, often at great personal expense. Wells was a staunch suffragette, and she urged the then radical concept of integration as the best solution to the racial problem. Since she advocated so many causes, she came into close contact with many white reformers, including Jane Addams.

Photograph courtesy of the *Chicago Defender.*

Wells, the daughter of slaves, began teaching in a Mississippi country school at the age of fourteen. Later she moved to Memphis to teach. In 1884 she filed a lawsuit against the Chesapeake and Ohio railroad when the conductor told her she would have to ride in the smoking car, the section set aside for African-American passengers. Wells steadfastly refused to budge. She was then forcibly removed. She sued the railroad and won a $500 settlement on the grounds that the accommodations violated the separate but equal law. In 1887, however, the Supreme Court of Tennessee reversed the decision, declaring that the smoking car could be considered first-class accommodation—by "colored" standards.

Wells began writing for church papers when she was invited to join the staff of the African-American weekly, the *Memphis Free Speech and Headlight.* Eventually she bought a one-third interest. An outspoken woman, she once publicly criticized the Memphis school system for their segregationist policies. As a result, she was dismissed from her teaching post in 1891.

By this time, Wells had discovered the power of the press. She shortened the name of the Memphis newspaper to the *Free Speech* and continued to write against discrimination. In 1892, after three young African-American businessmen—Thomas Moss, Calvin McDowell, and Lee Stewart—were lynched in Memphis, she initiated a newspaper campaign against the perpetrators and the white population that tacitly stood by in silence. She made many enemies in Memphis. When her newspaper office was burned to the ground, Wells moved to New York City where she became a staff writer for the *New York Age,* an African-American publication. She lectured throughout major American cities on the plight of the African-American and made two visits to Great Britain. In 1893 Wells visited Chicago to attend the World's Columbian Exposition. At that time the African-American population of the city, according to historian Allan H. Spear, numbered less than fifteen thousand. By 1915, however, the figure had risen to over fifty thousand and the first indications of a recognizable black community began to emerge on the South and West Sides.

Wells campaigned vigorously during the fair for a pavilion to honor the accomplishments of African-Americans. Her proposal was turned down. Thus, along with Frederick Douglass, Ferdinand L. Barnett, and I. Garland Penn, she authored a scathing eighty-one-page booklet, *Why the Colored American Is Not in the World's Columbian Exposition,* attacking city officials. Ten thousand copies were circulated at the fair.

In August of 1894, Wells settled permanently in Chicago, and on June 27, 1895, she married Ferdinand L. Barnett, a Chicago lawyer and the first black Cook County assistant state's attorney. She contributed to the *Conservator,* her husband's newspaper and the first African-American newspaper in the city. In 1895 she published *A Red Record: Tabulated Statistics and Alleged Causes of Lynchings in the United States, 1892–1893–1894.* In 1910 Wells founded and became president of the Negro Fellowship League, an organization with offices at 3005 South State Street, that found employment, coordinated social services, and provided housing for African-Americans, especially newly arrived migrants from the South. From 1913 to 1916, she was a probation officer of the Chicago municipal court.

When it came to justice, Wells refused to compromise. A critic of Booker T. Washington's "separate but equal" accommodationism theory, Wells instead encouraged integration. For this reason, too, she attacked the policies of W. E. B. DuBois's Niagara Movement and of the National Association for the Advancement of Colored People (NAACP) as being too moderate. Unlike Washington and DuBois, Wells believed it would take more than economic improvement to eradicate racism. "We must educate the white people out of their 250 years of slave history," she wrote in her autobiography.

In 1930 Wells became an independent candidate for state senator, running against Democrat Warren B. Douglas and Republican Adelbert H. Roberts. She placed a distant third.

Wells, who lived at 3624 South King Drive and later at 328 East Garfield Boulevard, died in Chicago of uremic poisoning in March of 1931. She was sixty-eight.

In December of 1989, public television broadcast *Ida B. Wells: A Passion for Justice*, a critically acclaimed one-hour documentary of her life and work.

See also: Robert S. Abbott, Jane Addams

Further reading: Duster, Alfreda M., ed. *Crusade for Justice: The Autobiography of Ida B. Wells* (1970); Spear, Allan H. *The Making of a Negro Ghetto 1890–1920* (1967).

William A. Wieboldt

Merchant

born: March 8, 1857
near Cuxhaven, Germany
died: December 9, 1954
Evanston, Illinois

William A. Wieboldt founded the chain of department stores that bore his name. Wieboldt parted with tradition when he became one of the first Chicago merchants to establish his stores in the neighborhoods away from the busy downtown shopping district. "My heart is in the neighborhood store," he once said. "Then I'm part of the community."

Photograph reprinted with permission from the *Chicago Sun-Times*.

Wieboldt's father, a farmer near Cuxhaven, Germany, died when William was two. As a youth, Wieboldt toiled long and hard on the farm, sometimes as much as fifteen hours a day. A letter from an uncle, W. R. Wieboldt, who had a store in Chicago, encouraged him to come to the New World to seek his fortune. He arrived in the United States in 1871 at the age of fourteen and found work at his uncle's store on Blue Island Avenue. Also employed in the store—in the millinery department—was another German-born youth, Anna Louisa Kruger. The couple courted and married in 1883.

Wieboldt's uncle then sent him to manage another store in Sheboygan, Wisconsin. The venture failed and Wieboldt returned to Chicago. After working for his uncle for twelve years, Wieboldt felt it was time for him to strike out on his own.

In 1883, with his wife as partner and $2,600 in savings, Wieboldt established a tiny general store—it was only twenty-five feet wide—on Indiana Avenue (now Grand Avenue) near Ashland Avenue and lived above the establishment in a small flat. The store turned a small profit during its first year. Encouraged, Wieboldt opened a larger store on Milwaukee Avenue at Paulina Street. That, too, prospered, and he established a chain of stores throughout Chicago, including a store at Lincoln and Belmont Avenues in 1912 and another outlet at Ashland Avenue and Monroe Street in 1925.

By locating stores in the neighborhoods, Wieboldt aimed to meet the needs of "the great middle millions of Chicagoland." Customers flocked to the full-service, budget-priced department stores.

In 1921 he and his wife established the Wieboldt Foundation, a charitable, civic, and educational organization that dispensed benefits to charitable institutions. He retired from active management of the store in 1923 but continued to attend board meetings. His son, Werner, succeeded him as president.

Wieboldt died in 1954 in Evanston Hospital. He was ninety-seven.

Faced with mounting financial problems and a rapidly dwindling customer base, Wieboldt Stores declared bankruptcy in 1987 and closed its remaining thirteen stores, including its flagship State Street store. The Wieboldt Foundation, the charitable wing of the company, is still in existence with offices at 53 West Jackson Boulevard.

See also: Marshall Field, Maurice Goldblatt

Further reading: Pacyga, Dominic A. and Ellen Skerrett. *Chicago: City of Neighborhoods* (1986).

Daniel Hale Williams

Physician

born: January 18, 1858
(other sources say January 18, 1856)
Hollidaysburg, Pennsylvania
died: August 4, 1931
Idlewild, Michigan

An eminent member of Chicago's African-American community in the 1890s, Daniel Hale Williams was the best known black physician in the country. Williams was also one of the founders of Provident Hospital in Chicago, the first interracial institution of its kind in the United States.

Photograph reprinted with permission from the *Chicago Sun-Times.*

Williams grew up in Pennsylvania, Illinois, and Wisconsin. Apprenticed to a shoemaker from the age of twelve, he held odd jobs until 1878 when he took up the study of medicine. He came to Chicago in 1880. Three years later he graduated from the Chicago Medical College (now a part of Northwestern University) and opened a practice at Michigan Avenue and 31st Street in a mixed black and white neighborhood on the South Side. The African-American population then numbered only ten thousand, according to Williams's biographer Helen Buckler. Williams treated both black and white patients.

At that time, black physicians were not permitted to work on the staffs of the city's hospitals so Williams co-founded a black hospital, Provident. Pleased with the interracial emphasis, such well-known and wealthy Chicagoans as Philip Danforth Armour, Marshall Field, and George Pullman contributed money to its construction. On May 4, 1891, Provident Hospital opened in a three-story, twelve-bed building on South Dearborn Street between 27th and 29th Streets. Families from throughout the neighborhood brought supplies—sheets, linen, sugar, soap, even loaves of bread. In 1896 the hospital moved to a larger building—it had sixty-five beds—at 36th and Dearborn Streets.

Williams considered Provident Hospital as a model, claims historian Allan H. Spear, "not of a Negro community institution, but of a venture in interracial cooperation." The advisory board consisted of mostly white Chicagoans, but the board of trustees and the hospital staff were predominantly African-American. In addition, Provident established the first nursing school for black women in the United States.

The first successful suture of the human heart occurred at Provident in 1893. Although there were reports of a similar operation performed in St. Louis two years before and perhaps even earlier by another physician, Williams is credited with being the first surgeon to conduct such an operation. In July of that year, a laborer, James Cornish, was brought to the hospital with a severe knife wound in his chest. Using primitive equipment and without the benefit of x-rays, Williams courageously entered the chest cavity and delicately sewed the lining of the heart with fine catgut. The operation made headlines across the world.

A perfectionist, Williams insisted on the highest of standards. Doctors and nurses were chosen solely on the basis of ability and included such outstanding physicians as Frank Billings and Christian Fenger, both white men. Unfortunately, this selectivity sometimes meant excluding African-American physicians, which caused some resentment in the black community. As a light-skinned African-American, Williams was sensitive to charges that Provident discriminated against darker-skinned blacks. Of mixed African-American, American Indian, and European ancestry, the light-skinned, red-haired Williams could have passed for white "as some of his relatives and forebears had," notes biographer Helen Buckler, yet, even so, he chose not to. He was never fully accepted by his fellow African-Americans, and he never could explain to his critics' satisfaction why virtually all of the staff appointments and nursing students were light-skinned. Provident physician and Williams's chief rival at the hospital, George Cleveland Hall, called Williams a "snob" who "doesn't seem to know what race he wants to belong to." Faced with mounting racial tension, white staff members

chose to leave so that by 1916 all the nurses and most of the physicians were black. Williams himself, weary of the situation, resigned in 1912.

From 1893 to 1898, Williams served as surgeon-in-chief of Freedman's Hospital in Washington, D.C. Here he established another school of nursing for African-Americans.

In 1898 Williams returned to Provident Hospital and simultaneously served on the staff of Cook County Hospital from 1900 to 1906 and at St. Luke's Hospital from 1907 to 1931. In 1895 he founded the National Medical Association, an organization for African-American physicians. Williams was the only black charter member of the American College of Surgeons. From 1899 until his death, he taught surgery ten days out of the year at Meharry Medical College, a black institution, in Nashville, Tennessee.

Williams died at his summer retreat in Idlewild, Michigan, in August of 1931.

In 1929 Provident Hospital relocated to 51st Street and Vincennes Avenue. In 1974 the trustees of Provident announced that the hospital would become an outpost of Cook County Hospital. In September of 1990 the Cook County Board purchased the three hundred-bed hospital—shuttered since September 1987, soon after it filed for bankruptcy—for $1 from the United States Department of Housing and Urban Development. Provident Hospital is scheduled to reopen in the fall of 1992.

See also: Frank Billings

Further reading: Buckler, Helen. *Doctor Dan: Pioneer in American Surgery* (1954); Spear, Allan H. *Black Chicago: The Making of a Negro Ghetto, 1890–1920* (1967).

Howlin' Wolf

Musician

born: June 10, 1910
West Point, Mississippi
died: January 10, 1976
Hines, Illinois

A character unique in the annals of blues music—indeed, any music—is Howlin' Wolf, a.k.a., Chester Arthur Burnett. Although his music was very much in the tradition of Charley Patton and Robert Johnson, nobody else sang quite like him. An energetic performer, a ferocious singer, this huge hulking man influenced a diverse group of white and black musicians, including the Paul Butterfield Blues Band, Cream, John Fogerty, the Rolling Stones, Johnny Shines, the Yardbirds, and Junior Wells. Like fellow Mississippian Muddy Waters, Wolf moved north to Chicago and helped forge a new sound in the blues—a sound that was loud, raucous, and brash. Although he never gained the level of Waters's fame, Howlin' Wolf helped shape the sound of post–World War II Chicago blues.

Photograph by Ray Flerlage.

One of six children, Wolf grew up on the Young and Mara plantation. He didn't pick up a guitar until he was almost eighteen. "At that time," he recalled, "I was working on the farm with my father, baling hay and driving tractors, fixing fences, picking cotton, and pulling corn. There was a lot of music around there, work songs." In the late twenties, Wolf met the enigmatic Charley Patton who lived on a nearby plantation and who gave him some rudimentary guitar lessons. Later he received informal coaching on the harmonica from Rice Miller (Sonny Boy Williamson II). Miller later married Wolf's stepsister, Mary. In the early 1930s Wolf traveled with legendary bluesman Robert Johnson.

In 1941 Wolf was drafted into the army. Based mostly in Seattle, Washington, he was frequently asked to entertain the troops, but he later admitted he never liked the experience.

After the war, Wolf returned to a life of farming until he formed his own band in the late forties. Popular around Arkansas and Mississippi, Wolf hosted his own radio broadcast on radio station KWEM in West Memphis, Arkansas, beginning in 1948. In the early 1950s, he recorded some sessions for Sam Phillips's Sun label and, then, with the Chicago-based Chess label. His early Chess recordings, "I Love My Baby" and "All Night Boogie," garnered little attention in the North but were popular in the South. Subsequent Chess records, which included "Evil Is Going On," "I'll Be Around," and "Forty Four"— all released in 1954—met much the same fate.

By the time Wolf had moved to Chicago, in late 1952, his style had matured. Critics have described it as a modern, almost jazzy style, accompanied by the singer's rough, intense vocals. Gradually his music began to soften. He experimented with a horn section and opted for slower rhythms. Wolf was a popular performer on the Chicago club circuit during the fifties and sixties. In 1968 he appeared at the University of Chicago Folk Festival and, by the mid-seventies, he was playing a double bill with another great bluesman, B. B. King, at the International Amphitheater, at 42nd and Halsted Streets.

Wolf recorded his first record, "Moanin' in the Midnight," in 1951. He enjoyed his first hit, the darkly brooding "No Place To Go," in 1954 and released "Smokestack Lightnin'" two years later, which remains a critical favorite. In the early 1960s, Wolf recorded a series of blues classics— many of them written by Willie Dixon—including "Wang Dang Doodle," "Back Door Man," "The Red Rooster," "I Ain't Superstitious," and "Goin' Down Slow."

In 1972 Wolf was awarded an honorary Doctor of Arts degree from Columbia College in Chicago.

In 1975 he entered the Veterans Administration Hospital in Hines, Illinois, and died of cancer early the next year. He was buried in Oakridge Cemetery in Hillside, Illinois.

See also: "Big" Bill Broonzy, Leonard Chess, Muddy Waters, Sonny Boy Williamson I [appendix]

Further reading: Guralnick, Peter. *Feel Like Going Home: Portraits in Blues and Rock 'n Roll* (1981); Harris, Sheldon. *Blues Who's Who: A Biographical Dictionary of Blues Singers* (1979); Palmer, Robert. *Deep Blues* (1981); Rowe, Mike. *Chicago Breakdown* (1975); Shaw, Arnold. *Honkers and Shouters: The Golden Years of Rhythm and Blues* (1978).

Frank Lloyd Wright

⚜

Architect

born: June 8, 1867
Richland Center, Wisconsin
died: April 9, 1959
Phoenix, Arizona

Frank Lloyd Wright, one of the great names of architecture, created a whole new style of American architecture that bore little resemblance to European models. Wright sought to achieve a natural balance between the landscape and manufactured materials. He adapted buildings to their environment. To Wright, everything was connected.

The son of William Wright and Anna Lloyd Jones, Frank Lloyd Wright was raised by his mother, who instilled in him an appreciation of art. After spending two years as a civil engineering student at the University of Wisconsin, he moved to Chicago to pursue a career in architecture. For five years he apprenticed with another great architect, Louis Sullivan. Wright worked with Sullivan on the design of the Auditorium Theater building.

In 1893 Wright opened his own practice in west suburban Oak Park, Illinois. His first project was the William H. Winslow house at 515 Auvergne Place in River Forest. Even then he utilized the innovative design that would make him famous. He used material in a new and exciting way—reinforced concrete, sheet metal, electric lighting, and stucco. Unlike the neoclassical styles of the nineteenth century or the steel and glass of the twentieth century, Wright chose to emphasize the organic foundation of architecture—the colors and textures of nature.

Wright developed a new type of architecture. The prairie style, characterized by overhanging eaves and wide roofs on low-lying houses, blended in with the flat, horizontal landscape of the Midwest. The prairie style produced a whole generation of architects. Among the most important Wright disciples are Walter Burley Griffin, George W. Maher, and George C. Nimmons.

In August of 1914, while working on the Midway Gardens entertainment center in Chicago, Wright received news that a deranged servant had burned Taliesin, his Spring Green, Wisconsin, retreat, to the ground and killed seven guests, including Wright's mistress.

In the aftermath of the tragedy, Wright found solace in his work. In 1915 he designed the Imperial Hotel in Tokyo, which was completed in 1922 and was the only major building to survive the earthquake of 1923. Other important Wright buildings include the Susan Lawrence Dana House in Springfield, Illinois (1903); Fallingwater, a private home in Bear Run, Pennsylvania (1936); Taliesin West in Scottsdale, Arizona (1938); the Johnson Wax Administration Building in Racine, Wisconsin (1936); and the Solomon R. Guggenheim Museum in New York City (1956).

As early as the 1920s Wright argued that modern cities were becoming filthy and uninhabitable places. During his last years, he made increasingly more outrageous remarks. "The modern city is a place for banking and prostitution and very little else," was a typical Wright comment of that period.

While such contemporary colleagues as Daniel H. Burnham and John Wellborn Root found fame designing commercial structures, Wright preferred to concentrate on private homes and experiment with interior design. Often the interior of a Wright-designed home was just as striking as its exterior, such as the innovative concept of confining the living and sleeping areas to one floor—without any doors or partitions—or his highly stylized dining room chairs. One of the most famous and universally admired residences in the world is the Robie House at 5757 South Woodlawn Avenue in Hyde Park (1909). With its broad overhanging roofs and long horizontal lines, the Robie House is considered the epitome of the prairie style.

West suburban Oak Park contains the largest concentration of Wright-designed buildings in the world. The Frank Lloyd Wright Historic District features a collection of twenty-five structures designed by the architect between 1895 and 1915. The Frank Lloyd Wright Home and Studio at Forest and Chicago Avenues, founded in 1974, sponsors lectures and walking tours, presents exhibitions, and operates the Gingko Bookshop. At Lake Street and Kenilworth Avenue is the Unity Temple, the only public building designed by Wright in Oak Park (1908). Some prominent Wright homes include the Edwin H. Cheney House, 520 North East Avenue in Oak Park (1904) and in Chicago, the James Charnley House at 1365 North Astor Street (1891), the Isadore Heller House at 5132 South Woodlawn Avenue (1896), and the Emil Bach House at 7415 North Sheridan Road (1915).

In the early 1930s Wright and his wife, Milanov, founded the Taliesin Fellowship, a residential architectural school, at their six-hundred-acre country estate in Spring Green, Wisconsin.

Wright died in 1959 at the age of ninety-one in Phoenix, Arizona. His work continues to inspire interest today. Reproductions of his tables and especially his tall-backed dining chairs remain popular while jewelry and scarves decorated with his designs find a ready market. Millionaire Thomas S. Monaghan, founder of the Domino's Pizza chain, reportedly owns the world's largest collection—approximately four hundred pieces—of Wright artifacts and decorative objects.

Among Wright's many books are *An Organic Architecture* (1939) and *An American Architecture* (1955).

See also: Daniel H. Burnham, Walter Burley Griffin [appendix], George W. Maher [appendix], Ludwig Mies van der Rohe, John Wellborn Root, Howard Van Doren Shaw, Louis Sullivan

Further reading: Eaton, Leonard K. *Two Chicago Architects and Their Clients: Frank Lloyd Wright and Howard Van Doren Shaw* (1969); Farr, Finis. *Frank Lloyd Wright: A Biography* (1961); Gill, Brendan. *Many Masks: A Life of Frank Lloyd Wright* (1987); Hoffman, Donald. *Frank Lloyd Wright's Robie House: The Illustrated Story of an Architectural Masterpiece* (1984); O'Gorman, James F. *Three American Architects: Richardson, Sullivan, and Wright, 1865–1915* (1991); Sprague, Paul E. *Guide to Frank Lloyd Wright & Prairie School Architecture in Oak Park* (1986); Twombly, Robert C. *Frank Lloyd Wright: An Interpretative Biography* (1973); Wright, Frank Lloyd. *An Autobiography* (1977).

John S. Wright

Pioneer

born: July 16, 1815
Sheffield, Massachusetts
died: September 26, 1874
Philadelphia, Pennsylvania

Called a visionary by his contemporaries, John Stephen Wright was an early Chicago booster. The city, he often wrote, was destined for greatness.

Born in Sheffield, Massachusetts, Wright was a precocious child. By the age of twelve he was studying algebra, Greek, and Latin at a nearby academy. At fourteen he was sent to a private school.

Wright first saw Chicago from the vantage point of a schooner when he and his father anchored near the mouth of the Chicago River in October of 1832. The boy envisioned a future city in the muddy squalor. His father was less optimistic, dismissed the frontier village—little more than a hamlet really—as a festering eyesore, and left it at that.

When the family eventually settled in the city, in 1833, the elder Wright built a general store and called it "The Prairie Store." Young Wright persuaded his father to let him buy several lots of land—forty-four acres south of 12th Street—for $35,000, according to Wright biographer Lloyd Lewis. Nearly two years later he was offered $50,000 for less than half the land. By the end of 1836, Wright owned 7,000 acres, worth an estimated $200,000. Twenty years later it was worth a whopping $1.7 million. In 1836 he purchased a warehouse on Water Street and engaged in the shipping business at the insistence of his father, who encouraged his son to acquire a proper vocation.

The winter of 1836–1837 brought word from Eastern financial markets of a possible credit crunch. Hard times, it was said, were on its way. Despite the dire warnings, Wright forged ahead with his plans and opened the warehouse on South Water Street in May 1837. When the Panic of 1837 struck with its full and devastating force, Wright, like many other Chicagoans, lost everything— his land, his business, and his newly acquired wealth.

In 1839 Wright formed the Union Agricultural Society "for the sole purpose of instruction and science, and improvements in scientific and practical agriculture and the mechanical arts in the counties of LaSalle, Will, Cook, McHenry, and Kane," and he embarked upon a career in public service.

Wright encouraged the trustees of the society to establish a farmers' newspaper—nonpolitical and nonpartisan. He, in turn, became a reporter, an editor, and the publisher of the agricultural monthly.

Wright also edited the weekly *Union Agriculturalist and Western Prairie Farmer,* which covered the usual farm news but also featured events and happenings in the city. Its slogan was "Farmers, Write for Your Paper." In 1843 the name was shortened to the *Prairie Farmer.* In 1870 he published his book, *Chicago: Past, Present, Future,* an early history of the city.

Wright was clearly a man ahead of his time. He campaigned for higher salaries for teachers—both male and female. He was an early advocate for developing Chicago as a railroad hub, and he worked tirelessly to improve Chicago's schools. He not only predicted that Chicago would one day be a great meatpacking center, but he also prophesied in 1837 that the city would eventually surpass the population of Pittsburgh. In less than a decade, that prediction proved true. In 1861 he declared that Chicago's population would even surpass Philadelphia's before the turn of the century. Wright was correct again.

By the early 1850s Wright was looking for other economic opportunities. He saw a future in the reaper and became convinced that this was the business for him. He built a factory and began manufacturing reapers; in so doing he became the chief rival of Cyrus H. McCormick, the "reaper king."

On the eve of the Civil War, Wright formed the Land Investment Company and resumed speculating in real estate. He felt the war would benefit the city greatly. "No earthly power," he wrote, "not even the dissolution of the Union, can divert from Chicago the business and the traffic of the great Northwest."

Even the Chicago Fire of 1871 could not quench Wright's enthusiasm. "Nothing of the least consequence to the future of the city perished in the flames," he claimed. "Only buildings and perishable property to be at once replaced." His optimistic vision, however, was not shared by Eastern capitalists.

Frustrated by the cold shoulder he received from Eastern businessmen, Wright fell into a deep depression. By Christmas of 1871 his mental condition had deteriorated so badly that he was placed in an asylum for the insane in Boston. Upon his release, he roamed around the city—he refused to return to Chicago—preaching that a promised land lay in the Midwest to anyone who would listen. Few did.

Wright spent his last days in and out of various insane asylums on the East Coast and in the Midwest. He died on September 26, 1874, in Philadelphia. His body was returned to Chicago and buried in Rosehill Cemetery.

See also: William Bross, Gurdon S. Hubbard, Cyrus H. McCormick

Further reading: Lewis, Lloyd. *John S. Wright: Prophet of the Prairies* (1941).

Richard Wright

Novelist

born: September 4, 1908
near Natchez, Mississippi
died: November 28, 1960
Paris, France

*Richard Wright began his writing career in Chicago and set his best known novel, **Native Son**, in his adopted city. He believed that good writing could make a difference, that good writing could change the world. From 1940 to 1960, Wright was the most famous African-American writer in the world.*

Photograph reprinted with permission from the *Chicago Sun-Times*.

Richard Wright was born on a Mississippi cotton plantation. His grandfather was a slave, and his father an illiterate sharecropper. Wright endured a harsh, poverty-stricken childhood in the rural South. His father left when he was five, and his mother became an invalid when he was ten. Consequently, Wright was shuffled from orphanage to orphanage until he struck out on his own at fifteen and moved to Memphis. For several years he roamed the country. When he arrived in Chicago in 1927, he lived briefly with his aunt in a South Side rooming house and found work as a clerk in the central post office, a dishwasher at a North Side cafe, and a porter at Michael Reese Hospital. He also attended writing classes and Communist party functions, but most of all he dreamed.

Wright joined the Chicago John Reed Club, a leftist literary group, and he eventually became the club's secretary. The club provided the emotional support that he and other like-minded writers could not find elsewhere. In 1935 Wright wrote guidebooks for the Illinois Federal Writers' Project and, for several months in 1936, he worked as a publicist for the Chicago Federal Negro Theater. In 1937 he moved to New York, and when World War II ended, he settled in Paris in 1947. "There is more freedom in one square block of Paris than in all of the United States," he declared.

His first book *Uncle Tom's Children: Four Novellas*, published in 1938, launched his writing career. In 1939 he received a Guggenheim fellowship that enabled him to complete a full-length novel, *Native Son*, in 1940. The book—based partly on his own experiences and partly on the true case of Robert Nixon, a black man electrocuted in 1938 for the murder of a white girl—is a bitter indictment of racial injustice in America. It was acclaimed as an intense, heartfelt, and brutally honest portrayal of a young African-American convicted of murder.

Native Son was an immediate success and the first novel by a black writer to be chosen as a Book-of-the-Month Club selection. Reactions to *Native Son* from the African-American community were mixed, however. Although proud that a member of their race had met with literary success, a number of blacks chafed at Wright's decision to make such a violent figure as Bigger Thomas the protagonist. They not only feared that his behavior confirmed—and fanned—the worst racist prejudice but also perpetuated the image of African-Americans as brutes. The response from the white mainstream press was less harsh. Fanny Butcher, literary critic of the *Chicago Tribune*, called *Native Son* "an astonishing piece of work."

The book spawned several stage and film versions. In 1941 a dramatization at New York's famous Mercury Theater, produced by John Houseman and directed by Orson Welles, opened on Broadway. In 1950 Wright himself portrayed the lead character in the film version. Shot on location in Chicago in 1949 by a French director, the movie received poor distribution in the United States. When it finally played Chicago two years later, it was panned as a well-intentioned but amateurish production. In 1978 the Goodman Theater, under the direction of newly installed artistic director Gregory Mosher, presented a critically acclaimed interpretation of Wright's book, and in 1987 another movie version was released featuring a stellar cast, including

Geraldine Page, Oprah Winfrey, Matt Dillon, and newcomer Victor Love as Bigger Thomas. Film exteriors were shot around 63rd Street and Greenwood Avenue.

The largely autobiographical *Black Boy*, published in 1945, further enhanced Wright's reputation as a major writer. But, like *Native Son*, it also inspired strong reactions.

Among Wright's other works were *The Outsider* (1953); *The Long Dream* (1958); and *Eight Men*, a posthumously released collection of short stories (1961), and *Lawd Today* (1963), a novel about an African-American postal worker in Chicago. Wright also wrote non-fiction, including *Twelve Million Black Voices* (1941), *Black Power* (1954), *The Color Curtain* (1956), *Pagan Spain* (1957), and *White Man, Listen!* (1957).

Wright lived a life of self-imposed exile on the periphery of society. Racial discrimination intensified his profound sense of isolation. Not only did he feel out of place within white mainstream society, he also felt alienated among his own people. An idealist at heart, he believed that somewhere on earth there was a land where men and women of all races and creeds lived together in peace and prosperity. Though he never found his utopia, he did find comfort in the permanence of the word and in his belief that the written word was the most powerful weapon of all because it could, in the right hands, effect social change. It was this sweet optimism that gave him hope and a sense of purpose even in his darkest moments.

Wright died of a heart attack complicated by dysentery in November of 1960 in Paris. He was fifty-two.

During the past decade there has been a renewal of interest in Wright's work. His novels are still considered classics of American literature.

See also: Nelson Algren, Jack Conroy, Willard Motley

Further reading: Drew, Bettina. *Nelson Algren: A Life On the Wild Side* (1989); Gayle, Addison. *Richard Wright, Ordeal of a Native Son* (1980); Webb, Constance. *Richard Wright: A Biography* (1968); Wright, Ellen and Michael Fabre. *Richard Wright Reader* (1978); Wright, Richard. *American Hunger* (1977).

William Wrigley, Jr.

Baseball Club Owner/ Entrepreneur

born: September 30, 1861
Philadelphia, Pennsylvania
died: January 26, 1932
Phoenix, Arizona

William Wrigley, Jr., founded a chewing gum empire, bought the Chicago Cubs, and built Wrigley Field. A classic underachiever during his early years in Philadelphia—he dropped out of grammar school—Wrigley nevertheless had ambition, smarts, and determination. A tireless promoter, the extroverted Wrigley once said, "anybody can make gum. Selling it is the problem."

Wrigley ran away from home at age eleven and got a job selling newspapers in New York before returning a few weeks later to his native Philadelphia. His father, a soap manufacturer, found him a job stirring a vat of soap in his factory at a salary of $1.50 a week. Although only thirteen, young Wrigley pleaded with his father to make him a traveling soap salesman. The older man reluctantly agreed.

Wrigley made a grand salesman—eager, aggressive, and hard-working. In 1901 he moved to Chicago to open a branch of the family firm and expanded his line to include lamps, clocks, guns, fountain pens, cameras, safety razors, accident insurance, and baking powder. Soon the baking power outsold everything else so that in 1892 Wrigley abandoned the soap line altogether. As an additional incentive, Wrigley offered two packs of chewing gum with each can of ten-cent baking powder. Encouraged by the positive response, Wrigley decided to discontinue the baking powder and began work on what would become a new empire—chewing gum.

Early brand names for the gum were Vassar, Lotta (as in "a lotta gum"), and Sweet Sixteen Orange. In 1893, operating out of a nondescript storeroom on East Kinzie Street, Wrigley introduced Juicy Fruit and Wrigley's Spearmint. In 1898 he formed the William Wrigley, Jr., Company.

In 1911 Wrigley moved into an elegant mansion, originally built for a wealthy brewer named Joseph Theurer, at 2466 North Lakeview Avenue. Previously the family had lived in rather makeshift quarters—in the Plaza hotel, located at the corner of North Avenue and Clark Street and in a small apartment on North Dearborn Street near Burton Place.

In 1921 Wrigley sold the house to his son, Philip. The Theurer/Wrigley house was designated a Chicago landmark in August 1979.

Wrigley was one of the first Chicago businessmen to advertise on a grand scale, using billboards, advertising space on streetcars, and ads in the major newspapers. The Wrigley ad campaign was deceptively simple, "Tell 'em quick and tell 'em often." He borrowed lavishly to fund his expensive campaign. Business eventually picked up with Spearmint sales increasing to well over the one million mark the first year. By 1910 Wrigley's Spearmint was on its way to becoming America's favorite gum.

In 1912 Wrigley moved the plant to 35th Street and Ashland Avenue—where it still stands—in the newly created Central Manufacturing District (CMD), a planned industrial community in the McKinley Park neighborhood. Its presence encouraged other industries to locate there.

In 1919 Wrigley purchased Catalina Island in California for $2 million, sight unseen, and spent millions more developing the fabled isle. Several years later, he hired Chicago's best architects to construct the Wrigley Building on North Michigan Avenue, completed in 1924, to house the burgeoning chewing gum empire. In 1921 Wrigley became principal stockholder of the Chicago Cubs baseball team. In 1926 the Cubs' stadium, formerly called Weeghman Park, was changed to Wrigley Field.

Wrigley was quite an innovator when it came to business. He was the first manufacturer to give employees Saturday off, he provided free medical care to workers for injuries sustained on the job, and he offered life insurance for every employee.

Wrigley died in 1932 at his winter home in Phoenix at the age of seventy without attaining his life's ambition: seeing his beloved Cubs win a world championship. He was buried on Catalina Island.

Upon his father's death, Philip K. Wrigley assumed control of both the chewing gum business and the Chicago Cubs baseball club. In 1981 the Tribune Company bought the team.

See also: Charles A. Comiskey, Bill Veeck

Further reading: Zimmerman, William, Jr. *William Wrigley Jr., The Man and His Business, 1861–1932* (1935).

Charles Tyson Yerkes

Financier

born: June 25, 1837
Philadelphia, Pennsylvania
died: December 29, 1905
London, England

Charles Tyson Yerkes, an unscrupulous railroad baron, was at the center of a controversy that plagued Chicago for many years: the traction problem—private versus public ownership of the streetcar and elevated lines. Yerkes bribed virtually everyone to obtain franchise rights. The very core of Yerkes's corrupt empire was based on bribery and shady deals. "Buy old junk, fix it up a little, unload it on the other fellow," he once said. That was the Yerkes's way of doing business.

The son of a Philadelphia bank president, Yerkes entered the brokerage business in Philadelphia as a clerk. In 1859 he opened a brokerage house and in 1862 a banking house. He built a sizable fortune until a recession struck in 1871. Yerkes was convicted and sent to prison for embezzlement over the alleged mishandling of Philadelphia municipal funds. He served seven months and then resumed his career by investing in Philadelphia railroads and transit companies.

In 1882 Yerkes, ready for a new life in another city, moved to Chicago. By 1886 he had gained control of the city's streetcar lines and organized his own line, the North Chicago Street Railway. He replaced horse cars with trolley cars and built new lines. Yerkes made the easy money while his stockholders were left holding the bag—usually an empty one. Through sly manueverings and shady deals with corrupt politicians, including the nefarious aldermen from the 1st Ward, "Bathhouse" John Coughlin and Michael "Hinky Dink" Kenna, Yerkes obtained franchises. In addition to Coughlin and Kenna, his allies in city hall included Republican chieftain William Lorimer and Johnny Powers, the powerful alderman from the 19th Ward.

In 1895 Yerkes tried to pass a plan through the city council to extend his franchise of the transit lines, which included the newly constructed elevated lines, for another fifty years with no compensation to the city. Yerkes's forces then introduced the bill—the Allen bill—in the state legislature. The *Chicago Tribune* estimated that the passage of such an ordinance would cost the city a massive $150 million.

The Allen bill became law in 1897, but the public outcry was so severe that Yerkes decided to wait before renewing his franchises. Two years later he tried again, and nearly succeeded, until Mayor Carter Harrison II and the city council finally turned against him, fueled by spirited attacks from the Municipal Voters League. Pressure mounted for municipal control of the city's transit lines. Protests occurred. Newspaper accounts report of marching in the streets and angry mobs converging on city hall, threatening death to any alderman who sided with the unscrupulous traction king. Succumbing to the will of the people, the Illinois legislature finally repealed the law. A sulking Yerkes blamed his defeat on "socialists, anarchists, and newspapers."

In 1892 Yerkes donated $1 million to the University of Chicago for the construction of the Yerkes Observatory—still the world's largest refracting telescope—in Lake Geneva, Wisconsin, and in 1897 he bought the *Chicago Inter-Ocean* newspaper. Yerkes, who lived in a mansion at Michigan Avenue and 32nd Street, was also a serious art collector. His attempts at respectability did not alter his corrupt image, however. Newspapers continued to condemn him as a ruthless and deceitful opportunist.

Writers were fascinated by Charles Yerkes's power and personality. Novelist Theodore Dreiser's Cowperwood trilogy was inspired by Yerkes's life. The series consists of *The Financier* (1912), *The Titan* (1914), and *The Stoic* (1947).

In 1899 Yerkes sold his interest in the traction franchises, and the following year he moved to London, where he played a significant role in the creation of that city's subway system. He died there in 1905, having squandered most of his wealth.

In 1907 the traction problem was finally resolved when the streetcar operators agreed to give the city the option to buy at any time. Eventually a single public agency—the Chicago Transit Authority—was created in 1947.

Yerkes's turbulent career continues to generate interest. In 1988 two local playwrights, Michael C. Dorf and Claudia Howard Queen, collaborated on a musical play entitled *Titan*. Based on Dreiser's book of the same name, *Titan* chronicled the life and times of the traction king.

See also: John Peter Altgeld, John Coughlin, Theodore Dreiser, Carter Harrison II, Michael Kenna

Further reading: Ginger, Ray. *Altgeld's America: The Lincoln Ideal Versus Changing Realities* (1958); Kogan, Herman and Lloyd Wendt. *Lords of the Levee: The Story of Bathhouse John and Hinky Dink* (1943).

Arthur Young

Accountant

born: circa December 1863
Glasgow, Scotland
died: April 3, 1948
Macon, South Carolina

Arthur Young was arguably the most important and influential accountant in the city's history. He entered the profession when accounting was still in its infancy, yet within a short time the public accounting firm he founded, Arthur Young and Company—a member of the "Big Eight"—became one of the largest accounting firms in the country.

Photograph courtesy of Ernst and Young.

Young was born in Scotland, the son of a Glasgow shipbuilder. Educated at the prestigious Glasgow Academy, he received a master's degree from Glasgow University in 1883. After serving a three-year apprenticeship as a clerk in a Glasgow law firm, he returned to the university and received his law degree in 1887.

Young had plans to move to Edinburgh to practice law when he began exhibiting the first signs of deafness, a condition that would grow progressively worse. Heeding the advice of his doctor, who suggested he find a less stressful profession, Young left Scotland. He spent some time in Switzerland and then traveled to the warmer climate of Algiers. There he met an American businessman, Gordon Bennett, who encouraged him to immigrate to the United States.

Young arrived in America in 1890 and settled in New York. He found work at J. Kennedy Tod and Company, an international banking firm on Wall Street, which was run by a fellow Scotsman. Young spent four years at the firm until he decided to pursue a new profession—accounting—in a new city—Chicago.

In Chicago, Young met Charles W. Stuart, a comptroller of a Boston-owned copper company, who had also just moved to the city. Together, in 1894, they established their own public accounting firm in a one-room office in the Monadnock Building at 53 West Jackson Boulevard, with a starting capital of $500 and a staff of one stenographer.

When Young started, the accounting profession in the United States was virtually nonexistent. "There was no legal recognition of accountancy; in fact, it was not until 1896 that New York state formally recognized accountancy as a profession," he recalled in his autobiography.

Accountancy originated in Young's native Scotland when the Society of Accountants was created by a royal charter in Edinburgh in 1854. The state of Illinois did not recognize accounting as a legitimate profession until 1903—almost ten years after Young entered the field. Young was one of the first people in the state to become a certified public accountant.

In 1906 the firm dissolved when Young parted with Stuart "who," he explained tersely, "had proved an unsatisfactory partner." With his brother Stanley—also a graduate of Glasgow University—Young founded Arthur Young and Company. In 1915 the firm moved into larger quarters in the Borland Building at 105 South Lasalle Street.

The firm grew slowly but steadily. Young's main obstacle was locating trained accountants. Since accounting was such a new profession in the United States, very few universities and colleges taught accounting classes. In addition most businesses were reluctant to hire outside employees to handle their bookkeeping tasks—managers preferred to handle accounting matters in-house. Thus, Young was compelled to return to Scotland to recruit good accountants.

Young secured important clients during those early years, including Swift and Company, Crane and Company, and the William Wrigley, Jr., Company. Others would follow: Montgomery Ward and Company, Encyclopaedia Britannica, and Rand McNally.

In 1911 Young opened a New York branch, which became the home office of the company when Young moved there in 1917. Prior to 1921, the various branches were run as local partnerships, operated independently from one another. In 1921 Young decided to merge all the branches into a single partnership under one firm with Young assuming the position of senior partner. In 1923 the first overseas branches opened in London and Paris.

The firm weathered the Great Depression, although not without some difficulty. The advent of World War II brought several significant changes. The firm hired its first women accountants for example, in 1943. In 1957, its first woman partner, Mary Lanigar came aboard.

Young died in April of 1948 of viral pneumonia in South Carolina at the age of eighty-four. A history of the company, *Arthur Young and the Business He Founded,* was published the same year.

In 1956 the firm moved to the Harris Bank Building at 111 West Monroe Street and, later, as business continued to expand, into the IBM Plaza at 420 North Wabash Avenue. During the eighties, additional emphasis was placed on the firm's thriving consulting practices. The firm specialized in the Entrepreneurial Services concept, providing business advice to companies in virtually every industry.

On June 22, 1989, Arthur Young and Company and Ernst and Whinney—two of the country's largest accounting firms—merged to form Ernst and Young, with branches in more than one hundred American cities and over one hundred countries around the world. Following the merger, the new firm emerged as the top-ranking accounting company in the city, according to a *Crain's Chicago Business* poll, edging out the historic leader and long-time rival, Arthur Andersen and Company.

See also: Arthur Andersen

Further reading: Burton J. C., ed. *Arthur Young and the Business He Founded* (1948); Stevens, Mark. *The Big Eight: Inside America's Largest Accounting Firms* (1984).

Ella Flagg Young

Educator

born: January 15, 1845
Buffalo, New York
died: October 26, 1918
Washington, D.C.

Ella Flagg Young was not only the first woman superintendent of the Chicago public school system, she was also one of the best educators in the Midwest. Fair and conscientious, Young served as a role model for a generation of young women. In her speeches and in the classroom, she told her students—both girls and boys—that they could be whatever they wanted to be.

In 1858 Young came to Chicago with her parents. Two years later she enrolled at the Chicago Normal School. Young secured her first teaching position in 1862 when she was assigned to the Foster School. On Saturday mornings she attended teacher training sessions to learn the latest instruction methods and theories. In 1863 she transferred to the Brown School as assistant principal, and in 1865 she began training neophyte teachers at the Scammon School.

An efficient and conscientious administrator, Young quickly advanced in her profession. In 1876 she was elected principal of the Scammon School, and several years later, in 1879, she became head of the much larger Skinner School on the West Side.

Although women dominated the teaching professions during the 1870s at both the elementary and high school levels, men still pulled the strings and determined hiring practices. In 1879 half of the city's high school teachers and half of the elementary school teachers were women, notes Young's biographer Joan A. Smith.

In 1887 Young became assistant superintendent of the Chicago Public Schools. Two years later she was appointed to the state board of education. At the same time she furthered her own education when, in the fall of 1895, she enrolled in a seminar at the University of Chicago, where her professor was the noted scholar, John Dewey.

Young's work as a member of the board of education had taken its toll, however, and her relationship with the reigning superintendent of schools Benjamin Andrews had become rather strained. In June of 1899 she resigned her position as assistant superintendent. After leaving the University of Chicago, she spent some time abroad, traveling and visiting the various school systems in Europe. Upon her return to the U.S., she received her Ph.D. from the University of Chicago in 1900 and was promoted soon thereafter from associate professional lecturer at the university to professor of education.

In 1900 the new superintendent, Edwin G. Cooley, chose Young as principal of the Chicago Normal School, a training school for teachers located at 68th Street and Stewart Avenue on the South Side. Young was influenced by the 'new humanism' promulgated by professors at her alma mater, the University of Chicago. Everything was connected, she believed. Nothing existed in isolation. She became determined to turn theory into practice.

As principal, Young was actively involved in the day-to-day activities of the school. Her influence grew. A progressive thinker, she opposed corporal punishment and allowed teachers flexibility when planning their day's work. She would make the rounds of the school, walking down the hallways, stepping into classrooms, and asking the students questions.

The teacher's aim, she insisted, "is the evolution of a character which, through thinking of the right and acting for the right, shall make for right conduct, rectitude, righteousness." She called for less punishment and more individual rewards in the classroom. In such a nurturing atmosphere, she believed, "the strong will be generous, the weak will dare to be true; the gifted and the lowly will strive for the good of all." Among the teaching staff, she attempted to instill a spirit of mutual cooperation.

When Supt. Cooley resigned in 1909, Young was considered a possible candidate. She had two strikes against her, however: her age—she was sixty-four years old—and her sex. "I only wish Mrs. Young were a man," mused one board member. Ultimately, however, she was elected.

Young took to the job with great energy and enthusiam. Immediately she announced that her door would always be open to teachers.

Her first two and one-half years in office were calm and fruitful. She introduced vocational courses in high schools and recommended courses in ethics and morality. Not one to dictate directives to either pupils or staff, she believed that children had the right to make their own choices when it came to their education and insisted that teachers have a say in determining school policy.

Rivalry on the school board disrupted her term in office and forced her, on two occasions, to resign her position as superintendent. In August of 1913 she stepped down, convinced that she was "the victim of political intrigue among board members." As evidence, she cited several examples: Salaries were approved by the board without her consultation, several of her recommendations for principal were rejected, and a committee was formed to suggest possible revisions in the curriculum from so-called fads and frills courses (sewing and crafts) to the "three R's." Bowing to public pressure—citizens, many of them women, held protest meetings throughout the city demanding that the popular superintendent be reinstated—the board voted to retain her, and she resumed her duties.

Young made many firsts. She was the first woman superintendent of a major American city; the first woman to earn a Ph.D. from the Department of Education at the University of Chicago; the first woman to attain the rank of full professor; the first woman president of the Illinois Teachers Association; and the first woman awarded an honorary LL.D. by the University of Illinois.

Young retired from the superintendency in December of 1915. On October 26, 1918, she died of pneumonia in Washington, D.C., while on a speaking tour. She was buried at Rosehill Cemetery.

See also: John Dewey [appendix], Margaret Haley, Francis W. Parker

Further reading: Counts, George S. *School and Society in Chicago* (1928); Herrick, Mary J. *The Chicago Schools: A Social and Political History* (1971); Smith, Joan A. *Ella Flagg Young: Portrait of a Leader* (1979).

Florenz Ziegfeld

Theatrical Producer

born: March 21, 1869
Chicago, Illinois
died: July 22, 1932
Hollywood, California

Florenz Ziegfeld was a native Chicagoan and a member of a prominent family who made a name for himself along Broadway. The Ziegfeld Follies, a lavish musical revue, represented good, old-fashioned, wholesome fare, while the Follies dancers came to epitomize the ideal American girl—virginal, sweet, and beautiful. "We do not select according to our own conception of beauty," Florenz once said. "No, we keep our finger on the public pulse and give it what it wants."

Photograph courtesy of the Chicago Historical Society.

Ziegfeld attended Chicago public schools. His father, a musician also named Florenz Ziegfeld, immigrated to the United States from Germany in 1858 and settled in Chicago in 1863. Four years later he founded the Chicago Academy of Music. In the Ziegfeld home at 1448 West Adams Street, young Florenz grew up listening to Beethoven and Bach and was active in amateur theater.

Ziegfeld entered show business in 1893, producing orchestras and musical shows at the World's Columbian Exposition. He brought a German band, Russian singers and dancers, a Hungarian string orchestra, and an English singer to the world's fair. He also introduced Eugene Sandow, the "perfect man," —named thus due to his athletic build—to the fair and acted as Sandow's manager for several years.

Like many Chicagoans who wanted to make a living in show business, Ziegfeld moved east to New York. In 1896 he introduced a French starlet, Anna Held, in *A Parlor Match.* Held appeared in many of his musical comedies. *The Follies of 1907* ushered in a new kind of musical variety program. The public, however, wasn't quite ready for it. One of his early musical comedies, *Mlle. Napoleon,* was an utter failure and left the showman on the brink of bankruptcy, but Ziegfeld didn't let hard times get in the way of success.

The *Follies* made their debut at the New York Theatre on July 8, 1907. The show was seen annually on Broadway, with three exceptions, until 1931.

The first *Follies* featured a bevy of beauties in a chorus line, personally chosen by Ziegfeld himself. Ziegfeld wished to "glorify the American girl." He selected not only the girls but also the music, approved the costumes, and directed the production numbers. Ziegfeld hired many eminent composers to write for his shows, including Irving Berlin and Jerome Kern. Entertainers Sophie Tucker, Eddie Cantor, Fannie Brice, W. C. Fields, Will Rogers, Bert Williams, and Ed Wynn got their start with Ziegfeld. Moreover, in his programs he introduced songs that became American standards, including "Shine On, Harvest Moon" (1908); "By the Light of the Silvery Moon" (1909); "My Man" (1921), sung by Fannie Brice; and "My Blue Heaven" (1927), performed by Eddie Cantor.

Other Ziegfeld shows included *Sally, Show Boat, Simple Simon, Show Girl,* and *Smiles.*

Critics accused Ziegfeld of provincialism and of lacking sophistication, to which he sniffed, "What is sophistication?" Americans, he claimed, preferred good, old-fashioned entertainment; and he, for one, would gladly supply it.

Ziegfeld always considered Chicago his home. Whenever he was in town, he would visit his parents and the old Victorian brick mansion on Adams Street.

In 1925 Ziegfeld announced plans to build a huge one-million-dollar playhouse on Michigan Avenue and 8th Street to be known simply as "The Ziegfeld." "I intend to inaugurate here an annual musical production, comparable to the *Follies,*" he told reporters. "Chicago is entitled to have just as good entertainment as New York. Any producer who tries to bring second-string casts here will be fooled. Chicago audiences are too wise." But it never came to pass. Neither did Ziegfeld's wish to produce another follies show starring Maurice Chevalier.

Weakened by a bout of pneumonia, Ziegfeld suffered a fatal heart attack in a Hollywood hospital in July of 1932. He was sixty-three. In 1936 a movie based on his career, *The Great Ziegfeld,* was released and in 1945, the *Ziegfeld Follies* starring Fred Astaire, Judy Garland, and Lena Horne, was made.

Several months before he died Ziegfeld produced a national weekly radio program, "Ziegfeld Follies of the Air," that aired locally on WGN on Sunday evenings. Ziegfeld hosted, arranged, and directed the program, which featured talent from past and contemporary Ziegfeld productions.

See also: Michael Todd [appendix]

Further reading: Hofmeister, Rudolph A. *The Germans of Chicago* (1976).

Appendix

Space prevents us from listing as many famous Chicagoans as we would like. Thus, we've put together brief sketches of other prominent figures who have contributed to the city's rich past.

Margaret C. Anderson (1891–1973); editor; b: Indianapolis, Indiana; d: Le Cannet, France; age: 82. Anderson edited the seminal literary magazine, the *Little Review,* during the heady days of the Chicago literary renaissance of the early twentieth century. She introduced the works of Sherwood Anderson and Ernest Hemingway and championed cubism, dada, surrealism, and anarchism. For a few brief but colorful years, Anderson was the toast of the town and the undisputed queen of the city's bohemian community. In 1917 she moved the magazine to New York, where she again caused a stir with the serialization of James Joyce's controversial masterpiece, *Ulysses.* Along with coeditor Jane Heap, Anderson was convicted of publishing obscenity and fined $100. In the late twenties she settled in France, which she had always considered her spiritual home. *Photograph courtesy of Charles H. Kerr Publishing Company.*

Ira J. Bach (1907–1985); city planner; b: Chicago, Illinois; d: Chicago, Illinois; age: 78. Bach, who served under five different mayors, left his mark on virtually every major Chicago building project during a thirty-year period. A native South Sider, Bach earned an architectural degree from the Massachusetts Institute of Technology in 1932. His first job in city government was with the Martin Kennelly administration in 1947 as executive director of the Land Clearance Commission. In 1957 he became planning commissioner under Richard J. Daley. In this capacity, he directed the planning of the controversial University of Illinois at Chicago on the Near West Side. The construction necessitated a massive urban renewal—approximately five thousand people were forced to relocate. Irate neighbors, led by Florence Scala, a resident and later a well-known Taylor Street restaurant owner, protested to the Daley administration and made several heated appearances at the city council—to no avail. The courts eventually sided with the city. In 1969 Bach left city government to head a private development consulting firm but returned two years later to serve as Daley's appointee to the Northeastern Illinois Planning Commission. Bach retired in 1984, although he continued to act as chairman of the Chicago Commission on Historical and Architectural Landmarks.

An ardent landmarks preservationist later in life, Bach helped save many of the city's most prominent buildings, including the Chicago Theatre. He authored several popular local guidebooks, including *Chicago on Foot, Chicago's Famous Buildings,* and *A Guide to Chicago's Public Sculpture. Photograph reprinted with permission from the* Chicago Sun-Times.

Jack Benny (1894–1974); comedian; b: Chicago, Illinois; d: Los Angeles, California; age: 80. Born in Chicago but raised in Waukegan, Illinois, Jack Benny (real name: Benjamin Kubelsky) was the son of Russian Jewish immigrants. He studied violin as a child and while a teenager played the Chicago-area theater circuit as part of a violin duo. Benny switched from musician to comedian when he discovered people were paying more attention to his jokes than to his music. For almost twenty-five years Benny was a fixture of Sunday night radio as the lovable miser who hated to part with his money. Benny made the successful transition from radio to television in 1951. Waukegan's favorite son continued to make public appearances until his death from stomach cancer in 1974.

Mother Frances Xavier Cabrini (1850–1917); saint; b: Lombardy, Italy; d: Chicago, Illinois; age: 67. Francesca Maria Cabrini founded the Institute of Missionary Sisters of the Sacred Heart of Jesus in 1880. In 1889 Pope Leo XIII assigned her to assist New York's poor Italian immigrants. Mother Cabrini traveled extensively throughout the United States and Europe as well as in Central and South America, establishing convents, schools, orphanages, and hospitals. In Chicago she founded two hospitals: Columbus Hospital in 1905 at 2520 North Lakeview Avenue and the Columbus Extension Hospital in 1910 at 811 South Lytle Street on the West Side, which was later renamed St. Cabrini Hospital in her honor. She was canonized by Pope Pius XII in 1946, the first American citizen to be so honored. Mother Cabrini died in Columbus Hospital in 1917.

Henry Crown (1896–1990); entrepreneur/philanthropist; b: Chicago, Illinois; d: Chicago, Illinois; age: 94. Born Henry Krinsky, Crown was cofounder of the sand and gravel company, Material Service Corporation, and was a member of one of Chicago's wealthiest families. The third of seven children born to an Eastern European immigrant peddler and match salesman, Crown lived with his family at 1309 North Ashland Avenue as a young boy. He made his fortune in many businesses, including the hotel, railroad, meatpacking, coal, sugar, and aerospace industries. Crown and his family contributed an estimated $100 million to charities and gave generously to various philanthropic and civic institutions, including the Illinois Institute of Technology, the Chicago Boys' Club, and Presbyterian-St. Luke's Medical Center. Several prominent buildings and cultural and educational institutions in the Chicago area bear his name such as the Henry Crown Space Center at the Museum of Science and Industry, the Henry Crown Sports Pavilion at Northwestern University, the Henry Crown Gallery at the Art Institute, and the Henry Crown Laboratory for computer science at DePaul University. *Photograph reprinted with permission from the* Chicago Sun-Times.

Floyd Dell (1887–1969); novelist/editor; b: Barry, Illinois; d: Bethesda, Maryland; age: 82. Dell cut a dashing figure in early twentieth-century Chicago. As editor of the influential *Friday Literary Review,* he furthered the careers of Sherwood Anderson, Robert Herrick, Vachel Lindsay, and other local writers. He hired a number of book reviewers who would become famous authors in their own right: Fanny Butcher, later the *Chicago Tribune's* literary critic, and Margaret Anderson, founder of the *Little Review* magazine. Dell moved to New York in the late teens and joined the staffs of two leftist publications, *The Masses* and *The Liberator.* His defense of conscientious objectors during World War I led to the suppression of *The Masses* and his indictment, in 1917, under the Sedition Act. The charges were later dropped. Dell wrote twenty-three books, several plays, and an autobiography, *Homecoming. Photograph courtesy of the Newberry Library.*

John Dewey (1859–1952) educator; b: Burlington, Vermont; d: New York, New York; age: 93. Considered one of America's greatest philosophers, John Dewey taught students to think for themselves and not merely memorize facts. He joined the faculty of the University of Chicago in 1894 as head of the department of philosophy, psychology, and pedagogy. Dewey profoundly influenced generations of educators. He established his experimental and pioneering Laboratory School on the Hyde Park campus in 1896. There the children learned by doing. Dewey believed that school should be an extension of everyday life. In a radical departure from traditional education, the children actually learned to work together and to cooperate in a nurturing, supportive atmosphere. Dewey argued that education was a process of accumulating experience—not a method of learning by rote. *Photograph courtesy of the University of Chicago Archives.*

Walt Disney (1901–1966); cartoonist/motion picture producer; b: Chicago, Illinois; d: Los Angeles, California; age: 65. Walt Disney revolutionized the art of animated film. Born in Chicago, Disney lived with his family at 1249 North Tripp Avenue (now 2156 North Tripp). He later moved to Missouri but returned to attend McKinley High School in Chicago and to study cartooning at the Chicago Academy of Fine Arts. Disney achieved his first commercial success with *Steamboat Willie,* which featured a character named Mickey Mouse. Over the years he introduced to the world such endearing figures as Donald Duck, Goofy, and Pluto. Some Disney classics include *Snow White and the Seven Dwarfs* (1938), the first feature-length cartoon motion picture; *Fantasia* (1940), a perennial favorite but, surprisingly, a commercial failure when first released; *Pinocchio* (1940); *Dumbo* (1941); *Bambi* (1953); and *Sleeping Beauty* (1959). He produced several television shows—*The Mickey Mouse Club* and *The Wonderful World of Disney*—and built the Disneyland amusement park in Anaheim, California, and Disney World in Orlando, Florida. *Photograph courtesy of the Chicago Historical Society.*

Michael Diversey (1810–1869); entrepreneur/philanthropist; b: Germany; d: Chicago, Illinois; age: 59. Diversey emigrated from Germany in 1836 and arrived in Chicago two years later. In 1841 he became a partner of a Chicago brewery, Lill and Diversey, located at the corner of Chicago and Pine (now Michigan Avenue). As the business prospered, Diversey contributed generously to the cultural and spiritual well-being of the German community. He donated land at the corner of North Avenue and Church Street (now Hudson Avenue) for the erection of a church that was dedicated to St. Michael, his patron saint. The present St. Michael's Church stands north of the original site. In 1863 he and his partner William Lill donated five acres for the

Presbyterian Theological Seminary of the Northwest, later the McCormick Theological Seminary. In 1844 Diversey was elected alderman of the old 6th Ward. *Photograph courtesy of the Chicago Historical Society.*

Mircea Eliade (1907–1986) educator; b: Bucharest, Romania; d: Chicago, Illinois; age: 79. One of the world's leading interpreters of myth and religion, Mircea Eliade was a professor at the University of Chicago for nearly thirty years. After earning his Ph.D. from the University of Bucharest with a dissertation in yoga, Eliade taught in his native city and at the Sorbonne in Paris before accepting a visiting professorship at the University of Chicago in 1957. Eliade encouraged his students to explore the divine within oneself or, to borrow his terminology, to find the sacred within the profane. In 1985 the Divinity School at the University of Chicago established the Mircea Eliade chair in the history of religions—the first ever awarded to a faculty member. At the time of his death Eliade was working as editor-in-chief of *Encyclopedia of Religion*, a sixteen-volume work published by Macmillan in 1986. Eliade wrote more than fifty books—nonfiction, novels, and plays—including a three-volume series on the history of religious ideas, *From the Stone Age to Eleusis, Buddha to the Triumph of Christianity*, and *From Mohammad to the Age of Reforms. Photograph courtesy of the University of Chicago Archives.*

Arthur J. Goldberg (1908–1990); judge; b: Chicago, Illinois; d: Washington, D. C.; age: 81. The son of Russian immigrant parents, Goldberg was raised in the Maxwell Street neighborhood on the Near West Side at Halsted and O'Brien Streets and later lived at 13th Street and Lawndale Avenue. After graduating first in his class from Northwestern University Law School in 1929, he joined the Chicago law firm of Pritzker and Pritzker and for two years edited the *Illinois Law Review.* In 1938 he began his own practice and from 1939 to 1948 served as a professor of law at the John Marshall Law School. Sympathetic to union causes, Goldberg represented several major unions in the thirties and forties and was instrumental in the formation of the merger of the Congress of Industrial Organizations (CIO) and the American Federation of Labor (AFL). Goldberg held many important positions on a national level, including U.S. Supreme Court justice, ambassador to the United Nations, and secretary of labor in the Kennedy administration. As a Supreme Court justice, Goldberg coauthored a landmark case in 1965 that struck down a Connecticut ban on birth control devices and laid the

foundation for the controversial *Roe v. Wade* decision in the early seventies that legalized abortion. In 1965 he resigned from the bench to serve as U.S. ambassador to the United Nations. He advocated the admission of China into the U.N. and urged the U.S. to adopt a harder line against apartheid in South Africa. Soon after moving his law firm to Washington, D. C., in 1971, he joined the faculty of American University as a professor of law and diplomacy. *Photograph reprinted with permission from the Chicago Sun-Times.*

Kenneth Sawyer Goodman (1883–1918); playwright; b: Chicago, Illinois; d: Chicago, Illinois; age: 35. Goodman, a promising playwright, worked in the family lumber business, yet theater and the arts were his passion. In 1911 Goodman and another up-and-coming playwright, Thomas Wood Stevens, were among the founders of the Chicago Theatre Society, an arts support group. Stevens, who established the influential Blue Sky Press and taught art at the Art Institute, met Goodman in 1908. The two friends established a publishing house, the Stage Guild, to distribute their own one-act plays and masques. Goodman's plays were performed by theater groups in Detroit, New York, and as far away as Manchester, England. In 1917 he enlisted in the United States Naval Reserve. He died while on leave at the family home on North Astor Street during the influenza epidemic of 1918 that swept through Chicago. In 1922 his parents proposed to the Board of Trustees of the Art Institute to create a memorial theater in their son's memory. The Goodman Memorial Theatre, designed by Chicago architect Howard Van Doren Shaw, opened on October 20, 1925. The theater's professional company, the Repertory Company, presented three Goodman plays at the dedication performance: *Back of the Yards, The Green Scarf,* and *The Game of Chess. Photograph courtesy of the Newberry Library.*

Walter Burley Griffin (1876–1937); architect; b: Maywood, Illinois; d: India; age: 60. As the planner of Canberra, Australia's capital city, Griffin's greatest achievement was carried out on another continent on the other side of the world. Yet Griffin was a local boy. He was educated in the Oak Park public schools and graduated from the University of Illinois. A disciple of Frank Lloyd Wright, Griffin's prairie-style homes are scattered throughout Evanston and in Elmhurst, Illinois, where he lived from 1893 to 1914. Yet the Beverly neighborhood on the Southwest Side has the largest concentration—twelve—of Griffin-designed houses. In 1912 Griffin submitted the winning entry in an international contest to plan the new capital city of Canberra, then little more than an oasis on the vast Australian continent. After seven years as director of design, he left the city when government officials introduced a plan of their own. With some minor alterations, his design was finally executed under his supervision. Griffin chose to stay in Australia and established a private practice, first in Melbourne and then in Sydney. He was killed during an accident at a construction site at the University of Lucknow in India, when he fell off a scaffold and ruptured his gall bladder. In 1963 Griffin made Australian history when he became the first American to appear on an Australian postage stamp. In 1981 the 1600 block of West 104th Place between Wood Street and Prospect Avenue—the site of seven of his commissions—was designated a Chicago landmark and renamed Walter Burley Griffin Place.

Albert Halper (1904–1984); novelist; b: Chicago, Illinois; d: Poughkeepsie, New York; age: 79. Best known for his proletarian novels of the thirties, Halper grew up on the West Side and, after graduating from high school, held a succession of blue-collar jobs. The mechanized nature of the work only reinforced his attitude that the majority of laborers toiled in dead-end jobs that offered little economic relief or mental sustenance. Several of his early novels were set in Chicago. They include *The Foundry* (1934), about workers in a Chicago electrotype plant on the eve of the stock market crash of 1929; *The Chute* (1937), set in the Sears, Roebuck and Company mail-order plant on the West Side; and *The Little People* (1942), about employees of a Chicago department store. *On The Shore* (1934), a collection of short stories, portrayed Jewish immigrant life in Chicago. Another Chicago novel is *Sons of the Fathers* (1940), an antiwar tract about the relationship between a Jewish immigrant and his son. *The Golden Watch* (1953) is a coming-of-age tale set in pre–World War I Chicago. His best known novel, *Union Square* (1933), takes place in Depression-era New York. Halper also edited two Chicago anthologies: *This Is Chicago* (1952), a collection of fiction and essays that featured the work of Nelson Algren, James T. Farrell, Ring Lardner, Meyer Levin, and Richard Wright; and *The Chicago Crime Book* (1967), which contains nonfictional accounts of the city's criminals and gangsters.

Dina Halpern (1910–1989); actress b: Warsaw, Poland; d: Chicago, Illinois; age: 79. Distinguished star of the Yiddish-speaking theater for more than half a century, Dina Halpern resided in Chicago from 1948 until her death. She began her career as a dancer and performed with the Warsaw Yiddish Art Theatre. By the time she came to the United States in 1938, she was a household name in Poland and the Baltic countries. After the end of World War II, Halpern directed and guest starred in Yiddish theater productions in England, France, Israel, Argentina, and Australia, and was featured in the films *The Dybbuk* and *The Vow*. She established all-time long-running records for Yiddish theater in Chicago with starring roles in *Anna Lucasta* in 1949 and *The Little Foxes* in 1950, both presented at the Douglas Park Theatre at Kedzie and Ogden Avenues. As founder and artistic director of the Chicago Yiddish Theater Association—now defunct—from 1960 to 1970, she produced productions of classic Yiddish works. In 1985 Israel's Bar-Ilan University established the Dina Halpern Institute for the Yiddish Performing Arts and in July of 1988 she received the Manger Prize, the most prestigious honor in Yiddish literature.

Alice Hamilton (1869-1970); scientist/ social reformer; b: New York, New York; d: Hadlyne, Connecticut; age: 101. Hamilton played a major role in the development of industrial health legislation in Illinois and contributed pioneering studies in the fields of public and industrial health. The New York–born, Indiana-raised Hamilton pursued a medical career because she felt the profession offered the best opportunity for women. She received her medical degree from the University of Michigan in 1893 and studied pathology and bacteriology in Germany and, later, at Johns Hopkins University. Hamilton first encountered slum living conditions while working at the New England Hospital for Women and Children in the outskirts of Boston, where she made frequent housecalls to patients living in tenements. In 1897 she moved to Chicago and became a resident at Hull-House, the famous settlement house cofounded by Jane Addams and Ellen Gates Starr. By day she was a professor of pathology at the Women's Medical College of Northwestern University; in the evening she would return to Hull-House, where she studied the sources of disease transmission and taught hygiene care to residents of the ethnically diverse neighborhood. Her published findings about the causes and transmission of tuberculosis provoked a public investigation and a reevaluation of the city's health department. From 1911 to 1921, Hamilton investigated industrial poisoning for the federal government while continuing to make occasional visits to Hull-House. In 1919 she became an assistant professor of industrial medicine at Harvard University, the first woman to hold a position on the Harvard medical faculty. Her autobiography *Exploring the Dangerous Trades* was published in 1943. *Photograph courtesy of the University of Illinois at Chicago, the University Library, Jane Addams Memorial Collection.*

Sydney J. Harris (1917–1986); journalist; b: London, England; d: Chicago, Illinois; age: 69. The sage of journalism known for his wise and philosophical writing style, Harris's "Strictly Personal" column was distributed to more than two hundred newspapers in the United States and Canada at the time of his death. Harris, who came to the United States with his family at age five, studied philosophy at the University of Chicago. In 1934 he began his journalism career with the *Chicago Herald and Examiner*. In 1941 he joined the *Chicago Daily News* as a columnist and drama critic until the newspaper's demise in 1978 when he moved to the *Chicago Sun-Times*. Harris was inducted into the Chicago Journalism Hall of Fame in 1982. His columns were collected into eleven books, including *Pieces of Eight, A Major-ity of One, Strictly Personal*, and *Clearing the Ground*. *Photograph reprinted with permission from the* Chicago Sun-Times.

William "Big Bill" Haywood (1869–1928); labor activist; b: Salt Lake City, Utah; d: Moscow, Russia; age: 59. William D. Haywood went to work in the mines of Utah and Nevada at fifteen. In 1894 he moved to Silver City, Idaho, where he joined the Western Federation of Miners (WFM). In 1900 he was named secretary-treasurer of the WFM, which had moved its headquarters to Denver. On June 27, 1905, Haywood was one of the organizers of the Industrial Workers of the World (IWW) in Chicago. Among the other delegates in attendance were Lucy Parsons, Mary Harris "Mother" Jones, and Eugene Debs. As head of the IWW, Haywood advocated "one big union" that encompassed all workers. In 1906 he was arrested for the murder of Frank Steunenberg, the antiunion former governor of Idaho. The case became a cause célèbre. Defended by Chicago attorney Clarence Darrow, Haywood was acquitted in 1907. With his authoritative presence and gruff manner, he came to symbolize the union cause and was considered one of the most effective labor leaders of his day. Convicted in 1917 for violating the Espionage Act—he denounced World War I as a capitalist conflict—Haywood

was imprisoned and sentenced by Judge Kenesaw Mountain Landis to twenty years in prison and fined $30,000. In 1921 he jumped bail and fled to the Soviet Union, where he died in 1928. In fulfillment of his wishes, half of his ashes were scattered at the site of the Haymarket Martyrs monument in Waldheim Cemetery in Forest Park, Illinois. *Photograph courtesy of Charles H. Kerr Publishing Company.*

Ernest Hemingway (1899–1961); novelist; b: Oak Park, Illinois; d: Ketchum, Idaho; age: 61. Oak Park has claimed Hemingway as its own, but for fifteen months in 1920 and 1921, the famous author lived on Chicago's North Side at several locations—1030 North State Street; 100 East Chicago Avenue; and in the 1300 block of North Clark Street—and edited an obscure magazine called *Cooperative Commonwealth*. Hemingway attended Oak Park and River Forest High School and delivered the *Oak Leaves* newspaper. Hemingway received his first taste of literary success in 1926 with the publication of *The Sun Also Rises*. Subsequent novels included *A Farewell to Arms* (1929); *To Have and Have Not* (1937); *For Whom the Bell Tolls* (1940); and *The Old Man and the Sea*, which earned him a Pulitzer prize in 1953 and a Nobel prize for literature the following year. Hemingway's image remains enigmatic, that of an essentially rootless man whose incurable wanderlust led him to adventures and places far from his native Midwest. Oak Park may never have appeared in his novels, but, as writer Michael Reynolds argues, it existed as a moral presence "beneath the surface, invisible, and inviolate." Hemingway remains a larger-than-life figure to this day. His name still sells books and magazines, and journalists and scholars still discuss his merits. The Ernest Hemingway Foundation of Oak Park is currently working to establish a Hemingway museum in the western suburb. In the meantime, Hemingway's boyhood home at 600 North Kenilworth Avenue remains a favorite stop of literary tourists. Hemingway died of a self-inflicted shotgun wound at his home in Idaho. *Photograph courtesy of the Ernest Hemingway Foundation of Oak Park.*

Sidney Hillman (1887–1946); labor activist; b: Zagare, Russia; d: Long Island, New York; age: 59. Called "the Rasputin of organized labor," Hillman rose from Chicago's West Side to the corridors of the White House and held several prominent positions in various labor organizations in both Chicago and New York. In the latter city he transformed the garment workers union into one of the country's most powerful.

The son of a merchant, Hillman initially studied to be a rabbi but for economic reasons accepted a position working in a chemical laboratory in Kovno, Russia. Hillman was imprisoned for eight months after his involvement in controversial labor activities. He fled to England upon his release and immigrated to the United States in 1907. He settled in Chicago and found menial work as a stock clerk at Sears, Roebuck and Company. Hillman then worked as a garment cutter at the clothing firm of Hart, Schaffner and Marx. He joined the United Garment Workers Union of America (UGW) and was an effective leader during the ground-breaking garment workers' strike of 1910, which essentially shut down the clothing industry—then Chicago's second-largest industry—for sixteen weeks. In 1914 Hillman moved to New York to head the International Ladies Garment Workers Union, one of the largest trade unions in the country. One of the original members of the Congress of Industrial Organizations (CIO), Hillman served as labor advisor to President Franklin D. Roosevelt. *Photograph courtesy of the Illinois Labor History Society.*

William Holabird (1854–1923); architect; b: Dutchess County, New York; d: Evanston, Illinois; age: 68. With its consistent, uniformly excellent designs, the firm of Holabird and Roche exemplified the mainstream approach of the Chicago school of architecture. "Individual buildings of Sullivan and Root are superior to anything they did; yet they discovered the simplest utilitarian and structural solutions to the problems of the big urban office block," wrote architectural historian Carl W. Condit. Born in New York State, William Holabird graduated from high school in St. Paul, Minnesota. He attended West Point for two years but resigned in 1875 and moved to Chicago, where he became a draftsman at William Le Baron Jenney's architectural firm. In 1880 Holabird formed a partnership with Ossian C. Simonds and the following year the firm changed its name to Holabird, Simonds and Roche. When Simonds left in 1883, the name became Holabird and Roche. The firm's first major commission, the Tacoma Building at the corner of LaSalle and Monroe Streets in 1889, was inspired by Jenney's Home Insurance Building, which was completed the previous year and is often acknowledged as the world's first skyscraper. The Tacoma improved and further developed Jenney's iron-and-steel skeleton method of construction. Indeed, the Tacoma was called one of the most advanced building designs of its time. Other important Holabird and Roche works in Chicago were the Caxton Building (1890); an addition to the Monadnock Building (1893); the Marquette Building (1894); the Congress Hotel (1907); the LaSalle Hotel

(1909); the Sherman Hotel (1912); and the John Crerar Library (1919). Holabird died in 1923 in Evanston, Illinois. He was buried in Graceland Cemetery. Today the firm that he founded is known as Holabird and Root and is located at 300 West Adams Street. *Photograph courtesy of Holabird and Root.*

Joseph Holmes (1948–1986); dancer; b: Chicago, Illinois; d: Chicago, Illinois; age: 38. Joseph Holmes was the founder and artistic director of the multiracial, multicultural Chicago-based modern dance company that bears his name and one of the first African-Americans to establish a dance company in Chicago. Born and raised on the South Side, Holmes spent several years in New York as a member of the Dance Theatre of Harlem and as a student in Alvin Ailey's Dance Theater before establishing the Joseph Holmes Dance Theatre in 1974. He began dancing at the age of seven when his mother sent him to ballet lessons near his home at 51st Street and South Park Avenue (now King Drive). At nineteen he was dancing with Darlene Blackburn's Afro Dance Company. Highlights from Holmes's repertory include "Aretha" (1983), a celebration of the music of singer Aretha Franklin; "He and She" (1983), a dramatization of first love; "Oh Mary Don't You Weep" (1974), a dance interpretation of the biblical story of Lazarus; and "Tradewind" (1981), an exploration of affairs of the heart. Following Holmes's death in 1986, Randy Duncan, a member of the troupe, became artistic director. Today the Joseph Holmes Dance Theatre, located at 1935 South Halsted Street in the Pilsen neighborhood, continues to combine jazz, modern dance, and ballet through performance, arts education, workshops, residencies, and outreach programs.

Jenkin Lloyd Jones (1843–1918); minister; b: Cardiganshire, Wales; d: Spring Green, Wisconsin; age: 74. An influential and outspoken Chicago preacher during the early years of this century, Jenkin Lloyd Jones was brought to America from Wales by his parents when he was an infant and originally settled in Wisconsin. He graduated from Meadville Theological Seminary in Pennsylvania in 1870 and entered the ministry of the Unitarian Church. Jones held his first church service in Chicago in 1882 at Vincennes Hall on Vincennes Avenue near 35th Street. Four years later he established his own church, the All Souls Church at Oakwood Boulevard and Langley Avenue. In 1905 he organized the Abraham Lincoln Centre, which offered classes in religion, citizenship, and literature. The center, located at

3858 South Cottage Grove Avenue, now serves the African-American community. A noted pacifist, Jones opposed the United States entry in World War I. Jones was the uncle of architect Frank Lloyd Wright.

Otto Kerner, Jr. (1908–1976); politician; b: Chicago, Illinois; d: Chicago, Illinois; age: 68. Kerner was a popular Chicago politician and judge who came from a prominent Chicago family—his father was also a judge. Kerner graduated from Brown University in Rhode Island, studied at Cambridge University in England, and graduated from Northwestern University Law School. After passing the Illinois bar in 1934, he began to practice law in Chicago. He joined the Illinois National Guard as a private during World War II. He resigned with the rank of major general after serving in Africa, Sicily, and the Pacific. In 1947 President Harry S. Truman named Kerner to the position of U.S. attorney for northern Illinois. In 1954 he secured the influential position of county judge of Cook County. In 1960 Kerner was elected governor of Illinois and won reelection to a second term in 1964. He resigned, however, in 1968 to accept an appointment to the U.S. Court of Appeals for the 7th Circuit Court. He was sentenced to three years in prison after a 1973 conviction for income tax evasion and conspiracy stemming from a racetrack stock scandal. Kerner became the first sitting judge of a U.S. appeals court to be convicted. Kerner suffered a fatal heart attack in the Edgewater Beach Hotel in 1976, shortly after his release from prison. *Photograph reprinted with permission from the* Chicago Sun-Times.

William W. Kimball (1828–1904); entrepreneur; b: Rumford, Maine; d: Chicago, Illinois; age: 76. Dean of the Chicago music trade, W. W. Kimball established a business that eventually became the world's largest manufacturer of pianos. Until Kimball, most pianos and organs were manufactured in New York or Boston. Kimball arrived in Chicago in 1857 to seek his fortune after spending several years in Iowa in the insurance and real estate fields. On his first day in town he struck up a conversation with a Yankee piano salesman who made him an offer. Kimball agreed to trade lots of land that he owned in Iowa for the salesman's four pianos that were sitting in a warehouse on South Water Street. His business prospered as the city grew and developed. Kimball pioneered the installment plan, which enabled families to purchase pianos, then a much-in-demand status symbol. By the late 1870s, Kimball had established outlets throughout the Midwest and had

imported highly skilled European-trained craftsmen to manufacture the instruments. To generations of music lovers across America, the Kimball name guaranteed quality.

Herman Kogan (1914–1989); journalist/historian; b: Chicago, Illinois; d: New Buffalo, Michigan; age: 75. Newsman and historian, Kogan was one of Chicago's most prolific—and respected—writers. Kogan started his journalism career in 1930 as a copy boy with the *Chicago Daily News* and the *Chicago Evening Post*. While still attending the University of Chicago, he worked as a police reporter for the City News Bureau. Then the *Chicago Tribune* hired him as a feature reporter. Before enlisting in the Marine Corps, he worked for the *Chicago Sun*. After completing his military duty, he returned to the paper, which, by that time, had changed its name to the *Chicago Sun-Times*. In 1961 he created and edited the *Chicago Daily News's* weekend magazine *Panorama*, and later moved to the *Sun-Times*, where he edited the *Sun-Times's Book Week* and *Show* sections. In 1969 he became editor of the *Sun-Times*. With Lloyd Wendt, he coauthored several classics of Chicago history: *Lords of the Levee*, a biography of the infamous 1st Ward aldermen John "Bathhouse" Coughlin and Michael "Hinky Dink" Kenna; *Give the Lady What She Wants*, a history of Marshall Field and Co.; and *Big Bill of Chicago*, a biography of mayor William Hale Thompson. Other books include *A Continuing Marvel*, a history of the Museum of Science and Industry and *The First Century: The Chicago Bar Association, 1874–1974*. Generous with his time and talent, Kogan was quick to offer advice and friendly encouragement to other writers. He died of a heart attack while walking near his home in Michigan. *Photograph courtesy of Rick Kogan.*

Rudy Lozano (1951–1983); community organizer; b: Harlingen, Texas; d: Chicago, Illinois; age: 31. Rudy Lozano dedicated his brief life to improving the quality of life in Chicago's Latino community. As a member of Harold Washington's transition team, he made aggressive efforts to unite African-American and Latino interests. Lozano was a trade union official, community activist, organizer, and Midwest director of the International Ladies Garment Workers Union. Born in South Texas, he moved with his family to Chicago in the early fifties and settled in the largely Mexican community of Pilsen. He was active in student activities at Harrison High School. In 1982 Lozano worked hard to register Latino voters in the 20th District in order to elect

Juan Soliz as state representative. When Soliz lost to incumbent Marco Domico, Lozano and Soliz joined forces and organized the Near West Side branch of the Independent Political Organization (IPO), a group that functioned as an alternative to the regular Democratic machine. In 1983 Lozano ran against incumbent Frank Stemberk for alderman of the 22nd Ward. On June 8 of that year, he was shot to death in his Pilsen apartment at 4035 West 25th Street shortly after losing the election. In 1984 an eighteen-year-old gang member, Gregory Escobar, was convicted of Lozano's murder and sentenced to forty years in prison. Motives for the slaying range from an argument over a possible drug deal gone bad to charges that Lozano employed rival gang members during his aldermanic campaign. Family and friends of the slain activist, however, called the murder "a political assassination" ordered by antiunion businessmen. In 1989 the Rudy Lozano branch of the Chicago Public Library opened at 1805 South Loomis Street. *Photograph reprinted with permission from the* Chicago Sun-Times.

Charles MacArthur (1895–1956); journalist/playwright; b: Scranton, Pennsylvania; d: New York, New York; age: 61. Along with his better known colleague Ben Hecht, Charles MacArthur wrote the plays *The Front Page* and *The Twentieth Century* and shared the best screenplay Oscar with Hecht for *The Scoundrel.* Despite his success in other fields, MacArthur was, at heart, a Chicago newspaperman. MacArthur began his journalism career as a reporter with the *Oak Leaves* in Oak Park, Illinois. In 1917 MacArthur worked briefly for the *Chicago Herald-Examiner* before joining the *Chicago Tribune.* MacArthur's cynical gallows humor fit in perfectly with the flippant, tongue-in-cheek world of Chicago journalism. Other MacArthur/Hecht collaborations include the screenplays of *Barbary Coast* (1935); *Gunga Din* (1939); and *Wuthering Heights* (1939). In 1928 MacArthur married Helen Hayes, the "first lady" of the theater. Although MacArthur lived on both coasts for many years, he always remembered Chicago fondly. A heavy drinker throughout most of his adult life, MacArthur died in a New York City hospital from kidney problems and anemia.

George W. Maher (1864–1926); architect; b: Mill Creek, West Virginia; d: Douglas, Michigan; age: 62. Like Louis Sullivan and John Wellborn Root, George W. Maher advocated indigenous American architecture. He laid out the villages of Kenilworth—including his own home at 424 Warwick Road—and Glencoe, Illinois, and built numerous mansions along the North Shore. Born in West Virginia, Maher moved with his family to New Albany, Indiana, in the late 1860s. When he was still a young boy his family settled in Chicago. At thirteen, Maher served as an apprentice at the architectural firm of Bauer and Hill but after a short stay moved to the office of Joseph L. Silsbee, where he received most of his architectural training. In 1888 he opened his own practice with Charles Corwin. A contemporary of Frank Lloyd Wright, Maher specialized in residential architecture and town planning. In the early 1890s he designed houses in the Edgewater community. Among his commissions are the John Farson house in Oak Park, the Patten gymnasium at Northwestern University on the Evanston campus, and the home of E. J. Magerstadt at 4930 South Greenwood Avenue in the Kenwood neighborhood on the South Side. In failing health, Maher committed suicide at his summer home in Michigan in 1926.

Mary E. Marcy (1877–1922); editor; b: Belleville, Illinois; d: Chicago, Illinois; age: 45. An important member of the editorial board of Charles H. Kerr's *International Socialist Review* (ISR), Mary Edna Marcy played a significant role in shaping and determining leftist attitudes in Chicago and beyond. Marcy first attracted public attention within radical circles when her scathing indictment of the meatpacking industry appeared in a 1904 issue of the ISR, the offical organ of the left wing of the Socialist party in the U. S. For nearly a decade, beginning in 1909, she served as the magazine's managing editor. The publication's circulation soared after she came aboard. It was one of the most widely read socialist journals in the U.S. until February 1918 when the government suppressed it because of its editorial opposition to American involvement in World War I. Contributors included Eugene Debs, John Reed, William Haywood, Joe Hill, Elizabeth Gurley Flynn, Jack London, Ralph Chaplin, and Carl Sandburg. Marcy studied philosophy and psychology briefly under John Dewey at the University of Chicago around the turn of the century. Acclaimed in her own day for her clear and lucid prose, Marcy authored a number of pamphlets that addressed pressing issues, including *Industrial Autocracy; Why Catholic Workers Should Be Socialists; How the Farmer Can Get His; The Right to Strike;* and *Shop Talks on Economics.* The latter sold over two million copies and was translated into several languages. Her theme, recalls her biographer, Jack Carney, was the "emancipation of the workers by the workers." She also wrote one-act plays, a novel, children's books, short stories, and poetry. She committed suicide in 1922. *Photograph courtesy of Charles H. Kerr Publishing Company.*

Jacques Marquette (1637–1675); missionary; b: Laon, France; d: Ludington, Michigan; age: 37. In 1673 Father Jacques Marquette left St. Ignace, Michigan, on a long and treacherous journey that took him through the wild Illinois prairie to a desolate spot near Lake Michigan that the Indians called Chicagou. The previous year Governor Frontenac of New France in what is now the province of Quebec in Canada commissioned a twenty-eight-year-old cartographer named Louis Jolliet to locate a great river that lay somewhere in the West. Marquette was chosen to accompany Jolliet on the expedition. Determining that the Mississippi River flowed into the Gulf of Mexico, Marquette and Jolliet traveled up the Illinois River, stopping at the Indian village of Kaskaskia, near present-day Utica, Illinois. Marquette promised the Indians that he would return one day to preach the Gospel. Journeying up the Des Plaines River, Marquette and his party floated down the south branch of the Chicago River to Lake Michigan before finally reaching Green Bay in the fall of 1673. Remembering his promise to the Illinois Indians, Marquette embarked on another journey. On December 4, 1674, he reached the mouth of the Chicago River. Too sick to continue—he was suffering from severe dysentery and chronic fever—he settled in a cabin at what is now Damen Avenue and the south branch of the Chicago River. Thus Marquette, along with his two French companions, became the first white men on record to live in Chicago. Marquette spent a blustery winter on the prairie before returning to Kaskaskia, where he was received by the Illinois Indians, according to his diary, like "an angel from heaven." His health rapidly deteriorating, Marquette died near Ludington, Michigan, on the return journey back to the mission at St. Ignace.

John McGreevy (1919–1990); musician; b: Chicago, Illinois; d: Chicago, Illinois; age: 70. An electrician by profession, John McGreevy was one of the finest traditional Irish fiddlers in the city. Of Irish descent, he served as secretary of the Irish Musicians Society and recorded more than ten albums of Irish folk music. His fiddling was characterized by a marked intensity and enthusiasm. As a child he listened to records of the great Irish fiddlers—Michael Coleman, Paddy Killoran, and Paddy Sweeney. In the days before the current Celtic music revival, McGreevy kept the tradition alive by performing at taverns or in the homes of fellow musicians and friends. With the growth of interest in traditional Irish music, McGreevy was a frequent figure on college campuses, at folk festivals, and in Irish pubs. *Photograph by Kevin O'Donnell.*

Vincente Minnelli (1903–1986); motion picture director; b: Chicago, Illinois; d: Los Angeles, California; age: 83. Vincente Minnelli (born Lester Anthony Minnelli) turned the movie musical into an art form. Born to an impoverished family of entertainers who performed under the name of the Minnelli Brothers' Tent Theater, Minnelli was raised in Chicago and took classes in design at the School of the Art Institute. Among his early jobs here were window dresser at Marshall Field and Company and set and costume designer for Balaban and Katz's stage shows at the Chicago Theater. In 1940 he moved to Hollywood to begin a long and illustrious career. His important films include *Cabin in the Sky* (1943); *Meet Me in St. Louis* (1944); *Ziegfeld Follies* (1944); *Madame Bovary* (1949); *An American in Paris* (1951); *The Bad and the Beautiful* (1952); *Brigadoon* (1954); *Lust for Life* (1956); *Gigi* (1958), for which he won an Academy Award as Best Director; *Some Came Running* (1958); *The Courtship of Eddie's Father* (1963); *The Sandpiper* (1965); and *On a Clear Day You Can See Forever* (1970). *Photograph courtesy of the Museum of Modern Art/Film Stills Archive, New York.*

William Vaughn Moody (1869–1910); poet/playwright/educator; b: Spencer, Indiana; d: Colorado Springs, Colorado; age: 41. William Vaughn Moody was considered one of the great poets of his day. He attended public schools in New Albany, Indiana, before entering the Pritchett Institute of Design in Louisville, Kentucky, in 1885 to study painting. In 1889 he enrolled at Harvard University and received his masters degree in 1894. That same year he joined the English department at Harvard. The following year he moved west to join the faculty of the new University of Chicago, where he remained until 1907. He wrote his best-known play *The Great Divide*, which was produced in Chicago in 1906 and enjoyed a successful two-year run, while at the university. In 1907 Moody resigned from the university to devote full time to writing. Among his other plays are *The Masque of Judgment* (1900), *The Fire-Bringer* (1904), and *The Faith Healer* (1909). In 1901 a collection of poetry, simply entitled *Poems*, was published. With fellow University of Chicago colleague Robert Morss Lovett, Moody wrote an introductory English textbook, *A First View of English Literature* (1905). *Photograph courtesy of the University of Chicago Archives.*

Joy Morton (1855–1934); entrepreneur; b: near Nebraska City, Nebraska; d: Lisle, Illinois; age: 79. Joy Morton founded the Morton Salt Company and established the Morton Arboretum in west suburban Lisle, Illinois. His parents were among the early settlers of the Nebraska Territory. Morton attended the Helmuth Institute in London, Ontario, for a short time before enrolling at the University of Michigan and then transferred to Mayhew Commercial College in Detroit. He worked for a bank in Nebraska City and for the Burlington railroad in Aurora, Illinois, before settling in Chicago. In 1880 Morton accepted the offer of a partnership in the firm of E. I. Wheeler and Company, a Chicago agent for the Michigan Salt Association. He was so successful that he was able to acquire a half interest by 1885. When Wheeler died the same year, Morton reorganized the firm as Joy Morton and Company. Chicago's meatpacking industry consumed massive quantities of salt. As the company prospered, Morton expanded into other areas. In 1889 he became a stockholder and director in the American Trust and Savings Bank of Chicago and in the Nebraska City National Bank. He also invested heavily in Chicago real estate. He expanded the salt company and acquired warehouses in cities throughout the Midwest. In 1910 the company, in an effort to promote its new moisture-proof salt container, created the now familiar image of a young girl coyly holding an umbrella, accompanied by the catchy slogan: "When It Rains, It Pours." The following year Morton purchased a farm in Lisle and in 1922 established the Morton Arboretum for scientific research in horticulture and agriculture. His father, J. Sterling Morton, was the founder of Arbor Day. Today the Morton Arboretum remains a popular spot for nature lovers.

William S. Paley (1901–1990); broadcaster; b: Chicago, Illinois; d: New York, New York; age: 89. Broadcaster. Called one of the giants of the American broadcast industry, Paley controlled the Columbia Broadcasting System (CBS) for almost fifty years in one capacity or another. Paley, the son of Ukrainian Jews, was born in an apartment in the rear of his father's storefront cigar shop at 1767 Odgen Avenue in the Maxwell Street neighborhood on the city's West Side. After graduating from Schurz High School on the Northwest Side, he enrolled at the Western Military Academy in Alton, Illinois, for college prep work. He attended the University of Chicago for one year but quit to move to Philadelphia to enter the family cigar manufacturing business, which by that time had grown into a successful company. After graduating from the Wharton School of Finance in 1922, Paley served as the company's advertising director. During the late twenties, he saw tremendous potential for the fledgling radio broadcast industry that had almost grown up overnight. In 1928 he purchased a small network of radio stations from a friend, left the cigar business altogether, and moved to New York and by September of that year became the president of the Columbia Broadcasting System. Paley made some bold moves in those early years. He hired Bing Crosby, then an untested singer with an unreliable reputation, and lured Jack Benny away from rival NBC. Regular television broadcasts were introduced in 1939. At first unsure of the new medium, Paley, an innovative programmer, turned CBS into one of the country's three major television networks by deliberately appealing to a mass audience. His reign at CBS was characterized, noted a colleague, by "creativity, energy, integrity, style, wit and an enormous sense of the public interest." Among the CBS programming that earned the network both critical raves and audience popularity during the Paley years were "The Ed Sullivan Show," "The Jackie Gleason Show," "I Love Lucy," "The Mary Tyler Moore Show," "All in the Family," and "M*A*S*H." In 1983 an unsuccessful hostile takeover attempt by cable television king Ted Turner forced Paley to retire. Lawrence Tisch of Loewes Corporation, one of CBS's biggest stockholders, assumed control. Three years later, however, Paley returned and was reelected chairman of the board. He died in his Manhattan home of a heart attack.

Irna Phillips (1901–1973); television writer; b: Chicago, Illinois; d: Chicago, Illinois; age: 72. Queen of the soap operas, Irna Phillips was largely responsible for successfully transferring the soap opera format from radio to television. A graduate of Senn High School, Phillips received her bachelor's degree in education from the University of Illinois and later pursued graduate work at Northwestern University and the University of Wisconsin. Phillips started her career at WGN radio in 1930 as a writer and actress. Her first show, *Painted Dreams,* premiered on WGN radio that year and was the first daytime serial aimed specifically at a female audience. Two years later she moved to the NBC radio network and created *Today's Children,* which was one of the most highly rated soap operas on radio. Other radio serials followed: *Road of Life; The Woman in White; The Right to Happiness;* and *The Guiding Light,* which was, in 1949, the first radio soap opera adapted to television. *These Are My Children,* the first soap opera created for television, premiered on WNBQ (now WMAQ-TV) the same year. Phillips wrote the scripts from her Near

North Side apartment at 1335 North Astor Street. Among the other soap operas that she created for television were *Young Doctor Malone, The Brighter Day, Another World,* and *As the World Turns. As the World Turns* is still a popular daytime show. *Photograph reprinted with permission from the* Chicago Sun-Times.

Leslee Reis (1943–1990); restaurant owner/chef; b: Chicago, Illinois; d: New Orleans, Louisiana; age: 47. Leslee Reis brought a touch of cosmopolitan dining to Chicago-area restaurants. As the genial host of Cafe Provençal in Evanston, Illinois, her ebullient personality was as much a part of the dining experience as the cuisine. Although born in Chicago, Reis grew up in Cincinnati and graduated from Carnegie-Mellon University in 1964 with degrees in biochemistry and bacteriology. While doing graduate work at Harvard University, Reis attended Julia Child's cooking classes and later studied cooking at the prestigious Cordon Bleu in Paris. In 1966 Reis moved to Evanston, where she opened a catering business. With her partner Lizann Bradshaw, she opened Cafe Provençal, a country-style French provincial restaurant at 1625 Hinman, in 1977. Cafe Provençal received stunning reviews in the local press for its exquisite food and its elegant ambiance. In 1988 Cafe Provençal was named the fifth best restaurant in America by the Zagat Survey. In 1982 Reis opened another restaurant in Evanston, Leslee's, which also featured jazz. Reis was a founding member of the American Institute of Wine and Food. She died of a heart attack while vacationing in New Orleans. *Photograph reprinted with permission from the* Chicago Sun-Times.

Hyman G. Rickover (1900–1986); naval officer; b: Makow, Russia (now Maków, Poland); d: Arlington, Virginia; age: 86. Hyman George Rickover, the father of the nuclear submarine and arguably the most renowned naval officer of the twentieth century, immigrated to the United States with his parents in 1906. The family initially settled in Brooklyn, but the following year they moved to Chicago, which the elder Rickover, a Polish Jew, felt offered better opportunity. Rickover grew up in humble surroundings at 3243 West Grenshaw Street in the Lawndale neighborhood on the West Side. A graduate of John Marshall High School, Rickover was accepted at the U.S. Naval Academy in Annapolis, Maryland, in 1922. Despite the prevalence of overt anti-Semitism at the time, Rickover succeeded through hard work and determination. He pursued graduate studies in electrical engineering at Annapolis and at Columbia

University, where he graduated with a master's degree in 1929. During World War II Rickover served as chief of the Navy's Bureau of Ships. He worked diligently to develop the atomic-powered submarine, which he considered a necessary ingredient of modern warfare. He was largely responsible for the design and development of the Nautilus, the world's first nuclear-powered submarine, in 1954. An outspoken iconoclast who had no patience for Navy bureaucracy, Rickover was passed over for promotion in the early fifties. The public outcry at such an injustice—Rickover was a famous and well-respected figure—was so intense that the Navy, under pressure, promoted him to rear admiral in 1953 and to vice-admiral in 1958. In 1982, at the age of eighty-two, the Reagan administration forced Rickover to retire from his position as director of naval nuclear propulsion. Rickover died four years later in 1986. *Photograph reprinted with permission from the* Chicago Sun-Times.

Knute Rockne (1888–1931); football coach; b: Voss, Norway; d: near Bazaar, Kansas; age: 43. The charismatic Rockne brought Notre Dame football to national prominence. Although closely identified with the University of Notre Dame—he coached there from 1918 to 1930—Rockne was actually raised in Chicago. Rockne was five when the family emigrated from Norway. He played sandlot football as a youth in the Logan Square neighborhood. After high school, he enrolled at the University of Notre Dame but, ironically, failed initially to make the football team (he was an excellent pole vaulter, however). Rockne developed gradually as a football player. In November 1913 everyone remembered his name when he led Notre Dame, then an unheralded team, to victory, trouncing the mighty Army 35 to 13. After graduation Rockne was retained as assistant coach. In 1918 he became head coach while doubling as a chemistry professor. During the Rockne era, the Fighting Irish won 105 games, lost 12, and tied 5. Rockne died in a plane crash over Kansas in 1931. *Photograph reprinted with permission from the* Chicago Sun-Times.

Carl R. Rogers (1902–1987); psychologist; b: Oak Park, Illinois; d: La Jolla, California; age: 85. The father of psychotherapy, Carl Rogers developed the client-centered approach to therapy and stressed a one-on-one relationship between the patient and the doctor.
Rogers grew up in a religious environment in Oak Park, Illinois. He attended the University of Wisconsin and studied at Union Theological Seminary in New York for two years but left to pursue psychology at

Columbia University, where he received his doctorate. Rogers was professor of psychology at the University of Chicago from 1945 to 1957. It was at the Hyde Park campus that Rogers first experimented with the client-centered approach to therapy. The counselor's chief function, he maintained, was to listen and emphathize with the patient. From 1957 to 1963, Rogers was professor of psychology and psychiatry at the University of Wisconsin. In 1963 he founded the Center for Studies of the Person in La Jolla, California. Among his books are *On Becoming a Person* (1961), *Personal Power* (1977), *A Way of Being* (1980), and *Freedom to Learn* (1983). *Photograph reprinted with permission from the* Chicago Sun-Times.

Ike Sewell (1903–1990); restaurant owner; b: Wills Point, Texas; d: Chicago, Illinois; age: 87. Ike Sewell is credited with inventing one of Chicago's most popular exports—deep-dish pizza. Sewell first achieved fame as an All-America football player at the University of Texas at Austin. He worked for American Airlines in the twenties and moved to Chicago in 1936 as a liquor salesman. Frequent visits to the city's restaurants and taverns led to a friendship with Ric Riccardo, Sr., owner of the popular Riccardo's restaurant on North Rush Street—and still a favorite of local journalists. Sewell proposed opening a Mexican restaurant as a sideline business. Riccardo, who did not like Mexican food, compromised and suggested a pizzeria instead. After some experimenting, they came up with the idea of a pizza that consisted of layers of cheese topped with a thick crust and then baked in a skillet. In 1943 Sewell and Riccardo opened Pizzeria Uno at 29 East Ohio Street. It met with such success that the pair opened a second pizzeria, Pizzeria Due, at 619 North Wabash Avenue, in 1955. In 1979 Sewell franchised the deep-dish pizza concept. There are now fifty Original Chicago Pizzeria Uno restaurants across the country. In 1963 Sewell finally did open the Mexican restaurant he had dreamed about decades earlier, Su Casa, at 49 East Ontario Street. Sewell died of leukemia in 1990. *Photograph reprinted with permission from the* Chicago Sun-Times.

Ellen Gates Starr (1859–1940); social reformer; b: Laona, Illinois; d: Suffern, New York; age: 80. Ellen Gates Starr, along with Jane Addams, cofounded Hull-House, the pioneering settlement institution located at 800 South Halsted Street. Starr met Addams in 1877 at Rockford Female Seminary. One year later Starr left to accept a teaching position at a country school in Mount Morris, Illinois. The following year she moved to Chicago to teach English and art appreciation at the Kirkland School, a wealthy girls' school on the North Side. Addams and Starr maintained their friendship through correspondence and occasional visits. A journey to Toynbee Hall, a settlement house located in the working-class Whitechapel section of London, in 1888 inspired Addams to establish a similar institution in Chicago. She asked Starr to join her in the new venture. In September of 1889 they moved into an old mansion at what is now Halsted and Polk Streets. The neighborhood consisted of a mix of Irish, Italians, Germans, and Eastern European Jews, who toiled in the nearby sweatshops and factories. Starr and Addams regarded themselves not as missionaries or as morally superior social reformers who lived and worked among the poor but as neighbors and colleagues who brightened their own lives and the lives of others through art, music, and literature. Starr's early years at Hull-House were spent organizing reading classes, reading clubs, and art classes and teaching bookbinding, a craft she learned in England. But as she aged, she grew more passionate and her political beliefs assumed a more radical nature. The pursuit of beauty—a lifelong interest—was accompanied by an intense desire for social justice. She defended organized labor and supported the unionization of women. It wasn't unusual to see the frail-looking Starr marching in picket lines. Gradually she embraced socialism and, in 1916, she ran unsuccessfully as the Socialist candidate for alderman of the 19th Ward. Starr retired from Hull-House in 1930. Raised in a Unitarian household, she converted to Catholicism in later years. Starr died in the Convent of the Holy Child in Suffern, New York.

Michael Todd (1907–1958); stage and motion picture producer; b: Bloomington, Minnesota; d: near Grants, New Mexico; age: 51. Though born in Minnesota, Michael Todd (born Avram Hirsch Goldbogen) launched his career in the city of his youth, Chicago. Later he would change his name, marry actress Elizabeth Taylor, and earn a reputation as a boy wonder. Todd believed that the secret of show business success was to give the audience its money's worth. Todd was called another Billy Rose, the New York theater impresario, but his real ambition was to be like a fellow Chicagoan, Florenz Ziegfeld. Todd grew up near the Wicker Park neighborhood. After a series of odd jobs, he made his theatrical debut in Chicago in 1933 as the impresario who introduced a flame dancer at the Century of Progress Exposition. Within two years he had moved to New York to try his hand at producing Broadway shows. His first two shows, *Call Me Ziggy* (1936) and *The Man From Cairo* (1938) flopped, but in 1939 he enjoyed his first success with *The Hot Mikado*, which led to one hit after another. In 1945 he formed Michael Todd Productions and began to produce films. His first movie, *Oklahoma!* (1955), introduced the new wide-screen technique called Cinerama and was a smash hit. His second film, *Around the World in Eighty Days,* did even better, winning five Oscars, including best picture of 1956. Two years later Todd was killed in a plane crash and was buried in Waldheim Cemetery in Forest Park, Illinois. *Photograph courtesy of the Chicago Historical Society.*

Thorstein B. Veblen (1857–1929); economist; b: Wisconsin; d: Menlo Park, California; age: 72. Veblen earned a reputation as a tough-minded and acerbic critic of American society. He pursued graduate studies in philosophy at Johns Hopkins University before transferring to Yale University, where he received his Ph.D. in 1884. Veblen then obtained a fellowship in economics at Cornell University before coming to the University of Chicago in 1892 as an assistant professor. He spent fourteen years in Hyde Park. Called one of America's few great original thinkers, Veblen completed his most significant work while teaching in Chicago. His books include *The Place of Science in Modern Civilization, The Theory of Business Enterprise, Higher Learning in America,* and probably his best known book, *The Theory of the Leisure Class,* an important work in which he divided the leisure class into those who produce goods and services and those who use them. *Photograph reprinted with permission from the* Chicago Sun-Times.

Frances E. Willard (1839–1898); educator/social reformer; b: Churchville, New York; d: New York, New York; age: 58. Frances Elizabeth Willard waged a lifelong battle against alcohol and its devastating effects. Alcohol, she said, weakened the fabric of society. As founder of the Women's Christian Temperance Union (WCTU), Willard's vigorous campaigning laid the groundwork that led to the eventual passage of the National Prohibition Act of 1919. In 1871 Willard was named president of the Evanston Ladies College and two years later became dean of women when the Ladies College became the Women's College of Northwestern University. Willard resigned from the university in 1874 to become secretary of the national WCTU. Her new position gave her the opportunity to assume a prominent role in the national crusade against alcohol, which was then sweeping the country. Five years later she was named president, a title she retained until her death. A powerful and forceful speaker, Willard toured the country speaking out against the evils of liquor. In addition, she promoted women's suffrage, insisted on stiffer penalties for sexual crimes against women, and advocated passage of the eight-hour day. Willard died in her sleep in a New York City hotel room. In 1965 the Willard House at 1730 Chicago Avenue in Evanston, Illinois, was placed on the National Register of Historic Places. *Photograph courtesy of the Women's Christian Temperance Union.*

Sonny Boy Williamson I (1914–1948); musician; b: Jackson, Tennessee; d: Chicago, Illinois; age: 34. One of the best-loved and most influential Chicago bluesmen, John Lee "Sonny Boy" Williamson I is credited with turning the blues harmonica, or blues harp, from an accompanying instrument to a prominent solo instrument. His ebullient style and forceful singing helped shape the course of Chicago blues during the 1940s and 1950s. Williamson moved to Chicago in 1934 and worked with such other important blues figures in town as "Big" Bill Broonzy and Muddy Waters. Several of his recordings, including "Good Morning Little Schoolgirl," "Bluebird Blues," and "Sugar Mama Blues," have become blues standards. On June 1, 1948, Williamson was robbed and severely beaten while walking toward his apartment at 3226 South Giles Avenue. He died at Michael Reese Hospital from a skull fracture. The crime remains unsolved. *Photograph by T. W. Utley, courtesy of the Jackson-Madison County Library, Jackson, Tennessee.*

Bibliography

Addams, Jane. *Twenty Years at Hull-House*. New York: Macmillan, 1910.

Addams, Jane. *The Second Twenty Years at Hull-House*. New York: Macmillan, 1930.

Ade, George. *Chicago Stories*. Chicago: Henry Regnery Co., 1963.

Adelman, Charlotte. "A History of Women Lawyers in Illinois," *Illinois Bar Journal* (May 1986).

Adelman, William J. *Touring Pullman*. Chicago: Illinois Labor History Society, 1972.

Adelman, William J. *Haymarket Revisited*. Chicago: Illinois Labor History Society, 1976.

Allen, Walter C. and Brian A. L. Rust. *King Joe Oliver*. New Mexico State University: Jazz Monographs, No. 1, 1955.

Allsop, Kenneth. *The Bootleggers and Their Era*. Garden City, N. Y.: Doubleday, 1961.

Allswang, John M. *A House for All Peoples: Ethnic Politics in Chicago*. Lexington, Ky.: University of Kentucky Press, 1971.

Allswang, John M. *Bosses, Machines, and Urban Voters: An American Symbiosis*. Port Washington, N.Y.: Kennikat Press, 1977.

Alter, Sharon Z. "A Woman for Mayor?" *Chicago History* (Fall 1986).

Anderson, Margaret. *My Thirty Years War: An Autobiography*. New York: Covici, Friede Publishers, 1930.

Anderson, Margaret. *The Fiery Fountains*. New York: Hermitage House, 1951.

Anderson, Sherwood. *Sherwood Anderson's Memoirs*. Edited by Paul Rosenfeld. New York: Harcourt, Brace, 1942.

Andreas, A. T. *History of Chicago from the Earliest Period to the Present Time*. 3 vols. Chicago: A. T. Andreas, 1884–86.

Andrews, Clarence A. *Chicago in Story: A Literary History*. Iowa City, Iowa: Midwest Heritage Publishing Co., 1983.

Andrews, Wayne. *Battle for Chicago*. New York: Harcourt, Brace, 1946.

Angle, Paul M. *Philip K. Wrigley: A Memoir of a Modest Man*. Chicago: Rand McNally, 1975.

Anson, Adrian Constantine. *A Ball Player's Career*. New York: Macmillan, 1900.

Arthur Andersen and Company. *The First Fifty Years, 1913–1963*. Chicago: Arthur Andersen & Co., 1963.

Asbury, Herbert. *Gem of the Prairie: An Informal History of the Chicago Underworld*. Garden City, N.Y.: Garden City Publishing Co., 1942.

Ashbaugh, Carolyn. *Lucy Parsons, American Revolutionary*. Chicago: Charles H. Kerr Publishing Co., 1976.

Ashe, Arthur R., Jr. *A Hard Road to Glory: A History of the African-American Athlete 1919–1945*. New York: Warner Books, 1988.

Asher, Louis E. and Edith Heal. *Send No Money*. Chicago: Argus Books, 1942.

Ashmore, Harry S. *Unseasonable Truths: The Life of Robert Maynard Hutchins*. Boston: Little, Brown & Co., 1989.

Asinof, Eliot. *Eight Men Out: The Black Sox and the 1919 World Series*. Chicago: Holt, Rinehart and Winston, 1963.

Avrich, Paul. *The Haymarket Tragedy*. Princeton, N. J.: Princeton University Press, 1984.

Axelson, Gustaf W. *"Commy": The Life Story of Charles Comiskey*. Chicago: Reilly & Lee Co., 1919.

Bach, Ira J. *Chicago's Famous Buildings: A Photographic Guide to the City's Architectural Landmarks and Other Notable Buildings*. Chicago: University of Chicago Press, 1980.

Bach, Ira J. *Chicago on Foot*. Revised 3rd ed. Chicago: Rand McNally, 1977.

Bach, Ira J. and Mary Lackritz Gray. *A Guide to Chicago's Public Sculpture*. Chicago: University of Chicago Press, 1983.

Badger, R. Reid. *The Great American Fair: The World's Columbian Exposition and American Culture*. Chicago: Nelson-Hall, Inc., 1979.

Baker, Carlos. *Ernest Hemingway: A Life Story*. New York: Charles Scribner's Sons, 1969.

Baker, Nina. *Big Catalogue: The Life of Aaron Montgomery Ward*. New York: Harcourt, Brace, 1956.

Bakish, David. *Richard Wright*. New York: Frederick Ungar Publishing Co., 1973.

Balaban, Carrie. *Continuous Performance: The Story of A. J. Balaban*. New York: A. J. Balaban Foundation, 1964.

Barnard, Harry. *Eagle Forgotten: The Life of John Peter Altgeld*. Indianapolis: Bobbs-Merrill, 1938.

Barrett, James R. *Work and Community in the Jungle: Chicago's Packinghouse Workers, 1894–1922*. Urbana, Ill.: University of Illinois Press, 1987.

Bartlett, Arthur Charles. *Baseball and Mr. Spalding*. New York: Farrar, Straus & Young, 1951.

Baum, Frank Joslyn and Russell P. MacFall. *To Please A Child: A Biography of L. Frank Baum*. Chicago: Reilly & Lee Co., 1961.

Beadle, Muriel. *The Fortnightly of Chicago: The City and Its Women, 1873–1973*. Chicago: Henry Regnery Co., 1973.

Beck, Frank. *Hobohemia*. West Rindge, N. H.: Richard R. Smith Publishers, 1956.

Bennett, James O'Donnell. *Joseph Medill, A Brief Biography and an Appreciation*. Chicago: Chicago Tribune, 1947.

Berkow, Ira. *Maxwell Street: Survival in a Bazaar*. Garden City, N. Y.: Doubleday, 1977.

Biles, Roger. "Jacob M. Arvey, Kingmaker: The Nomination of Adlai E. Stevenson in 1952," *Chicago History* (Fall 1979).

Biles, Roger. *Big City Boss in Depression and War: Mayor Edward J. Kelly of Chicago.* DeKalb, Ill.: Northern Illinois University Press, 1984.

Birrell, James. *Walter Burley Griffin.* Brisbane, Australia: University of Queensland Press, 1964.

Bishop, Glenn and Paul T. Gilbert. *Chicago's Accomplishments and Leaders.* Chicago: Bishop Publishing Co., 1932.

Black, Edwin. "Louis Farrakhan—would you buy a toothpaste from this man?" *Chicago Reader* (April 11, 1986).

Block, Jean F. *Hyde Park Houses: An Informal History, 1856–1910.* Chicago: University of Chicago Press, 1978.

Blumberg, Dorothy Rose. *Florence Kelley: The Making of a Social Pioneer.* New York: Augustus M. Kelley, 1966.

Boas, Maxwell and Steve Chain. *Big Mac: The Unauthorized Story of McDonald's.* New York: E. P. Dutton, 1976.

Bonner, Thomas Neville. *Medicine in Chicago 1850–1950, A Chapter in the Social and Scientific Development of a City.* Madison, Wis.: American History Research Center, Inc., 1957.

Bontemps, Arna and Jack Conroy. *Anyplace But Here.* New York: Hill and Wang, 1966.

Boorstin, Daniel. J. "A. Montgomery Ward's Mail-Order Business," *Chicago History* (Spring/Summer 1983).

Bordin, Ruth. *Frances Willard: A Biography.* Chapel Hill, N. C.: University of North Carolina Press, 1986.

Bowen, Louise DeKoven. *Open Windows: Stories of People and Places.* Chicago: Ralph Fletcher Seymour, Publisher, 1946.

Bowen, Louise DeKoven. *Growing Up With A City.* New York: Macmillan, 1962.

Bowron, Bernard R., Jr. *Henry B. Fuller of Chicago: The Ordeal of a Genteel Realist in Ungenteel America.* Westport, Conn.: Greenwood Press, 1974.

Bradley, Preston with Harry Barnard. *Along the Way: An Autobiography.* New York: David McKay Co., Inc., 1962.

Bradley, Van Allen. *Music for the Millions: The Kimball Piano and Organ Story 1857–1957.* Chicago: Henry Regnery Co., 1957.

Branch, Edgar Marquess. *James T. Farrell.* Minneapolis: University of Minnesota Press, 1963.

Breasted, Charles B. *Pioneer to the Past: The Story of James Henry Breasted, Archaeologist.* New York: Charles Scribner's Sons, 1943.

Bregstone, Philip P. *Chicago and Its Jews: A Cultural History.* Privately published, 1933.

Brommel, Bernard J. *Eugene V. Debs: Spokesman for Labor and Socialism.* Chicago: Charles H. Kerr Publishing Co., 1978.

Brooks, H. Allen. *The Prairie School: Frank Lloyd Wright and His Midwest Contemporaries.* New York: W. W. Norton & Co., 1976.

Brooks, H. Allen. *Frank Lloyd Wright and the Prairie School.* New York: George Braziller, Inc., 1984.

Brooks, Tim. *The Complete Directory to Prime Time TV Stars 1946–Present.* New York: Ballantine Books, 1987.

Broonzy, William and Yannick Bruynoghe. *Big Bill Blues: William Broonzy's Story.* London: Cassell, 1955.

Brown, Elijah. *The Real Billy Sunday.* New York: Fleming H. Revell Company, 1914.

Brown, Warren. *Rockne.* Chicago: Reilly & Lee Company, 1931.

Brown, Warren. *The Chicago Cubs.* New York: G. P. Putnam's Sons, 1946.

Browne, Maurice. *Too Late to Lament.* Bloomington, Ind.: Indiana University Press, 1956.

Brubaker, Robert L. "130 Years of Opera in Chicago," *Chicago History* (Fall 1979).

Bruns, Roger A. *The Damndest Radical: The Life and World of Ben Reitman, Chicago's Celebrated Social Reformer, Hobo King, and Whorehouse Physician.* Urbana, Ill.: University of Illinois Press, 1987.

Buckler, Helen. *Doctor Dan: Pioneer in American Surgery.* Boston: Little, Brown & Co., 1954.

Buder, Stanley. *Pullman: An Experiment in Industrial Order and Community Planning, 1880–1930.* New York: Oxford University Press, 1967.

Buhle, Mari Jo. *Women and American Socialism.* Urbana, Ill.: University of Illinois Press, 1979.

Buhle, Mari Jo, Paul Buhle, and Dan Georgakas. *Encyclopedia of the American Left.* New York: Garland Publishing, 1990.

Burg, David F. *Chicago's White City of 1893.* Lexington, Ill.: University of Kentucky Press , 1976.

Burton, J. C., ed. *Arthur Young and the Business He Founded.* New York: Arthur Young & Co., 1948.

Bushnell, George D., Jr. "When Jazz Came to Chicago," *Chicago History* (Spring 1971).

Butcher, Fanny. *Many Lives, One Love.* New York: Harper & Row, 1972.

Cahan, Richard. *Landmark Neighborhoods in Chicago.* Chicago: Commission on Chicago Historical and Architectural Landmarks, 1981.

Calmer, Alan. *Labor Agitator: The Story of Albert R. Parsons.* New York: International Publishers, 1937.

Campbell, Jack K. *Colonel Francis W. Parker: The Children's Crusader.* New York: Teachers College Press, 1967.

Carbutt, J., comp., *Biographical Sketches of the Leading Men of Chicago Written by the Best Talent of the Northwest.* Chicago: Wilson & St. Clair, 1868.

Carney, Jack. *Mary Marcy.* Chicago: Charles H. Kerr Publishing Co., 1923.

Carr, Clark E., *Stephen A. Douglas: His Life, Public Services, Speeches and Patriotism.* Chicago: A. C. McClurg, 1909.

Carson, Mina. *Settlement Folk: Social Thought and the American Settlement Movement 1885–1930.* Chicago: University of Chicago Press, 1990.

Carter, Steven R. *Hansberry's Drama: Commitment Amid Complexity.* Urbana, Ill.: University of Illinois Press, 1991.

Carwardine, William H. *The Pullman Strike.* Chicago: Charles H. Kerr Publishing Co., 1973.

Casey, Robert J. and W. A. S. Douglas. *Pioneer Railroad: The Story of the Chicago and North Western System.* New York: McGraw-Hill, 1948.

Cassin, Herbert N. *Cyrus Hall McCormick.* Chicago: A. C. McClurg, 1909.

Charters, Samuel B. *The Bluesmen.* New York: Oak Publications, 1967.

Charters, Samuel B. and Leonard Kunstadt. *Jazz: A History of the New York Scene.* New York: Da Capo Press, 1981.

Cheney, Anne. *Lorraine Hansberry.* Boston: Twayne Publishers, 1984.

Chilton, John. *Who's Who of Jazz: Storyville to Swing Street.* Philadelphia: Time-Life, 1978.

Clarke, Donald. *The Penguin Encyclopedia of Popular Music.* London: Penguin Books, 1989.

Collier, James Lincoln. *The Making of Jazz: A Comprehensive History.* New York: Dell Publishing Co., 1979.

Collier, James Lincoln. *Louis Armstrong: An American Genius.* New York: Oxford University Press, 1983.

Collier, James Lincoln. *Benny Goodman and the Swing Era.* New York: Oxford University Press, 1989.

Commission on Chicago Historical and Architectural Landmarks. "Black Metropolis Historic District." March 7, 1984.

Commission on Chicago Landmarks. "Chess Records Office and Studio." July 1989.

Condit, Carl W. *The Rise of the Skyscraper.* Chicago: University of Chicago Press, 1952.

Condit, Carl W. *The Chicago School of Architecture: A History of Commercial and Public Building in the Chicago Area, 1875–1925.* Chicago: University of Chicago Press, 1964.

Condit, Carl W. *Chicago 1910–29: Building, Planning, and Urban Technology.* Chicago: University of Chicago Press, 1973.

Condon, Eddie and T. Sugrue. *We Called it Music.* New York: Da Capo Press, 1987.

Cone, Fairfax M. *With All Its Faults: A Candid Account of Forty Years in Advertising.* Boston: Little, Brown & Co., 1969.

Cone, Fairfax M. *The Blue Streak: Some Observations, Mostly About Advertising.* Chicago: Crain Communications Inc., 1973.

Connor, D. Russell. *Benny Goodman: Listen to His Legacy.* Metuchen, N. J.: Scarecrow Press, 1988.

Conrow, Robert. *Field Days: The Life, Times and Reputation of Eugene Field.* New York: Charles Scribner's Sons, 1974.

Conroy, Joseph P. *Arnold Damen, S.J.: A Chapter in the Making of Chicago.* New York: Benziger Brothers, 1930.

Cook, Frederick Francis. *Bygone Days in Chicago: Recollections of the "Garden City" of the Sixties.* Chicago: A. C. McClurg, 1910.

Coombs, Sam and Bob West, eds. *America's National Game.* San Francisco: Halo Books, 1991.

Cortesi, Lawrence. *Jean duSable, Father of Chicago.* Philadelphia: Chilton Book Co., 1972.

Costin, Lela B. *Two Sisters for Social Justice: A Biography of Grace and Edith Abbott.* Urbana, Ill.: University of Illinois Press, 1983.

Counts, George S. *School and Society in Chicago.* New York: Harcourt, Brace, 1928.

Cox, Martha Heasley and Wayne Chatterton. *Nelson Algren.* Boston: Twayne, 1975.

Coyle, Lee. *George Ade.* New Haven, Conn.: College & University Press, 1964.

Crawford, Richard. *The Civil War Songbook.* New York: Dover Publications, 1977.

Cromie, Robert. *A Short History of Chicago.* San Francisco: Lexikos, 1984.

Currey, Josiah Seymour. *Chicago: Its History and Its Builders, A Century of Marvelous Growth.* Chicago: S. J. Clarke, 1912.

Currey, Josiah Seymour. *The Story of Old Fort Dearborn.* Chicago: A. C. McClurg, 1912.

Curtis, Richard K. *They Called Him Mister Moody.* Garden City, N.Y.: Doubleday, 1962.

Dance, Stanley. *The World of Earl Hines.* New York: Charles Scribner's Sons, 1977.

Dance, Stanley. *The World of Swing.* New York: Da Capo Press, 1979.

Darling, Sharon. *Chicago Furniture Art, Craft, & Industry 1833–1983.* New York: W. W. Norton & Co., 1984.

Darnell, Don. "Martie." *Chicago Tribune Sunday Magazine,* January 20, 1991.

Darrow, Clarence. *The Story of My Life.* New York: Charles Scribner's Sons, 1932.

Dart, Susan. *Evelyn Shaw McCutcheon and Ragdale.* Lake Forest, Ill.: Lake Forest–Lake Bluff Historical Society, 1980.

Davis, Allen F. *Spearheads of Reform: The Social Settlements and the Progressive Movement, 1890–1914.* New York: Oxford University Press, 1971.

Davis, Allen F. *American Heroine: The Life and Legend of Jane Addams.* Oxford: Oxford University Press, 1973.

Davis, Allen F. and Mary Lynn McCree, eds. *Eighty Years at Hull-House.* Bloomington, Ind.: Indiana University Press, 1969.

Davis, Ronald L. *Opera in Chicago.* New York: Appleton-Century, 1966.

Dawson, Warren R. *Who Was Who in Egyptology.* Oxford: Oxford University Press, 1972.

de Camp, L. Sprague. *Literary Swordsmen and Sorcerers: The Makers of Heroic Fantasy.* Sauk City, Wis.: Arkham House, 1976.

Dedmon, Emmett. *Fabulous Chicago.* New York: Atheneum, 1981.

deLatil, Pierre. *Enrico Fermi: The Man and His Theories.* New York: P. S. Eriksson, 1964.

Dell, Floyd. *Homecoming: An Autobiography.* New York: Farrar, 1933.

DeMuth, Jerry. *Small Town Chicago: The Comic Perspective of Finley Peter Dunne, George Ade, Ring Lardner.* Port Washington, N. Y.: Kennikat Press, 1980.

Dennis, Charles H. *Victor Lawson: His Time and His Work.* Chicago: University of Chicago Press, 1935.

Destler, Chester McArthur. *Henry Demarest Lloyd and the Empire of Reform.* Philadelphia: University of Pennsylvania, 1963.

Donnelly, Joseph P. *Jacques Marquette.* Chicago: Loyola University Press, 1985.

Drake, St. Clair and Horace R. Cayton. *Black Metropolis: A Study of Negro Life in a Northern City.* New York: Harper & Row, 1962.

Drew, Bettina. *Nelson Algren: A Life On the Wild Side.* New York: Putnam, 1989.

Duffey, Bernard. *The Chicago Renaissance in American Letters, A Critical History.* East Lansing, Mich.: The Michigan State College Press, 1954.

Duis, Perry. *Chicago: Creating New Traditions.* Chicago: Chicago Historical Society, 1976.

Duis, Perry. *The Saloon: Public Drinking in Chicago and Boston, 1880–1920.* Urbana, Ill.: University of Illinois Press, 1983.

Duis, Perry R. and Glen E. Holt. "Escape to Eagle's Nest," *Chicago* (September 1982).

Duncan, Hugh Dalziel. *The Rise of Chicago as a Literary Center.* Totawa, N. J.: Bedminster Press, 1964.

Duncan, Hugh Dalziel. *Culture and Democracy: The Struggle for Form in Society and Architecture in Chicago and the Middle West during the Life and Times of Louis H. Sullivan.* New Brunswick, N. J.: Transaction Publishers, 1989.

Duster, Alfreda M., ed. *Crusader for Justice: The Autobiography of Ida B. Wells.* Chicago: University of Chicago Press, 1970.

Eaton, Leonard K. *Two Chicago Architects and Their Clients: Frank Lloyd Wright and Howard Van Doren Shaw.* Cambridge, Mass.: MIT Press, 1969.

Ebner, Michael H. *Creating Chicago's North Shore: A Suburban History.* Chicago: University of Chicago Press, 1988.

Eckert, Allan. *Gateway to Empire.* Boston: Little, Brown & Co., 1982.

Eifert, Virginia S. *Louis Jolliet: Explorer of Rivers.* New York: Dodd, Mead & Co., 1961.

Elder, Donald. *Ring Lardner.* Garden City, N. Y.: Doubleday, 1956.

Elias, Robert H. *Theodore Dreiser: Apostle of Nature.* New York: Alfred A. Knopf, 1949.

Ellis, Elmer. *Mr. Dooley's America: A Life of Finley Peter Dunne.* New York: Alfred A. Knopf, 1941.

Ellis, W. T. *Billy Sunday: The Man and His Message.* Philadelphia: John C. Winston Co., 1936.

Ely, Melvin Patrick. *The Adventures of Amos 'n' Andy: A Social History of an American Phenomenon.* New York: The Free Press, 1991.

Enright, Jim. *Chicago Cubs.* New York: Macmillan, 1975.

Epstein, Dena J. *Music Publishing in Chicago before 1871: The Firm of Root & Cady.* Detroit: Harmonie Park Press, 1969.

Eskenazi, Gerald. *Bill Veeck: A Baseball Legend.* New York: McGraw-Hill, 1987.

Evans, Linda J. "Claude A. Barnett and the Associated Negro Press," *Chicago History* (Spring 1983).

Falk, Candace. *Love, Anarchy, and Emma Goldman.* New York: Holt, Rinehart and Winston, 1984.

Fanning, Charles, ed. *Mr. Dooley and the Chicago Irish: An Anthology.* New York: Arno Press, 1976.

Fanning, Charles. *Finley Peter Dunne and Mr. Dooley: The Chicago Years.* Lexington, Ky.: University of Kentucky Press, 1978.

Fanning, Charles and Ellen Skerrett. "James T. Farrell and Washington Park: The Novel as Social History," *Chicago History* (Summer 1979).

Farr, Finis. *Frank Lloyd Wright: A Biography.* New York: Charles Scribner's Sons, 1961.

Farr, Finis. *Black Champion: The Life and Times of Jack Johnson.* New York: Charles Scribner's Sons, 1964.

Farr, Finis. *Chicago: A Personal History of America's Most American City.* New Rochelle, N. Y.: Arlington House, 1973.

Farrell, James T. *Studs Lonigan.* New York: Random House, 1938.

Fehrenbacher, Don. *Chicago Giant: A Biography of "Long John" Wentworth.* Madison, Wis.: American History Research Center, 1957.

Fermi, Laura. *Atoms in the Family—My Life with Enrico Fermi.* Chicago: University of Chicago Press, 1954.

Fetherling, Doug. *The Five Lives of Ben Hecht.* Toronto: Lester and Orpen Ltd., 1977.

Ffrench, Charles, ed. *Biographical History of the American Irish in Chicago.* Chicago: American Biographical Publishing Co., 1897.

Fink, Gary M., ed. *Biographical Dictionary of American Labor Leaders.* Westport, Conn.: Greenwood Press, 1974.

Finks, P. David. *The Radical Vision of Saul Alinsky.* Mahwah, N. J.: Paulist Press, 1984.

Fischetti, John. *Zinga Zanga Za!* Chicago: Follett, 1973.

Fishbein, Leslie. *Rebels in Bohemia.* Chapel Hill, N. C.: University of North Carolina Press, 1982.

Fishbein, Morris. *Morris Fishbein, M.D.: An Autobiography*. Garden City, N.Y.: Doubleday, 1969.

Flinn, John J. *The Handbook of Chicago Biography*. Chicago: Standard Guide Co., 1893.

Flinn, John J. *History of the Chicago Police from the Settlement of the Community to the Present Time*. Chicago: Police Book Fund, 1887.

Foner, Eric and Olivia Mahoney. *A House Divided: America in the Age of Lincoln*. Chicago: Chicago Historical Society in association with W. W. Norton & Co., 1990.

Foner, Philip, ed. *Autobiographies of the Haymarket Martyrs*. Chicago: Charles H. Kerr Publishing Co., 1976.

Fortman, Edmund J. *Lineage: A Biographical History of the Chicago Province*. Chicago: Loyola University Press, 1987.

Fraser, Steven. *Labor Will Rule: Sidney Hillman and the Rise of American Labor*. New York: File Press, 1991.

Freeman, Bud, as told to Robert Wolf. *Crazeology: The Autobiography of a Chicago Jazzman*. Urbana, Ill.: University of Illinois Press, 1989.

Fremon, David K. *Chicago Politics Ward By Ward*. Bloomington, Ind.: Indiana University Press, 1988.

Fulk, David and Dan Riley, eds. *The Cubs Reader*. Boston: Houghton Mifflin Co., 1991.

Funchion, Michael F. *Chicago's Irish Nationalists, 1881–1890*. Salem, N. H.: Ayer Co. Pub., 1976.

Furer, Howard B. *Chicago: A Chronological & Documentary History, 1784–1970*. Dobbs Ferry, N. Y.: Oceana Publications, 1974.

Garden, Mary and Louis Biancolli. *Mary Garden's Story*. New York: Simon & Schuster, 1951.

Gardner, Martin and Russel B. Nye. *The Wizard of Oz and Who He Was*. East Lansing, Mich.: Michigan State University Press, 1957.

Garraghan, Gilbert J. *The Jesuits of the Middle United States*. Chicago: Loyola University Press, 1984.

Garvey, Timothy J. *Public Sculptor: Lorado Taft and the Beautification of Chicago*. Urbana, Ill.: University of Illinois Press, 1988.

Gayle, Addison. *Richard Wright, Ordeal of a Native Son*. Garden City, N. Y.: Anchor Press/Doubleday, 1980.

Gerstenberg, Alice. *Unquenched Fire*. Boston: Small, Maynard & Co., 1912.

Getz, Gene A. *MBI: The Story of the Moody Bible Institute*. Chicago: Moody Press, 1969.

Gies, Joseph. *The Colonel of Chicago: A Biography of the Chicago Tribune's Legendary Publisher, Colonel Robert McCormick*. New York: E. P. Dutton, 1979.

Gilbert, Gorman and Robert E. Samuels. *The Taxicab: An Urban Transportation Survivor*. Chapel Hill, N. C.: University of North Carolina Press, 1982.

Gilbert, Paul Thomas and Charles Lee Bryson. *Chicago and Its Makers*. Chicago: Felix Mendelsohn, 1929.

Gill, Brendan. *Many Masks: A Life of Frank Lloyd Wright*. New York: Ballantine Books, 1987.

Ginger, Ray. *The Bending Cross: A Biography of Eugene Victor Debs*. New Brunswick, N. J.: Rutgers University Press, 1949.

Ginger, Ray. *Altgeld's America: The Lincoln Ideal Versus Changing Realities*. New York: Funk and Wagnalls, 1958.

Gleason, Bill. *Daley of Chicago: The Man, the Mayor, and the Limits of Conventional Politics*. New York: Simon & Schuster, 1970.

Gold, Eddie and Art Ahrens. *The Golden Era Cubs 1876–1945*. Chicago: Bonus Books, 1985.

Golden, Harry. *Carl Sandburg*. Cleveland: World Publishing Co., 1961.

Goldmark, Josephine. *Impatient Crusader: Florence Kelley's Life Story*. Urbana, Ill.: University of Illinois Press, 1953.

Goler, Robert I. and Susan E. Hirsch. *A City Comes of Age: Chicago in the 1890s*. Chicago: Chicago Historical Society, 1990.

Goodman, Benny and Irving Kolodin. *The Kingdom of Swing*. New York: Stackpole Sons, 1939.

Goodspeed, Thomas Wakefield. *Gustavus Franklin Swift, 1839–1903*. Vol. 1. Chicago: University of Chicago Biographical Sketches, n.d.

Goodspeed, Thomas Wakefield. *A History of the University of Chicago, founded by John D. Rockefeller; the First-Quarter Century*. Chicago: University of Chicago Press, 1916.

Goodspeed, Thomas Wakefield. *The Story of the University of Chicago 1890–1925*. Chicago: University of Chicago Press, 1925.

Goreau, Laurraine. *Just Mahalia, Baby*. Gretna, La.: Pelican Publishing Co., 1975.

Gosnell, Harold F. *Negro Politicians: The Rise of Negro Politics in Chicago*. Chicago: University of Chicago Press, 1935.

Gottfried, Alex. *Boss Cermak of Chicago: A Study of Political Leadership*. Seattle: University of Washington, 1962.

Gove, Samuel K. and Louis H. Masotti. *After Daley: Chicago Politics in Transition*. Urbana, Ill.: University of Illinois Press, 1982.

Green, Paul M. and Melvin G. Holli, eds. *The Mayors: The Chicago Political Tradition*. Carbondale, Ill.: Southern Illinois University Press, 1987.

Greene, David L. and Dick Martin. *The Oz Scrapbook*. New York: Random House, 1977.

Greene, Victor. *For God and Country: The Rise of Polish and Lithuanian Ethnic Consciousness in America*. Madison, Wis.: State Historical Society of Wisconsin, 1975.

Griffin, Constance. *Henry Blake Fuller: A Critical Biography*. Oxford: Oxford University Press, 1939.

Grossman, James R. *Land of Hope: Chicago, Black Southerners, and the Great Migration*. Chicago: University of Chicago Press, 1989.

Grubb, Kevin Boyd. *Razzle Dazzle: The Life and Work of Bob Fosse.* New York: St. Martin's Press, 1989.

Guralnick, Peter. *Feel Like Going Home: Portraits in Blues and Rock 'n Roll.* New York: Vintage Books, 1981.

Guralnick, Peter. *The Listener's Guide to the Blues.* New York: Facts on File, Inc., 1982.

Guralnick, Peter. *Sweet Soul Music: Rhythm and Blues and the Southern Dream of Freedom.* New York: Harper & Row, 1986.

Guralnick, Peter. *Searching for Robert Johnson: The Life and Legend of the "King of the Delta Blues Singers."* New York: E. P. Dutton, 1989.

Gutstein, Morris A. *A Priceless Heritage, The Epic Growth of Nineteenth Century Chicago Jewry.* New York: Bloch Publishing Co., 1953.

Halas, George S. with Gwen Morgan and Arthur Veysey. *Halas: An Autobiography.* Chicago: Bonus Books, 1986.

Halker, Clark D. "Banding Together," *Chicago History* (September 1989).

Halper, Albert. *On the Shore.* New York: Viking Press, 1934.

Halper, Albert, ed. *This is Chicago.* New York: Holt, 1952.

Halpern, Martin. *William Vaughn Moody.* New Haven, Conn.: College & University Press, 1964.

Hamilton, Alice. *Exploring the Dangerous Trades: The Autobiography of Alice Hamilton.* Boston: Little, Brown & Co., 1943.

Hansberry, Lorraine. *To Be Young, Gifted and Black: An Informal Autobiography of Lorraine Hansberry.* Adapted by Robert Nemiroff. New York: Signet, 1969.

Hansen, Harry. *Midwest Portraits: A Book of Memories and Friendships.* New York: Harcourt, Brace, 1923.

Harding, Carroll Rede. *George M. Pullman, 1831–1897 and the Pullman Company.* New York: Newcomen Society in North America, 1951.

Harris, Frank. *The Bomb.* Chicago: University of Chicago Press, 1963.

Harris, Leon. *Merchant Princes: An Intimate History of Jewish Families Who Built Great Department Stores.* New York: Harper & Row, 1979.

Harris, Mark. *City of Discontent: An Interpretive Biography of Vachel Lindsay.* Sag Harbor, N. Y.: Second Chance Press, 1980.

Harris, Sheldon. *Blues Who's Who: A Biographical Dictionary of Blues Singers.* New York: Da Capo Press, 1979.

Harrison, Carter H., II. *Stormy Years: The Autobiography of Carter H. Harrison, Five Times Mayor of Chicago.* Indianapolis: Bobbs-Merrill, 1935.

Harrison, Carter H., II. *Growing Up with Chicago.* Chicago: Ralph Seymour, 1944.

Hart, John D. *The Oxford Companion to American Literature.* New York: Oxford University Press, 1983.

Hart, John E. *Floyd Dell.* New York: Twayne, 1971.

Harvey, Stephen. *Directed by Vincente Minnelli.* New York: The Museum of Modern Art and Harper & Row Publishers, 1989.

Hayden, Tom. *Trial.* New York: Holt, Rinehart and Winston. 1970.

Hayes, Alice and Susan Moon. *Ragdale: A History and Guide.* Berkeley, Calif., and Lake Forest, Ill.: Open Books and the Ragdale Foundation, 1990.

Hayner, Don and Tom McNamee. *Streetwise Chicago: A History of Chicago Street Names.* Chicago: Loyola University Press, 1988.

Hecht, Ben. *1001 Afternoons in Chicago.* Chicago: Covici-McGee, 1922.

Hecht, Ben. *A Child of the Century: An Autobiography.* New York: Simon & Schuster, 1954.

Hecht, Ben. *Charlie, The Improbable Life of Charles MacArthur.* New York: Harper & Bros., 1957.

Hecht, Ben. *Gaily, Gaily: The Memoirs of a Cub Reporter in Chicago.* New York: Doubleday, 1963.

Heffron, Ida Cassa. *Francis Wayland Parker: An Interpretative Biography.* Los Angeles: Ivan Deach, Jr., 1934.

Heim, Chris. "Riding the Waves: The Rise of Black Radio in Chicago." *Chicago Tribune Sunday Magazine* (February 12, 1989).

Heise, Kenan. *Alphonse: A One-Man Play on the Words of Al Capone.* Evanston, Ill.: Chicago Historical Bookworks, 1989.

Heise, Kenan and Michael Edgerton. *Chicago: Center for Enterprise.* 2 vols. Woodland Hills, Calif.: Windsor Publications, 1982.

Heise, Kenan and Mark Frazel. *Hands On Chicago: Getting Hold of the City.* Chicago: Bonus Books, 1987.

Henry, David D. *William Vaughn Moody: A Study.* Boston: Bruce Humphries, Publishers, 1934.

Herrick, Mary J. *The Chicago Schools: A Social and Political History.* Beverly Hills, Calif.: Sage Publications, 1971.

Higdon, Hal. *The Crime of the Century: The Leopold and Loeb Case.* New York: G. P. Putnam's Sons, 1975.

Hines, Thomas S. *Burnham of Chicago: Architect and Planner.* Chicago: University of Chicago Press, 1974.

Hirsch, Arnold R. *Making the Second Ghetto: Race & Housing in Chicago, 1940–1960.* New York: Cambridge University Press, 1983.

Hirsch, David E. *Rabbi Emil G. Hirsch: The Reform Advocate.* Chicago: Whitehall Company, 1968.

Hirsch, Edwin F. *Frank Billings: The Architect of Medical Education, an Apostle of Excellence in Clinical Practice, a Leader in Chicago Medicine.* Chicago: Edwin F. Hirsch, 1966.

Hirshey, Gerri. *Nowhere to Run: The Story of Soul Music.* New York: Times Books, 1984.

Hoffman, Donald. *The Architecture of John Wellborn Root.* Baltimore: Johns Hopkins University Press, 1973.

Hoffman, Donald. *Frank Lloyd Wright's Robie House: The Illustrated Story of an Architectural Masterpiece.* New York: Dover Publications, 1984.

Hofmeister, Rudolf A. *The Germans of Chicago.* Chicago: University of Illinois, 1976.

Hogan, Lawrence D. *A Black National News Service: The Associated Negro Press and Claude Barnett, 1919–1940.* Rutherford, N. J.: Fairleigh Dickinson University Press, 1984.

Holli, Melvin G. and Paul M. Green. *The Making of The Mayor, Chicago 1983: Harold Washington.* Grand Rapids, Mich.: William B. Eerdmans Publishing Co., 1983.

Holli, Melvin G. and Paul M. Green. *Bashing Chicago Traditions: Harold Washington's Last Campaign, Chicago 1987.* Grand Rapids, Mich.: William B. Eerdmans Publishing Co., 1989.

Holli, Melvin G. and Peter d'A. Jones, eds. *Biographical Dictionary of American Mayors, 1820–1980: Big City Mayors.* Westport, Conn.: Greenwood Press, 1981.

Holli, Melvin G. and Peter d'A. Jones, eds. *Ethnic Chicago.* Grand Rapids, Mich.: William B. Eerdmans Publishing Co., 1984.

Holloway, Jean. *Hamlin Garland.* Austin, Tex.: University of Texas Press, 1960.

Holt, Glen E. and Dominic A. Pacyga. *Chicago: A Historical Guide to the Neighborhoods, The Loop and South Side.* Chicago: Chicago Historical Society, 1979.

Honig, Donald. *Chicago Cubs: An Illustrated History.* New York: Prentice-Hall Press, 1991.

Horan, James D. *The Pinkertons: The Detective Dynasty That Made History.* New York: Crown Publishers, 1967.

Horowitz, Helen Lefkowitz. *Culture & The City: Cultural Philanthropy in Chicago From the 1880s To 1917.* Chicago: University of Chicago Press, 1976.

Horwitt, Sanford D. *Let Them Call Me Rebel: Saul Alinsky, His Life and Legacy.* New York: Alfred A. Knopf, 1989.

Howe, Irving. *Sherwood Anderson.* Stanford, Calif.: Stanford University Press, 1966.

Hutchinson, William T. *Cyrus Hall McCormick.* 2 vols. New York: The Century Co., 1930.

Hynek, J. Allen. *The UFO Experience: A Scientific Inquiry.* Chicago: Henry Regnery Co., 1972.

Inglehart, Babette, ed. *Walking with Women through Chicago History.* Chicago: Salsedo Press, 1981.

Jackson, Mahalia and E. M. Wylie. *Movin' On Up: The Mahalia Jackson Story.* New York: Hawthorn Books, 1966.

Jeuck, John E. and Boris Emmet. *Catalogues and Counters: A History of Sears, Roebuck & Co.* Chicago: University of Chicago Press, 1950.

Jewell, Frank. *Annotated Bibliography of Chicago History.* Chicago: Chicago Historical Society, 1979.

Johannsen, Robert W. *Stephen A. Douglas.* New York: Oxford University Press, 1973.

Johnson, Claudius O. *Carter Henry Harrison I: Political Leader.* Chicago: University of Chicago Press, 1928.

Johnson, Geoffrey. "Little Captain of the Ragged, the Mad Army of Poets," *Chicago Reader* (September 6, 1985).

Johnson, Geoffrey. "Edgar, the Ape-Man," *Chicago* (December 1989).

Johnson, Jack. *Jack Johnson is a Dandy, An Autobiography.* New York: Chelsea House Publishers, 1969.

Johnson, Mary Ann, ed. *The Many Faces of Hull-House.* Urbana, Ill.: University of Illinois Press, 1989.

Jones, Leroi. *Blues People.* New York: William Morrow, 1963.

Jones, Mary Harris. *The Autobiography of Mother Jones.* 3rd rev. ed. Chicago: Charles H. Kerr Publishing Co., 1976.

Jones, Max and John Chilton. *The Louis Armstrong Story, 1900–1971.* Boston: Little, Brown & Co., 1971.

Josephson, Matthew. *Sidney Hillman: Statesman of American Labor.* Garden City, N. Y.: Doubleday, 1952.

Kantowicz, Edward. *Polish-American Politics in Chicago.* Chicago: University of Chicago Press, 1972.

Kantowicz, Edward R. *Corporation Sole: Cardinal Mundelein and Chicago Catholicism.* Notre Dame, Ind.: University of Notre Dame Press, 1983.

Karl, Barry D. *Charles E. Merriam and the Study of Politics.* Chicago: University of Chicago Press, 1974.

Katz, Donald R. *The Big Store: Inside the Crisis & Revolution at Sears.* New York: Viking Press, 1987.

Keil, Charles. *Urban Blues.* Chicago: University of Chicago Press, 1966.

Kelly, Fred C. *George Ade: Warmhearted Satirist.* Indianapolis: Bobbs-Merrill Co., 1947.

Kennedy, Eugene. *Himself! The Life and Times of Richard J. Daley.* New York: Viking Press, 1978.

Kernfeld, Barry, ed. *The New Grove Dictionary of Jazz.* 2 vols. New York: Macmillan, 1988.

Kinsley, Philip. *The Chicago Tribune: Its First 100 Years.* 3 vols. New York: Alfred A. Knopf, 1943–46.

Kinzie, Juliette A. *Wau Bun, the "Early Days" of the Northwest.* Chicago: Caxton Club, 1901.

Kirkland, Caroline. *Chicago Yesterdays.* Chicago: Daughaday & Co., 1919.

Kirkland, Joseph. *The Story of Chicago: Bringing the History Up to December, 1894.* 2 vols. Chicago: Dibble, 1895.

Kleppner, Paul. *Chicago Divided: The Making of a Black Mayor.* DeKalb, Ill.: Northern Illinois University Press, 1988.

Klinkowitz, Jerome. *The Diaries of Willard Motley.* Ames, Iowa: Iowa State University Press, 1978.

Kobler, John. *Capone: The Life and World of Al Capone.* New York: G. P. Putnam's Sons, 1971.

Koenig, Rev. Msgr. Harry C., S.T.D. *A History of the Parishes of the Archdiocese of Chicago.* 2 vols. Chicago: Catholic Bishop of Chicago, 1980.

Kogan, Herman. *The Great EB: The Story of the Encyclopaedia Britannica.* Chicago: University of Chicago Press, 1958.

Kogan, Herman. *The Long White Line: The Story of Abbott Laboratories.* New York: Random House, 1963.

Kogan, Herman. *A Continuing Marvel, The Story of The Museum of Science and Industry.* Garden City, N. Y.: Doubleday, 1973.

Kogan, Herman. *The First Century: The Chicago Bar Association 1874–1974.* Chicago: Rand McNally, 1974.

Kogan, Herman and Robert Cromie. *The Great Fire: Chicago, 1871.* New York: G. P Putnam's Sons, 1971.

Kogan, Herman and Rick. *Pharmacist to the Nation: A History of Walgreen Co.* Deerfield, Ill.: Walgreen Co., 1989.

Kogan, Herman and Lloyd Wendt. *Lords of the Levee: The Story of Bathhouse John and Hinky Dink.* Indianapolis: Bobbs-Merrill Co., 1943.

Kogan, Herman and Lloyd Wendt. *Chicago: A Pictorial History.* New York: E. P. Dutton, 1958.

Kornbluh, Joyce, ed. *Rebel Voices.* Ann Arbor: University of Michigan Press, 1964.

Kornblum, William. *Blue Collar Community.* Chicago: University of Chicago Press, 1974.

Kramer, Dale. *Chicago Renaissance: The Literary Life of the Midwest 1900–1930.* New York: Appleton-Century, 1966.

Krassen, Miles and Larry McCullough. Liner notes to *Irish Traditional Instrumental Music from Chicago, Volume II.* Rounder Records 6006, 1978.

Kroc, Ray with Robert Anderson. *Grinding It Out: The Making of McDonald's.* Chicago: Henry Regnery Co., 1977.

Lait, Jack and Mortimer Lee. *Chicago Confidential: The Lowdown on the Big Town.* New York: Crown Publishers, 1950.

Lanctot, Barbara. *A Walk through Graceland Cemetery.* Chicago: Chicago Architecture Foundation, 1988.

Lane, George A. and Algimantas Kezys. *Chicago Churches and Synagogues: An Architectural Pilgrimage.* Chicago: Loyola University Press, 1981.

Langford, Jim. *The Game Is Never Over: An Appreciative History of the Chicago Cubs, 1948–1980.* South Bend, Ind.: Icarus Press, 1980.

Lardner, Ring. *The Best Short Stories of Ring Lardner.* New York: Charles Scribner's Sons, 1988.

Latham, Frank B. *1872–1972 A Century of Serving Customers: The Story of Montgomery Ward.* Chicago: Montgomery Ward & Co., 1972.

Lavine, Sigmund A. *Allan Pinkerton: America's First Private Eye.* New York: Dodd, Mead & Co., 1963.

Lawrence, Jerome. *Actor: The Life and Times of Paul Muni.* New York: G. P. Putnam's Sons, 1974.

Leach, Paul R. *That Man Dawes.* Chicago: Reilly & Lee Co., 1930.

Leech, Harper and John Charles Carroll. *Armour and His Times.* New York: Appleton-Century Co., 1938.

Leiter, Robert D. *The Musicians and Petrillo.* New York: Bookman Associates, 1953.

Levine, Edward M. *The Irish and Irish Politicians.* Notre Dame, Ind.: University of Notre Dame Press, 1966.

Levine, Mark L., George C. McNamee, and Daniel Greenberg, eds. *The Tales of Hoffman.* New York: Bantam Books, 1970.

Levine, Peter. *A. G. Spalding and the Rise of Baseball: The Promise of American Sport.* New York: Oxford University Press, 1985.

Levinsohn, Florence H. *Harold Washington: A Political Biography.* Chicago: Chicago Review Press, 1983.

Lewis, Lloyd. *John S. Wright: Prophet of the Prairies.* Chicago: Prairie Farmer Publishing Co., 1941.

Lewis, Lloyd and Henry Justin Smith. *Chicago: The History of its Reputation.* New York: Harcourt, Brace, 1929.

Lincoln, C. Eric. *The Black Muslims in America.* Boston: Beacon Press, 1961.

Lindberg, Richard. *Who's On 3rd?: The Chicago White Sox Story.* South Bend, Ind.: Icarus Press, 1983.

Lindberg, Richard. *Chicago Ragtime: Another Look at Chicago, 1880–1920.* South Bend, Ind.: Icarus Press, 1985.

Lindberg, Richard. *To Serve and Collect: Chicago Politics and Police Corruption from the Lager Beer Riot to the Summerdale Scandal.* New York: Praeger Publishers, 1991.

Lingeman, Richard. *Theodore Dreiser: At the Gates of the City 1871–1907.* New York: G. P. Putnam's Sons, 1986.

Lingeman, Richard. *Theodore Dreiser: An American Journey 1908–1945.* New York: G. P. Putnam's Sons, 1990.

Linn, James Weber. *Jane Addams, A Biography.* New York: Appleton-Century Co., 1935.

Lissak, Rivka Shpak. *Pluralism and Progressives: Hull House and the New Immigrants 1890–1919.* Chicago: University of Chicago Press, 1989.

Littlewood, Thomas B. *Horner of Illinois.* Evanston: Northwestern University Press, 1969.

Livermore, Mary A. *My Story of the War: A Woman's Narrative of Four Years' Personal Experience.* Hartford, Conn.: A. D. Worthington & Co., 1888.

Livermore, Mary A. *The Story of My Life, or the Sunshine and Shadow of Seventy Years.* Hartford, Conn.: A. D. Worthington & Co., 1889.

Livingston, Dorothy Michelson. *The Master of Light: A Biography of Albert A. Michelson.* New York: Charles Scribner's Sons, 1973.

Lloyd, Caro. *Henry Demarest Lloyd.* 2 volumes. New York: G. P. Putnam's Sons, 1912.

Logan, Nick and Bob Woffinden. *The Illustrated Encyclopedia of Rock.* New York: Harmony Books, 1977.

Logan, Rayford W. and Michael R. Winston, eds. *Dictionary of American Negro Biography*. New York: W. W. Norton & Co., 1982.

Longstreet, Stephen. *Chicago: An Intimate Portrait of People, Pleasures and Power, 1860–1919*. New York: David McKay Co., 1973.

Love, John F. *McDonald's Behind the Arches*. Toronto: Bantam Books. 1986.

Low, W. Augustus and Virgil A. Clift. *Encyclopedia of Black Americans*. New York: McGraw-Hill, 1981.

Lowe, David. *Lost Chicago*. Boston: Houghton, Mifflin Co., 1975.

Lucas, Carter. *History of Medicine and Surgery and Physicians and Surgeons of Chicago*. Chicago: Biographical Publishing Corp., 1922.

Lucia, Ellis. *Mr. Football, Amos Alonzo Stagg*. New York: A. S. Barnes, 1970.

Lupoff, Richard A. *Edgar Rice Burroughs: Master of Adventure*. New York: Ace Books, 1965.

Lyle, John H. *The Dry and Lawless Years*. Englewood Cliffs, N. J.: Prentice-Hall, 1960.

Maass, Alan. "The Little Red Book House," *Chicago Reader* (October 17, 1986).

MacAdams, William. *Ben Hecht: The Man Behind the Legend*. New York: Scribners, 1990.

MacDonald, J. Fred. *Don't Touch That Dial! Radio Programming in American Life from 1920 to 1960*. Chicago: Nelson-Hall, 1979.

Manguel, Alberto and Gianni Guadalupi. *The Dictionary of Imaginary Places*. San Diego: Harcourt, Brace & Jovanovich, 1987.

Marcy, Mary E. *You Have No Country!: Workers' Struggle Against War*. Edited by Franklin Rosemont. Chicago: Charles H. Kerr Publishing Co., 1984.

Martin, John. *Ruth Page: An Intimate Biography*. New York: M. Dekker, 1977.

Massa, Ann. *Vachel Lindsay: Fieldworker for the American Dream*. Bloomington, Ind.: Indiana University Press, 1970.

Masters, Edgar Lee. *Vachel Lindsay: A Poet in America*. New York: Biblo and Tannen, 1935.

Masters, Edgar Lee. *Across Spoon River*. New York: Farrar and Rinehart, 1936.

Mayer, Harold M. and Richard C. Wade. *Chicago: Growth of a Metropolis*. Chicago: University of Chicago Press, 1969.

Maynard, Theodore. *Too Small A World: The Life of Mother Cabrini*. Milwaukee: Bruce Publishing Co., 1945.

McCaffrey, Lawrence, Ellen Skerrett, Michael F. Funchion, and Charles Fanning. *The Irish in Chicago*. Urbana, Ill.: University of Illinois Press, 1987.

McCullough, Lawrence E. *Irish Music in Chicago: An Ethnomusicological Study*. Diss. Pittsburgh: University of Pittsburgh, 1978.

McCutcheon, John T. *Drawn from Memory, Containing Many of the Author's Famous Cartoons and Sketches*. Indianapolis: Bobbs-Merrill Co., 1950.

McDonald, Forrest. *Insull*. Chicago: University of Chicago Press, 1962.

McEwen, Joe. Edited by Greg Shaw. *Sam Cooke: A Biography in Words and Pictures*. New York: Sire Books, 1977.

McLoughlin, William G., Jr. *Billy Sunday Was His Real Name*. Chicago: University of Chicago Press, 1955.

McPhaul, John. *Deadlines and Monkeyshines: The Fabled World of Chicago Journalism*. Englewood Cliffs, N. J.: Prentice-Hall, 1962.

McPhaul, John. *Johnny Torrio: First of the Ganglords*. New Rochelle, N. Y.: Arlington House, 1970.

Meeker, Arthur. *Chicago With Love*. New York: Alfred A. Knopf, 1955.

Meites, Hyman L., ed. *History of the Jews of Chicago*. Chicago: Jewish Historical Society of Illinois, 1924.

Merriam, Charles E. *Chicago: A More Intimate View of Urban Politics*. New York: Macmillan, 1929.

Meyerowitz, Joanne. *Women Adrift: Independent Wage Earners in Chicago, 1880–1930*. Chicago: University of Chicago Press, 1988.

Mezzrow, Mezz and Bernard Wolfe. *Really the Blues*. Garden City, N. Y.: Anchor Books, 1972.

Miller, Alton. *Harold Washington: The Mayor, The Man*. Chicago: Bonus Books, 1989.

Miller, Jim, ed. *The Rolling Stone Illustrated History of Rock & Roll*. New York: Random House, 1976.

Minnelli, Vincente with Hector Arce. *I Remember It Well*. Garden City, N. Y.: Doubleday, 1974.

Molloy, Mary Alice. *Chicago Since the Sears Tower: A Guide to New Downtown Buildings*. Chicago: Inland Architect Press, 1990.

Monroe, Harriet. *A Poet's Life: Seventy Years in a Changing World*. New York: Macmillan, 1938.

Monroe, Harriet. *John Wellborn Root, A Study of His Life and Work*. Park Forest, Ill.: Prairie School Press, 1966.

Moody, Paul D. *My Father: An Intimate Portrait of Dwight Moody*. Boston: Little, Brown & Co., 1938.

Moore, Edward C. *Forty Years of Opera in Chicago*. New York: Horace Liveright, 1930.

Morgan, Anna. *My Chicago*. Chicago: R. F. Seymour, 1918.

Morgan, Gwen and Arthur Veysey. *Poor Little Rich Boy (and how he made good)*. Carpentersville, Ill.: Crossroads Communications, 1985.

Morn, Frank T. *The Eye That Never Sleeps: A History of the Pinkerton National Detective Agency*. Bloomington, Ind.: Indiana University Press, 1982.

Morris, Jeannie. *Brian Piccolo: A Short Season*. Chicago: Rand McNally, 1971.

Morrison, Hugh. *Louis Sullivan: Prophet of Modern Architecture*. Westport, Conn.: Greenwood Press, 1971.

Murray, George. *The Madhouse on Madison Street*. Chicago: Follett, 1965.

Names, Larry D. *Bury My Heart at Wrigley Field: The History of the Chicago Cubs—When the Cubs Were the White Sox*. Neshkoro, Wis.: Sportsbook Publishing Co., 1990.

Nash, Jay Robert. *Hustlers and Con Men*. New York: M. Evans & Co., 1976.

Nash, Jay Robert. *Makers & Breakers of Chicago from Long John Wentworth to Richard J. Daley*. Chicago: Academy Chicago, 1985.

Nelli, Humbert S. *Italians in Chicago, 1880–1930: A Study in Ethnic Mobility*. New York: Oxford University Press, 1970.

Nelson, Bruce C. *Beyond the Martyrs: A Social History of Chicago's Anarchists 1870–1900*. New Brunswick, N. J.: Rutgers University Press, 1988.

Ness, Eliot with Oscar Fraley. *The Untouchables*. New York: Award Books, 1969.

Nestor, Agnes. *Woman's Labor Leader*. Rockford, Ill.: Bellevue Books, 1954.

Nevius, Blake. *Robert Herrick: The Development of a Novelist*. Berkeley: University of California Press, 1962.

Newell, Barbara Warne. *Chicago and the Labor Movement Metropolitan Unionism in the 1930's*. Urbana, Ill.: University of Illinois Press, 1961.

Newman, Mark. *Entrepreneurs of Profit and Pride: From Black-Appeal to Radio Soul*. New York: Praeger, 1988.

Neyhart. Louise. *Giant of the Yards*. Boston: Houghton Mifflin Co., 1952.

Norris, James D. and James Livingston. "Jay Morton and the Conduct of Modern Business Enterprise." *Chicago History* (Spring 1981).

O'Connor, Len. *Clout—Mayor Daley and His City*. Chicago: Henry Regnery Co., 1975.

O'Connor, Len. *Requiem: The Decline and Demise of Mayor Daley and His Era*. Chicago: Contemporary Books, 1977.

O'Connor, Richard. *Sheridan the Inevitable*. Indianapolis: Bobbs-Merrill Co., 1953.

O'Gorman, James F. *Three American Architects: Richardson, Sullivan, and Wright, 1865–1915*. Chicago: University of Chicago Press, 1991.

Oliver, Paul, Max Harrison, and William Bolcom. *The New Grove Gospel, Blues and Jazz with Spirituals and Ragtime*. New York: W. W. Norton & Co., 1986.

Olson, James C. *J. Sterling Morton*. Lincoln, Neb.: Nebraska State Historical Society, 1972.

Otis, Philo Adams. *The Chicago Symphony Orchestra, Its Organization, Growth and Development 1891–1924*. Chicago: Clayton F. Summy Co., 1924.

Ottley, Roi. *The Lonely Warrior: The Life and Times of Robert S. Abbott*. Chicago: Henry Regnery Co., 1955.

Pacyga, Dominic A. and Ellen Skerrett. *Chicago: City of Neighborhoods*. Chicago: Loyola University Press, 1986.

Padilla, Felix M. *Latino Ethnic Consciousness: The Case of Mexican Americans and Puerto Ricans in Chicago*. Notre Dame, Ind.: University of Notre Dame Press, 1985.

Page, Ruth. *Page to Page*. Edited by Andrew Mark Wentink. Brooklyn, N. Y.: Dance Horizons, 1978.

Paley, William S. *As It Happened: A Memoir*. Garden City, N. Y.: Doubleday, 1979.

Palmer, Robert. *Deep Blues*. New York: Penguin Books, 1981.

Paper, Lewis J. *Empire: William S. Paley and the Making of CBS*. New York: St. Martin's Press, 1987.

Parot, Joseph. *Polish Catholics in Chicago, 1850–1920*. DeKalb, Ill.: Northern Illinois University, 1981.

Parry, Albert. *Garrets and Pretenders: A History of Bohemianism in America*. New York: Covici-Friede Publishers, 1933.

Parsons, Lucy E. *Life of Albert R. Parsons, with Brief History of the Labor Movement in America*. Chicago: Lucy E. Parsons, 1889.

Parton, Mary Field, ed. *Autobiography of Mother Jones*. Chicago: Charles H. Kerr Publishing Co., 1925.

Pasley, Fred D. *Al Capone: The Biography of a Self-Made Man*. New York: Ives Washburn, 1930.

Peck, Abe. *Uncovering the Sixties: The Life & Times of the Underground Press*. New York: Pantheon Books, 1985.

Peterson, Virgil W. *Barbarians In Our Midst: A History of Chicago Crime and Politics*. Boston: Little, Brown & Co., 1952.

Philpott, Thomas Lee. *The Slum and the Ghetto: Neighborhood Deterioration and Middle-Class Reform, Chicago 1880–1930*. New York: Oxford University Press, 1978.

Pierce, Bessie Louise. *As Others See Chicago: Impressions of Visitors, 1673–1933*. Chicago: University of Chicago Press, 1933.

Pierce, Bessie Louise. *A History of Chicago*. 3 vols. New York: Alfred A. Knopf, 1937–57.

Pienkos, Donald E. *P.N.A.: Centennial History of the Polish National Alliance of the United States of North America*. New York: Columbia University Press, 1984.

Pizer, Donald. *The Novels of Theodore Dreiser: A Critical Study*. Minneapolis: University of Minnesota Press, 1976.

Ploski, Harry A. and James Williams, eds. *The Negro Almanac: A Reference Work on the African American*. Detroit: Gale Research, 1989.

Pollock, John C. *Moody: A Biographical Portrait of the Pacesetter in Modern Mass Evangelism*. New York: Macmillan, 1963.

Poole, Ernest. *Giants Gone: Men Who Made Chicago*. New York: McGraw-Hill, 1943.

Pratt, William D. *The Abbott Almanac: 100 Years of Commitment to Quality Health Care*. Elmsford, N. Y.: Benjamin Co., 1987.

Preston, William, Jr. *Aliens and Dissenters: Federal Suppression of Radicals, 1903–1933*. Cambridge: Harvard University Press, 1963.

Quaife, Milo. *Chicago and the Old Northwest, 1673–1835*. Chicago: University of Chicago Press, 1913.

Quaife, Milo. *Checagou: From Indian Wigwam to Modern City, 1673–1835*. Chicago: University of Chicago Press, 1933.

Rakove, Milton. *Don't Make No Waves—Don't Back No Losers: An Insider's Analysis of the Daley Machine*. Bloomington, Ind.: Indiana University Press, 1975.

Rakove, Milton. *We Don't Want Nobody Nobody Sent: An Oral History of the Daley Years*. Bloomington, Ind.: Indiana University Press, 1979.

Randall, Ruth Painter. *Colonel Elmer Ellsworth: A Biography of Lincoln's Friend and First Hero of the Civil War*. Boston: Little, Brown & Co., 1960.

Rascoe, Burton. *Before I Forget*. New York: Doubleday, Doran, 1937.

Regnery, Henry. *The Cliff Dwellers: The History of a Chicago Cultural Institution*. Evanston, Ill.: Chicago Historical Bookworks, 1990.

Reid, Daniel G., ed. *Dictionary of Christianity in America*. Downers Grove, Ill.: InterVarsity Press, 1990.

Reid, Robert L., ed. *Battleground: The Autobiography of Margaret A. Haley*. Urbana, Ill.: University of Illinois Press, 1982.

Reisler, Mark. *By the Sweat of Their Brow: Mexican Immigrant Labor in the United States 1900–1940*. Westport, Conn.: Greenwood Press, 1976.

Reiss, Stephen A. *Touching Base*. Westport, Conn.: Greenwood Press, 1980.

Reiss, Stephen A. *City Games: The Evolution of American Urban Society and the Rise of Sports*. Urbana, Ill.: University of Illinois Press, 1989.

Rex, Frederick F. *The Mayors of the City of Chicago*. Chicago: Municipal Reference Library, 1934.

Reynolds, Gary A. and Beryl J. Wright. *Against The Odds: African-American Artists and the Harmon Foundation*. Newark, N. J.: The Newark Museum, 1989.

Reynolds, Michael. "The Young Man and the Suburb." *Chicago Reader* (March 30, 1990).

Reynolds, Patrick. "'Fra Lorado,' Chicago's Master Sculptor," *Chicago History* (Summer 1985).

Rice, Jon F. *Up on Madison, Down on 75th: A History of the Illinois Black Panther Party*. Evanston, Ill.: The Committee, 1983.

Riedy, James L. *Chicago Sculpture*. Urbana, Ill.: University of Illinois Press, 1981.

Roderick, Stella Virginia. *Nettie Fowler McCormick*. Rindge, N. H.: Richard R. Smith Publisher, 1956.

Roediger, Dave and Franklin Rosemont, eds. *Haymarket Scrapbook*. Chicago: Charles H. Kerr Publishing Co., 1986.

Root, George Frederick. *The Story of a Musical Life: An Autobiography*. Cincinnati: J. Church Co., 1891.

Ross, Barney with Martin Abramson. *No Man Stands Alone: The True Story of Barney Ross*. Philadelphia: J. B. Lippincott Co., 1957.

Ross, Ishbel. *Silhouette in Diamonds: The Life of Mrs. Potter Palmer*. New York: Harper & Brothers, 1960.

Rowan, Richard Wilmer. *The Pinkertons, a Detective Dynasty*. Boston: Little, Brown & Co., 1931.

Rowe, Mike. *Chicago Breakdown*. New York: Drake Publishers, 1975.

Royko, Mike. *Boss: Richard J. Daley of Chicago*. New York: E. P. Dutton, 1971.

Rubin, Steven J. *Meyer Levin*. Boston: Twayne Publishers, 1982.

Ruff, Allen M. "Socialist Publishing in Illinois: Charles H. Kerr & Company of Chicago, 1886–1928," *Illinois Historical Journal* (Spring 1986).

Russell, Charles. *The American Orchestra and Theodore Thomas*. Garden City, N. Y.: Doubleday, 1927.

Saliga, Pauline A., ed. *The Sky's the Limit, A Century of Chicago Skyscrapers*. New York: Rizzoli Books, 1990.

Salzman, Jack and David Ray, eds. *The Jack Conroy Reader*. New York: Burt Franklin & Co., 1979.

Sandburg, Carl. *The Chicago Race Riots, July 1919*. New York: Harcourt, Brace, 1919.

Sandburg, Carl. *Always the Young Strangers*. New York: Harcourt, Brace & Jovanovich, 1953.

Sayers, Gale with Al Silverman. *I Am Third*. New York: Viking Press, 1973.

Schabas, Ezra. *Theodore Thomas, America's Conductor and Builder of Orchestras, 1835–1905*. Urbana, Ill. : University of Illinois Press, 1989.

Schaff, Barbara C. *Mr. Dooley's Chicago*. Garden City, N. Y.: Anchor Press/Doubleday, 1977.

Schiavo, Giovanni. *The Italians in Chicago: A Study in Americanization*. Chicago: Italian American Publishing Co., 1928.

Schmidt, John R. *"The Mayor Who Cleaned Up Chicago": A Political Biography of William E. Dever*. DeKalb, Ill.: Northern Illinois University Press, 1989.

Schnell, J. Christopher. "Mary Livermore and the Great Northwestern Fair," *Chicago History* (Spring 1975).

Schoor, Gene with Henry Gilfond. *Red Grange Football's Greatest Halfback*. New York: Julian Messner, 1952.

Schulze, Franz. *Mies Van Der Rohe: A Critical Biography*. Chicago: University of Chicago Press, 1985.

Scroggs, Marilee Munger. *A Light in the City: The Fourth Presbyterian Church of Chicago*. Chicago: Fourth Presbyterian Church of Chicago, 1990.

Scully, Vincent, Jr. *Frank Lloyd Wright*. New York: George Braziller, 1960.

Seale, Bobby. *Seize the Time: The Story of the Black Panther Party and Huey P. Newton.* New York: Random House, 1970.

Segre, Emilio. *Enrico Fermi: Physicist.* Chicago: University of Chicago Press, 1970.

Sentinel Publishing Co. *The Sentinel's History of Chicago Jewry, 1911–1961.* Chicago: Sentinel Publishing Co., 1961.

Seymour, Ralph Fletcher. *Some Went This Way: A Forty-Year Pilgrimage among Artists, Bookmen and Printers.* Chicago: R. F. Seymour, 1945.

Shanabruch, Charles. *Chicago's Catholics: The Evolution of an American Identity.* Notre Dame, Ind.: University of Notre Dame Press, 1981.

Shapiro, Nat and Nat Hentoff, eds. *The Jazz Makers: Essays on the Greats of Jazz.* New York: Da Capo Press, 1957.

Shaw, Arnold. *Honkers and Shouters: The Golden Years of Rhythm and Blues.* New York: Macmillan, 1978.

Shaw, Arnold. *Black Popular Music in America.* New York: Schirmer Books, 1986.

Shay, Art. *Nelson Algren's Chicago.* Urbana, Ill.: University of Illinois Press, 1988.

Siebert, Wilbur Henry. *The Underground Railroad from Slavery to Freedom.* Chicago: Johnson Publishing Co., 1967.

Siegel, Arthur. *Chicago's Famous Buildings.* Chicago: University of Chicago Press, 1965.

Silber, Irwin, ed. *Songs of the Civil War.* New York: Columbia University Press, 1960.

Siry, Joseph. *Carson Pirie Scott, Louis Sullivan and the Chicago Department Store.* Chicago: University of Chicago Press, 1988.

Sklar, Kathryn Kish, ed. *The Autobiography of Florence Kelley: Notes of Sixty Years.* Chicago: Charles H. Kerr Publishing Co., 1986.

Slayton, Robert A. *Back of the Yards: The Making of a Local Democracy.* Chicago: University of Chicago Press, 1986.

Smith, Alson J. *Chicago's Left Bank.* Chicago: Henry Regnery Co., 1953.

Smith, Carl S. *Chicago and the American Literary Imagination, 1880–1920.* Chicago: University of Chicago Press, 1984.

Smith, Henry Justin. *Chicago's Great Century, 1833–1933.* Chicago: Consolidated, 1933.

Smith, Joan A. *Ella Flagg Young: Portrait of a Leader.* Ames, Iowa: Educational Studies Press and the Iowa State University Research Foundation, 1979.

Smith, Sally Bedell. *In All His Glory: The Life of William S. Paley The Legendary Tycoon and His Brilliant Circle.* New York: Simon & Schuster, 1990.

Sochen, June. *Movers and Shakers: American Women Thinkers and Activists 1900–1970.* New York: Quadrangle, 1973.

Sorenson, Lorin. *Sears, Roebuck and Co. 100th Anniversary 1886–1986.* St. Helena, Calif.: Silverado Publishing Co., 1985.

Spaeth, Sigmund. *A History of Popular Music in America.* New York: Random House, 1948.

Spear, Allan H. *Black Chicago: The Making of a Negro Ghetto 1890–1920.* Chicago: University of Chicago Press, 1967.

Special Collections Department of the Chicago Public Library. *Resetting the Stage: Theater Beyond the Loop 1960–1990.* Chicago: Chicago Public Library, 1990.

Spink, J. G. Taylor. *Judge Landis and Twenty-Five Years of Baseball.* New York: Thomas Y. Crowell, 1947.

Sprague, Paul E. *Guide to Frank Lloyd Wright & Prairie School Architecture in Oak Park.* Oak Park, Ill.: Village of Oak Park, 1986.

Stagg, Amos Alonzo, as told to Wesley Winans Stout. *Touchdown.* New York: Longmans, Green & Co., 1927.

Stambler, Irwin. *The Encyclopedia of Pop, Rock and Soul.* New York: St. Martin's Press, 1989.

Stevens, Mark. *The Big Eight: Inside America's Largest Accounting Firms.* New York: Macmillan, 1984.

Stone, Irving. *Clarence Darrow for the Defense.* Garden City, N. Y.: Doubleday, 1941.

Stone, Melville E. *Fifty Years a Journalist.* Garden City, N. Y.: Doubleday, Page, 1921.

Storr, Richard J. *Harper's University, The Beginnings.* Chicago: University of Chicago Press, 1966.

Strickland, Arvarh E. *The Chicago Urban League, 1916–1956.* Urbana, Ill.: University of Illinois Press, 1966.

Sullivan, Frank. *Legend: The Only Inside Story about Mayor Richard J. Daley.* Chicago: Bonus Books, 1989.

Sullivan, Louis H. *The Autobiography of an Idea.* New York: Dover Publications, 1924.

Sutton, William A. *The Road to Winesburg: A Mosaic of the Imaginative Life of Sherwood Anderson.* Metuchen, N. J.: Scarecrow Press, 1972.

Swanberg, W. A. *Dreiser.* New York: Charles Scribner's Sons, 1965.

Sweet, Jeffrey. *Something Wonderful Right Away.* New York: Avon Books, 1986.

Swift, Louis F. with Arthur Van Vlissingen, Jr. *The Yankee of the Yards: The Biography of Gustavus Franklin Swift.* Chicago: A. W. Shaw Co., 1927.

Taft, Ada Bartlett. *Lorado Taft: Sculptor and Citizen.* Greensboro, N. C.: Mary T. Smith, 1946.

Taylor, Graham. *Pioneering on Social Frontiers.* Chicago: University of Chicago Press, 1930.

Taylor, Graham. *Chicago Commons through Forty Years.* Chicago: Chicago Commons Association, 1936.

Teahan, Terence and Josh Dunson. *The Road to Glountane.* Chicago: Terence Teahan, 1980.

Tebbel, John W. *An American Dynasty: The Story of the McCormicks, Medills and Pattersons.* Garden City, N. Y.: Doubleday, 1947.

Tebbel, John W. *The Marshall Fields: A Study in Wealth.* New York: E. P. Dutton, 1947.

Thomas, John L. *Alternative America: Henry George, Edward Bellamy, Henry Demarest Lloyd and the Adversary Tradition.* Cambridge: Harvard University Press, 1983.

Thompson, Slason. *Eugene Field: A Study in Heredity and Contradictions.* 2 vols. New York: Charles Scribner's Sons, 1901.

Tierney, Kevin. *Darrow: A Biography.* New York: Thomas Y. Crowell Co., 1979.

Timmons, Bascom N. *Portrait of an American: Charles G. Dawes.* New York: Henry Holt and Company, 1953.

Townsend, Andrew. *The Germans of Chicago.* Chicago: University of Chicago Press, 1932.

Townsend, Kim. *Sherwood Anderson.* Boston: Houghton, Mifflin Co., 1987.

Travis, Dempsey J. *An Autobiography of Black Chicago.* Chicago: Urban Research Institute, 1981.

Travis, Dempsey J. *An Autobiography of Black Jazz.* Chicago: Urban Research Institute, 1983.

Travis, Dempsey J. *An Autobiography of Black Politics.* Chicago: Urban Research Institute, 1987.

Travis, Dempsey J. *Harold—The People's Mayor: An Authorized Biography of Mayor Harold Washington.* Chicago: Urban Research Institute, 1989.

Tucker, John I. "Tarzan Was Born in Chicago." *Chicago History* (Spring 1970).

Tuttle, William. *Race Riot: Chicago in the Red Summer of 1919.* New York: Atheneum, 1970.

Twombly, Robert C. *Frank Lloyd Wright: An Interpretative Biography.* New York: Harper & Row, 1973.

Twombly, Robert C. *Louis Sullivan, His Life and Work.* New York: Viking Press, 1986.

Twyman, Robert W. *History of Marshall Field & Co., 1852–1906.* Philadelphia: University of Pennsylvania Press, 1954.

Upton, George P., ed. *Theodore Thomas: A Musical Autobiography.* New York: Da Capo Press, 1964.

Van Doren, Charles. *Webster's American Biographies.* Springfield, Mass.: G. & C. Merriam Co., 1974.

Vass, George. *George Halas and the Chicago Bears.* Chicago: Henry Regnery Co., 1971.

Veeck, Bill with Ed Lynn. *Veeck—As in Wreck: The Autobiography of Bill Veeck.* New York: G. P. Putnam's Sons, 1962.

Wade, Louise Carroll. *Graham Taylor, Pioneer for Social Justice 1851–1938.* Chicago: University of Chicago Press, 1964.

Wade, Louise Carroll. *Chicago's Pride: The Stockyards, Packingtown, and Environs in the Nineteenth Century.* Urbana, Ill.: University of Illinois Press, 1987.

Waldman, Frank. *Famous American Athletes of Today,* 12th series. Boston: L. C. Page & Co., 1951.

Waldrop, Frank C. *McCormick of Chicago: An Unconventional Portrait of a Controversial Figure.* Englewood Cliffs, N. J.: Prentice-Hall, 1966.

Walgreen, Myrtle R. and Marguerite Harmon Bro. *Never A Dull Day.* Chicago: Henry Regnery Co., 1963.

Walljasper, Jay. "Those Vagabond Days." *Chicago Tribune Sunday Magazine* (August 15, 1982).

Walsh, Justin E. *To Print the News and Raise Hell: A Biography of Wilbur F. Storey.* Chapel Hill, N. C.: University of North Carolina, 1968.

Washburn, Charles. *Come Into My Parlor: A Biography of the Aristocratic Everleigh Sisters of Chicago.* New York: National Library, 1936.

Webb, Constance. *Richard Wright: A Biography.* New York: G. P. Putnam's Sons, 1968.

Weil, Gordon. *Sears, Roebuck, U.S.A.: The Great American Catalog Store and How It Grew.* New York: Stein and Day, 1977.

Weimann, Jeanne Madeline. *The Fair Women.* Chicago: Academy Press, 1981.

Weinberg, Arthur, ed. *Attorney for the Damned: Clarence Darrow in the Courtroom.* New York: Simon & Schuster, 1957.

Weinberg, Arthur and Lila. *Clarence Darrow: A Sentimental Rebel.* New York: G. P. Putnam's Sons, 1980.

Weissmuller, Johnny. *Water, World and Weissmuller.* Los Angeles: Vion Publishing Co., 1964.

Weller, Allen. *Lorado in Paris: The Letters of Lorado Taft, 1880–1885.* Urbana, Ill.: University of Illinois Press, 1985.

Wendt, Lloyd. *Chicago Tribune: The Rise of a Great American Newspaper.* Chicago: Rand McNally, 1979.

Wendt, Lloyd. *"Swift Walker": An Informal Biography of Gurdon Saltonstall Hubbard.* Chicago: Henry Regnery Co., 1986.

Wendt, Lloyd and Herman Kogan. *Give the Lady What She Wants! The Story of Marshall Field and Co.* Chicago: Rand McNally, 1952.

Wendt, Lloyd and Herman Kogan. *Big Bill of Chicago.* Indianapolis: Bobbs-Merrill Co., 1953.

Werner, Morris R. *Julius Rosenwald, The Life of a Practical Humanitarian.* New York: Harper & Brothers, 1939.

Wheeler, Adade M. with Marlene Wortman. *The Roads They Made: Women in Illinois History.* Chicago: Charles H. Kerr Publishing Co., 1977.

Willard, Frances. *Glimpses of Fifty Years: Autobiography of an American Woman.* Chicago: Woman's Temperance Publication Assoc., 1889.

Wille, Lois. *Forever Open, Clear and Free: The Historic Struggle for Chicago's Lakefront.* Chicago: Henry Regnery Co., 1972.

Williams, Ellen. *Harriet Monroe and the Poetry Renaissance: The First Ten Years of Poetry, 1912–22.* Urbana, Ill.: University of Illinois Press, 1977.

Williams, Kenny J. *In the City of Men: Another Story of Chicago.* Nashville: Townsend Press, 1974.

Williams, Kenny J. *Prairie Voices: A Literary History of Chicago from the Frontier to 1893.* Nashville: Townsend Press, 1980.

Williams, Kenny J. *A Storyteller and a City: Sherwood Anderson's Chicago.* DeKalb, Ill.: Northern Illinois University Press, 1988.

Williams, Martin. *Jazz Masters of New Orleans.* New York: Da Capo Press, 1967.

Wilson, Howard Eugene. *Mary McDowell, Neighbor.* Chicago: University of Chicago Press, 1928.

Wolseley, Roland E. *The Black Press, U.S.A.* Ames, Iowa.: Iowa State University Press, 1971.

Wood, David Ward. *Chicago and Its Distinguished Citizens or the Progress of Forty Years.* Chicago: M. George & Co., 1881.

Woodall, Elaine D. *Archibald J. Motley, Jr.: American Artist of the Afro-American People, 1891–1928.* Diss. University Park, Penn.: Pennsylvania State University, 1977.

Woodall, Elaine D. "Looking Backwards: Archibald J. Motley and the Art Institute of Chicago, 1914–1930," *Chicago History* (Spring 1979).

Woodward, Bob. *Wired: The Fast Times and Short Life of John Belushi.* New York: Simon & Schuster, 1984.

Wright, Ellen and Michael Fabre. *Richard Wright Reader.* New York: Harper & Row, 1978.

Wright, Frank Lloyd. *An Autobiography.* New York: Horizon Press, 1977.

Wright, Richard. *Native Son.* New York: Harper & Bros., 1940.

Wright, Richard. *American Hunger.* New York: Harper & Row, 1977.

Yardley, Jonathan. *Ring: A Biography of Ring Lardner.* New York: Random House, 1977.

Yatron, Michael. *America's Literary Revolt.* Freeport, N. Y.: Books for Libraries Press, 1959.

Zimmerman, William, Jr. *William Wrigley Jr., the Man and His Business, 1861–1932.* Chicago: R. R. Donnelley & Sons, 1935.

Zorbaugh, Harvey. *The Gold Coast and the Slum.* Chicago: University of Chicago Press, 1929.

Zukowsky, John, ed. *Mies Reconsidered: His Career, Legacy, and Disciples.* New York: Rizzoli Books, 1986.

Zukowsky, John, ed. *Chicago Architecture 1872–1922, Birth of a Metropolis.* Munich: Prestel-Verlag in association with the Art Institute of Chicago, 1987.

Index